McGraw-Hill

netw⦿rks™

A Social Studies Learning System

M000294097

MEETS YOU ANYWHERE —
TAKES YOU EVERYWHERE

McGraw-Hill networks™

**MEETS YOU ANYWHERE —
TAKES YOU EVERYWHERE**

GO online

1. Go to *connected.mcgraw-hill.com.*

2. Get your User Name and Password from your teacher and enter them.

3. Click on your **Networks** book.

4. Select your chapter and lesson.

HOW do you learn?

Read • Reflect • Watch • Listen • Connect • Discover • Interact

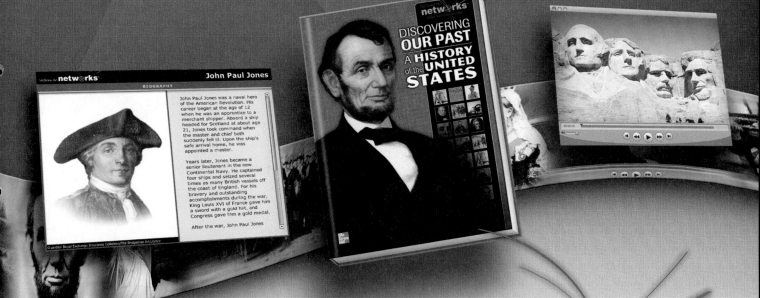

start netw✸rking

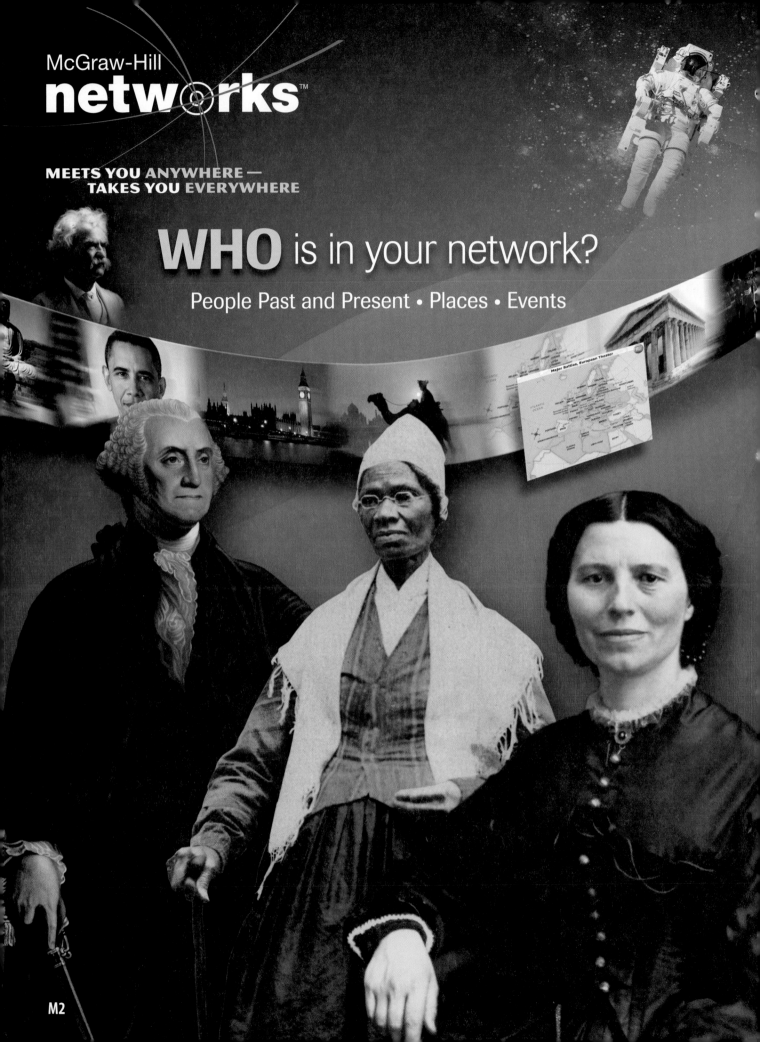

WHAT do you learn?

History • Geography • Economics • Government • Culture

start **network**ing

McGraw-Hill networks™

MEETS YOU ANYWHERE — TAKES YOU EVERYWHERE

HOW do you make **Networks** yours?

Organize • Take Notes • Study • Submit • Message

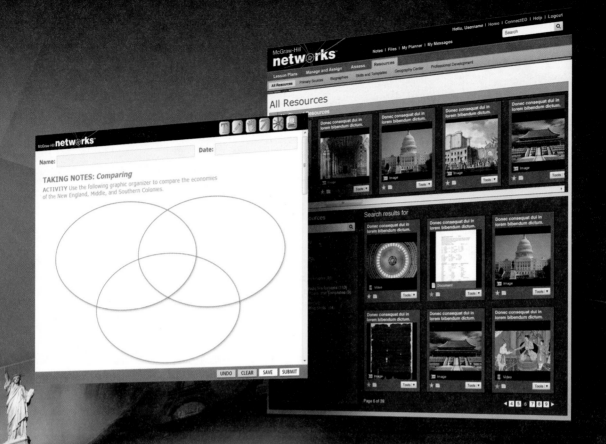

WHAT do you use?

Graphic Organizers • Primary Sources • Videos • Games • Photos

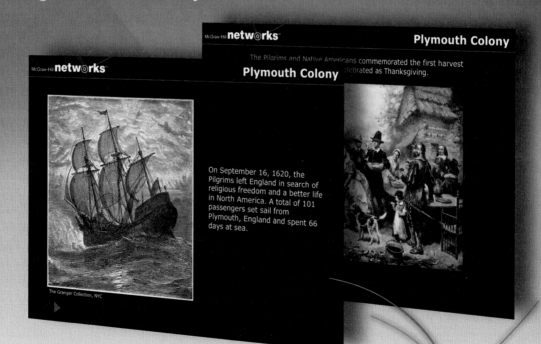

start**network**ing

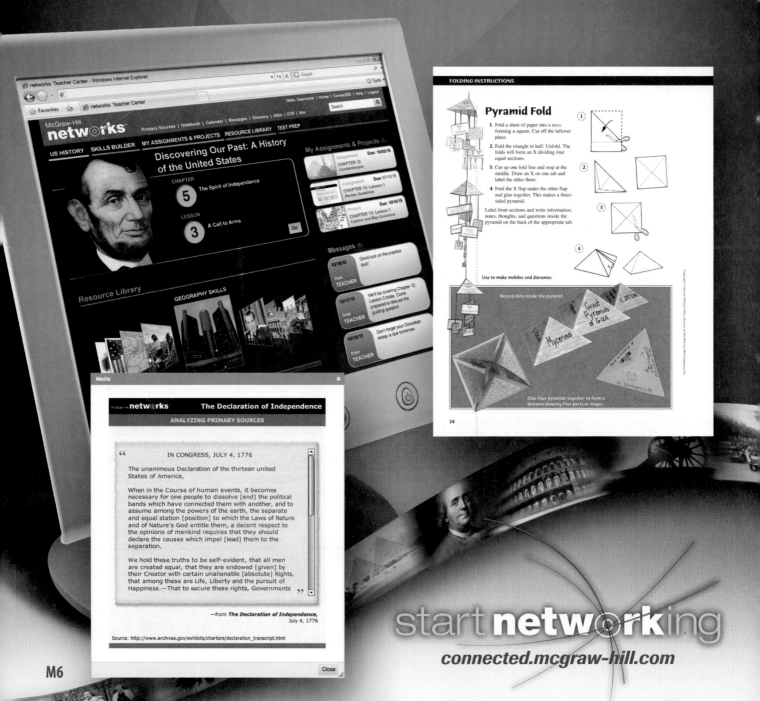

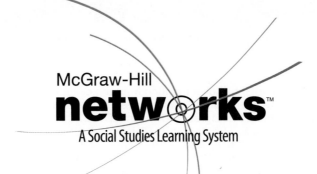

McGraw-Hill
netw⊕rks™
A Social Studies Learning System

DISCOVERING
OUR PAST

A **HISTORY**
of the **UNITED**
STATES

Early Years

Joyce Appleby, Ph.D.

Alan Brinkley, Ph.D.

Albert S. Broussard, Ph.D.

James M. McPherson, Ph.D.

Donald A. Ritchie, Ph.D.

McGraw Hill **Education**

Bothell, WA • Chicago, IL • Columbus, OH • New York, NY

Cover credits:
(main image) Sacagawea, William Ahrendt Inc./Cover painting from the collection of Mr. and Mrs. Frank Wylie
(thumbnails l to r, t to b) Royalty-Free/CORBIS, Library of Congress, Prints and Photographs Division (LC-
USZC4-6878), Library of Congress Prints & Photographs Division (LC-USZC4-4752), VisionsofAmerica/Joe Sohm/
Getty Images, Library of Congress, Prints and Photographs Division (LC-USW33-029971-C), Library of Congress,
Prints and Photographs Division (LC-USZC4-678), CORBIS/Punchstock, Library of Congress, Prints and Photographs
Division (LC-USZC4-11368), Library of Congress, Prints and Photographs Division (LC-USZ62-8422), Library of
Congress, Prints and Photographs Division (LC-USZC4-5801), Library of Congress, Prints and Photographs Division
(LC-USZC4-6877), Library of Congress, Prints and Photographs Division (LC-USZC4-6466), Library of Congress,
Prints and Photographs Division (LC-USZC4-1727), Ingram Publishing.

The *McGraw·Hill* Companies

www.mheonline.com/networks

 **Education**

Send all inquiries to:
McGraw-Hill Education
8787 Orion Place
Columbus, OH 43240

ISBN: 978-0-07-659685-0
MHID: 0-07-659685-0

Printed in the United States of America.

4 5 6 7 8 9 DOW 16 15 14 13

AUTHORS

Joyce Appleby, Ph.D., is Professor Emerita of History at UCLA. She is the author of several books, including her most recent, *The Relentless Revolution: A History of Capitalism.* She served as president of the Organization of American Historians and the American Historical Association, and she chaired the Council of the Institute of Early American History and Culture at Williamsburg. Appleby has been elected to the American Philosophical Society and the American Academy of Arts and Sciences, and she is a Corresponding Fellow of the British Academy.

Alan Brinkley, Ph.D., is Allan Nevins Professor of American History at Columbia University. His published works include *Voices of Protest: Huey Long, Father Coughlin, and the Great Depression,* which won the 1983 National Book Award. Other titles include *The End of Reform: New Deal Liberalism in Recession and War* and *Liberalism and Its Discontents.* He received the Levenson Memorial Teaching Prize at Harvard University.

Albert S. Broussard, Ph.D., is Professor of History at Texas A&M University, where he was selected as the Distinguished Faculty Lecturer for 1999–2000. He also served as the Langston Hughes Professor of American Studies at the University of Kansas in 2005. Before joining the Texas A&M faculty, Broussard was Assistant Professor of History and Director of the African American Studies Program at Southern Methodist University. Among the books he has published are *Black San Francisco: The Struggle for Racial Equality in the West, 1900–1954* and *African American Odyssey: The Stewarts, 1853–1963.* Broussard has also served as president of the Oral History Association.

James M. McPherson, Ph.D., is George Henry Davis Professor Emeritus of American History at Princeton University. He is the author of 11 books about the Civil War era, including *Tried by War: Abraham Lincoln as Commander in Chief,* for which he won a second Lincoln Prize in 2009. McPherson is a member of many professional historical associations, including the Civil War Preservation Trust.

Donald A. Ritchie, Ph.D., is Historian of the United States Senate. Ritchie received his doctorate in American history from the University of Maryland after service in the U.S. Marine Corps. He has taught American history at various levels, from high school to university. He edits the Historical Series of the Senate Foreign Relations Committee and is the author of several books, including *Press Gallery: Congress and the Washington Correspondents,* which received the Organization of American Historians' Richard W. Leopold Prize. Ritchie has served as president of the Oral History Association and as a council member of the American Historical Association.

Contributing Authors

Jay McTighe has published articles in a number of leading educational journals and has coauthored 10 books, including the best-selling *Understanding by Design* series with Grant Wiggins. McTighe also has an extensive background in professional development and is a featured speaker at national, state, and district conferences and workshops. He received his undergraduate degree from The College of William and Mary, earned a Masters degree from the University of Maryland, and completed post-graduate studies at the Johns Hopkins University.

Dinah Zike, M.Ed., is an award-winning author, educator, and inventor recognized for designing three-dimensional, hands-on manipulatives and graphic organizers known as Foldables®. Foldables are used nationally and internationally by teachers, parents, and other professionals in the education field. Zike has developed more than 150 supplemental educational books and materials. Her two latest books, *Notebook Foldables®* and *Foldables®, Notebook Foldables®, & VKV®s for Spelling and Vocabulary 4th–12th* were each awarded *Learning Magazine's* Teachers' Choice Award for 2011. In 2004, Zike was honored with the CESI Science Advocacy Award. She received her M.Ed. from Texas A&M, College Station, Texas.

Doug Fisher, Ph.D., and Nancy Frey, Ph.D., are professors in the School of Teacher Education at San Diego State University. Fisher's focus is on literacy and language, with an emphasis on students who are English Learners. Frey's focus is on literacy and learning, with a concentration in how students acquire content knowledge. Both teach elementary and secondary teacher preparation courses, in addition to their work with graduate and doctoral programs. Their shared interests include supporting students with diverse learning needs, instructional design, and curriculum development. They are coauthors of numerous articles and books, including *Better Learning Through Structured Teaching, Checking for Understanding, Background Knowledge,* and *Improving Adolescent Literacy.* They are coeditors (with Diane Lapp) of the NCTE journal *Voices from the Middle.*

CONSULTANTS AND REVIEWERS

ACADEMIC CONSULTANTS

David Berger, Ph.D.
Ruth and I. Lewis Gordon
  Professor of Jewish History
Dean, Bernard Revel Graduate
  School
Yeshiva University
New York, New York

Stephen Cunha, Ph.D.
Professor of Geography
Humboldt State University
Arcata, California

Tom Daccord
Educational Technology Specialist
Co-Director, EdTechTeacher
Boston, Massachusetts

Sylvia Kniest
Social Studies Teacher
Tucson Unified School District
Tucson, Arizona

Bernard Reich, Ph.D.
Professor of Political Science and
  International Affairs
George Washington University
Washington, D.C.

Justin Reich
Educational Technology Specialist
Co-Director, EdTechTeacher
Boston, Massachusetts

TEACHER REVIEWERS

Laura Abundes
Jefferson Middle School
Waukegan, Illinois

Debbie Clay
Brink Junior High
Moore, Oklahoma

Wendy Blanton
Berkeley Middle School
St. Louis, Missouri

Michael Frint
Fort Riley Middle School
Fort Riley, Kansas

Brian M. Gibson
Highland East Junior High School
Moore, Oklahoma

Carol V. Gimondo
Jefferson Middle School
Waukegan, Illinois

Mark Hamann
Perrysburg Junior High School
Perrysburg, Ohio

Norman Jackson
Frontier Middle School
O'Fallon, Missouri

Connie K. Simmonds
Ferguson Middle School
Ferguson, Missouri

Mary Beth Whaley
Highland West Junior High School
Moore, Oklahoma

CONTENTS

CHAPTER 1
The First Americans 1

CHAPTER 2
Exploring the Americas 25

There's More Online . . .

BIOGRAPHIES Malinche • Dekanawidah
GRAPHIC ORGANIZERS Reasons Early Peoples Migrated
• Early Civilizations of the Americas • Information
About Ancient Native Americans
INTERACTIVE MAPS Native American Cultures • Routes
to the Americas • Civilizations of Mexico and Central
America • The Inca Empire • Significant Adena,
Hopewell, and Mississippian Sites
VIDEOS
SELF-CHECK QUIZZES Lesson 1 • Lesson 2 • Lesson 3

There's More Online . . .

BIOGRAPHIES Vasco da Gama • Queen Isabella • Sor
Juana Inés de la Cruz • Christopher Columbus
GRAPHIC ORGANIZERS Technological Advances
• Explorers and Their Sponsors • The Northwest
Passage
INTERACTIVE MAPS European Exploration • Trade Routes
to Asia • West African Trading Kingdoms
• Early Portuguese Exploration • European Voyages of
Exploration • Spanish Explorers • Spanish Missions in
California
PRIMARY SOURCES Vasco da Gama • Cortés and the
Aztecs • Sor Juana Inés de la Cruz • Cabeza de Vaca
VIDEOS
SLIDE SHOWS Mansa Musa
SELF-CHECK QUIZZES Lesson 1 • Lesson 2 • Lesson 3
• Lesson 4

There's More Online . . .

INTERACTIVE CHARTS/GRAPHS The Golden Crop • The Mystery of the Lost Colony • King Philip's War • Middle Colonies • Indentured Servants and Enslaved Africans

GRAPHIC ORGANIZERS Listing • Cooperation and Conflict Between Colonists and Native Americans • Dividing Colonies • Cause and Effect of Bacon's Rebellion

INTERACTIVE MAPS Land Claims • The New England Colonies • The Middle Colonies • The Southern Colonies

PRIMARY SOURCES Attack on New Amsterdam • Bacon's Rebellion

SLIDE SHOWS The Pilgrims

VIDEOS

SELF-CHECK QUIZZES Lesson 1 • Lesson 2 • Lesson 3 • Lesson 4

There's More Online . . .

BIOGRAPHIES Olaudah Equiano • George Washington

INTERACTIVE CHARTS/GRAPHS The African Slave Trade • Literacy Rates • Great Awakening and the Enlightenment

GRAPHIC ORGANIZERS The Triangular Trade • Principles of Government • Colonial Government • Great Awakening and the Enlightenment • Native American Relations With the Europeans

INTERACTIVE MAPS The Colonial Economy • The Triangular Trade • The French and Indian War

PRIMARY SOURCES Life on a Plantation • Conditions on a Slave Ship • Freedom of the Press • Political Cartoon: Unite or Die

TIME LINES Principles of British Government

VIDEOS

SLIDE SHOWS A Child's Life in the Colonies

SELF-CHECK QUIZZES Lesson 1 • Lesson 2 • Lesson 3 • Lesson 4

(l) W. Langdon Kihn/National Geographic Society/Corbis, (r) Burstein Collection/CORBIS

CHAPTER **5**
The Spirit of Independence
. . . . 109

CHAPTER **6**
The American Revolution
. . . . 141

There's More Online . . .

BIOGRAPHIES Patrick Henry • Thomas Paine
GRAPHIC ORGANIZERS British Policies • The Intolerable Acts • Key Actions of the Continental Congress • Declaration of Independence
INTERACTIVE MAPS North America 1775 • The Proclamation of 1763 • Battles of Lexington and Concord • The Siege of Boston
PRIMARY SOURCES The Boston Tea Party • Battles of Lexington and Concord • Reaction to Declaration of Independence
VIDEOS
SELF-CHECK QUIZZES Lesson 1 • Lesson 2 • Lesson 3 • Lesson 4

There's More Online . . .

INTERACTIVE CHARTS/GRAPHS Native American Alliances
BIOGRAPHIES Franklin and the Revolution • Martha Washington • John Paul Jones • Rochambeau
GRAPHIC ORGANIZERS Early Battles • Sources of Aid to Patriots • British Defeats in the South • Treaty of Paris
INTERACTIVE MAPS The War for Independence • The Revolutionary War • The Revolutionary War in the West and South • Siege at Yorktown
PRIMARY SOURCES Abigail Adams • Winter at Valley Forge • Political Cartoon: British Rider
TIME LINES Thaddeus Kósciuszko • Bernardo de Gálvez
VIDEOS
SLIDE SHOWS Famous Women of the Revolutionary War
SELF-CHECK QUIZZES Lesson 1 • Lesson 2 • Lesson 3 • Lesson 4

CHAPTER 7
A More Perfect Union 173

CHAPTER 8
The Constitution
. . . . 203

There's More Online . . .

INTERACTIVE CHARTS/GRAPHS Capitals of the United
States • Articles of Confederation and the
Constitution • Leaders and Their Roles • Framers of
the Constitution
GRAPHIC ORGANIZERS Identifying • Comparing and
Contrasting • Categorizing
INTERACTIVE MAPS The Northwest Territory
PRIMARY SOURCES Plantation Life • Political Cartoon:
The Ninth Pillar Erected!
VIDEOS
SLIDE SHOWS State Constitutions
SELF-CHECK QUIZZES Lesson 1 • Lesson 2 • Lesson 3

There's More Online . . .

INTERACTIVE CHARTS/GRAPHS Amending the
Constitution • The Federal Court System • Landmark
Supreme Court Cases
BIOGRAPHIES Sandra Day O'Connor
GRAPHIC ORGANIZERS Major Principles of the
Constitution • Branches of Government
INTERACTIVE MAPS Washington, D.C.
VIDEOS
SLIDE SHOWS The Oval Office
SELF-CHECK QUIZZES Lesson 1 • Lesson 2

CHAPTER **9**
The Federalist Era

CHAPTER **10**
The Jefferson Era

There's More Online . . .

INTERACTIVE CHARTS/GRAPHS The First Cabinet
  • Jefferson and Hamilton
BIOGRAPHIES John Jay
GRAPHIC ORGANIZERS Leaders and Roles • Effects of
  Treaties • Role of Federal Government
INTERACTIVE MAPS The United States 1790 • Native
  American Campaigns
PRIMARY SOURCES Treaty of Greenville • Political
  Cartoon: Jefferson and the Constitution
VIDEOS
SLIDE SHOWS The Supreme Court • The Two-Party System
SELF-CHECK QUIZZES Lesson 1 • Lesson 2 • Lesson 3

There's More Online . . .

BIOGRAPHIES Toussaint L'Ouverture • Zebulon Pike
  • Stephen Decatur • Dolley Madison
GAMES Lesson Vocabulary
INTERACTIVE CHARTS/GRAPHS The Supreme Court–
  Then and Now • Alexander Hamilton and Aaron Burr
  • U.S. Policies Leading to the War of 1812
GRAPHIC ORGANIZERS Republicans and the Role of
  Government • Exploring the West • U.S. Actions
  • Battles and Outcomes
INTERACTIVE MAPS The Expanding Nation • The Election
  of 1800 • Exploring the Louisiana Territory • The War
  of 1812
VIDEOS
SLIDE SHOWS Monticello • Lewis and Clark
SELF-CHECK QUIZZES Lesson 1 • Lesson 2 • Lesson 3
  • Lesson 4

The Granger Collection, NYC

CHAPTER 11
Growth and Expansion
. 293

CHAPTER 12
The Jackson Era. 321

There's More Online . . .

INTERACTIVE CHARTS/GRAPHS Mississippi River Basin
BIOGRAPHIES Henry Clay
GRAPHIC ORGANIZERS Free Enterprise System
  • Transportation Developments • Effects of the
  Missouri Compromise
INTERACTIVE MAPS Growing Industrial Cities • The
  National Road • Canals 1820–1860 • The Missouri
  Compromise • Acquisition of Florida
PRIMARY SOURCES *Lowell Offering*
TIME LINES Henry Clay
VIDEOS
SLIDE SHOWS The Erie Canal
SELF-CHECK QUIZZES Lesson 1 • Lesson 2 • Lesson 3

There's More Online . . .

BIOGRAPHIES Andrew Jackson
GRAPHIC ORGANIZERS Democrats and National
  Republicans • Seminole and Cherokee Resistance
  • The Bank War
INTERACTIVE MAPS The Removal of Native Americans
  •The Election of 1824 • Elections of 1836 and 1840
PRIMARY SOURCES Osceola • Political Cartoon: King
  Andrew the First • Political Cartoon: Panic of 1837 •
  Harrison Campaign Poster
VIDEOS
SELF-CHECK QUIZZES Lesson 1 • Lesson 2 • Lesson 3

CHAPTER **13**
Manifest Destiny
. . . . 345

CHAPTER **14**
North and South
. 373

There's More Online . . .

INTERACTIVE CHARTS/GRAPHS Oregon Trail Facts • Florida's
   Capitol Buildings • San Francisco Population Growth
BIOGRAPHIES Davy Crockett • John C. Frémont
   • Mariano G. Vallejo
GRAPHIC ORGANIZERS Event Time Line 1819–1846
   • Texas History Time Line • Individual Achievements
   • Roles in the West
INTERACTIVE MAPS Territorial Expansion • Oregon
   Country • Texas War for Independence • Santa Fe
   Trail • War With Mexico
PRIMARY SOURCES Osborne Russell, Trapper • The Bear
   Flag • Gold Rush Letter
VIDEOS
SLIDE SHOWS The Alamo
SELF-CHECK QUIZZES Lesson 1 • Lesson 2 • Lesson 3
   • Lesson 4

There's More Online . . .

INTERACTIVE CHARTS/GRAPHS Immigration Sources
   • Immigration, 1820–1860
BIOGRAPHIES John Deere • Harriet Tubman
GRAPHIC ORGANIZERS Phases of Industrialization
   • Growth of Cities • The Southern Economy • Working
   on a Plantation
INTERACTIVE MAPS Territorial Expansion • Major
   Railroads • Cotton Production
PRIMARY SOURCES Life in Lowell • *American Slavery As
   It Is*
VIDEOS
SLIDE SHOWS Child Labor
SELF-CHECK QUIZZES Lesson 1 • Lesson 2 • Lesson 3
   • Lesson 4

The Granger Collection, NYC

CHAPTER **15**
The Spirit of Reform......401

CHAPTER **16**
Toward Civil War..........425

There's More Online . . .

INTERACTIVE CHARTS/GRAPHS Slavery in the United States

BIOGRAPHIES Gallaudet and Dix • Sojourner Truth

GRAPHIC ORGANIZERS Prominent Abolitionists • Women's Rights Leaders

INTERACTIVE MAPS Routes of the Underground Railroad • Liberia

PRIMARY SOURCES A Sermon about Slavery • William Lloyd Garrison on Frederick Douglass • Seneca Falls Convention Declaration of Sentiments

TIME LINES Opportunity and Achievement for Women

VIDEOS

SLIDE SHOWS Farm Labor in the United States

SELF-CHECK QUIZZES Lesson 1 • Lesson 2 • Lesson 3

There's More Online . . .

BIOGRAPHIES Abraham Lincoln • Jefferson Davis

GRAPHIC ORGANIZERS The Kansas-Nebraska Act • Political Parties 1848–1856 • November 1860 to April 1861

INTERACTIVE MAPS A Nation Divided • New Territories of the United States • The Compromise of 1850 • The Kansas-Nebraska Act 1854 • The Election of 1856 • Seceding States 1860–1861

PRIMARY SOURCES A Defense of the Kansas-Nebraska Act • The *Dred Scott* Decision • "A Plea for Captain John Brown" • Political Cartoon: Secessionists Leaving the Union

VIDEOS

SELF-CHECK QUIZZES Lesson 1 • Lesson 2 • Lesson 3

There's More Online . . .

INTERACTIVE CHARTS/GRAPHS Army Salaries • The Cost of U.S. Wars
INTERACTIVE MAPS The Civil War • War in the West • War in the East • The Battle of Gettysburg, Day 3 • The Final Battles
PRIMARY SOURCES Report on the Ironclads • Obituary of Stonewall Jackson • Union Recruitment Poster • Grant's Strategy for Spring 1864
SLIDE SHOWS Civil War Casualties • The Battle of Antietam • Civil War Political Cartoons • Women in the War • Women and Social Reform • Dorothea Dix • Richmond
VIDEOS
SELF-CHECK QUIZZES Lesson 1 • Lesson 2 • Lesson 3 • Lesson 4 • Lesson 5

There's More Online . . .

INTERACTIVE CHARTS/GRAPHS Radical Republicans • Illiteracy Rates • African Americans in Congress
GRAPHIC ORGANIZERS Reconstruction Plans • The Fourteenth and Fifteenth Amendments • Improvements in Education • The New South
INTERACTIVE MAPS The United States in the Reconstruction Era • Reconstruction Military Districts • Election of 1876
PRIMARY SOURCES Sharecropper Contract
VIDEOS
SLIDE SHOWS Reconstruction in the South • Lincoln's Funeral Procession • Violence in the South • Southern Textile Industry
SELF-CHECK QUIZZES Lesson 1 • Lesson 2 • Lesson 3 • Lesson 4

(l) Library of Congress/LC-DIG-ppmsca-19241, (r) Bettmann/CORBIS

MAPS, CHARTS, AND GRAPHS

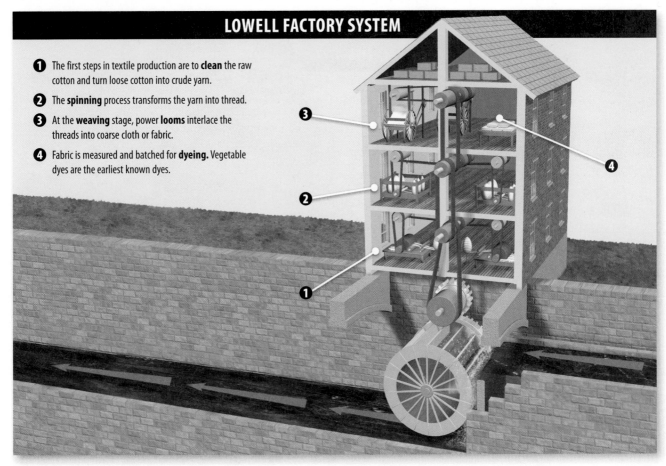

LOWELL FACTORY SYSTEM

❶ The first steps in textile production are to **clean** the raw cotton and turn loose cotton into crude yarn.

❷ The **spinning** process transforms the yarn into thread.

❸ At the **weaving** stage, power **looms** interlace the threads into coarse cloth or fabric.

❹ Fabric is measured and batched for **dyeing**. Vegetable dyes are the earliest known dyes.

MAPS, CHARTS, AND GRAPHS

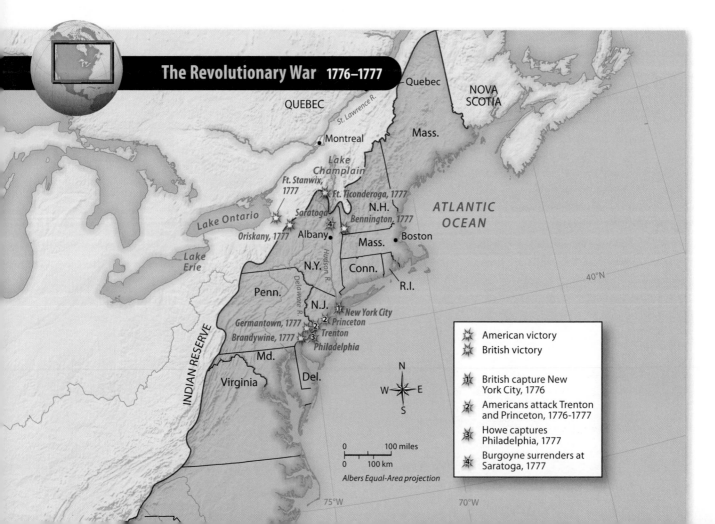

The Revolutionary War 1776–1777

American victory
British victory

1 British capture New York City, 1776
2 Americans attack Trenton and Princeton, 1776–1777
3 Howe captures Philadelphia, 1777
4 Burgoyne surrenders at Saratoga, 1777

0   100 miles
0   100 km
Albers Equal-Area projection

MAPS, CHARTS, AND GRAPHS

PRIMARY SOURCES AND POLITICAL CARTOONS

PRIMARY SOURCES AND POLITICAL CARTOONS

COME AND JOIN US BROTHERS.

PUBLISHED BY THE SUPERVISORY COMMITTEE FOR RECRUITING COLORED REGIMENTS
1210 CHESTNUT ST. PHILADELPHIA.

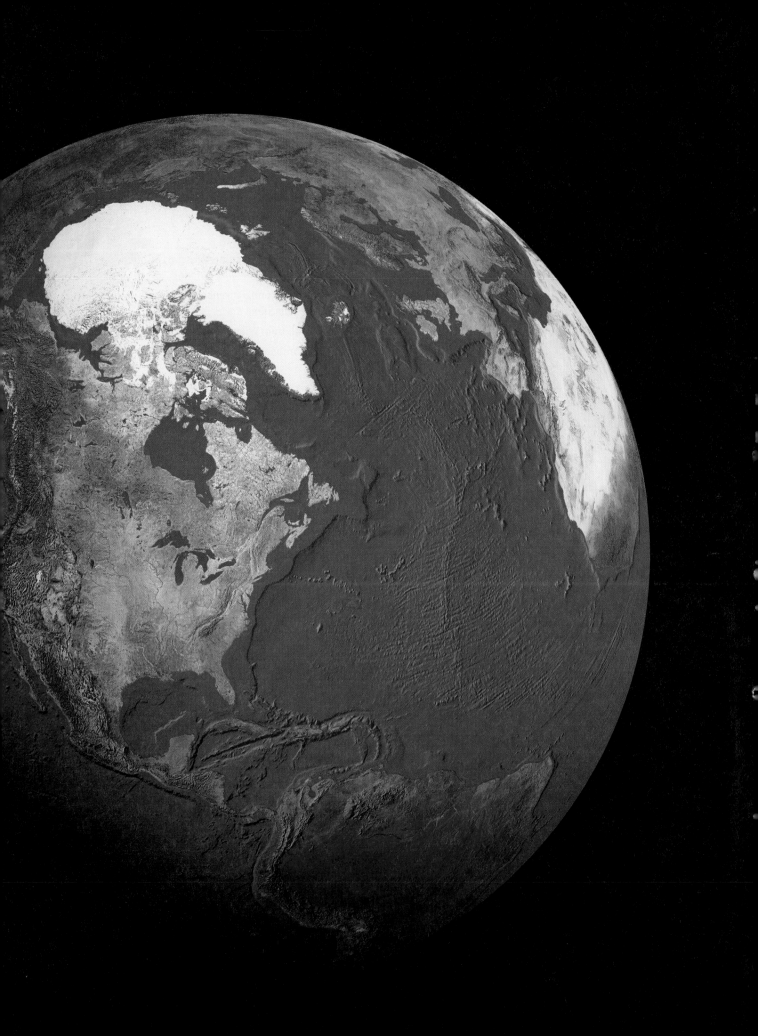

REFERENCE ATLAS

ATLAS KEY

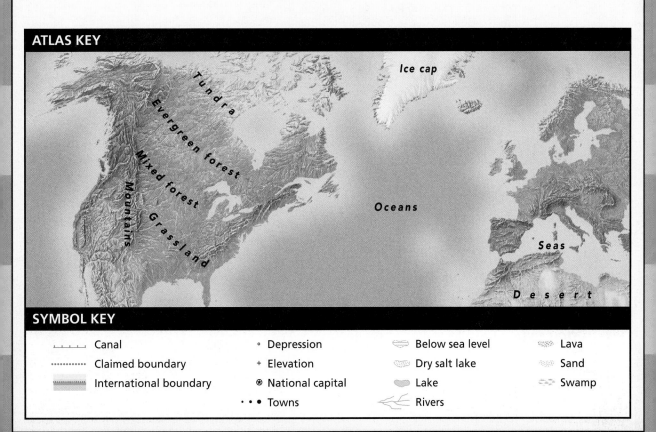

Tundra

Ice cap

Evergreen forest

Mixed forest

Mountains

Grassland

Oceans

Seas

Desert

SYMBOL KEY

- ⊥⊥⊥⊥ Canal
- ·········· Claimed boundary
- International boundary
- ° Depression
- + Elevation
- ⊛ National capital
- • • Towns
- Below sea level
- Dry salt lake
- Lake
- Rivers
- Lava
- Sand
- Swamp

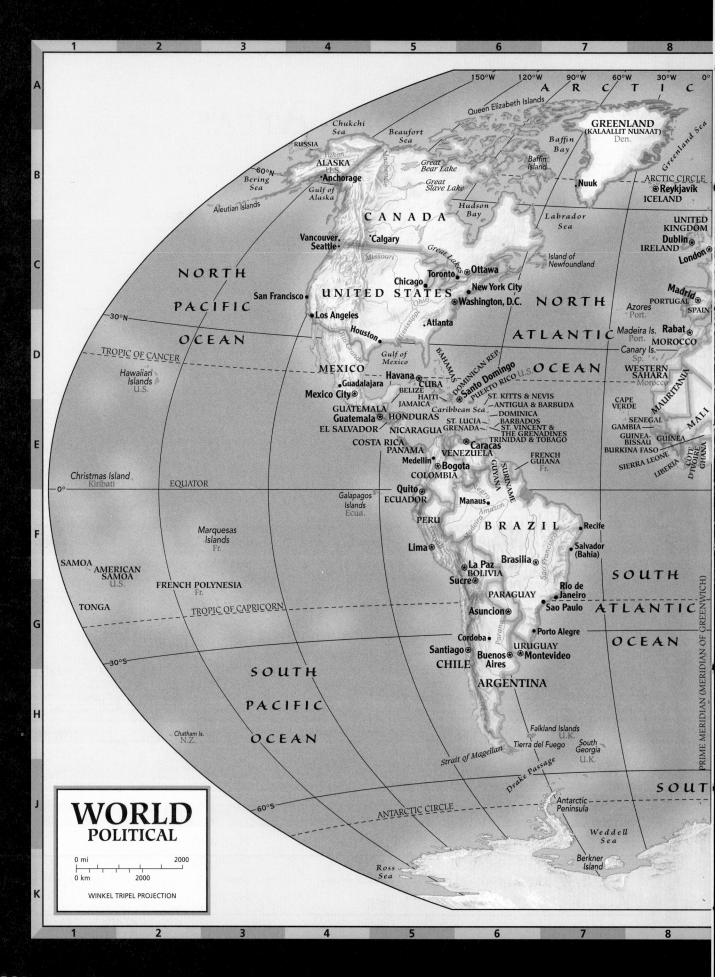

WORLD
POLITICAL

0 mi   2000

0 km   2000

WINKEL TRIPEL PROJECTION

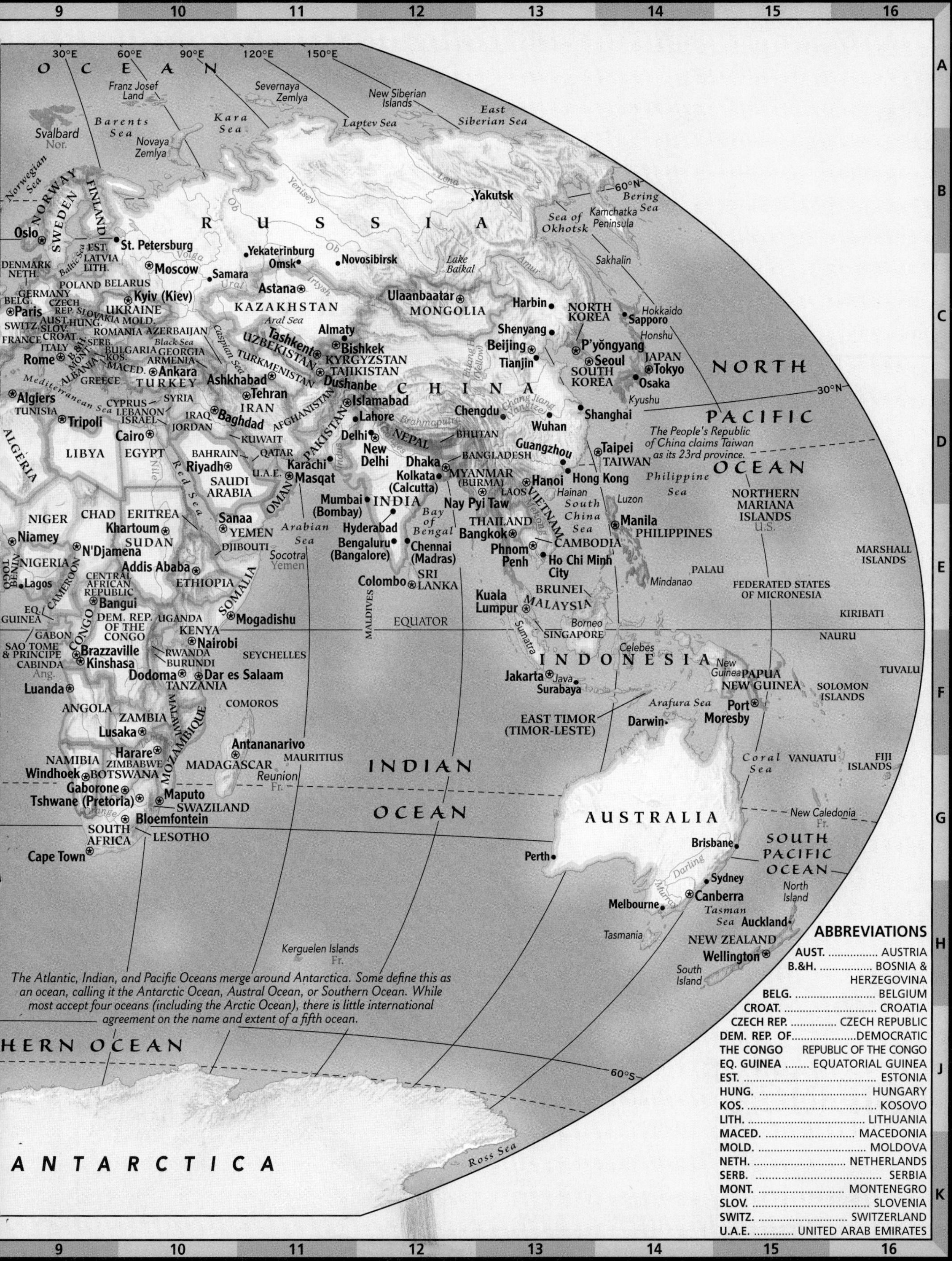
9
10
11
12
13
14
15
16
A
B
C
D
E
F
G
H
J
K
30°E
60°E
90°E
120°E
150°E
OCEAN
Franz Josef Land
Severnaya Zemlya
New Siberian Islands
East Siberian Sea
Laptev Sea
Kara Sea
Barents Sea
Svalbard Nor.
Novaya Zemlya
Norwegian Sea
NORWAY
SWEDEN
FINLAND
Oslo
St. Petersburg
EST.
LATVIA
LITH.
Baltic Sea
DENMARK
NETH.
Moscow
POLAND
BELARUS
GERMANY
BELG.
Paris
CZECH REP.
SLOVAKIA
UKRAINE
Kyiv (Kiev)
MOLD.
SWITZ.
AUST.
SLOV.
HUNG.
FRANCE
CROAT.
ITALY
SERB.
B.&H.
MONT.
KOS.
ROMANIA
BULGARIA
ALBANIA
MACED.
GREECE
Rome
AZERBAIJAN
GEORGIA
ARMENIA
Black Sea
Ankara
TURKEY
Mediterranean Sea
CYPRUS
LEBANON
ISRAEL
SYRIA
Algiers
TUNISIA
Tripoli
ALGERIA
LIBYA
Cairo
EGYPT
Nile
Red Sea
RUSSIA
Yekaterinburg
Omsk
Novosibirsk
Samara
Volga
Ural
Ob
Yenisey
Irtysh
Lena
Yakutsk
60°N
Bering Sea
Sea of Okhotsk
Kamchatka Peninsula
Sakhalin
Lake Baikal
Amur
Astana
KAZAKHSTAN
Aral Sea
Caspian Sea
UZBEKISTAN
TURKMENISTAN
Tashkent
Bishkek
Almaty
KYRGYZSTAN
TAJIKISTAN
Dushanbe
Ashkhabad
Tehran
IRAN
IRAQ
Baghdad
JORDAN
KUWAIT
BAHRAIN
QATAR
U.A.E.
Riyadh
SAUDI ARABIA
Masqat
OMAN
AFGHANISTAN
PAKISTAN
Islamabad
Lahore
Karachi
Indus
Ulaanbaatar
MONGOLIA
CHINA
Huang He (Yellow)
Chang Jiang (Yangtze)
Brahmaputra
Ganges
Beijing
Tianjin
Harbin
Shenyang
NORTH KOREA
P'yŏngyang
Seoul
SOUTH KOREA
JAPAN
Tokyo
Osaka
Hokkaido
Sapporo
Honshu
Kyushu
Shanghai
Wuhan
Chengdu
Guangzhou
Hong Kong
Taipei
TAIWAN
The People's Republic of China claims Taiwan as its 23rd province.
30°N
NORTH PACIFIC OCEAN
Delhi
New Delhi
NEPAL
BHUTAN
BANGLADESH
Dhaka
Kolkata (Calcutta)
MYANMAR (BURMA)
Nay Pyi Taw
INDIA
Mumbai (Bombay)
Hyderabad
Bengaluru (Bangalore)
Chennai (Madras)
Bay of Bengal
Arabian Sea
Colombo
SRI LANKA
MALDIVES
LAOS
Hanoi
VIETNAM
Hainan
THAILAND
Bangkok
Mekong
CAMBODIA
Phnom Penh
Ho Chi Minh City
South China Sea
Philippine Sea
Luzon
Manila
PHILIPPINES
Mindanao
PALAU
NORTHERN MARIANA ISLANDS U.S.
MARSHALL ISLANDS
FEDERATED STATES OF MICRONESIA
KIRIBATI
NAURU
TUVALU
BRUNEI
MALAYSIA
Kuala Lumpur
Borneo
SINGAPORE
Sumatra
Celebes
INDONESIA
Jakarta
Java
Surabaya
New Guinea
PAPUA NEW GUINEA
Port Moresby
SOLOMON ISLANDS
Arafura Sea
EAST TIMOR (TIMOR-LESTE)
Darwin
Coral Sea
VANUATU
FIJI ISLANDS
New Caledonia Fr.
AUSTRALIA
Perth
Brisbane
Darling
Murray
Sydney
Canberra
Melbourne
Tasmania
Tasman Sea
SOUTH PACIFIC OCEAN
North Island
Auckland
NEW ZEALAND
Wellington
South Island
EQUATOR
NIGER
Niamey
CHAD
N'Djamena
ERITREA
Khartoum
SUDAN
Sanaa
YEMEN
DJIBOUTI
Socotra Yemen
NIGERIA
BENIN
TOGO
Lagos
CAMEROON
CENTRAL AFRICAN REPUBLIC
Bangui
Addis Ababa
ETHIOPIA
SOMALIA
Mogadishu
EQ. GUINEA
GABON
SAO TOME & PRINCIPE
CONGO
DEM. REP. OF THE CONGO
UGANDA
KENYA
Nairobi
RWANDA
BURUNDI
Brazzaville
Kinshasa
CABINDA Ang.
SEYCHELLES
Dodoma
Dar es Salaam
TANZANIA
Luanda
ANGOLA
COMOROS
ZAMBIA
MALAWI
Lusaka
Zambezi
MOZAMBIQUE
Antananarivo
MADAGASCAR
MAURITIUS
Reunion Fr.
NAMIBIA
ZIMBABWE
Harare
Windhoek
BOTSWANA
Gaborone
Tshwane (Pretoria)
Orange
Maputo
SWAZILAND
Bloemfontein
SOUTH AFRICA
LESOTHO
Cape Town
INDIAN OCEAN
Kerguelen Islands Fr.
The Atlantic, Indian, and Pacific Oceans merge around Antarctica. Some define this as an ocean, calling it the Antarctic Ocean, Austral Ocean, or Southern Ocean. While most accept four oceans (including the Arctic Ocean), there is little international agreement on the name and extent of a fifth ocean.
HERN OCEAN
60°S
ANTARCTICA
Ross Sea
ABBREVIATIONS
AUST. .... AUSTRIA
B.&H. .... BOSNIA & HERZEGOVINA
BELG. .... BELGIUM
CROAT. .... CROATIA
CZECH REP. .... CZECH REPUBLIC
DEM. REP. OF THE CONGO .... DEMOCRATIC REPUBLIC OF THE CONGO
EQ. GUINEA .... EQUATORIAL GUINEA
EST. .... ESTONIA
HUNG. .... HUNGARY
KOS. .... KOSOVO
LITH. .... LITHUANIA
MACED. .... MACEDONIA
MOLD. .... MOLDOVA
NETH. .... NETHERLANDS
SERB. .... SERBIA
MONT. .... MONTENEGRO
SLOV. .... SLOVENIA
SWITZ. .... SWITZERLAND
U.A.E. .... UNITED ARAB EMIRATES

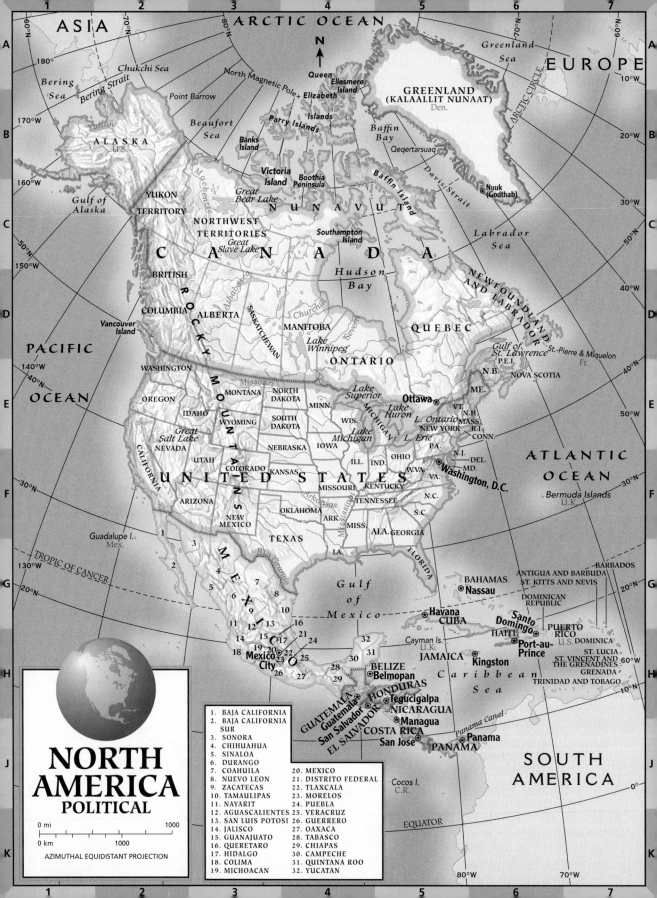

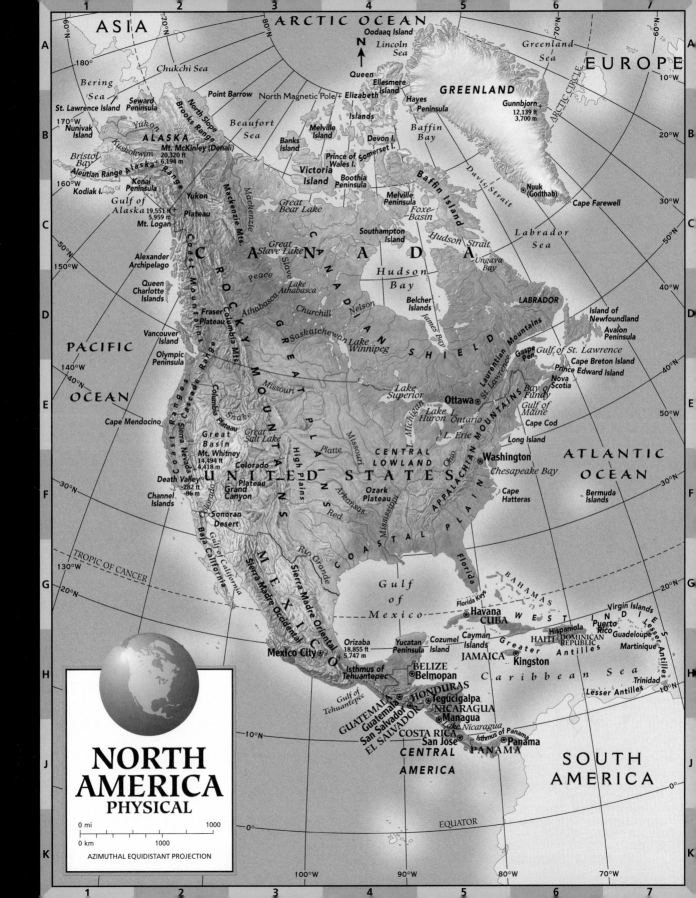

NORTH AMERICA
PHYSICAL

0 mi _____ 1000
0 km _____ 1000

AZIMUTHAL EQUIDISTANT PROJECTION

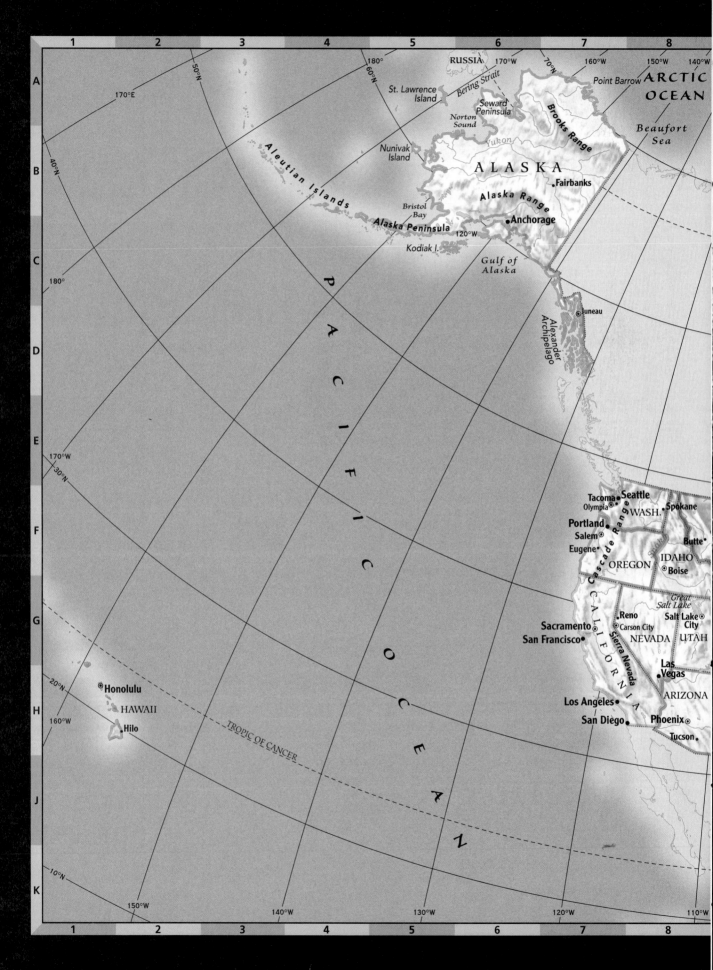

A B C D E F G H J K

1 2 3 4 5 6 7 8

170°E 50°N 60°N 180° RUSSIA 170°W 70°W 160°W 150°W 140°W

ARCTIC OCEAN

Point Barrow

40°N St. Lawrence Island Bering Strait Seward Peninsula Brooks Range Beaufort Sea

Norton Sound Yukon

ALASKA

Nunivak Island Fairbanks

Alaska Range

180° Aleutian Islands Bristol Bay Anchorage

Alaska Peninsula 120°W

Kodiak I. Gulf of Alaska

170°W 30°N Juneau

Alexander Archipelago

P A C I F I C

Tacoma Seattle
Olympia WASH. Spokane
Portland
Salem Butte
Eugene IDAHO
OREGON Boise

Cascade Range

Great Salt Lake

Reno Salt Lake City
Sacramento Carson City
San Francisco NEVADA UTAH

Sierra Nevada

C A L I F O R N I A

Las Vegas

ARIZONA

20°N Honolulu
HAWAII Los Angeles

O C E A N

160°W Hilo San Diego Phoenix

TROPIC OF CANCER Tucson

N

10°N

150°W 140°W 130°W 120°W 110°W

1 2 3 4 5 6 7 8

GREENLAND
(KALAALLIT NUNAAT)
Den.

UNITED
STATES
POLITICAL

0 mi 600
0 km 600

OBLIQUE AZIMUTHAL EQUIDISTANT PROJECTION

ARCTIC CIRCLE

C A N A D A

MAINE

MONTANA
Helena
Billings

NORTH
DAKOTA
Bismarck

MINNESOTA

Lake Superior

MICHIGAN

Lake Huron

Montpelier
VT.
Augusta
Portland
Concord, N.H.
Boston, MASS.
Providence, R.I.
Hartford, CONN.

NEW
YORK
Albany

Lake
Ontario

Minneapolis
St. Paul

WISCONSIN

L. Michigan

Detroit
Erie
Cleveland
Buffalo

Pierre

SOUTH
DAKOTA

Milwaukee
Madison
Lansing

PA.

New York City

WYOMING
Casper
Cheyenne

Sioux City
Des Moines

IOWA

Chicago

ILLINOIS

Toledo

IND.

Columbus
OHIO
Dayton

Pittsburgh

Harrisburg

Trenton, N.J.
Philadelphia

Baltimore

Dover, DEL.

Denver

NEBRASKA

Lincoln
Omaha

Indianapolis

Cincinnati

Annapolis, MD.
Washington, D.C.

COLORADO

Kansas City

Topeka
MISSOURI

Springfield
St. Louis

W. VA.

Charleston

Richmond

KANSAS
Jefferson City

Louisville

VIRGINIA

Virginia Beach

Santa Fe

KENTUCKY

Raleigh

Nashville

NORTH CAROLINA

Charlotte

Tulsa

TENNESSEE

SOUTH
CAROLINA

Columbia

Albuquerque
Oklahoma City
OKLAHOMA

ARKANSAS
Little Rock

Memphis

Atlanta

Charleston

NEW
MEXICO

Fort
Worth
Dallas

Birmingham
ALABAMA
MISS.

GEORGIA

Savannah

El Paso

TEXAS

LOUISIANA

Jackson

Montgomery

Jacksonville

Austin

Baton Rouge

Tallahassee

Rio Grande

San Antonio
Houston

New Orleans

FLORIDA

Tampa

M E X I C O

Gulf of
Mexico

Miami

BAHAMAS

Bermuda Is.
U.K.

A T L A N T I C   O C E A N

Straits of Florida

CUBA

Caribbean

Sea

JAMAICA

DOMINICAN
REPUBLIC
HAITI

PUERTO
RICO
U.S.

San Juan

ANTIGUA
& BARBUDA
ST. KITTS
& NEVIS

DOMINICA

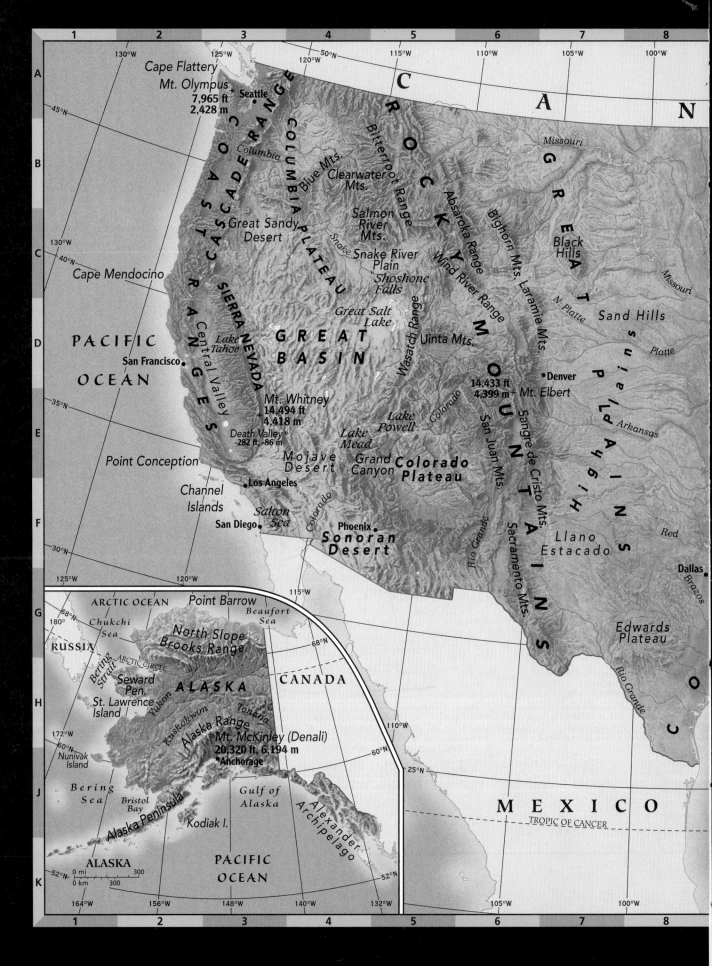

UNITED STATES
STATES
PHYSICAL

0 mi — 300
0 km — 300

ALBERS CONIC EQUAL-AREA PROJECTION

Map labels:

Lake of the Woods

Isle Royale
Lake Superior
Upper Peninsula
Lake Michigan
Lower Peninsula
Lake Huron

Minneapolis
Mississippi
Milwaukee
Chicago
Detroit
Lake Erie
Cleveland

Lake Ontario
Niagara Falls

Lake Champlain
Adirondack Mts.
Green Mts.
White Mts.
Gulf of Maine
Connecticut
Boston
Cape Cod

CENTRAL LOWLAND

Indianapolis
Ohio
St. Louis
Wabash

Pittsburgh
Appalachian Plateau
Allegheny Mts.
Cumberland Plateau
APPALACHIAN MOUNTAINS
Blue Ridge
Piedmont

Philadelphia
Baltimore
Washington
Delaware Bay
Chesapeake Bay
Hudson
New York City
Long Island

ATLANTIC OCEAN

Flint Hills
Ozark Plateau
Boston Mts.
Memphis
Ouachita Mts.
Tennessee
Cumberland

Mt. Mitchell
6,684 ft
2,037 m

Cape Hatteras

Atlanta
Black Belt
Mississippi
Red
Savannah

COASTAL PLAIN

Houston
New Orleans
Mississippi River Delta

Gulf of Mexico

Jacksonville

Cape Canaveral

Lake Okeechobee
The Everglades
Miami

Florida Keys
Straits of Florida
TROPIC OF CANCER

CUBA

Inset — Hawaiian Islands:

Niihau
Kauai
Oahu
Honolulu
Molokai
Lanai
Kahoolawe
Maui—21°N
Hawaii
PACIFIC OCEAN

Mauna Kea
13,796 ft
4,205 m

PRINCIPAL HAWAIIAN ISLANDS

0 mi — 100
0 km — 100

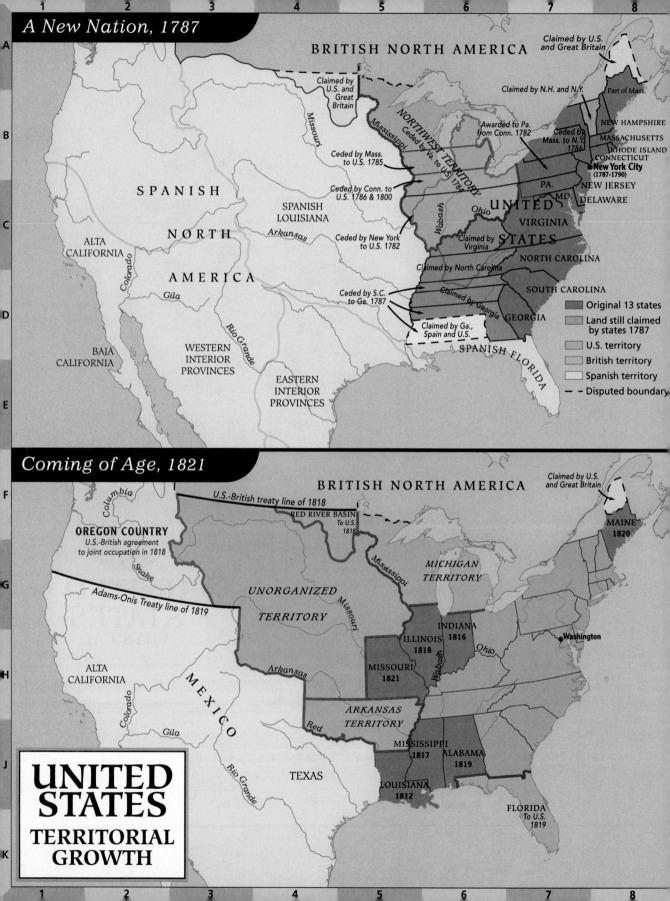

A New Nation, 1787

BRITISH NORTH AMERICA

Claimed by U.S. and Great Britain

Claimed by U.S. and Great Britain

Claimed by N.H. and N.Y.

Part of Mass.

Missouri

NORTHWEST TERRITORY

Mississippi

Ceded by Va. to U.S. 1784

Awarded to Pa. from Conn. 1782

Ceded by Mass. to N.Y. 1786

NEW HAMPSHIRE

MASSACHUSETTS

RHODE ISLAND

CONNECTICUT

Ceded by Mass. to U.S. 1785

New York City (1787-1790)

SPANISH

PA.

NEW JERSEY

NORTH

SPANISH LOUISIANA

Ceded by Conn. to U.S. 1786 & 1800

Arkansas

Wabash

Ohio

UNITED

MD.

DELAWARE

ALTA CALIFORNIA

AMERICA

Ceded by New York to U.S. 1782

VIRGINIA

STATES

Claimed by Virginia

NORTH CAROLINA

Claimed by North Carolina

Colorado

Gila

Ceded by S.C. to Ga. 1787

Claimed by Georgia

SOUTH CAROLINA

BAJA CALIFORNIA

WESTERN INTERIOR PROVINCES

Rio Grande

GEORGIA

Claimed by Ga., Spain and U.S.

EASTERN INTERIOR PROVINCES

SPANISH FLORIDA

■	Original 13 states
■	Land still claimed by states 1787
■	U.S. territory
■	British territory
□	Spanish territory
- - -	Disputed boundary

Coming of Age, 1821

BRITISH NORTH AMERICA

Claimed by U.S. and Great Britain

Columbia

U.S.-British treaty line of 1818

RED RIVER BASIN To U.S. 1818

OREGON COUNTRY
U.S.-British agreement to joint occupation in 1818

MAINE 1820

Snake

Mississippi

MICHIGAN TERRITORY

UNORGANIZED

Adams-Onis Treaty line of 1819

TERRITORY

Missouri

ALTA CALIFORNIA

M E X I C O

Arkansas

ILLINOIS 1818

INDIANA 1816

Wabash

Ohio

•Washington

MISSOURI 1821

Colorado

Gila

ARKANSAS TERRITORY

Red

MISSISSIPPI 1817

ALABAMA 1819

Rio Grande

TEXAS

LOUISIANA 1812

FLORIDA To U.S. 1819

UNITED STATES TERRITORIAL GROWTH

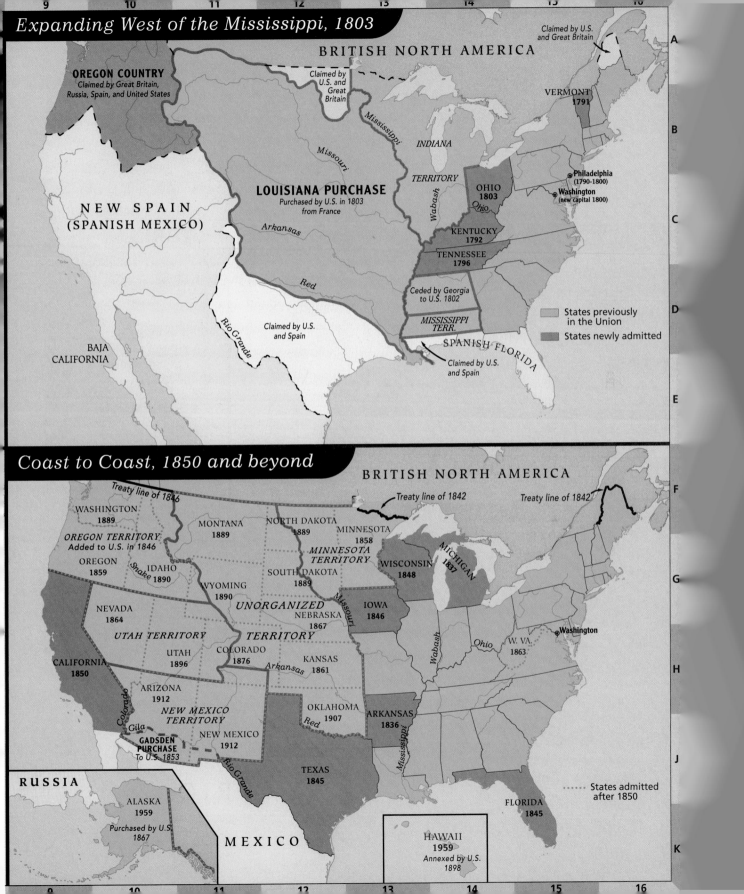

Expanding West of the Mississippi, 1803

BRITISH NORTH AMERICA

Claimed by U.S. and Great Britain

OREGON COUNTRY
Claimed by Great Britain, Russia, Spain, and United States

Claimed by U.S. and Great Britain

VERMONT **1791**

Mississippi

Missouri

INDIANA

TERRITORY

OHIO **1803**

Ohio

Philadelphia (1790–1800)

Washington (new capital 1800)

LOUISIANA PURCHASE
Purchased by U.S. in 1803 from France

NEW SPAIN
(SPANISH MEXICO)

Arkansas

Wabash

KENTUCKY **1792**

TENNESSEE **1796**

Ceded by Georgia to U.S. 1802

Red

Rio Grande

Claimed by U.S. and Spain

MISSISSIPPI TERR.

SPANISH FLORIDA

BAJA CALIFORNIA

Claimed by U.S. and Spain

| | States previously in the Union |
| | States newly admitted |

Coast to Coast, 1850 and beyond

BRITISH NORTH AMERICA

Treaty line of 1846

Treaty line of 1842

Treaty line of 1842

WASHINGTON **1889**

MONTANA **1889**

NORTH DAKOTA **1889**

MINNESOTA **1858**

MINNESOTA TERRITORY

MICHIGAN **1837**

OREGON TERRITORY
Added to U.S. in 1846

OREGON **1859**

Snake

IDAHO **1890**

WYOMING **1890**

SOUTH DAKOTA **1889**

WISCONSIN **1848**

NEVADA **1864**

UTAH TERRITORY

UNORGANIZED

NEBRASKA **1867**

Missouri

IOWA **1846**

Washington

TERRITORY

W. VA. **1863**

CALIFORNIA **1850**

UTAH **1896**

COLORADO **1876**

KANSAS **1861**

Arkansas

Wabash

Ohio

ARIZONA **1912**

NEW MEXICO TERRITORY

OKLAHOMA **1907**

Red

ARKANSAS **1836**

Colorado

Gila

GADSDEN PURCHASE
To U.S. 1853

NEW MEXICO **1912**

Mississippi

RUSSIA

ALASKA **1959**

Purchased by U.S. 1867

Rio Grande

TEXAS **1845**

MEXICO

FLORIDA **1845**

HAWAII **1959**
Annexed by U.S. 1898

| States admitted after 1850 |

EUROPE

Black Sea

Sea of Marmara

Istanbul

ANATOLIA

★ **Ankara**

TURKEY

TUNISIA

★ **Tunis**

Taurus Mountains

CYPRUS

• **Aleppo**

SYRIA

LEBANON — **Damascus** ★

Beirut

Tripoli ★

Mediterranean Sea

ISRAEL

Syrian Desert

Jerusalem ★

★ **Amman**

•**Alexandria**

★ **Cairo**

JORDAN

• **El Giza**

Sinai Pen.

See inset below

LIBYA

EGYPT

Nile R.

Hejaz

Eastern Mediterranean Area

TURKEY

N ↑

CYPRUS

• **Aleppo**

SYRIA

Mediterranean Sea

LEBANON

Beirut ★

★ **Damascus**

Sea of Galilee

Golan Heights

Jordan River

Tel Aviv–Jaffa

West Bank

Suez Canal

Jerusalem ★

★ **Amman**

Gaza Strip

Dead Sea

ISRAEL

JORDAN

El Giza • ★ **Cairo**

30°N

EGYPT

SAUDI ARABIA

Aswan High Dam

SAHARA

Boundary claimed by Sudan

Red Sea

Nile River

Gulf of Suez

Gulf of Aqaba

SUDAN

AFRICA

0 mi   100

0 km   100

★ **Khartoum**

Red Sea

30°E

Aral Sea

UZBEKISTAN

⊛ Tashkent

TAJIKISTAN

TURKMENISTAN

Dushanbe

Caucasus Mountains

GEORGIA
Tbilisi ⊛

Yerevan ⊛
ARMENIA

Baku ⊛

Caspian Sea

A S I A

⊛ Ashkhabad

Kabul ⊛

Mt. Ararat
(16,854 ft
5,137 m)

AZERBAIJAN

Mashhad ●

AFGHANISTAN

Elburz Mountains

⊛ Tehran

Plateau
of Iran

Tigris R.

Zagros Mountains

IRAQ

⊛ Baghdad

IRAN

PAKISTAN

Euphrates R.

Al Basrah ●

KUWAIT

Kuwait ⊛

Persian Gulf
(Arabian Gulf)

Gulf of Oman

TROPIC OF CANCER

Arabian
Sea

Manama
BAHRAIN

QATAR
⊛ Doha

Abu
Dhabi

Masqat ⊛

SAUDI
ARABIA

⊛ Riyadh

UNITED
ARAB
EMIRATES

OMAN

ARABIAN
PENINSULA

Makkah
(Mecca) ●

Asir

Rub al Khali
(Empty Quarter)

YEMEN

Sanaa ⊛

N

⊛

MIDDLE EAST

PHYSICAL / POLITICAL

0 mi   500

0 km   500

AZIMUTHAL EQUIDISTANT PROJECTION

Aden ●

Gulf of Aden

Thinking Like a
HIST◉RIAN

WHAT DOES A HISTORIAN DO?

A historian is a person who studies and writes about the people and events of the past. Historians find out how people lived, what happened to them, and what happened around them. They look for the causes of events and the effects of those events.

We study history so we can understand what happened in the past. Understanding what happened to others can help us make sense of current events—things taking place today. It can also help us predict what might happen in the future so we can make better decisions about today and tomorrow.

Have you ever wondered if you could be a historian? To answer that question, you will need to find out how historians conduct research and write about history. Historians use a number of tools to research, or collect information about, their subjects. They also use special tools to organize information. You will learn about these tools in the next few pages and throughout this textbook.

By studying sites where people lived and examining the objects they made and used, we can learn about the lives of people who lived in the past.

MEASURING TIME

One challenge when studying history is knowing when events took place. Which event happened first? How far apart in time did events take place? We use different tools to measure time.

Calendars A calendar is a system for breaking time into units and keeping track of those units. With a calendar, you can measure how much time has passed between events. You can describe that time, for example, in months and years.

The dates in this book are based on the Western calendar. In the Western calendar, a year is 365 days. The calendar begins at the birth of Jesus. The years before this date are known as B.C., or "before Christ." Years after are called A.D., or *anno domini*, which is Latin for "in the year of the Lord." Some people also use C.E., or "common era," and B.C.E., or "before common era."

To date events that took place before B.C., historians count backward from A.D. 1. There is no year 0. The year before A.D. 1 is 1 B.C. The year before that is 2 B.C. To date events after "A.D.," historians count forward. The year after A.D. 1 is A.D. 2.

Throughout history, different cultures have developed different calendars.

Reading a Time Line Historians are interested in chronology, or the order in which events happen. An easy way to keep track of chronology is to use or make a time line. A *time line* is a diagram showing the order of events within a period of time.

Along a time line, each section represents a period of time. A time line also has labels for events. The labels appear near the date on the time line when the event took place.

Gianni Dagli Orti/CORBIS

U.S. AND WORLD HISTORY 1855–1870

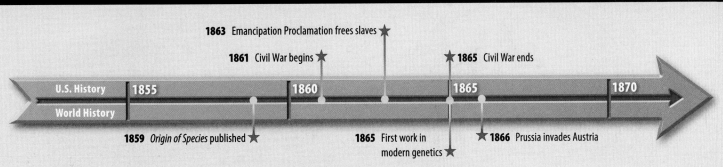

1863 Emancipation Proclamation frees slaves ★

1861 Civil War begins ★

1865 Civil War ends

U.S. History | 1855 | 1860 | 1865 | 1870

World History

1859 *Origin of Species* published ★

1865 First work in modern genetics ★

★ **1866** Prussia invades Austria

ANALYZING SOURCES

Suppose a teacher has asked you to write a paper about the space program. Where would you get the information you need to begin writing? You would look for two types of information—primary and secondary sources.

Primary sources are descriptions or pictures of an event by someone who actually saw or lived through that event. In other words, if you see a rocket launch in person and then write about it, you are creating a primary source. Written impressions of any others who watched at the same time are primary sources, too. Diaries, journals, photographs, and eyewitness reports are examples of primary sources.

Secondary sources usually come from people who were not present at an event. A book about the history of the space program is a secondary source. The author of the book collected information from many sources. He or she then combined this information into something new. Textbooks, biographies, and histories are secondary sources.

Note that a secondary source may use primary sources. In this textbook, you will see and read excerpts from many primary sources. The book itself, however, is a secondary source.

To analyze primary sources, try to answer the five "W" questions:

CLASSIFYING PRIMARY SOURCES

- **Printed publications** include newspapers, magazines, and books. Web sites and e-mails are also printed publications that appear in electronic format.
- **Songs and poems** are often good sources of information because they describe events and reactions to them.
- **Visual materials** include original paintings, drawings, photographs, films, and maps. Political cartoons and other types of cartoons are also visual primary sources.
- **Oral histories** are interviews that are recorded to collect people's memories and observations about their lives and experiences.
- **Personal records** include diaries, journals, and letters.
- **Artifacts** are tools or ornaments that were used by people in the past.

1. **Who** created the primary source?
2. **Why** was the source created—what was its purpose and its intended audience?
3. **What** is the source about?
4. **Where** was the source created?
5. **When** was the source created?

Answering these questions can help you find the historical significance of a primary source. Ask yourself these questions as you look at the following primary sources.

Personal Records and Artifacts

The Native Americans of the Plains used the skins of the animals they hunted to make a number of everyday items. This Sioux deerskin bag (above) is decorated with beads. The mortar, a vessel used for grinding, and the serpent figure (right) are other artifacts left behind by ancient cultures.

The letters from Abraham Lincoln (above right) and Dr. Martin Luther King, Jr., are personal records. The photographs are also examples of primary sources.

Letters and Visual Materials

66 We have waited for more than 340 years for our constitutional and God-given rights. . . . [W]e still creep at horse and buggy pace toward gaining a cup of coffee at a lunch counter. Perhaps it is easy for those who have never felt the stinging darts of segregation to say, 'Wait.' . . . Let us all hope that the dark clouds of racial prejudice will soon pass away. 99

—Dr. Martin Luther King, Jr., "Letter from Birmingham Jail," April 1963

As Dr. Martin Luther King, Jr., sat in an Alabama cell, he wrote his famous "Letter from Birmingham Jail."

During the Great Depression of the 1930s, people struggled to survive. This photo shows one example of people affected by tough economic times.

CHARTS, DIAGRAMS, AND GRAPHS

Charts, diagrams, and graphs are ways of displaying types of information such as percentages, numbers, and amounts. They help organize this information and make it easier to read.

Charts Charts present facts and numbers in an organized way. One type of chart is a table. A table arranges data, especially numbers, in rows and columns for easy reference. People also use charts to summarize ideas or main points of broader topics. This allows you to review material and compare main ideas easily.

Chart Skill

Rank	Civil War	World War II 1942	Vietnam War 1965	Iraq War 2007
Private	*$13	$50	$85	$1,203–1,543
Corporal	$14	$66	$210	$1,700
Sergeant	$17	$78	$261	$1,854–2,339
Sergeant Major	$21	$138	$486	$4,110

*Until 1864, African Americans in the Civil War were paid $7 per month.
Source: Bureau of Economic Analysis; *Princeton Review*; www.militaryfactory.com

This chart shows information about monthly army salaries.

▶ **CRITICAL THINKING**
Comparing What two types of comparisons are possible using this chart?

Diagram Skill

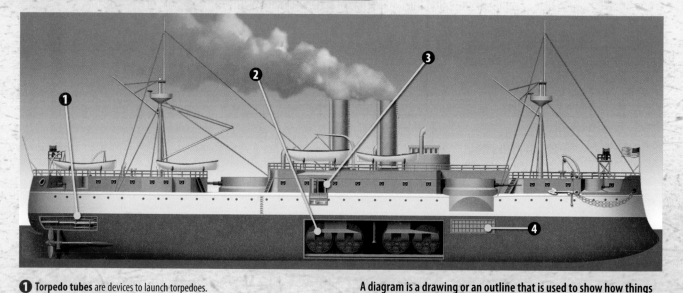

1 **Torpedo tubes** are devices to launch torpedoes.
2 **Steam boilers** power the engines.
3 **Munitions** are stored in the magazine.
4 **Cowls** provide fresh air below deck.

A diagram is a drawing or an outline that is used to show how things work or to show how parts relate to each other. This diagram shows an old U.S. warship, the USS *Maine* (1895).

▶ **CRITICAL THINKING**
Analyzing Why is a diagram a better choice for displaying this information than a chart?

Diagrams Diagrams are drawings that show steps in a process, point out the parts of an object, or explain how something works. Diagrams are sometimes called "infographics."

Graphs Graphs present numbers visually. This makes the numbers easier to understand. The types of graphs you will find in this textbook are described and displayed below:

- Circle graphs show how the whole of something is divided.
- Bar graphs use bars to compare numbers visually. They compare different items or groups. Bar graphs can also compare items at different points in time.
- Line graphs can be used to show how something changes over time. Rather than showing data for only specific points in time, line graphs show a continuous line of data.

Graph Skill

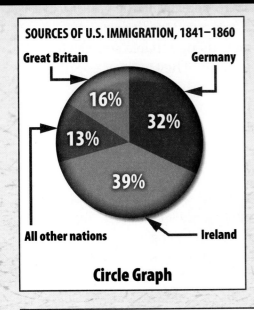

SOURCES OF U.S. IMMIGRATION, 1841–1860

Great Britain — 16%
Germany — 32%
All other nations — 13%
Ireland — 39%

Circle Graph

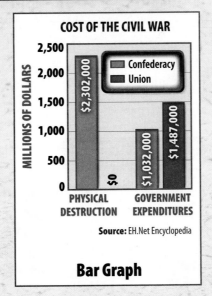

COST OF THE CIVIL WAR

MILLIONS OF DOLLARS

Confederacy
Union

PHYSICAL DESTRUCTION: $2,302,000 / $0
GOVERNMENT EXPENDITURES: $1,032,000 / $1,487,000

Source: EH.Net Encyclopedia

Bar Graph

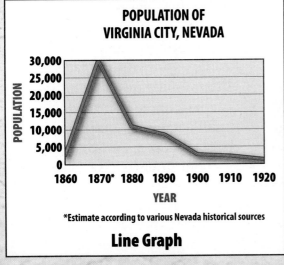

POPULATION OF VIRGINIA CITY, NEVADA

POPULATION

30,000
25,000
20,000
15,000
10,000
5,000
0

1860 1870* 1880 1890 1900 1910 1920

YEAR

*Estimate according to various Nevada historical sources

Line Graph

CRITICAL THINKING SKILLS

Studying history is about more than reading sources and viewing pictures or graphs. Historians use many thinking skills.

Understanding Cause and Effect A *cause* is an action or a situation that produces an event. What happens as a result of a cause is an *effect*. Understanding cause and effect means thinking about *why* an event occurred. It helps you see how one thing can lead to another. Such an understanding can help you plan to encourage or prevent the same event in the future.

Predicting Consequences Predicting future events is difficult. Sometimes, though, you can use knowledge of how certain causes led to certain effects in the past to make a prediction. For example, if you know that conflicts over borders have often led to war, you might be able to predict the outcome of a current border dispute.

Distinguishing Fact from Opinion To determine the validity of sources and find answers in a text, you need to distinguish facts from opinions. You can check facts using reliable sources to determine whether or not they are accurate. They answer specific questions such as: What happened? Who did it?

Opinions are based on values and beliefs. They are not true, and they are not false. Opinions often begin with phrases such as *I believe . . .* , or they contain words such as *should, ought, best, worst,* or *greatest.*

Drawing Inferences and Conclusions

When you make an *inference*, you "read between the lines" to figure out something that is not stated directly. A *conclusion* is an understanding based on details or facts you read or hear.

Follow these steps to draw inferences and conclusions from a piece of writing:

- Read carefully for key facts and ideas, and list them.
- Summarize the information.
- Recall what you already know about the topic.
- Use your knowledge and insight to develop some inferences and conclusions about the passage.

In 1983, 20 years after Dr. Martin Luther King, Jr.'s March on Washington, a huge crowd gathered once again in the nation's capital. Comparing photographs of the two events can help you see how they were similar and how they were different.

MAKING COMPARISONS

When making comparisons, you examine two or more things. Among the things to compare are documents, events, and images. Compare these two photographs.

▶ **CRITICAL THINKING**
Comparing and Contrasting What similarities do you see? How are the images different?

Making Comparisons To make a comparison, look for similarities among ideas or objects. You can also examine contrasts—qualities that make each of the ideas or objects unique. Making comparisons can help you choose among several possible alternatives.

To make comparisons and contrasts, examine the texts, images, or other items and follow these steps:

- Select the items to compare.
- Determine what you are comparing. For example, you might compare a topic or a point of view. Look for similarities within these categories.
- Look for differences that set the items apart from each other.

Thinking Like a HISTORIAN

Review Vocabulary

1. Use the terms *calendar* and *chronology* in a sentence that explains their role in the study of history.

Answer the Guiding Questions

2. *Describing* Describe the role and purpose of the historian.

3. *Explaining* Why is it important to understand the order in which events occurred?

4. *Defining* Give three examples of primary sources.

5. *Describing* What is the purpose of graphs, charts, and diagrams?

6. **PERSONAL WRITING** Write a short essay in which you express why you think it is important to read about, study, and understand the past.

WHAT IS GEOGRAPHY?

Geography is the study of Earth and its people. A geographer tries to understand a place—not just where it is, but what it is like, what takes place there, and how the people there live.

To help them build this understanding, geographers organize their study into themes, or subjects. For example, geographers often speak of the five themes of geography: location, place, regions, movement, and human-environment interaction.

- **Location** describes where something is. Geographers describe location in two ways. Absolute location is the exact position on Earth where a geographic feature, such as a city or mountain, is found. Relative location describes where a geographic feature is located in relation to another feature.

- **Place** explores the physical and human features that make a city, state, or country unique. The Grand Canyon and the Hoover Dam are examples of features that make Arizona a special place.

- **Regions** are areas that share common features. A region may be land, water, or a specific area in a city or state. For instance, New England is a region in the northeastern United States. The West Coast is a region bordering the Pacific Ocean and includes the states of California, Oregon, and Washington.

The technology used for navigation has changed a lot over the centuries. The compass and astrolabe (below right) have given way to the global positioning system (GPS), below.

George Rose/Getty Images Entertainment/Getty Images

Geography explores different places and the people who live in those places.

- **Movement** explains how and why people, things, and ideas move. For instance, a group of people might move for various reasons. Ideas spread from one place to another. Both types of movement lead to change.

- **Human-environment interaction** explores the relationship between people and their environments. For example, early Native Americans in the southwestern United States used materials from plants, animals, and the land to build their homes and to clothe and feed themselves.

MAPS AND GLOBES

The tools of the geographer include maps and globes. These help us learn more about Earth. Globes and maps serve different purposes, and each has its advantages and disadvantages.

A globe is a round model of Earth. It shows the Earth's shape, its lands, and its bodies of water. The shapes, sizes, and locations of the lands and seas are accurate.

A map is a flat drawing of all or part of Earth's surface. Cartographers, or mapmakers, use complex mathematics to transfer shapes from the round globe to a flat map. Still, all maps distort the shapes of the places they show. Maps can show small areas such as a college campus. They can show the streets in a city, whole continents, or the entire world. Some show places as they exist now. Historical maps show the features of a place at some time in the past.

Understanding Parts of a Map Maps can contain a large amount of information in a small space. In order to understand this information, however, you need to know how to read a map. To read a map, you need to understand the different parts, what they represent, and how they work together. The map on the next page shows some of the most basic map parts.

Studying geography helps us understand Earth—its people, its natural features, and the ways they interact with each other.

CHART SKILL

Maps and globes do similar things, but each has advantages and disadvantages.

1 IDENTIFYING Do maps or globes give a more accurate representation of the shape, size, and location of places on Earth?

2 CRITICAL THINKING
Explaining Why are maps able to show information in greater detail than globes in many cases?

MAPS AND GLOBES

	Advantages	Disadvantages
Globes	• Represent true land shapes, distances, and directions	• Cannot show detailed information • Difficult to carry or transport
Maps	• Show small areas in great detail • Display different types of information, such as population densities or natural resources • Easy to transport	• Distort, or change, the accuracy of shapes and distances

NASA/Corbis

Physical and Political Maps Maps are useful tools. You can use them to show information and make connections between different facts, such as how the location of towns and cities relates to the location of waterways.

Geographers use many different kinds of maps. Maps that show a wide range of information about an area are known as general purpose maps. Two of the most common general purpose maps are physical maps and political maps.

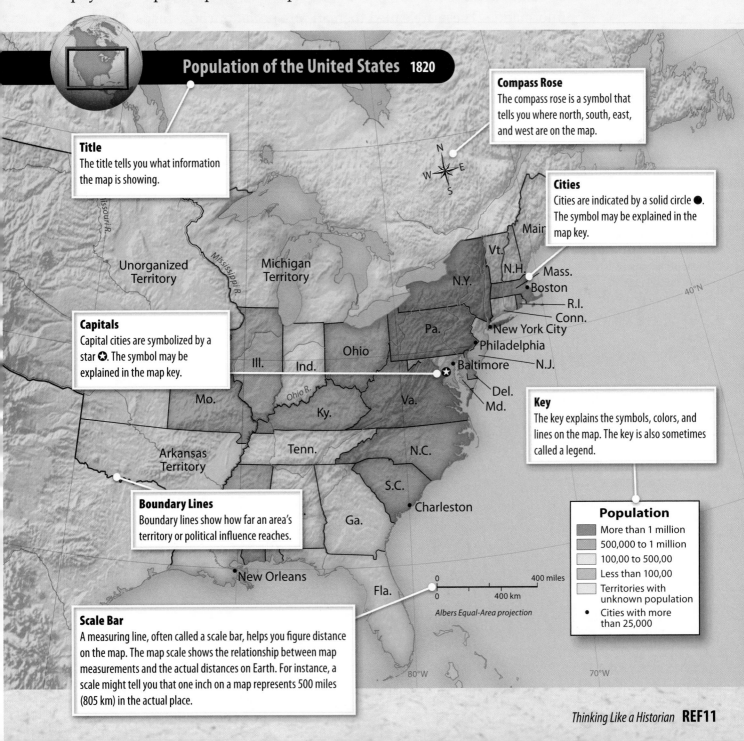

Population of the United States 1820

Title
The title tells you what information the map is showing.

Compass Rose
The compass rose is a symbol that tells you where north, south, east, and west are on the map.

Cities
Cities are indicated by a solid circle ●. The symbol may be explained in the map key.

Capitals
Capital cities are symbolized by a star ✪. The symbol may be explained in the map key.

Key
The key explains the symbols, colors, and lines on the map. The key is also sometimes called a legend.

Boundary Lines
Boundary lines show how far an area's territory or political influence reaches.

Population
	More than 1 million
	500,000 to 1 million
	100,00 to 500,00
	Less than 100,00
	Territories with unknown population
•	Cities with more than 25,000

Scale Bar
A measuring line, often called a scale bar, helps you figure distance on the map. The map scale shows the relationship between map measurements and the actual distances on Earth. For instance, a scale might tell you that one inch on a map represents 500 miles (805 km) in the actual place.

Albers Equal-Area projection

0 — 400 miles
0 — 400 km

Unorganized Territory, Michigan Territory, Missouri R., Mississippi R., Ill., Ind., Ohio, Mo., Ohio R., Ky., Arkansas Territory, Tenn., Va., N.C., S.C., Ga., Fla., New Orleans, Charleston, Pa., N.Y., Vt., N.H., Maine, Mass., Boston, R.I., Conn., New York City, Philadelphia, Baltimore, N.J., Del., Md., 40°N, 80°W, 70°W

Physical maps show landforms and water features. Landforms are natural features on Earth such as deserts, mountains, plains, and plateaus. Physical maps may also show relief, or ups and downs of the Earth's surface, and elevation, the height of an area above sea level.

Political maps show the names and political boundary lines, or borders, of a place. Political maps may also show human-made features, such as cities or transportation routes.

Special Purpose Maps Some maps present specific kinds of information. These are called thematic or special purpose maps. They usually show themes or patterns, or emphasize one subject. For example, special purpose maps may present information on climate or natural resources. They may display where different Native American languages are spoken, what industries are found in an area, or what kind of vegetation grows there.

One type of special purpose map shows population density. A population density map is shown below. Population density refers to how thickly a place is settled—how many people live in each square mile. Cities have a high population density. Rural areas have a low population density. These maps use different colors or dots to show this.

Special purpose maps may also display events that occurred over time. Maps that display historical information, such as voting rights for women (shown top right), are called historical maps. In this textbook, you will study many historical maps.

The special purpose map explores a specific theme. The one below uses red dots to show the population density of the United States.

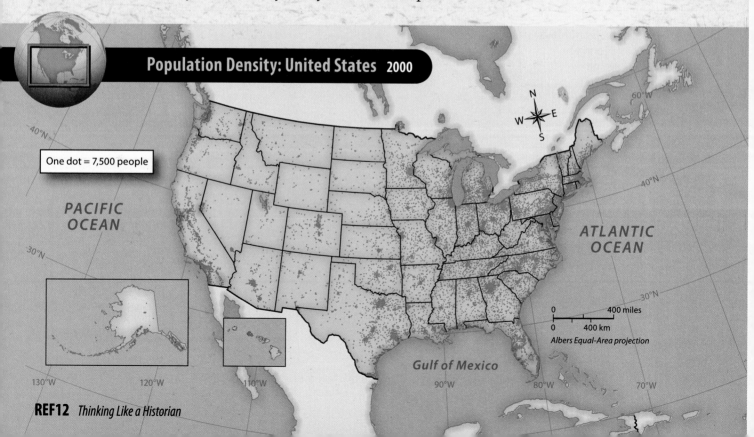

Population Density: United States 2000

One dot = 7,500 people

PACIFIC OCEAN

ATLANTIC OCEAN

Gulf of Mexico

0 — 400 miles
0 — 400 km
Albers Equal-Area projection

40°N
30°N
130°W 120°W 110°W 90°W 80°W 70°W
60°W
40°N
30°N

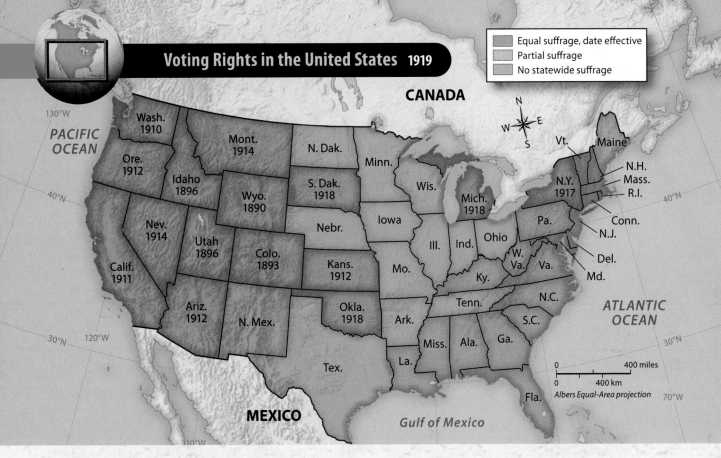

Voting Rights in the United States 1919

Legend:
- Equal suffrage, date effective
- Partial suffrage
- No statewide suffrage

CANADA

PACIFIC OCEAN

130°W

Wash. 1910

Ore. 1912

Mont. 1914

Idaho 1896

N. Dak.

Minn.

S. Dak. 1918

Wis.

Mich. 1918

Vt.

Maine

N.H.
Mass.
R.I.

N.Y. 1917

Wyo. 1890

Nev. 1914

Utah 1896

Colo. 1893

Nebr.

Iowa

Ill.

Ind.

Ohio

Pa.

Conn.

N.J.

Calif. 1911

Kans. 1912

Mo.

Ky.

W. Va.

Va.

Del.

Md.

Ariz. 1912

N. Mex.

Okla. 1918

Ark.

Tenn.

N.C.

S.C.

ATLANTIC OCEAN

Miss.

Ala.

Ga.

Tex.

La.

Fla.

MEXICO

Gulf of Mexico

40°N

30°N

120°W

110°W

70°W

0   400 miles
0   400 km
Albers Equal-Area projection

The historical map above gives data about a time in the past and is a type of special purpose map. This map also includes political information about state borders in 1919.

A physical map (below) calls out landforms and water features.

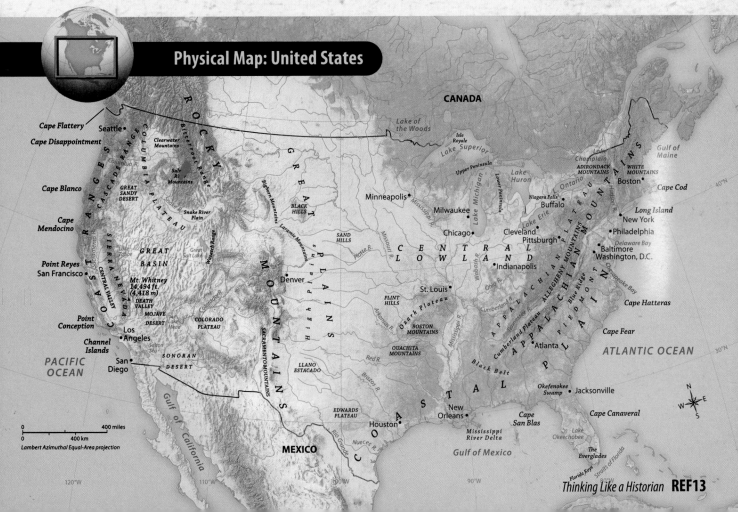

Physical Map: United States

CANADA

Cape Flattery

Seattle

Cape Disappointment

ROCKY

Clearwater Mountains

Bitterroot Range

Columbia R.

Columbia Plateau

GREAT

Lake of the Woods

Isle Royale

Lake Superior

Upper Peninsula

Lower Peninsula

Lake Champlain

ADIRONDACK MOUNTAINS

WHITE MOUNTAINS

Gulf of Maine

Cape Blanco

GREAT SANDY DESERT

Salmon River Mountains

Snake River Plain

Bighorn Mountains

BLACK HILLS

SAND HILLS

Minneapolis

Mississippi R.

Lake Michigan

Milwaukee

Lake Huron

Niagara Falls

L. Ontario

Buffalo

Lake Erie

Boston

Cape Cod

Cape Mendocino

Lake Tahoe

GREAT BASIN

Great Salt Lake

Wasatch Range

Laramie Mountains

PLAINS

Chicago

Cleveland

Pittsburgh

PLATEAU

Long Island

New York

Philadelphia

Point Reyes

San Francisco

SIERRA NEVADA

CENTRAL VALLEY

Mt. Whitney 14,494 ft. (4,418 m)

DEATH VALLEY

Snake R.

Platte R.

Missouri R.

Wabash R.

CENTRAL LOWLAND

Indianapolis

APPALACHIAN MOUNTAINS

ALLEGHENY MOUNTAINS

Delaware Bay

Baltimore

Washington, D.C.

Chesapeake Bay

Point Conception

MOJAVE DESERT

Lake Mead

COLORADO PLATEAU

Colorado R.

FLINT HILLS

St. Louis

Ohio R.

Cumberland R.

Cumberland Plateau

Blue Ridge

PIEDMONT

Cape Hatteras

Channel Islands

Los Angeles

SONORAN DESERT

Salton Sea

High Plains

BOSTON MOUNTAINS

Ozark Plateau

Arkansas R.

Mississippi R.

OUACHITA MOUNTAINS

Tennessee R.

Atlanta

Black Belt

Cape Fear

PACIFIC OCEAN

San Diego

SACRAMENTO MOUNTAINS

LLANO ESTACADO

Red R.

COASTAL

Okefenokee Swamp

Jacksonville

ATLANTIC OCEAN

COAST

RANGES

CASCADE RANGE

MOUNTAINS

EDWARDS PLATEAU

Brazos R.

Houston

New Orleans

Cape San Blas

Lake Okeechobee

PLAIN

Cape Canaveral

MEXICO

Nueces R.

Rio Grande

Gulf of Mexico

Mississippi River Delta

The Everglades

Florida Keys

Straits of Florida

40°N

30°N

0   400 miles
0   400 km
Lambert Azimuthal Equal-Area projection

120°W   110°W   100°W   90°W

Thinking Like a Historian **REF13**

THE ELEMENTS OF GEOGRAPHY

You have read about the five themes of geography. Geographers have also broken down the study of their subject into six essential elements. Thinking about these six elements is another good way to organize your study and understanding of geography.

Several U.S. cities, such as New York and San Francisco (above), have "Chinatowns"—districts heavily influenced by Chinese culture and immigrants. Canadian cities such as Vancouver and Toronto also have Chinatowns.

The World in Spatial Terms When studying a place, geographers are interested in where it is located. Every place has an absolute location and a relative location. *Absolute location* refers to the exact spot of a place on the Earth's surface. For example, the city of St. Louis, Missouri, is located at a specific spot on the Earth—38°37' N latitude and 90°13' W longitude. No other place on Earth has the same absolute location as St. Louis.

Relative location tells where a place is compared with one or more other places. St. Louis is located in the Midwest of the United States, in eastern Missouri, about 295 miles (475 km) southwest of Chicago, Illinois.

Knowing a place's relative location may help a historian understand how it was settled and how its culture developed. For example, Miami, Florida, is the closest large U.S. city to Cuba. This fact helps explain why Miami is home to such a large population of Cuban Americans.

Places and Regions *Place* describes all the characteristics that give an area its own special quality. These can be physical features such as mountains, waterways, climate, and plant or animal life. Places can also be described by human features. These include language, religion, and architecture. If you were trying to tell someone about the town where you live, you would be describing place.

Each place is unique. Still, many places share features in common with others. A *region* is a group of places that share common features.

Physical features, such as a type of landform or plant life, can define regions. Human features, such as religion, language, or industry, also shape regions. For example, the South during the early 1800s was a largely agricultural region. The economy was based on trading agricultural products. The widespread use of slavery also defined the region.

Mitchell Funk/Photographer's Choice/Getty Images

Physical Systems Have you ever wondered where mountains come from or how the oceans formed? What are the factors that cause storms? Earth is subject to powerful forces. These physical systems have shaped the planet.

Physical systems include the complex forces that create weather—wind, rain, snow, and storms. Physical systems make the surface of Earth move and change shape. These forces build mountain ranges, cause earthquakes, and form volcanoes.

Physical systems affect where and how humans live. For example, people will not live on the slopes of an active volcano that could erupt at any time. Almost every place that people choose to live suffers some sort of negative impact from storms, earthquakes, fires, or other physical systems.

Ecosystems are a type of physical system. An ecosystem is a community of living beings and the surroundings in which they live. A lake is an example of an ecosystem. The ecosystem includes the plants, animals, water, and everything that lives beneath the water. Other major ecosystems in the United States include forests, wetlands, grasslands, and deserts.

In an ecosystem, all the creatures and features are connected. A change to one part affects other parts.

Human Systems Geographers are also interested in human systems. A human system includes all the things humans create as they build their lives together on Earth. It includes all the people and their settlements, as well as the cultures they form. It also includes the way different groups of people interact with each other, how they work to get along, and how they settle conflicts when they occur.

Human systems are always changing. Movements of people, ideas, and goods shape the world. At all times of day, people are flying across oceans and continents, delivering goods to distant cities. They are piloting boats filled with goods across the ocean or learning about other cultures through textbooks and the Internet. People move to new places and start new lives. As a result, cultures spread into new areas.

Volcanoes show the powerful impact of physical systems.

ROMEO RANOCO/Reuters/Corbis

Cities like New York City are one form of human system that affects the world. The city has grown significantly over its long history.

Environment and Society

As people, we shape the world in which we live. In turn, the world shapes us. People settle in certain places and change their environment to suit them. For example, people create cities with buildings, streets, and homes. People tunnel through mountains to create roads, and they use nonrenewable resources such as coal to make electricity. People also adapt to the world around them. For example, people drive less when gas prices rise. They use renewable energy sources to heat homes during cold weather.

The relationship between people and their surroundings is an important one. Landforms, waterways, climate, and natural resources have helped and hindered human activities.

People respond to their surroundings in different ways. Sometimes they adjust to them. At other times, people change their environment to meet their needs, such as by planting trees to absorb highway noise.

Human beings have a significant impact on the ecosystem they live in. For instance, your school is a building that took a great amount of time and energy to build. The ground had to be leveled. Workers built walls with wood and concrete. Roads were laid to allow people to come and go from the school. These actions affected the environment, destroying plants and forcing animals to find new places to live.

In April 2010, an explosion on an oil-drilling platform in the Gulf of Mexico killed 11 workers. The blast also triggered the worst oil spill—and the worst human-made environmental disaster—in the nation's history. The spill fouled shorelines from Louisiana to the Florida Panhandle.

Even before the spill, pollution, overexploitation, natural disasters, and environmental changes had taxed the Gulf's ecosystems. These factors impacted the region's environment, marine life, and wildlife, as well as the health and well-being of residents. The disaster added to these effects and threatened the people who relied on the Gulf for their livelihood. Jobs and industry in fishing, agriculture, oil, and trade are at risk. Restoration efforts continue, but long-term effects are still unknown.

The Uses of Geography The story of the United States begins with geography—the study of Earth and all of its variety. Geographic factors—including landforms, waterways, and natural resources—have shaped the history of the nation. Wherever people have lived, their lives have been shaped by the geography around them.

Studying geography introduces you to all the elements of geography—people, places, and environments—and how geographers look at our world. The study of geography allows us to make sense out of varied physical environments, diverse cultural systems, why people live where they do, and how they earn a living.

Knowledge of geography helps people understand the relationships among people, places, and the environment. Just as Native Americans and European explorers used knowledge of geography to live in and explore our land, your ability to understand geography and the tools and technology available for its study will equip you for life in our modern world.

An important part of studying geography is learning about the new technologies available for mapping and understanding where and how we live. These technologies have advanced greatly in recent years. You only need to watch automobile television ads to see how Global Positioning Systems (GPS's) and Geographic Information Systems (GIS's) have made their way into our everyday lives. These tools give geographers and students new ways of expanding their knowledge.

Thinking Like a HISTORIAN

Review Vocabulary

1. Use the following terms in a sentence that explains the relationship between the terms.

   a. globe   **b.** map

2. Use the following terms in a sentence that explains the relationship among the terms.

   a. landforms   **b.** relief   **c.** elevation

Answer the Guiding Questions

3. *Identifying* What are the five themes of geography? Why are they important?

4. *Listing* What are the different disadvantages of globes and maps?

5. *Applying* What is the absolute location of your community? What is the relative location?

6. *Assessing* How do physical systems affect humans?

7. *Speculating* What are two examples of ways that people shape the world they live in? Why do you think people do this?

8. *Explaining* Why is it important to protect our ecosystems?

9. **EXPOSITORY WRITING** What is the definition of a place? Give two examples of places you are familiar with.

SCAVENGER HUNT

NETWORKS contains a wealth of information. The trick is to know where to look to access all the information in the book. If you complete this scavenger hunt exercise with your teachers or parents, you will see how the textbook is organized and how to get the most out of your reading and studying time. Let's get started!

1 How many chapters are in this book?

2 Where in the front of the book can you find a physical map of the United States?

3 What time period does Chapter 3 cover?

4 What is the 21st Century Skills Activity for Chapter 5?

5 Where can you find the Thinking Like a Historian activity in each chapter?

6 What is the title of Chapter 9?

7 What Essential Questions will you answer in Chapter 11?

8 What are the Academic Vocabulary words in Lesson 3, Chapter 12?

9 Where in the back of the book can you find the meaning of vocabulary words such as *mercenary*?

10 Where in the back of the book can you find page numbers for information about Frederick Douglass?

The First Americans

Prehistory to 1492

ESSENTIAL QUESTIONS • What are characteristics that make up a culture? • How do civilizations rise and fall? • What makes a culture unique?

The Story Matters . . .

The year is 1905, but this woman and the rest of her Acoma community are living much as their people did in 1305. The Acoma's culture is shaped by the environment that surrounds them. Their mesa-top village provides natural protection from ancient enemies they have outlasted. In the fields below, they grow crops using methods that have sustained their people in this dry land for hundreds of years. Their artwork—in particular their finely crafted pottery—shows the influences of the shapes and colors of the American Southwest that is their home.

The Acoma are just one example of the hundreds of Native American cultures that developed in the time before Europeans arrived. Their story is part of the rich history of the Americas.

◄ *This Acoma woman lived in what is today western New Mexico.*

Buyenlarge/Archive Photos/Getty Images

1

Place and Time: The Americas c. 1492

By the late 1400s, Native American groups had spread out across most of North America. Groups adapted to the different climates and conditions to form unique cultures.

Step Into the Place

MAP FOCUS Each Native American group had its own features, yet groups within certain areas often shared similar characteristics.

1 REGION How many different culture groups are shown on the map?

2 PLACE According to this map, which part of North America was not populated by Native Americans?

3 CRITICAL THINKING
Speculating What geographic factors do you think might have defined the different culture areas shown on this map?

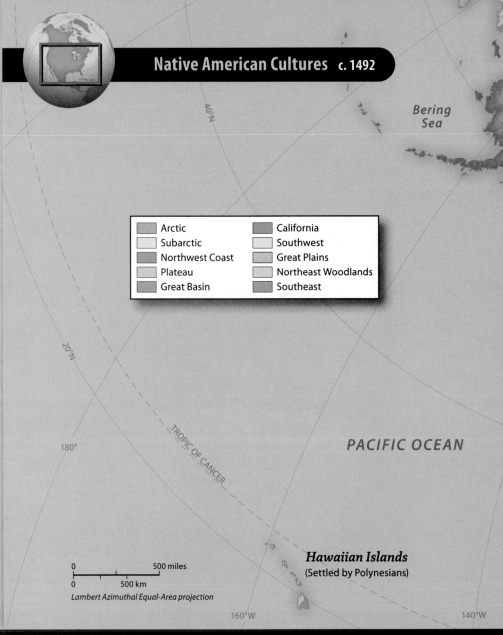

Native American Cultures c. 1492

Bering Sea

- Arctic
- Subarctic
- Northwest Coast
- Plateau
- Great Basin
- California
- Southwest
- Great Plains
- Northeast Woodlands
- Southeast

PACIFIC OCEAN

Hawaiian Islands
(Settled by Polynesians)

40°N
20°N
180°
TROPIC OF CANCER
160°W
140°W

0 — 500 miles
0 — 500 km
Lambert Azimuthal Equal-Area projection

Step Into the Time

TIME LINE Look at the time line. Had human beings reached North America before the end of the last Ice Age? How long after the likely date of human arrival in the Americas did the Olmec civilization emerge?

c. 18,000 B.C. Humans have likely reached the Americas

c. 1200 B.C. Olmec civilization develops in Mexico

AMERICAS
WORLD
PREHISTORY

c. 8,000 B.C.
Ice Age ends

c. 600s B.C.
Construction of Great Wall of China begins

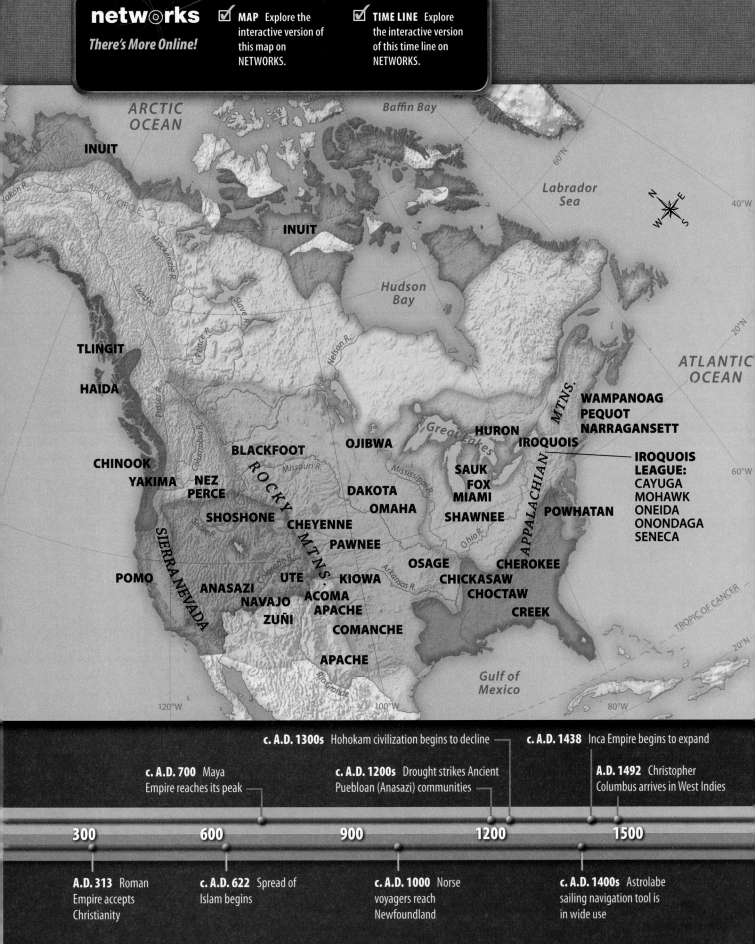

netw✷rks
There's More Online!

☑ **MAP** Explore the interactive version of this map on NETWORKS.

☑ **TIME LINE** Explore the interactive version of this time line on NETWORKS.

ARCTIC OCEAN

Baffin Bay

INUIT

INUIT

Labrador Sea

60°N

40°W

Yukon R.

ARCTIC CIRCLE

Mackenzie R.

Liard R.

Slave R.

Peace R.

Nelson R.

Hudson Bay

20°N

TLINGIT

HAIDA

ATLANTIC OCEAN

Fraser R.

WAMPANOAG
PEQUOT
NARRAGANSETT

Great Lakes

HURON

IROQUOIS

APPALACHIAN MTNS.

CHINOOK

BLACKFOOT

OJIBWA

IROQUOIS
LEAGUE:
CAYUGA
MOHAWK
ONEIDA
ONONDAGA
SENECA

60°W

Columbia R.

Missouri R.

Mississippi R.

YAKIMA

NEZ
PERCE

ROCKY

SAUK
FOX
MIAMI

DAKOTA

Snake R.

SHOSHONE

OMAHA

POWHATAN

CHEYENNE

SHAWNEE

Ohio R.

MTNS.

PAWNEE

SIERRA NEVADA

Colorado R.

Arkansas R.

OSAGE

CHEROKEE

POMO

UTE

KIOWA

CHICKASAW

ANASAZI

ACOMA

CHOCTAW

NAVAJO

APACHE

CREEK

ZUÑI

COMANCHE

TROPIC OF CANCER

APACHE

20°N

Rio Grande

Gulf of Mexico

120°W

100°W

80°W

c. A.D. 1300s Hohokam civilization begins to decline

c. A.D. 700 Maya Empire reaches its peak

c. A.D. 1200s Drought strikes Ancient Puebloan (Anasazi) communities

c. A.D. 1438 Inca Empire begins to expand

A.D. 1492 Christopher Columbus arrives in West Indies

300   600   900   1200   1500

A.D. 313 Roman Empire accepts Christianity

c. A.D. 622 Spread of Islam begins

c. A.D. 1000 Norse voyagers reach Newfoundland

c. A.D. 1400s Astrolabe sailing navigation tool is in wide use

netw⊙rks

There's More Online!

☑ **GRAPHIC ORGANIZER**
Reasons Early Peoples
Migrated

☑ **MAP** Routes to the
Americas

☑ **VIDEO**

NORTH
AMERICA

Lesson 1
Migration to the Americas

ESSENTIAL QUESTION *What are characteristics that make up a culture?*

IT MATTERS BECAUSE
Human history in the Americas began thousands of years ago.

The Migration Begins

GUIDING QUESTION *Who were the first Americans and how did they live?*

The written history of the Americas is several hundred years old, yet human beings have been living on these continents for thousands of years. Where did these people come from? How and when did they get here? How did the different corners of North and South America get settled?

Today, scientists are still seeking answers to these questions. Experts in **archaeology** (AHR•kee•ah•luh•jee), the study of ancient peoples, continue to piece together evidence that tells the story of the first Americans.

Archaeologists have learned a lot about the past from **artifacts** (AHR•tih•fakts)—the tools, weapons, and other objects that early people left behind. Based on this and other types of evidence, archaeologists have offered some possible answers to questions about the first Americans. A widely held theory of recent times is that the first humans might have come to the Americas perhaps 20,000 or more years ago. This theory maintains that early people traveled along a strip of land that once linked Asia and the Americas.

A Land Bridge Revealed

Throughout Earth's history, the climate has changed. Several periods of extreme cold have occurred. The most recent of these ice ages began 100,000 years ago and ended about 12,000 years

(c)Gianni Dagli Orti/CORBIS, (r)Kenneth Garrett

Reading HELPDESK

Taking Notes: *Identifying*

As you read, use a chart like this one to record reasons early peoples migrated from place to place.

Reasons Early Peoples Migrated
1.
2.

Content Vocabulary

• archaeology   • migration   • carbon dating
• artifact   • nomad   • culture
• strait   • maize

4   *The First Americans*

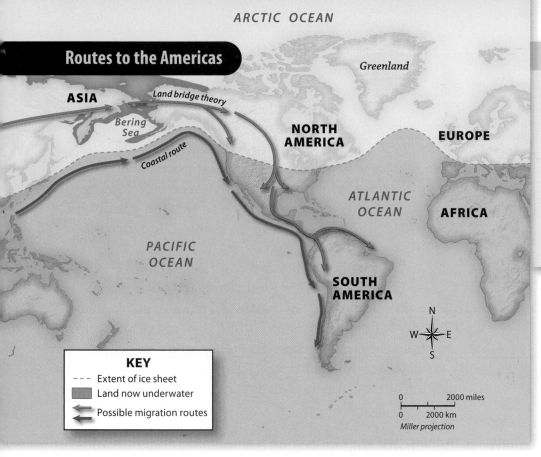

Routes to the Americas

ARCTIC OCEAN

Greenland

ASIA

Land bridge theory

Bering Sea

Coastal route

NORTH AMERICA

EUROPE

ATLANTIC OCEAN

AFRICA

PACIFIC OCEAN

SOUTH AMERICA

KEY
- - - Extent of ice sheet

Land now underwater

Possible migration routes

0   2000 miles
0   2000 km
Miller projection

GEOGRAPHY CONNECTION

Over thousands of years, prehistoric people migrated to and then throughout the Americas.

1 MOVEMENT Based on this map, how did prehistoric people get to North America from Asia?

2 CRITICAL THINKING
Analyzing Why do you think prehistoric people moved from one place in the Americas to another?

ago. During these years, a large share of Earth's water formed huge sheets of ice, or glaciers. The glaciers held so much water that ocean levels were lower. The lower sea level exposed a strip of land—a "land bridge"—connecting northeastern Asia to what is now Alaska. Scientists today call this land bridge Beringia. It now lies beneath the Bering Strait, a body of water named for explorer Vitus Bering. A **strait** is a narrow body of water that connects two larger ones.

Many scientists believe early people traveled from Asia to North America across the land bridge. Yet not all scientists agree on how or when this might have happened. For example, some think people might have come to the Americas by boat. This might have allowed humans to spread faster throughout the Americas. As archaeologists discover new artifacts and evidence, new theories emerge to challenge old ones.

Searching for Hunting Grounds

It is clear, of course, that humans arrived in the Americas. Over centuries, they traveled throughout both continents. In time, settlements stretched as far east as the Atlantic Ocean and as far south as the tip of South America.

archaeology the study of the material remains of ancient peoples
artifact a tool, weapon, or other object left behind by early peoples

strait a narrow passage of water between two larger bodies of water

A single mammoth, which averaged 12 feet (3.7 m) tall, could provide tons of meat, enough to feed a group of people for months.

What is the reason for this **migration** (my•GRAY•shuhn), or movement of people from one area to another? Why did these early Americans travel such distances? The answer may lie in the search for food. Early peoples were **nomads** (NOH•madz), people who moved from place to place in search of hunting grounds. Although they also ate wild grains and fruits, they depended on hunting for much of their food.

The first Americans did, indeed, find huge mammals to hunt. These included giant, shaggy beasts that resembled modern elephants: mastodons and mammoths. Early Americans were skilled at hunting these and other animals. They stalked herds of bison, mastodons, or mammoths, charging at the animals with spears.

Earth Warms

About 15,000 years ago, the Ice Age began to end. Temperatures started to rise, and the glaciers began to melt. Ocean levels rose, and Beringia disappeared beneath the waves, cutting off the land route between Asia and the Americas.

Around the same time, the large mammals on which humans depended for food began to disappear. This might have been the result of overhunting or changes in the climate. The decline in game populations meant that early Americans had to find other **sources** of food.

☑ **PROGRESS CHECK**

Explaining How did the Ice Age expose a land bridge between Asia and the Americas?

Settlement

GUIDING QUESTION *How did agriculture change the way of life for early Americans?*

The constant search for food meant trying new methods. Early Americans caught fish and hunted smaller animals, while also gathering berries and grains. Farming was another new option that began to emerge. Its development would change the nomadic way of life of many groups.

Gianni Dagli Orti/CORBIS

migration the movement of people into a new area
nomad person who moves from place to place

maize a variety of corn
carbon dating a scientific method of determining the age of an artifact
culture a people's shared values, beliefs, traditions, and behaviors

Academic Vocabulary

source a supply
estimate a rough calculation of a number

Learning to Farm

Around 10,000 years ago, people in the area now known as Mexico learned to plant an early form of **maize** (MAYZ), which is a type of corn. These early farmers also planted pumpkins, beans, and squash. The crops provided a steady, reliable source of food. The farming people no longer had to move from place to place to find things to eat. Farming also allowed the people to spend time on activities other than finding food. This resulted in an improvement in the lives of early Americans.

Establishing Unique Cultures

Although some early Americans remained nomadic hunters, many others began to settle down. They built permanent shelters from clay, stone, or wood. They also made pottery and cloth.

Scientists have a method of determining how old an artifact is. Using a process called **carbon dating,** scientists can measure the amount of radioactive carbon in an artifact. They can use this measurement to come up with an **estimate** of the artifact's age. Carbon dating has helped scientists to date some settled North American villages to about 5,000 years ago.

Through the study and dating of artifacts from these villages, scientists know that agriculture changed the lives of early Americans. Common customs and beliefs also grew over time. Eventually, the groups of people living in the Americas developed their own **cultures** (KUHL•churz), or shared traditions and behaviors.

☑ **PROGRESS CHECK**

Identifying What were some changes that affected the nomadic way of life?

─Thinking Like a─
HISTORIAN

Drawing Inferences

Studying artifacts such as this antler or bone tool helps scientists learn about early cultures. Items like this give important clues about the way ancient people lived. For example, scientists may be able to use this tool to infer how early people worked, what foods they ate, and what other tools they may have used. To learn more about Drawing Inferences, review *Thinking Like a Historian.*

By studying tools such as this, archaeologists can learn about the skills and ways of living of the people who made it.

LESSON 1 REVIEW

Review Vocabulary

1. Examine the three terms below. Then write a sentence explaining what the terms have in common.

   a. archaeology

   b. artifact

   c. carbon dating

2. Use the following terms in a sentence about the ancient history of the Americas.

   a. nomad b. migration

Answer the Guiding Questions

3. ***Explaining*** Why might people have migrated from Asia to the Americas?

4. ***Explaining*** What factors likely led some early Americans to change from hunting to farming?

5. ***Describing*** How does carbon dating help scientists learn about early cultures?

6. **EXPOSITORY WRITING** Write a short essay describing how farming changed the lives of early people. Include examples of the types of food they grew.

networks
There's More Online!

☑ **BIOGRAPHY** Malinche

☑ **GRAPHIC ORGANIZER**
Early Civilizations of the Americas

☑ **MAP**
• Civilizations of Mexico and
Central America
• The Inca Empire

☑ **VIDEO**

Lesson 2
Cities and Empires

ESSENTIAL QUESTION *How do civilizations rise and fall?*

IT MATTERS BECAUSE
Early Americans developed rich cultures and complex civilizations in several locations.

Great Civilizations of Mexico, Central America, and South America

GUIDING QUESTION *What civilizations in Mexico, Central America, and South America predated the arrival of Europeans?*

Centuries before the Europeans arrived, great **civilizations** (sih•vuh•luh•ZAY•shuhnz), or highly developed societies, thrived in Mexico, Central America, and South America. The largest and most advanced of these were the Olmec, Maya, Aztec, and Inca.

Each of these civilizations controlled areas covering hundreds of square miles. They included millions of people and lasted for several centuries. The accomplishments of the Olmec, Maya, Aztec, and Inca rivaled any of the great civilizations in other parts of the world. Their people built grand cities in dense forests and on high mountains. They created spectacular works of art and developed advanced tools. They also came up with **complex** methods for tracking time, counting, and writing.

The Olmec
Along the Gulf Coast of what is now Mexico, a people called the Olmec (OHL•mehk) once flourished. Between 1200 B.C. and 800 B.C., the Olmec built stone houses, monuments, and drainage systems. Their farmers grew food for thousands of people. For

(l) Gianni Dagli Orti/CORBIS, (cl) Getty Images, (c) North Wind Picture Archives,
(c) The British Museum/Heritage-Images/The Image Works,
(cl) Manuel Cohen/Getty Images News/Getty Images
(r) Science and Society Picture Library/SSPL/Getty Images

Reading **HELP**DESK

Taking Notes: *Listing*

As you read, use a chart like this to make note of the features of each of the following civilizations. Include when and where they existed, what they accomplished, and other features of their societies.

OLMEC	MAYA	AZTEC	INCA

Content Vocabulary
• civilization
• theocracy
• hieroglyphic
• terrace

8 *The First Americans*

reasons that are not fully understood, the Olmec civilization declined. By about 300 B.C., it had collapsed. Yet the Olmec had a strong influence on the cultures that followed.

The Maya

The Maya (MY•uh) civilization followed the Olmec and reached its peak between A.D. 250 and A.D. 900. Maya farmers planted maize, beans, squash, and other vegetables. These crops helped feed a large population, which may have peaked at 2 million people. These people lived in one of the many large cities the Maya built in the steamy rain forests of present-day Mexico, Guatemala, Honduras, and Belize.

Maya civilization was a **theocracy** (thee•AH•kruh•see), a society ruled by religious leaders. Powerful Maya priests believed the gods were visible in the stars, sun, and moon. Their understanding of astronomy and their advanced mathematics helped them predict eclipses and develop a 365-day calendar. The Maya also developed a system of writing that used **hieroglyphics** (HY•ruh•glih•fihks), symbols or pictures that represent things, ideas, and sounds.

Maya Transport and Trade

The Maya were active traders. Farmers brought maize and vegetables to city markets. They exchanged their goods for items such as cotton cloth, pottery, deer meat, and salt.

Without wheeled vehicles or horses, the Maya carried goods on their backs. Traders traveled on a network of roads that were carved out of the jungle. They also used canoes to ship goods, such as jade statues, turquoise jewelry, and cacao beans used for making chocolate, up and down Mexico's east coast.

Maya Civilization Declines

In time the Maya civilization declined. By about 1200, its once-great cities were nearly deserted. The reason is a mystery. One theory holds that the soil became exhausted and unable to produce enough food for large populations.

Though their civilization declined, the Mayan people did not disappear entirely. Descendants of this great civilization still live in parts of Mexico and Central America today.

This Aztec calendar played an important role in religious as well as daily life. The Maya also had complex calendars.

Each Maya city had at least one stone pyramid, some of which reached about 200 feet (61 m)—the height of a 20-story building. The temples on top of the pyramids were religious and governmental centers.

▶ **CRITICAL THINKING**
Drawing Conclusions What can you conclude about Mayan society based on their ability to build such large structures?

(t) Gianni Dagli Orti/CORBIS, (b) Manuel Cohen/Getty Images News/Getty Images

civilization highly developed society
theocracy a society that is ruled by religious leaders
hieroglyphic a form of writing that uses symbols or pictures to represent things, ideas, and sounds

Academic Vocabulary
complex highly detailed

Malinche (c. 1501–1550)

Much of what we know about individual Native Americans comes from Europeans. Malinche is one example. In 1519 she was enslaved and living under harsh Aztec rule. When the Spanish arrived in 1519, she gave them information about Aztec culture. She also learned Spanish quickly and served as a translator for the Spanish, who called her Doña Marina. Malinche helped build ties between the Spanish and the many unhappy Aztec subjects in the region.

▶ **CRITICAL THINKING**
Making Inferences Why might Malinche have been willing to help the Spanish?

The Aztec Empire

In 1325, centuries after the fall of the Maya, a group of hunters called the Aztec (AZ•tehk) were wandering through central Mexico. They were searching for a permanent home for their people. One day, they came upon an island in Lake Texcoco (tehs•KOH•koh). There they saw what they thought was a sign from their god: an eagle with a snake in its beak sitting on a cactus. According to Aztec legend, this sign indicated that the island was to be their home. It was on this site that the Aztec would build their capital city, Tenochtitlán (tay•NAWCH•teet•LAHN). Today it is the site of Mexico City.

At its height, Tenochtitlán was the largest city in the Americas— and one of the largest in the world. The city was a center of trade, attracting thousands of merchants to its outdoor marketplaces.

Tenochtitlán's construction was a marvel of building skill, knowledge, and human labor. Workers toiled day and night under the direction of priests and nobles. They dug soil from the bottom of the lake to make causeways, or bridges of earth. These causeways **linked** the island and the shore. Elsewhere, they used earth to fill in parts of the lake, creating fields for growing crops.

Aztec Culture

The Aztec created a military empire. In the 1400s, the Aztec army conquered many neighboring communities. Conquered people had to pay tribute in food and other goods. Some were also forced to work as slaves in Aztec cities and villages.

Like Mayan culture, Aztec culture revolved around its religious beliefs. The Aztec believed they must perform human sacrifices to please the gods and ensure abundant harvests. They sacrificed prisoners of war by the thousands for this purpose.

A Great City Remembered

The Aztec Empire was still going strong when Europeans arrived in the Americas in 1492. The first Europeans to see Tenochtitlán were awed by its splendor. In 1519 Hernán Cortés led 550 Spanish soldiers into the Aztec capital. Cortés wrote:

PRIMARY SOURCE

66 There are forty towers at the least, all of stout construction and very lofty. . . . The workmanship both in wood and stone could not be bettered anywhere. 99

—from *Five Letters*

Northwind Picture Archives

Civilizations of Mexico and Central America

MEXICO

Gulf of Mexico

Chichén Itzá •

Lake Texcoco ○ Tenochtitlán

YUCATÁN PENINSULA

Palenque •

• Tikal

PACIFIC OCEAN

100°W 95°W 90°W

20°N

15°N

N W E S

☐ Olmec, c. 900 B.C.
☐ Maya, c. A.D. 750
☐ Aztec, c. A.D. 1500

0 _____ 250 miles
0 _____ 250 km
Lambert Azimuthal Equal-Area projection

GEOGRAPHY CONNECTION

The civilizations that developed in modern-day Mexico and Central America rivaled those that grew in other parts of the world.

1 **PLACE** Which of the empires shown covered the largest area?

2 **CRITICAL THINKING**
Drawing Conclusions
Given what you have read about the Aztec, what do you think is the explanation for the small areas within the Aztec Empire that were not under Aztec control?

Bernal Díaz del Castillo, one of the soldiers, marveled at the "great towers and cues [temples] and buildings rising from the water." Some of the Spanish soldiers thought Tenochtitlán was more magnificent than Rome and the other great European capitals of the time.

☑ **PROGRESS CHECK**

Identifying What was the capital city of the Aztec Empire, and where was it located?

The Great Inca Civilization

GUIDING QUESTION *Why were the Inca considered a highly developed culture?*

In the western highlands of South America, the largest of all early American civilizations grew—the Inca. The Inca people founded their capital city of Cuzco (KOOS•koh) around 1200.

In 1438 the emperor Pachacuti (PAH•chah•KOO•tee) came to the throne. He and his son, Topa Inca, expanded the empire by conquering others with their powerful army. At its peak, the Inca Empire stretched for more than 3,000 miles (4,828 km), from present-day Colombia to northern Argentina and Chile.

This double-headed serpent is an Aztec wood carving covered in turquoise tiles. It may have been worn as a chest decoration during important occasions.

The Inca Empire was divided into four provinces along the western coast of South America. Modern-day countries are bordered and labeled in black.

1 LOCATING In which modern-day countries did the Inca Empire have territory?

2 CRITICAL THINKING
Analyzing How do you think the Andes Mountains shaped and affected the Inca Empire?

The Inca Empire 1532

Fearsome Warriors

The Inca state was built around war. All men between 25 and 50 years old could be drafted to serve in the army for up to five years. Their weapons included clubs, spears, and spiked copper balls on ropes. Using slings, Inca soldiers could throw stones 30 yards (27 m).

Rather than fight this fearsome force, many neighboring areas accepted Inca rule. The Inca allowed those who cooperated to take part in the empire's government. Those who resisted or rebelled faced harsh treatment.

Inca Culture

The Inca people believed their emperor was a descendant of the sun god. The Inca made magnificent gold jewelry and temple ornaments as gifts to the sun god. Inca workers also built great cities devoted to religious ceremonies, including Machu Picchu (MAH•choo PEE•choo), a site hidden high in the Andes Mountains.

Reading **HELP**DESK

terrace a broad platform of flat land cut into a slope

Supporting the large Inca population required a lot of food. In order to farm their mountainous lands, the Inca cut **terraces,** or broad platforms, into steep slopes. Stone walls on the terraces held the soil and plants in place. Inca farmers grew maize, squash, tomatoes, peanuts, chili peppers, cotton, and potatoes.

Managing and ruling over such a large territory was a great challenge. The Inca built at least 10,000 miles (16,093 km) of stone-paved roads to link distant parts of their empire. The roads crisscrossed mountains, deserts, and dense forests. To cross deep canyons or river valleys, the Inca built rope bridges. Runners carried messages to and from the emperor and linked outposts of the empire to Cuzco. The Inca language, Quechua (KEH•chuh•wuh), became the official language for the entire empire. The Inca had no written language, but they did develop a system of recordkeeping using string called quipus (KEE•poos). By knotting different colors of string in special patterns, quipus helped the Inca record and keep track of information about resources, such as grain supplies.

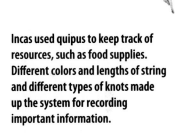

Incas used quipus to keep track of resources, such as food supplies. Different colors and lengths of string and different types of knots made up the system for recording important information.

Like the Aztec, the Inca were thriving in the early 1500s. They, too, would soon come face to face with Spanish soldiers and experience a dramatic change in fortunes.

✓ **PROGRESS CHECK**

Explaining How did the Inca Empire grow so large?

Science and Society Picture Library/SSPL/Getty Images

LESSON 2 REVIEW

Review Vocabulary

1. Use the following terms in a paragraph about the Maya.

   a. civilization

   b. theocracy

   c. hieroglyphic

Answer the Guiding Questions

2. ***Sequencing*** In what chronological order did the great civilizations of Mexico, Central America, and South America appear?

3. ***Describing*** What key features did the great civilizations of Mexico, Central America, and South America have in common?

4. ***Contrasting*** In what ways were the great civilizations of Mexico, Central America, and South America different?

5. **EXPOSITORY WRITING** Consider each of the four civilizations detailed in the lesson. Write a short essay discussing what life might have been like in one of these societies. Use facts from the chapter to add details to your writing.

netw⊙rks
There's More Online!

☑ **BIOGRAPHY**
Dekanawidah

☑ **GRAPHIC ORGANIZER**
Describing Ancient Native
Americans

☑ **GAME**

☑ **MAP** Significant Adena, Hopewell,
and Mississippian Sites

☑ **VIDEO**

Lesson 3
North American Peoples

ESSENTIAL QUESTION *What makes a culture unique?*

IT MATTERS BECAUSE
Early Native American groups of North America adapted to their environments.

Early North American Cultures

GUIDING QUESTION *What did the Adena, Hopewell, Mississippian, Hohokam, and Ancient Puebloan cultures have in common?*

As in Mexico, Central America, and South America, advanced cultures developed in parts of North America that are now the United States long before Europeans arrived in the 1500s. Among these cultures were the Adena, Hopewell, and Mississippians in the central and eastern regions of the present-day United States. The Hohokam and the Ancient Puebloans emerged in the southwestern region.

The Adena, Hopewell, and Mississippian Cultures

In central and eastern North America, prehistoric Native Americans built thousands of earthen mounds, or earthworks. The earthworks were not created by a single group but by many different peoples. Scientists have sometimes referred to these different peoples together as the Mound Builders.

The ancient earthworks take many different forms. One famous example is in the shape of a serpent. Some resemble the pyramids of the Maya and the Aztec. Some contained burial chambers, and others were topped with temples. This seems to indicate that cultures of Mexico and Central America, such as the Maya and Aztec, may have influenced some of these cultures.

(l) Doug Pensinger/Getty Images Sport/Getty Images, (cl) SSPL/Getty Images, (c) Chris Cheadle/All Canada Photos/Corbis, (cr) Peabody Essex Museum, Salem, MA/Bridgeman Art Library, (r) Stock Montage/Alamy Images

Reading **HELP**DESK

Taking Notes: *Describing*

As you read, use a chart like this one to make notes about each of the ancient cultures given.

Adena, Hopewell, and Mississippians	Hohokam	Ancient Puebloans

Content Vocabulary
• **irrigate**
• **federation**
• **clan**

14 *The First Americans*

Archaeologists have classified these earthwork-building cultures into three groups: the Adena, Hopewell, and Mississippian cultures. Modern-day scientists named the groups. No one knows what these early peoples called themselves.

The Adena were hunters and gatherers who lived in the Ohio River valley from about 800 B.C. to A.D. 100. The Hopewell people came later, between 200 B.C. and A.D. 500. The Hopewell were farmers and traders who built huge burial earthworks in the shapes of birds, bears, and snakes. Within these earthworks, archaeologists have discovered freshwater pearls, shells, cloth, and copper. These finds indicate that the Hopewell trade networks extended for hundreds of miles.

Cahokia

Sometime after A.D. 900, a people now called the Mississippians built the largest known earthworks complex in present-day Illinois. Later named Cahokia (kuh•HOH•kee•uh), the complex might have had 20,000 or more residents. Surrounded by farms and settlements, Cahokia became the center of Mississippian culture.

Cahokia appears to have resembled the ancient cities of Mexico. A great pyramid-shaped earthwork dominated Cahokia. Known as Monks Mound, it rose nearly 100 feet (30 m).

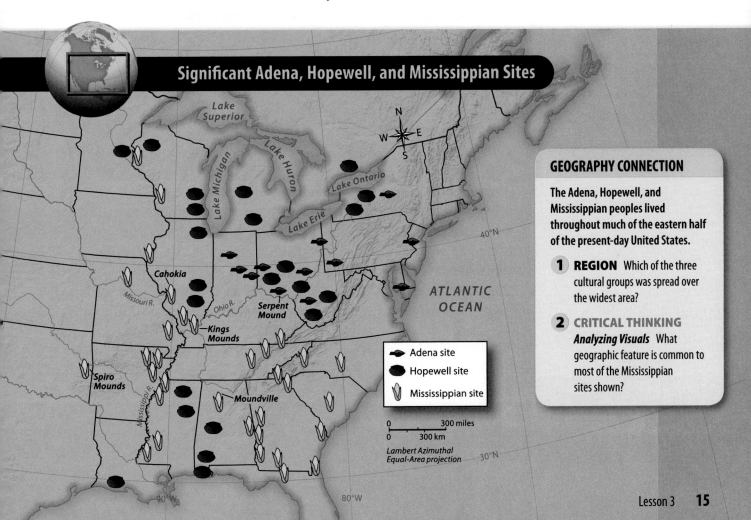

Significant Adena, Hopewell, and Mississippian Sites

Lake Superior
Lake Michigan
Lake Huron
Lake Ontario
Lake Erie
Cahokia
Missouri R.
Ohio R.
Serpent Mound
Kings Mounds
Spiro Mounds
Mississippi R.
Moundville
ATLANTIC OCEAN
40°N
30°N
90°W
80°W

Adena site
Hopewell site
Mississippian site

0   300 miles
0   300 km
Lambert Azimuthal Equal-Area projection

GEOGRAPHY CONNECTION

The Adena, Hopewell, and Mississippian peoples lived throughout much of the eastern half of the present-day United States.

1 REGION Which of the three cultural groups was spread over the widest area?

2 CRITICAL THINKING
Analyzing Visuals What geographic feature is common to most of the Mississippian sites shown?

Ancient cliff dwellings are preserved at Mesa Verde National Park in Colorado. The largest cliff dwelling is Cliff Palace, which could shelter up to 250 people.

A temple crowned the summit of Monks Mound. A legend of the Natchez people, descendants of the Mississippians, hints of a direct link to Mexico:

PRIMARY SOURCE

❝ Before we came into this land, we lived yonder, under the sun. [the speaker pointed toward Mexico] . . . Our entire nation extended along the great water [the Gulf of Mexico] where this great river (the River St. Louis) loses itself. ❞

—Natchez legend

The Hohokam

From about A.D. 200 to A.D. 1400, the Hohokam (hoh•hoh•KAHM) culture flourished in the dry, hot desert of present-day Arizona. As with the Adena, Hopewell, and Mississippian cultures, the name *Hohokam* was given to this culture in modern times.

As desert dwellers, the Hohokam were experts at maximizing their few sources of water. They **irrigated** (IHR•uh•gayt•uhd), or brought water to, their corn, cotton, and other crops by digging hundreds of miles of **channels.** The Hohokam also produced pottery, carved stone, and etched shells with acid. The shells serve as evidence of trade with coastal peoples.

The Ancient Puebloans

The Four Corners is the place where the modern-day states of Utah, Colorado, Arizona, and New Mexico meet. It was in this region that the Ancient Puebloans (PWEH•bloh•uhnz) lived at about the same time as the Hohokam—from about A.D. 1 to A.D. 1300. In the past, these people were called the Anasazi, but descendants of the Ancient Puebloans dislike that name.

The Ancient Puebloans built great stone dwellings that Spanish explorers later called **pueblos** (PWEH•blohs), or villages. Visitors to New Mexico today can still see one of the most spectacular of these ancient settlements, Pueblo Bonito. The huge **structure** was at least four stories high and had hundreds of rooms. Around Pueblo Bonito, archaeologists have found traces of a complex network of roads. These roads linked the pueblo with other villages. They suggest that Pueblo Bonito may have been a center for trade or religion.

(t) Doug Pensinger/Getty Images Sport/Getty Images, (b) Tom Bean/CORBIS

Reading **HELP**DESK

irrigate to supply water to crops by artificial means

Academic Vocabulary

channel a long, narrow gutter or groove through which water can flow

structure a building

Visual Vocabulary

pueblo a communal Native American structure with a flat roof; a type of Native American village

The Ancient Puebloans also built dwellings in the walls of steep cliffs. Cliff dwellings were easy to defend and offered protection from winter weather. One of the largest cliff dwellings is Mesa Verde (MAY•suh VUHR•dee) in Colorado. This ancient, complex structure was home to several thousand people.

The Ancient Puebloans began leaving their pueblos and cliff dwellings for smaller communities in about 1300. They might have abandoned their large villages when drought, a long period of little rainfall, destroyed their crops.

☑ **PROGRESS CHECK**

Describing Name two types of dwellings for which the Ancient Puebloans are known.

The Native Americans Circa 1492

GUIDING QUESTION *How did early Native Americans adapt to their environment?*

While the Hohokam, Ancient Puebolan, and the Adena, Hopewell, and Mississippian civilizations eventually faded away, other Native American cultures arose to take their place. In the time before European arrival in the late 1400s, many unique societies flourished throughout North America. Within different regions, different groups shared common features. These features reflected the conditions within each region.

Northern Peoples

A people called the Inuit (IH•noo•wuht) settled the frigid lands at the northernmost part of North America, near the Arctic Ocean. Some scientists believe the Inuit were the last migrants to come from Asia to North America.

The Inuit may have originally come from the Asian region of Siberia, bringing with them the skills needed to survive the cold climate. In the winter, the Inuit built igloos, low-lying structures of snow blocks, which protected them from severe weather.

The Inuit were skilled hunters and fishers. In the coastal waters, they hunted whales, seals, and walruses in small, skin-covered boats called kayaks. On land they hunted caribou, large deerlike animals that lived in the far North. The Inuit made warm, waterproof clothing from caribou skins and seal skins. They burned seal oil in lamps.

The Inuit people of the far North developed tools and techniques for living in a frozen and watery land.

Build Vocabulary: *Word Origins*

The words *igloo* and *kayak* are two examples of the many English-language words that come from Native American languages. Other examples include the words *tomahawk, moose,* and *moccasin.*

Western Peoples

The western coast of North America has a mostly mild climate and dependable food sources. Such favorable conditions helped many native groups in this region thrive.

The Tlingit (TLIHNG•kuht), Haida (HY•duh), and Chinook (shuh•NUK) lived on the northwestern coast of North America in what are now Canada, southern Alaska, Washington, and Oregon. The cultures of this region depended on the forest and the sea for food and materials needed for living. Forests provided wood for houses and canoes as well as tree bark for making baskets and clothing. The rivers and coastal waters were filled with salmon, a main food source. Native Americans preserved salmon by smoking it over fires.

The area between the Cascade Mountains and the Rocky Mountains is known as the plateau region. There, the Nez Perce (NEHZ PUHRS) and Yakima (YAH•keh•muh) peoples also depended on the land, fishing the rivers, hunting deer in forests, and gathering roots and berries. The Native Americans of the plateau region lived in earthen houses.

Present-day California was home to a great variety of cultures. Along the northern coast, Native Americans fished for their food. In the central valley of California, the Pomo (poh•moh) gathered acorns and pounded them into flour. In the more barren southern deserts, nomadic groups collected roots and seeds.

Between the Sierra Nevada and the Rocky Mountains lies the Great Basin region. There, the soil was too hard and rocky for farming. This meant that peoples such as the Ute (YOOT) and Shoshone (shuh•SHOHN) had to travel in search of food. They hunted and gathered small game, pine nuts, juniper berries, roots, and some insects. They crafted temporary shelters from branches and reeds.

Southwestern Peoples

In the Southwest region, descendants of the Ancient Puebloans formed the Hopi (HOH•pee), the Acoma (uh•KOH•muh), the Zuni (ZOO•nee), and other peoples. Farming was central to their cultures, with maize serving as their basic food source.

Totem poles are carved wooden pillars made by Native American groups of the Pacific Northwest. Totem poles typically include symbols that represent the history and experience of a family or clan.

Chris Cheadle/All Canada Photos/Corbis

Reading **HELP**DESK

Reading Strategy: *Categorizing*

When you categorize information, you organize it into clearly identified categories. As you read the section on Native American Groups Circa 1492, identify the categories of groups presented, such as Northern, Western, or Southwestern peoples. Use these headings to organize notes you take as you read the material.

They built their homes from dried mud bricks called adobe (uh•DOH•bee). They also used irrigation to grow beans, squash, melons, pumpkins, and fruit. Their trade network spread throughout the Southwest and into Mexico.

The Apache (uh•PAH•chee) and the Navajo (NAH•vuh•hoh) settled in the Southwest region about 1,000 years ago. These new groups were primarily hunters and gatherers. In time, the Navajo settled in villages and built square houses called hogans. They also began to grow maize and beans, and they raised sheep as well.

Plains Peoples

The peoples of the Great Plains were nomadic. Their villages were temporary, lasting only for a growing season or two. The women planted maize, squash, and beans. The men hunted antelope, deer, and buffalo. When the people moved from place to place, they dragged their homes—cone-shaped skin tents called tepees—behind them.

Buffalo were central to the lives of the people of the Plains. Native Americans used buffalo to supply many basic needs. Buffalo meat was a good source of food, and people used the bones to make tools and weapons. Buffalo skins provided shelter and clothing.

Today many people associate Native Americans of the Plains with the use of horses. These animals would transform Plains life—but not until the 1600s, after their arrival from Europe.

Eastern Peoples

Complex societies existed in the woodlands of eastern North America. A similar language connected the many Algonquian (al•GAHN•kwee•uhn) groups. The Cherokee (CHEHR•uh•kee) and Iroquois (IHR•uh•kwoy) had formal law codes and formed **federations** (feh•duh•RAY•shuhnz), agreements among different groups to join together.

federation a government that links and unites different groups

Peabody Essex Museum, Salem, MA/Bridgeman Art Library

Connections to
TODAY

Native American Languages

Many Native American groups still speak their native languages today, though the number of native-language speakers is small. It is estimated that approximately 150,000 people still speak Navajo (nah vuh HO), while only about 2,000 still speak Cherokee.

For centuries, Native American groups of the Great Plains hunted buffalo. Native Americans often painted buffalo skins and made them into robes.

The Iroquois lived in bark-covered longhouses. Each building could shelter several families.

The Iroquois lived near Canada in what is now northern New York. The original five Iroquois groups, or nations, were the Onondaga (ah•nuhn•DAW•guh), the Seneca (SEH•nih•kuh), the Mohawk (MOH•hawk), the Oneida (oh•NY•duh), and the Cayuga (kay•YOO•guh).

These groups often warred with each other. Then, in the 1500s, they established the Great Peace, an alliance called the Iroquois League. According to Iroquoian tradition, Dekanawidah (deh•kah•nuh•WEE•duh), a tribal elder, and a chief of the Mohawk named Hiawatha (hi•uh•WAH•thuh) founded the league. Worried that war was tearing the nations apart, they urged the people to unite in the spirit of friendship and peace.

The five nations agreed to the Great Binding Law, an oral constitution that defined how the league worked and established the Grand Council. This group of leaders met regularly to settle disputes among the various peoples.

Although Grand Council members were men, women played an important part in choosing delegates to the council.

clan a group of people who have a common ancestor

The different members of the Iroquois League were organized according to **clans,** or groups of related families. The women in each clan chose a clan mother. These clan mothers then chose the male members of the Grand Council.

The Tuscarora (tus•kuh•ROR•uh) people joined the league in 1715. With their addition, the five nations became six.

Southeastern Peoples

The Southeast was also a woodlands area, but with a warmer climate than the Eastern Woodlands. Among the Native American groups of the Southeast were the Creek, Cherokee, and Chickasaw (CHIH•kuh•saw). Farming was essential for each of these groups. The Creek lived in loosely knit farming communities in what is now Georgia and Alabama. There they grew corn, squash, tobacco, and other crops. The Cherokee farmed in the mountains of what is now Georgia, Tennessee, and the Carolinas. The Chickasaw spread out across the Southeast, but most of their largest settlements were in present-day Mississippi. There they farmed the fertile river bottomlands.

A Changing World

In whichever part of North America they lived, Native Americans developed rich and varied cultures, and ways of living that were suited to their environments. In the 1500s, however, a new people with vastly different cultures and ways of life would arrive in the Americas: the Europeans. Their arrival would change the Native Americans' world forever.

☑ **PROGRESS CHECK**

Describing How did location affect the culture of different native peoples? Give examples from the text to support your answer.

BIOGRAPHY

Dekanawidah (1500s)

Legend has it that a leader named Dekanawidah founded the Iroquois League. A Huron by birth, Dekanawidah sought an end to the terrible fighting among Native Americans in the Northeast. He drew up the "Great Law," which created a system for making decisions and settling disputes in an orderly manner. The agreement helped the Iroquois become one of the most powerful Native American groups in North America.

▶ **CRITICAL THINKING**
Drawing Conclusions Why do you think Iroquois groups were willing to join together in a federation?

LESSON 3 REVIEW

Review Vocabulary

1. Examine the two terms below. Then write a sentence explaining how the words are related.

   a. federation   b. clan

Answer the Guiding Questions

2. *Describing* Describe the cliff dwellings of the Ancient Puebloans, and explain the advantages those dwellings may have offered.

3. *Explaining* How did the Inuit adapt to the cold Arctic climate?

4. *Explaining* What was the significance of the Iroquois League?

5. **NARRATIVE WRITING** Consider the different groups discussed in the lesson. Write a paragraph that describes what life might have been like for a young member of one of these groups. Use details from the lesson to illustrate how your chosen group adapted to the environment where they lived.

Write your answers on a separate piece of paper.

1 Exploring the Essential Questions

EXPOSITORY WRITING Geography played an important part in the development of North America's Native American cultures. Write an essay in which you explain how factors of geography helped shape cultures. Use specific examples from the chapter in making your argument.

2 21st Century Skills

CRITICAL THINKING AND PROBLEM SOLVING Use the Internet to research the Iroquois constitution. Read parts 1 and 2 only. Then rewrite these parts of the constitution in your own words, using modern English. Share and compare your rewrites with those of other members of the class. How are they similar? How do they differ?

3 Thinking Like a Historian

DRAWING INFERENCES AND CONCLUSIONS Consider what you have read about the great Native American civilizations that existed in the Americas prior to the arrival of Europeans. What became of those civilizations? What conclusions can you draw about the nature of civilizations and cultures based on the history of the Native American civilizations?

4 Visual Literacy

ANALYZING IMAGES Petroglyphs are paintings or carvings on rock. What can you determine about the cultures that created these petroglyphs in southern Utah?

REVIEWING THE GUIDING QUESTIONS
Choose the best answer for each question.

1 Which of the following has been a leading theory about how human beings first came to the Americas?
A. They crossed a land bridge from Asia to North America.
B. They swam across the Pacific Ocean from small islands.
C. They sailed from Europe to explore new lands.
D. They crossed glaciers that once linked Antarctica to South America.

2 Why do scientists think people first migrated to the Americas?
F. to escape from harsh rule in their homeland
G. to seek out other ancient peoples for wisdom
H. to search for hunting grounds for food
I. to map the land for future generations

3 Which city was the center of the Aztec Empire?
A. Montezuma
B. Machu Picchu
C. Cuzco
D. Tenochtitlán

4 Which of the following is an example of a key feature of the Inca civilization?
F. farming their land by cutting terraces into the mountainsides
G. building their capital city in the middle of Lake Texcoco
H. creating enormous stone monuments that were up to nine feet tall
I. predicting eclipses and creating a 365-day calendar

5 Which of the following correctly describes the Adena, Hopewell, and Mississippian cultures, and the Hohokam and Ancient Puebloans?
A. These were the dominant cultures of North America in 1492.
B. These cultures thrived and then faded before the arrival of Europeans.
C. These cultures influenced the development of the great empires of Mexico, Central America, and South America.
D. These cultures were competitors that eventually destroyed one another.

6 The Native American groups living in North America around 1492
F. varied according to the environments in which they lived.
G. were remarkably similar.
H. had developed advanced farming techniques.
I. were dependent on hunting and gathering for all their food.

DBQ DOCUMENT-BASED QUESTIONS

This excerpt is from the Iroquois constitution.

> *"I am Dekanawidah and with the Five Nations' Confederate Lords I plant the Tree of Great Peace. … Roots have spread out from the Tree of the Great Peace, one to the north, one to the east, one to the south, and one to the west."*
>
> —From the Iroquois constitution

7 **Analyzing** What do you think the roots mentioned in the excerpt represent?

   A. a peace that grows and spreads out in all directions

   B. each of the Five Nations' confederate lords

   C. the desire to start wars with other peoples in different areas

   D. the separation that keeps the Five Nations apart

8 **Drawing Conclusions** The main purpose of the Iroquois constitution as explained in the excerpt is to

   F. appoint the leader of the confederate lords.

   G. plant trees that will create a forest.

   H. establish peace among the Five Nations.

   I. begin a war with other cultures.

SHORT RESPONSE

Spaniard Bernal Díaz del Castillo was among the first Europeans to meet Montezuma, the ruler of the Aztec Empire. This excerpt describes how Montezuma was treated by his subjects.

> *"[T]here were … Lords who walked before the Great Montezuma, sweeping the ground where he would tread and spreading cloths on it, so that he should not tread on the earth. Not one of these chieftains dared even to think of looking him in the face, but kept their eyes lowered with great reverence."*
>
> —From *The True History of the Conquest of New Spain*

9 Why did the lords spread cloths on the ground where Montezuma was to walk?

10 How did the Aztec people apparently feel about Montezuma? Give specific details to support your response.

EXTENDED RESPONSE

11 **Expository Writing** Write an essay exploring how the quest for food and the way it was obtained helped shape and define various Native American civilizations. Use examples from the chapter to make your argument.

Need Extra Help?

If You've Missed Question	❶	❷	❸	❹	❺	❻	❼	❽	❾	🔟	⓫
Review Lesson	1	1	2	2	3	3	3	3	2	2	1–3

Exploring the Americas

1400–1625

ESSENTIAL QUESTIONS • *How do new ideas change the way people live?*
• *Why do people trade?* • *What are the consequences when cultures interact?*

The Story Matters . . .

The year is 1492—a good year for Queen Isabella. After centuries of struggle, Catholic forces have driven the Muslim invaders from Spain. She is grateful to God—and determined to use her power for God's glory.

Full of these thoughts, Isabella recalls a visit she received the year before. A sailor named Christopher Columbus said he knew of a new route to faraway Asia. She ignored him then. Now she is ready to listen. She knows if Columbus succeeds, it will bring glory to God—and untold wealth to Spain.

Queen Isabella agrees to give Columbus the ships and sailors he needs. Before long, he is ready to set sail. The European exploration of the Americas is about to begin.

◀ *Queen Isabella of Spain supported early explorations of the Americas.*

The Art Archive / General Archive of the Indies Seville / Gianni Dagli Orti

CHAPTER 2

Place and Time: The Americas 1400 to 1625

Starting in the late 1400s, Europeans explored the oceans, hoping to find a direct sea route to the East Indies. Instead, they found what to them was a "New World." Over the next few centuries, they explored and settled the Americas.

Step Into the Place

MAP FOCUS This map shows the different routes taken by different explorers.

1 **MOVEMENT** How many European nations made explorations of North and South America?

2 **CRITICAL THINKING**
Drawing Conclusions Why do you think so many nations sent out voyages of exploration at this time?

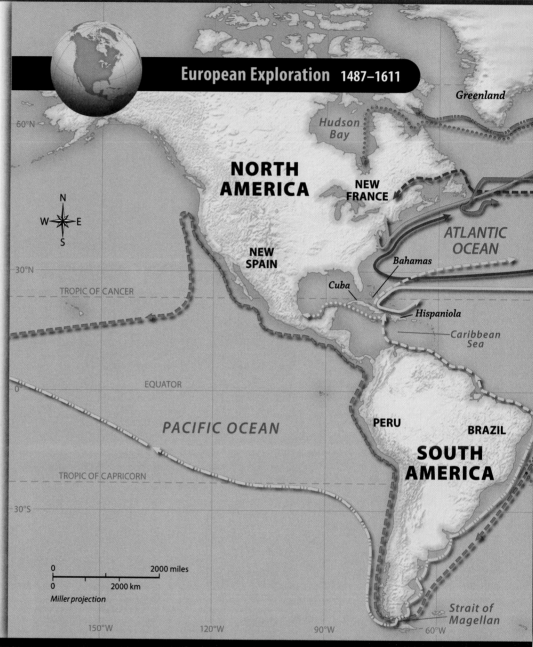

European Exploration 1487–1611

Greenland

Hudson Bay

NORTH AMERICA

NEW FRANCE

ATLANTIC OCEAN

NEW SPAIN

Bahamas

Cuba

Hispaniola

Caribbean Sea

60°N

30°N

TROPIC OF CANCER

EQUATOR

PACIFIC OCEAN

PERU

BRAZIL

SOUTH AMERICA

0

30°S

TROPIC OF CAPRICORN

Strait of Magellan

0   2000 miles
0   2000 km
Miller projection

150°W   120°W   90°W   60°W

Step Into the Time

TIME LINE Study the time line. How much time passed after Europeans first arrived in the Americas before they explored Florida?

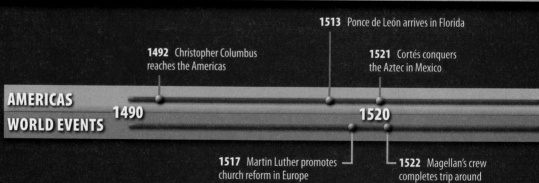

1513 Ponce de León arrives in Florida

1492 Christopher Columbus reaches the Americas

1521 Cortés conquers the Aztec in Mexico

AMERICAS   1490

WORLD EVENTS   1520

1517 Martin Luther promotes church reform in Europe

1522 Magellan's crew completes trip around the world

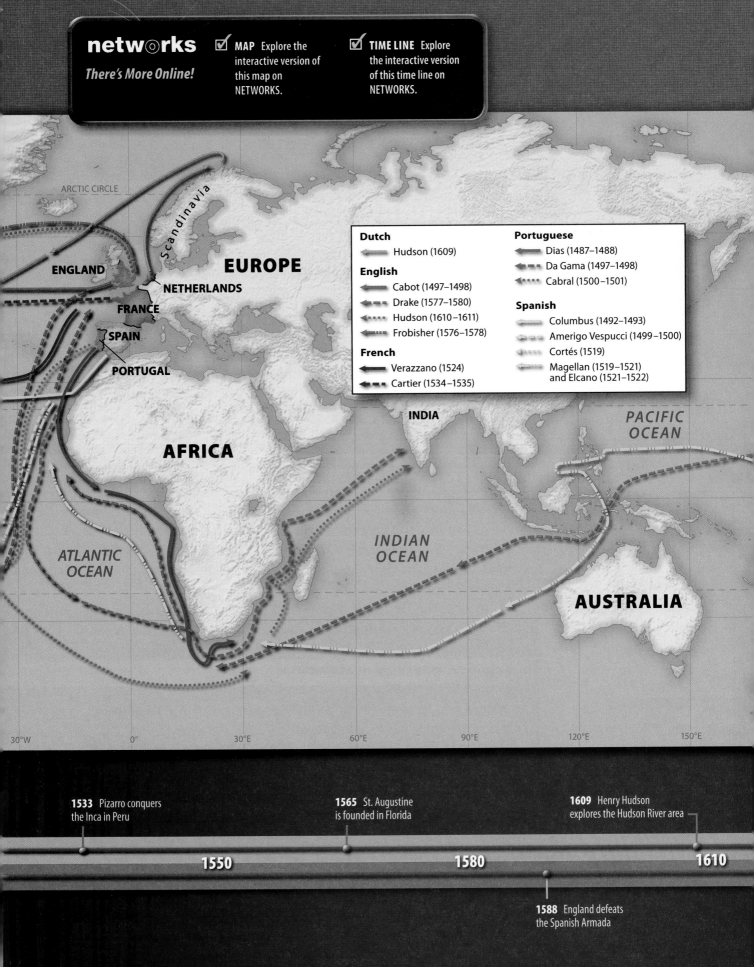

ARCTIC CIRCLE

Scandinavia

ENGLAND

EUROPE

NETHERLANDS

FRANCE

SPAIN

PORTUGAL

AFRICA

INDIA

PACIFIC OCEAN

ATLANTIC OCEAN

INDIAN OCEAN

AUSTRALIA

Dutch
Hudson (1609)

English
Cabot (1497–1498)
Drake (1577–1580)
Hudson (1610–1611)
Frobisher (1576–1578)

French
Verazzano (1524)
Cartier (1534–1535)

Portuguese
Dias (1487–1488)
Da Gama (1497–1498)
Cabral (1500–1501)

Spanish
Columbus (1492–1493)
Amerigo Vespucci (1499–1500)
Cortés (1519)
Magellan (1519–1521)
and Elcano (1521–1522)

30°W   0°   30°E   60°E   90°E   120°E   150°E

1533 Pizarro conquers the Inca in Peru

1565 St. Augustine is founded in Florida

1609 Henry Hudson explores the Hudson River area

1550   1580   1610

1588 England defeats the Spanish Armada

Lesson 1

A Changing World

ESSENTIAL QUESTION *How do new ideas change the way people live?*

IT MATTERS BECAUSE
Europe was aware of the riches of Asia and Africa. Attempts to increase trade with these lands eventually developed into an era of European exploration that reached far beyond Europe's borders.

New Ideas, New Nations

GUIDING QUESTION *Where did the Renaissance take place?*

For centuries after the Roman Empire fell in A.D. 476, the people of Western Europe were cut off from the rest of the world. Western Europe was made up of small kingdoms and city-states dominated by the Catholic Church. Then, in the early A.D. 600s, a new religion, Islam, began to spread rapidly in the Middle East and Africa. This rise of Islam would soon end Western Europe's isolation.

In 1095 the Europeans launched the first of nine expeditions, known as the **Crusades.** Their purpose was to take back control of Christian holy sites in the Middle East from the Muslims—followers of Islam. The Crusades also had an unplanned result. In the Middle East, Europeans met Arab merchants, who sold them spices, sugar, silk, and other goods from China and India. European interest in Asia grew.

That interest grew even more after Italian explorer Marco Polo returned from China. In the late 1200s, Polo wrote about Asia's people, great riches, and splendid cities in his book, *Travels,* which was widely read in Europe. Two hundred years later, his *Travels* would inspire another Italian explorer—Christopher Columbus.

Reading **HELP**DESK

Taking Notes: *Identifying*

As you read, use a diagram like this one to identify the advances in technology that paved the way for European voyages of exploration.

Technological Advances

Content Vocabulary

• **Crusade**
• **classical**
• **Renaissance**
• **technology**
• **astrolabe**
• **compass**
• **pilgrimage**
• **mosque**

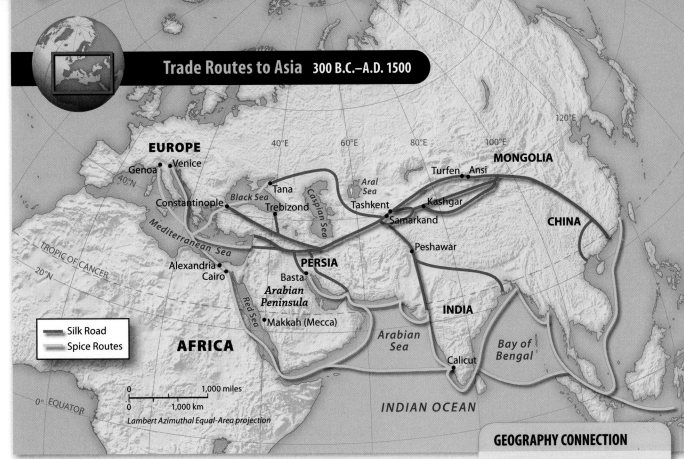

Trade Routes to Asia 300 B.C.–A.D. 1500

EUROPE
Genoa • Venice
Black Sea
Tana
Constantinople
Trebizond
Mediterranean Sea
Caspian Sea
Aral Sea
Tashkent
Samarkand
Kashgar
Turfen • Ansi
MONGOLIA
CHINA
Peshawar
TROPIC OF CANCER
Alexandria
Cairo
PERSIA
Basta
Arabian Peninsula
Makkah (Mecca)
Red Sea
Arabian Sea
INDIA
Bay of Bengal
Calicut
AFRICA

Silk Road
Spice Routes

0   1,000 miles
0   1,000 km
Lambert Azimuthal Equal-Area projection

EQUATOR
INDIAN OCEAN

40°E 60°E 80°E 100°E 120°E
40°N
20°N

The Growth of Trade

Merchants in Europe knew they could make a lot of money selling goods from Asia. Wealthy Europeans were eager to buy Asian spices, perfumes, silks, and precious stones.

Merchants first bought these goods from Arab traders in the Middle East. The merchants then sent the goods overland by caravan to the Mediterranean Sea. From there, the goods traveled by ship to Italian ports in Venice, Genoa, and Pisa. These cities prospered as centers of the growing trade. However, Arab traders charged high prices. This led Europeans to look for a route to the East that would not require them to buy from Arab merchants.

The Growth of Ideas

By the 1300s, several Italian city-states had become strong economic and cultural centers. Their influence spread across Europe. Newly powerful bankers and merchants in Pisa, Venice, and Genoa studied **classical** works—those of ancient Greece and Rome.

Science was another area in which change occurred. Many scholars tested new and old theories of science. They performed experiments and evaluated the results.

GEOGRAPHY CONNECTION

Caravans, or groups of travelers, from Asia carried silks and spices overland to markets in the West. At the shores of the Mediterranean and Black Seas, the goods were loaded onto ships and transported to Europe.

1 **LOCATION** How would you describe the location of Genoa and Venice?

2 **CRITICAL THINKING**
Making Connections Based on the information on this map, why do you think European traders charged high prices for silks and spices?

Crusade one of a series of expeditions Europeans made to regain control of Christian holy sites in the Middle East from the A.D. 1000s to the 1200s
classical related to the culture of ancient Greece and Rome

Reading in the Content Area: *Understanding Visuals*

When a map shows a historical event or era, you will not always find present-day boundaries. Sometimes you can identify where things are taking place today by using natural features, such as bodies of water. Historical maps provide a sense of time and help us to understand which cities and countries existed hundreds of years ago and which still exist today.

The arts were also influenced by classical forms and new ideas. Authors wrote about the individual's place in the universe. Artists studied classical sculpture and architecture. They admired the harmony and balance in Greek art.

The Renaissance

This period of intellectual and artistic creativity is known as the **Renaissance** (reh•nuh•SAHNTS). The word *renaissance* means "rebirth" in French. It refers to the rebirth of interest in classical Greek and Roman ideas. As the Renaissance spread across Europe over the next two centuries, it changed the way Europeans thought about themselves and the world. It also set the stage for an age of exploration and discovery.

The Rise of Powerful Nations

For centuries, Europe had been a patchwork of small states. By the 1400s, however, a new, larger type of state had developed in Western Europe. Strong monarchs rose to power in Spain, Portugal, England, and France. They began to establish national laws, courts, taxes, and armies to replace those of the local rulers. These ambitious monarchs sought ways to increase trade and make their countries even stronger and wealthier.

As early as the mid-1400s, powerful countries such as Portugal and Spain began to search for sea routes to Asia. They, too, wanted to engage in foreign trade. This placed them in direct competition with the Italian port cities that had become so powerful a century earlier. As a result, a new era of exploration began.

✅ **PROGRESS CHECK**

Drawing Conclusions In what way did trade help to bring about the Renaissance?

The Effects of New Technology

GUIDING QUESTION *What technological advancements paved the way for European voyages of exploration?*

Advances in **technology**—the use of scientific knowledge for practical purposes—helped to make European voyages of exploration possible. In the 1450s, the introduction of the printing press made it much easier to print books. More people had access to books and to new information. Many Europeans read Marco

The Mona Lisa, painted by Leonardo da Vinci, is a masterpiece of the Renaissance. From what we know, the portrait features a woman from Florence who was 24 years old when da Vinci began the painting.

Renaissance a reawakening of culture and intellectual curiosity in Europe from the 1300s to the 1600s
technology the use of scientific knowledge for practical purposes

astrolabe an instrument used to plan a course, using the stars
compass an instrument that shows the direction of magnetic north

Compass

Astrolabe

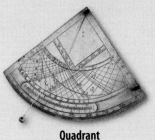

Quadrant

With the compass, sailors could tell which direction they were sailing. The astrolabe and quadrant (QWAH • druhnt) allowed sailors to measure the angle of a star to the horizon, which helped them find their location on the sea.

INFOGRAPHIC

1 DRAWING CONCLUSIONS Explain how the compass, astrolabe, and quadrant could make a long ocean voyage possible.

2 CRITICAL THINKING *Making Connections* What tools might sailors use to find their position at sea today?

Polo's *Travels* when it appeared in printed form in 1477. This book gave people descriptions of faraway places, such as modern-day areas of Iraq, Siberia, Japan, India, Ethiopia, and Madagascar. Whether the descriptions were entirely accurate is open to debate. However, Polo's *Travels* led European readers to realize that there were many spectacular sights beyond their immediate world.

Better Maps and Instruments

Most early maps were not accurate. This was because they were drawn based on the points of view of traders and travelers. Little by little, cartographers, or mapmakers, improved their accuracy. Using reports of explorers and information from Arab and Chinese scholars and astronomers, mapmakers made more accurate land and sea maps. These maps showed the directions of ocean currents. They also showed lines of latitude, which measured the distance north and south of the Equator.

People also improved instruments for navigating the seas. Sailors could find their latitude with an **astrolabe** (AS•truh•layb), which measured the positions of stars. In the 1200s, Europeans **acquired** the magnetic **compass** from China. The compass allowed sailors to accurately determine their direction.

Better Ship Design

Advances in ship design allowed sailors to make long ocean voyages. The stern rudder and triangular sail enabled ships to sail into the wind. The Portuguese three-masted caravel (KER•uh•vehl) became the most famous ship of the European age of exploration. Caravels could sail faster and carry more cargo and supplies than earlier ships. These advances and competition for foreign trade led countries such as Portugal and Spain to search for sea routes to Asia. Portugal began its explorations along the west coast of Africa, an area Europeans had never visited before.

✓ **PROGRESS CHECK**

Determining Cause and Effect How did the caravel affect exploration in a positive way?

GEOGRAPHY CONNECTION

Trade routes across Earth's largest desert, the Sahara, provided West African kingdoms with access to the Mediterranean coast.

1 LOCATION What West African kingdom extended the farthest west?

2 CRITICAL THINKING
Draw Conclusions Other than the information on trade routes, what key historic information does the map show?

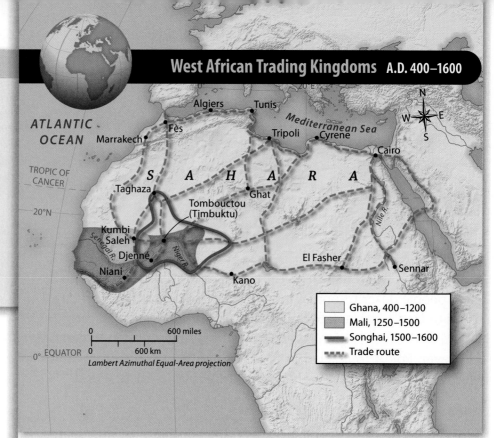

West African Trading Kingdoms A.D. 400–1600

Kingdoms and Empires in Africa

GUIDING QUESTION *What were the most powerful empires in Africa?*

Between A.D. 400 and 1600, powerful kingdoms and city-states flourished in Africa south of the Sahara. Much of their power and wealth came from mining and trade.

Arab traders traveled Africa's east coast exchanging cotton, silk, and porcelain for African ivory and metals. West Africans mined and traded gold, copper, and iron ore. Trade with North Africa's Islamic societies brought wealth and Islamic customs to the West African kingdoms. The kingdoms also traded directly with Europe. The Portuguese set up trading posts along Africa's western coast in the mid-1400s.

Ghana—A Trading Empire

Between A.D. 400 and 1100, a vast trading empire known as Ghana emerged in West Africa. Ghana grew wealthy from the taxes it placed on trade. Caravans carrying gold, ivory, and enslaved people crossed the desert to North Africa and returned with salt, cloth, and brass. Such trading contacts led many West Africans to become Muslim.

Reading **HELP**DESK

pilgrimage a journey to a holy place
mosque a Muslim house of worship

Academic Vocabulary

acquire to get possession or control of

In 1076 North African people called Almoravids (al•muh•RAH•vihdz) attacked Ghana, disrupting the trade routes in the region. Soon new trade routes bypassed Ghana altogether. The drop in trade led to Ghana's decline, and new kingdoms emerged in the region.

Mali—Wealth and Power

Mali, one of the new kingdoms, grew very powerful. Mali developed trade routes across the desert to North Africa. By the late 1200s, Mali's territory was huge. One traveler reported that it took four months to cross it from north to south.

In 1324 Mali's great king, Mansa Musa, a Muslim, traveled to the Muslim holy city of Makkah (Mecca) in what is now Saudi Arabia. He returned from this religious journey, or **pilgrimage** (PIHL•gruh•mihj), with an Arab architect. The architect built great **mosques** (MAHSKS), Muslim houses of worship, in Timbuktu, Mali's capital. Timbuktu became a center of Islamic art and learning.

The Songhai Empire

In time, the Songhai (sawng•GEYE) people, who lived along the Niger River, overthrew Mali rule. They captured Timbuktu in 1468. Askìya Muhammad, leader of the Songhai Empire, divided Songhai into provinces, each with its own officials. Everyone in the empire followed a legal system based on the teachings of Islam. In the late 1500s, North Africa's kingdom of Morocco defeated—and ended—the Songhai Empire.

✓ **PROGRESS CHECK**

Drawing Conclusions What did the Middle East and Africa have that Europeans wanted?

Gold was one of the valuable trade items that helped enrich the great trading empires of West Africa.

C squared Studios/ Photodisc/ Getty Images

LESSON 1 REVIEW

Review Vocabulary

1. Examine the two terms that follow. Then write a sentence based on what you have read that explains the connection between the terms.

   a. astrolabe   **b.** technology

2. Write a sentence about the classical ideas that were rediscovered during the Renaissance.

Answer the Guiding Questions

3. ***Explaining*** How did the rise of Italian city-states help lead to the Renaissance?

4. ***Identifying*** How did new technology pave the way for European voyages of exploration?

5. ***Listing*** What were the three most powerful empires in West Africa between the 400s and 1500s?

6. **PERSUASIVE WRITING** Which of the following do you think was the most important innovation, and why?
   • the compass
   • improved maps
   • the printing press

networks

There's More Online!

☑ **BIOGRAPHY**
 • Vasco da Gama
 • Queen Isabella
 • Christopher Columbus

☑ **GRAPHIC ORGANIZER**
 Explorers and Their Sponsors

☑ **MAP** Early Portuguese Exploration

☑ **PRIMARY SOURCE**
 Vasco da Gama

☑ **VIDEO**

Lesson 2
Early Exploration

ESSENTIAL QUESTION *Why do people trade?*

IT MATTERS BECAUSE

The arrival of the Europeans in the Americas in the fifteenth century changed the lives of people in both the Americas and Europe forever.

The Search for New Trade Routes

GUIDING QUESTION *Which country took the lead in finding a trade route to India?*

In 1492 Christopher Columbus led 90 sailors in three ships on a voyage into the unknown. As the voyage dragged on, the sailors grew angry. Columbus wrote: "I am told … that if I persist in going onward, the best course of action will be to throw me into the sea some night." Before that could happen, a lookout from the ship *Pinta* made the signal that he had spotted land. On October 12, 1492, Columbus left his ship, the *Santa María*, and went ashore.

Columbus believed he had arrived in the Indies—islands located southeast of China. Actually, he had reached North America. How did Columbus get it so wrong? The maps that he and other European explorers used at the time did not include the Americas because no one in Europe knew they existed. All maps showed three continents—Europe, Asia, and Africa—merged into a huge landmass and bordered by oceans. Some explorers thought that the Western (Atlantic) and Eastern (Pacific) Oceans ran together to form what they called the "Ocean Sea." No one realized the true size of the oceans or the existence of other continents.

Reading **HELP**DESK

Taking Notes: *Identifying*

As you study the lesson, use a diagram such as this one to identify the explorers who were sponsored by Portugal and those who were sponsored by Spain.

Explorers

Sponsored by Portugal | Sponsored by Spain

Content Vocabulary
• **cape**
• **circumnavigate**

Columbus was sailing on behalf of Spain, but Portugal was the first European power to explore the boundaries of the known world by sea. Unlike Spain, Portugal did not have a port on the Mediterranean Sea. This meant the Portuguese could not use the existing trade routes between Asia and Europe. Portugal's rulers wanted to find a new route to China and India.

The Portuguese also knew about the great riches in the West African kingdoms. These riches were carried by caravan across the desert to North Africa and then by ship across the Mediterranean. Portuguese traders needed a better route so that they, too, could get West African gold and other riches.

The Beginning of Portuguese Exploration

Portugal's Prince Henry laid the groundwork for the era of exploration. In about 1420, he set up a center for exploration at Sagres (SAW•grish), on the southwestern tip of Portugal, "where endeth land and where beginneth sea."

Known as Henry the Navigator, the prince never intended to become an explorer himself. Instead, he planned the voyages and then analyzed the reports that his crews brought home. At Sagres, Prince Henry set up a school of navigation. There, astronomers, geographers, and mathematicians came to share their knowledge with Portuguese sailors, shipbuilders, and mapmakers. As each successful voyage brought back new information, Henry's expert mapmakers updated the charts.

Portuguese ships sailed south along the coast of West Africa. As they went south, they traded for gold and ivory and set up trading posts in the region. Because of its abundance of gold, Africa's west coast came to be known as the "Gold Coast." In the mid-1400s, Portuguese traders began to buy enslaved Africans there as well.

King John II of Portugal launched new efforts to create a Portuguese trading empire in Asia. All the Portuguese had to do was find a sea route around Africa. If they succeeded, they would be able to trade directly with India and China. They could bypass the North African and Asian caravans and Mediterranean merchants. With that goal in mind, in the 1480s King John urged Portuguese sea captains to explore farther south along the African coast.

The *Santa María* was a sturdy vessel built to survive a long ocean voyage.

▶ CRITICAL THINKING
Making Inferences What traits would make a person a good crew member on the *Santa María*?

CORBIS

Reading Strategy: *Reading in the Content Area*

Answers to the questions "What happened?" and "Why did it happen?" fill the pages of history books. Look for the answers to these questions as you read. It can help your understanding of history to think of the situations you encounter as a series of cause-and-effect relationships.

In order to reach Asia, ships from Europe had to sail south, all the way around Africa, and then north again to Asia.

1 MOVEMENT Study the map. Trace da Gama's route with your finger. Then describe where it began, the oceans through which it passed, and where it ended.

2 CRITICAL THINKING
Speculating What can you conclude from the fact that Bartolomeu Dias's route hugged the coast of Africa and Vasco da Gama's route did not?

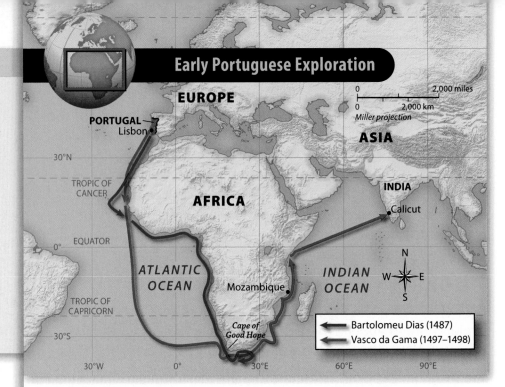

Early Portuguese Exploration

Bartolomeu Dias

In 1487 Bartolomeu Dias set out from Lisbon with two small caravels and a supply ship. King John had sent Dias to explore the southernmost part of Africa. From there, Dias was to sail northeast into the Indian Ocean. This expedition included some of Portugal's best pilots.

They sailed for days, staying close to the coast of Africa. After passing the mouth of the Orange River in South Africa, the expedition met with a fierce storm that carried it southward, off course, and out of sight of land. When the winds finally died down, Dias steered east and then north until he found land again. Excitedly, Dias realized that he had already sailed past the southernmost part of Africa. On the way, he had passed a landform called a **cape,** a piece of land that juts into the water.

Dias set a course back to Portugal. On the return journey, after passing that piece of land again, he wrote that he had been around the "Cape of Storms." King John renamed it the "Cape of Good Hope." The king hoped that the passage around Africa might provide a new route to India.

Vasco da Gama

Portugal's voyages to India began years later. In July 1497, after much preparation, Vasco da Gama set sail from Portugal with four ships, headed for Africa. Da Gama's ships did not hug the

cape a point of land that sticks out into water, much like a peninsula

Word Origins: *Changing Meanings*

The word *pilot* used to mean *navigator*. What does it mean today?

African coast, as Dias's ships had. Instead, they sailed in a wide arc south and west of Africa. They were out of sight of land for more than three months. The purpose of this detour was to reach ocean currents that would help the sailors travel safely around the Cape of Good Hope.

After rounding the cape on November 22, da Gama was on Africa's eastern coast. He made many stops, including one at Mombasa (mahm•BAH•suh), part of present-day Kenya. There, he met a pilot from India who guided him the rest of the way. Da Gama reached the port of Calicut, in India, in May 1498. Portugal's long-held dream of a sea route to Asia was now reality.

Portugal's Trading Empire

Events moved quickly. Within six months of da Gama's return to Portugal, 13 ships set sail out of Lisbon and headed for India. The ships were commanded by a nobleman, Pedro Álvares Cabral (PEH•droo AWL•vuh ruhsh kuh•BRAWL).

Cabral planned to follow da Gama's westward-then-southward course. Instead, he went so far west that he reached Brazil. Cabral claimed Brazil for his king and sent one of the ships back to Portugal with the good news that Portugal now had a foothold in the Americas.

Cabral then continued to India and returned with spices, porcelain, and other valuable cargo. Other Portuguese fleets soon made the journey to India, where Portugal set up permanent forts. Portuguese fleets began to make yearly voyages to India. Their cargoes made the Portuguese capital of Lisbon the marketplace of Europe.

✓ **PROGRESS CHECK**

Analyzing What was the importance of the voyages of Dias and da Gama?

Columbus Crosses the Atlantic

GUIDING QUESTION *How did Spain and Portugal protect their claims in the Americas?*

Born in Genoa, Italy, in 1451, Christopher Columbus became a sailor for Portugal. He traveled as far north as the Arctic Circle and as far south as Africa's Gold Coast. To reach Asia, Christopher Columbus had a different route in mind than the one used by his Portuguese comrades. He planned to sail west.

In the 1400s, most educated people believed the world was round. People were less certain about the Earth's size. Columbus was among those who based their estimates on the works of Ptolemy (TAHL•uh•mee), an ancient Greek astronomer. Columbus believed Asia was about 2,760 miles (4,441 km) from Portugal—a voyage of about two months by ship. However, Ptolemy had underestimated Earth's size and, by using Ptolemy's estimate, Columbus did, too.

BIOGRAPHY

Vasco da Gama (c. 1460–1524)

Vasco da Gama, who was the son of a Portuguese noble, led two voyages of exploration for Portugal. During the second, he landed at Goa, which later became Portugal's base of power in India. In 1524 the king of Portugal made da Gama Portugal's viceroy, or governor, in India, and he returned to Goa.

▶ **CRITICAL THINKING**
Making Inferences Why do you think the king appointed Vasco da Gama his viceroy in India?

The triangular **lateen sail** caught wind that blew perpendicular to, or at a right angle to, the ship, making the ship easier to maneuver.

A **bilge pump**, operating from the main deck, removed water from storage areas.

Ballast stones were placed in the hull of the ship to provide better balance.

DIAGRAM SKILL

Caravels ranged in length from 75 to 90 feet (23 to 27 m) and were suited for sailing along shallow coastlines.

▶ **CRITICAL THINKING**
Explaining How did the caravel's lateen sail help sailors?

Vikings in North America

Several centuries before the voyages of da Gama, Cabral, and Columbus, northern Europeans had sailed to North America. Known as Vikings, or Norsemen, their ships sailed from present-day Scandinavia to Iceland and Greenland in the 800s and 900s, and established settlements there for a brief period of time. According to Norse sagas, or traditional stories, a Viking sailor named Leif Eriksson explored lands west of Greenland in about the year 1000. The sagas refer to this land as "Vinland." Ruins from around that period exist in northeastern Canada, which could support the sagas. The Vikings' voyages were not well-known throughout Europe, however. Other Europeans did not "discover" the Americas until Columbus made his historic voyage.

Columbus and Queen Isabella

Columbus had a plan for reaching Asia, but he still needed money to finance his expedition. He visited European monarchs, looking for support. Finally, he found a sponsor in Spain.

For most of the 1400s, Spanish monarchs **devoted,** or committed, their energy to driving the Muslims out of Spain. Muslims had invaded Spain in the 700s, but their power had been declining for centuries. The last Muslim kingdom in Spain

Reading HELPDESK

Academic Vocabulary

devote to commit oneself or one's resources to something
alter to change

Reading Strategy: *Reading a Diagram*

Diagrams may include a cutaway view. This provides a view of the outside and part of the inside of an object at the same time.

fell in 1492. This freed Spain's monarchs to focus on other goals. The Spanish observed the seafaring and trading successes of neighboring Portugal with envy. They, too, wanted the riches of Asian trade.

King Ferdinand and Queen Isabella of Spain agreed to support Columbus's expedition for two reasons. One reason was that Columbus promised to bring Christianity to any lands he found. As a devout Catholic, this was important to Isabella. Another reason was that if he succeeded in finding a route to Asia, Spain would become wealthy from trade with that region. Queen Isabella promised Columbus a share of any riches gained from lands he discovered on his way to Asia.

Columbus's First Voyage

On August 3, 1492, Columbus set sail from Palos, Spain. He had two small ships, the *Niña* and the *Pinta*, and a larger one, the *Santa María*. Columbus was captain of the *Santa María*, his lead ship, or flagship. The three ships carried about 90 sailors and a six-month supply of food and water.

The small fleet stopped at the Canary Islands off the coast of West Africa for repairs and supplies. Columbus then began the difficult voyage westward across unknown and mysterious stretches of the Atlantic Ocean.

After a few weeks at sea, the sailors grew nervous about the distance they had traveled. Columbus refused to **alter** his course. Instead, he encouraged the crew by describing the riches he believed they would find. He urged them on, saying that, "with the help of our Lord" they would arrive in the Indies.

On October 12, 1492, at two o'clock in the morning, a lookout shouted, *"Tierra! Tierra!"* "Land! Land!" He had spotted a small island in the chain now called the Bahamas. Columbus went ashore, claimed the island for Spain, and named it "San Salvador." Although he did not know it, Columbus had reached the Americas.

Columbus believed he had arrived in the East Indies, the islands off the coast of Asia. This is why today we call the Caribbean Islands "the West Indies." It also explains why Columbus called the local people "Indians." He noted that the natives regarded the Europeans with wonder and often touched the crew members to find out "if they were flesh and bones like themselves."

When Columbus returned to Spain, Queen Isabella and the Spanish king, Ferdinand, received him with great honor. They made him Admiral of the Ocean Sea, and agreed to provide funds for his future voyages.

BIOGRAPHY

Queen Isabella (1451–1504)

Queen Isabella was a Catholic of strong faith. She insisted Columbus treat Native Americans fairly and ordered him to release several enslaved Native Americans he brought to Spain. Isabella hoped to convert the Native Americans to Christianity. She also wanted their labor. She ordered that the Native Americans be forced "to work on ... buildings, to mine and collect gold ... and to work on ... farms and crop fields."

Christopher Columbus (1451–1506)

Columbus proved himself to be a great navigator and sailor. He believed he would discover great riches and new lands. He also knew he could win rich rewards for himself. Columbus wrote in 1492: "Your Highnesses commanded me ... [to] go to ... India, and for this accorded me great rewards and ennobled me [raised me to the rank of nobility]."

▶ **CRITICAL THINKING**
Comparing and Contrasting How were the goals of Queen Isabella and Columbus similar and different?

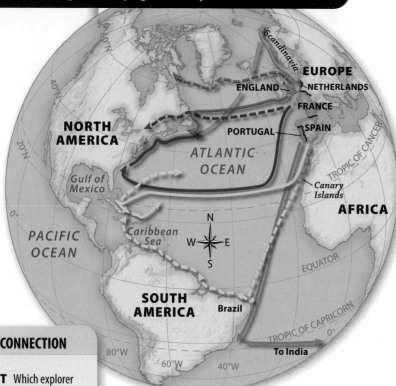

Spanish
- Christopher Columbus (1492–1493)
- Amerigo Vespucci (1499–1500)

Portuguese
- Pedro Cabral (1500)

English
- John Cabot (1497–1498)
- Martin Frobisher (1576–1578)

French
- Giovanni da Verrazano (1524)
- Jacques Cartier (1535)

Dutch
- Henry Hudson (1609)

0   1,000 miles
0   1,000 km
Orthographic projection

GEOGRAPHY CONNECTION

1 **MOVEMENT** Which explorer traveled along the northern coast of South America? For which country did he sail?

2 **CRITICAL THINKING**
Analyzing Visuals Study Cabral's route. Based on what you know about Portugal and the information in the map key, explain why his route is labeled, "To India."

Columbus's Achievements

Columbus made three more voyages for Spain, in 1493, 1498, and 1502. He explored the Caribbean islands of Hispaniola (present-day Haiti and the Dominican Republic), Cuba, and Jamaica. He also sailed along the coasts of Central America and northern South America. He claimed these lands for Spain and started settlements. He also mapped the coastline of Central America.

Columbus had not reached Asia, but instead had found a part of the world that was unknown to Europeans, Asians, and Africans. In the years that followed, the Spanish went on to explore most of the Caribbean, and to establish the Spanish Empire in the Americas.

Dividing the Americas

Both Spain and Portugal wanted to protect their claims in the Americas. They turned to Pope Alexander VI for help. In 1493 he ordered a line of demarcation, an imaginary line that reached from the North Pole to the South Pole, and cut through the middle of the Atlantic Ocean. Spain was to control all lands west of the line, and Portugal would control all lands east of the line.

Reading **HELP**DESK

circumnavigate to travel completely around something, usually by water

Portugal objected, saying that the division gave more land to Spain. In 1494 the two countries signed an agreement called the Treaty of Tordesillas (tohr•day•SEE•yuhs), which moved the line farther west. The two countries had divided the entire unexplored world between themselves.

Further Explorations

After Columbus, other voyagers explored the Americas. In 1499 Italian Amerigo Vespucci (veh•SPOO•chee) led a voyage funded by Spain. On this and a later journey for Portugal, he explored the coast of South America. Vespucci realized South America was a separate continent, and not part of Asia. European geographers began to call the continent "America" in his honor.

A Spaniard, Vasco Núñez de Balboa (bal•BOH•uh), heard stories of the "great waters" beyond the mountains of Panama, in Central America. He hiked through steamy rain forests to find them. At the coast in 1513, Balboa saw a vast body of water, which he claimed for Spain, along with the adjoining lands. Balboa was the first European to see the Pacific Ocean from the Americas.

Sailing Around the World

In 1520 Ferdinand Magellan, a Portuguese explorer who was sailing for Spain, reached the southernmost tip of South America. He sailed through the stormy waters of a narrow sea passage, or strait. The strait led him into a calm ocean—the same one Balboa had seen. The waters were so peaceful—*pacifico* in Spanish—that Magellan named the ocean the Pacific Ocean. Magellan died in the Philippine Islands, but his crew continued to sail westward, arriving back in Spain in 1522. Magellan's crew were the first people known to **circumnavigate,** or sail around, the world.

✓ **PROGRESS CHECK**

Evaluating What did Spain have to gain by supporting Columbus and his voyage?

The strait that led Magellan (above) from the Atlantic to the Pacific Ocean is now called the Strait of Magellan.

North Wind Picture Archive /North Wind Picture Archives

LESSON 2 REVIEW

Review Vocabulary

1. Use the term *cape* in a sentence about the explorations of Portugal in the late 1800s.

2. Write a sentence about why it was such an achievement for someone to circumnavigate the globe.

Answer the Guiding Questions

3. *Describing* Describe the geographic factors that led Portugal to begin its ocean explorations.

4. *Explaining* What was the purpose of the Treaty of Tordesillas?

5. **EXPOSITORY WRITING** Write a paragraph explaining why Americans might celebrate Eriksson Day rather than Columbus Day.

netw◉rks
There's More Online!

☑ **BIOGRAPHY**
   Sor Juana Inés de la Cruz

☑ **MAP**
   • Spanish Explorers
   • California's Missions

☑ **PRIMARY SOURCE**
   • Cortés and the Aztecs
   • Sor Juana Inés de la Cruz
   • Cabeza de Vaca

☑ **VIDEO**

Lesson 3

Spain in America

ESSENTIAL QUESTION *What are the consequences when cultures interact?*

IT MATTERS BECAUSE

Spanish explorers in the Americas conquered people and searched for gold. Spain became richer, while many Native Americans suffered from harsh treatment at the hands of the Spaniards.

European Explorers and Conquerors

GUIDING QUESTION *What were the goals of early Spanish explorers?*

When Spanish explorers reached the Americas, natives told tales of gold, silver, and kingdoms wealthy beyond belief. The Spanish listened eagerly, and they traveled far and wide in search of these riches.

These explorers, known as **conquistadors** (kahn•KEES•tah•dohrz), got encouragement from Spanish rulers. The rulers gave conquistadors the right to explore and create settlements in the Americas. In return, the conquistadors agreed to give Spain one-fifth of any treasure they found. This deal allowed Spanish rulers to explore the Americas with little risk. If a conquistador failed, he lost his own fortune. If he succeeded, both he and Spain gained wealth and glory.

The Conquest of Mexico and Peru

Although many of the tales of gold and riches proved to be false, some were true. Two wealthy empires—the Aztec in what is now Mexico and Central America and the Inca in South America— were among the richest prizes the conquistadors claimed.

Reading **HELP**DESK

Taking Notes: *Describing*

As you study the lesson, use a graphic organizer like this one to identify three Spanish conquistadors and describe the regions they explored.

Explorer	Region Explored

Content Vocabulary

• **conquistador**
• **immunity**
• **pueblo**
• **mission**
• **presidio**
• **plantation**

In 1519 Hernán Cortés landed on the east coast of present-day Mexico. Within two years, Cortés conquered the Aztec Empire that had ruled the region. Huge amounts of Aztec gold made Cortés and Spain wealthy.

Cortés's success encouraged other conquistadors. Twelve years after the Aztec conquest, Francisco Pizarro led an army into the Inca capital in Cuzco, Peru. The Spanish arrested and later executed the Inca ruler. Without their leader, the Inca were not able to fight effectively. Pizarro soon controlled most of the vast and wealthy Inca Empire.

Why Spain Won

The conquistadors' victories over the Aztec and Inca were quick and lasting. How did Cortés and Pizarro conquer such mighty empires with their small forces?

First, the Spanish had weapons and animals the Aztec and Inca had never seen. The Spanish had guns and cannons. They rode horses and had huge, ferocious dogs. To the Native Americans, the Spanish seemed almost like gods. One Aztec recalled the fear that spread at the soldiers' approach: "[T]heir weapons clashed and rattled. ... [T]hey terrified everyone who saw them." Cortés received help from some native people who disliked their harsh rulers and were happy to help overthrow them. Finally, disease played a large role. For many native groups, **contact** with the Europeans was deadly. With no **immunity,** or resistance, to European diseases, the Aztec and the Inca suffered terrible epidemics. Illnesses weakened them in their struggle against the Spanish.

✓ PROGRESS CHECK

Analyzing How were the Spanish able to defeat Native American empires?

Spain in North America

GUIDING QUESTION *What did Spain hope to find in the Americas?*

Mexico and Peru were lands rich in silver and gold. Hoping to find similar wealth to the north, conquistadors explored the southeastern and southwestern parts of what is today the United States.

conquistador Spanish explorer
immunity resistance, such as to disease

Cortés accepts the surrender of the Aztec ruler.

Thinking Like a HISTORIAN

Analyzing Primary Sources

In 1519 Hernán Cortés prepared to leave Cuba for Mexico with 11 ships carrying about 550 Spanish soldiers and 16 horses. Before setting off, Cortés said to his men:

"I know in my heart that we shall take vast and wealthy lands, people such as have never before been seen. ... If you do not abandon me, as I shall not abandon you, I shall make you in a very short time the richest of all men who have crossed the seas."

—from *The Life of the Conqueror by His Secretary,* trans. Lesley Byrd Simpson

Based on this quote, what inspired the conquistadors?

For more about analyzing primary sources, review *Thinking Like a Historian.*

Sor Juana Inés de la Cruz (1651?–1695)

Juana Inés de la Cruz was born in New Spain, the daughter of a Spanish father and a Creole mother. She became a famous writer in a culture where most women were not taught to read. Her intelligence and thirst for learning led her to seek religious training, which allowed her time to study and write. Her private library was one of the largest in the Americas. In addition to books, she also collected musical and scientific instruments. Recognized as a great writer in her own lifetime, her poems, plays, and stories were published in the Americas and in Spain. Today, de la Cruz is seen as one of the greatest Mexican colonial writers.

▶ **CRITICAL THINKING**

Speculating Why do you think it might have been difficult for de la Cruz to become a successful writer?

Juan Ponce de León (pahn•suh day lee•OHN) made the first Spanish landing on the east coast of present-day Florida in 1513. According to legend, Ponce de León was not looking only for gold. He also hoped to find the legendary fountain of youth. This had been described by a historian of that time as, "a spring of running water of such marvelous virtue" that drinking it "makes old men young again." Ponce de León's exploration led to the first Spanish settlement in what is now the United States—a fort the Spanish built at St. Augustine, Florida, in 1565.

The Seven Cities of Gold

Still other conquistadors searched for quick riches, and several lost their lives in the process. Álvar Núñez Cabeza de Vaca (cuh•BAY•suh duh VAH•cuh) was part of a Spanish expedition to Florida in 1528. After coming into conflict with Native Americans in Florida, the expedition sailed south toward Mexico in November, led by Pánfilo de Narváez (nahr•VAH•ays). Three of its five boats were lost in a storm.

The two boats that made it through the storm became stuck on a beach on an island near present-day Texas. Within a few months, only a handful of the Spanish explorers were still alive. To survive among the Native Americans, de Vaca and an enslaved African named Estevanico (es•TAY•vahn•EE•koh) persuaded the Native Americans that they had healing powers. Cabeza de Vaca later wrote that their method of healing was "to bless the sick, breathing upon them," and to recite Latin prayers.

In 1533 the Spaniards set off on a long trek across the Southwest. While traveling, they often heard stories about seven rich cities in the region. When Cabeza de Vaca finally arrived in Mexico in 1536, he told eager listeners about the "Seven Cities of Cíbola"—seven cities of gold.

De Soto Searches for Gold

Excited by these stories, Hernando de Soto led an expedition to explore Florida and what is today the southeastern United States. For three years they traveled, following stories of gold. Their encounters with the native people often turned violent.

De Soto crossed the Mississippi River in 1541, describing it as "swift, and very deep." After traveling as far west as present-day Oklahoma, de Soto died of fever. His men buried him in the waters of the Mississippi.

© Alfredo Dagli Orti/The Art Archive/Corbis

Reading HELPDESK

Academic Vocabulary

contact when two or more groups or objects come together

Reading in the Content Area: *Map Keys*

A map key shows what symbols and colors on the map mean. In the map on the next page, the key explains the colors of the lines on the map. For example, the yellow line represents Ponce de León's route in 1513.

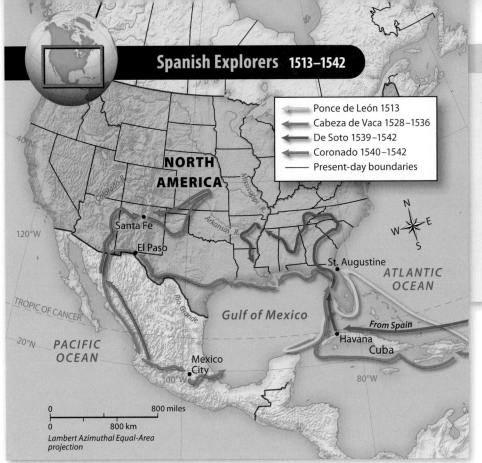

Spanish Explorers 1513–1542

Ponce de León 1513
Cabeza de Vaca 1528–1536
De Soto 1539–1542
Coronado 1540–1542
Present-day boundaries

NORTH AMERICA

120°W
40°N
Santa Fe
El Paso
Colorado R.
Arkansas R.
Mississippi R.

St. Augustine
ATLANTIC OCEAN

TROPIC OF CANCER
Rio Grande
Gulf of Mexico
From Spain
Havana
Cuba
80°W

20°N
PACIFIC OCEAN
Mexico City
100°W

0   800 miles
0   800 km
Lambert Azimuthal Equal-Area projection

The Granger Collection, NYC

Coronado Takes Up the Search

Another conquistador who searched for the Seven Cities of Cíbola was Francisco Vásquez de Coronado (kawr•oh•NAH•doh). His travels took him through northern Mexico and present-day Arizona and New Mexico, until his expedition reached a Zuni (ZOO•nee) settlement in 1540. Finally convinced that there was no gold, members of the expedition traveled west to the Colorado River and east into what is now Kansas. They found no gold— only "windswept plains" and strange "shaggy cows" (buffalo).

☑ PROGRESS CHECK

Speculating Why do you think that the encounters between de Soto's party and Native Americans were sometimes violent?

Life Under Spanish Rule

GUIDING QUESTION *What effect did Spanish rule have on society?*

Spanish law set up three kinds of settlements in the Americas— pueblos, missions, and presidios. **Pueblos,** or towns, were centers of trade. **Missions** were religious communities.

They included a church, a small town, and fields for crops. A **presidio** was a type of fort, and was usually built near a mission.

Juan de Oñate (day ohn•YAH•tay) traveled up from Mexico to establish a Spanish presence in the lands to the north. He was also assigned to convert the native people to Christianity.

Mission Santa Clara de Asís was California's eighth mission. All missions had the same basic plan and were located near wood, water, and land for farming and grazing. There was a church, housing for the priests and Native American converts, grain fields with irrigation ditches, and corrals for cattle, sheep, and goats.

In 1598 Oñate **founded,** or established, the province of New Mexico. He introduced cattle and horses to the Pueblo people. The first Spanish city in the southwest, Santa Fe, was established in 1607. Santa Fe became the capital of the province in 1610.

Spanish Colonial Society

There was a very clear class system in Spanish colonial society. The highest level of society was made up of the *peninsulares,* people who were born in Spain. They were the landowners, leaders of government, and heads of the Catholic Church. Next in rank were the Creoles, people born in the Americas whose parents were Spanish. The next level below were the mestizos (meh•STEE•zohs), people with one Spanish and one Native American parent. Still lower were the Native Americans, most of whom lived in great poverty, and enslaved Africans.

The Spanish government granted conquistadors who settled in the Americas the right to demand either taxes or labor from Native Americans living on the land. This system forced the Native Americans into a form of slavery.

For example, in the 1540s, when the Spanish discovered silver ore in northern Mexico, they set up mining camps. They then forced Native Americans to dig for silver. The damp mineshafts were a grueling environment in which to work. Many Native Americans died there from malnutrition and disease.

Lake County Museum/CORBIS

pueblo a town in the Spanish-ruled lands
mission a religious community where farming was carried out and Native Americans were converted to Christianity

presidio a fort
plantation a large farm

Academic Vocabulary

found to start, to establish

A Spanish priest, Bartolomé de Las Casas, spoke out against such cruel treatment of Native Americans and pleaded for laws to protect them. He claimed that millions had died because the Spanish "made gold their ultimate aim, seeking to load themselves with riches in the shortest possible time."

Las Casas's reports convinced Spanish leaders to pass the New Laws in 1542. These laws forbade enslaving Native Americans. Unfortunately, the laws were not always enforced.

The Plantation System

Not all Spaniards sought gold. Some found wealth shipping crops to Spain. In the West Indies, key exports were tobacco and sugarcane. The Spanish developed the **plantation** system to raise these crops. A plantation is a large farm.

The Spanish first used Native American labor to work their plantations. Las Casas suggested that they be replaced by enslaved Africans—a suggestion he bitterly regretted later. As a result, thousands of enslaved Africans were brought from West Africa to the Americas. Those who survived the brutal voyage were sold to plantation owners. By the late 1500s, slave labor was an essential part of the economy of the colonies.

Spanish Missions in California

■ Missions begun by Serra
■ Other Missions
═ El Camino Real

San Francisco de Asís (1776)
Santa Clara de Asís (1777)
San Carlos Borroméo de Carmelo (1770)
San Antonio de Padua (1771)
San Luís Obispo de Tolosa (1772)
San Buenaventura (1782)
San Gabriel Arcángel (1771)
San Juan Capistrano (1776)
San Diego de Alcalá (1769)

SIERRA NEVADA
COAST RANGE
California
PACIFIC OCEAN

0   100 miles
0   100 km
Albers Equal-Area projection

GEOGRAPHY CONNECTION

By 1820 there were 21 missions along the California portion of *El Camino Real*, "the royal road."

1 LOCATION What was the southernmost Spanish mission?

2 CRITICAL THINKING *Drawing Conclusions* Why do you think so many missions were located along waterways?

The Spanish influence in the United States is strong. Many Spanish words have been incorporated into the language, such as fiesta and canyon. The Spanish, who were expert ranchers, introduced animals such as horses, sheep, pigs, and beef cattle into the American Southwest. Many place names in the United States today are Spanish in origin. Some examples in the text are Santa Fe and San Diego. Can you think of any others?

Spanish Settlement in the Southwest

In the 1600s and 1700s, the Spanish, with much help from Native Americans, settled the Southwest, including present-day New Mexico, Texas, and California.

The Spanish explorer Juan Cabrillo (kuh•BREE•yoh) first sighted what is now California in 1542. However, for 200 years the Spanish had left the area alone. Around 1769, that policy changed. California was the northern frontier of the Spanish Empire in North America, and Spain needed a large number of colonists to solidify its hold on the region. Spain also wanted to convert more Native Americans to Christianity.

Spanish settlement in California consisted mostly of mission building. The Spaniards trained Native Americans who lived on the mission as farmers. They learned how to grow crops, irrigate farmland, and perform other tasks usually carried out on a ranch. Eventually, the missions became economically profitable enough to sell some of their goods, such as wine, olive oil, and leather.

Effect on Native American Life

California's many Native American groups had well-ordered societies before the Spanish arrived. They hunted, fished, and gathered plants for food. The arrival of the Spanish disrupted this way of life. The Spanish forced native peoples to convert to Christianity and to live and work at the missions.

✓ PROGRESS CHECK

Summarizing What kinds of settlements did the Spanish build in the Americas?

LESSON 3 REVIEW

Review Vocabulary

1. Use the following content vocabulary terms to write a short paragraph about Spanish settlement in the Americas.

   a. pueblo   b. mission

   c. presidio   d. plantation

Answer the Guiding Questions

2. *Summarizing* What did most conquistadors hope to accomplish in the Americas?

3. *Explaining* Why was 1513 a significant year in the history of the United States?

4. *Making Generalizations* What effect do you think Spanish settlement had on Native Americans?

5. **EXPOSITORY WRITING** The conquistadors are often described as possessing both good and bad qualities. Write a paragraph in which you express what you think were the qualities, both good and bad, of the Spanish conquistadors.

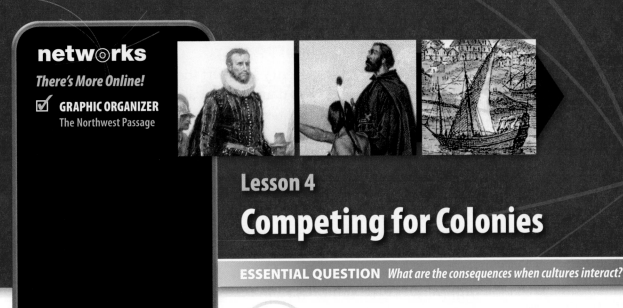

Lesson 4
Competing for Colonies

ESSENTIAL QUESTION *What are the consequences when cultures interact?*

IT MATTERS BECAUSE
The European competition for colonies in the Americas led to settlement and exploration in many parts of North America.

Religious Rivalries

GUIDING QUESTION *What were the religious motives behind the Age of Exploration?*

The Europeans who explored and settled in North America in the 1500s sought wealth. They also wanted to spread their Christian faith. The first to arrive were Roman Catholics—the only Christian church in the western part of Europe at that time. Not long after Columbus made his first voyage across the Atlantic, however, religious conflict shook Europe. New rivalries based on religious beliefs emerged.

Luther and the Reformation

In 1517 a German priest named Martin Luther nailed a list of complaints on the door of a local Catholic church, questioning the power and authority of Catholic leaders—including the pope, the head of the Catholic Church. Luther hoped to spark reform within the Church, but Pope Leo X rejected his ideas. Others agreed with Luther. His ideas helped launch a movement called the **Reformation** (reh•fuhr•MAY•shuhn). The movement led to a new form of Christianity called **Protestantism** (PRAH•tuhs•tuhn•tih•zuhm). Among the differences between Protestants and Catholics was that Protestants did not accept the leadership of the pope. The Reformation led to **widespread** conflict within and between the nations of Europe.

(l) Bettmann/CORBIS, (c) PoodlesRock/Corbis, (r) The Granger Collection, NYC

Reading **HELP**DESK

Taking Notes: *Listing*

As you study the lesson, use a diagram like this to list the explorers who tried to find a Northwest Passage.

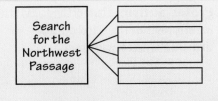

Search for the Northwest Passage

Content Vocabulary
- **Reformation**
- **Protestantism**
- **armada**
- **Northwest Passage**
- **tenant farmer**

In 1639 a French woman named Marie Guyard, or Marie of the Incarnation, arrived in Quebec, New France's first colony. Later, she wrote religious books in the languages of the native peoples she met there. In a letter, Guyard wrote:

"You will perhaps laugh that at the age of fifty years I am beginning to study a new tongue [language], but one must undertake all things for the service of God and the salvation of one's neighbour."

—from *Word From New France*, by Marie Guyard

From her letter, what do you know about the person and character of Marie Guyard?

For more about analyzing primary sources, review *Thinking Like a Historian*.

Religious Rivalry in Europe

In 1533 the English king, Henry VIII, left the Catholic Church. Later, during the rule of his daughter Elizabeth I, further reforms established England as a Protestant nation. At that time, it was common for kings and queens to insist that their subjects follow their religion. Subjects who did not could lose their lands and fortunes. In England, many people were unhappy about leaving the Catholic Church, but they had little power to resist.

England's Protestantism caused conflict with Spain. Beginning in 1585, King Philip of Spain made plans to invade England. A successful invasion could mean the overthrow of Protestantism. In May 1588, Philip sent an **armada** (ahr•MAH•duh), or war fleet, of 132 ships to England. With 30,000 troops and more than 2,000 guns, the Spanish Armada was the mightiest naval force in the world. Yet the smaller, faster English ships quickly gained the upper hand.

The defeat of Spain's armada marked the end of Spanish control of the seas. Now the way was clear for the English to start colonies in North America.

Religious Rivalries in the Americas

Catholics from Spain and France worked to spread their faith among the Native Americans. The Spanish settled in the southwestern and southeastern regions of North America, and the French settled in the northeast. Dutch and English Protestants set up colonies along the Atlantic coast between the French and the Spanish settlements. Religious differences contributed to the rivalries between these settlements.

Search for a Northwest Passage

In the 1500s and early 1600s, England, France, and the Netherlands sent explorers to map the coast of North America and, later, establish trade and colonies. Explorers also hoped to discover a **Northwest Passage** to Asia, a direct water route through the Americas.

England sent John Cabot, an Italian, to look for a northern sea route to Asia in 1497. Cabot probably landed on the coast of present-day Newfoundland. In 1524 France hired another Italian, Giovanni de Verrazano, to look for a northern route. Verrazano explored the coast of North America from present-day Nova Scotia down to the Carolinas.

Reading HELPDESK

Reformation a sixteenth-century religious movement rejecting or changing some Roman Catholic teachings and practices and establishing the Protestant churches

Protestantism a form of Christianity that was in opposition to the Catholic Church
armada a fleet of warships

Academic Vocabulary

widespread over a wide area

In 1609 Henry Hudson and his crew landed on the shores of Delaware Bay. The native people offered goods for trade.

In 1535 French explorer Jacques Cartier (kahr•tee•AY) sailed up the St. Lawrence River, hoping it would lead to the Pacific. Cartier did not make it to the Pacific, but he discovered a mountain peak that he named Mont-Royal, which means "royal mountain." This is the site of the present-day city of Montreal.

The Netherlands also wanted to find a passage through the Americas. The Dutch hired English sea explorer and navigator Henry Hudson to look for it. In 1609 he discovered the river that now bears his name. In his ship, the *Half Moon*, Hudson sailed north on the Hudson River as far as the site of present-day Albany, New York. Deciding that he had not found a passage to India, he turned back.

The following year England sent Hudson to try again. On this trip, Hudson discovered a huge bay—now called Hudson Bay. Thinking he had reached the Pacific, Hudson spent months looking for an outlet. His crew became impatient and rebelled. They set Hudson, his son, and a few sailors adrift in a small boat, never to be seen again.

☑ **PROGRESS CHECK**

Analyzing Why did nations want to find a Northwest Passage?

Northwest Passage a sea passage between the Atlantic and the Pacific along the north coast of North America

Bettmann/CORBIS

In 1673 Father Jacques Marquette and Louis Joliet located the great Mississippi River. They hoped to find that the river led to the Pacific Ocean.

▶ **CRITICAL THINKING**

Explaining In what way was Marquette and Joliet's expedition successful? Unsuccessful?

French and Dutch Settlements

GUIDING QUESTION *How did French and Dutch settlements compare to the Spanish colonies?*

French explorers and settlers trailed the Spanish by many years, but the French did establish settlements in North America. At first, the French were most interested in natural resources, including fish and furs. French trappers went far into the interior of North America and traded with Native Americans. France built forts to protect their trade. French missionaries followed the traders.

In 1663 New France became a royal colony. The new royal governor supported expanded exploration.

Exploring the Mississippi River

In the 1670s, two French explorers—a fur trader, Louis Joliet, and a priest, Jacques Marquette—traveled the Mississippi River by canoe. Joliet and Marquette hoped to find precious metals. They were also looking for a Northwest Passage. When they realized that the Mississippi flowed south into the Gulf of Mexico rather than west into the Pacific, they headed back upriver.

In 1682 Robert Cavelier de La Salle followed the Mississippi all the way to the Gulf of Mexico. He claimed the region for France, calling it Louisiana in honor of Louis XIV. In 1718 the French founded New Orleans. French explorers and missionaries traveled west to the Rocky Mountains and the Rio Grande.

PoodlesRock/Corbis

Reading **HELP**DESK

tenant farmer settler who pays rent or provides work to a landowner in exchange for the right to use the landowner's land

Academic Vocabulary

pose to present; to offer

New France and New Netherland

French settlement in North America advanced slowly. New France was made up of estates along the St. Lawrence River. Estate holders brought in settlers in exchange for land. These **tenant** (TEH•nuhnt) **farmers** paid rent and worked for their lord for a set period each year.

The French got along well with the Native Americans. French trappers and missionaries lived among them, learned their languages, and respected their ways. The missionaries had come to convert Native Americans to Catholicism, but they did not try to change their customs. Because the French colony grew slowly, it did not seem to **pose** a threat to the Native Americans and their lands.

The Netherlands was a small country with few natural resources and limited farmland. This is why the Dutch were anxious to set up a North American colony. After Hudson's voyage in 1609, the Dutch began to explore North America.

The Netherlands also had a large fleet of trading ships that sailed all over the world. In 1621 the Netherlands created the Dutch West India Company to run its trade between the Americas and Africa. In 1623 the company took over control of the Dutch colony in North America, called "New Netherland."

The heart of the colony was New Amsterdam. The town was built on the tip of Manhattan Island. In 1626 governor Peter Minuit bought the island from the Manhattoes people for 60 Dutch guilders (about $24) worth of trade goods.

The Dutch hoped New Amsterdam, located where the Hudson River enters what is now New York Harbor, would become an important center for their trade.

▶ **CRITICAL THINKING**

Analyzing Which characteristics of the region of New Amsterdam might encourage trade for the Dutch settlers?

The Granger Collection, NYC

☑ PROGRESS CHECK

Explaining What were France's goals in North America?

LESSON 4 REVIEW

Review Vocabulary

1. Explain the meaning of the terms *armada* and *Protestantism* by using both in a sentence.

2. Explain the significance of the term *tenant farmer*.

Answer the Guiding Questions

3. *Explaining* What were the key religious differences between the European nations that explored the Americas?

4. *Analyzing* What was the effect on England of the defeat of the Spanish Armada?

5. *Contrasting* How did the French attitude toward Native Americans differ from that found in the Spanish colonies?

6. **PERSONAL WRITING** Write a letter to a relative in Europe from the point of view of an early French or Dutch settler in North America. Describe what life is like and what your goals are in North America.

Write your answers on a separate piece of paper.

1 **Exploring the Essential Question**

EXPOSITORY WRITING Choose one of the main topics discussed in this chapter: the Renaissance, the trading empires of Africa, the Age of Exploration, Spain in the Americas, the Protestant Reformation, or the colonization of the Americas by France or the Netherlands. For the topic you chose, identify one new idea and one way in which it caused a change for people living at that time. Explain whether it was a positive or a negative change, and why. Use examples from the text to support your opinion.

2 **21st Century Skills**

INFORMATION LITERACY Working in small groups, research the factors and events that contributed to the decline in the population of Native Americans. Then, research the factors and events that contributed to the increase in the population of Africans in the Americas. Create a time line or other kind of diagram that charts the development of these two historical trends. Present your findings to the class.

3 **Thinking Like a Historian**

UNDERSTANDING CAUSE AND EFFECT Create a diagram like the one to the right to examine how the exploration and conquest of the Americas may have affected Europe.

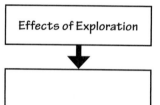

Effects of Exploration

4 **Visual Literacy**

ANALYZING PAINTINGS In the painting below, Coronado heads an expedition into New Mexico. What does this image suggest about the way the Spanish conquistadors viewed their role in the lands they explored? Explain your answer.

REVIEW THE GUIDING QUESTIONS

Choose the best answer for each question.

1 The tool of navigation that showed the direction of magnetic north was the

A. caravel.

B. compass.

C. carrack.

D. quadrant.

2 Between A.D. 400 and 1100, many West Africans decided to become Muslim through trading contact with

F. Asia.

G. Europe.

H. North Africa.

I. North America.

3 Vasco da Gama fulfilled Portugal's goal of a sea route to Asia when he reached

A. the coast of Brazil.

B. the Cape of Good Hope.

C. Calicut in India.

D. Mombasa in eastern Africa.

4 Spanish settlements that served as centers for teaching Native Americans the Spanish religion and ways of living were called

F. pueblos.

G. missions.

H. presidios.

I. plantations.

5 What was one result from the defeat of the armada sent by Spain?

A. The Reformation began.

B. Spain controlled the world's sea trade.

C. France became the world's largest empire.

D. The way was clear for England to start colonies in North America.

6 Joliet and Marquette

F. condemned the treatment of Native Americans.

G. founded the settlement of New Amsterdam.

H. explored the Mississippi River for France.

I. led the battle against the Spanish Armada.

DBQ DOCUMENT-BASED QUESTIONS

7 Locating According to the map, St. Augustine is located in

A. New Spain.

B. New Granada.

C. Peru.

D. the Rio de la Plata.

8 Analyzing Visuals Spanish settlements in North America include

F. Lima.

G. La Paz.

H. Santiago.

I. Santa Fe.

Map labels:
- 120°W 100°W 80°W 60°W 40°W 20°W
- 40°N
- Santa Fe • Taos
- St. Augustine
- Rio Grande
- *Gulf of Mexico* TROPIC OF CANCER
- **VICEROYALTY OF NEW SPAIN**
- Cuba Puerto Rico 20°N
- Mexico City
- Veracruz Hispaniola
- *Caribbean Sea* **ATLANTIC OCEAN**
- Panama Caracas
- **VICEROYALTY OF NEW GRANADA**
- Bogotá
- Guayaquil EQUATOR 0°
- Amazon
- **PACIFIC OCEAN**
- **VICEROYALTY OF PERU** **BRAZIL**
- Lima
- Cuzco
- La Paz
- **VICEROYALTY OF RÍO DE LA PLATA** São Paulo 20°S
- TROPIC OF CAPRICORN Rio de Janeiro
- 0 1000 miles
- 0 1000 km Valparaíso Santiago Rio Grande
- Lambert Azimuthal Equal-Area projection Buenos Aires
- 40°S

SHORT RESPONSE

In 1541, the Spanish priest Bartolomé de Las Casas wrote:

"The pattern established at the outset has remained unchanged to this day, and the Spaniards still do nothing save tear the natives to shreds, murder them and inflict upon them untold misery, suffering and distress, tormenting ... and persecuting them mercilessly."

—from *A Short Account of the Destruction of the Indies* by Bartolomé de Las Casas

9 What does this passage suggest about Spanish attitudes toward the Native Americans they encountered?

10 Why did the Spanish treat the Native Americans as described here?

EXTENDED RESPONSE

11 Narrative Writing Write a letter to a friend from the perspective of a Native American living in lands that the French have recently settled. How has life changed for you and your people since the French arrived? What are they doing to your people? What appears to be their purpose?

Need Extra Help?

If You've Missed Question	1	2	3	4	5	6	7	8	9	10	11
Review Lesson	1	1	2	3	4	4	3	3	3	3	4

Colonial America

1587–1770

ESSENTIAL QUESTIONS • *How does geography influence the way people live?*
• *How do new ideas change the way people live?*

The Story Matters . . .

She has three names, and she lives in two worlds. She is born Matoak, daughter of the chief of the Powhatan people. Yet she is such a fun-loving child that she is called "Pocahontas," or "playful one."

In 1607, bold Pocahontas—not yet a teenager—befriends the English colonists who settle nearby. She convinces her father to aid the colonists. In time she receives the English name Rebecca and marries a Briton. Their son is Thomas. The family travels to England, where Rebecca is presented to King James as a princess. Sadly, before her return to America, she falls ill. "Tis enough that [our] child liveth," she tells her husband before she dies.

◀ *Pocahontas played a key role in the early history of colonial Virginia.*

W. Langdon Kihn/National Geographic Society/Corbis

57

CHAPTER 3

Place and Time: Colonial America 1587 to 1770

Although several European nations had claims in North America, it was the British who eventually dominated the continent. England's early attempts at colonizing ended in failure, but by 1750, British colonies stretched for hundreds of miles along the Atlantic Coast.

Step Into the Place

MAP FOCUS Several European powers claimed parts of North America in the mid-1700s.

1 **PLACE** Which European power claimed the largest territory in North America?

2 **HUMAN-ENVIRONMENT INTERACTION** Which nation's land claims seem to be the most settled and populated?

3 **CRITICAL THINKING**
Predicting What effect do you think these nations' land claims in North America might have on relations between them?

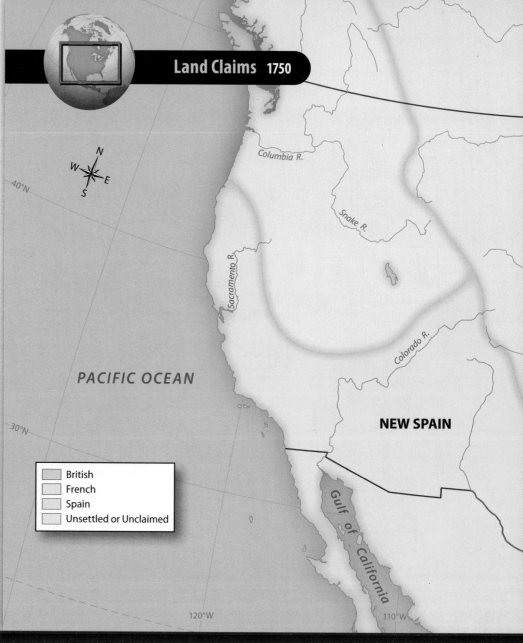

Land Claims 1750

Columbia R.

Snake R.

Sacramento R.

Colorado R.

PACIFIC OCEAN

NEW SPAIN

Gulf of California

	British
	French
	Spain
	Unsettled or Unclaimed

40°N

30°N

120°W   110°W

Step Into the Time

TIME LINE Look at the time line. The Spanish Armada was a fleet of warships Spain sent to attack England. How might this event be related to what happened in North America at about that time?

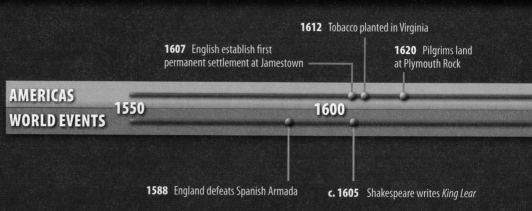

1612 Tobacco planted in Virginia

1607 English establish first permanent settlement at Jamestown

1620 Pilgrims land at Plymouth Rock

AMERICAS

WORLD EVENTS   1550   1600

1588 England defeats Spanish Armada   **c. 1605** Shakespeare writes *King Lear*

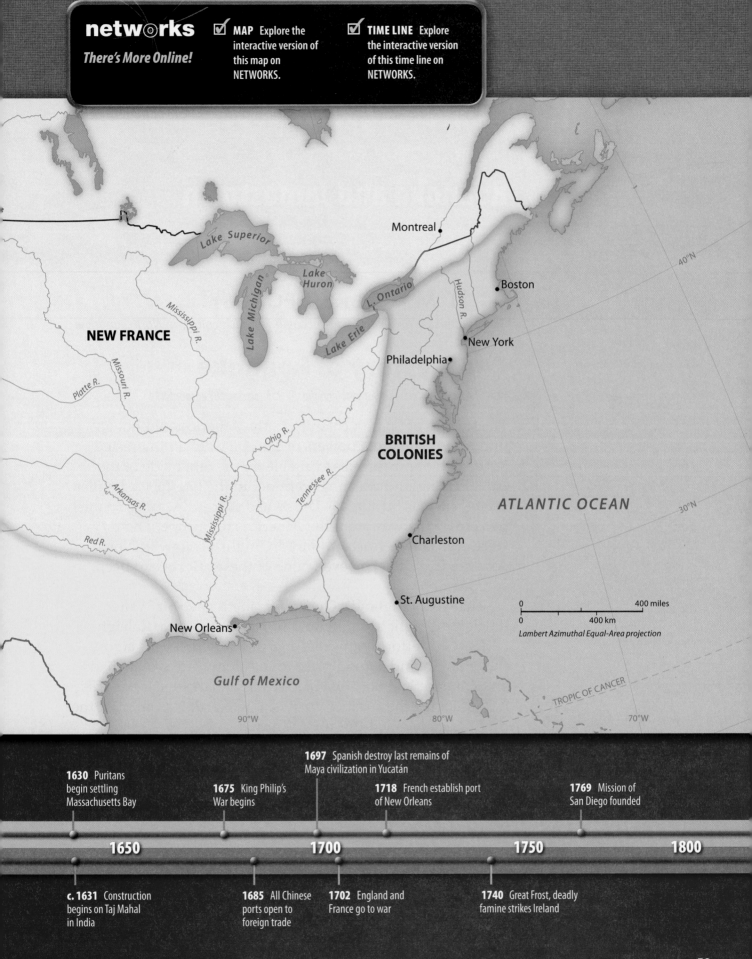

networks

There's More Online!

☑ **MAP** Explore the interactive version of this map on NETWORKS.

☑ **TIME LINE** Explore the interactive version of this time line on NETWORKS.

Montreal

Boston

NEW FRANCE

Lake Superior

Lake Michigan

Lake Huron

L. Ontario

Lake Erie

Hudson R.

New York

Philadelphia

Mississippi R.

Missouri R.

Platte R.

Ohio R.

Tennessee R.

Arkansas R.

Mississippi R.

Red R.

BRITISH COLONIES

ATLANTIC OCEAN

40°N

30°N

Charleston

St. Augustine

New Orleans

0   400 miles
0   400 km

Lambert Azimuthal Equal-Area projection

Gulf of Mexico

TROPIC OF CANCER

90°W   80°W   70°W

1697 Spanish destroy last remains of Maya civilization in Yucatán

1630 Puritans begin settling Massachusetts Bay

1675 King Philip's War begins

1718 French establish port of New Orleans

1769 Mission of San Diego founded

1650   **1700**   **1750**   **1800**

c. 1631 Construction begins on Taj Mahal in India

1685 All Chinese ports open to foreign trade

1702 England and France go to war

1740 Great Frost, deadly famine strikes Ireland

Lesson 1
Roanoke and Jamestown

ESSENTIAL QUESTION *How does geography influence the way people live?*

IT MATTERS BECAUSE
Jamestown was the first successful English colony in North America.

The Mystery of Roanoke

GUIDING QUESTION *What problems did the Roanoke settlers encounter?*

The success of Spain's colonies in the Americas did not go unnoticed. The great powers of Europe were all interested in the rich opportunities available on the other side of the Atlantic. England was no exception. In the late 1500s, English pirates such as Sir Francis Drake had success stealing Spanish treasure on its way from the Americas to Europe. There were even some efforts to start an English colony in North America. By 1584, however, none of these efforts had been successful.

That year, England's Queen Elizabeth gave Sir Walter Raleigh the right to claim land in North America. Raleigh took up this effort with great energy. He sent scouts across the ocean to find a good place for a colony. The scouts made an enthusiastic report of a place called Roanoke Island. This island lies off the coast of what is now North Carolina. At the time, Raleigh called this area Virginia.

Raleigh sent settlers to Roanoke Island twice. The first group arrived in 1585. While they were there, artist John White explored the area and drew pictures of what he saw. In a book illustrated by White, another colonist described the Native American towns:

Reading **HELP**DESK

Taking Notes: *Listing*

As you read, use a diagram like this one to list hardships the people of Jamestown faced.

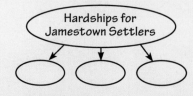

Content Vocabulary
• **charter**
• **joint-stock company**
• **headright**
• **burgess**

❝ Their townes are but small, & neere the sea coast but few, some containing but 10 or 12 houses: some 20, the greatest that we [have] seene [have] bene but of 30 houses: if they be walled it is only done with barks of trees made fast to stakes. ❞

—from *A Briefe and True Report of the New Found Land of Virginia*, 1588

The 1585 expedition produced some valuable information about the people and places of Virginia. Their colony, however, did not survive. After suffering through a difficult winter, the colonists gave up and returned to England.

Then, in 1587 Raleigh sent 91 men, 17 women, and 9 children to Roanoke. John White led this group. Shortly after arriving on the island, White's daughter, who was part of the expedition, gave birth. Virginia Dare was the first English child born in North America.

Nine days after his granddaughter's birth, White returned to England for supplies. Although he had hoped to be back within a few months, White was delayed. His country was at war with Spain. This war featured England's great naval battle with the Spanish Armada. The fighting between England and Spain made it impossible for White to sail back to Roanoke for nearly three years.

When he returned to Roanoke, White found his colony deserted. The only clue he found was a tree with the word *Croatoan* carved on it. White thought perhaps the colonists had gone to Croatoan Island, about 50 miles (80 km) to the south. Bad weather kept White from **investigating**. The Roanoke colonists were never seen again.

✓ PROGRESS CHECK

Explaining Why did the English decide to settle in Roanoke?

Success at Jamestown

GUIDING QUESTION *Why did the Jamestown settlement succeed?*

For a time, the failure at Roanoke discouraged the English from settling in North America. The idea emerged again in 1606. By then, England had a new king, James I. He wanted to renew England's quest for a colony in North America. Several merchants pressed him for a **charter**—a document that granted the right to form a colony.

Thinking Like a HISTORIAN

Analyzing Primary Sources

John White drew pictures of the plants, animals, and people of the region in order to help educate Europeans about North America. For more information about analyzing primary sources, read *Thinking Like a Historian.*

▶ CRITICAL THINKING

Analyzing Visuals Do you think John White's sketches are a primary source? Why or why not?

The Granger Collection, NYC.

---

charter a document granting the recipient the right to settle a colony

Academic Vocabulary

investigate to try to discover facts and other information about something

The Virginia Company

The Virginia Company was a **joint-stock company**, in which investors bought shares, or part ownership. Investors bought shares hoping the company would make money and that they would share in the profits. The plan was for the company's settlers to find gold and establish trade in fish and furs.

James I granted a charter to the Virginia Company of London. In December 1606, the company sent 144 settlers in three ships to build a new colony in North America. In April 1607, the ships entered Chesapeake Bay. They sailed up a river flowing into the bay. The colonists named the river the James and their new settlement Jamestown to honor their king.

Jamestown Survives

The colonists did not find gold or riches in Virginia. Instead they faced severe hardships, including disease and hunger. The colony survived its first two years in part because of 27-year-old Captain John Smith. Smith forced the settlers to work. He also built ties with—and got food from—the local Powhatan people and their chief, who was also named Powhatan.

In late 1609, Smith was injured and had to return to England. The colony struggled. The Powhatan stopped providing food. The winter of 1609–1610 was called "the starving time."

National Park Service.

Soon after landing, the Jamestown colonists began building a fort for protection. The surrounding forest provided the materials they needed for this project.

joint-stock company a company in which investors buy stock in return for a share of its future profits

headright a 50-acre grant of land given to colonial settlers who paid their own way
burgess elected representative to an assembly

Academic Vocabulary

expand to increase in size or number

Somehow Jamestown survived this terrible time. More colonists arrived to replace those who had died. The colonists also found a way to make money for the investors. They began growing a type of tobacco using seeds from the West Indies. Soon planters all along the James River were raising this valuable crop.

More Settlers Come to Virginia

The colony of Virginia began to **expand**. Relations with the Powhatan improved after a colonist, John Rolfe, married the chief's daughter, Pocahontas. The Virginia Company sent women to Jamestown. As a result, marriage and children became a part of life in the colony. The Virginia Company also began giving a **headright** (HEHD•RYT), or land grant, of 50 acres to settlers who paid their own way to the colony. The headright system helped the colony succeed. The chance to own land lured many settlers to Virginia and gave them a reason to work hard.

Pocahontas, shown here in English-style clothes for a visit to England, served as a link between the colonists and the Native Americans of Virginia.

The Virginia Company also gave the colonists the right to take part in their own government. In 1619 land-owning male colonists cast ballots for **burgesses** (BUHR•juhs•uhz), or representatives. The burgesses helped make laws for the colony. The House of Burgesses was the first legislature in North America elected by the people.

The Virginia Colony was growing in size, but it was not making any money for the shareholders of the Virginia Company. In fact, the company faced financial troubles. In 1624 King James took away the company's charter. Virginia became a royal colony, meaning it was directly under the control of the government in England.

☑ PROGRESS CHECK

Analyzing Why was the House of Burgesses important?

LESSON 1 REVIEW

Review Vocabulary

1. Examine the meaning of *charter* and *joint-stock company* by using each term in a sentence.

2. Write a sentence about the early years of the Virginia colony that use the following terms.

    a. headright   **b.** burgess

Answer the Guiding Questions

3. *Describing* What did John White find when he returned to Roanoke after several years in England?

4. *Explaining* Why was the Jamestown colony able to prosper in spite of many hardships?

5. **PERSUASIVE WRITING** Using primary and secondary source images and descriptions in this lesson, write an advertisement for a newspaper in England that encourages people to come to America in the 1600s.

networks

There's More Online!

☑ **CHART/GRAPH**
King Philip's War

☑ **GRAPHIC ORGANIZER**
Cooperation and Conflict between Colonists and Native Americans

☑ **MAP** The New England Colonies

☑ **SLIDE SHOW** The Pilgrims

Lesson 2
The New England Colonies

ESSENTIAL QUESTION *How do new ideas change the way people live?*

IT MATTERS BECAUSE

Seeking freedom to pursue their own religion, English settlers started colonies in New England. Many people still come to the Americas in search of religious freedom.

Seeking Religious Freedom

GUIDING QUESTION *Why did the Puritans settle in North America?*

The Jamestown settlers had come to America in search of wealth. The next wave of English colonists arrived in search of religious freedom.

England had been a Protestant country since 1534, when the king, Henry VIII, broke away from the Roman Catholic Church and formed the Anglican Church. Not everyone in England was happy with the new church. Many people **dissented** (dih•SEHNT•uhd), disagreeing with Anglican beliefs or practices. Some English people remained Catholic. Others were Protestants who wanted to reform the Anglican Church. Still others wanted to break away from it altogether. The Protestants who wished to reform the Anglican Church were called Puritans. Those who sought to set up their own churches were known as Separatists.

The Separatists were **persecuted** (PUHR•sih•kyoot•uhd)—mistreated because of their beliefs—in England. Some fled to the Netherlands. There they found freedom to practice their religion, but they had difficulty finding work. They also worried that their children were losing their religious values and their English way of life.

(c) Swerve/Alamy Images, (r) Bettmann/CORBIS.

Reading **HELP**DESK

Taking Notes: *Describing*

Use a diagram like this one to describe examples of cooperation and conflict between Native Americans and English colonists.

Content Vocabulary
• **dissent**
• **persecute**
• **tolerance**

The Pilgrims Settle Plymouth

In 1620 a group of Separatists decided to move to America. They became known as the Pilgrims. A pilgrim is someone who undertakes a religious journey. The Pilgrims were able to get grants of land from the Virginia Company. They got permission to settle in Virginia and to practice their religion freely. They boarded a ship called the *Mayflower* and left to begin new lives.

The *Mayflower* drifted off course on its journey across the Atlantic. The first land the Pilgrims sighted was Cape Cod, well north of their target. It was November, and winter was fast approaching. The colonists decided to drop anchor in Cape Cod Bay. They went ashore on a cold, bleak day in December at a place they called Plymouth.

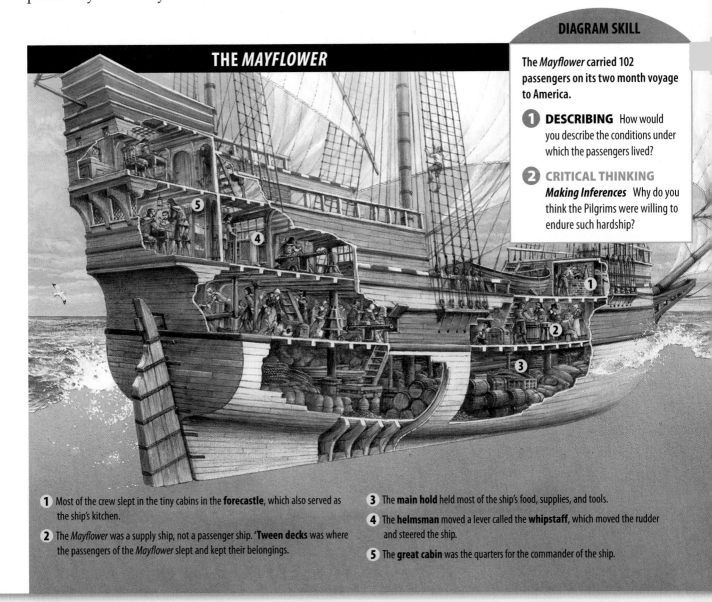

THE *MAYFLOWER*

DIAGRAM SKILL

The *Mayflower* carried 102 passengers on its two month voyage to America.

1 DESCRIBING How would you describe the conditions under which the passengers lived?

2 CRITICAL THINKING
Making Inferences Why do you think the Pilgrims were willing to endure such hardship?

1 Most of the crew slept in the tiny cabins in the **forecastle**, which also served as the ship's kitchen.

2 The *Mayflower* was a supply ship, not a passenger ship. **'Tween decks** was where the passengers of the *Mayflower* slept and kept their belongings.

3 The **main hold** held most of the ship's food, supplies, and tools.

4 The **helmsman** moved a lever called the **whipstaff**, which moved the rudder and steered the ship.

5 The **great cabin** was the quarters for the commander of the ship.

dissent to disagree with or oppose an opinion
persecute to mistreat a person or group on the basis of their beliefs

Build Vocabulary: *Word Origins*

The term *pilgrim* refers to someone who travels to a shrine or sacred place. It can also mean simply "a traveler."

The Mayflower Compact

Plymouth was outside the territory of the Virginia Company and its laws. While they were still onboard ship, the Pilgrims signed a document they called the Mayflower Compact. This document set up an organized, orderly government. Each signer promised to obey the laws passed "for the general good of the colony." The Mayflower Compact was a key step in the development of representative, democratic government in America.

Native American Help

During their first winter in America, almost half the Pilgrims died. Illness, hunger, and cold took a terrible toll. In the spring, however, two Native Americans, Squanto and Samoset, befriended the colonists. They taught the Pilgrims to grow corn, beans, and pumpkins and showed the colonists where to hunt and fish. Without their help, the Pilgrims might not have survived.

Squanto and Samoset also helped the Pilgrims make peace with the Wampanoag people who lived in the area. For a time, the two groups lived together in harmony. In the fall of 1621, the Pilgrims included their new Wampanoag friends in a feast of thanksgiving.

☑ PROGRESS CHECK

Analyzing What was the significance of the Mayflower Compact?

New Colonies

GUIDING QUESTION *What role did religion play in founding the various colonies?*

In 1629 a group of Puritans formed the Massachusetts Bay Company. They received a royal charter to establish a colony north of Plymouth. The company chose John Winthrop to be the colony's governor. In 1630 Winthrop led about 900 men, women, and children to Massachusetts Bay. Most of them settled in a place they called Boston.

More settlers followed. During the 1630s, more than 15,000 Puritans journeyed to Massachusetts to escape religious persecution and economic hard times in England. This movement of people became known as the Great Migration.

At first Winthrop and his assistants made the colony's laws. In 1634 settlers demanded a larger role in the government. Adult male church members were allowed to vote for the governor and for representatives to the government. Later, property ownership became a requirement for voting.

Connections to
TODAY

Plimoth Plantation

Plimoth Plantation, shown here, is an outdoor museum and a popular tourist site. Located in present-day Plymouth, Massachusetts, it uses actors to portray life as it was in 1627.

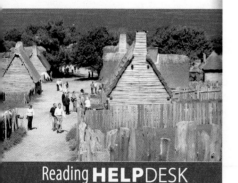

Reading **HELP**DESK

Reading Strategy: *Sequencing*

Sequencing means arranging events in the order in which they occur. Create a time line for the years 1620 to 1700, then place the events discussed in this lesson in their proper place along this line.

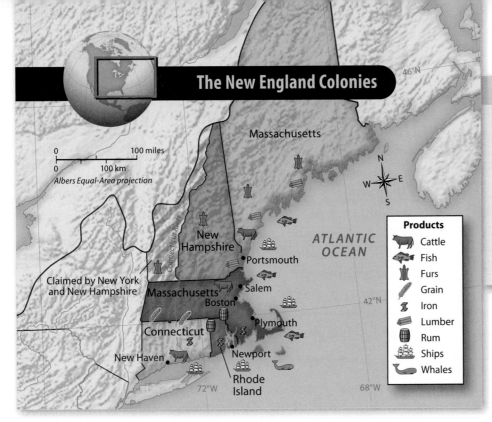

The New England Colonies

Massachusetts

New Hampshire

ATLANTIC OCEAN

Portsmouth
Salem
Massachusetts
Boston
Plymouth
Connecticut
New Haven
Newport
Rhode Island

Claimed by New York and New Hampshire

0   100 miles
0   100 km
Albers Equal-Area projection

46°N
42°N
72°W   68°W

Products
Cattle
Fish
Furs
Grain
Iron
Lumber
Rum
Ships
Whales

GEOGRAPHY CONNECTION

English settlers formed the New England colonies.

1 MOVEMENT What colonies were founded after the settling of Massachusetts?

2 CRITICAL THINKING
Identifying In what part of New England was farming a significant industry?

The Puritans came to America to put their religious beliefs into practice. At the same time, they themselves had little **tolerance** (TAH•luh•ruhnts) for different beliefs. They criticized or persecuted people who did not agree with their views. They strictly **enforced** their own religious rules. This lack of tolerance led people to form new colonies.

Connecticut and Rhode Island

To the west of Boston is land we now call the Connecticut River Valley. This rich land is better for farming than the stony soil around Boston. In the 1630s colonists began to settle this area.

A leader of this movement was Massachusetts minister Thomas Hooker. He did not like how Winthrop and other Puritan leaders ran the colony. In 1636 Hooker led his congregation to the Connecticut River Valley. There he founded the town of Hartford. Other nearby towns were soon established. Three years later these towns formed a colony called Connecticut. In 1639 they adopted a plan of government called the Fundamental Orders of Connecticut. This was the first written constitution in America. The document described the organization of representative government in detail. Like the Mayflower Compact, it reflected a belief in democratic principles.

tolerance the ability to accept or put up with different views or behaviors

Academic Vocabulary

enforce to apply a rule or law
policy a statement of ideals or plan of action

Anne Hutchinson held meetings in her home to discuss and give her views on religious teachings. Puritan leaders charged her with "dishonoring" the Massachusetts Bay Colony. They banished Hutchinson in 1637.

A minister named Roger Williams founded the colony of Rhode Island. Williams felt that government should not force people to worship in a certain way. He also believed it was wrong for settlers to take land away from the Native Americans. Forced by Massachusetts leaders to leave the colony, Williams found refuge with the Narragansett, a Native American people. They later sold him land, where Williams founded the town of Providence. With its **policy** of religious toleration, Rhode Island became a safe place for dissenters. It was the first place in America where people of all faiths could worship freely.

Others followed Williams's example. In 1638 John Wheelwright led a group of dissidents from Massachusetts to found the town of Exeter in New Hampshire. New Hampshire became an independent colony in 1679.

Conflict With Native Americans

As settlers spread across New England, they met the Native Americans who lived there—Wampanoags, Narragansett, and other groups. Native Americans traded furs for settlers' goods, but conflicts arose. Usually settlers moved onto Native American lands without permission or payment. Throughout the colonial period, settlers and Native Americans competed fiercely for land.

In 1675 Wampanoag leader Metacomet waged war against the New England colonies. Known to settlers as King Philip, Metacomet enlisted the help of other Native American groups. King Philip's War raged for 14 months. In the end, the colonists defeated Metacomet. The war destroyed the power of the Native Americans in New England. Colonial settlement expanded.

☑ **PROGRESS CHECK**

Identifying Which colony was first to let people of all faiths worship freely?

Bettmann/CORBIS.

LESSON 2 REVIEW

Review Vocabulary

1. Examine the words below. Then write a paragraph explaining what the words have in common.

   a. dissent   **b.** persecute   **c.** tolerance

Answer the Guiding Questions

2. *Explaining* Why did the Separatists and Puritans leave England and settle in North America?

3. *Comparing* What did the colonies of Connecticut, Rhode Island, and New Hampshire have in common?

4. **EXPOSITORY WRITING** Write a paragraph describing the importance of the search for religious freedom in the settling of America. Describe the founding of at least two colonies.

netw⊙rks

There's More Online!

- ☑ **CHART/GRAPH** The Middle Colonies
- ☑ **GRAPHIC ORGANIZER** Dividing Colonies
- ☑ **MAP** The Middle Colonies
- ☑ **PRIMARY SOURCE** Attack on New Amsterdam

Lesson 3

The Middle Colonies

ESSENTIAL QUESTION *How does geography influence the way people live?*

IT MATTERS BECAUSE

The Middle Colonies drew a diverse population to North America.

New York and New Jersey

GUIDING QUESTION *Why did the Middle Colonies grow?*

By 1660, England had two groups of colonies in North America. In the north were the New England colonies. In the south was Virginia, and also the colony of Maryland, which was settled in 1634. Between these two groups of colonies were lands under Dutch control. This area was called New Netherland.

The main settlement of New Netherland was New Amsterdam, on Manhattan Island. This location combined a good seaport with access to the Hudson River. The river served as a major transportation link to a rich land of farms, forests, and furs. As a result, New Amsterdam became a center of shipping to and from the Americas.

The Dutch West India Company controlled New Netherland. It wanted to increase the colony's population. To do this, the company offered large grants of land to anyone who could bring at least 50 settlers to work the land. The landowners who received these grants were called **patroons** (puh•TROONS). The patroons ruled like kings. They had their own courts and laws. Settlers owed the patroons labor and a share of their crops.

(tl) Bloomberg/Getty Images, (cl) Allan Baxter/The Image Bank/Getty, (r) Art Resource, NY.

Reading **HELP**DESK

Taking Notes: *Identifying*

As you read, use a diagram like this one to illustrate how the New York and Pennsylvania colonies split to form the four middle colonies under British rule.

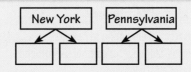

Content Vocabulary
- **patroon**
- **pacifist**

New Amsterdam, which later became New York City, was a prosperous and diverse city. Its population was around 8 thousand in 1664. Today, the city is home to 8 million people. The population is still diverse. Some 3 million New York City residents were born in another country.

NOW

▶ **CRITICAL THINKING**
Speculating Why do you think New York City draws such a diverse population?

New Netherland Becomes New York

New Netherland's success did not go unnoticed. The English wanted to gain control of the valuable Dutch colony. England insisted it had a right to the land based on John Cabot's explorations in the late 1400s. In 1664 the English sent a fleet to attack New Amsterdam. Peter Stuyvesant, governor of the colony, surrendered it to the English forces without a fight.

England's King Charles gave the colony to his brother, the Duke of York, who renamed it New York. New York was a proprietary colony. This was a colony in which an owner, or proprietor, owned all the land and controlled the government. Not until 1691 did the English government allow citizens of New York to elect their legislature.

New York continued to prosper under English control. It had a diverse population made up of Dutch, German, Swedish, and Native American people. Also among the population were people of the Jewish religion. They were the first Jews to settle in North America.

In 1664 New York had about 8,000 residents, including at least 300 enslaved Africans. By 1683 the population had swelled to about 12,000 people. New Amsterdam, which had been renamed New York City, was one of the fastest-growing places in the colonies.

Founding New Jersey

The Duke of York decided to divide his colony. He gave the land between the Hudson and Delaware Rivers to Lord John Berkeley and Sir George Carteret. The two proprietors named their colony New Jersey, after the English Channel island of Jersey, where Carteret was born. To attract settlers, the proprietors offered large tracts of land and also promised freedom of religion, trial by jury, and a representative assembly.

Like New York, New Jersey had a diverse population. There were people of many different racial, religious, and national backgrounds—that is, many different **ethnic** groups. New Jersey had no natural harbors, so it did not develop a major port or city like New York. New Jersey's proprietors made few profits. Both eventually sold their shares in the colony. By 1702, New Jersey had become a royal colony. However, the colonists continued to make local laws.

☑ **PROGRESS CHECK**

Explaining Why did no major city develop in New Jersey?

Reading **HELP**DESK

patroon landowner in the Dutch colonies who ruled over large areas of land

Academic Vocabulary

ethnic of or relating to national, tribal, racial, religious, language, or cultural background

Pennsylvania and Delaware

GUIDING QUESTION *How did Pennsylvania differ from the other English colonies?*

The Quakers, a Protestant group that had been persecuted in England, founded the colony of Pennsylvania. In 1680 William Penn, a wealthy English Quaker, received the land in payment for a debt King Charles owed Penn's father. Pennsylvania, or "Penn's Woods," stretched inland from the Delaware River. The new colony was nearly as large as England.

William Penn saw Pennsylvania as a "holy experiment," a chance to put his Quaker ideals into practice. The Quakers, or Society of Friends, believed that everyone was equal. People could follow their own "inner light" rather than the teachings of a religious leader. Quakers were also **pacifists** (PA•suh•fihsts), or people who refuse to use force or fight in wars.

Penn was an active proprietor. In 1682 he sailed to America to supervise the building of Philadelphia, a name that means "city of brotherly love." Penn designed the city himself. He also wrote Pennsylvania's first constitution. Penn believed that the land belonged to the Native Americans and that settlers should pay for it. He negotiated several treaties with local Native Americans.

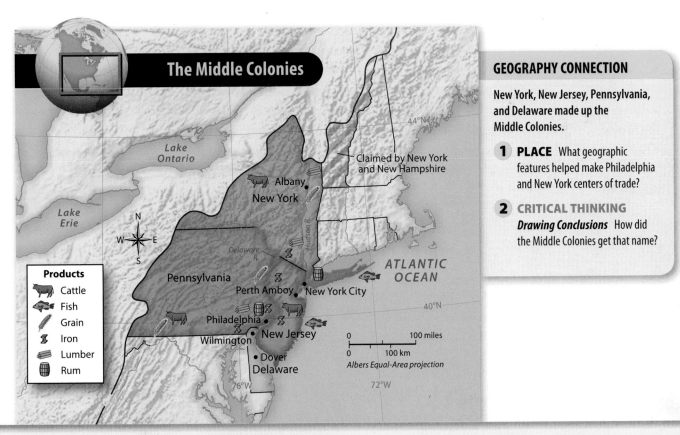

The Middle Colonies

Products
- Cattle
- Fish
- Grain
- Iron
- Lumber
- Rum

Lake Ontario

Lake Erie

Albany
New York

Claimed by New York and New Hampshire

Hudson R.

Delaware R.

Pennsylvania

Perth Amboy

New York City

ATLANTIC OCEAN

Philadelphia

New Jersey

Wilmington

Dover

Delaware

44°N

40°N

76°W

72°W

0   100 miles
0   100 km
Albers Equal-Area projection

GEOGRAPHY CONNECTION

New York, New Jersey, Pennsylvania, and Delaware made up the Middle Colonies.

1 **PLACE** What geographic features helped make Philadelphia and New York centers of trade?

2 **CRITICAL THINKING** *Drawing Conclusions* How did the Middle Colonies get that name?

pacifists people opposed to the use of war or violence to settle disputes

Academic Vocabulary

function to be in action; to operate

Rich farmland lured immigrants from throughout Europe to the Middle Colonies. These colonists produced important agricultural exports.

▶ CRITICAL THINKING

Identifying What farm products were important in Pennsylvania.

Penn advertised his colony throughout Europe. By 1683, more than 3,000 English, Welsh, Irish, Dutch, and German settlers had arrived. In 1701, in the Charter of Privileges, Penn granted colonists the right to elect representatives to the legislature. Philadelphia quickly became America's most prosperous city and its most popular port.

People from Sweden had settled land in southern Pennsylvania before the Dutch and then the English took over the area. Penn allowed these southern counties to form their own legislature. The counties then **functioned**, or worked, as a separate colony known as Delaware. However, Delaware remained under the authority of Pennsylvania's governor.

☑ PROGRESS CHECK

Inferring What was William Penn's main purpose for founding the colony of Pennsylvania?

Art Resource, NY

LESSON 3 REVIEW

Review Vocabulary

1. Explain the significance of the words.

   a. patroon **b.** pacifist

Answer the Guiding Questions

2. *Describing* How was the colony of New York governed?

3. *Summarizing* What policies of Pennsylvania reflected Quaker beliefs?

4. **NARRATIVE WRITING** Think about what you read about New Amsterdam: It was a bustling seaport with many different types of people. Write a paragraph that describes what it might have been like to walk down one of its busy streets. What might you have seen? Heard? Felt?

Lesson 4
The Southern Colonies

ESSENTIAL QUESTION *How does geography influence the way people live?*

IT MATTERS BECAUSE
A warm climate, long growing season, and rich soil spurred the growth of large-scale agriculture in the Southern Colonies.

Virginia and Maryland

GUIDING QUESTION *What problems faced Maryland and Virginia?*

The settlement of Jamestown marked the beginning of English colonization in North America—and of the Virginia Colony. After its difficult beginnings, Virginia began to grow. The demand for workers was high. It took a great deal of labor to plant, tend, and harvest the tobacco crop on which the colony depended.

White landowners helped meet this need through the use of enslaved Africans. The first group of 20 Africans arrived in 1619 aboard a Dutch trading vessel. In the years to follow, many more shiploads of this human cargo would arrive in North America. You will learn more about this terrible trade in enslaved Africans in other chapters.

The story of Virginia's first Africans shows that not all people came to work in the colonies of their own free will. England also shipped criminals and prisoners of war to the colonies. They could earn their release by working for a period of time—usually seven years.

Many people also came to the colonies as **indentured servants** (ihn•DEHN•shuhrd SIR•vuhnts). To pay for their passage to America, they agreed to work without pay for a certain length of time.

(l) The Granger Collection, NYC, (cl) Bettmann/CORBIS,(r) akg-images.

Reading **HELP**DESK

Taking Notes: *Determining Cause and Effect*
Use a diagram like this one to list the causes and effects of Bacon's Rebellion.

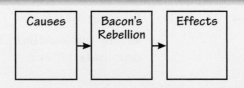

Content Vocabulary
• **indentured servant**
• **constitution**
• **debtor**

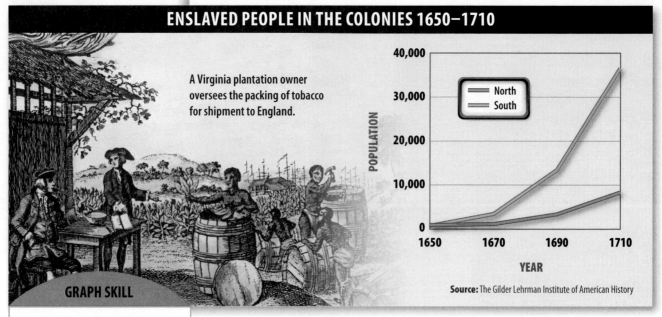

ENSLAVED PEOPLE IN THE COLONIES 1650–1710

A Virginia plantation owner oversees the packing of tobacco for shipment to England.

GRAPH SKILL

POPULATION / YEAR

Legend: North, South

Source: The Gilder Lehrman Institute of American History

Most enslaved Africans lived in the Southern Colonies, where they were forced to work on plantations. Northern Colonies had fewer enslaved people but also profited from the international slave trade.

1 IDENTIFYING In about what year did the South begin relying on slavery in a much larger way than the North?

2 CRITICAL THINKING *Comparing and Contrasting* Describe how the number of enslaved people in the South compared to those in the North during the time period shown in this graph.

Founding Maryland

Maryland arose from the dream of Sir George Calvert, Lord Baltimore. Calvert wanted a safe place for his fellow Catholics who faced persecution in England. England's king, Charles I, gave Calvert a proprietary colony north of Virginia. Soon after receiving this grant, Calvert died. His son, Cecilius, inherited the colony and named it Maryland. Cecilius sent two of his brothers to start the colony. They reached America in 1634.

Cecilius gave large **estates** to English aristocrats. He also granted smaller pieces of land to other settlers. As the number of plantations grew, so did the need for workers. The colony imported indentured servants and enslaved Africans.

For years the Calvert and Penn families argued over the boundary between Maryland and Pennsylvania. In the 1760s, they hired two men named Charles Mason and Jeremiah Dixon to map the boundary between the colonies. This boundary line became known as the Mason-Dixon Line.

Religion was another source of conflict. The Calverts welcomed Protestants as well as Catholics. Protestant settlers outnumbered Catholics. To protect Catholics, the colony established the Act of Toleration in 1649. The act ensured Protestants and Catholics the right to worship freely.

Tensions, however, continued. In 1692 Maryland—now a royal colony—established an official Protestant church. As a result, Catholics faced the same restrictions they had in England.

The Granger Collection, NYC.

Reading **HELP**DESK

indentured servant laborer who agrees to work without pay for a certain period of time in exchange for passage to America

Academic Vocabulary

estate large area of land that has one owner
dominate to control

Rebellion in Virginia

Virginia also experienced conflict. As the colony grew, settlers moved west—and onto Native American lands. In the 1640s, Virginia governor William Berkeley made a pledge to Native Americans. In exchange for a large piece of land, he agreed to keep settlers from pushing farther into their territory. Berkeley's goal was to prevent the outbreak of a war with the Native Americans.

Nathaniel Bacon was a young planter in western Virginia. He opposed the colonial government because it was **dominated** by easterners. Many westerners also resented Berkeley's pledge to stay out of Native American territory. Some settled in the forbidden areas. They then blamed the government for not clearing the colony of Native Americans.

In 1676 Bacon led attacks on Native American villages. His army also marched to Jamestown to drive out Berkeley, and they burned the town to the ground. Bacon seemed on the verge of taking over the colony when he suddenly became ill and died. With his death, the rebellion faded. England recalled Berkeley and sent troops to restore order. Bacon's Rebellion showed that government could not ignore the demands of its people.

☑ **PROGRESS CHECK**

Analyzing Why did Nathaniel Bacon oppose the colonial government?

Bettmann/CORBIS

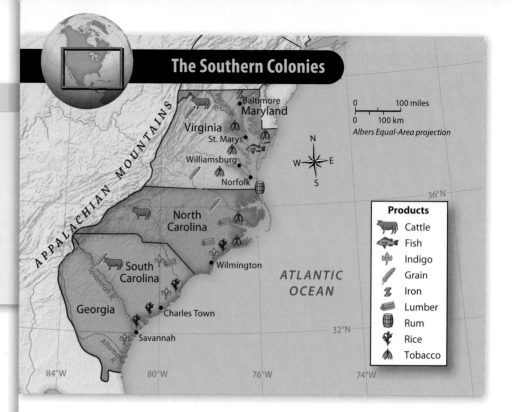

GEOGRAPHY CONNECTION

The Southern Colonies were Maryland, Virginia, North and South Carolina, and Georgia.

1 **LOCATION** Which was the southernmost colony?

2 **CRITICAL THINKING**
Analyzing Visuals How does the map show the importance of tobacco in the Southern Colonies?

Products
- Cattle
- Fish
- Indigo
- Grain
- Iron
- Lumber
- Rum
- Rice
- Tobacco

The Carolinas and Georgia

GUIDING QUESTION *What factors contributed to the growth of the Carolinas?*

In 1663 King Charles II created a proprietary colony south of Virginia called Carolina—Latin for "Charles's land." The king gave the colony to eight nobles. The proprietors set up estates and sold or rented land to settlers brought from England.

John Locke, an English philosopher, wrote a **constitution** (kahn•stuh•TOO•shuhn), a plan that outlined the jobs and powers of the colony's government. The constitution covered topics such as land divisions and social rank. Locke stated, "Every man has a property in his own person. ... The labour of his body, and the work of his hands ... are properly his."

Two Carolinas

Carolina did not develop as planned. It split into northern and southern Carolina.

Farmers from inland Virginia settled northern Carolina. They grew tobacco and sold timber and tar. Northern Carolina lacked a good harbor, so farmers used Virginia's ports.

Settlers in southern Carolina took advantage of fertile land and the harbor at Charles Town (later Charleston). Settlements there spread, and trade in deerskin, lumber, and beef thrived.

constitution a list of fundamental laws to support a government
debtor person or country that owes money

Visual Vocabulary

indigo The *indigofera* plant, often called just indigo, was used to make indigo dye.

Two crops came to dominate Carolina agriculture. In the 1680s planters discovered that rice grew well in the wet coastal lowlands. Growing rice required much labor, and the demand for slave labor rose. Another important crop was **indigo**. A young English woman named Eliza Lucas developed this crop in the 1740s. Indigo, a blue flowering plant, was used to dye cloth.

By the early 1700s, Carolina's settlers were growing tired of proprietor rule. In 1719 settlers in southern Carolina took control from the proprietors. In 1729 Carolina became two royal colonies—North Carolina and South Carolina.

Georgia

Georgia, founded in 1733, was the last British colony set up in America. James Oglethorpe received a charter from George II for a colony where debtors and poor people could make a fresh start. In Britain, **debtors** (DEH•tuhrs)—those who had debts—could be imprisoned if they were unable to pay what they owed.

The British also hoped Georgia would block any Spanish attack on the colonies from Florida. Oglethorpe and his settlers built the forts and town of Savannah to discourage such attacks.

Georgia did not develop as Oglethorpe planned. Hundreds of poor people came from Britain, but few debtors settled there. Religious refugees from Central Europe and a small group of Jews also arrived. Many settlers complained about Oglethorpe's rules, especially the limits on landholding and the bans on slave labor and rum. A frustrated Oglethorpe finally agreed to their demands. Disappointed with the colony's slow growth, he gave up and turned Georgia over to the king in 1751.

By that time, the British had been in eastern North America for almost 150 years. They had lined the Atlantic coast with colonies.

☑ **PROGRESS CHECK**

Explaining Why was Georgia founded?

LESSON 4 REVIEW

Review Vocabulary

1. Examine the terms below. Write a sentence explaining what the terms have in common.

   a. indentured servant   **b.** debtor

2. Use the word *constitution* in a sentence.

Answer the Guiding Questions

3. *Explaining* Why did George Calvert establish the colony of Maryland?

4. *Analyzing* Why did demand for enslaved workers increase in the Carolinas?

5. **PERSUASIVE WRITING** Take the role of James Oglethorpe. Write a letter to the king asking for a charter for a colony. Explain why you are founding Georgia and how it might benefit England.

Write your answers on a separate piece of paper.

① Exploring the Essential Questions

EXPOSITORY WRITING Write an essay in which you answer this question: How did geography, religion, and government affect how people in the English colonies lived? Use examples from the chapter to help you organize your essay.

② 21st Century Skills

ORGANIZING IDEAS Working with a small group, read the Mayflower Compact. Rewrite the Compact in your own words. Then compare the rewritings done by various groups of your classmates. How do they differ from the original document?

③ Thinking Like a Historian

UNDERSTANDING CAUSE AND EFFECT In about 150 years, the population of the English colonies in America increased from about 100 to about 1,000,000. What is one reason the population may have increased? What are two effects this increase may have had?

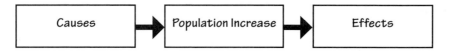

| Causes | → | Population Increase | → | Effects |

④ Visual Literacy

ANALYZING PAINTINGS This painting shows William Penn meeting with Native Americans in the colony of Pennsylvania. What details in the painting give you clues about the Native Americans' relationship with William Penn?

William Penn's Treaty with the Indians by Edward Hicks, 1830–1840

REVIEW THE GUIDING QUESTIONS

Choose the best answer for each question.

1 A document that grants the right to organize a settlement in an area is called a

   A. charter.

   B. compact.

   C. headright.

   D. policy.

2 What crop was important in making Jamestown and early Virginia an economic success?

   F. indigo

   G. tobacco

   H. potatoes

   I. rice

3 Roger Williams clashed with Massachusetts Puritans because

   A. he converted to Roman Catholicism.

   B. he did not think government should require certain religious beliefs.

   C. he wanted Native American land.

   D. his views were considered too intolerant.

4 In which type of colony does a person or persons own all the land and control the colony's government?

   F. a royal colony

   G. a charter colony

   H. a proprietary colony

   I. a joint-stock colony

5 Men and women who signed contracts to pay for their passage to the Americas were called

   A. Separatists.

   B. burgesses.

   C. indentured servants.

   D. tenant farmers.

6 What role did Eliza Lucas play in the Southern Colonies?

   F. She wrote a constitution.

   G. She divided the Carolinas into two colonies.

   H. She developed indigo as an important crop.

   I. She founded Charles Town (later Charleston).

DBQ DOCUMENT-BASED QUESTIONS

7 **Analyzing Visuals** The map at the right shows the settlement of the British Colonies. Which colony was the most heavily settled before 1660?

A. Virginia

B. North Carolina

C. Massachusetts

D. New Hampshire

8 **Analyzing Visuals** Which of the following best describes what happened to English settlement over time?

F. It spread to the north.

G. It spread to the south.

H. It spread to the east.

I. It spread to the west.

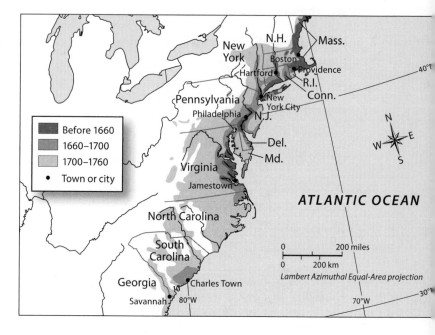

SHORT RESPONSE

William Bradford was governor of the Plymouth Colony in 1621.

"[I]n two or three months' time half of their company died, especially in ... the depth of winter, and wanting houses and other comforts; being infected with the scurvy and other diseases. ... there died sometimes two or three of a day ... of 100 and odd persons, scarce 50 remained. And of these ... there was but six or seven sound persons who to their great commendation [took care of the sick people] ... and ... willingly and cheerfully ... showing herein their true love unto their friends.

—from *Of Plymouth Plantation,* by William Bradford, c. 1650

9 Why do you think Bradford recorded this information about the Pilgrims?

10 Do you think this scene is typical of the hardships early colonists faced? Why or why not?

EXTENDED RESPONSE

11 **Expository Writing** What role did religion play in the establishment and life of the English colonies? Write your answer in a one-page paper.

Need Extra Help?

If You've Missed Question	1	2	3	4	5	6	7	8	9	10	11
Review Lesson	1	1	2	3	4	4	1–4	1–4	2	2	2

Life in the American Colonies

1607–1770

ESSENTIAL QUESTIONS • How does geography influence the way people live?
• How do new ideas change the way people live? • Why does conflict develop?

Burstein Collection/CORBIS

networks

There's More Online about life in the American colonies.

CHAPTER 4

Lesson 1
Colonial Economy

Lesson 2
Colonial Government

Lesson 3
Culture and Society

Lesson 4
Rivalry in North America

The Story Matters . . .

At first glance, the painting is simple—just a woman and her small baby. Look deeper, however, and you can see more.

The portrait dates from the 1670s, just 50 years after the Pilgrims first arrived in New England. It shows Elizabeth Freake, wife of a Boston merchant and lawyer John Freake, with baby Mary. Notice the fine fabrics mother and child are wearing.

For many colonial Americans such as the Freakes, life is no longer a struggle for survival. In fact, it is increasingly prosperous and comfortable.

Place and Time: America 1607 to 1770

Colonial America was rich in natural resources, such as lumber, fish, and furs. In many of the colonies, the land was well-suited to agriculture, producing crops like wheat, corn, tobacco, rice, and indigo. In some colonies, industries developed to process and transport the wealth of the new land.

The kitchen was the heart of the American home in colonial times. Maintaining the fire was an important task. The fire was used to cook the food, provide warmth, and boil the water for washing the clothes.

Step Into the Place

MAP FOCUS The Colonial Economy map shows the different regions of the thirteen colonies along with their major industries.

1 PLACE Where was shipbuilding a major industry?

2 REGION What crops were common to both the Middle Colonies and the Southern Colonies?

3 CRITICAL THINKING
Drawing Conclusions Why do you think the New England Colonies developed industries that were not based in agriculture?

Perhaps no other person represented the rise of the American colonies better than Benjamin Franklin. A successful businessperson, a scientific genius, and a skilled political leader—Franklin showed many of the best traits of the growing colonial society.

Step Into the Time

TIME LINE Which events on the time line hint at conflict in colonial North America?

c. 1570 Iroquois Confederacy forms

1619 The first Africans arrive in Virginia

AMERICAS

WORLD EVENTS

1550

1600

(b) Topham/The Image Works, (l) The Granger Collection, NYC.

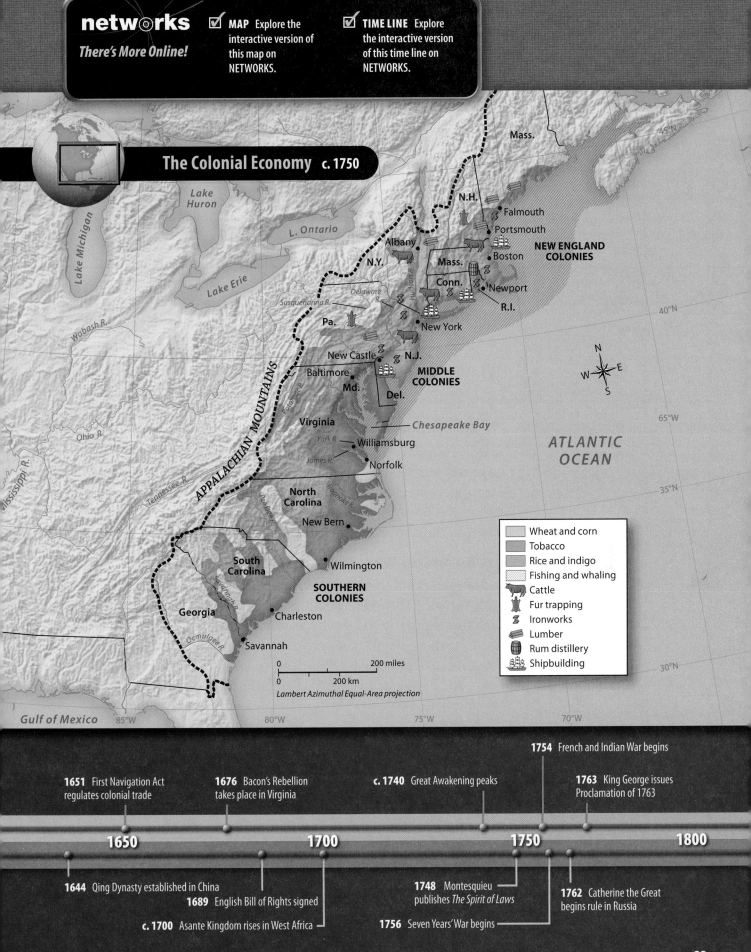

networks

There's More Online!

☑ **MAP** Explore the interactive version of this map on NETWORKS.

☑ **TIME LINE** Explore the interactive version of this time line on NETWORKS.

The Colonial Economy c. 1750

Lake Huron

Lake Michigan

L. Ontario

Lake Erie

Mass.

N.H.

Falmouth

Portsmouth

Albany

N.Y.

Mass.

Boston

Conn.

Newport

R.I.

NEW ENGLAND COLONIES

Delaware R.

Susquehanna R.

Hudson R.

New York

Pa.

New Castle

N.J.

MIDDLE COLONIES

Baltimore

Md.

Del.

Wabash R.

Ohio R.

Virginia

Chesapeake Bay

Williamsburg

York R.

James R.

Norfolk

Mississippi R.

Tennessee R.

APPALACHIAN MOUNTAINS

Roanoke R.

North Carolina

Pee Dee R.

New Bern

South Carolina

Wilmington

SOUTHERN COLONIES

Savannah R.

Georgia

Charleston

Ocmulgee R.

Savannah

ATLANTIC OCEAN

N E W S

65°W

45°N

40°N

35°N

30°N

85°W 80°W 75°W 70°W

Gulf of Mexico

	Legend
	Wheat and corn
	Tobacco
	Rice and indigo
	Fishing and whaling
	Cattle
	Fur trapping
	Ironworks
	Lumber
	Rum distillery
	Shipbuilding

0   200 miles
0   200 km
Lambert Azimuthal Equal-Area projection

1754 French and Indian War begins

1651 First Navigation Act regulates colonial trade

1676 Bacon's Rebellion takes place in Virginia

c. 1740 Great Awakening peaks

1763 King George issues Proclamation of 1763

1650   **1700**   **1750**   **1800**

1644 Qing Dynasty established in China

1689 English Bill of Rights signed

1748 Montesquieu publishes *The Spirit of Laws*

1762 Catherine the Great begins rule in Russia

c. 1700 Asante Kingdom rises in West Africa

1756 Seven Years' War begins

netw⊙rks
There's More Online!

☑ **BIOGRAPHY**
Olaudah Equiano

☑ **CHART/GRAPH**
The African Slave Trade

☑ **GRAPHIC ORGANIZER**
The Triangular Trade

☑ **MAP** The Triangular Trade

☑ **PRIMARY SOURCE**
• Life on a Plantation
• Conditions on a Slave Ship

Lesson 1

Colonial Economy

ESSENTIAL QUESTION *How does geography influence the way people live?*

IT MATTERS BECAUSE
The unique resources and conditions that existed in each colony helped shape colonial economies and ways of living.

Making a Living in the Colonies

GUIDING QUESTION *How did the economic activity of the three regions reflect their geography?*

Life in colonial America was based largely on agriculture. Most colonists farmed or made their livings from businesses related to farming, such as milling flour. Geography played an important role in the colonies' economic development. Colonists learned to adapt to the climate and terrain of the region where they lived.

Commercial New England

In New England, long winters and thin, rocky soil made large-scale farming difficult. Most farmers here practiced **subsistence farming** (suhb•SIS•tuhns)—producing enough to meet the needs of their families, with little left over to sell or trade. New England farmers often depended on their children for labor. Everyone in the family worked—spinning yarn, milking cows, fencing fields, and sowing and harvesting crops. Women made cloth, garments, candles, and soaps for their families.

Throughout New England were many small businesses. Nearly every town had a mill for grinding grain or sawing lumber. People used waterpower from streams to run the mills. Large towns attracted skilled craftspeople. Among them were blacksmiths, shoemakers, furniture makers, and gunsmiths.

(l) Collection of the New-York Historical Society/Bridgeman Art Library, (c, c) The Granger Collection, (r) Getty Images

Reading **HELP**DESK

Taking Notes: *Describing*

As you read, use a diagram like this one to describe the triangular trade routes.

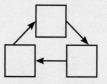

Content Vocabulary
• **subsistence farming**   • **triangular trade**
• **cash crop**   • **slave code**
• **diversity**

Shipbuilding was an important New England industry. The lumber for building ships came from the region's forests. Workers floated the lumber down rivers to shipyards in coastal towns. The Northern coastal cities served as centers of the colonial shipping trade, linking the Northern Colonies with the Southern Colonies—and America with other parts of the world.

Fishing was also important. Some New Englanders ventured far out to sea to hunt whales for oil and whalebone.

The Middle Colonies

Most people in the Middle Colonies were farmers. This region enjoyed more fertile soil and a slightly milder climate than New England. Farmers here plowed and planted larger areas of land and produced bigger harvests than did New Englanders. In New York and Pennsylvania, farmers grew large quantities of wheat and other **cash crops**—crops that could be sold easily in markets in the colonies and overseas.

Farmers sent wheat and livestock for shipment to New York City and Philadelphia, which became busy ports. By 1760, New York, with 14,000 people, and Philadelphia, with 19,000 people, were two of the largest cities in the American colonies.

Like the New England Colonies, the Middle Colonies also had industries. Some were home-based crafts, such as carpentry and flour making. Others were larger businesses—lumber mills, mines, ironworks, small-scale manufacturing, and so on.

The Middle Colonies attracted many Scotch-Irish, German, Dutch, and Swedish settlers. Using agricultural methods developed in Europe, these immigrants became successful farmers. They gave the Middle Colonies a cultural **diversity** (duh•VUHR•suh•tee), or variety, not found in New England.

New York City, shown here in the late 1750s, was a bustling center of trade and population in the American colonies.

▶ **CRITICAL THINKING**
Analyzing What geographic features helped New York thrive as a seaport?

Life in the Southern Colonies

The Southern Colonies had rich soil and a warm climate well suited to certain kinds of farming. Southern farmers could plant large areas and produce harvests of cash crops, such as tobacco or rice. Most settlers in the Southern Colonies made their living from farming.

subsistence farming producing just enough to meet immediate needs
cash crop a crop that can be sold easily in markets

diversity variety, such as of ethnic or national groups

Little commerce or industry developed there. For the most part, London merchants rather than local merchants from the colonies managed Southern trade.

Most large plantations were located in the Tidewater, a region of flat, low-lying plains along the seacoast. Planters built their plantations on rivers so they could ship their crops to market by boat. A plantation was like a small village. It had fields stretching out around a cluster of buildings, including cabins, barns, and stables, as well as carpenter and blacksmith shops, storerooms, and kitchens. A large plantation might have its own chapel and school. Small plantations often had fewer than 50 enslaved workers. Large ones typically had 200 or more.

Between the Tidewater and the Appalachian Mountains lay a region of hills and forests known as the backcountry. Its settlers included hardy newcomers to the colonies. They grew corn and tobacco on small family farms. Some had one or two enslaved Africans to help with the work. Backcountry farmers greatly outnumbered large plantation owners. Still, the plantation owners were wealthier and more powerful. They controlled the economic and political life of the region.

Tobacco and Rice

Tobacco was the **principal** cash crop in Maryland and Virginia. Growing tobacco and preparing it for sale required a lot of labor. At first, planters used indentured servants to work in the fields. These servants worked for a time and then went free. When indentured servants became scarce and expensive, Southern planters began using enslaved Africans instead.

Slaveholders with large farms grew wealthy by growing tobacco. They sold most of it in Europe. Sometimes, though, there was too much tobacco on the market—more than buyers wanted. To sell the extra tobacco, planters had to lower their prices. As a result, their profits fell. Some planters switched to other crops, such as corn and wheat.

The geography of South Carolina and Georgia helped make rice the main cash crop there. In low-lying areas along the coast, planters built dams to create rice fields, called paddies. Planters flooded the fields when the rice was young and drained them when the rice was ready to harvest.

Work in the rice paddies was very hard. It involved standing knee-deep in the mud with no protection from the blazing sun or biting insects. To do this hard work, rice growers **relied** on slave labor.

Reading **HELP**DESK

Academic Vocabulary

principal most important
rely to depend upon

Build Vocabulary: *Related Words*

If the word *principal* means "most important," what can you say about the principal of your school?

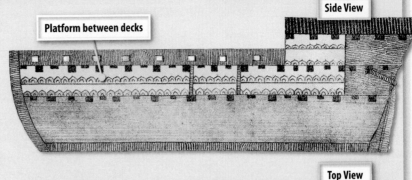

Destination	Total
British America/United States	427,000
Mexico and Central America	224,000
West Indies	4,040,000
Spanish South America	522,000
Guianas	531,000
Brazil	3,647,000
Europe	175,000

Side View

Platform between decks

Top View

Captives crowded together

Captains of slave ships added platforms between decks to fit more captives onto their ships. In the filthy, crowded slave compartments, disease—and rebellion—spread rapidly. On some ships, as many as half of the Africans died.

INFOGRAPHIC

Millions of Africans were victims of the slave trade.

1 CALCULATING
What was the total number of Africans shipped from Africa to the countries and regions shown?

2 CRITICAL THINKING
Drawing Conclusions What do you think was the impact of the slave trade on African cultures?

Rice proved to be an even more profitable crop than tobacco. Prices rose steadily as rice became popular in Europe. By the 1750s, South Carolina and Georgia had the fastest-growing economies in the colonies.

☑ **PROGRESS CHECK**

Summarizing Why was agriculture so important to the economy of the Southern Colonies?

The Growth of Slavery

GUIDING QUESTION *Why were enslaved Africans brought to the colonies?*

By the time Europeans were sailing to the Americas, slavery was widely practiced in West Africa. Many West African kingdoms enslaved those they defeated in war. Slave traders from Arab lands bought some of these enslaved people. Others were forced to work in gold mines or farm fields.

The arrival of Europeans in the Americas created a huge new demand for enslaved workers. Colonists needed a large labor force to work on their plantations. West African slave traders met this need. They sold captives they gained through wars and raids. Slavery and the slave trade became major parts of the colonial economy.

For enslaved Africans, the voyage to America usually began with a march to a European fort on the West African coast. There, they were sold to Europeans, who loaded them on ships.

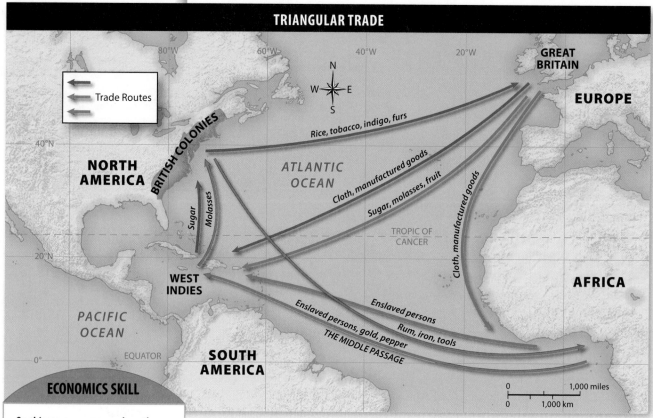

TRIANGULAR TRADE

Trade Routes

GREAT BRITAIN

EUROPE

NORTH AMERICA

BRITISH COLONIES

ATLANTIC OCEAN

Rice, tobacco, indigo, furs

Cloth, manufactured goods

Sugar, molasses, fruit

Cloth, manufactured goods

TROPIC OF CANCER

AFRICA

Sugar

Molasses

WEST INDIES

PACIFIC OCEAN

Enslaved persons, gold, pepper

Enslaved persons

Rum, iron, tools

THE MIDDLE PASSAGE

EQUATOR

SOUTH AMERICA

0   1,000 miles
0   1,000 km

ECONOMICS SKILL

On this map, you can see how the trade routes between the colonies, Great Britain, and Africa formed triangles. The triangular trade supported the economies of all three regions—though at a terrible human cost. The map shows which goods and products came from which locations.

1 **IDENTIFYING** From where did the American colonies receive molasses?

2 **CRITICAL THINKING** *Analyzing* What was the main role of Great Britain in the triangular trade?

The Middle Passage

The trip across the ocean was called the "Middle Passage." This name came from the fact that it was often the second, or middle, leg of the three-part route known as the **triangular trade** (try•ANG•gyuh•luhr). People called this route "triangular" because, as the ships traveled between their destinations, their paths formed the three sides of a triangle.

The Middle Passage was a terrible ordeal. Chained together for more than a month, prisoners could hardly sit or stand. They received little food or water. Africans who died or became sick were thrown overboard. Those who refused to eat were whipped.

Those who survived the Middle Passage faced another terror when they reached American ports—the slave market. There they were put up for sale as laborers to plantation owners.

The Life of the Slave

Some enslaved Africans on plantations did housework, but most worked in the fields. Many enslaved workers suffered great cruelty. Owners of large plantations hired overseers, or bosses, to keep the enslaved Africans working hard.

Reading HELPDESK

triangular trade trade route between three destinations, such as Britain, West Africa, and the West Indies

slave code rules focusing on the behavior and punishment of enslaved people

Many colonies had **slave codes**, rules governing the behavior and punishment of enslaved people. Some did not allow enslaved workers to leave the plantation without the slaveholder's written permission. Some made it illegal to teach enslaved people to read or write. Enslaved people were seldom allowed to move about freely or gather in large groups. Punishments ranged from whipping for even minor misdeeds to hanging or burning to death for more serious crimes. Enslaved workers who ran away were punished severely when caught.

Although enslaved Africans had strong family ties, their families were often torn apart when a slaveholder sold a spouse, parent, or child. Many of the enslaved found strength in their African roots. They developed a culture that drew on the languages, customs, and religions of their African homelands.

Some enslaved Africans learned trades, such as carpentry, blacksmithing, or weaving. Skilled workers could sometimes set up shops, sharing their profits with the slaveholders. Those lucky enough to be able to buy their freedom joined the small population of free African Americans.

On large plantations, the owner or a hired overseer looked on while enslaved workers worked in the fields from sunrise to sunset.

Critics of Slavery

Not all colonists believed in slavery. Many Puritans, for example, refused to hold enslaved people. In Pennsylvania, Quakers and Mennonites condemned slavery. Eventually, the debate over slavery would spark a bloody war between North and South.

✓ PROGRESS CHECK

Describing What role did Africans play in the economy of the Southern Colonies?

LESSON 1 REVIEW

Review Vocabulary

1. Define the following terms by using them in a sentence about colonial farming.

   a. subsistence farming   b. cash crop

2. Explain the significance of the following terms by using each in a sentence.

   a. triangular trade   b. diversity
   c. slave code

Answer the Guiding Questions

3. ***Comparing and Contrasting*** How did agriculture differ in the three colonial regions?

4. ***Identifying Main Ideas*** What was the Middle Passage, and what made it so horrible?

5. **NARRATIVE WRITING** As a New England farmer, write a letter to relatives in Europe describing your family's daily life as subsistence farmers.

The Interesting Narrative of the Life of Olaudah Equiano

by Olaudah Equiano

Most of what we know about Equiano comes from his autobiography. According to his writings, Olaudah Equiano was born in Nigeria. At age 11, he was kidnapped, separated from his family, and sold into slavery.

In this excerpt, Equiano tells about his life in Nigeria and the day he was kidnapped.

66 *When we went to rest the following night, they offered us some victuals, but we refused it; and the only comfort we had was in being in one another's arms all that night, and bathing each other with our tears.* 99

Olaudah Equiano

—*The Interesting Narrative of the Life of Olaudah Equiano; or, Gustavus Vassa, the African, Written by Himself*

Enslaved Africans were transported across the ocean and sold in the Americas.

      Generally, when the grown people in the neighborhood were gone far in the fields to labor, the children assembled together in some of the neighboring premises to play; and commonly some of us used to get up a tree to look out for any assailant, or kidnapper, that might come upon us, for they sometimes took those opportunities of our parents' absence to attack and carry off as many as they could seize. . . . One day, when all our people were gone out to their works as usual, and only I and my dear sister were left to mind the house, two men and a woman got over our walls, and in a moment seized us both, and, without giving us time to cry out, or make resistance, they stopped our mouths, and ran off with us into the nearest wood. Here they tied our hands, and continued to carry us as far as they could, till night came on, when we reached a small house, where the robbers halted for refreshment, and spent the night. We were then unbound, but were unable to take any food; and, being quite overpowered by fatigue and grief, our only relief was some sleep, which **allayed** our misfortune for a short time. The next morning we left the house, and continued travelling all the day. For a long time we had kept [to] the woods, but at last we came into a road which I believed I knew. I had now some hopes of being delivered; for we had advanced but a little way before I discovered some people at a distance, on which I began to cry out for their assistance; but my cries had no other effect than to make them tie me faster and stop my mouth, and then they put me into a large sack. They also stopped my sister's mouth, and tied her hands; and in this manner we proceeded till we were out of sight of these people. When we went to rest the following night, they offered us some **victuals**, but we refused it; and the only comfort we had was in being in one another's arms all that night, and bathing each other with our tears. But alas! we were soon deprived of even the small comfort of weeping together. The next day proved a day of greater sorrow than I had yet experienced, for my sister and I were then separated while we lay clasped in each other's arms. It was in vain that we besought them not to part us; she was torn from me and immediately carried away, while I was left in a state of distraction not to be described. I cried and grieved continually, and for several days I did not eat anything but what they forced into my mouth. 99

Chicago History Museum/The Bridgeman Art Library

Literary Element

Point of View is the vantage point from which a story is told. This passage is told from the first-person point of view. In it, you learn the narrator's thoughts and feelings. As you read, think about how the story's point of view affects your reading experience.

Vocabulary

allay
to reduce in strength

victual
food

Kidnappers chained their captives together in pairs—right leg to left leg.

Analyzing Literature DBQ

❶ *Drawing Conclusions* Why is a first-person narrative of an enslaved person valuable?

❷ *Speculating* What kind of person did the kidnappers target? Why do you think that might be?

❸ *Predicting* What do you think will happen to Equiano and his sister?

networks
There's More Online!

☑ **CHART/GRAPH**
Literacy Rates

☑ **GRAPHIC ORGANIZER**
• Principles of Government
• Colonial Government

☑ **TIME LINE** Principles of British Government

☑ **VIDEO**

Lesson 2

Colonial Government

ESSENTIAL QUESTION *How do new ideas change the way people live?*

IT MATTERS BECAUSE

Using ideas from England and their own experiences, American colonists began developing their beliefs about the proper form and role of government.

English Principles of Government

GUIDING QUESTION *Why are protected rights and representative government important principles?*

When English colonists came to North America, they brought with them English ideas about government. These ideas had been developing in England over hundreds of years. By the 1600s, the English people had won political liberties, such as trial by jury, that were largely unknown elsewhere.

At the heart of the English system were two principles of government—protected rights and representative legislatures. These two principles greatly influenced the development of the United States and are important parts of the U.S. Constitution.

Protected Rights

The colonists believed that government must respect civil liberties, or rights. In fact, the protection of people's rights was a central idea in the English system of government. It first appeared in the Magna Carta, or Great Charter, which King John signed on June 15, 1215. This document gave English people protection against unjust treatment or punishment. For the English, even kings and queens were bound by the law.

(l and r) The Granger Collection, NYC, (c) Erin Paul Donovan / Alamy

---

Reading **HELP**DESK

Taking Notes: *Explaining*

As you read, use a diagram like this one to explain protected rights and representative government.

Protected Rights ⇨ ☐

Representative Government ⇨ ☐

Content Vocabulary
• **representative government** • **import**
• **mercantilism**
• **export**

Representative Government

The English had a tradition of **representative government**, in which people elect delegates to make laws and conduct government. The English Parliament was a representative assembly. It had the power to legislate, or make laws.

Parliament had two chambers, or houses: the House of Lords and the House of Commons. Only the eldest sons of England's aristocracy—the upper, ruling class—could sit in the House of Lords. The House of Commons included commoners—mostly merchants or property owners elected by other property owners. American legislatures grew in part from this English model.

In the mid-1600s, Parliament and King James II began a struggle for power. In 1688, Parliament removed King James II from power and crowned William and Mary to rule. William and Mary promised to govern England according to the "statutes [laws] in Parliament agreed upon, and the laws and customs of the same." The English called this peaceful transfer of power the Glorious Revolution. It brought a major change in the idea of government in England. From that time forward, no ruler would have more power than the legislature.

The English Bill of Rights

To set clear limits on a ruler's powers, Parliament drew up the English Bill of Rights in 1689. The Bill of Rights stated that the ruler could not **suspend** Parliament's laws, **impose** taxes, or raise an army without Parliament's consent. Members of Parliament had to be freely elected. Citizens of England had the right to a fair trial by jury in court cases. The Bill of Rights also banned cruel and unusual punishments.

Government in America

The thirteen colonies began as either charter or proprietary colonies. Charter colonies were based on a charter, a grant of rights by the English monarch to a company. Massachusetts was a charter colony.

Established in 1619, the Virginia House of Burgesses was the first legislature in the English Colonies. It became a foundation for the principle of self-government in colonial America and, later, the United States.

The Granger Collection, NYC

---

representative government
a system by which people elect delegates to make laws and conduct government

Academic Vocabulary

suspend to set aside or temporarily stop operation of something
impose to force on others

In New England, town meetings were held in meeting houses like this one in Pelham, Massachusetts. Built in 1743, Pelham's Old Meeting House is the oldest town hall in continuous use in the nation.

Proprietary colonies were the property of an owner or group of owners. These proprietors ruled more or less as they wished. For example, they named their own governors and many other colonial officials. Pennsylvania was a proprietary colony.

Some colonies later became royal colonies, under direct English control. Virginia became the first royal colony in 1624. In a royal colony, Parliament appointed a governor and council, known as the upper house. The colonists selected an assembly, or lower house. The governor and council usually did as the English king and Parliament told them. This often led to conflicts with the assembly. For example, colonists got angry when officials enforced tax or trade laws.

Not all colonists had a voice in government. In general, only white men who owned property could vote. Most women, indentured servants, landless poor, and African Americans could not vote. Still, compared to Europe, the share of the colonial population taking part in government was large. This training proved valuable when the colonies became independent.

Local Government in the Colonies

Over time, townspeople began discussing local issues at town meetings. These developed into local governments, with landowners holding the right to vote and pass laws. Because colonists in many areas took part in local government, they developed a strong belief in their right to govern themselves. Town meetings helped set the stage for the American Revolution.

✓ PROGRESS CHECK

Making Connections How did the Magna Carta influence government in the colonies?

English Economic Policies

GUIDING QUESTION *How did the colonists react to England's economic policies?*

Beginning in the 1600s, many European nations followed a theory known as **mercantilism** (MUHR•kuhn•tuh•lih•zuhm). Mercantilism holds that a country builds wealth and power by building its supplies of gold and silver. To achieve this goal, a country must **export**, or sell to other countries, more than it

Erin Paul Donovan / Alamy

Reading **HELP**DESK

mercantilism an economic theory whose goal is building a state's wealth and power by increasing exports and accumulating precious metals in return

export to sell abroad
import to bring in from foreign markets

imports, or buys from other countries. A country must also seek colonies, which could supply raw materials and serve as a market for exports.

The English followed a mercantilist policy. They looked to the American colonies for raw materials, such as tobacco, rice, indigo, wheat, lumber, fur, leather, fish, and whale products. They also wanted the colonists to buy English manufactured goods, such as tools, clothing, and furniture.

To control this trade, England began passing a series of laws called Navigation Acts in the 1650s. The laws forced colonists to sell their raw materials to England even if they could get a better price elsewhere. Goods bought by the colonies from other countries in Europe had to go to England first and be taxed. All trade goods had to be carried on ships built in England or the colonies. The crews on the ships had to be English as well.

Colonial Resistance

The colonists at first accepted the Navigation Acts because the laws guaranteed them a place to sell their raw materials. Later, the colonists came to resent English restrictions. With their population growing, colonists wanted to manufacture their own goods rather than import them from England. They also wanted to sell their products to buyers other than England. Colonial merchants began smuggling, or shipping goods without government permission or payment of taxes. Controls on trade would later cause conflict between the American colonies and England.

✓ **PROGRESS CHECK**

Making Generalizations What was the purpose of the Navigation Acts?

Many items in a colonial kitchen were tinware imported from England. Because of its silvery color, tinware was often called "poor man's silver." Although it was thought to be inferior to china or silver, tinware goods were less breakable than china and easier to clean than silverware.

The Granger Collection, NYC

LESSON 2 REVIEW

Review Vocabulary

1. Use the words *import, export,* and *mercantilism* in a paragraph about the colonies.

2. Write a sentence about the political ideas of the English colonists using the term *representative government.*

Answer the Guiding Questions

3. ***Analyzing*** Where did the colonists get their ideas and attitudes about government?

4. ***Explaining*** How did the colonists react to Britain's economic policies?

5. **PERSUASIVE WRITING** Write a speech from the perspective of a merchant, urging colonists to support your idea of free trade with countries other than Britain.

networks

There's More Online!

☑ **CHART/GRAPH** Great Awakening and the Enlightenment

☑ **GRAPHIC ORGANIZER** Great Awakening and the Enlightenment

☑ **PRIMARY SOURCE** Freedom of the Press

☑ **SLIDE SHOW** A Child's Life in the Colonies

Lesson 3
Culture and Society

ESSENTIAL QUESTION *How do new ideas change the way people live?*

IT MATTERS BECAUSE
An American culture, influenced by religion and education, began to develop in the colonies.

Life in the Colonies

GUIDING QUESTION *What was life like for people living in the thirteen colonies?*

The number of people living in the thirteen colonies rose from about 250,000 in 1700 to approximately 2.5 million by the mid-1770s. The population of African Americans increased at an even faster rate—from about 28,000 to more than 500,000.

Immigration (im•ih•GRAY•shuhn)—the permanent moving of people into one country from other countries—was important to this growth. Between 1607 and 1775, an estimated 690,000 Europeans came to the colonies. Also during this time, traders brought in 278,000 enslaved Africans to the colonies.

There was another reason for the growing population. Colonial women tended to marry early and have large families. In addition, the colonies—especially New England—turned out to be a very healthy place to live compared to other parts of the world.

Still, compared to today, life was fragile. For example, women often died in childbirth. Outbreaks of serious diseases such as smallpox were common. Many people died in **epidemics** (eh•puh•DEH•mihks), outbreaks that affect large numbers of people. In 1721, for example, a smallpox epidemic in the city of Boston killed about 850 people, or 15 percent of the city's population.

(l) Bettmann/Corbis, (cl) The Granger Collection, NYC, (cr) Francis G. Mayer/Corbis, (r) MPI/Stringer/Getty Images

Reading **HELP**DESK

Taking Notes: *Determining Cause and Effect*

As you read, use a diagram like this one to explain how the Great Awakening and the Enlightenment affected the colonists.

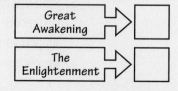

Content Vocabulary

• **immigration** • **civic virtue**
• **epidemic**
• **apprentice**

A New American Spirit

Many Americans were born in other countries. They brought with them different languages and ways of thinking. Yet in the colonies, immigrants became something new and different—they became Americans. In 1782 French writer J. Hector St. John De Crèvecoeur (krev•KUHR) described this new type of person:

PRIMARY SOURCE

66 He is an American, who, leaving behind him all his ancient prejudices and manners, receives new ones from the new mode of life he has embraced, the new government he obeys, and the new rank he holds. . . . Here individuals of all races are melted into a new race of man, whose labors and posterity will one day cause great changes in the world. 99

—from *Letters from an American Farmer*

In 1721, Boston clergyman Cotton Mather suggested a daring answer to smallpox—inoculation, or injecting smallpox virus into healthy people. Often, inoculation causes only mild disease and leaves the body protected from illness in the future. In 1796, Edward Jenner, shown inoculating a child, developed a safer smallpox vaccine.

A spirit of independence developed early in the history of the American people. Far from the rules and limits of their home countries, settlers began to develop their own ways of doing things. Throughout the colonies, people **adapted** their traditions to the new conditions of life.

Religion, education, and the arts contributed to a new American culture. The family, however, formed the basic foundation of colonial society—for those who were not enslaved, at least.

Family Roles

Men were the formal heads of the households. They managed the farm or business and represented the family in the community. On the farm, men worked in the fields and built barns, houses, and fences. Sons might work as indentured servants for local farmers or become apprentices. An **apprentice** (uh•PREHN•tuhs) agrees to work with a skilled craftsperson as a way of learning a trade.

Women ran their households and cared for children. Many worked in the fields with their husbands. Married women had few rights. Unmarried women might work as maids or cooks.

Bettmann/Corbis

---

immigration the permanent movement of people into one country from other nations
epidemic an illness that affects large numbers of people

apprentice a young person who learns a trade from a skilled craftsperson

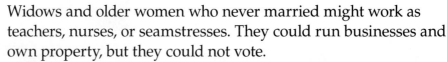

Connections to
TODAY

Colleges and Universities

Several colleges and universities founded in colonial times are still educating students today. For example, Harvard University in Massachusetts got its start in 1636 as a school for training ministers. Next came Virginia's College of William and Mary, founded in 1693. Yale University in Connecticut started as a school in 1701. The University of Pennsylvania in Philadelphia began as a charity school in 1740.

A hornbook, made of a wooden paddle with lessons tacked onto it, helped young students learn to read.

Widows and older women who never married might work as teachers, nurses, or seamstresses. They could run businesses and own property, but they could not vote.

Even children as young as four or five often had jobs. When they played, they enjoyed simple games, such as hopscotch or leap frog. Their toys were usually made from common objects.

✅ **PROGRESS CHECK**

Finding the Main Idea What was the role of the family in colonial life?

American Beliefs

GUIDING QUESTION *What values and beliefs were important to the American colonists?*

The American spirit and the family served as a foundation for life in the colonies. In addition, Americans shared a commitment to education, strong religious beliefs, and openness to new ideas.

Colonial Education

Most colonists valued education. Parents often taught their children to read and write at home. In New England and Pennsylvania, in particular, people set up schools to make sure everyone could read and study the Bible. In 1647 the Massachusetts Puritans passed a public education law requiring communities with 50 or more homes to have a public school.

The result was a high level of literacy in New England. By 1750, about 85 percent of the men and about half of the women were able to read. Many learned from *The New England Primer*.

Most schools in the Middle Colonies were private. Widows or unmarried women ran many of those schools. Quakers and other religious groups ran others. In towns and cities, craftspeople often set up night schools for their apprentices. The earliest colleges in the colonies were founded to train ministers.

The Great Awakening

Religion had a strong influence in colonial life. In the 1730s and 1740s, a religious revival called the Great Awakening swept through the colonies. In New England and the Middle Colonies, ministers called for "a new birth," a return to the

The Granger Collection, NYC

Reading in the Content Area: *Percentages*

Many social studies texts give information in percentages. A percentage gives information as a fraction—how many out of 100. For instance, 12 percent, which may also be written 12%, means 12 out of every 100. Twelve percent of 200 would be 24, and twelve percent of 1,000 would be 120. Percentages allow for easy comparison of different numbers.

strong faith of earlier days. One of these was Jonathan Edwards of Massachusetts, who gave powerful and convincing sermons. George Whitefield, an English preacher who arrived in the colonies in 1739, inspired worshipers in churches and open fields from New England to Georgia.

The Great Awakening inspired greater religious freedom. It led to the formation of many new types of churches. The new churches placed an **emphasis** on having personal faith rather than on church rituals. More colonists began choosing their own faiths, and the strength of established official churches declined. As a Baptist preacher noted soon after the Great Awakening, "The common people now claim as good a right to judge and act in matters of religion as civil rulers or the learned clergy."

The Great Awakening also united colonists from north to south in a common experience. The colonists overcame regional barriers, and this helped pave the way for the rapid spread of revolutionary ideas and excitement during the struggle for independence.

Ministers such as George Whitefield (shown below) and Jonathan Edwards swayed crowds with their vivid, emotional style of preaching.

The Enlightenment

By the middle of the 1700s, many educated colonists were also influenced by the Enlightenment. This movement, which began in Europe, spread the idea that knowledge, reason, and science could improve society. In the colonies, the Enlightenment increased interest in science. People observed nature, staged experiments, and published their findings, much as Benjamin Franklin did. The Enlightenment also promoted freedom of thought and expression, a belief in equality, and the idea of popular government.

Ideas of Freedom

Freedom of the press became an important issue in colonial America. Newspapers in colonial cities, such as Boston and Philadelphia, carried political news and often faced government censorship. Censorship is the banning of printed materials because they contain unpopular or offensive ideas.

Academic Vocabulary

emphasis a special stress or indication of importance

In 1733 publisher John Peter Zenger, in his newspaper the *New-York Weekly Journal*, accused New York's governor of corruption. For criticizing the governor, officials charged Zenger with a crime and threw him in jail. Zenger argued that the statements written about the governor were true. Therefore, he claimed, he had the right to publish them. Zenger's lawyer, Andrew Hamilton, made a stirring defense:

PRIMARY SOURCE

66 The loss of liberty in general would soon follow the suppression of the liberty of the press; for it is an essential branch of liberty, so perhaps it is the best preservative of the whole. 99

—from *The Trial of John Peter Zenger and the Birth of Freedom of the Press*, by Doug Linder

The jury found Zenger not guilty. The case is seen as a key step in the development of a free press in this country.

Civic Virtue

Colonists were beginning to form new ideas of freedom. They began thinking in terms of **civic virtue** (SI•vihk VUHR•choo)—democratic ideas, practices, and values that form a truly free society. De Crèvecoeur was writing about these ideals when he described the spirit of the new American. Benjamin Franklin was a shining example of civic virtue at its best. Colonists would soon put their belief in civic virtue into action. These ideas and actions would become the building blocks of a new nation.

✓ **PROGRESS CHECK**

Analyzing In what ways did the Great Awakening influence culture in the colonies?

John Peter Zenger's newspaper, the *New-York Weekly Journal,* was the battleground in an early case about freedom of the press.

civic virtue the democratic ideas, practices, and values that are at the heart of citizenship in a free society

MPI/Stringer/Getty Images

LESSON 3 REVIEW

Review Vocabulary

1. Describe how each of the following terms relates to culture and society in the thirteen colonies.

   a. immigration   **b.** epidemic
   c. apprentice   **d.** civic virtue

Answer the Guiding Questions

2. *Summarizing* How did the size of the colonial population change in the 1700s, and what contributed to this development?

3. *Explaining* Describe some of the central values and beliefs that helped shape the emerging culture of the American colonies.

4. **PERSONAL WRITING** Imagine you are a student in a colonial town. Write three journal entries that describe a typical day in school.

netw✸rks

There's More Online!

☑ **BIOGRAPHY**
George Washington

☑ **GRAPHIC ORGANIZER**
Native American Relations
With the Europeans

☑ **MAP** The French and Indian War

☑ **PRIMARY SOURCE**
Political Cartoons

☑ **VIDEO**

Lesson 4
Rivalry in North America

ESSENTIAL QUESTION *Why does conflict develop?*

IT MATTERS BECAUSE
Rivalry between Great Britain and France led to a war for control of North America and set the stage for a dispute between the colonists and Great Britain.

Rivalry Between the French and the British

GUIDING QUESTION *How did competition for land in North America lead to the French and Indian War?*

In the 1700s, Britain and France were leading European powers. They competed for wealth and empire in different parts of the world. In North America, their rivalry was very strong.

This rivalry turned especially bitter in the mid-1700s. The British began to show interest in the Ohio River valley. This vast land beyond the Appalachian Mountains was rich in resources. The British believed they had a right to this land. The French also viewed the valley as theirs. The French enjoyed a thriving fur trade with the Native Americans of the region. They did not want to share this business with British settlers.

To protect their claims in the valley, the French built a chain of forts from Lake Ontario south to the Ohio River. The British responded by starting to build a fort in what is now western Pennsylvania. Before they could finish, the French seized the site. On it, they built their own fort, calling it Fort Duquesne (doo•KAYN).

Reading **HELP**DESK

Taking Notes: *Summarizing*

As you read, use a diagram like this one to summarize why Native Americans had better relations with the French than with the British.

Native Americans

| Relations With the British | Relations With the French |

Content Vocabulary

- **militia**
- **Iroquois Confederacy**
- **alliance**

(l) Artist Robert Griffing/ Paramount Press Inc., (c) Art Archive, (cl) Art Archive/General Wolfe Museum, Quebec House/Eileen Tweedy, (r) The Granger Collection, NYC

Although Washington suffered defeat at Fort Necessity, the colonists viewed him as the hero who had struck the first blow against the French.

In spring 1754, the governor of Virginia sent a **militia** (muh•LIH•shuh)—a military force made up of ordinary citizens—to drive out the French. Leading this force was a young Virginian. His name was George Washington.

After marching to Fort Duquesne, Washington set up a small fort of his own nearby. He called it Fort Necessity. Washington's outpost soon came under attack by the French and their Native American allies. This combined army won the battle and forced Washington's soldiers to surrender. The French later released the soldiers, who returned to Virginia.

Native American Alliances

As the conflict got underway, the French and the British both sought Native American help. The French had a big advantage. They already had many Native American allies. Native Americans generally distrusted the British and their hunger for land. In contrast, the French were more interested in fur trading than in land. French trappers and fur traders often married Native American women. French missionaries **converted** many Native Americans to Catholicism. For these reasons, Native Americans helped the French and raided British settlements.

To counter the threat of the French and their Native American friends, the British colonists tried to make a treaty with the Iroquois. The **Iroquois Confederacy** (EER•uh•kwoy kuhn•FEH•duh•ruh•see) was the most powerful group of Native Americans in eastern North America. At that time, the confederacy included six nations—the Mohawk, Seneca, Cayuga, Onondaga, Oneida, and Tuscarora. Delegates—representatives—from seven colonies met with Iroquois leaders at Albany, New York, in June 1754. The Iroquois refused an **alliance** (uh•LY•uhns), or partnership, with the British. They did, however, promise to remain **neutral**—that is, to take no side.

The Albany delegates also talked about how the colonies might work together more closely against the French. They decided to adopt Benjamin Franklin's Albany Plan of Union for a united colonial government. To form a colonial government, each colony would have to give up some of its powers. Not one

Artist Robert Griffing/ Paramount Press Inc.

Reading **HELP**DESK

militia a military force made up of ordinary citizens
Iroquois Confederacy a group of Native American nations in eastern North America joined together under one general government

alliance partnership

Academic Vocabulary

convert to change the religious beliefs of someone
neutral taking no side

colonial assembly was willing to do so. Disappointed, Franklin wrote, "Everybody cries, a Union is absolutely necessary; but when they come to the manner and form of the union, [they] are perfectly distracted."

The Albany meeting failed to unify the colonists. Meanwhile, the conflict between the British and the French expanded into full-scale war—the French and Indian War.

✓ PROGRESS CHECK

Determining Cause and Effect Why did hostilities between the French and British increase during the mid-1700s?

The French and Indian War

GUIDING QUESTION *What was the turning point in the French and Indian War?*

The French enjoyed early success in the war. They captured several British forts. Meanwhile, their Native American allies carried out raids on the frontier, or edges, of the colonies. They killed colonists, burned farmhouses and crops, and drove many families back toward the coast.

The turning point came in 1757, when William Pitt became prime minister, the head of the British government. Pitt was a great military planner. He sent more trained British troops to fight in North America. To stop colonial complaints about the cost of the war, Pitt decided that Britain would pay for it. He knew that, after the war, the British would raise colonists' taxes to help pay the large bill. Pitt had only delayed the time when the colonists would have to pay their share of the military costs.

Pitt's goal was not just to open the Ohio River valley. He also wanted to conquer French Canada. In 1758 British forces won a key victory at Fort Louisbourg, in present-day Nova Scotia.

(t) Art Archive, (b) Art Archive/General Wolfe Museum, Quebec House/Eileen Tweedy

After a month-long siege, Major General James Wolfe ordered British forces to cross the St. Lawrence River and climb the cliffs near the city of Quebec. In less than an hour, French troops fled, and the city fell.

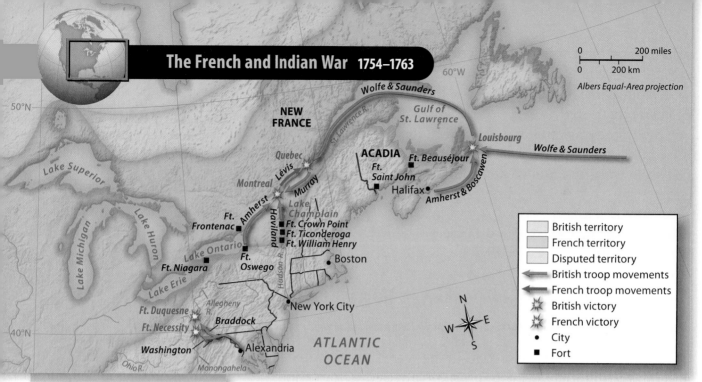

The French and Indian War 1754–1763

0 — 200 miles
0 — 200 km
Albers Equal-Area projection

NEW FRANCE

Wolfe & Saunders

Gulf of St. Lawrence

Louisbourg

Wolfe & Saunders

ACADIA

Ft. Beauséjour

Ft. Saint John

Halifax

Amherst & Boscawen

Quebec

Lévis

Montreal

Murray

Amherst

Lake Champlain

Ft. Crown Point

Ft. Ticonderoga

Ft. William Henry

Ft. Frontenac

Haviland

Lake Ontario

Ft. Niagara

Ft. Oswego

Boston

Lake Superior

Lake Michigan

Lake Huron

Lake Erie

Hudson R.

New York City

ATLANTIC OCEAN

Allegheny R.

Ft. Duquesne

Braddock

Ft. Necessity

Washington

Alexandria

Ohio R.

Monongahela

	British territory
	French territory
	Disputed territory
←	British troop movements
←	French troop movements
✸	British victory
✸	French victory
•	City
■	Fort

GEOGRAPHY CONNECTION

During the French and Indian War, the British and the French fought for control of the lands between their North American territories.

1 LOCATION Where are the cities of Quebec and Montreal located?

2 CRITICAL THINKING
Analyzing Why do you think Quebec and Montreal were related to French dominance in the Ohio River valley?

The same year a British force, made up mostly of New York and New England militia, captured Fort Frontenac at Lake Ontario. Another British force finally took Fort Duquesne. The British renamed it Fort Pitt.

Quebec, the capital of New France, sat on a cliff above the St. Lawrence River. Because of its position, Quebec was thought to be impossible to attack. In September 1759, British scouts spotted a poorly guarded path along the back of the cliff. At night, Wolfe's soldiers overwhelmed the French guards and scrambled up the path. The British troops then surprised and defeated the French army on a field called the Plains of Abraham. The fall of Quebec and of Montreal the next year marked the defeat of France in North America.

The war in Europe finally ended with the Treaty of Paris of 1763. This treaty forced France to give Canada and most of its lands east of the Mississippi River to Great Britain. Great Britain also received Florida from France's ally, Spain. Spain acquired French lands west of the Mississippi River—called Louisiana— as well as the port of New Orleans.

The Treaty of Paris marked the end of France as a power in North America. In its aftermath, North America was in the hands of two European powers—Great Britain and Spain.

✓ PROGRESS CHECK

Explaining Why was William Pitt successful at managing the war for Britain?

Reading **HELP**DESK

Reading Strategy: *Identifying the Main Idea*

In most paragraphs, the main idea appears near the beginning. The rest of the paragraph often gives examples or details to help you understand the main idea. Read the first paragraph under the Guiding Question on the next page. Identify the main idea of the paragraph and three supporting details.

New British Policies

GUIDING QUESTION *How did the American colonists react to new British policies?*

The French defeat was a blow to Native Americans in the Ohio River Valley. They had lost their French allies and trading partners and now had to deal with the British. The British raised the prices of their goods. Unlike the French, the British refused to pay Native Americans to use their land. Worst of all, more colonists began settling in Native American lands.

Many Native Americans saw the settlers as a threat to their way of life. One of these was Pontiac, the chief of an Ottawa village near Detroit. In 1763, Pontiac and his forces captured the British fort at Detroit and other British outposts. During Pontiac's War, Native Americans killed settlers along the Pennsylvania and Virginia frontiers.

The same year as Pontiac's War began, Britain's King George declared that colonists were not to settle west of the Appalachian Mountains. To enforce the new rule, the British planned to keep 10,000 troops in America. The Proclamation of 1763 helped removed a source of conflict with Native Americans. It also kept colonists on the coast—where the British could control them.

Colonists believed the proclamation limited their freedom of movement. They feared that the large number of British troops might interfere with their liberties. As a result, distrust began to grow between Britain and its American colonies.

Britain's financial problems also led to trouble. Deeply in debt as a result of the war with France, the British government made plans to tax the colonies and tighten trade rules. These efforts would lead to conflict—and eventually revolution.

The Granger Collection, NYC

☑ PROGRESS CHECK

Examining Why did the Proclamation of 1763 anger colonists?

Pontiac, c. 1720–1769

Pontiac became an Ottawa chief while still a young man. A born leader, he brought together three tribes—the Ottawa, the Potawatomi, and the Ojibwa—in an alliance. As more British settlers moved into their lands, he convinced more tribes to join. Based on Pontiac's plans, these tribes attacked British forts and settlements. Pontiac himself led the successful attack on the fort at Detroit. Pontiac agreed to peace with the British in July 1766. Afterward, his allies turned against him.

▶ **CRITICAL THINKING**
Drawing Conclusions Why do you think Pontiac's former allies turned against him?

LESSON 4 REVIEW

Review Vocabulary

1. Write a sentence using the terms *alliance* and *Iroquois Confederacy*.

2. Write a sentence about the colonies using the word *militia*.

Answer the Guiding Questions

3. ***Explaining*** What was the role of the Ohio River valley in the growing conflict between the French, Native Americans, and British in the mid-1700s?

4. ***Identifying*** What was the role of William Pitt in the French and Indian War?

5. ***Summarizing*** Why were the American colonists dissatisfied with the outcome of the war?

6. **EXPOSITORY WRITING** Write a paragraph that summarizes the Albany Plan of Union, including the problems it was meant to address and the response it received among the colonies.

Write your answers on a separate piece of paper.

① Exploring the Essential Questions

EXPOSITORY WRITING How did geography shape the lives of the American colonists? Write a summary essay in which you consider how geographic factors shaped the development of life in the colonies, but also how it led to conflict, including conflicts with Great Britain.

② 21st Century Skills

CREATE AND GIVE A PRESENTATION Use presentation software or a poster to create a presentation that illustrates how life in colonial America was influenced and shaped by geography. Use illustrations of life in the different colonies and colonial regions, and include explanations of how the illustrations show geographic differences and factors.

③ Thinking Like a Historian

DRAWING INFERENCES AND CONCLUSIONS Create a diagram such as the one here to identify the factors in colonial America that caused conflict with Great Britain.

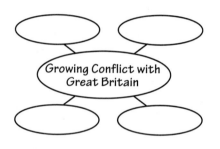

Growing Conflict with Great Britain

④ Visual Literacy

ANALYZING IMAGES This painting shows methods used in whaling in colonial times. Explain how this picture demonstrates the effects of geography on the economy of the colonies.

REVIEW THE GUIDING QUESTIONS

Choose the best answer for each question.

1 The Middle Colonies were known for
- A. poor farmland.
- B. a diverse population.
- C. plantations.
- D. their whaling industry.

2 The success of the large plantations of the Southern Colonies depended upon
- F. the region's many large ports.
- G. large families.
- H. slavery.
- I. rocky soil.

3 The concept of protected rights began with the
- A. Magna Carta.
- B. Enlightenment.
- C. English Bill of Rights.
- D. Great Awakening.

4 Merchants in the American colonies began smuggling goods because
- F. the Navigation Act allowed merchants to choose the buyer.
- G. Britain always offered the colonists the best price.
- H. they had more goods than Britain could buy.
- I. they could sometimes get better prices from customers in other countries.

5 The Great Awakening resulted in a renewed interest in
- A. science.
- B. religion.
- C. mercantilism.
- D. conflict.

6 Benjamin Franklin is an example of an American colonist strongly influenced by
- F. traditional medicine.
- G. the Great Awakening.
- H. the unfairness of censorship.
- I. the Enlightenment.

7 The Albany Plan of Union was not approved by the colonies because
- A. it called for the colonies to declare their independence from Britain.
- B. most colonists did not consider the western lands valuable.
- C. it diminished the strength of the united colonial government.
- D. colonies were not willing to give up any of their power.

8 How did the British victory over the French affect the Native Americans of the Ohio River valley?
- F. It helped them because the British, unlike the French, paid Native Americans for the use of their land.
- G. It hurt them because so many French refugees fled to their lands.
- H. It hurt them because they lost their French allies and trading partners.
- I. It helped them because the British lowered the prices of their goods.

DBQ DOCUMENT-BASED QUESTIONS

9 **Identifying** This map illustrates trade and industry in the American colonies around 1750. Based on the map, what trade and industry was found only in the Southern Colonies?

A. lumber

B. fur and skins

C. rice and indigo

D. fishing

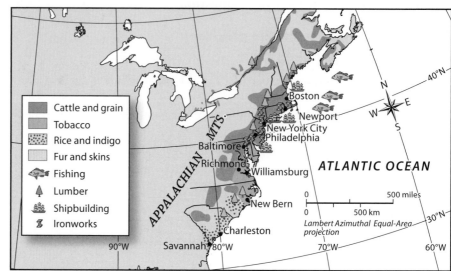

Source: *Historical Atlas of the United States*

10 **Locating** Near which major city were ironworks found?

F. Philadelphia

G. Richmond

H. Williamsburg

I. Savannah

SHORT RESPONSE

"It is proposed that humble application be made for an act of Parliament of Great Britain, by virtue of which one general government may be formed in America, including all the said colonies, within and under which government each colony may retain its present constitution."

—from *Albany Plan of Union*

11 What is being proposed here?

12 How would the resulting government have affected the individual colonies?

EXTENDED RESPONSE

13 **Expository Writing** Benjamin Franklin served a number of roles in the American colonies in the 1700s. Write an essay about the way he represented key qualities of the colonies.

Need Extra Help?

If You've Missed Question	**1**	**2**	**3**	**4**	**5**	**6**	**7**	**8**	**9**	**10**	**11**	**12**	**13**
Review Lesson	1	1	2	2	3	3	4	4	1	1	4	4	2,3,4

The Spirit of Independence

1763–1776

ESSENTIAL QUESTIONS · *Why does conflict develop?*
· *What motivates people to act?*

networks

There's More Online about the events that drove the colonies and the British apart.

CHAPTER 5

The Story Matters . . .

He stands proud and tall, this minuteman, part of a colonial militia. Citizen soldiers like him were the first responders of their time. A call to arms could come day or night. The minutemen were out the door on a minute's notice, ready to protect their communities.

Few would doubt the minutemen's bravery. But if the growing tension between the colonies and Great Britain led to war, how would these farmers, clerks, and shopkeepers stand up to a force of skilled British soldiers? This was one of many troubling questions that the colonies faced as they moved closer to declaring their independence.

◀ *This portrait of a minuteman was created in 1876 to celebrate 100 years of American independence.*

Bettmann/CORBIS

Place and Time: The British Colonies 1763 to 1776

The British colonies extended along the coast of the Atlantic Ocean. In the middle of this strip was Philadelphia. This city would become a gathering place for colonial leaders as they discussed the growing conflict with Great Britain.

Step Into the Place

MAP FOCUS By 1775, British policies had caused unrest in the colonies and a growing movement toward independence.

1 REGION Which colonial region appears to have the largest area of Loyalist support?

2 LOCATION What lay beyond the borders of British territory in North America?

3 CRITICAL THINKING
Making Connections In which colonies do you think the movement for independence might have been the strongest? What makes you think so?

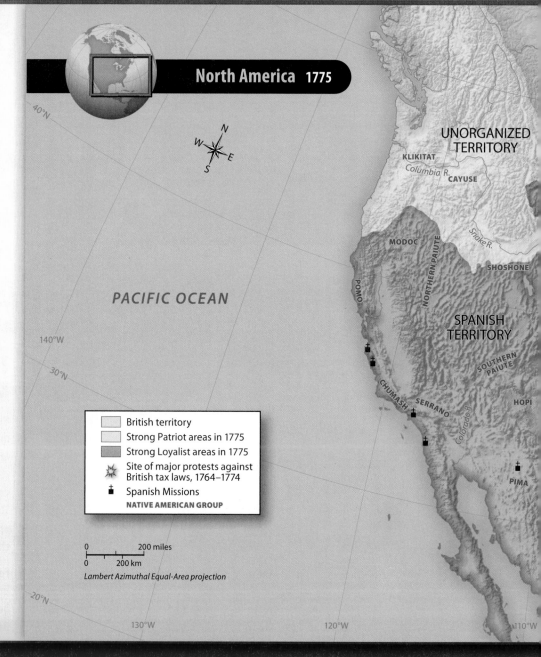

North America 1775

UNORGANIZED TERRITORY

KLIKITAT
Columbia R.
CAYUSE

MODOC

NORTHERN PAIUTE

Snake R.

SHOSHONE

POMO

PACIFIC OCEAN

SPANISH TERRITORY

SOUTHERN PAIUTE

CHUMASH

SERRANO

Colorado R.

HOPI

PIMA

British territory
Strong Patriot areas in 1775
Strong Loyalist areas in 1775
Site of major protests against British tax laws, 1764–1774
Spanish Missions
NATIVE AMERICAN GROUP

0   200 miles
0   200 km
Lambert Azimuthal Equal-Area projection

Step Into the Time

TIME LINE Review the time line. What was taking place in Europe at about the same time the First Continental Congress met in America?

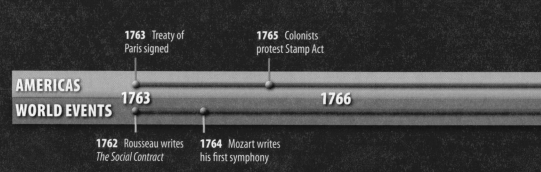

1763 Treaty of Paris signed

1765 Colonists protest Stamp Act

AMERICAS

WORLD EVENTS

1763

1766

1762 Rousseau writes *The Social Contract*

1764 Mozart writes his first symphony

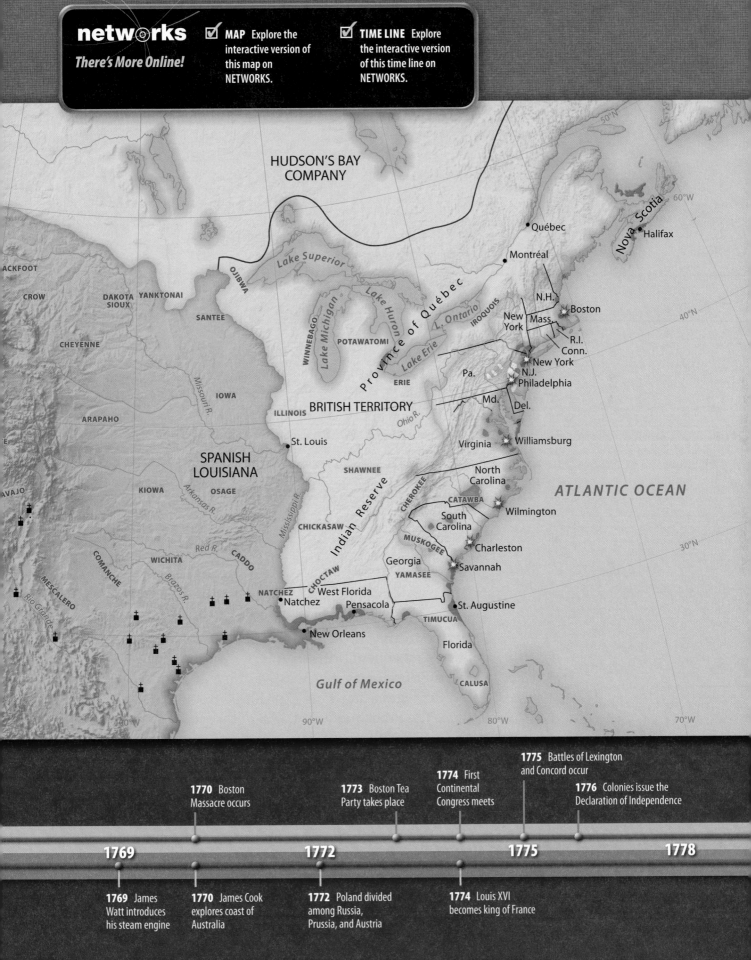

networks
There's More Online!

☑ **MAP** Explore the interactive version of this map on NETWORKS.

☑ **TIME LINE** Explore the interactive version of this time line on NETWORKS.

HUDSON'S BAY COMPANY

BLACKFOOT
CROW
DAKOTA SIOUX
YANKTONAI
SANTEE
CHEYENNE
ARAPAHO
KIOWA
OSAGE
WICHITA
CADDO
COMANCHE
MESCALERO
NAVAJO

OJIBWA
WINNEBAGO
POTAWATOMI
IOWA
ILLINOIS
SHAWNEE
CHICKASAW
NATCHEZ
CHOCTAW

Lake Superior
Lake Michigan
Lake Huron
Lake Erie
L. Ontario
ERIE
IROQUOIS

Province of Québec
BRITISH TERRITORY

SPANISH LOUISIANA
St. Louis

Indian Reserve

Missouri R.
Ohio R.
Mississippi R.
Arkansas R.
Red R.
Brazos R.
Rio Grande

CHEROKEE
CATAWBA
MUSKOGEE
YAMASEE
TIMUCUA
CALUSA

Québec
Montréal
Nova Scotia
Halifax
N.H.
Boston
New York
Mass.
R.I.
Conn.
New York
N.J.
Philadelphia
Pa.
Md.
Del.
Virginia
Williamsburg
North Carolina
South Carolina
Wilmington
Charleston
Georgia
Savannah
West Florida
Natchez
Pensacola
New Orleans
St. Augustine
Florida

ATLANTIC OCEAN

Gulf of Mexico

50°N
60°W
40°N
30°N
70°W
80°W
90°W
100°W

1775 Battles of Lexington and Concord occur

1774 First Continental Congress meets

1773 Boston Tea Party takes place

1770 Boston Massacre occurs

1776 Colonies issue the Declaration of Independence

1769   **1772**   **1775**   **1778**

1769 James Watt introduces his steam engine

1770 James Cook explores coast of Australia

1772 Poland divided among Russia, Prussia, and Austria

1774 Louis XVI becomes king of France

networks

There's More Online!

☑ **GRAPHIC ORGANIZER**
British Policies

☑ **MAP** The Proclamation
of 1763

Lesson 1

No Taxation Without Representation

ESSENTIAL QUESTION *Why does conflict develop?*

IT MATTERS BECAUSE

Conflict between the American colonies and the British began to deepen in the years after the French and Indian War.

Dealing with Great Britain

GUIDING QUESTION *Why did the British government establish new policies?*

After their victory in the French and Indian War, the British controlled much of North America. Now they had to protect all this territory. To meet this challenge, King George III issued the Proclamation of 1763. This order **prohibited**, or barred, colonists from living west of the Appalachian Mountains, on Native American land. For the British, the proclamation offered several advantages. It helped keep peace between Native Americans and settlers. It also kept colonists near the Atlantic Coast, where British authority was stronger. Finally, it allowed Britain to control westward expansion and the fur trade in the region. The king sent 10,000 troops to the colonies to enforce the Proclamation of 1763 and keep the peace with Native Americans.

Enforcing Trade Laws

Great Britain needed new **revenue**, or income, to pay for the troops. The British also had large debts from the French and Indian War. The king and Parliament felt the colonists should pay part of these

(r) The Granger Collection, NYC

Taking Notes: *Identifying*

As you read, identify British policies that affected the colonists. Record each policy in a chart like this one. Then record the colonists' views of each policy.

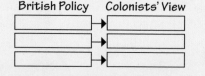

British Policy   Colonists' View

Content Vocabulary

• revenue
• writ of assistance
• resolution

• effigy
• boycott
• repeal

costs, so the British government issued new taxes on the colonies. It also enforced old taxes more strictly. To avoid taxes, some colonists resorted to smuggling. This caused British revenues to fall.

In 1763 Britain's prime minister, George Grenville, set out to stop the smuggling. Parliament passed a law to have accused smugglers tried by royally appointed judges rather than local juries. Grenville knew that American juries often found smugglers innocent. Parliament also empowered customs officers to obtain **writs of assistance**. These documents allowed the officers to search almost anywhere—shops, warehouses, and even private homes—for smuggled goods.

The Sugar Act

In 1764 Parliament passed the Sugar Act, which lowered the tax on the molasses the colonists imported. Grenville hoped this change would convince the colonists to pay the tax instead of smuggling. The act also allowed officers to seize goods from accused smugglers without going to court.

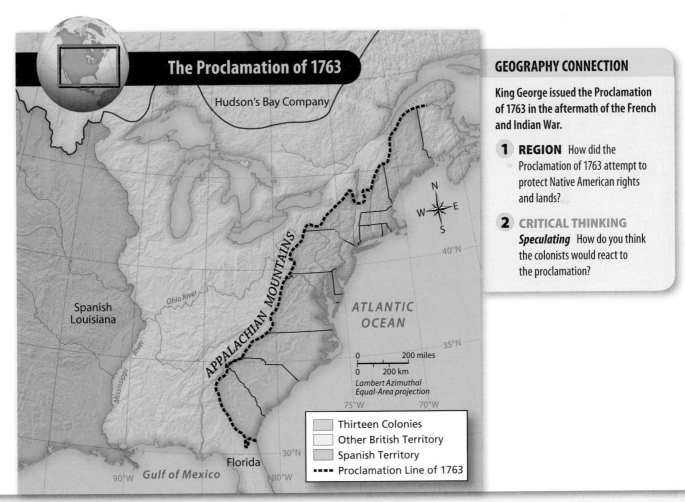

The Proclamation of 1763

Hudson's Bay Company

Spanish Louisiana

Ohio River

Mississippi River

APPALACHIAN MOUNTAINS

ATLANTIC OCEAN

Florida

Gulf of Mexico

0   200 miles
0   200 km
Lambert Azimuthal Equal-Area projection

☐ Thirteen Colonies
☐ Other British Territory
☐ Spanish Territory
---- Proclamation Line of 1763

GEOGRAPHY CONNECTION

King George issued the Proclamation of 1763 in the aftermath of the French and Indian War.

1 REGION How did the Proclamation of 1763 attempt to protect Native American rights and lands?

2 CRITICAL THINKING
Speculating How do you think the colonists would react to the proclamation?

revenue incoming money from taxes or other sources
writ of assistance court document allowing customs officers to enter any location to search for smuggled goods

Academic Vocabulary

prohibit to prevent or forbid

A GROWING DEBT

1 **CALCULATING** Did British or colonial subjects pay more toward the debt? What was the difference in pounds and shillings?

2 **CRITICAL THINKING**
Identifying Central Issues
How did residents of Britain and the American colonists pay their shares of the debt?

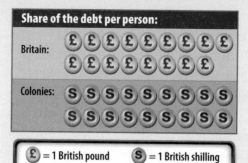

Share of the debt per person:

Britain: £ £ £ £ £ £ £ £ £
£ £ £ £ £ £ £ £

Colonies: S S S S S S S S
S S S S S S S S

£ = 1 British pound   S = 1 British shilling
1 Pound (£) = 20 Shillings

Great Britain's national debt soared as a result of the French and Indian War. Subjects living in Great Britain paid more on this debt per person than people living in the colonies. British efforts to get colonists to pay a bigger share of war-related debt led to sharp conflict.

Source: Don Cook. *The Long Fuse: How England Lost the American Colonies, 1760–1785*

The Sugar Act angered many colonists. They believed this and other new laws **violated** their rights. As British citizens, colonists argued, they had a right to a trial by jury and to be viewed as innocent until proved guilty, as stated in British law. Colonists also believed they had the right to be secure in their homes—without the threat of officers barging in to search for smuggled goods.

British taxes also alarmed the colonists. James Otis, a lawyer in Boston, argued:

PRIMARY SOURCE

❝ No parts of [England's colonies] can be taxed without their consent … every part has a right to be represented. ❞

—from *The Rights of the British Colonies*, 1763

☑ **PROGRESS CHECK**

Explaining Why did Parliament pass the Sugar Act?

New Taxes on the Colonies

GUIDING QUESTION *How did the American colonists react to British policies?*

In 1765 Parliament passed the Stamp Act. This law taxed almost all printed materials. Newspapers, wills, and even playing cards needed a stamp to show that the tax had been paid.

Opposition to the Stamp Act

The Stamp Act outraged the colonists. They argued that only their own assemblies could tax them. Patrick Henry, a member of the Virginia House of Burgesses, got the burgesses to take

Reading **HELP**DESK

resolution an official expression of opinion by a group
effigy a mocking figure representing an unpopular individual

boycott to refuse to buy items in order to show disapproval or force acceptance of one's terms
repeal to cancel an act or law

Academic Vocabulary

violate to disregard or go against

action. The assembly passed a **resolution**—a formal expression of opinion—declaring that it had "the only and sole exclusive right and power to lay taxes" on its citizens.

In Boston, Samuel Adams helped start the Sons of Liberty. Its members took to the streets to protest the Stamp Act. Protesters burned **effigies** (EH•fuh•jeez)—stuffed figures—made to look like unpopular tax collectors.

Colonial leaders decided to work together. In October, delegates from nine colonies met in New York at the Stamp Act Congress. They sent a statement to the king and Parliament declaring that only colonial assemblies could tax the colonists.

People in colonial cities urged merchants to **boycott**—refuse to buy—British goods in protest. As the boycott spread, businesses in Britain lost so much money that they demanded Parliament **repeal**, or cancel, the Stamp Act. In March 1766, Parliament repealed the law. However, it also passed the Declaratory Act, stating that it had the right to tax and make decisions for the British colonies "in all cases."

The Townshend Acts

The Stamp Act taught the British that the colonists would resist internal taxes—those paid inside the colonies. As a result, in 1767 Parliament passed the Townshend Acts to tax imported goods, such as glass, tea, and paper. The tax was paid when the goods arrived—before they were brought inside the colonies.

By then, *any* British taxes angered the colonists. Protests of the Townshend Acts began immediately. In towns throughout the colonies, women protested by supporting another boycott of British goods. They also urged colonists to wear homemade fabrics rather than buying fabric made in Britain. Some women's groups called themselves the Daughters of Liberty.

A British government official placed this seal, or stamp, on certain paper items in the colonies to show that the tax on them had been paid.

☑ PROGRESS CHECK

Contrasting How did the Townshend Acts differ from the Stamp Act?

The Granger Collection, NYC

LESSON 1 REVIEW

Review Vocabulary

1. Write a paragraph about the 1760s in the American colonies in which you use these vocabulary words:

   a. revenue   **b.** resolution   **c.** effigy
   d. boycott   **e.** repeal

Answer the Guiding Questions

2. *Describing* What advantages did the British hope to gain by limiting westward settlement in 1763?

3. *Explaining* Why did some colonists smuggle goods in the 1760s?

4. *Identifying* Why did colonists oppose the Stamp Act?

5. **NARRATIVE WRITING** Write a conversation between two colonists who disagree over Britain taxing the colonies to help pay off its debts from the French and Indian War.

networks
There's More Online!

☑ **GRAPHIC ORGANIZER**
The Intolerable Acts

☑ **PRIMARY SOURCE** The
Boston Tea Party

☑ **VIDEO**

Lesson 2
Uniting the Colonists

ESSENTIAL QUESTION *Why does conflict develop?*

IT MATTERS BECAUSE
Harsh British actions aimed at controlling the colonies united them instead.

Trouble in Massachusetts

GUIDING QUESTION *How did the American colonists react to the Boston Massacre?*

Protests continued to flare in the colonies, making British officials nervous. In 1768 they sent word to Britain that the colonies were on the brink of **rebellion**—a rejection of British authority. Parliament sent troops to Boston. As angry colonists jeered, the "redcoats" set up camp in the center of the city.

For many colonists, this British act went too far. First the colonists were convinced that the British had passed laws that violated colonial rights. Now Britain had sent an army to **occupy,** or take control of, colonial cities.

To make matters worse, the soldiers in Boston acted rudely. The redcoats, who were mostly poor men, earned little pay. Some stole from local shops and got into fights with colonists. Also, in their off-hours, the soldiers competed for jobs that Bostonians wanted.

Tension in the Streets

On March 5, 1770, violence erupted. A fight broke out between some Bostonians and soldiers. As British officers tried to calm the crowd, a man shouted, "We did not send for you. We will not have you here. We'll get rid of you, we'll drive you away!"

Reading **HELP**DESK

Taking Notes: *Describing*

As you read, use a diagram like this one to record how the Intolerable Acts changed life for the colonists.

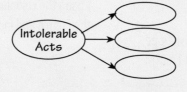

Intolerable Acts

Content Vocabulary
• **rebellion**
• **propaganda**
• **committee of correspondence**

The angry townspeople surged forward. They began throwing sticks and stones at the soldiers. "Come on, you rascals, you bloody backs, you lobster scoundrels, fire, if you dare," someone in the crowd shouted.

After one soldier was knocked down, the nervous redcoats did fire. They killed five colonists. Among the dead was Crispus Attucks, a dockworker who was part African, part Native American. One Bostonian cried: "Are the inhabitants to be knocked down in the streets? Are they to be murdered … ?" The colonists called the tragic **encounter** "the Boston Massacre."

Spreading the News

Colonial leaders used the killings as **propaganda**—information designed to influence opinion. Samuel Adams put up posters that described the Boston Massacre as a slaughter of innocent Americans by bloodthirsty redcoats. Paul Revere made an engraving that showed a British officer giving the order to open fire on an orderly crowd.

Crispus Attucks was the first colonist killed by the British in the Boston Massacre.

The Boston Massacre led colonists to call for stronger boycotts of British goods. Troubled by the growing opposition in the colonies, Parliament repealed all the Townshend Acts taxes on British imported goods, except the one on tea. In response, the colonists ended their boycotts, except on tea. Trade with Britain resumed.

Still, some colonists continued to call for resistance to British rule. In 1772 Samuel Adams revived the Boston **committee of correspondence**, a group used in earlier protests. The group circulated calls for action against Britain. Soon committees of correspondence sprang up throughout the colonies, bringing together protesters opposed to British measures.

☑ PROGRESS CHECK

Explaining How did the Boston Massacre affect the relations between the colonists and Britain?

Crisis in Boston

GUIDING QUESTION *How did the British government react to the actions of the colonists?*

The British East India Company was vital to the British economy. Colonial refusal to import British East India tea had nearly driven the company out of business. To help save the company and protect the British economy, Parliament passed the Tea Act.

---

rebellion open defiance of authority
propaganda ideas or information intentionally spread to harm or help a cause
committee of correspondence an organization that spread political ideas and information through the colonies

Academic Vocabulary

occupy to move into and take control of a place, especially by force
encounter a sudden, often violent clash

Build Vocabulary: *Multiple Meaning Words*

As a verb, the word *encounter* means "to come across or meet." As a noun, *encounter* can mean "a chance meeting" or "a sudden, often violent, meeting between hostile people."

Colonists angry at the restrictions of the Tea Act staged a dramatic protest. They threw three shiploads of British tea into Boston Harbor.

▶ CRITICAL THINKING
Analyzing Why were American colonists especially angry with the Tea Act?

It gave the company nearly total control of the market for tea in the colonies. The Tea Act also removed some—but not all—of the taxes on tea, making it less expensive for colonists. Yet the colonists remained angry. They did not want to pay any tax, and they did not want to be told what tea they could buy.

Colonial merchants called for a new boycott. Colonists vowed to stop East India Company ships from unloading. The Daughters of Liberty issued a pamphlet declaring that rather than part with freedom, "We'll part with our tea."

A Tea Party

Despite warnings of trouble, the East India Company continued shipping tea to the colonies. Colonists in New York and Philadelphia forced the tea ships to turn back. In 1773, three ships loaded with tea arrived in Boston Harbor. The royal governor ordered that they be unloaded. The Boston Sons of Liberty acted swiftly. At midnight on December 16, colonists dressed as Native Americans boarded the ships and threw 342 chests of tea overboard. As word of the "Boston Tea Party"

Time & Life Pictures/Getty Images

Reading **HELP**DESK

Reading Strategy: *Determining Cause and Effect*

A cause is an event or action that makes something else happen. That something else that happens is an effect. Determining causes and effects can help you see relationships between events and find patterns in history. As you read, identify one cause and one effect of the Boston Tea Party.

spread, colonists gathered to celebrate the bold act. Yet no one spoke out against British rule itself. Most colonists still saw themselves as loyal British citizens.

The Intolerable Acts

When news of the Boston Tea Party reached London, King George III realized that Britain was losing control of the colonies. He declared, "We must either master them or totally leave them to themselves."

In 1774 Parliament responded by passing a series of laws called the Coercive Acts. *Coercive* (co•UHR•sihv) means to force someone to do something. These laws were meant to punish the colonists for resisting British authority. One Coercive Act applied to all the colonies. It forced the colonies to let British soldiers live among the colonists. Massachusetts, though, received the harshest treatment.

One of the Coercive Acts banned town meetings in Massachusetts. Another closed Boston Harbor until the colonists paid for the ruined tea. This stopped most shipments of food and other supplies to the colony. Parliament was trying to cut Massachusetts off from the other colonies. Instead, the Coercive Acts drew the colonies together. Other colonies sent food and clothing to support Boston.

Following the Coercive Acts, Parliament also passed the Quebec Act. This law created a government for Canada and extended its territory south all the way to the Ohio River. This action ignored the colonies' claims to that region.

The colonists believed all of these new laws violated their rights as English citizens. They expressed their feelings about the laws by calling them the Intolerable Acts. *Intolerable* means painful and unbearable.

King George's determination to take a firm stand against the colonies after the Boston Tea Party failed to resolve the growing crisis. In fact, colonial anger grew.

☑ **PROGRESS CHECK**

Summarizing List the effects of the Coercive Acts on the citizens of Boston.

LESSON 2 REVIEW

Review Vocabulary

1. Explain the significance of the following terms:

   a. rebellion   **b.** propaganda
   c. committee of correspondence

Answer the Guiding Questions

2. *Sequencing* List the events leading up to and following the Boston Massacre in the order that they occurred.

3. *Analyzing* How did Samuel Adams and Paul Revere use propaganda to rally colonists after the Boston Massacre?

4. *Explaining* How did the British punish the colonists for the Boston Tea Party?

5. **NARRATIVE WRITING** Write an account of the Boston Massacre from the point of view of a British soldier involved in the event.

networks

There's More Online!

☑ **BIOGRAPHY**
Patrick Henry

☑ **GRAPHIC ORGANIZER**
Key Actions of the
Continental Congress

☑ **MAP** Battles of Lexington
and Concord

Lesson 3
A Call to Arms

ESSENTIAL QUESTION *What motivates people to act?*

IT MATTERS BECAUSE

As anger toward the British grew, Americans began to consider the possibility of independence.

A Meeting in Philadelphia

GUIDING QUESTION *What role did key individuals play in the movement toward independence?*

In September 1774, fifty-five delegates gathered in Philadelphia. They had come to set up a political body that would represent Americans and challenge British control. The delegates called this body the Continental Congress.

Leaders from twelve of the thirteen colonies attended the meeting. Only Georgia did not send a representative. Massachusetts sent fiery Samuel Adams and his lawyer cousin, John Adams. New York sent John Jay, another lawyer. Virginia sent George Washington as well as Richard Henry Lee and Patrick Henry, two outspoken defenders of colonial rights. Patrick Henry wanted the colonies to unite in firm resistance to Britain. He summed up the meaning of the meeting when he addressed the delegates on its second day:

PRIMARY SOURCE

66 The distinctions between Virginians, Pennsylvanians, New Yorkers, and New Englanders are no more. I am not a Virginian, but an American. 99

—Patrick Henry, at the Continental Congress, 1774

(l) © Kevin Fleming/CORBIS, (cl) National Portrait Gallery, Smithsonian Institution/Art Resource, NY, (c) North Wind Picture Archives, (cr) Library of Congress, Prints and Photographs Division, LC-USZC4-4971, (r) Bettmann/CORBIS

Reading **HELP**DESK

Taking Notes: *Summarizing*

As you read, use a diagram like this one to list three key actions of the Continental Congress.

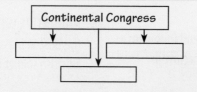

Content Vocabulary

- **minuteman**
- **Loyalist**
- **Patriot**

The Delegates Vote

The delegates discussed complaints against the British. Then they voted. In a statement of grievances, the delegates called for the repeal of 13 acts of Parliament. They believed these laws violated the "laws of nature, the principles of the English constitution, and the several charters" of the colonies. The delegates also voted to boycott British trade. The colonies would not import or use any British goods, nor would they sell their goods in Great Britain.

Continental Congress delegates also decided to endorse the Suffolk Resolves, prepared by the people of Boston and other Suffolk County towns in Massachusetts. These resolutions declared the Coercive Acts to be illegal. They called on the county's residents to arm themselves against the British. After delegates endorsed the resolves, other colonies also organized militias—groups of citizen soldiers.

The Colonial Militias

American colonists had a long tradition of serving and protecting their communities in militias. Members of a militia were an important part of each town's defense. Militia members trained and had drills with the other citizen soldiers. They practiced using muskets and cannons. Each member was required to provide his own weapon—usually a musket—and ammunition. Later, as tension between Britain and the colonies grew, towns began to gather and store military supplies.

✓ **PROGRESS CHECK**

Explaining What was the purpose of the Continental Congress?

Kevin Fleming/CORBIS

A MASSACHUSETTS COMMUNITY PREPARES

Purchases authorized by Salem Provincial Congress, October 1774	
20 tons grape- and round shot, from 3 to 24 lb. @ £15	£300
10 tons bomb shells @ £20	£200
5 tons lead balls @ £33	£165
1,000 barrels of powder @ £8	£8,000
5,000 arms and bayonets @ £2	£10,000
75,000 flints	£100

CHART SKILL

This chart shows military supplies that the town of Salem, Massachusetts, purchased for its militia in 1774.

1 IDENTIFYING About how many soldiers does Salem appear prepared to equip?

2 CRITICAL THINKING *Making Inferences* What does this list suggest about this community's expectations about relations with the British?

Build Vocabulary: *Multiple Meaning Words*

The word *resolves*, as used on this page, means "something that is decided." As a noun, the word *resolve* can also mean "firmness of purpose," as in "The Patriots showed resolve against the British." As a verb, *resolve* can mean "to decide something" or "to solve a problem."

Patrick Henry (1736–1799)

Henry was one of the first members of the Virginia House of Burgesses to argue for independence from Britain. His speaking ability inspired many colonists. In a debate over whether the Virginia Colony should form a militia, he said, "Give me liberty or give me death!" His stirring cry gave voice to the independence movement.

▶ **CRITICAL THINKING**
Analyzing Is good speaking ability an important quality of a leader? Explain.

Fighting Begins

GUIDING QUESTION *Why were the battles at Lexington and Concord important?*

Many colonists believed that if fighting with the British were to break out, it would happen in New England. Militias in Massachusetts held drills, made bullets, and stockpiled weapons. Some militias were known as **minutemen** because they boasted they would be ready to fight at a minute's notice. In the winter of 1774–1775, a British officer stationed in Boston noted in his diary:

PRIMARY SOURCE

❝ The people are evidently making every preparation for resistance. They are taking every means to provide themselves with Arms. ❞

—from *Diary of Frederick Mackenzie*, 1775

Great Britain Sends Troops

The British also got ready for a fight. King George told Parliament that the New England Colonies were "in a state of rebellion" and that "blows must decide" who would control America. By April 1775, several thousand British troops were in and around Boston, with more on the way. British general Thomas Gage had orders to seize the weapons from the Massachusetts militia and arrest the leaders.

Gage learned that the militia stored arms and ammunition at Concord, a town about 20 miles (32 km) northwest of Boston. He ordered 700 troops under Lieutenant Colonel Francis Smith "to Concord, where you will seize and destroy all the artillery and ammunition you can find."

The British on the Move

On the night of April 18, 1775, colonial protest leader Dr. Joseph Warren walked through Boston. Watching for any unusual activity by the British, he saw troops marching out of the city.

Warren alerted Paul Revere and William Dawes, members of the Sons of Liberty. Revere and Dawes rode to Lexington, a town east of Concord, to spread the word that the British were coming. Revere galloped across the countryside, shouting his warning of the approaching troops. Hearing the news, Samuel Adams said, "What a glorious morning this is!" He was ready to fight. A British patrol later captured Dawes and Revere. Another rider named Samuel Prescott carried the warning to Concord.

National Portrait Gallery, Smithsonian Institution/Art Resource, NY

Reading HELPDESK

minuteman during Revolutionary era, civilian sworn to be ready to fight with only one minute's notice

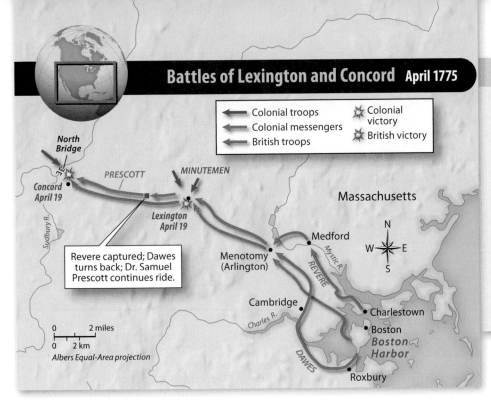

Battles of Lexington and Concord April 1775

Legend:
→ Colonial troops
→ Colonial messengers
→ British troops
✷ Colonial victory
✷ British victory

North Bridge
Concord April 19
PRESCOTT
MINUTEMEN
Lexington April 19
Revere captured; Dawes turns back; Dr. Samuel Prescott continues ride.
Menotomy (Arlington)
Medford
Massachusetts
Mystic R.
REVERE
Cambridge
Charles R.
Charlestown
Boston
Boston Harbor
DAWES
Roxbury
Sudbury R.

0   2 miles
0   2 km
Albers Equal-Area projection

N W E S

GEOGRAPHY CONNECTION

The first fighting between British troops and the colonial militia took place at Lexington and Concord, Massachusetts.

1 **MOVEMENT** Which towns did Paul Revere warn on his ride to Lexington?

2 **CRITICAL THINKING** *Analyzing* How might the starting point of the British forces in Boston have affected the outcome of these battles?

Lexington and Concord

Meanwhile, the British continued their march. At dawn, the redcoats **approached** Lexington. There they ran into about 70 waiting minutemen. Led by Captain John Parker, the minutemen stood on the town common with muskets in hand. Badly outnumbered, the minutemen were about to give way to the redcoats. Just then, a shot was fired—from where is still not clear. Both sides let loose an exchange of bullets. When the shooting ended, eight minutemen lay dead.

The British continued on to Concord. While some troops burned the few weapons they found, the others met a group of minutemen waiting at the North Bridge. In a short battle, the British took heavy losses. They began to make their way back to Boston.

All along the road, colonists hid behind trees and fired on the soldiers. By the time the redcoats reached Boston, at least 174 were wounded and 73 were dead.

About 60 years later, poet Ralph Waldo Emerson wrote in "The Concord Hymn" that the Americans at Lexington and Concord had fired the "shot heard 'round the world." The battle for independence had begun.

☑ **PROGRESS CHECK**

Explaining Why did British troops march to Concord?

Academic Vocabulary

approach to draw near to something

This painting shows the British charge at what historians call the Battle of Bunker Hill—which actually took place on Breed's Hill.

More Military Action

GUIDING QUESTION *What were the beliefs of the Loyalists and Patriots?*

After the battles at Lexington and Concord, armed conflict with British forces quickly spread. Benedict Arnold, a captain in the Connecticut militia, raised a force of 400 to seize Fort Ticonderoga near Lake Champlain in New York. Ticonderoga occupied a key location. It was also rich in military supplies. Arnold learned that Ethan Allen of nearby Vermont also planned to attack the fort. So Arnold joined forces with Allen's men—the **so-called** Green Mountain Boys. Together, they took the British by surprise. Fort Ticonderoga surrendered on May 10, 1775.

Later, Arnold became a traitor to the Patriot cause. He sold military information to the British. When his crime was discovered in September 1780, he fled to British-controlled New York City. There he commanded British troops and led raids against the Americans in Virginia and Connecticut.

The Battle of Bunker Hill

Following Lexington and Concord, more volunteers joined the colonial militias. Soon militia around Boston numbered about 20,000 strong.

The British remained in control of the city, with the militia camped nearby. On June 16, 1775, militia commanded by Colonel William Prescott set up posts on Bunker Hill and Breed's Hill, across the harbor from Boston.

North Wind Picture Archives

Reading **HELP**DESK

Loyalist American colonist who remained loyal to Britain and opposed the war for independence
Patriot American colonist who favored American independence

Academic Vocabulary
so-called known as

The next day, the redcoats assembled at Breed's Hill. Bayonets drawn, they charged. Low on ammunition, Prescott reportedly ordered, "Don't fire until you see the whites of their eyes." The Americans opened fire, forcing the British to retreat. Twice more the redcoats charged, receiving furious fire from above. Finally, the Americans ran out of gunpowder and had to withdraw.

The battle on Breed's Hill—which became known as the Battle of Bunker Hill—was a British victory. Yet the British suffered heavy losses of more than 1,000 dead and wounded. They were learning that defeating the Americans on the battlefield would be neither quick nor easy.

Choosing Sides

As news spread about these battles, the colonists each faced a major decision—to join the rebels or remain loyal to Great Britain.

Those who sided with Britain, the **Loyalists**, did not think unfair taxes and laws justified a rebellion. Some were officeholders who felt a responsibility to uphold British rule. Others had not suffered from British policies and saw no reason to break with Britain. Still others believed Britain would win the war and did not want to be on the losing side.

The **Patriots**, on the other hand, supported the war. They believed that the colonists should have the right to govern themselves. The Patriots were determined to fight the British until American independence was won.

The American Revolution was not just a war between America and Britain. It was also a civil war—Patriots against Loyalists.

✔ PROGRESS CHECK

Describing What did the British learn from the Battle of Bunker Hill?

Thinking Like a HISTORIAN

Making Predictions

Loyalists came from all parts of American society. Political differences divided communities and even split families. Benjamin Franklin's son, William, served as Royal Governor of New Jersey. When the Revolution began, William remained loyal to Britain and quarreled with his father. Do you think Benjamin Franklin and William Franklin resolved their differences? For more about making predictions, review *Thinking Like a Historian.*

LESSON 3 REVIEW

Review Vocabulary

1. Write a paragraph explaining what the words below have in common.

   a. minuteman   **b.** Loyalist   **c.** Patriot

Answer the Guiding Questions

2. *Explaining* How did support for the Suffolk Resolves by the Continental Congress push the colonies closer to war?

3. *Describing* What fighting methods did the colonists use against the British troops marching back to Boston from Concord?

4. *Interpreting* Reread Patrick Henry's quote about the Continental Congress. What change was taking place in how the colonists saw themselves?

5. **NARRATIVE WRITING** Write a scene from a play in which colonists in a small town react to the news of the Battle of Lexington. Remember, not all colonists wanted independence from Britain.

What Do You Think?

Should the Colonies Declare Their Independence From Great Britain?

Some Americans did not think that independence was the right path for the colonies. They wanted to remain under British rule. These colonists were called Loyalists. Colonists who believed the colonies should become an independent nation were called Patriots.

In these excerpts, Patriot Thomas Paine and Loyalist Charles Inglis express different points of view about the fight for American Independence.

Yes

PRIMARY SOURCE

66 Volumes have been written on the subject of the struggle between England and America ... and the period of debate is closed. ...

... I challenge the warmest **advocate** for **reconciliation** to show a single advantage that this continent can reap by being connected with Great Britain. ...

But the injuries and disadvantages ... are without number; and our duty to mankind at large, as well as to ourselves, instruct us to **renounce** the alliance. ...

... Every thing that is right or reasonable pleads for separation. The blood of the slain, the weeping voice of nature cries, 'TIS TIME TO PART. 99

—Thomas Paine, *Common Sense*, 1776

THOMAS PAINE

Tension between British authorities and the colonists grew during the 1770s.

Not every colonist agreed with the behavior of the protesters involved with the Boston Tea Party.

No

CHARLES INGLIS

PRIMARY SOURCE

❝ I think it no difficult matter to point out many advantages which will certainly attend our reconciliation and connection with Great-Britain. . . . The blood of the slain, the weeping voice of nature cries—*It is time to be reconciled;* it is time to lay aside those **animosities** which have pushed on Britons to shed the blood of Britons . . .

. . . A Declaration of Independency would **infallibly** disunite and divide the colonists. . . .

. . . **Torrents** of blood will be spilt, and thousands reduced to beggary and wretchedness. . . .

America is far from being yet in a desperate situation. I am confident she may obtain honourable and advantageous terms from Great-Britain. ❞

—Charles Inglis, *The True Interest of America Impartially Stated,* 1776

Vocabulary

advocate
supporter

reconciliation
settlement, understanding

renounce
to give up, to abandon

animosity
hostility, ill will, hatred

infallibly
without fail

torrent
fast-moving liquid

What Do You Think? DBQ

❶ *Interpreting* What is Paine's argument in favor of independence?

❷ *Analyzing* What did Inglis believe would result from declaring independence from Great Britain?

❸ *Evaluating* In your opinion, which of the two writers makes a more powerful appeal to emotions? Explain your answer in a short essay.

Lesson 4
Declaring Independence

ESSENTIAL QUESTION *What motivates people to act?*

IT MATTERS BECAUSE
The decision to declare independence came only after all other options had been exhausted.

The Second Continental Congress

GUIDING QUESTION *How did individuals and events impact efforts for independence?*

In 1774 the Continental Congress agreed to meet again if the British did not address their complaints. In fact, as the battles at Lexington and Concord in 1775 showed, the dispute between the British and the colonies had worsened.

Distinguished Leaders

The Second Continental Congress met on May 10, 1775. The delegates included some of the greatest leaders in the colonies. Among them were John and Samuel Adams, Patrick Henry, Richard Henry Lee, and George Washington—all delegates to the First Continental Congress. Several new delegates came as well.

Benjamin Franklin, one of the most respected men in the colonies, had been a leader in the Pennsylvania legislature. In 1765 he represented the colonies in London and helped win repeal of the Stamp Act. John Hancock of Massachusetts was a wealthy merchant. He funded many Patriot groups, including the Sons of Liberty. The delegates chose Hancock to be president of the Second Continental Congress. Thomas Jefferson, only 32, was also a delegate. He served in the Virginia legislature. Jefferson was already known as a brilliant thinker and writer.

(cl) North Wind Picture Archives, (c) MPI/Archive Photos/Getty Images, (cr) SuperStock (r) © Bettmann/CORBIS

Reading **HELP**DESK

Taking Notes: *Organizing*

As you read, use a diagram like this one to describe the parts of the Declaration of Independence.

Declaration of Independence

| Part 1: |
| Part 2: |
| Part 3: |
| Part 4: |

Content Vocabulary
• **petition**
• **preamble**

The delegates at the Second Continental Congress had much to discuss. Though American and British blood had been spilled, they were not ready to vote for a break from Britain. It would be another year before Jefferson would write the Declaration of Independence.

Key Actions

The Continental Congress did take steps to begin governing the colonies. It authorized the printing of money and set up a post office, with Franklin in charge. The Congress also formed committees to handle relations with Native Americans and foreign countries. Most important, it created the Continental Army. Unlike local militias, such a force could form and carry out an overall strategy for fighting the British. The Congress unanimously chose George Washington to command this army. Washington was an experienced soldier and a respected Southern planter. He left Philadelphia at once to take charge of the forces in Boston.

The delegates then offered Britain a last chance to avoid war. They sent a **petition**, or formal request, to George III. Called the Olive Branch Petition, it assured the king that the colonists wanted peace. It asked him to protect the colonists' rights. The king rejected the petition. Instead, he prepared for war. He hired more than 30,000 German troops, called Hessians (HEH•shuhnz), to fight alongside British troops.

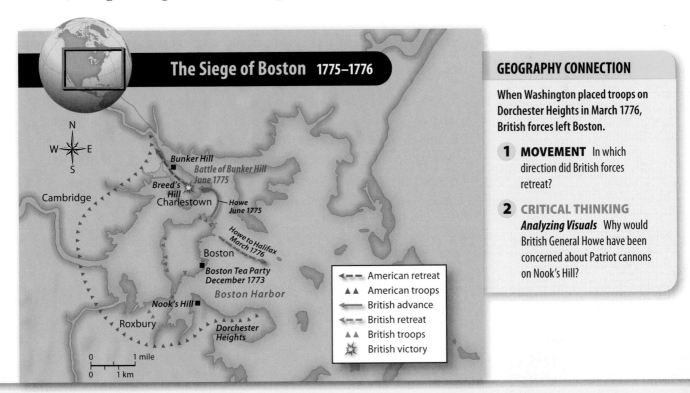

The Siege of Boston 1775–1776

- N
- Bunker Hill
  Battle of Bunker Hill June 1775
- Breed's Hill
- Charlestown — Howe June 1775
- Cambridge
- Howe to Halifax March 1776
- Boston
- Boston Tea Party December 1773
- Boston Harbor
- Nook's Hill
- Roxbury
- Dorchester Heights

Legend:
- ◄--- American retreat
- ▲▲ American troops
- ◄— British advance
- ◄--- British retreat
- ▲▲ British troops
- ✸ British victory

0   1 mile
0   1 km

GEOGRAPHY CONNECTION

When Washington placed troops on Dorchester Heights in March 1776, British forces left Boston.

1 MOVEMENT In which direction did British forces retreat?

2 CRITICAL THINKING *Analyzing Visuals* Why would British General Howe have been concerned about Patriot cannons on Nook's Hill?

petition a formal request

General George Washington commanded the Continental Army in their battles with the British.

Thomas Paine's *Common Sense* had a great influence on public opinion in the colonies.

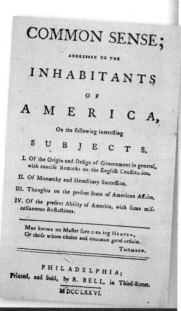

The War Heats Up

Congress learned that British troops in Canada were planning to invade New York. The Americans decided to strike first. A unit of Patriots marched north from Fort Ticonderoga and captured Montreal. However, an American attack on Quebec, led by Benedict Arnold, failed.

Washington reached the Boston area in July 1775, a few weeks after the Battle of Bunker Hill. The British held Boston, but Patriot militia ringed the city. Although the size of the colonial force grew every day, Washington realized that the men were disorganized and lacked **discipline**—the ability to follow strict rules and procedures. Washington began the task of turning armed civilians into soldiers.

Washington also needed weapons. He arranged to have dozens of cannons hauled 300 miles (483 km) from Fort Ticonderoga. Moving the heavy guns was a huge effort.

In March 1776, Washington believed his army was ready to fight. Under the cover of darkness, he moved soldiers and cannons into position overlooking Boston, while the redcoats slept.

The move surprised the British, who realized they were now within easy reach of Washington's big guns. British General William Howe commanded his soldiers to board ships and withdraw from Boston. On March 17, Washington led his jubilant troops into the city. They watched as the British troops sailed away to Halifax, Nova Scotia, a part of Canada.

Moving Toward Independence

Many colonists held on to hope that the colonies could remain part of Great Britain. Still, support for independence was growing. It was inspired in no small part by writer Thomas Paine. Paine arrived in the colonies from England in 1774. He soon caught the revolutionary spirit. In January 1776, he published a pamphlet called *Common Sense*. In bold language, Paine called for a complete break with British rule.

> **PRIMARY SOURCE**
>
> 66 Every thing that is right or reasonable pleads for separation. The blood of the slain, the weeping voice of nature cries, 'TIS TIME TO PART. 99
>
> —from *Common Sense*, 1776

Reading **HELP**DESK

Academic Vocabulary

discipline the ability to follow strict rules and procedures
debate a discussion of opposing points of view

Common Sense listed powerful reasons why Americans would be better off free from Great Britain. The pamphlet greatly influenced opinions throughout the colonies.

✅ **PROGRESS CHECK**

Explaining What was the significance of the Olive Branch Petition?

Declaring Independence

GUIDING QUESTION *Why did the American colonies declare independence?*

The Second Continental Congress was filled with spirited **debate**: Should the colonies declare themselves an independent nation or stay under British rule? In June 1776, Virginia's Richard Henry Lee offered a bold resolution:

PRIMARY SOURCE

❝ That these United Colonies are, and of right ought to be, free and independent States … and that all political connection between them and the State of Great Britain is, and ought to be, totally dissolved. ❞

—Richard Henry Lee, resolution for independence, 1776

The Congress debated Lee's resolution. Some delegates still thought the colonies should not form a separate nation. Others argued that war had already begun and they should be free from Great Britain. Still others feared Britain's power to crush the rebellion.

Writing the Declaration

While delegates debated, Congress chose a committee to write a declaration of independence. John Adams, Benjamin Franklin, Thomas Jefferson, Robert Livingston, and Roger Sherman formed the committee. Adams asked Jefferson to write the first draft. Jefferson hesitated, but Adams persuaded him, saying:

PRIMARY SOURCE

❝ Reason first—You are a Virginian, and a Virginian ought to appear at the head of this business. Reason second—I am obnoxious, suspected, and unpopular. You are very much otherwise. Reason third—you can write ten times better than I can. ❞

—from *The Writings of Thomas Jefferson*, 1822

Jefferson agreed that he would do the writing for the great project. He drew on ideas from English philosopher John Locke to explain why the 13 colonies were proclaiming their freedom. In the

Committee members Benjamin Franklin, Thomas Jefferson, and John Adams examine Jefferson's changes to his draft of the Declaration.

1690s Locke expressed the idea that people are born with certain natural rights to life, liberty, and property. Locke wrote that people form governments to protect those rights, and that a government interfering with those rights could rightfully be overthrown. Jefferson and other Patriots agreed with Locke. On July 2, 1776, the Second Continental Congress voted on Lee's resolution for independence. Twelve colonies voted for independence. New York did not vote but later announced its support.

Jefferson and the rest of the committee present the completed Declaration of Independence to the Second Continental Congress.

Next, the delegates discussed Jefferson's draft of the Declaration of Independence. After making some changes, delegates approved the document on July 4, 1776. John Hancock signed the Declaration first. He remarked that he wrote his name large enough for King George to read without his glasses. Eventually 56 delegates signed the document announcing the birth of the United States.

Copies of the Declaration of Independence were printed and sent out to people in the newly declared states. George Washington had the Declaration read to his troops in New York City on July 9. In Worcester, Massachusetts, a public reading of the Declaration of Independence led to "repeated [cheers], firing of musketry and cannon, bonfires, and other demonstrations of joy."

The Declaration of Independence

The Declaration has four major sections. The **preamble**, or introduction, states that people who wish to form a new country should explain their reasons for doing so. The next two sections of the Declaration list the rights that the colonists believed they should have and their complaints against Great Britain. The final section proclaims the existence of the new nation.

John Adams expected the day Congress voted on Lee's resolution for independence to be celebrated as a national holiday. He wrote, "The Second Day of July 1776 … ought to be

© Bettmann/CORBIS

solemnized with Pomp and Parade ... and Illuminations from one End of this Continent to the other." Instead, July 4, the date the delegates actually adopted the Declaration of Independence, is celebrated as Independence Day.

The Declaration of Independence states what Jefferson and many Americans thought were universal principles—that is, principles that apply to all people in all situations. It begins by describing what had long been viewed as basic English rights:

PRIMARY SOURCE

❝ We hold these truths to be self-evident, that all men are created equal, that they are endowed by their Creator with certain unalienable [not to be denied] Rights, that among these are Life, Liberty, and the pursuit of Happiness. ❞

—*Declaration of Independence*, 1776

The Declaration states that government exists to protect these rights. If government fails, "it is the Right of the People to alter or to abolish it and to institute new Government." The document goes on to list grievances against the king and Parliament. These include "cutting off our trade with all parts of the world" and "imposing taxes on us without our consent." Americans had "Petitioned for Redress" of these grievances. The British had ignored or rejected these petitions.

Finally, the Declaration announces America's new **status** (STAY•tuhs). Pledging "to each other our Lives, our Fortunes, and our sacred Honor," the Americans declared themselves a new nation. The struggle for independence—the American Revolution—had begun.

☑ **PROGRESS CHECK**

Summarizing According to John Locke, what is the purpose of government?

LESSON 4 REVIEW

Review Vocabulary

1. Use the term *petition* in a sentence about the colonists' struggles with Britain.

2. Use *preamble* in a sentence that helps explain its meaning.

Answer the Guiding Questions

3. *Explaining* What actions did the Second Continental Congress take to begin governing the colonies?

4. *Summarizing* What grievances against King George III were included in the Declaration of Independence?

5. *Interpreting* Reread the Primary Source quote from the Declaration of Independence above. Rewrite this quote in your own words and explain its significance.

6. **EXPOSITORY WRITING** Who did the most to promote the cause of independence: George Washington, Thomas Jefferson, or Thomas Paine? Give reasons for your choice.

Write your answers on a separate piece of paper.

1 Exploring the Essential Questions

EXPOSITORY WRITING The conflict that led to the Declaration of Independence took many years to develop. Write a brief summary of the events leading up to the Declaration that explains the basic views of the British and of the colonists. Use examples from the chapter to support your answer.

2 21st Century Skills

RECOGNIZING BIAS Look at this poster, which was created after the Boston Massacre. Create an alternative version that describes the event from the British point of view. Write a brief explanation of how your poster differs from the one shown here.

> AMERICANS!
> BEAR IN REMEMBRANCE
> The HORRID MASSACRE!
> Perpetrated in King-street, BOSTON,
> New-England,
> On the Evening of March the Fifth, 1770.
> When FIVE of your fellow countrymen,
> GRAY, MAVERICK, CALDWELL, ATTUCKS,
> and CARR,
> Lay wallowing in their Gore!
> Being *basely*, and most *inhumanly*
> MURDERED!
> And SIX others...

3 Thinking Like a Historian

DRAWING INFERENCES AND CONCLUSIONS The Declaration of Independence guarantees "unalienable rights" to life, liberty, and "the pursuit of happiness. "What exactly does "pursuit of happiness" mean? Does it mean that you can do anything you want to as long as it makes you happy? Take a survey of friends and neighbors. Ask them what it means to them. Prepare a short report on your findings for the class.

4 Visual Literacy

ANALYZING POLITICAL CARTOONS This 1774 cartoon shows some Patriots pouring tea down the throat of John Malcolm, a British tax collector. What message is the artist trying to send? How do the Patriots seem to feel toward the tax collector?

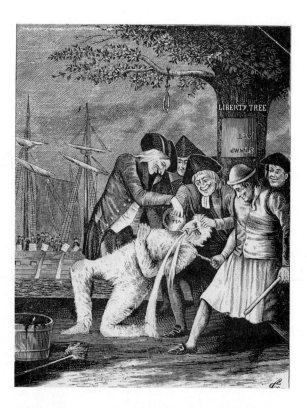

REVIEW THE GUIDING QUESTIONS
Choose the best answer for each question.

1 What British regulation prohibited colonists from moving west of the Appalachian Mountains?

A. Townshend Acts

B. Coercive Acts

C. Proclamation of 1763

D. Stamp Act

2 Why did colonists object to the Sugar Act?

F. It prevented colonists from trading with other nations.

G. It violated colonists' right to be secure in their homes.

H. It taxed colonists with their consent.

I. It made sugar much more expensive.

3 What was the purpose of the committees of correspondence?

A. to write protests to the king

B. to oversee trials in British courts

C. to handle problems with Native Americans

D. to share information among the colonies

4 What resulted from the Coercive Acts?

F. Boston Harbor was closed until the colonists paid for tea dumped at the Boston Tea Party.

G. The area west of the Appalachians and north of the Ohio River became part of Quebec.

H. The tax on molasses imported into the colonies was raised.

I. A tax was collected on almost all printed material sold in the colonies.

5 What name was given to American colonists who sided with Great Britain during the American Revolution?

A. Sons of Liberty

B. minutemen

C. Loyalists

D. Patriots

6 What did the preamble to the Declaration of Independence say?

F. It spelled out the colonists' complaints against Britain.

G. It listed the rights the colonists believed they should have.

H. It proclaimed the existence of the new nation.

I. It stated that people who wish to form a new country should explain their reasons for doing so.

DBQ DOCUMENT-BASED QUESTIONS

7 **Drawing Conclusions**
According to the map, the battles of Lexington and Concord were fought

A. three days apart.

B. at the same location.

C. on the same day.

D. in New York.

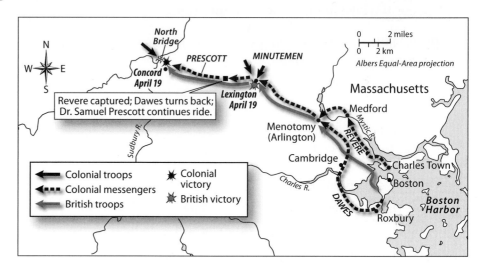

Revere captured; Dawes turns back; Dr. Samuel Prescott continues ride.

Colonial troops
Colonial messengers
British troops
Colonial victory
British victory

8 **Identifying** Based on the map, who traveled in a southeasterly direction to the battle at Concord?

F. the Loyalists

G. the British troops

H. the colonial messengers

I. the colonial troops

SHORT RESPONSE

British writer Samuel Johnson said in his 1775 pamphlet, Taxation No Tyranny:

"He who goes voluntarily to America, cannot complain of losing what he leaves in Europe. ... By his own choice he has left a country where he had a vote and little property, for another where he has great property, but no vote."

—*The Works of Samuel Johnson*

9 What complaint does Johnson's statement appear to address?

10 How might colonists respond to Johnson's statement?

EXTENDED RESPONSE

11 **Personal Writing** It is the 1770s and you are visiting the colonies from a country other than Great Britain. How would you describe the conflict between the colonists and the British? Write a letter to a friend back in your country giving your impressions of the disagreement.

Need Extra Help?

If You've Missed Question	**1**	**2**	**3**	**4**	**5**	**6**	**7**	**8**	**9**	**10**	**11**
Review Lesson	1	1	2	2	3	4	3	3	1,2,3	1,2,3	2,3,4

THE DECLARATION of INDEPENDENCE

In Congress, July 4, 1776. The unanimous Declaration of the thirteen United States of America,

[Preamble]

When in the Course of human events, it becomes necessary for one people to dissolve the political bands which have connected them with another, and to assume among the Powers of the earth, the separate and equal station to which the Laws of Nature and of Nature's God entitle them, a decent respect to the opinions of mankind requires that they should declare the causes which **impel** them to the separation.

[Declaration of Natural Rights]

We hold these truths to be self-evident, that all men are created equal, that they are **endowed** by their Creator with certain unalienable Rights, that among these are Life, Liberty, and the pursuit of Happiness.

That to secure these rights, Governments are instituted among Men, deriving their just powers from the consent of the governed,

That whenever any Form of Government becomes destructive of these ends, it is the Right of the People to alter or to abolish it, and to institute new Government, laying its foundation on such principles and organizing its powers in such form, as to them shall seem most likely to effect their Safety and Happiness. Prudence, indeed, will dictate that Governments long established should not be changed for light and transient causes; and accordingly all experience hath shown, that mankind are more disposed to suffer, while evils are sufferable, than to right themselves by abolishing the forms to which they are accustomed. But when a long train of abuses and **usurpations**, pursuing invariably the same Object evinces a design to reduce them under absolute **Despotism**, it is their right, it is their duty, to throw off such Government, and to provide new Guards for their future security.

[List of Grievances]

Such has been the patient sufferance of these Colonies; and such is now the necessity which constrains them to alter their former Systems of Government. The history of the present King of Great Britain is a history of repeated injuries and usurpations, all having in direct object the establishment of an absolute Tyranny over these States. To prove this, let Facts be submitted to a candid world.

Getty Images

Words are spelled as originally written.

The Preamble The Declaration of Independence has four parts. The Preamble explains why the Continental Congress drew up the Declaration.

impel: force

Natural Rights The second part, the Declaration of Natural Rights, lists the rights of the citizens. It goes on to explain that, in a republic, people form a government to protect their rights.

endowed: provided

usurpations: unjust uses of power

despotism: unlimited power

List of Grievances The third part of the Declaration lists the colonists' complaints against the British government. Notice that King George III is singled out for blame.

He has refused his Assent to Laws, the most wholesome and necessary for the public good.

He has forbidden his Governors to pass Laws of immediate and pressing importance, unless suspended in their operation till his Assent should be obtained; and when so suspended, he has utterly neglected to attend to them.

He has refused to pass other Laws for the accommodation of large districts of people, unless those people would **relinquish** the right of Representation in the Legislature, a right **inestimable** to them and formidable to tyrants only.

He has called together legislative bodies at places unusual, uncomfortable, and distant from the depository of their Public Records, for the sole purpose of fatiguing them into compliance with his measures.

He has dissolved Representative Houses repeatedly, for opposing with manly firmness his invasions on the rights of the people.

He has refused for a long time, after such dissolutions, to cause others to be elected; whereby the Legislative Powers, incapable of **Annihilation**, have returned to the People at large for their exercise; the State remaining in the mean time exposed to all the dangers of invasion from without, and **convulsions** within.

He has endeavoured to prevent the population of these States; for that purpose obstructing the **Laws for Naturalization of Foreigners;** refusing to pass others to encourage their migrations hither, and raising the conditions of new Appropriations of Lands.

He has obstructed the Administration of Justice, by refusing his Assent to Laws for establishing Judiciary Powers.

He has made Judges dependent on his Will alone, for the **tenure** of their offices, and the amount and payment of their salaries.

He has erected a multitude of New Offices, and sent hither swarms of Officers to harass our people, and eat out their substance.

He has kept among us, in times of peace, Standing Armies without the Consent of our legislature.

He has affected to render the Military independent of and superior to the Civil Power.

He has combined with others to subject us to a jurisdiction foreign to our constitution, and unacknowledged by our laws; giving his Assent to their acts of pretended legislation: For **quartering** large bodies of troops among us:

relinquish: give up
inestimable: priceless

annihilation: destruction

convulsions: violent disturbances

Laws for Naturalization of Foreigners: process by which foreign-born persons become citizens

tenure: term

quartering: lodging

For protecting them, by a mock Trial, from Punishment for any Murders which they should commit on the Inhabitants of these States:

For cutting off our Trade with all parts of the world:

For imposing taxes on us without our Consent:

For depriving us in many cases, of the benefits of Trial by Jury:

For transporting us beyond Seas to be tried for pretended offences:

For abolishing the free System of English Laws in a neighbouring Province, establishing therein an Arbitrary government, and enlarging its Boundaries so as to **render** it at once an example and fit instrument for introducing the same absolute rule into these Colonies:

For taking away our Charters, abolishing our most valuable Laws, and altering fundamentally the Forms of our Governments:

For suspending our own Legislature, and declaring themselves invested with Power to legislate for us in all cases whatsoever.

He has **abdicated** Government here, by declaring us out of his Protection and waging War against us.

He has plundered our seas, ravaged our Coasts, burnt our towns, and destroyed the lives of our people.

He is at this time transporting large armies of foreign mercenaries to compleat the works of death, desolation and tyranny, already begun with circumstances of Cruelty & **perfidy** scarcely paralleled in the most barbarous ages, and totally unworthy the Head of a civilized nation.

He has constrained our fellow Citizens taken Captive on the high Seas to bear Arms against their Country, to become the executioners of their friends and Brethren, or to fall themselves by their Hands.

He has excited domestic **insurrections** amongst us, and has endeavoured to bring on the inhabitants of our frontiers, the merciless Indian Savages, whose known rule of warfare, is an undistinguished destruction of all ages, sexes and conditions.

In every stage of these Oppressions We have **Petitioned for Redress** in the most humble terms: Our repeated Petitions have been answered only by repeated injury. A Prince, whose character is thus marked by every act which may define a Tyrant, is unfit to be the ruler of a free People.

Nor have We been wanting in attention to our British brethren. We have warned them from time to time of attempts by their legislature to extend an **unwarrantable jurisdiction** over us. We have reminded them of the circumstances of our emigration and settlement here. We have appealed to their native justice and magnanimity, and we have conjured them by the ties of our common kindred to disavow these usurpations, which, would inevitably interrupt our connections and correspondence. They too have been deaf to the voice of justice and of **consanguinity**.

render: make

abdicated: given up

perfidy: violation of trust

insurrections: rebellions

petitioned for redress: asked formally for a correction of wrongs

unwarrantable jurisdiction: unjustified authority

consanguinity: originating from the same ancestor

We must, therefore, acquiesce in the necessity, which denounces our Separation, and hold them, as we hold the rest of mankind, Enemies in War, in Peace Friends.

[Resolution of Independence by the United States]

We, therefore, the Representatives of the united States of America, in General Congress, Assembled, appealing to the Supreme Judge of the world for the **rectitude** of our intentions, do, in the Name, and by Authority of the good People of these Colonies, solemnly publish and declare, That these United Colonies are, and of Right ought to be Free and Independent States; that they are Absolved from all Allegiance to the British Crown, and that all political connection between them and the State of Great Britain, is and ought to be totally dissolved; and that as Free and Independent States, they have full Power to levy War, conclude Peace, contract Alliances, establish Commerce, and to do all other Acts and Things which Independent States may of right do.

And for the support of this Declaration, with a firm reliance on the Protection of Divine Providence, we mutually pledge to each other our Lives, our Fortunes and our sacred Honor.

Resolution of Independence The final section declares that the colonies are "Free and Independent States" with the full power to make war, to form alliances, and to trade with other countries.

rectitude: rightness

Signers of the Declaration The signers, as representatives of the American people, declared the colonies independent from Great Britain. Most members signed the document on August 2, 1776.

John Hancock
    President from
    Massachusetts

Georgia
Button Gwinnett
Lyman Hall
George Walton

North Carolina
William Hooper
Joseph Hewes
John Penn

South Carolina
Edward Rutledge
Thomas Heyward, Jr.
Thomas Lynch, Jr.
Arthur Middleton

Maryland
Samuel Chase
William Paca
Thomas Stone
Charles Carroll
    of Carrollton

Virginia
George Wythe
Richard Henry Lee
Thomas Jefferson
Benjamin Harrison
Thomas Nelson, Jr.
Francis Lightfoot Lee
Carter Braxton

Pennsylvania
Robert Morris
Benjamin Rush
Benjamin Franklin
John Morton
George Clymer
James Smith
George Taylor
James Wilson
George Ross

Delaware
Caesar Rodney
George Read
Thomas McKean

New York
William Floyd
Philip Livingston
Francis Lewis
Lewis Morris

New Jersey
Richard Stockton
John Witherspoon
Francis Hopkinson
John Hart
Abraham Clark

New Hampshire
Josiah Bartlett
William Whipple
Matthew Thornton

Massachusetts
Samuel Adams
John Adams
Robert Treat Paine
Elbridge Gerry

Rhode Island
Stephen Hopkins
William Ellery

Connecticut
Samuel Huntington
William Williams
Oliver Wolcott
Roger Sherman

Bettmann/CORBIS

The American Revolution

1776–1783

ESSENTIAL QUESTION · *Why does conflict develop?*

The Story Matters . . .

It is December 25, 1776. General George Washington is preparing to lead 2,400 troops across the Delaware River to launch a surprise attack on the British troops stationed in Trenton. The river is filled with huge chunks of ice. The weather is terrible, and hurricane-force winds pound at Washington's troops. After crossing the Delaware River, General Washington and his troops will have to march 9 miles (14 km) to meet their enemy. General Washington is well aware how important a victory in Trenton could be. The young United States is in desperate need of some battlefield success in its war against the British.

◀ *General George Washington led the Continental Army in the War for Independence.*

Place and Time: Revolutionary America 1775 to 1783

After a period of growing tension, the American colonies rebelled against the British. Soon, Patriot soldiers were fighting against British redcoats up and down the East Coast as well as in the West. The map on the next page shows many of the major battles of the Revolutionary War.

1776 Nathan Hale (standing, left) was an officer of the Continental Army, but his greatest contribution was as a spy—and as a symbol of the Patriot spirit of freedom. Captured by the British during a mission and sentenced to die, Hale is said to have declared, "I only regret that I have but one life to lose for my country."

Step Into the Place

MAP FOCUS This map shows some of the major battles fought during the American Revolution.

1 **PLACE** Which two battles were fought in New Jersey?

2 **LOCATION** Which was the southernmost battle?

3 **CRITICAL THINKING**
Identifying Where did most of the battles in the Revolutionary War take place?

1778 Most women did not have the opportunity to fight for the Patriot cause. Mary Ludwig Hays McCauley—known to history as Molly Pitcher—was one woman who did. The wife of a Patriot soldier, she had followed her husband to the battlefield when he went off to war. She earned her nickname carrying pitchers of water to weary troops. She won fame for helping her husband fire a cannon during the Battle of Monmouth.

Step Into the Time

TIME LINE This era is dominated by war between Britain and its American colonies. Why do you think Great Britain hired German mercenaries in 1775?

1776 Thomas Jefferson writes the Declaration of Independence

1777 Americans and British fight Battle of Saratoga

U.S. EVENTS		
1774		**1776**

WORLD EVENTS

1774 Joseph Priestley discovers oxygen

1775 The British hire German soldiers to fight for them in North America

1776 Adam Smith publishes *Wealth of Nations*

(t) The Granger Collection, NYC, (b) Bettmann/CORBIS

networks
There's More Online!

☑ **MAP** Explore the interactive version of this map on NETWORKS.

☑ **TIME LINE** Explore the interactive version of this time line on NETWORKS.

The War for Independence 1775–1781

Lake Superior

Lake Michigan

Lake Huron

Lake George

L. Ontario

Lake Erie

St. Lawrence R.

Lake Champlain
Ft. Ticonderoga

N.H.

Saratoga

Bennington

New York

Bunker Hill
Mass. Boston

Conn.

Lexington & Concord

R.I.

Delaware R.

Susquehanna R.

Hudson R.

New York City

Pa.

Trenton

Long Island

Princeton

N.J.

Md.

Philadelphia

Del.

Virginia

Potomac R.

York R.

James R.

Chesapeake Bay

Yorktown

ATLANTIC OCEAN

APPALACHIAN MOUNTAINS

Wabash River

Ohio River

Cahokia

Vincennes

Kaskaskia

Mississippi River

Tennessee River

Guilford Courthouse

North Carolina

Kings Mtn.

Cowpens

Camden

South Carolina

Georgia

Charles Town

Savannah

Gulf of Mexico

0   200 miles
0   200 km

Lambert Azimuthal Equal-Area projection

	Original 13 Colonies
✳	Major battle

60°W
45°N
40°N
35°N
30°N
95°W 90°W 85°W 80°W 75°W 70°W 65°W

N E S W

1778 Act of Congress prohibits import of enslaved people into U.S.

1780 British forces capture Charles Town, South Carolina

1781 British surrender at Yorktown

1782 Spain completes conquest of Florida

1783 Treaty of Paris is signed

1778   **1780**   **1782**   **1784**

1779 Spain declares war on Great Britain

1780 Great Britain declares war on Holland

1783 Japan suffers famine

networks

There's More Online!

☑ **GRAPHIC ORGANIZER**
Early Battles

☑ **SLIDE SHOW**
Famous Women of the
Revolutionary War

Lesson 1
The War for Independence

ESSENTIAL QUESTION *Why does conflict develop?*

IT MATTERS BECAUSE

The Patriots used skill, cunning, and determination to survive early defeats and win a key victory at Saratoga.

The Two Armies Face Off

GUIDING QUESTION *Who were the opposing sides in the American Revolution?*

In April 1776, colonial leader John Adams predicted "We shall have a long ... and bloody war to go through." Few people agreed with him. Each side thought they would win the war quickly. The British planned to crush the colonists by force. Most Patriots—Americans who supported independence— believed the British would give up after losing one or two major battles.

British Advantages

As the war began, the British seemed to have a big advantage. They had the strongest navy in the world. The British also had a well-trained army. They were supported by the wealth of their empire. Great Britain also had more people. More than 8 million people lived in Britain. There were only 2.5 million Americans.

The Patriots did not seem to be a match for the British. They had no regular army and a weak navy. American soldiers also lacked experience and weapons for fighting. Much of the Patriot military force was in the form of militia groups. These volunteer soldiers fought only for short periods of time and then returned home.

(l) Painting by Don Troiani, courtesy of Historical Art Prints, Ltd. (cl) Bob Krist/CORBIS, (c) Blend Images / SuperStock, (cr) The Granger Collection, NYC, (r) SuperStock

---

Reading **HELP**DESK

Taking Notes: *Categorizing*

Use a diagram like this one to list the Patriot defeats and victories during the early years of the American Revolution.

Content Vocabulary
• **mercenary**
• **recruit**

In addition, not all Americans supported the struggle for independence. Some Americans remained loyal to Britain. Others, such as the Quakers, were neutral. They would not take part in the war because they opposed all armed conflict.

Loyalists in the Colonies

At least one in five Americans was thought to be a "Loyalist" or "Tory." The number may have been as high as one in three. These Americans remained loyal to Britain and opposed independence. Some Americans changed sides during the war. Loyalist support also varied from region to region. In general, support for Britain was strongest in the Carolinas and Georgia and weakest in New England.

Loyalists had reasons to support Britain. Some depended on the British for their jobs. Some feared the Revolution would throw America into chaos. Others simply could not understand why the colonies wanted independence. For them, Patriot complaints seemed minor and not worth fighting over.

The British actively sought the support of African Americans. Virginia's royal governor, Lord Dunmore, promised freedom to those African Americans who joined the British cause. Many men answered his call. Eventually some of them ended up free in Canada. Others settled in the British colony of Sierra Leone in Africa.

Loyalty to Britain divided friends and family. For example, William Franklin, son of Patriot Benjamin Franklin, was a Loyalist who had served as a royal governor of New Jersey. This disagreement caused lasting damage to their relationship. As one Connecticut man observed: "Neighbor [was] … against neighbor, father against son and son against father, and he that would not thrust his own blade through his brother's heart was called an infamous villain."

Advantages of the Patriots

The Patriots did hold some advantages. They were fighting on their own ground. The British, on the other hand, had to fight from thousands of miles across the Atlantic Ocean. It took time and money to ship soldiers and supplies.

(t) Bob Krist/CORBIS
(b) Painting by Don Troiani; courtesy of Historical Art Prints, Ltd.

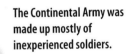

The Continental Army was made up mostly of inexperienced soldiers.

Thinking Like a HISTORIAN

Drawing Inferences and Conclusions

Made in the 1750s, the Liberty Bell hung in the Pennsylvania State House (now Independence Hall). Legend has it that on July 8, 1776, the bell's ringing announced the first public reading of the Declaration of Independence. The Liberty Bell also rang every Fourth of July and for many public events until a crack appeared in about 1846. Today, the Liberty Bell stands as a symbol of freedom. Why do you think such symbols are important to the people of a country? For more about drawing inferences and conclusions, review *Thinking Like a Historian.*

Build Vocabulary: *Word Parts*

The suffix *-ist* means "one who is." Adding this suffix to an adjective creates a noun. Adding *-ist* to the word *loyal* makes the word *loyalist*—one who is loyal. During the Revolution, Loyalists were Americans who were loyal to Great Britain.

During the Revolutionary War, women could not officially join the army. A few managed to fight in disguise. Many more served as cooks, nurses, or even spies.

NOW

Today, about 400,000 women serve openly in the American armed forces, reserves, and National Guard.

▶ **CRITICAL THINKING**
Comparing and Contrasting How have attitudes about women in the military changed since the 1770s?

The Patriot soldier also had greater motivation, or sense of purpose. The British relied on **mercenaries** (MUHR•suh•nehr•eez) to fight for them. The Americans called these mercenaries "Hessians" (HEH•shuhnz) after the region in Germany from which most of them came. The Patriots fought for the freedom of their own land. This gave them a greater stake in the war's outcome than soldiers who fought for money. The Americans also lured the Hessians away with promises of land.

The Patriots' greatest advantage was probably their leader, George Washington. Few could match him for courage and determination. The war might have taken a different turn without Washington.

The Continental Army

After the Declaration of Independence, the Continental Congress served as the national government. However, the Congress lacked the power to raise money through taxes. Delegates led by James Madison of Virginia called for a stronger national government to bind the colonies together. They believed that winning independence was possible only under a strong national government.

Not every American agreed. They placed great value on liberty and personal freedom. After rejecting the rule of the British Parliament, they were unwilling to **transfer** power to their own Continental Congress. As a result, the American Revolution was in some ways 13 separate wars, with each state fighting for its own interests. This made it hard for the Congress to get soldiers and raise money.

Local militia made up a key part of the Patriot forces. These troops were limited. Many were farmers who needed to provide for their families and did not want to leave their fields unattended. The Patriots also needed well-trained soldiers who could fight the British throughout the colonies. To meet this need, the Congress established the Continental Army, which depended on the states to **recruit** (ree•KROOT) soldiers.

At first, soldiers signed up for just one year, but General Washington asked for longer terms. "If we ever hope for success," he said, "we must have men enlisted for the whole term of the war." Eventually the Continental Congress invited soldiers to sign up for three years or until the war ended. Most soldiers, however, still signed up for only one year.

Reading **HELP**DESK

mercenary hired soldier
recruit to enlist in the military

Academic Vocabulary

transfer to move
previous earlier

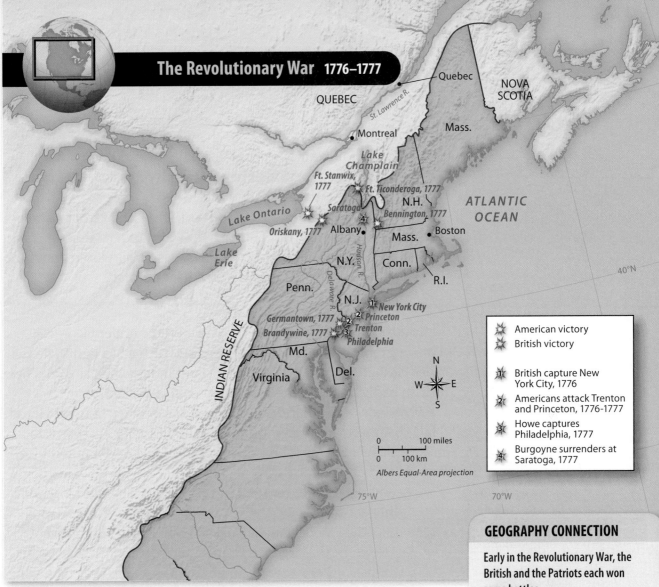

The Revolutionary War 1776–1777

QUEBEC
Quebec
NOVA SCOTIA
Montreal
St. Lawrence R.
Mass.
Lake Champlain
Ft. Stanwix, 1777
Ft. Ticonderoga, 1777
Saratoga
N.H.
ATLANTIC OCEAN
Bennington, 1777
Lake Ontario
Oriskany, 1777
Albany
Mass.
Boston
Lake Erie
Hudson R.
N.Y.
Conn.
R.I.
40°N
Penn.
Delaware R.
N.J.
New York City
Germantown, 1777
Princeton
Brandywine, 1777
Trenton
Philadelphia
Md.
Virginia
Del.
INDIAN RESERVE

N W E S

0   100 miles
0   100 km
Albers Equal-Area projection

75°W   70°W

American victory
British victory
① British capture New York City, 1776
② Americans attack Trenton and Princeton, 1776-1777
③ Howe captures Philadelphia, 1777
④ Burgoyne surrenders at Saratoga, 1777

GEOGRAPHY CONNECTION

Early in the Revolutionary War, the British and the Patriots each won some battles.

1 LOCATION In what area were most battles on this map fought?

2 CRITICAL THINKING
Sequencing According to this map, which British victory occurred just before the Battle of Saratoga?

The Continental Army also had a hard time finding officers—qualified military commanders. Some were young men who were recruited from the ranks. The best officers had experience from **previous**, or earlier, wars.

Men did all the fighting—with a few exceptions. For example, Margaret Corbin of Pennsylvania went with her husband when he joined the Continental Army. After he died in battle, she took his place. Mary Ludwig Hays McCauley joined her husband in battle as well. The soldiers called her "Moll of the Pitcher," or "Molly Pitcher," because she carried water pitchers to the soldiers. Legend has it she also took part in combat. On February 21, 1822, Pennsylvania recognized Molly Pitcher's service by granting her an annual payment of $40. Deborah Sampson of Massachusetts took a different route to the battlefield. She joined up as a soldier by disguising herself as a man.

✓ PROGRESS CHECK

Summarizing What disadvantages did the Patriots face in fighting the British?

Early Campaigns

GUIDING QUESTION *What were significant battles in the early years of the American Revolution?*

Relatively few soldiers fought in the war's early battles. At Bunker Hill, for example, about 2,200 British soldiers fought 1,200 Americans. The British had not yet won a clear victory. They realized they were going to need more troops.

During the summer of 1776, Britain sent 32,000 troops across the Atlantic to New York. The British commander, General William Howe, hoped the sheer size of his army would convince the Patriots to give up. He was soon disappointed.

Patriot Defeat on Long Island

Only 20,000 soldiers made up the Patriot force under George Washington. Yet the Americans were determined to fight. The two sides clashed in the Battle of Long Island in late August 1776. The British badly defeated the outnumbered Continental Army.

One Patriot, Nathan Hale, showed his bravery at Long Island. Hale disguised himself as a Dutch schoolteacher and went to spy on British troops. The British caught Hale and hanged him as punishment. According to legend, Hale went to his death saying, "I only regret that I have but one life to lose for my country."

The Patriots fought hard on Long Island but could not overcome the larger and better-equipped British army. A British officer wrote that many Patriot soldiers killed on Long Island had not been wearing shoes, socks, or jackets. "They are also in great want of blankets," he said, predicting that the rebels would suffer during the winter.

After the defeat, Washington retreated from New York, which became a Loyalist stronghold. The British chased the Continental Army across New Jersey into Pennsylvania. Satisfied that Washington was beaten, the British let him go.

A Low Point for the Patriots

Washington and his forces had managed to escape the British. As winter approached, however, the Patriots' cause was near collapse. The Continental Army had fewer than 5,000 soldiers. Many had completed their terms. Others had run away.

▶ **CRITICAL THINKING**

Analyzing What is the approximate ratio of British army forces to the Continental Army and colonial militias?

THE FIGHTING FORCES 1777

20,000

42,000

British regular army

Continental Army and colonial militias

Enslaved African American Peter Salem appears in the far right of this painting of the Battle of Bunker Hill.

Washington wrote his brother that if new soldiers were not found soon, "I think the game is pretty near up." Yet he remained hopeful that the fight for freedom would succeed.

Washington begged the Continental Congress for more troops. He suggested allowing free African Americans to enlist, but many Americans opposed this idea. Early in the war, the Southern Colonies had persuaded the Congress not to take this step. Many white people in the South worried about giving guns and training to African Americans. They feared the possibility of revolt among the enslaved population.

African Americans in Battle

The growing need for soldiers led some states to ignore the ban on African Americans. Rhode Island raised an all-African American regiment in 1778. By the war's end, every state except South Carolina enlisted African Americans to fight.

Historians believe that as many as 5,000 African Americans joined the Patriots. One example was Peter Salem, an enslaved African American from Massachusetts. Salem fought at Concord and at the Battle of Bunker Hill, and he served the Patriot cause throughout the war. In return for his service, Salem won his freedom.

African Americans had many reasons to fight. Some fought because they believed in the Patriot cause. Others may have joined up for the chance to earn money. Some were enslaved Africans who had run away or who, like Salem, were allowed by their owners to enlist.

Washington's forces made a daring crossing of the icy Delaware River, surprising the enemy at Trenton and delivering a key Patriot victory.

The Battles of Trenton and Princeton

While the Patriots were struggling through the winter, the main British force was settled in New York. The British also left some troops in Princeton and Trenton, New Jersey. Washington saw a chance to catch the British by surprise.

Washington was camped in Pennsylvania, across the Delaware River from the British camp in New Jersey. On Christmas night 1776, Washington led 2,400 troops across the icy river to surprise the enemy at Trenton the next day. Washington then escaped and marched to Princeton; his army scattered the British force there.

✓ PROGRESS CHECK

Explaining Why was the winter of 1776–1777 significant?

British Strategy

GUIDING QUESTION *Was the British plan for victory successful?*

In early 1777, the British began a three-pronged battle plan. Their goal was to seize Albany, New York, and gain control of the Hudson River. If they controlled the Hudson, they would cut off New England from the Middle Colonies.

SuperStock

Reading **HELP**DESK

Build Vocabulary: *Multiple Meaning Words*

Some words have more than one meaning. *Late* most commonly means "not on time." It can also mean "recent."

First, General John Burgoyne would lead troops south from Canada. At the same time, Lieutenant Colonel Barry St. Leger would move east from Lake Ontario. A third group, under General Howe, would move north up the Hudson. The three British forces would then attack Patriot troops at Albany.

The British Capture Philadelphia

Before the attack on Albany, Howe sought to capture Philadelphia—the home of the Continental Congress. Howe won battles in September 1777 at Brandywine and Paoli, near Philadelphia. Then Howe's troops captured Philadelphia, forcing the Continental Congress to flee. By now, winter was coming. Howe decided to stay in Philadelphia instead of going to Albany.

The Battle of Saratoga

Meanwhile, the British plan for taking Albany was in trouble. In August, American soldiers led by Benedict Arnold stopped St. Leger at Fort Stanwix, New York.

General Burgoyne's army hadn't reached Albany either. In July he captured Fort Ticonderoga, but he needed supplies. He sent a force to the American supply base at Bennington, Vermont. A local militia group, the Green Mountain Boys, defeated them. Burgoyne retreated to Saratoga, New York.

Here Burgoyne found himself in serious trouble—and alone. Patriots had stopped St. Leger at Fort Stanwix. Howe was still in Philadelphia. Now American troops under General Horatio Gates blocked and surrounded Burgoyne's army. Burgoyne made a desperate attack on October 7. The Patriots held firm.

On October 17, 1777, General Burgoyne surrendered. The British plan had failed. The Continental Army had won an enormous victory that changed the course of the war.

✓ PROGRESS CHECK

Analyzing Why did Howe's Philadelphia victory lead to defeat at Saratoga?

LESSON 1 REVIEW

Review Vocabulary

1. Use each of the following words in a sentence that demonstrates its meaning.

   a. mercenary   **b.** recruit

Answer the Guiding Questions

2. *Contrasting* How did the two sides in the American Revolution differ?

3. *Summarizing* How did the Continental Army fare in the early battles of the war?

4. *Explaining* What key factors led to the American victory at Saratoga?

5. **PERSUASIVE WRITING** As a Patriot, write a letter to the editor of your local newspaper. Point out the Patriot strengths and why you think the Patriots will win the war for independence.

networks

There's More Online!

☑ **BIOGRAPHY**
 • Franklin and the Revolution
 • Martha Washington

☑ **GRAPHIC ORGANIZER**
 Sources of Aid to Patriots

☑ **PRIMARY SOURCE**
 • Abigail Adams
 • Winter at Valley Forge

☑ **TIME LINE**
 Thaddeus Kościuszko

Lesson 2

The War Continues

ESSENTIAL QUESTION *Why does conflict develop?*

IT MATTERS BECAUSE
The ideals of liberty and freedom helped attract key support and helped the colonists overcome difficult challenges.

Gaining Allies

GUIDING QUESTION *How did America gain allies?*

By late 1777, Benjamin Franklin had been in France for a year. He was trying to get the French to support the Americans' fight for independence. With his skill and charm, Franklin gained many friends for the United States. The French had secretly given the Americans money, but they had not entered the war.

The Continental Congress sent Jonathan Austin of Boston to France to deliver the news of the American victory at Saratoga. As soon as Austin arrived, Franklin asked if the British had taken Philadelphia. Austin answered, "Yes sir. … But sir, I have greater news than that. General Burgoyne and his whole army are prisoners of war!"

Franklin surely understood the importance of this news. The victory at Saratoga was a turning point in the American Revolution. France and other nations now realized that the Americans might actually win their war against Great Britain. France decided to help the Americans. In February 1778, France declared war on Britain and sent money, equipment, and troops to **aid** the American Patriots.

Like France, Spain also decided to help the Americans. Spain did not form an alliance with the United States, but it did declare war on Great Britain in 1779. Spanish forces fought the British

(tl) North Wind Picture Archives, (cl) SuperStock, (c) SuperStock, (cr) North Wind Picture Archives, (r) Bettmann/CORBIS

Taking Notes: *Identifying*

Use a diagram like the one here to determine what aid the Patriots received during the American Revolution.

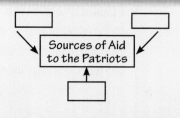

Sources of Aid
to the Patriots

Content Vocabulary
• inflation

Academic Vocabulary
aid to help
desert to leave without permission

in present-day Louisiana, Mississippi, Alabama, and Florida. This fighting kept many British troops out of action against the Americans.

Winter at Valley Forge

In 1778 news traveled slowly across the Atlantic. People in the United States did not learn of the French-American alliance until the spring. Meanwhile, British general Howe and his forces spent the winter in comfort in Philadelphia. Washington set up camp at Valley Forge, about 20 miles (32 km) to the west. There, Washington and his troops suffered through a terrible winter. They lacked decent food, clothing, shelter, and medicine. Washington's greatest challenge at Valley Forge was keeping the Continental Army together.

Snowstorms and damaged roads slowed delivery of supplies. The Continental Army built huts and gathered supplies from the countryside. Several volunteers—including Washington's wife, Martha—made clothes for the troops and cared for the sick. Washington declared that no army had ever put up with "such uncommon hardships" with such spirit. "Naked and starving as they are," he wrote, "we cannot enough admire the incomparable patience and fidelity [faithfulness] of the soldiery."

North Wind Picture Archives

Thinking Like a
HISTORIAN

Understanding Cause and Effect

Benjamin Franklin served as America's first ambassador to France. French nobles and thinkers greatly admired the American. Much like a singer or actor today, Franklin became a star in America and Europe. Fashionable women even wore a hairstyle meant to look like a fur cap Franklin wore. How might Franklin's popularity have helped the Patriot cause? For more about understanding cause and effect, review _Thinking Like a Historian._

Martha Washington, shown here on the arm of George Washington, helped lift the spirits of the army during the bitter winter at Valley Forge.

Washington and the Continental Army lived through a terrible winter at Valley Forge.

▶ **CRITICAL THINKING**
Determining Cause and Effect How did the difficult winter at Valley Forge affect the Continental Army?

Joseph Martin, a young soldier from Connecticut, spent the winter at Valley Forge. "We had hard duty to perform," he wrote years later, "and little or no strength to perform it with." Most of the men lacked blankets, shoes, and shirts. Martin made a pair of rough shoes for himself out of a scrap of cowhide, which hurt his feet.

PRIMARY SOURCE

66 [T]he only alternative I had, was to endure this inconvenience or to go barefoot, as hundreds of my companions had to, till they might be tracked by their blood upon the rough frozen ground. 99

—Joseph Martin, in *A Narrative of a Revolutionary Soldier*

Many soldiers became sick and died. Other men **deserted** (duh•ZERT•ed), or left without permission. Some officers quit. The Continental Army seemed to be falling apart.

Yet the Continental Army did survive the winter. Spring came, and conditions gradually improved. New soldiers joined the ranks. "The army grows stronger every day," one officer wrote. "There is a spirit of discipline among the troops that is better than numbers."

Then, in April 1778, Washington told his troops of France's help. Everyone's spirits rose at the thought. The Continental Army celebrated with a religious service and a parade.

SuperStock

Reading **HELP**DESK

Academic Vocabulary

desert to leave without permission or intent to come back

Build Vocabulary: *Related Words*

Some words sound the same despite different spellings and meanings. Still, *aid* and *aide* have related meanings. The word *aide* is a noun meaning "helper." The Academic Vocabulary *aid* is a verb meaning "to help."

Foreigners Help on the Battlefield

The Patriot cause had supporters around the world. A number of individuals from other nations gave their talents to the cause.

One leader at Valley Forge was Marquis de Lafayette (lah•fee• EHT) of France. He had come to the United States as a 19-year-old volunteer in June 1777. Lafayette was excited about the ideas expressed in the Declaration of Independence, and he wanted to join the battle for freedom. He believed that the American cause represented the future of humankind.

When he reached the United States, Lafayette offered his services to General Washington. He agreed to serve without pay and became a trusted aide to Washington.

Other Europeans volunteered to work for the Patriot cause. Two Polish men—Thaddeus Kościuszko (THAD•ee• uhs kawsh•CHUSH•KOH) and Casimir Pulaski (KAH• sih•meer poo•LAHS•kee)—supported American efforts. Kościuszko helped build important defenses for the Americans. Pulaski won promotion to the rank of general. He died in 1779, fighting for the Continental Army.

Friedrich von Steuben (FREE•drihk vahn STOO•buhn) also came to help Washington. Von Steuben had been an officer in the Prussian army. He helped to train the Patriot troops at Valley Forge and shape the ragged Continental Army into a more effective fighting force.

In 1778 Spaniard Juan de Miralles (mee•RAH•yays) arrived in Philadelphia. He had persuaded Spain, Cuba, and Mexico to send money to the United States. Miralles became friends with many Patriot leaders and loaned money to the cause.

Europeans who had recently moved to the United States also joined the Patriot cause. For example, almost two-thirds of the Pennsylvania regiments were foreign-born.

Even with the help of foreign nations and individuals, the Patriots faced a huge challenge. The Continental Army still needed large amounts of money to fight the war and defeat the British.

Thaddeus Kościuszko of Poland was a big contributor to the Patriot cause.

Baron von Steuben trained American recruits at Valley Forge, 1778.

✓ PROGRESS CHECK

Describing How did Lafayette help the Patriot cause?

Life on the Home Front

GUIDING QUESTION *What was life like on the home front during the American Revolution?*

The hardships of the soldiers involved in fighting the war were considerable. However, the war changed the lives of all Americans, even those who stayed at home. For example, wives of soldiers had to take care of families by themselves. They had to run a farm or a business without a husband's help. Children had to make do without a father present.

Problems in the Economy

For the young United States, getting the money to pay for the war was a great challenge. The Continental Congress had no power to raise money through taxes. The Congress did get some money from the states and from foreign countries. Yet this amount fell far short of the need.

To meet this need, the Congress and the states simply printed hundreds of millions of dollars' worth of paper money. The paper money quickly lost its value. The amount of bills was greater than the supply of gold and silver backing them. This led to **inflation** (in•FLAY•shun), which means that it took more and more money to buy the same amount of goods. People began to have doubts about how much their paper bills were worth. Congress stopped printing paper money because no one would use it. This left the Americans with no way to finance their fight for independence.

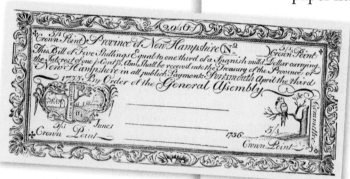

During the war, Congress and the states printed paper money. Over time, people came to question the value of this paper money, and the amounts required to make purchases rose.

▶ **CRITICAL THINKING**
Determining Cause and Effect What happened when people began to question the value of the paper money?

New Ways of Thinking

The ideals of liberty and freedom inspired the American Revolution. These same ideals also caused some women to question their role in American society.

Abigail Adams was one example. She wrote to her husband, John Adams, a member of Congress:

PRIMARY SOURCE

❝ I can not say that I think you [are] very generous to the Ladies, for whilst you are proclaiming peace and good will to Men, Emancipating all Nations, you insist upon retaining an absolute power over Wives. ❞

—from *Adams Family Papers*

North Wind Picture Archives

Questioning Slavery

The revolutionary quest for freedom and liberty led some white Americans to question slavery. In 1778 Governor William Livingston of New Jersey asked his government to free all enslaved people. He said slavery was "utterly inconsistent with the principles of Christianity and humanity."

African Americans made similar arguments. In New Hampshire enslaved people asked the government for their freedom so "that the name of slave may not be heard in a land gloriously contending for the sweets of freedom."

As you have read, African Americans fought for the American cause and hoped the Revolution would help end slavery. The Pennsylvania legislature in 1780 adopted a plan to gradually free enslaved people—the first legislature in the world to take such action against slavery. Other northern states soon took similar measures. Still, the **issue** of slavery would remain unsettled for many years.

Treatment of Loyalists

Not all Americans supported the Patriot cause. During the war, thousands of Loyalists fought on the side of the British. Some Loyalists spied on the Patriots. Many Loyalists fled, packing their belongings and selling whatever they could. Some left hurriedly for England. Others took off for Spanish-owned Florida.

Known Loyalists who remained in the United States faced difficult times. Their neighbors often shunned them. Some became victims of violence. Loyalists who actively helped the British faced arrest. In a few rare cases, Patriots executed Loyalists.

✅ **PROGRESS CHECK**

Describing How were Loyalists treated by the Patriots during the war?

Bettmann/CORBIS

BIOGRAPHY

Abigail Adams (1744–1818)

Abigail Adams was the wife of John Adams, delegate to the Continental Congress. She had a close relationship with her husband, and the two wrote often about the political issues of the day. Abigail Adams famously argued for women's rights in a letter to her husband, telling him, "If [particular] care and attention is not paid to the Ladies we are determined to [start] a [rebellion], and will not hold ourselves bound by any Laws in which we have no voice, or Representation."

▶ **CRITICAL THINKING**
Analyzing Primary Sources On what basis did Abigail Adams suggest women might not hold themselves bound by laws?

LESSON 2 REVIEW

Review Vocabulary

1. Explain the significance of the following terms from this lesson.

   a. desert **b.** inflation

Answer the Guiding Questions

2. *Identifying* Who were the key European allies of the Patriots?

3. *Explaining* Explain some of the ways that the war affected women.

4. **PERSUASIVE WRITING** Take the perspective of a foreign soldier volunteering to serve in the United States in the fight against the British. Write a letter to family back home explaining why you have decided to risk your life in this cause.

Lesson 3
Battlegrounds Shift

ESSENTIAL QUESTION *Why does conflict develop?*

IT MATTERS BECAUSE
Important battles of the War for Independence took place along the western frontier, at sea, and in the South.

Fighting in the West

GUIDING QUESTION *How did the war in the West develop?*

The Revolutionary War was of great interest to many Native American groups living in and around the 13 states. Some Native Americans helped the Patriots. More sided with the British. For them, the British seemed less of a threat than the Americans, who lived in their midst and took their land.

West of the Appalachian Mountains, the British and their Native American allies raided American settlements. Mohawk war chief Joseph Brant led a number of brutal attacks in southwestern New York and northern Pennsylvania. Farther west, Henry Hamilton, British commander at Detroit, paid Native Americans for settlers' scalps. This practice earned him the nickname, the "hair buyer."

Virginia militia leader George Rogers Clark set out to end attacks in the West. In July 1778, Clark led a force of 175 westward down the Ohio River and over land. The Patriots captured a British post at Kaskaskia (ka•SKAS•kee•uh) in present-day Illinois. They then took the British town of Vincennes (vin•SEHNZ) in present-day Indiana. British troops under Hamilton recaptured Vincennes that December. Clark vowed to get it back. In February 1779, Clark and his troops

(l) Painting by Don Troiani, Military & Historical Image Bank, (c) Guardian Royal Exchange Insurance Collection/The Bridgeman Art Library, (cr) Bettmann/CORBIS, (cr) Richard Cummins/SuperStock, (r) SuperStock

Reading **HELP**DESK

Taking Notes: *Determining Cause and Effect*

Use a diagram like the one here to show why the British lost control in the South.

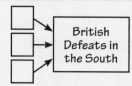

Content Vocabulary
• **blockade**
• **privateer**

braved harsh winter conditions to surprise the British and force their surrender. Clark's victory strengthened the American position in the West.

✓ **PROGRESS CHECK**

Summarizing What victories did the American forces win in the West?

The War at Sea

GUIDING QUESTION *What was the result of the war at sea?*

The Revolutionary War also took place at sea. Here Great Britain's powerful navy enjoyed a major advantage. British vessels formed an effective **blockade** (blo•KAYD), keeping ships from entering or leaving American harbors. The blockade limited delivery of supplies and troops to Patriot forces.

Privateers

To break the blockade, Congress ordered 13 warships, but only two of the ships made it to sea. Several were quickly captured by the British. The American navy was too weak to operate well.

Congress also authorized some 2,000 ships to sail as privateers. A **privateer** (pry•vuh•TEER) is a privately owned merchant ship outfitted with weapons. The goal of the privateer is to capture enemy merchant ships and cargo.

Finding crews for these ships was not difficult. Sailors from the whaling and fishing ports of New England signed on eagerly for the profitable privateering trade. During the war, privateers captured more British ships than the American navy did.

At the time of the Revolution, about 200,000 Native Americans lived along the western frontier. Here they attack an American settlement in Pennsylvania's Wyoming Valley in 1778.

▶ **CRITICAL THINKING**
Speculating Why do you think many Native Americans supported the British rather than the Americans?

blockade measure that keeps a country from communicating and trading with other nations
privateer privately owned ship outfitted with weapons

The warships *Bonhomme Richard* and *Serapis* meet in one of the most famous naval battles of the war. American naval officer, John Paul Jones, led the crew of the *Bonhomme Richard* in the conflict.

An American Naval Hero

The war at sea produced one of the war's great heroes. A daring American naval officer, John Paul Jones, won his first successes raiding British ports. Near the coast of Great Britain in September 1779, Jones's ship, *Bonhomme Richard*, met the British warship *Serapis*. The *Bonhomme Richard* and the *Serapis* fought for hours. The British captain asked whether Jones wished to surrender. Jones is said to have answered, "I have not yet begun to fight."

In the end, it was the *Serapis* that surrendered. The naval victory made John Paul Jones a hero to the Patriots.

✓ PROGRESS CHECK

Describing How did privateers contribute to the American war effort?

Fighting in the South

GUIDING QUESTION *What was the result of the war in the South?*

In the early years of the war, the Americans had won several battles in the South. In 1776 Patriot forces crushed Loyalists at the Battle of Moore's Creek, near Wilmington, North Carolina. They also saved the key port of Charles Town, South Carolina, from the British. Although this was a small battle, its **impact** on the rest of the war was great.

Reading **HELP**DESK

Academic Vocabulary
impact an effect

By 1778, these results, along with Patriot victories such as Saratoga, had convinced the British that bringing their old colonies back into the empire would not be easy. As a result, the British came up with a new plan to finish the war.

The new British plan focused on the South, where there were many Loyalists. The British hoped to use sea power and the support of the Loyalists to win important victories in the Southern states. At first, the strategy worked.

Early British Success

In late 1778, British general Henry Clinton sent 3,500 troops from New York to take Savannah, Georgia. The British occupied the coastal city and controlled most of the state.

Clinton himself led a force into the South in early 1780. In May, he led a second British attack on Charles Town. This time the South Carolina city surrendered, and the British took thousands of prisoners. It marked the worst American defeat of the war.

After Clinton's victory, he returned to New York. He left General Charles Cornwallis in command of British forces in the South. The Continental Congress sent forces under General Horatio Gates to face Cornwallis. The two armies met at Camden, South Carolina, in August 1780. The British won this first encounter. Yet Cornwallis soon found that he could not control the area he had conquered. He and his troops faced a new kind of warfare.

GEOGRAPHY CONNECTION

Starting in 1778, many Revolutionary War battles took place in the West and the South.

1 **LOCATION** Based on this map, what was the southernmost battle between the Patriots and the British?

2 **CRITICAL THINKING**
Analyzing Visuals Why do you think the British wanted to capture ports at Savannah and Charles Town?

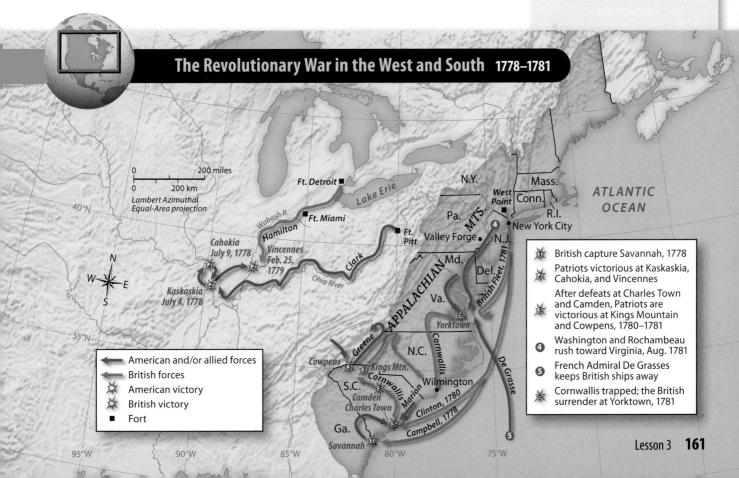

The Revolutionary War in the West and South 1778–1781

0 200 miles
0 200 km
Lambert Azimuthal Equal-Area projection

Ft. Detroit
Lake Erie
N.Y.
Mass.
West Point
Conn.
R.I.
ATLANTIC OCEAN
Pa.
New York City
Ft. Miami
Wabash R.
Hamilton
Ft. Pitt
Valley Forge
N.J.
Cahokia July 9, 1778
Vincennes Feb. 25, 1779
Clark
Ohio River
Md.
Del.
British Fleet, 1781
Kaskaskia July 4, 1778
APPALACHIAN MTS.
Va.
Greene
Yorktown
Cornwallis
De Grasse
Cowpens
Kings Mtn.
N.C.
Cornwallis
Marion
Wilmington
S.C.
Camden
Charles Town
Clinton, 1780
Ga.
Campbell, 1778
Savannah

Legend:
- American and/or allied forces
- British forces
- American victory
- British victory
- ■ Fort

1 British capture Savannah, 1778

2 Patriots victorious at Kaskaskia, Cahokia, and Vincennes

3 After defeats at Charles Town and Camden, Patriots are victorious at Kings Mountain and Cowpens, 1780–1781

4 Washington and Rochambeau rush toward Virginia, Aug. 1781

5 French Admiral De Grasses keeps British ships away

6 Cornwallis trapped; the British surrender at Yorktown, 1781

Hit-and-Run Tactics

The British had counted on strong Loyalist support in the South. They received less help than expected. Instead, as British forces moved through the countryside, small forces of Patriots attacked them. These bands of soldiers appeared suddenly, fired their weapons, and then disappeared. This hit-and-run technique caught the British off guard.

Francis Marion was one successful Patriot leader. Marion, who was known as the "Swamp Fox," operated out of the swamps of eastern South Carolina. He was quick and smart. One British colonel grumbled that "the devil himself" could not catch Marion.

Spain's Help

Great Britain also found itself with another new enemy. Spain declared war on Britain in 1779. The Spanish governor of Louisiana, Bernardo de Gálvez (GAHL•ves), had tons of supplies and ammunition shipped up the Mississippi River to American troops in the Northwest Territory. It was with this help that George Rogers Clark captured the key posts of Kaskaskia and Vincennes. Gálvez also raised an army to fight the British. Gálvez's forces drove the British out of the Gulf of Mexico region.

American Successes

After their victory at Camden, South Carolina, the British moved northward through the Carolinas in September 1780. Along the way, the British warned the local people to give up the fight for independence and join the British. If they refused, the British threatened to "hang their leaders, and lay their country waste ..."

The Americans who received this warning were mountain people. Fiercely independent, they had been neither Patriots nor Loyalists until the British warning angered them. They formed a militia army and set out to force the British from their land. At Kings Mountain, the American militia force killed or captured a British-led Loyalist force of about 1,000. The Patriot victory brought new support for independence from Southerners.

In October 1780, Nathanael Greene replaced Gates as commander of the Continental forces in the South. Rather than lead one attack on Cornwallis's forces, Greene split his army in two. In January 1781, one section defeated the British at Cowpens, South Carolina. Another section joined Francis Marion's raids. Greene combined his forces in March. Then, he

Spaniard Bernardo de Gálvez fought against the British during the American Revolution.

Richard Cummins / SuperStock

Academic Vocabulary

sustain to suffer or experience

Build Vocabulary: *Word Origins of Sayings*

Today, people refer to the hit-and-run tactics used by some patriot forces as guerrilla warfare.

This British cartoon dates from 1779, before the American Revolution ended. It shows a rider being thrown off a horse. The horse represents the former colonies. The rider represents Great Britain, and the man on the ground represents a Revolutionary War soldier.

▶ CRITICAL THINKING
Analyzing Political Cartoons
What outcome of the war does the cartoonist predict?

met Cornwallis's army at Guilford Courthouse, in present-day Greensboro, North Carolina. Greene's army was forced to retreat, but the British **sustained** great losses in the process. General Cornwallis gave up the campaign to conquer the Carolinas.

Cornwallis Retreats

Cornwallis realized the British had to act quickly to win the war. More French troops were coming to North America, and the Patriots held Virginia. Troops and supplies were moving south.

In April 1781, Cornwallis marched north to Virginia. His troops carried out raids throughout the region. General Washington sent Lafayette and General Anthony Wayne south to push Cornwallis back. Meanwhile, Cornwallis took shelter at Yorktown, on the Virginia coast. The battle for the South was entering its final phase.

☑ PROGRESS CHECK

Evaluating What effect did the Patriot victory at Kings Mountain produce?

LESSON 3 REVIEW

Review Vocabulary

1. Use each of the following words in a sentence about the Revolutionary War.

   a. blockade   **b.** privateer

Answer the Guiding Questions

2. *Describing* What role did many Native Americans take during the war in the West?

3. *Identifying* Who was John Paul Jones, and what was his significance in the war?

4. *Summarizing* What happened during the British campaign in the South?

5. EXPOSITORY WRITING You read about several military leaders in this lesson. Which leader do you think most helped the Patriot cause? Write a short essay to explain your answer.

There's More Online!

☑ **BIOGRAPHY**
Rochambeau

☑ **GRAPHIC ORGANIZER**
Treaty of Paris

☑ **VIDEO**

Lesson 4
The Final Years

ESSENTIAL QUESTION *Why does conflict develop?*

IT MATTERS BECAUSE

The Patriots' and their allies' cleverness and commitment led to final victory in the Revolutionary War.

Victory at Yorktown

GUIDING QUESTION *What events occurred in the victory at Yorktown?*

While the British were carrying out their southern campaign, key events were taking place in the North. In July 1780, French warships appeared off Newport, Rhode Island. The ships carried French aid: thousands of soldiers commanded by Comte de Rochambeau (row•sham•BOH).

Eventually, Rochambeau joined up with General Washington, who was camped north of New York City. There the two leaders waited for the arrival of a second fleet of French ships. If and when the second French fleet arrived, Washington planned to attack the British army base in New York, which was under the command of General Clinton.

As it turned out, the second French fleet never did arrive in the North. Washington and Rochambeau would never launch the attack on Clinton. Instead, both the ships and the troops would find a better opportunity to strike at the British. That opportunity would come farther south—at Yorktown, Virginia.

Washington Leaves for Virginia

As he waited outside New York, Washington had followed reports of fighting in the South. In 1781 he sent Lafayette and Anthony Wayne to Virginia to stop Cornwallis. The results were

(l) Archivo Iconografico, SA/CORBIS,
(c) Library of Congress, Prints & Photographs Division, LC-DIG-ppmsca-05936,
(cr) Buyenlarge/Archive Photos/Getty Images, (r) Bettmann/CORBIS

Reading **HELP**DESK

Taking Notes: *Describing*

Use a diagram like this one to show what the United States and Great Britain agreed to in the Treaty of Paris.

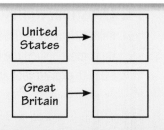

Content Vocabulary

• **siege**
• **ratify**
• **ambush**

positive. Lafayette had Cornwallis pinned down on a peninsula, a piece of land surrounded by water on three sides. The place was called Yorktown.

Washington also got important news about the French fleet he was waiting for: The ships were heading toward Chesapeake Bay instead of New York. They were going to join in the fight to defeat Cornwallis. With this news, Washington quickly changed his plans. He and Rochambeau would advance on the British at Yorktown rather than at New York.

Washington kept his new **strategy**, or plan of action, secret. He wanted Clinton to think the Patriots still planned to attack at New York. This, he hoped, would keep Clinton from sending aid to Cornwallis.

Washington and Rochambeau then rushed south with their armies. Secrecy was strict. Most soldiers did not know where they were going. Wrote one, "We do not know the object of our march, and are in perfect ignorance whether we are going against New York, or … Virginia."

The French and American troops marched 200 miles (322 km) in 15 days. General Clinton did not learn they were gone until it was too late. There was nothing he could do to stop the three forces—Lafayette's troops, Washington's and Rochambeau's army, and the French fleet—from meeting at Yorktown.

A Trap at Yorktown

Washington's plan worked perfectly. By the end of September, 14,000 American and French troops stood against Cornwallis's 8,000 British and Hessian troops at Yorktown. Meanwhile, the French fleet kept guard at Chesapeake Bay. British ships could not get in to help Cornwallis escape by sea. General Clinton and the rest of the British army sat helplessly in New York. They were unable to help Cornwallis. The British were trapped. American and French forces began a **siege** (SEEJ)—they blocked off the British supply and escape routes. In this way, they hoped to force the British to surrender.

In August 1781, Comte de Rochambeau joined Washington's Continental Army in its march to Yorktown.

Thinking Like a HISTORIAN

Predicting Consequences

Throughout the Revolutionary War, Washington succeeded in holding his army together, despite many difficulties. One of these difficulties was political meddling. The Continental Congress often interfered with his military operations. During the gloomy winter at Valley Forge, some members of Congress and army officers plotted to replace Washington as commander in chief. How might Washington's removal or resignation have affected the war? For more about predicting consequences, review *Thinking Like a Historian*.

siege an attempt to force surrender by blocking the movement of people or goods into or out of a place

Academic Vocabulary

strategy a plan of action

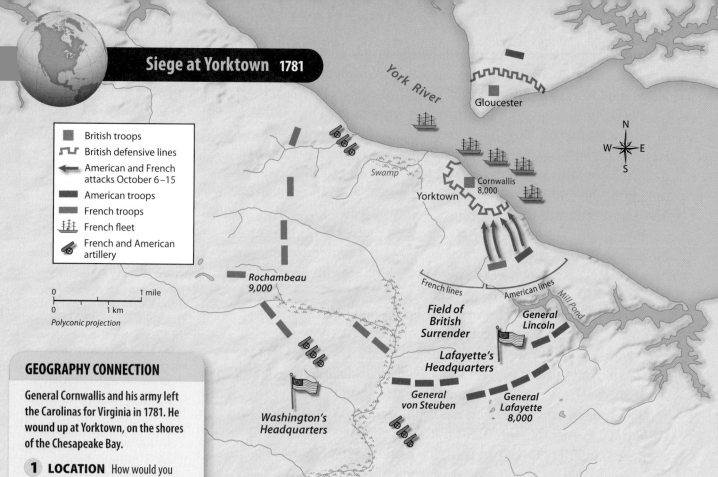

Map Legend

- British troops
- British defensive lines
- American and French attacks October 6–15
- American troops
- French troops
- French fleet
- French and American artillery

0 _____ 1 mile
0 _____ 1 km
Polyconic projection

Gloucester
York River
Swamp
Cornwallis 8,000
Yorktown
French lines
American lines
Mill Pond
Rochambeau 9,000
Field of British Surrender
General Lincoln
Lafayette's Headquarters
General von Steuben
General Lafayette 8,000
Washington's Headquarters

GEOGRAPHY CONNECTION

General Cornwallis and his army left the Carolinas for Virginia in 1781. He wound up at Yorktown, on the shores of the Chesapeake Bay.

1 LOCATION How would you describe the type of land on which Cornwallis and his forces camped at Yorktown?

2 CRITICAL THINKING
Analyzing Does this location seem like it would be easy or difficult to defend? Explain.

Victory Over Cornwallis

The siege began to take effect. The British ran low of supplies and many soldiers were wounded or sick. On October 14, Washington's aide, Alexander Hamilton, led an attack that captured key British defenses. Cornwallis could see that the situation was hopeless. On October 19, he surrendered his troops. The Patriots had won the Battle of Yorktown. They took nearly 8,000 British prisoners and captured more than 200 guns.

At the surrender ceremony, the British marched between rows of French and American troops. A French band played "Yankee Doodle." This was a song the British had used to taunt the Americans. A British band responded with a children's tune, "The World Turned Upside Down." With the mighty British surrendering to the upstart Americans, it seemed a fitting song for the situation.

☑ **PROGRESS CHECK**

Explaining Why did Washington advance on Yorktown?

Reading **HELP**DESK

Reading Strategy: *Sequence of Events*

Describe the sequence of events from October 9 to October 19 that led to the victory over Cornwallis.

Independence Achieved

GUIDING QUESTION *What helped the Patriots win independence?*

The Patriot victory at Yorktown was a terrible blow to the British and their war effort. Still, the fighting went on after Cornwallis surrendered. The British still held Savannah, Charles Town, and New York. There would be a few more clashes on land and sea. However, the defeat at Yorktown convinced the British that the war was too costly to **pursue**, or proceed with.

The Americans and British sent delegates to Paris to work out a treaty. Benjamin Franklin, John Adams, and John Jay represented the United States. The American Congress **ratified** (RAT•ih•fyed), or approved, the first draft of the treaty in April 1783. The final Treaty of Paris was signed on September 3, 1783. By that time Britain had also made peace with France and Spain.

Under the Treaty of Paris, Great Britain recognized the United States as an independent nation. The British also promised to withdraw all their troops from American territory. They gave Americans fishing rights to the waters off the coast of nearby Canada.

In turn, the United States promised that Americans would pay to British merchants what they owed. The treaty also stated that the Congress would advise the new states to return property taken from Loyalists.

A Conspiracy Against Congress

Many months passed between the end of fighting in the Revolutionary War and the signing of the peace treaty. During that time, Washington was unwilling to dissolve the army. Instead, he camped his idle troops in Newburgh, New York.

Many of these soldiers believed they were owed pay from the Congress. When this pay did not come, the soldiers grew angry. Some officers sent a letter around in March 1783. If their demands were not met, the letter said, the army should use force against the Congress.

Washington realized that this threat of revolt was dangerous. The new nation could be destroyed. In a dramatic speech, he asked the angry soldiers to be patient. Then Washington urged the Congress to meet their just demands.

British forces first sang "Yankee Doodle" to poke fun at what they considered the awkward ways of the Americans. The Americans, however, quickly made "Yankee Doodle" their own. They created new verses that made fun of the British and praised George Washington.

▶ CRITICAL THINKING
Explaining Why might songs and other forms of music be important in fighting a war? Explain.

ratify to approve officially

Academic Vocabulary
pursue to proceed with

After the war, Washington looked forward to a return to his home, Mount Vernon, in Virginia. He planned to take no role in the new government.

▶ **CRITICAL THINKING**
Speculating Why do you think Washington hoped to get away from public life?

The Congress agreed. Washington's leadership ended the threat to the new nation.

Washington Returns Home

In late November 1783, the war truly ended. The last British troops left New York City. Washington could at last give up his command. The soldiers could return to their homes and their lives.

On December 4, Washington said farewell to his troops. Three weeks later he formally resigned, or gave up his position, at a meeting of the Congress. Washington said, "Having now finished the work assigned me, I retire . . . and take my leave of all the employments of public life."

Washington returned home to Mount Vernon, Virginia. There he planned to remain and live quietly with his family.

Why the Americans Won

How did the Americans defeat powerful Great Britain? Remember, the Americans had several advantages in the war. First, they fought on their own land. The British had to move troops and supplies across an ocean. It was harder for them to get reinforcement, as the siege of Yorktown showed. When their ships were blocked, the British troops had no support.

Also, the Americans knew the land. They knew where to lay an **ambush** (AM•bush), or surprise attack. They were expert at wilderness fighting. The British, in contrast, had much difficulty controlling the American countryside once they occupied the cities. The Battle of Kings Mountain, which you read about in Lesson 3, illustrates this point. The rural people did not like being told what to do. They also had wilderness fighting skills that could defeat their new enemies.

Help from other countries contributed to the American victory. The success at Yorktown would not have been possible without French soldiers and ships. Spain gave aid when they

Buyenlarge/Archive Photos/Getty Images

Reading **HELP**DESK

ambush an attack in which the attacker hides and surprises the enemy

attacked the British. Individuals, such as Lafayette and von Steuben, came to America to provide vital services to the Patriot cause.

Perhaps most important, the American Revolution was a people's movement. Its outcome depended not on any one battle or event but on the determination and spirit of all Patriots. As Washington remarked about the patriotic crowds, "Here is an army they [the British] will never conquer."

In 1776 the American colonists began a revolution. In the Declaration of Independence they outlined the principles of freedom and the rights they felt all peoples and nations should have. These ideas inspired people in other parts of the world. For example, French rebels in 1789 fought a revolution in defense of "Liberty, Equality, and Fraternity." The French upheld these principles: "Men are born and remain free and equal in rights."

In 1791 there was revolution in the French colony of Saint Domingue. Inspired by the ideals of the American and French revolutions, enslaved Africans took up arms. They were led by a man named Toussaint L'Ouverture (too•SAN loo•vuhr•TOOR) and soon shook off French rule. In 1804 Saint Domingue—present-day Haiti—became the second nation in the Americas to achieve independence from colonial rule. "We have asserted our rights," declared the revolutionaries. "We swear never to yield them to any power on earth."

The ideals of the American Revolution helped inspire the enslaved people of Haiti, who fought for the independence of their French colony.

✓ PROGRESS CHECK

Explaining Why did Washington take action to end the Newburgh Conspiracy?

LESSON 4 REVIEW

Review Vocabulary

1. Define each of the following terms and use it in a sentence.

   a. siege **b.** ratify **c.** ambush

Answer the Guiding Questions

2. *Sequencing* Describe Washington's actions leading up to and during the Patriot victory at Yorktown.

3. *Listing* What elements were key to the Patriots' victory in the war?

4. **PERSONAL WRITING** Take the perspective of Deborah Sampson, who joined the Patriots in the conflict by disguising herself as a man. Write a short autobiography describing what you went through to become a soldier and why taking part in the war was important to you.

CHAPTER 6 Activities

Write your answers on a separate piece of paper.

1 **Exploring the Essential Question**

EXPOSITORY WRITING How did the experiences of the Patriots and the experiences of the British differ in the war? How did these differences contribute to the outcome? Use examples from the chapter to help you organize your essay.

2 **21st Century Skills**

COMPARING AND CONTRASTING Working in small groups, use the Internet or other sources to research the French Revolution, which began not long after the American Revolution and which involved the key Patriot ally, France. Together, create a poster that compares and contrasts the features of these two revolutions. Present the poster to the class.

3 **Thinking Like a Historian**

DRAWING INFERENCES AND CONCLUSIONS Use a diagram like the one at the right to explain why Loyalists supported Britain rather than the Patriot cause.

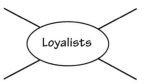

4 **Visual Literacy**

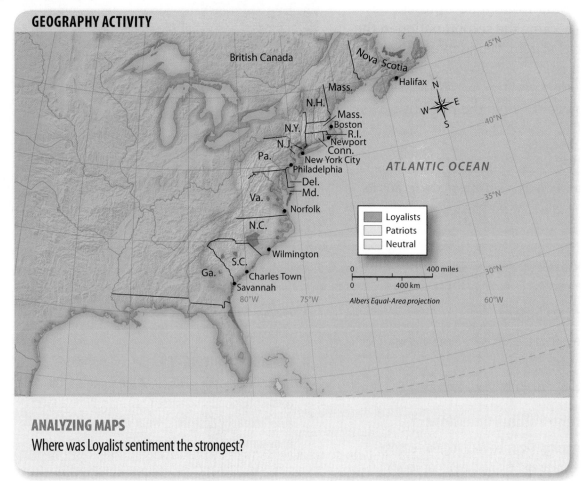

GEOGRAPHY ACTIVITY

ANALYZING MAPS
Where was Loyalist sentiment the strongest?

REVIEW THE GUIDING QUESTIONS
Choose the best answer for each question.

1 Washington's surprise attack across the Delaware River on Christmas night
   A. was the last battle of the Revolutionary War.
   B. boosted the morale of the Patriots.
   C. was followed by calls for his resignation.
   D. was successful but caused a great number of American casualties.

2 Americans had problems getting enough money to finance the war because
   F. Congress did not have the power to raise money through taxes.
   G. the states were against the war.
   H. no foreign countries would help the Patriots pay for the war.
   I. the British closed all colonial banks at the start of the war.

3 Why were African Americans at first banned from serving in the army?
   A. General Washington had forbidden African Americans from serving.
   B. All African Americans were loyal to the British.
   C. African Americans were needed to serve the war effort in factories.
   D. Some Southern colonies feared arming African Americans.

4 How did the war affect attitudes toward slavery in the United States?
   F. African Americans were seen as too valuable as soldiers to be enslaved people.
   G. Loyalists had to free enslaved people as punishment for supporting the British.
   H. Slavery was outlawed in the United States immediately following the war.
   I. The ideals of freedom and liberty led some white Americans to question slavery.

5 During the war, Native Americans generally supported the
   A British because the British promised to free enslaved African Americans.
   B British because the British seemed less of a threat to their way of life.
   C Patriots because the Patriots seemed less of a threat to their way of life.
   D Patriots because the Patriots promised to return Native American lands.

6 What role did the French play in the Patriot victory at Yorktown?
   F. They prevented the British navy from leaving New York.
   G. They tricked the British into fighting them before arriving at Yorktown.
   H. They provided troops and ships to help contain the British at Yorktown.
   I. They sank British ships in Newport Harbor.

DBQ **DOCUMENT-BASED QUESTIONS**

"And we not only groan under our own Burden, but with Concern, & Horror, look forward, & Contemplate, the miserable Condition of our Children, who are training up, and kept in Preparation, for a like State of Bondage, and Servitude. [We ask] your Honours serious Consideration, whether it is consistent with the present Claims, of the united States to hold so many Thousands . . . in perpetual Slavery."

—from *Connecticut Slaves Petition for Freedom*, 1779

7 **Analyzing** According to the writer, what did enslaved Africans look upon with "horror"?

A. their own burdens

B. perpetual slavery

C. the condition of their children

D. the consideration of his audience

8 **Summarizing** Which of the following best summarizes this excerpt?

F. Enslaved Africans have been fighting alongside the Patriots during the war.

G. Enslaved Africans should be freed after the war is over.

H. Slavery is not in agreement with the ideals of freedom on which the United States is based.

I. The Patriots need enslaved Africans in order to win the war.

SHORT REPONSE

"I was not yet fourteen years of age. . . . The boys were employed in waiting on the officers, but in time of action a boy was quartered [assigned] to each gun to carry cartridges."

—from Andrew Sherburne's *Experiences on a Privateer During the Revolutionary War*

9 How old was Sherburne, and what were his duties aboard the ship?

10 What dangers do you think Andrew Sherburne faced while on a privateer?

EXTENDED RESPONSE

11 **Personal Writing** Write a letter to a famous Patriot of your choice who helped the United States win the Revolution. Thank the Patriot for his or her service, and ask questions about the war effort. Finally, tell him or her about America in the modern era. State your view about whether the United States has lived up to the ideals upon which it was founded.

Need Extra Help?

If You've Missed Question	❶	❷	❸	❹	❺	❻	❼	❽	❾	❿	⓫
Review Lesson	1	2	1	2	3	4	1	1	3	3	1–4

A More Perfect Union

1777–1790

ESSENTIAL QUESTIONS • *Why do people form governments?*
• *How do new ideas change the way people live?* • *How do governments change?*

netw⌀rks

There's More Online about the first years of the United States.

CHAPTER 7

Lesson 1
The Articles of Confederation

Lesson 2
Forging a New Constitution

Lesson 3
A New Plan of Government

The Story Matters . . .

The story goes that in June 1776, Betsy Ross is mourning her husband, a member of the militia killed that year in the line of duty. A seamstress, Ross is also trying to run her husband's furniture-covering business. One day, she gets a visit from none other than George Washington and two other men. The men ask Ross to make a special flag. They show her their ideas for the flag, and Ross offers some of her own. Then, the seamstress gets to work.

That story may or may not be true. It is a fact, however, that on June 14, 1777, the Continental Congress voted to make the Stars and Stripes the national flag of the United States. This was just one of the many decisions facing the leaders of the young United States.

◀ *Legend has it that Betsy Ross sewed the first flag of the independent United States.*

The Granger Collection, NYC.

A few years after achieving independence, the United States made plans to expand into some of the land to the west. Leaders put forward a plan to settle the Northwest Territory and, over time, form new states.

Step Into the Place

MAP FOCUS The British gave up their claim to the Northwest Territory in the Treaty of Paris.

1 **REGION** What geographical features made this territory desirable for settlement by people from the United States?

2 **PLACE** What present-day states were made from the Northwest Territory?

3 **CRITICAL THINKING**
Drawing Conclusions Which areas of the territory do you think were likely to be settled first? Explain your answer.

The Land Ordinance of 1785 set up a plan for dividing and selling western lands. The new grid system worked well and was later used across the nation. You can still see traces of this system from the air.

Many American settlers moved to the Northwest Territory by sailing on flatboats along the Ohio River. At anywhere from 8 to 20 feet wide (2 to 6 m) and sometimes 100 feet long (30 m), the flatboat was capable of carrying large amounts of cargo.

(t) George Rose/Getty Images News/Getty Images
(b) Archive Photos/George Eastman House/Getty Images

Step Into the Time

Time Line Review the time line. What years are covered in this time line? Identify two world events that might have been influenced by the Revolutionary War.

U.S. PRESIDENTS

U.S. EVENTS

WORLD EVENTS

1776

1779

1781 Maryland ratifies Articles of Confederation; document is "in force"

1778 France goes to war against Britain

1780 League of Armed Neutrality is formed

The Northwest Territory 1787

Lake Superior

Lake Michigan

Lake Huron

Lake Erie

■ Fort Mackinac

Wisconsin

Michigan

Fort Detroit ■

Illinois

Indiana

Ohio

St. Louis

SPANISH LOUISIANA

Minnesota R.

Mississippi R.

Des Moines R.

Illinois R.

Missouri R.

Wabash R.

Ohio R.

St. Lawrence R.

ATLANTIC OCEAN

N W E S

90°W

80°W

| ☐ | Northwest Territory |
| --- | Present-day state boundaries |

0 — 200 miles
0 — 200 km

Lambert Azimuthal Equal-Area projection

1785 • Congress moves to New York City, temporary capital of U.S.
• Congress passes Land Ordinance of 1785

1782 The Great Seal of the United States adopted by Congress of the Confederation

1786 • Meeting in Maryland to discuss Articles of Confederation
• Rebellion in Massachusetts led by Daniel Shays

1788 U.S. Constitution ratified

George Washington
1789–1797

1782   **1785**   **1788**   **1791**

1782 • Rama I starts new dynasty in Siam
• Japan experiences famine

1784 Russians establish colony on Kodiak Island, Alaska

1786 Mozart's opera *The Marriage of Figaro* is performed

1788 British establish penal colony in Australia

1789 French Revolution begins

1787 • Shays's Rebellion is suppressed
• Congress approves meeting to revise Articles of Confederation
• U.S. introduces dollar currency

netw⊙rks
There's More Online!

☑ **CHART/GRAPH**
  • Capitals of the United
    States
  • Articles of Confederation
    and the Constitution

☑ **GAME** Concentration Game

☑ **GRAPHIC ORGANIZER**
  Identifying

☑ **MAP** The Northwest Territory

☑ **SLIDE SHOW** State Constitutions

Lesson 1
The Articles of Confederation

ESSENTIAL QUESTION *Why do people form governments?*

IT MATTERS BECAUSE
After gaining independence, Americans faced the task for forming independent governments at both the state and national levels.

The Making of a Republic

GUIDING QUESTION *What kind of government was created by the Articles of Confederation?*

After throwing off British rule, the independent states faced the challenge of governing themselves. The 13 states needed a plan of government that would satisfy all their needs. Would the states be able to work together and still maintain their independence? How would each individual state govern itself?

States Write Constitutions

The Continental Congress took up this last question even before declaring independence. In May 1776, Congress asked the states to organize their governments. Each state adopted a state constitution, or plan of government. Eight states had drafted constitutions before the end of the year. New York and Georgia followed in 1777 and Massachusetts in 1780. Connecticut and Rhode Island decided to use their colonial charters as state constitutions.

Limits on Power

After years of British rule, Americans were determined not to place too much power in the hands of one ruler or body. They crafted constitutions that limited the power of the governor. Pennsylvania's constitution replaced the office entirely with an elected 12-person council.

(l) Kevin W./HMdb.org, (cl) The Granger Collection, NYC, (c) North Wind Picture Archives, (cr) StockBrazil/Alamy Images, (r) Time & Life Pictures/Getty Images

Reading **HELP**DESK

Taking Notes: *Identifying*

As you read, use a diagram like the one shown to identify the powers of the national government under the Articles of Confederation.

Powers of National Government

Content Vocabulary
• bicameral   • depreciate
• republic
• ordinance

States also divided power between the governor (or council) and the legislature. Most states set up two-house, or **bicameral** (bye•KAM•ruhl), legislatures to divide the work of government even further.

The first state constitutions aimed to keep power in the hands of the people. For example, voters chose the state legislators, and states held elections often. In most states, only white males who were at least 21 years old could vote. These men also had to own a certain amount of property or pay a certain amount of taxes. Some states allowed free African American males to vote.

Because state constitutions limited the powers of the governors, the legislatures became the most powerful branch of government. The state legislatures tried to make taxes fair for everyone, but disagreements arose. The shift from British colonies to self-governing states held many challenges.

A New Republic

In addition to forming state governments, the American people had to form a national government. People agreed the new country should be a **republic**, a government in which citizens rule through elected representatives. They could not agree, however, on what powers the new republic's government should have.

CAPITALS OF THE UNITED STATES

City	Length of Time as U.S. Capital
Philadelphia, Pennsylvania	May 10, 1775 to December 12, 1776
Baltimore, Maryland	December 20, 1776 to February 27, 1777
Philadelphia, Pennsylvania	March 4, 1777 to September 18, 1777
Lancaster, Pennsylvania	September 27, 1777 (one day)
York, Pennsylvania	September 30, 1777 to June 27, 1778
Philadelphia, Pennsylvania	July 2, 1778 to June 21, 1783
Princeton, New Jersey	June 30, 1783 to November 4, 1783
Annapolis, Maryland	November 26, 1783 to August 13, 1784
Trenton, New Jersey	November 1, 1784 to December 24, 1784
New York City, New York	January 11, 1785 to August 12, 1790
Philadelphia, Pennsylvania	December 6, 1790 to May 14, 1800
Washington, D.C.	November 17, 1800 to present

Kevin W./HMdb.org

CHART SKILL

Nine different cities have served as capitals of the United States.

1 **IDENTIFYING** What was the first capital of the United States?

2 **CRITICAL THINKING** *Making Inferences* Why do you think the United States had so many different capital cities during the period shown?

MARYLAND STATE HOUSE
BUILT 1772-1779

CAPITOL OF THE UNITED STATES
NOVEMBER 26, 1783 - AUGUST 13, 1784

IN THIS STATE HOUSE, OLDEST IN THE NATION STILL IN LEGISLATIVE USE, GENERAL GEORGE WASHINGTON RESIGNED HIS COMMISSION BEFORE THE CONTINENTAL CONGRESS DECEMBER 23, 1783. HERE, JANUARY 14, 1784, CONGRESS RATIFIED THE TREATY OF PARIS TO END THE REVOLUTIONARY WAR AND, MAY 7, 1784, APPOINTED THOMAS JEFFERSON MINISTER PLENIPOTENTIARY. FROM HERE, SEPTEMBER 14, 1786, THE ANNAPOLIS CONVENTION ISSUED THE CALL TO THE STATES THAT LED TO THE CONSTITUTIONAL CONVENTION.

A REGISTERED NATIONAL HISTORIC LANDMARK
MARYLAND HISTORICAL SOCIETY

bicameral having two separate lawmaking chambers

republic a government in which citizens rule through elected representatives

At first, most Americans wanted a weak central government. They expected each state would remain free to act independently on most issues. The states would rely on a central government only to wage war and handle relations with other countries.

The Articles of Confederation

In 1776 the Second Continental Congress appointed a committee to draw up a plan for a new central government. The result of this committee's work was the Articles of Confederation. After much discussion, Congress adopted the Articles—the nation's first constitution—in November 1777.

The Articles of Confederation established a weak central government. The states kept most of their power. For the states, the Articles of Confederation were "a firm league of friendship" in which each state retained "its sovereignty, freedom and independence."

The Articles of Confederation gave the Congress limited powers. Congress could conduct foreign affairs, maintain armed forces, borrow money, and issue currency. Congress did not have the power to regulate trade, force citizens to join the army, or impose taxes. If Congress needed to raise money or troops, it had to ask the states. States were not required to contribute.

The new central government had no chief executive. This is an official, such as a president or a governor, who carries out the laws and leads the government in its day-to-day operations. Under the Articles of Confederation government carried on its business, such as selling western lands, through congressional committees.

All the states had to approve the Articles and any amendments. Yet not every state supported the Articles of Confederation at first. Under the new plan, each state had one vote regardless of population. States with large populations believed they should have more votes.

Disputes over land also threatened to block approval of the Articles. By the 1780s, seven of the original states lay claim to areas in the West. Maryland refused to approve the Articles until New York, Virginia, and other states **abandoned** their land claims west of the Appalachian Mountains. This done, Maryland joined the other 12 states in approving the Articles. On March 1, 1781, the Confederation formally became the government of the United States of America.

On June 7, 1776, Virginia's Richard Henry Lee moved that "a plan of confederation be prepared and transmitted to the respective colonies, for their consideration and approbation [approval]."

The Granger Collection, NYC

Reading **HELP**DESK

Academic Vocabulary

abandon to give up

WEAKNESSES OF THE ARTICLES OF CONFEDERATION

CHART SKILL

Congress had no authority to raise money by collecting taxes.
Congress had no control over foreign trade.
Congress could not force states to carry out its laws.
All 13 states had to agree to any amendments, making it nearly impossible to correct problems.

The Articles of Confederation had several key weaknesses.

1 SUMMARIZING
Summarize the basic problem with the Articles of Confederation.

2 CRITICAL THINKING
Speculating Why do you think getting 13 states to agree on decisions and actions was so difficult?

The Confederation Government

The next several years were critical ones for the young republic. It soon became clear that the new national government was too weak to handle the problems facing the United States. The weak Congress could not pass a law unless nine states voted in favor of it. Changing the Articles required the approval of all 13 states. This made it hard for Congress to pass laws when there was any disagreement.

Even with these challenges, the new government managed some key achievements. Under the Confederation government, Americans negotiated a peace treaty with Britain and expanded the country's foreign trade. The Confederation also helped with settling and governing the country's western lands.

✓ PROGRESS CHECK

Specifying How many votes did each state have in the new Congress?

Policies for Western Lands

GUIDING QUESTION *What process allowed new states to join the union?*

The Articles of Confederation did not propose a way to add new states to the United States. Yet there were settlers living west of the Appalachian Mountains, outside the existing states. These Western settlers wanted to organize their lands as states and join the Union.

Under the terms of the Treaty of Paris, the British gave up control of the land north of the Ohio River and west of the Appalachian Mountains. Many Americans were eager to settle in this region. The new United States government had to establish policies for settlement of these western lands. Another challenge was to come up with an orderly process by which new territories could achieve the status of statehood.

Reading in the Content Area: *Charts*

Charts can take many forms. The simple chart on this page lists a series of statements or facts. It presents a clear, short summary of key information. The title of the chart indicates the common theme that unites the items in the chart.

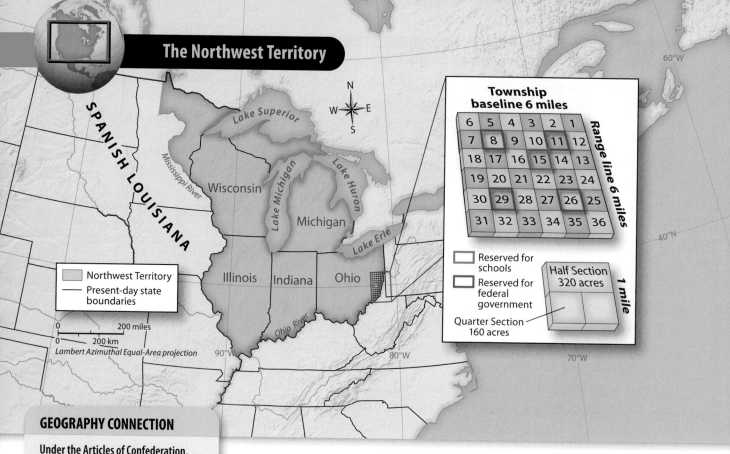

The Northwest Territory

SPANISH LOUISIANA

Lake Superior

Mississippi River

Wisconsin

Lake Michigan

Lake Huron

Michigan

Lake Erie

Illinois   Indiana   Ohio

Ohio River

Township baseline 6 miles

6	5	4	3	2	1
7	8	9	10	11	12
18	17	16	15	14	13
19	20	21	22	23	24
30	29	28	27	26	25
31	32	33	34	35	36

Range line 6 miles

☐ Reserved for schools
☐ Reserved for federal government

Half Section 320 acres

Quarter Section 160 acres

1 mile

- Northwest Territory
- Present-day state boundaries

0   200 miles
0   200 km
Lambert Azimuthal Equal-Area projection

60°W
40°N
90°W   80°W   70°W

GEOGRAPHY CONNECTION

Under the Articles of Confederation, Congress could not tax citizens directly. Congress raised money by selling land in the Northwest Territory. The Ordinance divided land into townships, 6 miles (10 km) to a side. This created 36 square miles, or "sections."

1 PLACE Which rivers acted as borders for the Northwest Territory?

2 CRITICAL THINKING
Explaining Why do you think Congress set up such a precise system for measuring out and dividing up the land?

The Ordinance of 1785

In 1785 the Confederation Congress passed an **ordinance**, or law, that set up a process to survey and sell the lands north of the Ohio River. The new law divided this large area into townships 6 miles long (9.7 km) and 6 miles wide (9.7 km). These townships were to be further divided into 36 sections of 640 acres (259 ha). The government would sell each section at public auction, or sale, for at least a dollar an acre. Concerned about lawless people moving into western lands, Richard Henry Lee, the president of the Congress, urged that "the rights of property be clearly defined" by the government. Congress drafted another law to protect the interests of hardworking settlers.

The Northwest Ordinance

The Northwest Ordinance, passed in 1787, created a single Northwest Territory from lands north of the Ohio River and east of the Mississippi River. The lands were to be divided into three to five smaller territories. When a territory had 60,000 residents, the people could seek statehood. Each new state would have the same standing as the original 13 states.

Reading **HELP**DESK

ordinance law

Academic Vocabulary

clause a special condition in a formal document

The Northwest Ordinance had a bill of rights for the settlers in the territory. It guaranteed freedom of religion and trial by jury. It also stated, "There shall be neither slavery nor involuntary servitude in said territory." This **clause**, or condition added to a document, marked the first attempt to stop the spread of slavery in the United States. The Ordinance of 1785 and the Northwest Ordinance attempted to make possible the settlement of the Northwest Territory in a peaceful and orderly way. In general, the laws were successful.

The United States Congress would later take a similar step in the South. In 1798 it created the Mississippi Territory from land west of Georgia. Congress organized the government of the territory in the same basic way as in the Northwest Territory—except that slavery was allowed.

Land Act of 1800

The Ordinance of 1785 and the Northwest Ordinance aimed to encourage settlement in the Northwest Territory. In time it became clear that people needed even more help. In 1800 Congress passed the Land Act. This law made it easier for people to buy land in the territory. For example, the act made it possible for people to pay for land a little at a time. Under the terms of this law, a person was required to buy at least 320 acres of land at a price of $2 per acre. The buyer could pay half of the money at the time of purchase and the rest in four yearly payments.

☑ **PROGRESS CHECK**

Explaining What did the Northwest Ordinance say about slavery?

Much of the land in the West was sold to pay off debts from the Revolutionary War. The sale of these lands also provided opportunity for many settlers, who eagerly moved West.

North Wind Picture Archives

THEN

Money is any object widely accepted as payment. Tobacco leaves were once used as money in colonial Virginia. Colonists also used other goods as well as coins as money. Eventually, governments began issuing paper money to make exchanges of goods and business dealings easier.

NOW

▶ **CRITICAL THINKING**
Drawing Conclusions Why is it important to have a system of money that is recognized, agreed upon, and used by all people?

Problems at Home and Abroad

GUIDING QUESTION *In what ways was the Confederation government weak?*

Because of its weakness, the Confederation government had trouble with financial issues. Continentals, paper bills the Continental Congress printed during the war, did not hold their value. By 1781, the currency had **depreciated** (dih•PREE•shee•ayt•ed), or fallen in value, so far that it was worth almost nothing. As more continentals appeared, people realized that Congress could not exchange or trade in the bills for gold or silver. The public began to doubt the money was worth anything. In 1779 it took 40 continentals to buy a single Spanish silver dollar. By 1781, a person needed 146 continentals to buy that Spanish coin. "Not worth a continental" became a common saying. At the same time, the price of food and other goods soared. In Boston and some other areas, high prices led to food riots.

In the 1780s, the Continental Congress faced a large debt. During the Revolutionary War, Congress had borrowed money from American citizens and foreign governments. It still owed Revolutionary soldiers pay for their military service. Without the power to tax, the Confederation could not easily raise money to pay its debts. The Continental Congress asked the states for money, but it could not force the states to pay. In fact, the states provided less than half of the money the federal government asked them to contribute.

Plan for Import Tax

Congress faced a collapse of the country's finances. In 1781 it created a department of finance led by Philadelphia merchant Robert Morris. While serving in Congress, Morris had proposed a 5 percent tax on imported goods to help pay the national debt. The plan required a change to the Articles of Confederation. Twelve states approved the plan, but Rhode Island opposed it. Under the Articles, the single "no" vote was enough to block the plan. A second effort in 1783 also failed to win approval by all the states. The financial crisis grew worse.

Relations With Britain

Trouble with foreign governments also revealed the weaknesses of the American government. For example, American merchants complained that the British were blocking Americans from the West Indies and other British markets. In the Treaty of Paris

(tl) StockBrazil/Alamy Images, (tr) Time & Life Pictures/Getty Images, (b) Westend61/SuperStock

Reading **HELP**DESK

depreciate to fall in value

of 1783, Britain had promised to withdraw from the lands east of the Mississippi River. British troops, however, continued to occupy several forts in the Great Lakes region.

In 1785 Congress sent John Adams to London to discuss these problems. Adams found the British unwilling to talk. They pointed to the failure of the United States to honor its promises made in the Treaty of Paris. The British claimed that Americans had agreed to pay Loyalists for the property taken from them during the Revolutionary War. Congress had proposed that the states pay the Loyalists. The states simply refused, and Congress could do nothing about it.

Relations With Spain

The United States had even greater problems with Spain. This European power, which controlled Florida as well as lands west of the Mississippi River, wanted to stop American expansion into its territory. To do this, Spain closed the lower Mississippi River to American shipping in 1784. Western settlers could no longer use the Mississippi River, which they relied on to ship goods to market.

In 1786 American diplomats reached a new trade agreement with Spain. Representatives from the Southern states, however, blocked the agreement because it did not include the right to use the Mississippi River.

The weakness of the Confederation and its inability to deal with problems worried many leaders, including George Washington. Americans began to agree that the country needed a stronger government.

During the early years of the republic, John Adams served as an ambassador to Great Britain. Adams was unable to convince the British to honor their promises made in the Treaty of Paris of 1783.

☑ **PROGRESS CHECK**

Analyzing Why did Spain close the lower Mississippi River to American shipping in 1784?

Time & Life Pictures/Getty Images

LESSON 1 REVIEW

Review Vocabulary

1. Use each of these words in a sentence about the newly independent United States.

   a. bicameral b. republic

2. Explain the significance of the following words:

   a. ordinance b. depreciate

Answer the Guiding Questions

3. *Explaining* Why did most states limit the power of their governors and divide their legislatures into two bodies?

4. *Specifying* What were some of the successes of the Articles of Confederation?

5. *Explaining* What were the weaknesses of the Confederation government?

6. **PERSUASIVE WRITING** You are a delegate to the Second Continental Congress. Congress is debating whether to allow the central government to impose taxes. Take a stand on this issue, and write a short essay defending your position. Give specific reasons for your opinion.

Lesson 2
Forging a New Constitution

ESSENTIAL QUESTION *How do new ideas change the way people live?*

IT MATTERS BECAUSE
Bold action helped the nation overcome the serious shortcomings of the Articles of Confederation.

The Need for Change

GUIDING QUESTION *What problems did the government face under the Articles of Confederation?*

A growing number of Americans became convinced that the government under the Articles of Confederation was too weak to deal with the country's problems. Among these problems were serious economic difficulties.

After the Revolutionary War, the United States went through a **depression**, a period when economic activity slows and unemployment increases. Wartime damage to Southern plantations led to a sharp drop in rice exports. Trade also fell off when the British closed the West Indies market to American merchants. The little money the government did have went to pay debts to foreign countries. This resulted in a serious shortage of money in the United States.

Shays's Rebellion

Economic troubles hit farmers hard. Unable to sell their goods, they could not pay their taxes and debts. This led state officials to seize farmers' lands and throw them in jail. This treatment angered many farmers. Some began to view the new government as just another form of tyranny. They wanted the

(l) Bettmann/CORBIS,(cl and c) The Granger Collection, NYC, (cr) Tom Grill/Corbis, (r) VisionsofAmerica/Joe Sohm/ Getty Images.

Reading **HELP**DESK

Taking Notes: *Comparing and Contrasting*

As you read, use a diagram like the one shown to take notes about each individual's plan for creating a new government.

Leader	Role
Edmund Randolph	
James Madison	
Roger Sherman	
Gouverneur Morris	

Content Vocabulary

• **depression**   • **compromise**
• **manumission**
• **proportional**

government to issue paper money and make new policies to help those in debt. A group of farmers in Massachusetts made this plea to state officials:

PRIMARY SOURCE

❝ Surely your honours are not strangers to the distresses [problems] of the people but . . . know that many of our good inhabitants are now confined in [jail] for debt and taxes. ❞

—from "Petition from the Town of Greenwich, Massachusetts"

Resentment boiled in Massachusetts. In 1786 angry farmers led by former Continental Army captain Daniel Shays forced courts in the western part of the state to close. The goal was to stop judges from legally taking away farmers' lands.

The farmers' revolt grew. In January 1787, Shays led a force of about 1,200 supporters toward the federal arsenal, or weapons storehouse, in Springfield, Massachusetts. The farmers wanted to seize guns and ammunition. The state militia ordered the advancing farmers to halt and then fired over their heads. The farmers did not stop. The militia fired again, killing four farmers.

Shays and his followers fled, and the uprising was over. Still, Shays's Rebellion frightened Americans. Concern grew that the government could not handle unrest and prevent violence. On hearing of the rebellion, George Washington wondered whether "mankind, when left to themselves, are unfit for their own government."

Shays's Rebellion divided the young country during the difficult 1780s.

Slavery in the New Republic

The Revolutionary War called attention to the clash between the American belief in liberty and the practice of slavery. Between 1776 and 1786, 11 states—all except South Carolina and Georgia—outlawed or taxed the importation of enslaved people.

Slavery existed and was legal in every state. In the North, however, it was not a major source of labor. People in that region began working to end slavery in America. In 1774 Quakers in Pennsylvania founded the first American antislavery society.

Bettmann/CORBIS

depression a period when economic activity slows and unemployment increases

In the South, much of the wealth came from large plantations that used slave labor to grow valuable crops such as tobacco, rice, and later, cotton. The reliance on slavery tended to keep Southern states from investing in other parts of their economy. Southern cities remained smaller than those in the North because there were fewer businesses in the South. The South also did not devote itself to improving its transportation systems or training its people to build new businesses and industries.

▶ **CRITICAL THINKING**

Identifying Central Issues Why do you think the white South was so committed to keeping a slave-based economy?

The Granger Collection, NYC

Six years later Pennsylvania passed a law that provided for the gradual freeing of enslaved people. Between 1783 and 1804, Connecticut, Rhode Island, New York, and New Jersey passed laws that gradually ended slavery there.

Still, free African Americans faced discrimination. They were barred from many public places. Only a few states gave them the right to vote. Most of their children had to attend separate schools from white children. In response, free African Americans set up their own churches, schools, and aid groups.

Slavery continued to spread south of Pennsylvania. The plantation system depended on slave labor, and many white Southerners feared their economy could not survive without it.

That fear did not stop a number of slaveholders from freeing enslaved people. The number of free African Americans increased in Virginia after that state passed a law that encouraged **manumission** (man•yuh•MIH•shuhn), the freeing of individual enslaved persons.

Around this time, American leaders were deciding that the Articles of Confederation needed to be strengthened. The question of slavery would make those discussions more difficult.

✓ **PROGRESS CHECK**

Explaining Why did farmers in Massachusetts rebel in 1787?

Reading **HELP**DESK

manumission the freeing of individual enslaved persons

The Constitutional Convention

GUIDING QUESTION *How did leaders reshape the government?*

Although the American Revolution led to a union of 13 states, it had not yet created a nation. Some leaders were satisfied with independent state governments that were similar to the old colonial governments. Others wanted a strong national government. They demanded a change in the Articles of Confederation. Among the leading Americans supporting reform were James Madison, a Virginia planter, and Alexander Hamilton, a New York lawyer.

The Convention Begins

In September 1786, Hamilton called for a **convention**, or meeting, in Philadelphia to discuss trade issues. He also suggested that this convention consider what possible changes were needed to make "the Constitution of the Federal Government adequate to the exigencies [needs] of the Union."

George Washington at first was not enthusiastic about the meeting. Then, news of Shays's Rebellion made Washington change his mind. He agreed to attend the Philadelphia convention, and the meeting took on greater importance.

The Convention began in May 1787 and continued through one of the hottest summers on record. The 55 delegates included planters, merchants, lawyers, physicians, generals, governors, and a college president. Three of the delegates were under 30 years of age, and one, Benjamin Franklin, was over 80. Many of the delegates were well educated. At a time when few people went to college, 26 of the delegates had college degrees. Native Americans, African Americans, and women were not represented at the Convention. These groups were not considered part of the political process at that time.

Having Washington and Franklin at the Convention guaranteed public trust.

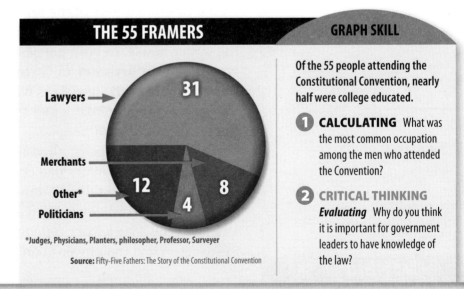

THE 55 FRAMERS

Lawyers → 31

Merchants →

Other* → 12

Politicians → 4

8

*Judges, Physicians, Planters, philosopher, Professor, Surveyor

Source: Fifty-Five Fathers: The Story of the Constitutional Convention

GRAPH SKILL

Of the 55 people attending the Constitutional Convention, nearly half were college educated.

1 CALCULATING What was the most common occupation among the men who attended the Convention?

2 CRITICAL THINKING *Evaluating* Why do you think it is important for government leaders to have knowledge of the law?

Reading in the Content Area: *Circle Graphs*

Circle or pie graphs show how a whole is divided into different parts. To read a circle graph, imagine that the circle is a pie. Compare the different sizes of the different pieces. Use any numbers or labels to help you measure and compare the sizes of each piece.

Academic Vocabulary

convention meeting

Trust was important, because the convention did not just **amend,** or revise, the Articles of Confederation. It produced an entirely new constitution. Some questioned whether the Convention had such authority.

Yet the work went on. Two men from Philadelphia also had key roles. James Wilson did important work on the details of the Constitution, and Gouverneur Morris polished the final draft. James Madison, who was a keen supporter of a strong national government, kept a record of the convention's work. Madison is often called the "Father of the Constitution" because he was the author of the basic plan of government that the Convention adopted.

The Convention Organizes

The delegates chose George Washington to lead the meetings. Delegates also decided that each state would have one vote on all questions. Decisions would be based on a majority vote of the states present. Sessions were not open to the public. In fact, the windows were closed in the sweltering heat to keep anyone from listening in. This made it possible for the delegates to talk freely.

The Virginia Plan

Edmund Randolph of Virginia opened the Convention with a surprise. He proposed the Virginia Plan that called for a strong national government. The plan, which was largely the work of James Madison, created a government with three branches: a two-house legislature, a chief executive chosen by the legislature, and a court system. The legislature would have powers to tax, regulate trade, and veto state laws. Voters would elect members of the lower house of the legislature. The members of the lower house would then choose members of the upper house. In both houses the number of representatives would be **proportional**, or corresponding in size, to the population of each state. This would give a state such as Virginia many more delegates than Delaware, the state with the fewest number of people.

Delegates from the small states objected. They preferred a system in which all states had equal representation. Opponents of the Virginia Plan rallied around William Paterson of New Jersey. On June 15, he presented another plan. This plan amended the Articles of Confederation, which was all the Convention had the power to do.

proportional having the proper size in relation to other objects or items

Academic Vocabulary

amend to change or revise

VIRGINIA AND NEW JERSEY PLANS

Virginia Plan	New Jersey Plan
Edmund Randolph proposed the Virginia Plan.	William Paterson proposed the New Jersey Plan.
Legislative Branch	**Legislative Branch**
• Powerful legislature • Two houses, with membership proportional to state's population • Lower house elected by the people • Upper house elected by lower house	• One house with equal representation from all states • Legislature could collect taxes from states
Executive Branch	**Executive Branch**
• Chosen by legislature • Limited power • Could veto legislation, subject to override	• Chosen by Congress • Would serve a single term • Subject to recall on request of state governors
Judicial Branch	**Judicial Branch**
• Would serve for life • Could veto legislation, subject to override	• Appointed by executive branch • Would serve for life
Both Plans	
Were federal systems with three branches—legislative, executive, and judicial	
Gave the federal government more powers than it had under the Articles of Confederation	

The New Jersey Plan

Under this plan, the legislature would have a single house, with each state having one vote. Paterson argued that the Convention should not deprive smaller states of the equality they had under the Articles. The New Jersey plan gave Congress the power to set taxes, regulate trade, and elect an executive branch made up of more than one person. In sum, the New Jersey Plan favored a more powerful government than existed under the Articles—but a less powerful government than the Virginia Plan proposed.

☑ **PROGRESS CHECK**

Explaining Why did New Jersey's delegates object to the Virginia Plan?

CHART SKILL

Delegates at the Constitutional Convention considered different plans.

1 **COMPARING** In what ways were the two plans similar?

2 **CRITICAL THINKING**
Explaining Explain how proportional representation favored larger states.

George Washington
(1732–1799)

George Washington's military service is well known. He also became a key political leader in his later years. Washington did not want to attend the Constitutional Convention, but he did because he worried that the nation would not survive under the weak Articles of Confederation. The delegates unanimously chose him as the presiding officer, or leader, of the Convention. Washington said very little during the debates but later became one of the new Constitution's strongest supporters. He argued that later generations could make any changes necessary.

▶ CRITICAL THINKING
Making Inferences What can you infer from the fact that the other delegates chose Washington as the leader of the Convention?

compromise a settlement of a dispute by each party giving up some demands

Agreeing to Compromise

GUIDING QUESTION *What compromises were reached in the new Constitution?*

The delegates had to decide whether to revise the Articles of Confederation or write a new constitution. On June 19, the states voted to work toward a new constitution based on the Virginia Plan. They still had to deal with the difficult issue of representation that divided the large and small states.

The Great Compromise

The Convention appointed a committee to settle the disagreement. Roger Sherman of Connecticut suggested what would later be called the Great Compromise. A **compromise** is a settlement of a dispute by each party giving up some demands. Sherman's compromise proposed different representation in the two-house legislature. In the upper house—the Senate—each state would have two members. That is, the states would be equal in representation. In the lower house—the House of Representatives—the number of seats for each state would vary based on the state's population. Larger states would have more representation.

The Three-Fifths Compromise

Delegates from the South and North disagreed on whether—and how—to count each state's enslaved population. Including enslaved people as part of a state's population would increase each Southern state's size. This would give Southern states more seats in Congress. The Southern states liked this, and the Northern states did not. At the same time, larger populations would increase each Southern state's taxes, because states were to be taxed based on their populations. The South was not happy about this.

As a solution to this dispute, delegates agreed to what was called the Three-Fifths Compromise. As part of this compromise, every five enslaved persons would count as three persons in the state's population total. This population total would be the basis for setting taxes and representation in Congress.

The Question of the Slave Trade

The Northern states had already banned the slave trade. They wanted to prohibit it nationwide. Southern states considered slavery central to their economy. Northerners agreed to keep the new Congress from interfering with the slave trade until 1808.

Debating a Bill of Rights

State constitutions such as those of Virginia and Massachusetts had a listing of key rights and freedoms. These are known as a declaration of rights, or a bill of rights. At the Convention, some delegates worried that without a bill of rights, the new national government might abuse its power. George Mason of Virginia proposed a bill of rights to be included in the Constitution. The delegates defeated this idea. Most of the delegates believed that the Constitution carefully defined government powers and provided enough protection of individual rights.

Approving the Constitution

On September 17, 1787, the delegates assembled to sign the Constitution they had created. Three delegates refused to sign—Elbridge Gerry of Massachusetts, and Edmund Randolph and George Mason of Virginia. Gerry and Mason would not sign because the Constitution did not have a bill of rights. Randolph, who had put forth the Virginia Plan, felt the final document strayed too far from his own beliefs.

The other delegates did sign the document. The approved draft of the Constitution went out to the states for their approval. Under the Articles of Confederation, all 13 states would have had to accept any change. The drafters of the new Constitution decided, however, that the document would go into effect with the approval of just 9 of the 13 states.

☑ **PROGRESS CHECK**

Explaining What compromises were reached concerning enslaved people?

LESSON 2 REVIEW

Review Vocabulary

1. Use each of the two words below in a sentence that shows their meaning in this lesson.

   a. depression   **b.** manumission

2. Write a sentence about the Constitutional Convention that uses both of these terms.

   a. proportional   **b.** compromise

Answer the Guiding Questions

3. *Specifying* What weaknesses in the national government did Shays's Rebellion reveal?

4. *Contrasting* What was the difference between the Virginia Plan and the New Jersey Plan concerning the legislature?

5. *Describing* On what key issues did delegates have to compromise in order to create a Constitution that most states would accept?

6. **EXPOSITORY WRITING** You have been asked to write a short announcement to inform your community about the Great Compromise. Summarize the key points of the agreement. Include any other details you think are important.

What Do You Think?

Should the Constitution Be Ratified?

After the delegates in Philadelphia wrote the U.S. Constitution, it went before the American people for approval. Delegates in each state met at special conventions to decide whether to accept or reject the Constitution. In order for the Constitution to become the new plan for the government of the United States, nine of the 13 states had to ratify, or approve, it.

Those who opposed the Constitution were called Anti-Federalists. They feared a strong national government that would be able to take away the rights of citizens. Federalists supported the Constitution. They believed that the Constitution would give the national government power to manage the problems facing the United States. At the same time, the Federalists argued, the Constitution would protect the right of the individual.

The Constitutional Convention met at Independence Hall.

No

PRIMARY SOURCE

MERCY OTIS WARREN

❝ Our situation is truly delicate & critical. On the one hand we are in need of a strong federal government founded on principles that will support the prosperity & union of the colonies. On the other we have struggled for liberty & made lofty sacrifices at her shrine: and there are still many among us who **revere** her name too much to **relinquish** (beyond a certain medium) the rights of man for the Dignity of Government. ❞

TEXT: Mercy Otis Warren to Catherine Macauly, 28 September 1787, GLC01800.03, Courtesy of the Gilder Lehrman Collection, The Gilder Lehrman Institute of American History. Not to be reproduced without written permission.
PHOTO: (t) Kean Collection/Staff/Archive Photos/Getty Images, (b) Tom Grill/Corbis

This is the Assembly Room, where delegates signed the United States Constitution.

Yes

PRIMARY SOURCE

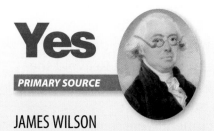

JAMES WILSON

❝ I am satisfied that anything nearer to perfection could not have been accomplished. If there are errors, it should be remembered, that the seeds of **reformation** are sown in the work itself, and the **concurrence** of two-thirds of the Congress may at any time introduce alterations and amendments. . . . I am bold to assert, that it is the BEST FORM OF GOVERNMENT WHICH HAS EVER BEEN OFFERED TO THE WORLD. ❞

Vocabulary

revere deeply love and respect
relinquish give up
reformation change
concurrence agreement

What Do You Think?   DBQ

1 **Making Inferences** What does Warren suggest is more important than the "dignity of government"?

2 **Identifying** According to Wilson, how can the Constitution be changed?

3 **Contrasting** How would you summarize the difference between Warren's and Wilson's views on the risks involved with ratifying the Constitution?

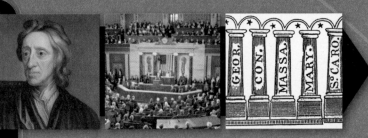

Lesson 3

A New Plan of Government

ESSENTIAL QUESTION *How do governments change?*

IT MATTERS BECAUSE
The Constitution contains features that came from the best political thinkers and that have helped the nation survive and thrive.

The Constitution's Sources

GUIDING QUESTION *From where did the Framers of the Constitution borrow their ideas about government?*

Although an American document, the Constitution has roots in other civilizations. The delegates who wrote the document studied the history of political thought in an effort to avoid the mistakes of the past. Many ideas found in the Constitution came from European political institutions and writers.

The Framers who shaped the document were familiar with the parliamentary system of Britain. Many had taken part in their colonial or state assemblies. They valued the individual rights guaranteed by the British judicial system. Although the Americans broke away from British rule, they respected many British **traditions**, or cultural beliefs and practices.

European Influences

The English Magna Carta (1215) placed limits on the power of the monarch. Parliament, England's lawmaking body, became a force that the king or queen had to depend on to pay for wars and the royal government. Like Parliament, colonial assemblies controlled their colonies' funds. The assemblies had some control over colonial governors.

(l) DEA PICTURE LIBRARY/Getty Images, (c) Brooks Kraft/Corbis, (r) The Granger Collection, NYC

Reading **HELP**DESK

Taking Notes: *Categorizing*

As you read, use a chart like this one to identify the powers of each branch of the federal government.

Branch	Example
Executive	
Legislative	
Judicial	

Content Vocabulary

- **federalism**
- **legislative branch**
- **executive branch**
- **Electoral College**
- **judicial branch**
- **checks and balances**
- **amendment**

The English Bill of Rights of 1689 was another model for Americans. In fact, many people in the United States felt the Constitution also needed a bill of rights. The Framers believed in the ideas about the nature of people and government put forth by European writers of the Enlightenment. The Enlightenment was a movement of the 1700s that promoted knowledge, reason, and science as a means of improving society. James Madison and other Framers of the Constitution were familiar with the work of John Locke and Baron de Montesquieu (mahn•tuhs•KYOO), two philosophers of the Enlightenment.

The English philosopher Locke wrote that all people have natural rights. He stated that these natural rights include the rights to life, liberty, and property. In his *Two Treatises of Civil Government* (1690), he wrote that government is based on an agreement, or contract, between the people and the ruler. Americans interpreted natural rights to mean the rights of Britons defined in the Magna Carta and the English Bill of Rights. The Framers viewed the Constitution as a contract between the American people and their government. The contract protected people's natural rights by limiting government power.

The French writer Montesquieu declared in *The Spirit of Laws* (1748) that the powers of government should be separated and balanced against each other. This separation would prevent any one person or group from gaining too much power. The Framers of the Constitution carefully spelled out and divided the powers of government.

John Locke influenced many of the Framers of the Constitution. His views on natural rights are reflected in the Constitution.

Federalism

The Constitution created a federal system of government that divided powers between the national, or federal, government and the states. In the Articles of Confederation, the states held most powers. Under the Constitution, the states gave up some powers to the federal government and kept others. **Federalism** (FE•duh•ruh•lih•zuhm), or sharing power between the federal and state governments, is one of the key features of the United States government. Under the Constitution, the federal government gained wide-ranging powers to tax, regulate trade, control the currency, raise an army, and declare war. It could also pass laws that were "necessary and proper" for carrying out its responsibilities. This power would allow Congress to make laws as needed to deal with new situations.

federalism sharing power between the federal and state governments

Academic Vocabulary

tradition longstanding cultural belief and practice

The Constitution left some important powers to the states. The states kept the power to control trade inside their borders. They also could set up local governments and schools and establish marriage and divorce laws.

The Constitution also called for the sharing of some powers between the federal and state governments. Both federal and state governments would have the power to tax and to establish criminal justice.

While states had powers and shared others with the federal government, the Constitution and the laws of Congress were to be "the supreme law of the land." No state could make laws or take actions that went against the Constitution. Federal courts would settle disputes between the federal government and the states on the basis of the Constitution.

☑ **PROGRESS CHECK**

Describing What is the principle of federalism?

Government Structure

GUIDING QUESTION *How does the Constitution limit the power of the government?*

The Framers of the Constitution used Montesquieu's idea of a division of powers. They divide the federal government into three branches—legislative, executive, and judicial. The first three articles, or parts, of the Constitution describe each branch's powers and responsibilities. They detail the methods for electing or selecting key members of each branch.

CHART SKILL

The Constitution gives exclusive powers to the state and federal governments, and it also calls for some powers to be shared.

1 IDENTIFYING What is an example of a power shared by the federal and state governments?

2 CRITICAL THINKING
Explaining Why do you think both the national and state governments have the power to collect taxes?

FEDERAL AND STATE POWERS

National Government	National and State Governments	State Governments
Coin money	Establish courts	Regulate trade within a state
Maintain army and navy	Enforce laws	Protect public welfare and safety
Declare war	Collect taxes	Conduct elections
Regulate trade between states and with foreign nations	Borrow money	Establish local governments
Carry out all expressed powers	Provide for general welfare	

Reading **HELP**DESK

legislative branch lawmaking branch of government

executive branch branch of government that executes, or carries out, the law; headed by the president

Electoral College special group of electors chosen to vote for president and vice president

Congress, shown here listening to the president deliver the State of the Union speech, consists of both the House of Representatives and the Senate. Congress currently has 100 senators and 435 representatives.

Government Branches

Article I of the Constitution declares Congress to be the **legislative** (LEH•juhs•lay•tiv) **branch**, or lawmaking branch, of the government. Congress is made up of the House of Representatives and the Senate. The powers of Congress include establishing taxes, coining money, and regulating trade.

Article II of the Constitution sets up the **executive branch**, to carry out the nation's laws and policies. At the head of this branch are the president and vice president. A special group called the **Electoral** (ee•lehk•TAWR•uhl) **College** elects the president and vice president. Voters in each state choose the electors who make up the Electoral College.

Article III deals with the **judicial** (joo•DIH•shuhl) **branch**, or court system. The nation's judicial power **resides** in "one supreme Court" and any lower federal courts Congress creates. The Supreme Court and other federal courts hear cases involving the Constitution, federal laws, and disputes between states.

Checks and Balances

The Constitution contains a system of **checks and balances**. This means each branch of government has ways to check, or limit, the power of the other branches. With this system, no single branch can gain too much power in the government. You will learn more about this system in another chapter.

✓ PROGRESS CHECK

Explaining Why does the Constitution divide power among branches of government?

Brooks Kraft/Corbis

---

judicial branch the branch of government that includes the courts that settle disputes and questions of the law

checks and balances a system by which each branch of government limits power of other branches

Academic Vocabulary

reside to exist in

Debate and Adoption

GUIDING QUESTION *How was the Constitution ratified?*

Before the Constitution could go into effect, nine states had to ratify, or approve, it. Americans debated the arguments for and against the Constitution in newspapers, at meetings, and in everyday conversations.

Federalists and Anti-Federalists

People who supported the new Constitution were called Federalists. They took this name to stress that the Constitution would create a system of federalism, a government in which power is divided between the national government and the states. Among them were George Washington and Benjamin Franklin. James Madison, Alexander Hamilton, and John Jay wrote a series of essays explaining and defending the Constitution. Called the Federalist Papers, these essays were later published in newspapers and sent to delegates at state conventions. They made a powerful argument in favor of ratification.

Those who opposed the Constitution were called Anti-Federalists. They wrote their own essays, which later came to be known as the Anti-Federalist Papers. Anti-Federalists argued that a strong national government would take away liberties Americans had fought for in the American Revolution. They warned that the government would ignore the will of the states and favor the wealthy few over the common people. Anti-Federalists favored local government that was controlled more closely by the people.

A Bill of Rights

The strongest criticism of the Constitution may have been that it lacked a bill of rights to protect individual freedoms. Several state conventions announced that they would not ratify it unless a bill of rights was included. George Mason expressed the problem:

PRIMARY SOURCE

❝ There is not a declaration of rights, and the laws of the general government being paramount to the laws and constitutions of the several States, the declarations of rights in the separate States are no security. ❞

Connections to
TODAY

The Bill of Rights

Various groups have drafted their own specialized versions of the Bill of Rights. For instance, in 2010 New Jersey lawmakers drafted an "Anti-Bullying Bill of Rights." This legislation was designed to protect students from bullying and cyberbullying. The bill calls for anti-bullying training for teachers and gives school administrators tools for responding to bullying.

▶ **CRITICAL THINKING**
Drawing Conclusions Why do you think lawmakers today refer to the Bill of Rights when proposing and promoting legislation?

Reading **HELP**DESK

amendment a change, correction, or improvement added to a document

The Ninth PILLAR erected!

"The Ratification of the Conventions of nine States, shall be sufficient for the establishment of this Constitution, between the States so ratifying the same." *Art.* vii.

INCIPIENT MAGNI PROCEDERE MENSES.

If it is not up it will rise.

The Attraction must be irresistible

DEL. PEN. N.JER. GEOR. CON. MASSA. MARY. S°CARO. N.HAMP. VIRG. N.YORK

The pillars in this cartoon represent the ratifying vote by each state convention.

▶ CRITICAL THINKING
Drawing Conclusions Why is the ninth pillar significant?

Ratifying the Constitution

On December 7, 1787, Delaware became the first state to approve the Constitution. By June 21, 1788, the ninth state—New Hampshire—ratified it. In theory, this made the Constitution law. However, without the support of the largest states—New York and Virginia—the new government could not succeed.

In Virginia, Patrick Henry claimed the Constitution did not place enough limits on government power. Still, Virginia did ratify the document after promises that there would be a bill of rights **amendment** (uh•MEHND•muhnt)—something added to a document. This promise was met in 1791. In July 1788, New York ratified the Constitution, followed by North Carolina in November 1789 and Rhode Island in May 1790.

✓ PROGRESS CHECK

Explaining Why was it important that the largest states ratify the Constitution?

LESSON 3 REVIEW

Review Vocabulary

1. Explain the relationship between the following terms.

   a. Electoral College   b. executive branch

2. Explain the significance of the following terms.

   a. federalism
   b. legislative branch
   c. judicial branch
   d. checks and balances
   e. amendment

Answer the Guiding Questions

3. *Identifying* What features of the Constitution developed from the ideas of Montesquieu?

4. *Explaining* What is the purpose of the first three articles of the Constitution?

5. *Specifying* Why did Virginia finally ratify the Constitution?

6. **PERSUASIVE WRITING** Take the role of James Madison. Write an essay for the Federalist Papers, urging states to ratify the Constitution. Use details about the Constitution to support your argument.

Write your answers on a separate piece of paper.

① Exploring the Essential Questions

EXPOSITORY WRITING How would you explain the behavior of the people of the United States in the period between 1776 and 1783? Write a summary that explains the goals of the people in throwing off British rule, forming the Articles of Confederation, and then establishing the Constitution. Be sure to explain how these actions relate to the question of why people form governments, how governments affect people's lives, and how governments change.

② 21st Century Skills

MAKING AN ARGUMENT Reread the discussion of Shays's Rebellion from Lesson 2 of this chapter. Write a letter to the editor of your local newspaper in which you explain what the incident reveals about the nation and its system of government at that time.

③ Thinking Like a Historian

UNDERSTANDING CAUSE AND EFFECT In a chart, identify at least three reasons Americans believed the Articles of Confederation needed to be strengthened.

④ VISUAL LITERACY

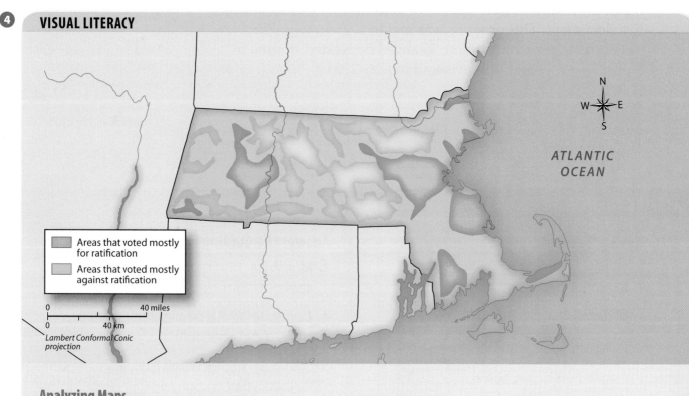

Analyzing Maps

MAKING AN ARGUMENT This map shows areas of Massachusetts that voted for or against the ratification of the U.S. Constitution. Based on the map, where was Federalist support in Massachusetts weakest?

REVIEW THE GUIDING QUESTIONS

Choose the best answer for each question.

1 Under the Articles of Confederation, Congress did not have the authority to

    A. conduct foreign affairs.

    B. maintain armed forces.

    C. borrow money.

    D. force citizens to join the army.

2 The Northwest Ordinance

    F. allowed for the spread of slavery.

    G. encouraged the sale of land to speculators.

    H. provided a method for petitioning for statehood.

    I. denied a bill of rights for settlers.

3 Shays's Rebellion demonstrated the

    A. strength of the Articles of Confederation.

    B. weakness of the Virginia Plan.

    C. weakness of the Articles of Confederation.

    D. strength of the United States Constitution.

4 At the Constitutional Convention, the New Jersey Plan proposed

    F. a two-house legislature.

    G. a court system.

    H. one vote for each state.

    I. a chief executive chosen by the legislature.

5 The Framers of the Constitution wanted to protect people's natural rights. This idea was reflected in the work of

    A. English philosopher John Locke.

    B. French writer Baron de Montesquieu.

    C. King George III.

    D. Italian philosopher Niccolo Machiavelli.

6 In the debate over the ratification of the Constitution, the Anti-Federalists most feared

    F. government oppression.

    G. the establishment of a state religion.

    H. disorder without a strong central government.

    I. a national sales tax.

DBQ DOCUMENT-BASED QUESTIONS

"That [the Constitution] will meet the full and entire approbation [approval] of every state is not perhaps to be expected; but each will doubtless consider, ... that [the Constitution] may promote the lasting welfare of that country so dear to us all, and secure her freedom and happiness."

—George Washington, 1787

7 **Summarizing** Which most closely reflects Washington's main point?

A. The Constitution gives too much power to the legislative branch.

B. The Constitution is not popular and will never win approval.

C. The Constitution takes away too much power from the states.

D. The Constitution is good for the nation overall.

8 **Analyzing** Which idea is not part of Washington's response?

F. All states will eventually approve it.

G. Serving one state's interests would be harmful to the other states.

H. The approval of every state is not expected.

I. The welfare of the country is important to all the states.

SHORT RESPONSE

"There shall be neither slavery nor involuntary servitude in the said territory. ... Provided, always, that any person escaping into the same ... such fugitive may be lawfully reclaimed and conveyed [transferred] to the person claiming his or her labor or service as aforesaid."

—Article 6 of Northwest Ordinance, 1787

9 What practices were not allowed in the Northwest Territory?

10 What was the legal status of escaped enslaved people in the Northwest Territory?

EXTENDED RESPONSE

11 **Persuasive Writing** Write an essay in which you:

• defend the Constitution as a model of democracy; or

• express criticism of the Constitution based on differences between its ideals and the status of enslaved people and women in the 1700s.

Need Extra Help?

If You've Missed Question	**1**	**2**	**3**	**4**	**5**	**6**	**7**	**8**	**9**	**10**	**11**
Review Lesson	1	1	2	2	3	3	1	1	1	1	2, 3

The Constitution

1788–Today

ESSENTIAL QUESTIONS • *Why do people form governments?*
• *How do new ideas change the way people live?*

Lesson 1
Principles of the Constitution

Lesson 2
Government and the People

The Story Matters . . .

The early years of the United States and the Constitution produced many great leaders and heroes. Of that group, none stands taller than James Madison.

It is Madison's Virginia Plan that provides the basic framework and many of the central ideas of the Constitution. It is his detailed notes taken throughout the months of debate that serve as a record of the convention. Then, as the nation debates ratification, Madison's contributions to the *Federalist Papers* help persuade many to accept the new document. Later, he sponsors the Bill of Rights, the first 10 amendments to the Constitution, which help protect the basic liberties Americans enjoy to this day.

◄ *James Madison earned the nickname "Father of the Constitution."*

Place and Time: The Nation's Capital 1788 to Today

The Constitution established a strong central government. The home of that government is the District of Columbia—Washington, D.C.

Step Into the Place

MAP FOCUS Washington, D.C. serves as the capital of the United States and the home to many important buildings and offices.

1 LOCATION Between what two states is the district located?

2 PLACE What are some of the buildings or institutions of national importance located in Washington, D.C.?

3 CRITICAL THINKING
Drawing Conclusions One of the reasons that the site of Washington, D.C., was chosen as the capital was that it was in the center of the country as it existed in 1790. What are the advantages of such a location?

A joint session of Congress—including both the House and the Senate—listens to the president deliver the State of the Union Address.

In the United States, immigrants can become citizens—and accept the rights and responsibilities that go along with it.

(t) Time & Life Images/Getty Images, (c) JIM LO SCALZO/epa/Corbis, (b) White House Historical Association

Step Into the Time

TIME LINE What two amendments protect the right to vote? When were they ratified?

George Washington
1789–1797

U.S. PRESIDENTS

U.S. EVENTS

WORLD EVENTS

| 1770 | 1810 | 1850 |

1788 United States Constitution ratified

1789 George Washington elected first president

1789 French Revolution begins

1803 *Marbury v. Madison* decision establishes judicial review

1791 Bill of Rights ratified

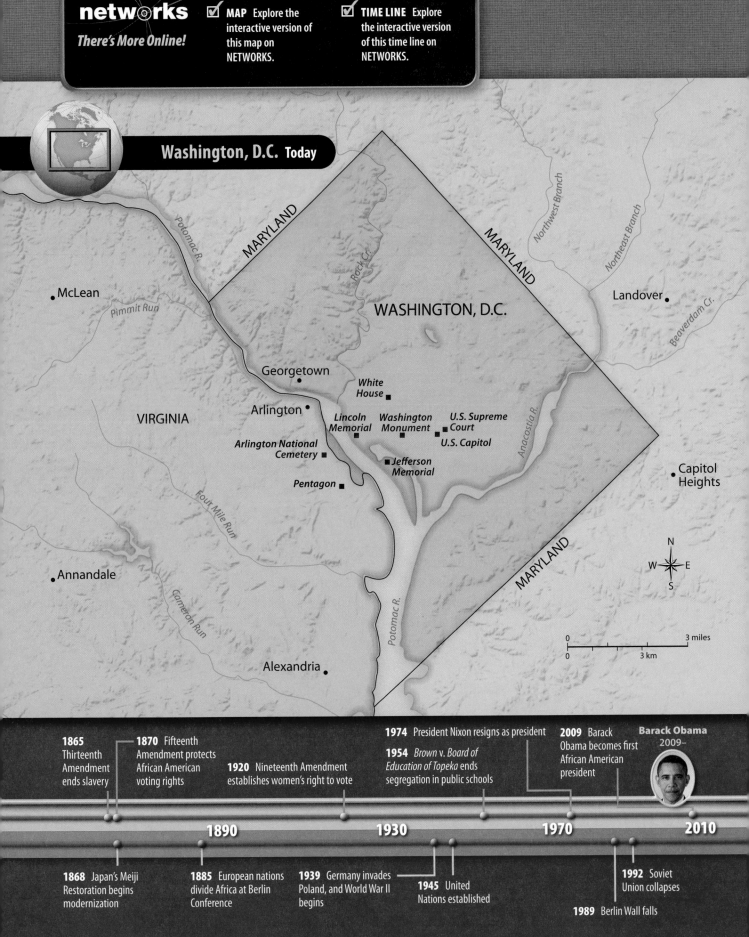

networks
There's More Online!

☑ **MAP** Explore the interactive version of this map on NETWORKS.

☑ **TIME LINE** Explore the interactive version of this time line on NETWORKS.

Washington, D.C. Today

MARYLAND

MARYLAND

Northwest Branch

Northeast Branch

WASHINGTON, D.C.

Potomac R.

Rock Cr.

Beaverdam Cr.

McLean

Landover

Pimmit Run

Georgetown

White House

Arlington

VIRGINIA

Lincoln Memorial

Washington Monument

U.S. Supreme Court

U.S. Capitol

Anacostia R.

Arlington National Cemetery

Jefferson Memorial

Capitol Heights

Pentagon

Four Mile Run

Annandale

Cameron Run

MARYLAND

N W E S

0 ___ 3 miles
0 ___ 3 km

Potomac R.

Alexandria

1865 Thirteenth Amendment ends slavery

1870 Fifteenth Amendment protects African American voting rights

1920 Nineteenth Amendment establishes women's right to vote

1974 President Nixon resigns as president

1954 *Brown v. Board of Education of Topeka* ends segregation in public schools

2009 Barack Obama becomes first African American president

Barack Obama 2009–

1890

1930

1970

2010

1868 Japan's Meiji Restoration begins modernization

1885 European nations divide Africa at Berlin Conference

1939 Germany invades Poland, and World War II begins

1945 United Nations established

1992 Soviet Union collapses

1989 Berlin Wall falls

Lesson 1
Principles of the Constitution

ESSENTIAL QUESTION *Why do people form governments?*

IT MATTERS BECAUSE
The Constitution is the foundation of our country's government.

Our Constitution

GUIDING QUESTION *What basic principles of government are set forth by the Constitution?*

The United States Constitution presents the American solution to the challenge of government. This solution is based on seven key principles: (1) popular sovereignty, (2) a republican form of government, (3) limited government, (4) federalism, (5) separation of powers, (6) checks and balances, and (7) individual rights.

Popular Sovereignty

The Constitution begins with an introduction, or preamble. With its first words—"We the People"—the preamble lays the foundation of the American system of government: **popular sovereignty** (PAH•pyuh•luhr SAHV•rihn•tee), or the authority of the people. The preamble makes clear that it is the people of the United States who hold the power and who establish a system of government for their own well-being.

The Nation Is a Republic

How do the people rule in the United States? The Constitution establishes a republican form of government. A republic is a government in which the people rule through elected representatives. Those representatives make laws and conduct government on behalf of the people. In general, the terms *republic* and *representative government* mean the same thing.

*(tl) James Leynse/CORBIS
(tcl) WireImage/Getty Images*

Reading **HELP**DESK

Taking Notes: *Listing*

As you read, use a diagram like the one shown to identify the seven major principles on which the Constitution was based.

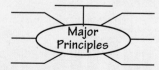

Major Principles

Content Vocabulary

• popular sovereignty
• limited government
• enumerated power
• reserved power

• concurrent power
• separation of powers
• implied power

Limited Government

The Framers were wary of a government that might take away people's rights or favor certain groups. At the same time, they realized that the nation needed a stronger government than the Articles of Confederation had provided. Their goal was to establish **limited government**, in which the powers of government are strictly defined. A limited government has only those powers that are given to it by the people.

Federalism

The original thirteen states had fought hard to win independence from Great Britain. The Articles of Confederation protected that independence, but it failed to create a national government strong enough to deal with many challenges the young nation faced. The United States has a federal government, where the many state governments and the single federal government share power. This system is known as federalism.

The Constitution creates the federal system. It explains how powers are distributed among different levels of government. The Constitution spells out the powers given to Congress and establishes the executive and judicial branches.

The Constitution lists **enumerated** (ee•NOO•muh•ray•tuhd) **powers,** or those powers that are specifically given to Congress. Enumerated powers include the power to coin money, regulate interstate and foreign trade, maintain the armed forces, and create federal courts. The states cannot exercise these powers.

Reserved powers are those powers that belong to the states. The Constitution does not specifically list the reserved powers. The Tenth Amendment declares that all powers not specifically granted to the federal government "are reserved to the States." The reserved powers include the power to establish schools, pass marriage and divorce laws, and regulate trade within a state.

Under the Constitution, the federal government and the state governments share certain powers. These are the **concurrent** (kuhn•KUHR•hnt) **powers.** Examples of concurrent powers are the right to raise taxes, borrow money, provide for public welfare, and carry out criminal justice. Each state and the federal government can exercise these powers at the same time.

The power to coin money is an enumerated power. Congress also has the power to print currency, such as the paper bills shown here.

James Leynse/CORBIS

popular sovereignty the belief that government is subject to the will of the people

limited government government with limited powers strictly defined by law

enumerated power power specifically given Congress in the Constitution

reserved power power belonging only to the states

concurrent power power shared by the states and federal government

While states have their own laws and powers, the Constitution is "the supreme Law of the Land." If a state law **contradicts** the Constitution or federal law, the Constitution or federal law prevails. This is stated in Article VI, Clause 2, of the Constitution—the "Supremacy Clause."

Separation of Powers

To make sure no person or group in government has too much power, the Constitution provides for a **separation of powers**. This means the Constitution separates the legislative, executive, and judicial powers of government. It then places these powers in three different branches of government. Each branch has different—and limited—powers, duties, and responsibilities.

Checks and Balances

The Framers did more than separate the powers of government. They set up a system of checks and balances. Under this system, each branch of government can check, or limit, the power of the other branches. This system helps maintain a balance in the power of the three branches.

Here is an example of how the system of checks and balances works: Congress (legislative branch) has the power to pass a law. If the president (executive branch) disagrees with the law, he or she can reject it through the presidential power of the veto. This veto power checks the power of Congress. At the same time, Congress can override the veto. This checks the power of the executive branch.

The United States Supreme Court (judicial branch) also has important checks on the other branches. The Supreme Court has the power to interpret the Constitution and to decide whether or not actions by the legislative and executive branches are allowed.

Congress can check decisions made by the courts by beginning the process of changing the Constitution itself. For example, the Supreme Court ruled in the 1857 *Dred Scott* v. *Sandford* decision that enslaved African Americans were not citizens. In 1866 Congress proposed the Fourteenth Amendment. The amendment was meant to grant full citizenship to formerly enslaved African Americans. When ratified by the states in 1868, the Fourteenth Amendment had the effect of overruling the *Dred Scott* decision.

There are several other ways in which the branches of government check and balance one another. The diagram on the next page shows the system in detail.

The right to carry out criminal justice is a concurrent power, and the federal government and the states have their own justice systems.

WireImage/Getty Images

Reading **HELP**DESK

separation of powers a principle by which powers are divided among different branches of government to make sure no one branch has too much power

Academic Vocabulary

contradict to go against or state the opposite

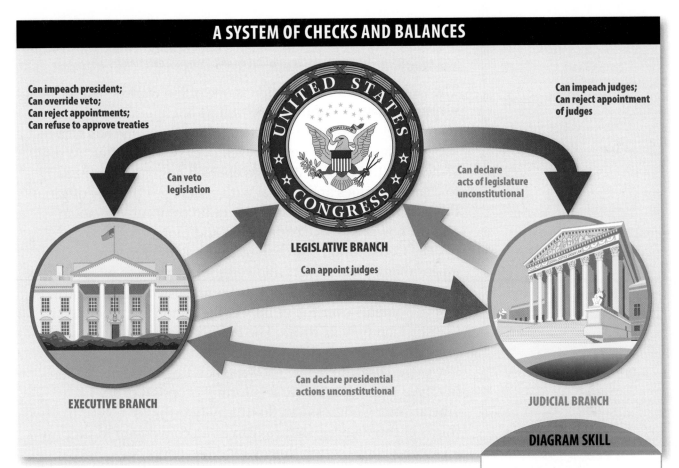

Can impeach president;
Can override veto;
Can reject appointments;
Can refuse to approve treaties

Can impeach judges;
Can reject appointment of judges

Can veto legislation

Can declare acts of legislature unconstitutional

LEGISLATIVE BRANCH

Can appoint judges

Can declare presidential actions unconstitutional

EXECUTIVE BRANCH

JUDICIAL BRANCH

DIAGRAM SKILL

Each branch of government can check and balance the power of the other branches in several ways.

1 IDENTIFYING What is an example of a legislative branch check on the judicial branch?

2 CRITICAL THINKING
Analyzing Do you think the different branches of government are truly balanced? Why or why not?

Individual Rights

The Constitution that the Framers wrote in Philadelphia in 1787 did not have a Bill of Rights. These ten amendments became part of the Constitution in 1791. They guarantee basic freedoms and liberties including:

- Freedom of religion
- Freedom of speech and of the press
- Freedom to assemble in groups and to protest against the government
- The right to bear arms
- The right to a speedy and public trial by jury
- The right to be free from unreasonable searches and seizures by the government
- Freedom from "cruel and unusual" punishments.

Since 1791, other constitutional amendments have expanded on the rights of the American people. For example, amendments have abolished slavery, defined citizenship, guaranteed "equal protection of the law" for all people, and guaranteed the right to vote for people aged 18 and older. Amendments have also authorized the direct, popular election of senators.

✓ PROGRESS CHECK

Describing What is the purpose of the system of checks and balances?

Amending the Constitution

GUIDING QUESTION *How is the Constitution able to change over time?*

The United States Constitution is one of the world's oldest written Constitutions. It is also a short document compared to many other constitutions. Its clear, direct language has helped support stable government for well over two centuries. At the same time, the Constitution has enabled government to adapt to changing times and to deal with challenges that the original Framers never dreamed of—from radio communications to nuclear power to space exploration and more.

The Constitution has changed as a result of formal amendment. The Framers allowed for this process when they wrote the Constitution. People have suggested many hundreds of amendments over the years. Yet the nation has amended its Constitution only 27 times. The Framers deliberately made the amendment process difficult.

As the diagram below shows, amending the Constitution **involves** two steps. The first is formal proposal of an amendment. Congress can do this by two-thirds' vote. Also, two-thirds of the state legislatures can call a convention to propose an amendment, though this method has never been used.

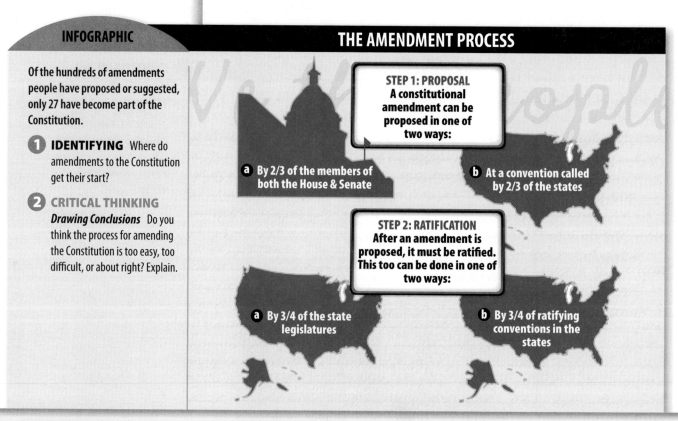

INFOGRAPHIC

THE AMENDMENT PROCESS

Of the hundreds of amendments people have proposed or suggested, only 27 have become part of the Constitution.

1 **IDENTIFYING** Where do amendments to the Constitution get their start?

2 **CRITICAL THINKING**
Drawing Conclusions Do you think the process for amending the Constitution is too easy, too difficult, or about right? Explain.

STEP 1: PROPOSAL
A constitutional amendment can be proposed in one of two ways:

ⓐ By 2/3 of the members of both the House & Senate

ⓑ At a convention called by 2/3 of the states

STEP 2: RATIFICATION
After an amendment is proposed, it must be ratified. This too can be done in one of two ways:

ⓐ By 3/4 of the state legislatures

ⓑ By 3/4 of ratifying conventions in the states

implied power power not enumerated in the Constitution but suggested in its language

Academic Vocabulary

involve to include

The second step in the amendment process is ratification. Ratification of an amendment requires approval by three-fourths of the states. States can ratify the amendment at either a state convention or through a vote by the state legislature.

Amendments have brought significant changes to the nation. In addition to protecting our rights, amendments have extended the right to vote to a larger share of the population. The Fifteenth Amendment sought to ensure that African American men would have the right to vote. The Nineteenth Amendment extended voting rights to women. The Twenty-Fourth Amendment outlawed poll taxes, giving more people the ability to vote. The Twenty-Sixth Amendment lowered the voting age to 18.

Formal amendment is one way the Constitution has changed. The language of the Constitution has also been subject to different interpretations.

For example, over history, Congress has claimed for itself certain **implied** (ihm•PLYD) **powers**. These are powers that are suggested but not directly stated in the Constitution. The source of the implied powers is Article I, Section 8 of the Constitution. Here is found the "necessary and proper clause," or the "elastic clause." This clause directs Congress to "make all Laws which shall be necessary and proper" for carrying out its duties.

Also in Article I, Section 8, is the "commerce clause." This gives Congress power to "regulate Commerce with foreign Nations, and among the several States." Congress has used this clause to expand its powers into areas, such as the regulation of television, that do appear in the Constitution.

☑ **PROGRESS CHECK**

Calculating How many constitutional amendments have been ratified?

Thinking Like a HISTORIAN

Understanding Cause and Effect

Over the course of American history, some unwritten customs of government have become so strong that they seem to have the effect of law. For example, until the 25th Amendment, which was ratified in 1967, the Constitution did not specify that the vice president would assume the office of president in the event of a president's death. Yet on eight occasions, that is exactly what happened. Each time the custom was applied, it acquired more force. For more information about understanding cause and effect, read *Thinking Like a Historian.*

LESSON 1 REVIEW

Review Vocabulary

1. Write a paragraph in which you explain the difference between the following:
   a. enumerated power   b. reserved power
   c. concurrent power   d. implied power

2. Explain the significance of the following terms:
   a. popular sovereignty   b. limited government

Answer the Guiding Questions

3. *Explaining* What was the challenge that the Framers faced when setting out to write the Constitution, and how did they meet it?

4. *Discussing* Why do you think the Framers made the Constitution difficult to amend? .

5. **PERSUASIVE WRITING** Should Congress have the power to interpret the Constitution? Write a paragraph in which you argue for or against the wide application of the implied powers.

netw⊙rks

There's More Online!

☑ **BIOGRAPHY**
Sandra Day O'Connor

☑ **CHART/GRAPH** Landmark
Supreme Court Cases

☑ **GAME** Crossword Puzzle

☑ **GRAPHIC ORGANIZER** Branches of
Government

☑ **SLIDE SHOW** The Oval Office

Lesson 2

Government and the People

ESSENTIAL QUESTION *How do new ideas change the way people live?*

IT MATTERS BECAUSE

In a nation where the people rule, citizens must understand their government and their rights and responsibilities.

The Federal Government

GUIDING QUESTION *What are the three branches of government?*

To achieve a separation of powers, the Constitution divides the federal government into three branches. They are called the legislative, executive, and judicial branches.

The Nation's Legislature

Congress is the legislative branch of government. It has two houses—the House of Representatives and the Senate. Currently the House has 435 voting members and 6 nonvoting delegates from the District of Columbia, Puerto Rico, Guam, American Samoa, the Virgin Islands, and the Northern Mariana Islands. Representatives, who must be at least 25 years old, serve two-year terms. There is no limit to the number of terms a person can serve.

The number of representatives from each state is based on the state's population. States with more people have more representatives in Congress, though every state has at least one representative. The federal government resets each state's share of the 435 House seats every 10 years. A state's number of representatives may go up or down depending on population changes.

*(tl) AFP/Getty Images, (tcr) Wally McNamee/CORBIS
(tcr) William Hogarth, (tr) Zach Boyden-Holmes/Getty Images*

Reading **HELP**DESK

Taking Notes: *Summarizing*

Write a short summary of the job of each branch of government as you read along. Then compare how each branch differs from the other two.

Content Vocabulary

• **judicial review**   • **naturalization**
• **due process**
• **equal protection**

The Senate has 100 senators, two from each state. Senators must be 30 years old, and they serve six-year terms. Only a third of the seats come up for election every two years. As with House members, there are no term limits for Senators.

Article I of the Constitution describes the role of Congress. Congress makes the nation's laws. These laws are not just rules for behavior. Congress passes laws that impose taxes, authorize the spending of money, and create government programs. Congress also has the job of declaring war.

Both houses of Congress must agree on a bill, or proposed law. Once both houses do this, the bill goes to the president. If the president signs the bill, it becomes law.

The Executive Branch

The executive branch is led by the president and vice president, who each serve four-year terms. It also includes the president's cabinet, or top advisers, and many other offices, departments, and agencies. The executive branch's main job is to **administrate,** or carry out, the laws passed by Congress. The president does, however, propose laws to Congress.

The president has many other powers laid out in Article II of the Constitution. These include directing foreign policy, naming ambassadors, and negotiating treaties with other nations. The president is also the commander-in-chief of the armed forces.

The Oval Office is the official office of the president of the United States.

The Judicial Branch

Article III of the Constitution establishes a Supreme Court and allows for Congress to create lower courts. Congress has established district courts, which are the main trial courts for the federal government, and appeals courts, which hear cases on appeal from lower courts. There are several other types of federal courts as well. For example, there are special federal courts for hearing bankruptcy cases. Bankruptcy is a legal process for people or businesses that cannot pay off their debts.

The Supreme Court is at the top of the United States legal system. It rules on only the most difficult legal questions, and its rulings are never appealed.

The Supreme Court also has the power of **judicial review.** This means that the Court can review the actions of the executive and legislative branches to determine whether or not they violate the Constitution.

judicial review power of the court to judge whether or not actions of other branches are constitutional

Academic Vocabulary

administrate to carry out

**Sandra Day O'Connor
(1930 –   )**

In his 1980 election campaign, Ronald Reagan promised to name the first woman justice to the Supreme Court. During his first year in office, a vacancy opened on the Court. Reagan chose Sandra Day O'Connor, an Arizona appeals court judge, to fill the vacancy. O'Connor served as a justice until 2006. In an interview, she discussed the increased opportunities for women she had witnessed: "When I went to law school, about 1 percent of all law students were women. And last year, over 50 percent were."

► **CRITICAL THINKING**
Describing What view does Sandra Day O'Connor express about the progress of women's opportunities? Explain.

Members are nominated by the president and approved by Congress. Today the Supreme Court is made up of nine justices—the chief justice and eight associate justices. The Constitution gave Congress the power to set this number. Justices serve no fixed term. Unless removed for bad behavior, they stay on the bench until they retire or die.

The main duties of the justices are to hear and rule on cases they choose from among the thousands that are presented to them each year. They listen to arguments, and then they must present and explain their decision—called the Court's opinion. This opinion is then used by lower courts in making their rulings.

✓ PROGRESS CHECK

Identifying What parts of the Constitution discuss the establishment and duties of the three branches of our federal government?

What it Means to be a Citizen

GUIDING QUESTION *What are the rights and elements of participation of American citizens?*

Citizens of the United States enjoy certain rights and liberties. Being a citizen also involves some responsibilities.

Our Rights

Our rights fall into three main categories: The right to be protected from unfair government actions, the right to be treated equally with others, and the right to enjoy basic freedoms.

Our government must treat people fairly and according to clear rules. This is spelled out in the Fifth Amendment, which says no one shall "be deprived of life, liberty, or property, without due process of law." **Due process** means the government must follow established procedures in taking action against a citizen.

The Fourteenth Amendment guarantees all people **equal protection** of the laws. This principle means all people, regardless of race, religion, or political beliefs, must receive the same treatment under the law.

The First Amendment outlines many of our basic freedoms. These include freedom of religion, freedom of speech and of the press, freedom of assembly, and freedom to petition the government. The Framers knew that in a free society in which the people rule, people must be able to share ideas.

Wally McNamee/CORBIS

Reading **HELP**DESK

due process the legal rules and procedures the government must observe before depriving a person of life, liberty, or property
equal protection the equal application of the law regardless of a person's race, religion, political beliefs, or other qualities

naturalization
the process of becoming a citizen of another country

Academic Vocabulary

diminish reduce, make smaller

Our rights and freedoms have some limits. For example, government can limit our freedom of speech or our right to hold a protest if it threatens public health or safety. Also, one person's exercise of his or her rights cannot take away the rights of other people. Limits on rights and freedoms must be applied equally to all people.

The Duties and Responsibilities of Citizenship

A citizen is a person who owes loyalty to a nation and is entitled to its protection. For the most part, anyone born on U.S. soil is automatically a U.S. citizen. U.S. soil includes American territories and military bases around the world.

Citizenship is also granted to anyone born outside of the United States if one parent is a U.S. citizen. A person who was born in another country can become a citizen through the process called **naturalization** (NA•chuh•ruh•lih•ZAY•shuhn).

With citizenship comes duties and responsibilities. Duties are things we must do, while responsibilities are things we should do. Citizens have a duty to obey the law, to pay taxes, and to sit on a jury if called. Another key duty is defending the country. All males 18 and older must register with the government in case they are needed to serve in the military.

Responsibilities are things a person should do, though they may not be required by law. However, if people do not fulfill their responsibilities as citizens, the quality of our government and communities is **diminished.** Exercising the right to vote is probably the most important responsibility of a citizen. Voting allows you to participate in government and guide its direction.

Early in United States history, voting was generally limited to white men who owned property. Today, the right to vote is available to most citizens 18 years of age or older.

▶ **CRITICAL THINKING**

Drawing Conclusions Why do you think the people of the United States have steadily expanded the eligibility to vote?

✓ PROGRESS CHECK

Contrasting What is the difference between a duty and a responsibility? Why should citizens fulfill both?

LESSON 2 REVIEW

Review Vocabulary

1. Write a brief paragraph that includes the following terms:
   a. due process **b.** equal protection
2. Explain the significance of these terms:
   a. judicial review **b.** naturalization

Answer the Guiding Questions

3. ***Summarizing*** How does a person become a citizen of the United States?
4. ***Describing*** What are the three branches of government, and what are their roles in the government?
5. ***Explaining*** Explain how our freedoms help people become more effective and knowledgeable citizens.
6. **PERSONAL WRITING** In the United States, voting is considered a responsibility. Should the United States make voting a duty and require all citizens to vote? Write a short essay that supports your position.

CHAPTER 8 Activities

Write your answers on a separate piece of paper.

1 Exploring the Essential Questions

EXPOSITORY WRITING After gaining independence, Americans were concerned about the new government having too much power. Write an essay in which you explain the measures taken by the Framers of the Constitution to prevent the government from becoming too powerful. Consider different features of the Constitution and Bill of Rights.

2 21st Century Skills

CREATING A PUBLIC SERVICE ANNOUNCEMENT Recall what you have read about the duties and responsibilities of citizenship. Write a public service announcement that stresses the key role citizens play in our society. Address the difference between duties and responsibilities, and explain why both are important. Link the need for all citizens to do their part with the idea that in the United States, the people rule.

3 Thinking Like a Historian

ANALYZING AND INTERPRETING INFORMATION Create a graphic organizer such as the one shown that shows the three branches of the federal government. Add details about how one branch acts as a check for the other two.

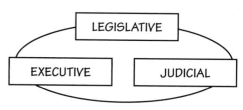

4 Visual Literacy

ANALYZING MAPS The Constitution authorized the federal government to determine the population, or take a census, every 10 years. This map shows the results of the first census in 1790. The count included states and future states. Under the Constitution, what states or future states would have the fewest representatives in Congress based on the 1790 population figures? Explain how you arrived at your answer.

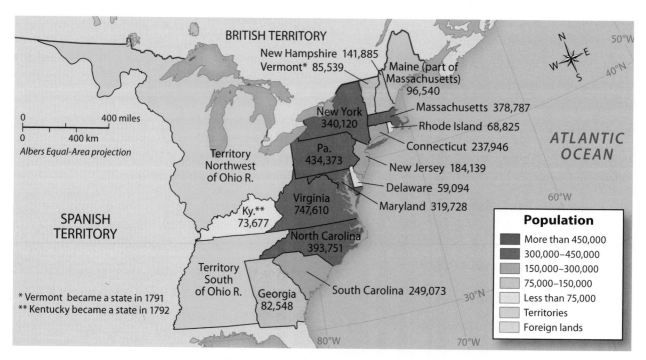

REVIEW THE GUIDING QUESTIONS

Choose the best answer for each question.

1 What is federalism?

    A. a series of articles written in response to the *Federalist Papers*

    B. a major political party in the early years of the United States

    C. a set of powers that belong only to the federal government

    D. a system in which state and national governments share power

2 What are enumerated powers?

    F. powers belonging only to the states

    G. powers not directly mentioned in the Constitution

    H. powers belonging to Congress listed in the Constitution

    I. powers shared between the states and federal government

3 What is the name used for the first 10 constitutional amendments?

    A. the Articles of Confederation

    B. the Preamble

    C. the Declaration of Independence

    D. the Bill of Rights

4 Which are the two houses of Congress?

    F. the House of Commons and the House of Lords

    G. the Senate and the National Assembly

    H. the House of Representatives and the Senate

    I. the Legislative Council and the City Council

5 The way that two branches keep the third from gaining too much power is known as

    A. federalism.

    B. checks and balances.

    C. due process.

    D. naturalization.

6 What is due process?

    F. procedures the government must follow when taking any action against a person

    G. requirements a foreign-born person must fulfill to become a citizen of the United States

    H. procedures the federal government must follow when selecting a Supreme Court justice

    I. steps the members of the legislative branch must follow when creating laws

DBQ DOCUMENT-BASED QUESTIONS

"It has been … remarked that it seems to have been reserved to the people of this country … to decide … whether societies of men are really capable or not of establishing good government from reflection and choice, or whether they are forever destined to depend for their political constitutions on accident and force. If there be any truth in the remark, the crisis at which we are arrived may … be regarded as the era in which that decision is to be made; and a wrong election of the part we shall act may … deserve to be considered as the general misfortune of mankind."

Source: *The Federalist,* No. 1

7 **Identifying Central Issues** According to the authors, what is the alternative to support for the Constitution?

A. good government based on reflection and choice

B. a return to the status of a British colony

C. government based on accident and force

D. the rise of an American Empire

8 **Inferring** What can you infer about the beliefs of the authors?

F. They thought the U.S. would be an example for the world.

G. They thought the British Empire was the worst in history.

H. They thought the people were not capable of making rational decisions.

I. They thought all mankind shared the same misfortunes.

SHORT RESPONSE

As Benjamin Franklin was leaving the last session of the Constitutional Congress, a woman asked, "Well, Doctor, what have we got: a republic or a monarchy?" Franklin answered, "A republic, if you can keep it."

9 What do you think Franklin meant by his remark?

10 What does he suggest about citizen rights and responsibilities in a republic?

EXTENDED RESPONSE

11 **Persuasive Writing** The Constitution contains features that allow for it to be changed and to be interpreted. Do you consider this to be a strength or a weakness of the Constitution? Write an essay to explain your view.

Need Extra Help?

If You've Missed Question	1	2	3	4	5	6	7	8	9	10	11
Review Lesson	1	1	1	2	2	2	1	1	2	2	1, 2

THE CONSTITUTION
of the UNITED STATES

The Constitution of the United States is truly a remarkable document. It was one of the first written constitutions in modern history. The Framers wanted to devise a plan for a strong central government that would unify the country, as well as preserve the ideals of the Declaration of Independence.

The entire text of the Constitution and its amendments follows. For easier study, those passages that have been set aside or changed by the adoption of amendments are printed in blue. Also included are explanatory notes that will help clarify the meaning of each article and section.

The Preamble introduces the Constitution and sets forth the general purposes for which the government was established. The Preamble also declares that the power of the government comes from the people.

The printed text of the document shows the spelling and punctuation of the parchment original.

Preamble

We the People of the United States, in Order to form a more perfect Union, establish Justice, insure domestic Tranquility, provide for the common defence, promote the general Welfare, and secure the Blessings of Liberty to ourselves and our Posterity, do ordain and establish this Constitution for the United States of America.

Article I

Section 1

All legislative Powers herein granted shall be vested in a Congress of the United States, which shall consist of a Senate and House of Representatives.

Article I. The Legislative Branch
The Constitution contains seven divisions called articles. Each article covers a general topic. For example, Articles I, II, and III create the three branches of the national government—the legislative, executive, and judicial branches. Most of the articles are divided into sections.

Section 2

[1.] The House of Representatives shall be composed of Members chosen every second Year by the People of the several States, and the Electors in each State shall have the Qualifications requisite for Electors of the most numerous Branch of the State Legislature.

[2.] No person shall be a Representative who shall not have attained the Age of twenty five Years, and been seven Years a Citizen of the United States, and who shall not, when elected, be an Inhabitant of that State in which he shall be chosen.

Representation The number of representatives from each state is based on the size of the state's population. Each state is entitled to at least one representative. *What are the qualifications for members of the House of Representatives?*

[3.] Representatives and direct Taxes shall be apportioned among the several States which may be included within this Union, according to their respective Numbers, which shall be determined by adding to the whole Number of free Persons, including those bound to Service for a Term of Years, and excluding Indians not taxed, three fifths of all other Persons. The actual Enumeration shall be made within three Years after the first Meeting of the Congress of the United States, and within every subsequent Term of ten Years, in such Manner as they shall by Law direct. The Number of Representatives shall not exceed one for every thirty Thousand, but each State shall have at Least one Representative; and until such enumeration shall be made, the State of New Hampshire shall be entitled to chuse three; Massachusetts eight, Rhode-Island and Providence Plantations one, Connecticut five, New-York six, New Jersey four, Pennsylvania eight, Delaware one, Maryland six, Virginia ten, North Carolina five, South Carolina five, and Georgia three.

Vocabulary

preamble: introduction

constitution: principles and laws of a nation

enumeration: census or population count

[4.] When vacancies happen in the Representation from any State, the Executive Authority thereof shall issue Writs of Election to fill such Vacancies.

[5.] The House of Representatives shall chuse their Speaker and other Officers; and shall have the sole Power of Impeachment.

Section 3

[1.] The Senate of the United States shall be composed of two Senators from each State, chosen by the Legislature thereof, for six Years; and each Senator shall have one Vote.

[2.] Immediately after they shall be assembled in Consequence of the first Election, they shall be divided as equally as may be into three Classes. The Seats of the Senators of the first Class shall be vacated at the Expiration of the second Year, of the second Class at the Expiration of the fourth Year, and of the third Class at the Expiration of the sixth Year, so that one third may be chosen every second Year; and if Vacancies happen by Resignation, or otherwise, during the Recess of the Legislature of any State, the Executive thereof may make temporary Appointments until the next Meeting of the Legislature, which shall then fill such Vacancies.

[3.] No Person shall be a Senator who shall not have attained to the Age of thirty Years, and been nine Years a Citizen of the United States, and who shall not, when elected, be an Inhabitant of that State for which he shall be chosen.

[4.] The Vice President of the United States shall be President of the Senate, but shall have no Vote, unless they be equally divided.

[5.] The Senate shall chuse their other Officers, and also a President pro tempore, in the Absence of the Vice President, or when he shall exercise the Office of the President of the United States.

[6.] The Senate shall have the sole Power to try all Impeachments. When sitting for that Purpose, they shall be on Oath or Affirmation. When the President of the United States is tried, the Chief Justice shall preside: And no Person shall be convicted without the Concurrence of two thirds of the Members present.

[7.] Judgment in Cases of Impeachment shall not extend further than to removal from Office, and disqualification to hold and enjoy any Office of honor, Trust or Profit under the United States: but the Party convicted shall nevertheless be liable and subject to Indictment, Trial, Judgment and Punishment, according to Law.

Electing Senators Originally, senators were chosen by the state legislators of their own states. The Seventeenth Amendment changed this, so that senators are now elected by the people. There are 100 senators, 2 from each state. The vice president serves as president of the Senate.

Impeachment One of Congress's powers is the power to impeach—to accuse government officials of wrongdoing, put them on trial, and if necessary remove them from office. *Which body has the power to decide the official's guilt or innocence?*

Vocabulary

impeachment: bringing charges against an official

president pro tempore: presiding officer of Senate who serves when the vice president is absent

indictment: charging a person with an offense

Section 4

[1.] The Times, Places and Manner of holding Elections for Senators and Representatives, shall be prescribed in each State by the Legislature thereof; but the Congress may at any time by Law make or alter such Regulations, except as to the Places of chusing Senators.

[2.] The Congress shall assemble at least once in every Year, and such Meeting shall be on the first Monday in December, unless they shall by Law appoint a different Day.

Section 5

[1.] Each House shall be the Judge of the Elections, Returns and Qualifications of its own Members, and a Majority of each shall constitute a Quorum to do Business; but a smaller Number may adjourn from day to day, and may be authorized to compel the Attendance of absent Members, in such Manner, and under such Penalties as each House may provide.

[2.] Each House may determine the Rules of its Proceedings, punish its Members for disorderly Behaviour, and, with the Concurrence of two thirds, expel a Member.

[3.] Each House shall keep a Journal of its Proceedings, and from time to time publish the same, excepting such Parts as may in their Judgment require Secrecy; and the Yeas and Nays of the Members of either House on any question shall, at the Desire of one fifth of those Present, be entered on the Journal.

[4.] Neither House, during the Session of Congress, shall, without the Consent of the other, adjourn for more than three days, nor to any other Place than that in which the two Houses shall be sitting.

Section 6

[1.] The Senators and Representatives shall receive a Compensation for their Services, to be ascertained by Law, and paid out of the Treasury of the United States. They shall in all Cases, except Treason, Felony and Breach of the Peace, be privileged from Arrest during their Attendance at the Session of their respective Houses, and in going to and returning from the same; and for any Speech or Debate in either House, they shall not be questioned in any other Place.

[2.] No Senator or Representative shall, during the Time for which he was elected, be appointed to any civil Office under the Authority of the United States, which shall have been created, or the Emoluments whereof shall have been encreased during such time; and no Person holding any Office under the United States, shall be a Member of either House during his Continuance in Office.

Congressional Salaries To strengthen the federal government, the Founders set congressional salaries to be paid by the United States Treasury rather than by members' respective states. Originally, members were paid $6 per day. In 2006, all members of Congress received a base salary of $165,200.

Vocabulary

quorum: minimum number of members that must be present to conduct sessions

adjourn: to suspend a session

immunity privilege: members cannot be sued or prosecuted for anything they say in Congress

emoluments: salaries

Section 7

[1.] All Bills for raising Revenue shall originate in the House of Representatives; but the Senate may propose or concur with Amendments as on other Bills.

[2.] Every Bill which shall have passed the House of Representatives and the Senate, shall, before it become a Law, be presented to the President of the United States; If he approve he shall sign it, but if not he shall return it, with his Objections to that House in which it shall have originated, who shall enter the Objections at large on their Journal, and proceed to reconsider it. If after such Reconsideration two thirds of that House shall agree to pass the Bill, it shall be sent, together with the Objections, to the other House, by which it shall likewise be reconsidered, and if approved by two thirds of that House, it shall become a Law. But in all such Cases the Votes of both Houses shall be determined by yeas and Nays, and the Names of the Persons voting for and against the Bill shall be entered on the Journal of each House respectively. If any Bill shall not be returned by the President within ten Days (Sundays excepted) after it shall have been presented to him, the Same shall be a Law, in like Manner as if he had signed it, unless the Congress by their Adjournment prevent its Return, in which Case it shall not be a Law.

[3.] Every Order, Resolution, or Vote to which the Concurrence of the Senate and House of Representatives may be necessary (except on a question of Adjournment) shall be presented to the President of the United States; and before the Same shall take Effect, shall be approved by him, or being disapproved by him, shall be repassed by two thirds of the Senate and House of Representatives, according to the Rules and Limitations prescribed in the Case of a Bill.

Section 8

[1.] The Congress shall have the Power To lay and collect Taxes, Duties, Imposts and Excises, to pay the Debts and provide for the common Defence and general Welfare of the United States; but all Duties, Imposts and Excises shall be uniform throughout the United States;

[2.] To borrow Money on the credit of the United States;

[3.] To regulate Commerce with foreign Nations, and among the several States, and with the Indian Tribes;

[4.] To establish an uniform Rule of Naturalization, and uniform Laws on the subject of Bankruptcies throughout the United States;

[5.] To coin Money, regulate the Value thereof, and of foreign Coin, and fix the Standard of Weights and Measures;

[6.] To provide for the Punishment of counterfeiting the Securities and current Coin of the United States;

[7.] To establish Post Offices and post Roads;

Where Tax Laws Begin All tax laws must originate in the House of Representatives. This ensures that the branch of Congress that is elected by the people every two years has the major role in determining taxes.

How Bills Become Laws A bill may become a law only by passing both houses of Congress and by being signed by the president. The president can check Congress by rejecting—vetoing—its legislation. *How can Congress override the president's veto?*

Powers of Congress Expressed powers are those powers directly stated in the Constitution. Most of the expressed powers of Congress are listed in Article I, Section 8. These powers are also called enumerated powers because they are numbered 1–18. *Which clause gives Congress the power to declare war?*

Vocabulary

bill: draft of a proposed law

revenue: income raised by government

resolution: legislature's formal expression of opinion

naturalization: procedure by which a citizen of a foreign nation becomes a citizen of the United States.

Elastic Clause The final enumerated power is often called the "elastic clause." This clause gives Congress the right to make all laws "necessary and proper" to carry out the powers expressed in the other clauses of Article I. It is called the elastic clause because it lets Congress "stretch" its powers to meet situations the Founders could never have anticipated.

What does the phrase "necessary and proper" in the elastic clause mean? Almost from the beginning, this phrase was a subject of dispute. The issue was whether a strict or a broad interpretation of the Constitution should be applied. The dispute was first addressed in 1819, in the case of *McCulloch* v. *Maryland*, when the Supreme Court ruled in favor of a broad interpretation.

Habeas Corpus A writ of habeas corpus issued by a judge requires a law official to bring a prisoner to court and show cause for holding the prisoner. A bill of attainder is a bill that punished a person without a jury trial. An "ex post facto" law is one that makes an act a crime after the act has been committed. *What does the Constitution say about bills of attainder?*

Vocabulary
tribunal: a court
insurrection: rebellion

[8.] To promote the Progress of Science and useful Arts, by securing for limited Times to Authors and Inventors the exclusive Right to their respective Writings and Discoveries;

[9.] To constitute Tribunals inferior to the supreme Court;

[10.] To define and punish Piracies and Felonies committed on the high Seas, and Offences against the Law of Nations;

[11.] To declare War, grant Letters of Marque and Reprisal, and make Rules concerning Captures on Land and Water;

[12.] To raise and support Armies, but no Appropriation of Money to that Use shall be for a longer Term than two Years;

[13.] To provide and maintain a Navy;

[14.] To make Rules for the Government and Regulation of the land and naval Forces;

[15.] To provide for calling forth the Militia to execute the Laws of the Union, suppress Insurrections and repel Invasions;

[16.] To provide for organizing, arming, and disciplining, the Militia, and for governing such Part of them as may be employed in the Service of the United States, reserving to the States respectively, the Appointment of the Officers, and the Authority of training the Militia according to the discipline prescribed by Congress;

[17.] To exercise exclusive Legislation in all Cases whatsoever, over such District (not exceeding ten Miles square) as may, by Cession of particular States, and the Acceptance of Congress, become the Seat of Government of the United States, and to exercise like Authority over all Places purchased by the Consent of the Legislature of the State in which the Same shall be, for the Erection of Forts, Magazines, Arsenals, dock-Yards, and other needful Buildings, —And

[18.] To make all Laws which shall be necessary and proper for carrying into Execution the foregoing Powers, and all other Powers vested by this Constitution in the Government of the United States, or in any Department or Officer thereof.

Section 9

[1.] The Migration or Importation of such Persons as any of the States now existing shall think proper to admit, shall not be prohibited by the Congress prior to the Year one thousand eight hundred and eight, but a Tax or duty may be imposed on such Importation, not exceeding ten dollars for each Person.

[2.] The Privilege of the Writ of Habeas Corpus shall not be suspended, unless when in Cases of Rebellion or Invasion the public Safety may require it.

[3.] No Bill of Attainder or ex post facto Law shall be passed.

[4.] No Capitation, or other direct, Tax shall be laid, unless in Proportion to the Census or Enumeration herein before directed to be taken.

[5.] No Tax or Duty shall be laid on Articles exported from any State.

[6.] No Preference shall be given by any Regulation of Commerce or Revenue to the Ports of one State over those of another: nor shall Vessels bound to, or from, one State, be obliged to enter, clear, or pay Duties in another.

[7.] No Money shall be drawn from the Treasury, but in Consequence of Appropriations made by Law; and a regular Statement and Account of the Receipts and Expenditures of all public Money shall be published from time to time.

[8.] No Title of Nobility shall be granted by the United States: And no Person holding any Office of Profit or Trust under them, shall, without the Consent of the Congress, accept of any present, Emolument, Office, or Title, of any kind whatever, from any King, Prince, or foreign State.

Section 10

[1.] No State shall enter into any Treaty, Alliance, or Confederation; grant Letters of Marque and Reprisal; coin Money; emit Bills of Credit; make any Thing but gold and silver Coin a Tender in Payment of Debts; pass any Bill of Attainder, ex post facto Law, or Law impairing the Obligation of Contracts, or grant any Title of Nobility.

[2.] No State shall, without the Consent of the Congress, lay any Imposts or Duties on Imports or Exports, except what may be absolutely necessary for executing its inspection Laws: and the net Produce of all Duties and Imposts, laid by any State on Imports and Exports, shall be for the Use of the Treasury of the United States; and all such Laws shall be subject to the Revision and Controul of the Congress.

[3.] No State shall, without the Consent of Congress, lay any Duty of Tonnage, keep Troops, or Ships of War in time of Peace, enter into any Agreement or Compact with another State, or with a foreign Power, or engage in War, unless actually invaded, or in such imminent Danger as will not admit of delay.

Article II

Section 1

[1.] The executive Power shall be vested in a President of the United States of America. He shall hold his Office during the Term of four Years, and, together with the Vice President, chosen for the same Term, be elected, as follows.

[2.] Each State shall appoint, in such Manner as the Legislature thereof may direct, a Number of Electors, equal to the whole Number of Senators and Representatives to which the State may be entitled in the Congress: but no Senator or Representative, or Person holding an Office of Trust or Profit under the United States, shall be appointed an Elector.

Limitations on the States Section 10 lists limits on the states. These restrictions were designed, in part, to prevent an overlapping in functions and authority with the federal government.

Article II. The Executive Branch Article II creates an executive branch to carry out laws passed by Congress. Article II lists the powers and duties of the presidency, describes qualifications for office and procedures for electing the president, and provides for a vice president.

Vocabulary

appropriations: funds set aside for a specific use

emolument: payment

impost: tax

duty: tax

[3.] The Electors shall meet in their respective States, and vote by Ballot for two Persons, of whom one at least shall not be an Inhabitant of the same State with themselves. And they shall make a List of all the Persons voted for, and of the Number of Votes for each; which List they shall sign and certify, and transmit sealed to the Seat of the Government of the United States, directed to the President of the Senate. The President of the Senate shall, in the Presence of the Senate and House of Representatives, open all the Certificates, and the Votes shall then be counted. The Person having the greatest Number of Votes shall be the President, if such Number be a Majority of the whole Number of Electors appointed; and if there be more than one who have such Majority, and have an equal Number of Votes, then the House of Representatives shall immediately chuse by Ballot one of them for President; and if no person have a Majority, then from the five highest on the List the said House shall in like Manner chuse the President. But in chusing the President, the Votes shall be taken by States, the Representation from each State having one Vote; A quorum for this Purpose shall consist of a Member or Members from two thirds of the States, and a Majority of all the States shall be necessary to a Choice. In every Case, after the Choice of the President, the Person having the greatest Number of Votes of the Electors shall be the Vice President. But if there should remain two or more who have equal Votes, the Senate shall chuse from them by Ballot the Vice President.

[4.] The Congress may determine the Time of chusing the Electors, and the Day on which they shall give their Votes; which Day shall be the same throughout the United States.

[5.] No Person except a natural born Citizen, or a Citizen of the United States, at the time of the Adoption of this Constitution, shall be eligible to the Office of President; neither shall any Person be eligible to that Office who shall not have attained to the Age of thirty five Years, and been fourteen Years a Resident within the United States.

[6.] In Case of the Removal of the President from Office, or of his Death, Resignation, or Inability to discharge the Powers and Duties of the said Office, the Same shall devolve on the Vice President, and the Congress may by Law provide for the Case of Removal, Death, Resignation or Inability, both of the President and Vice President, declaring what Officer shall then act as President, and such Officer shall act accordingly, until the Disability be removed, or a President shall be elected.

[7.] The President shall, at stated Times, receive for his Services, a Compensation, which shall neither be encreased nor diminished during the Period for which he shall have been elected, and he shall not receive within that Period any other Emolument from the United States, or any of them.

[8.] Before he enter on the Execution of his Office, he shall take the following Oath or Affirmation:—"I do solemnly swear (or affirm) that I will faithfully execute the Office of President of the United States, and will to the best of my Ability, preserve, protect and defend the Constitution of the United States."

Section 2

[1.] The President shall be Commander in Chief of the Army and Navy of the United States, and of the Militia of the several States, when called into the actual Service of the United States; he may require the Opinion, in writing, of the principal Officer in each of the executive Departments, upon any Subject relating to the Duties of their respective Offices, and he shall have Power to grant Reprieves and Pardons for Offences against the United States, except in Cases of Impeachment.

[2.] He shall have Power, by and with the Advice and Consent of the Senate, to make Treaties, provided two thirds of the Senators present concur; and he shall nominate, and by and with the Advice and Consent of the Senate, shall appoint Ambassadors, other public Ministers and Consuls, Judges of the supreme Court, and all other Officers of the United States, whose Appointments are not herein otherwise provided for, and which shall be established by Law: but the Congress may by Law vest the Appointment of such inferior Officers, as they think proper, in the President alone, in the Courts of Law, or in the Heads of Departments.

[3.] The President shall have Power to fill up all Vacancies that may happen during the Recess of the Senate, by granting Commissions which shall expire at the End of their next Session.

Section 3

He shall from time to time give to the Congress Information of the State of the Union, and recommend to their Consideration such Measures as he shall judge necessary and expedient; he may, on extraordinary Occasions, convene both Houses, or either of them, and in Case of Disagreement between them, with Respect to the Time of Adjournment, he may adjourn them to such Time as he shall think proper; he shall receive Ambassadors and other public Ministers; he shall take Care that the Laws be faithfully executed, and shall Commission all the Officers of the United States.

The Cabinet Mention of "the principal officer in each of the executive departments" is the only suggestion of the president's cabinet to be found in the Constitution. The cabinet is an advisory body, and its power depends on the president. Section 2, Clause 1 also makes the president—a civilian—the head of the armed services. This established the principle of civilian control of the military.

Presidential Powers An executive order is a command issued by a president to exercise a power which he or she has been given by the U.S. Constitution or by a federal statute. In times of emergency, presidents sometimes have used the executive order to override the Constitution and Congress. During the Civil War, President Lincoln suspended many fundamental rights, such as closing down newspapers that opposed his policies and imprisoning people who disagreed with him. Lincoln said that these actions were justified to preserve the Union.

Article III. The Judicial Branch The term judicial refers to courts. The Constitution set up only the Supreme Court, but provided for the establishment of other federal courts. The judiciary of the United States has two different systems of courts. One system consists of the federal courts, whose powers derive from the Constitution and federal laws. The other includes the courts of each of the 50 states, whose powers derive from state constitutions and laws.

Statute Law Federal courts deal mostly with "statute law," or laws passed by Congress, treaties, and cases involving the Constitution itself.

The Supreme Court A Court with "original jurisdiction" has the authority to be the first court to hear a case. The Supreme Court has "appellate jurisdiction" and mostly hears cases appealed from lower courts.

Vocabulary

original jurisdiction: authority to be the first court to hear a case

appellate jurisdiction: authority to hear cases that have been appealed from lower courts

Section 4

The President, Vice President and all civil Officers of the United States, shall be removed from Office on Impeachment for, and Conviction of, Treason, Bribery, or other high Crimes and Misdemeanors.

Article III
Section 1

The judicial Power of the United States, shall be vested in one supreme Court, and in such inferior Courts as the Congress may from time to time ordain and establish. The Judges, both of the supreme and inferior Courts, shall hold their Offices during good Behaviour, and shall, at stated Times, receive for their Services, a Compensation, which shall not be diminished during their Continuance in Office.

Section 2

[1.] The judicial Power shall extend to all Cases, in Law and Equity, arising under this Constitution, the Laws of the United States, and Treaties made, or which shall be made, under their Authority;—to all Cases affecting Ambassadors, other public Ministers and Consuls;—to all Cases of admiralty and maritime Jurisdiction;—to Controversies to which the United States shall be a Party;—to Controversies between two or more States;—between a State and Citizens of another State;—between Citizens of different States,—between Citizens of the same State claiming Lands under Grants of different States, and between a State, or the Citizens thereof, and foreign States, Citizens or Subjects.

[2.] In all Cases affecting Ambassadors, other public Ministers and Consuls, and those in which a State shall be Party, the supreme Court shall have original Jurisdiction. In all the other Cases before mentioned, the supreme Court shall have appellate Jurisdiction, both as to Law and Fact, with such Exceptions, and under such Regulations as the Congress shall make.

[3.] The Trial of all Crimes, except in Cases of Impeachment, shall be by Jury; and such Trial shall be held in the State where the said Crimes shall have been committed; but when not committed within any State, the Trial shall be at such Place or Places as the Congress may by Law have directed.

Section 3

[1.] Treason against the United States, shall consist only in levying War against them, or in adhering to their Enemies, giving them Aid and Comfort. No Person shall be convicted of Treason unless on the Testimony of two Witnesses to the same overt Act, or on Confession in open Court.

[2.] The Congress shall have Power to declare the Punishment of Treason, but no Attainder of Treason shall work Corruption of Blood, or Forfeiture except during the Life of the Person attainted.

Article IV

Section 1

Full Faith and Credit shall be given in each State to the public Acts, Records, and judicial Proceedings of every other State. And the Congress may by general Laws prescribe the Manner in which such Acts, Records and Proceedings shall be proved, and the Effect thereof.

Section 2

[1.] The Citizens of each State shall be entitled to all Privileges and Immunities of Citizens in the several States.

[2.] A Person charged in any State with Treason, Felony, or other Crime, who shall flee from Justice, and be found in another State, shall on Demand of the executive Authority of the State from which he fled, be delivered up, to be removed to the State having Jurisdiction of the Crime.

[3.] No Person held to Service of Labour in one State, under the Laws thereof, escaping into another, shall, in Consequence of any Law or Regulation therein, be discharged from such Service or Labour, but shall be delivered up on Claim of the Party to whom such Service or Labour may be due.

Section 3

[1.] New States may be admitted by the Congress into this Union; but no new State shall be formed or erected within the Jurisdiction of any other State; nor any State be formed by the Junction of two or more States, or Parts of States, without the Consent of the Legislatures of the States concerned as well as of the Congress.

[2.] The Congress shall have Power to dispose of and make all needful Rules and Regulations respecting the Territory or other Property belonging to the United States; and nothing in this Constitution shall be so construed as to Prejudice any Claims of the United States, or of any particular State.

Article IV. Relations Among the States Article IV explains the relationship of the states to one another and to the national government. This article requires each state to give citizens of other states the same rights as its own citizens, addresses admitting new states, and guarantees that the national government will protect the states.

New States Congress has the power to admit new states. It also determines the basic guidelines for applying for statehood. Two states, Maine and West Virginia, were created within the boundaries of another state. In the case of West Virginia, President Lincoln recognized the West Virginia government as the legal government of Virginia during the Civil War. This allowed West Virginia to secede from Virginia without obtaining approval from the Virginia legislature.

Vocabulary

treason: violation of the allegiance owed by a person to his or her own country, for example, by aiding an enemy

Section 4

The United States shall guarantee to every State in this Union a Republican Form of Government, and shall protect each of them against Invasion; and on Application of the Legislature, or of the Executive (when the Legislature cannot be convened) against domestic Violence.

Article V

The Congress, whenever two thirds of both Houses shall deem it necessary, shall propose **Amendments** to this Constitution, or, on the Application of the Legislatures of two thirds of the several States, shall call a Convention for proposing Amendments, which, in either Case, shall be valid to all Intents and Purposes, as Part of this Constitution, when ratified by the Legislatures of three fourths of the several States, or by Conventions in three fourths thereof, as the one or the other Mode of **Ratification** may be proposed by the Congress; Provided that no Amendment which may be made prior to the Year One thousand eight hundred and eight shall in any Manner affect the first and fourth Clauses in the Ninth Section of the first Article; and that no State, without its Consent, shall be deprived of its equal Suffrage in the Senate.

Article V. The Amendment Process
Article V spells out the ways that the Constitution can be amended, or changed. All of the 27 amendments were proposed by a two-thirds vote of both houses of Congress. Only the Twenty-first Amendment was ratified by constitutional conventions of the states. All other amendments have been ratified by state legislatures. *What is an amendment?*

Article VI

[1.] All Debts contracted and Engagements entered into, before the Adoption of this Constitution, shall be as valid against the United States under this Constitution, as under the Confederation.

[2.] This Constitution, and the Laws of the United States which shall be made in Pursuance thereof; and all Treaties made, or which shall be made, under the Authority of the United States, shall be the supreme Law of the Land; and the Judges in every State shall be bound thereby, any Thing in the Constitution or Laws of any State to the Contrary notwithstanding.

[3.] The Senators and Representatives before mentioned, and the Members of the several State Legislatures, and all executive and judicial Officers, both of the United States and of the several States, shall be bound by Oath or Affirmation, to support this Constitution; but no religious Test shall ever be required as a Qualification to any Office or public Trust under the United States.

Article VI. National Supremacy
Article VI contains the "supremacy clause." This clause establishes that the Constitution, laws passed by Congress, and treaties of the United States "shall be the supreme Law of the Land." The "supremacy clause" recognized the Constitution and federal laws as supreme when in conflict with those of the states.

Vocabulary

amendment: a change to the Constitution

ratification: process by which an amendment is approved

Article VII

The Ratification of the Conventions of nine States, shall be sufficient for the Establishment of this Constitution between the States so ratifying the Same.

Done in Convention by the Unanimous Consent of the States present the Seventeenth Day of September in the Year of our Lord one thousand seven hundred and Eighty seven and of the Independence of the United States of America the Twelfth. In witness whereof We have hereunto subscribed our Names,

> **Article VII. Ratification** Article VII addresses ratification and declares that the Constitution would take effect after it was ratified by nine states.

Signers

George Washington,
President and Deputy
from Virginia

New Hampshire
John Langdon
Nicholas Gilman

Massachusetts
Nathaniel Gorham
Rufus King

Connecticut
William Samuel Johnson
Roger Sherman

New York
Alexander Hamilton

New Jersey
William Livingston
David Brearley
William Paterson
Jonathan Dayton

Pennsylvania
Benjamin Franklin
Thomas Mifflin
Robert Morris
George Clymer
Thomas FitzSimons
Jared Ingersoll
James Wilson
Gouverneur Morris

Delaware
George Read
Gunning Bedford, Jr.
John Dickinson
Richard Bassett
Jacob Broom

Maryland
James McHenry
Daniel of St. Thomas Jenifer
Daniel Carroll

Virginia
John Blair
James Madison, Jr.

North Carolina
William Blount
Richard Dobbs Spaight
Hugh Williamson

South Carolina
John Rutledge
Charles Cotesworth
Pinckney
Charles Pinckney
Pierce Butler

Georgia
William Few
Abraham Baldwin

Attest: *William Jackson,*
Secretary

Bill of Rights The first 10 amendments are known as the Bill of Rights (1791). These amendments limit the powers of government. The First Amendment protects the civil liberties of individuals in the United States. The amendment freedoms are not absolute, however. They are limited by the rights of other individuals. *What freedoms does the First Amendment protect?*

Amendment I

Congress shall make no law respecting an establishment of religion, or prohibiting the free exercise thereof; or abridging the freedom of speech, or of the press; or the right of the people peaceably to assemble, and to petition the Government for a redress of grievances.

Amendment II

A well regulated Militia, being necessary to the security of a free State, the right of the people to keep and bear Arms, shall not be infringed.

Amendment III

No Soldier shall, in time of peace be **quartered** in any house, without the consent of the Owner, nor in time of war, but in a manner to be prescribed by law.

Amendment IV

The right of the people to be secure in their persons, houses, papers, and effects, against unreasonable searches and seizures, shall not be violated, and no **Warrants** shall issue, but upon **probable cause**, supported by Oath or affirmation, and particularly describing the place, to be searched, and the persons or things to be seized.

Rights of the Accused This amendment contains important protections for people accused of crimes. One of the protections is that government may not deprive any person of life, liberty, or property without due process of law. This means that the government must follow proper constitutional procedures in trials and in other actions it takes against individuals. *According to Amendment V, what is the function of a grand jury?*

Amendment V

No person shall be held to answer for a capital, or otherwise infamous crime, unless on a presentment or indictment of a Grand Jury, except in cases arising in the land or naval forces, or in the Militia, when in actual service in time of War or public danger; nor shall any person be subject for the same offence to be twice put in jeopardy of life or limb; nor shall be compelled in any criminal case to be a witness against himself, nor be deprived of life, liberty, or property, without due process of law; nor shall private property be taken for public use without just compensation.

Vocabulary

quarter: to provide living accommodations

warrant: document that gives police particular rights or powers

probable cause: a reasonable basis to believe a person is linked to a crime

common law: law established by previous court decisions

bail: money that an accused person provides to the court as a guarantee that he or she will be present for a trial

Amendment VI

In all criminal prosecutions, the accused shall enjoy the right to a speedy and public trial, by an impartial jury of the State and district wherein the crime shall have been committed, which district shall have been previously ascertained by law, and to be informed of the nature and cause of the accusation; to be confronted with the witnesses against him; to have compulsory process for obtaining Witnesses in his favor, and to have the assistance of counsel for his defence.

Rights to a Speedy, Fair Trial A basic protection is the right to a speedy, public trial. The jury must hear witnesses and evidence on both sides before deciding the guilt or innocence of a person charged with a crime. This amendment also provides that legal counsel must be provided to a defendant. In 1963, the Supreme Court ruled, in *Gideon* v. *Wainwright*, that if a defendant cannot afford a lawyer, the government must provide one to defend him or her. *Why is the right to a "speedy" trial important?*

Amendment VII

In Suits at common law, where the value in controversy shall exceed twenty dollars, the right of trial by jury shall be preserved, and no fact tried by a jury, shall be otherwise reexamined in any Court of the United States, than according to the rules of common law.

Amendment VIII

Excessive bail shall not be required, nor excessive fines imposed, nor cruel and unusual punishments inflicted.

Powers of the People This amendment prevents government from claiming that the only rights people have are those listed in the Bill of Rights.

Amendment IX

The enumeration in the Constitution, of certain rights, shall not be construed to deny or disparage others retained by the people.

Powers of the States The final amendment of the Bill of Rights protects the states and the people from an all-powerful federal government. It establishes that powers not given to the national government—or denied to the states—by the Constitution belong to the states or to the people.

Amendment X

The powers not delegated to the United States by the Constitution, nor prohibited by it to the States, are reserved to the States respectively, or to the people.

Amendment XI

The Judicial power of the United States shall not be construed to extend to any suit in law or equity, commenced or prosecuted against one of the United States by Citizens of another State, or by Citizens or Subjects of any Foreign State.

Suits Against States The Eleventh Amendment (1795) limits the jurisdiction of the federal courts. The Supreme Court had ruled that a federal court could try a lawsuit brought by citizens of South Carolina against a citizen of Georgia. This case, *Chisholm* v. *Georgia*, decided in 1793, raised a storm of protest, leading to passage of the Eleventh Amendment.

Amendment XII

The electors shall meet in their respective states and vote by ballot for President and Vice-President, one of whom, at least, shall not be an inhabitant of the same state with themselves; they shall name in their ballots the person voted for as President, and in distinct ballots the person voted for as Vice-President, and they shall make distinct lists of all persons voted for as President, and of all persons voted for as Vice-President, and of the number of votes for each, which lists they shall sign and certify, and transmit sealed to the seat of the government of the United States, directed to the President of the Senate;—The President of the Senate shall, in the presence of the Senate and House of Representatives, open all the certificates and the votes shall then be counted;—The person having the greatest number of votes for President, shall be the President, if such number be a majority of the whole number of Electors appointed; and if no person have such majority, then from the persons having the highest numbers not exceeding three on the list of those voted for as President, the House of Representatives shall choose immediately, by ballot, the President. But in choosing the President, the votes shall be taken by states, the representation from each state having one vote; a quorum for this purpose shall consist of a member or members from two-thirds of the states, and a majority of all the states shall be necessary to a choice. And if the House of Representatives shall not choose a President whenever the right of choice shall devolve upon them, before the fourth day of March next following, then the Vice-President shall act as President, as in the case of the death or other constitutional disability of the President. The person having the greatest number of votes as Vice-President, shall be the Vice-President, if such number be a majority of the whole number of Electors appointed, and if no person have a majority, then from the two highest numbers on the list, the Senate shall choose the Vice-President; a quorum for the purpose shall consist of two-thirds of the whole number of Senators, and a majority of the whole number shall be necessary to a choice. But no person constitutionally ineligible to the office of President shall be eligible to that of Vice-President of the United States.

Vocabulary

common law: law established by previous court decisions

bail: money that an accused person provides to the court as a guarantee that he or she will be present for a trial

majority: more than half

devolve: to pass on

Amendment XIII

Section 1

Neither slavery nor involuntary servitude, except as a punishment for crime whereof the party shall have been duly convicted, shall exist within the United States, or any place subject to their jurisdiction.

Section 2

Congress shall have power to enforce this article by appropriate legislation.

Amendment XIV

Section 1

All persons born or naturalized in the United States, and subject to the jurisdiction thereof, are citizens of the United States and of the State wherein they reside. No State shall make or enforce any law which shall abridge the privileges or immunities of citizens of the United States; nor shall any State deprive any person of life, liberty, or property, without due process of law; nor deny to any person within its jurisdiction the equal protection of the laws.

Section 2

Representatives shall be apportioned among the several States according to their respective numbers, counting the whole number of persons in each State, excluding Indians not taxed. But when the right to vote at any election for the choice of electors for President and Vice President of the United States, Representatives in Congress, the Executive and Judicial officers of a State, or the members of the Legislature thereof, is denied to any of the male inhabitants of such State, being twenty-one years of age, and citizens of the United States, or in any way abridged, except for participation in rebellion, or other crime, the basis of representation therein shall be reduced in the proportion which the number of such male citizens shall bear to the whole number of male citizens twenty-one years of age in such State.

Section 3

No person shall be a Senator or Representative in Congress, or elector of President and Vice President, or hold any office, civil or military, under the United States, or under any State, who, having previously taken an oath, as a member of Congress, or as an officer of the United States, or as a member of any State legislature, or as an executive or judicial officer of any State, to support the Constitution

Abolition of Slavery Amendments Thirteen (1865), Fourteen (1868), and Fifteen (1870) often are called the Civil War amendments because they grew out of that great conflict. The Thirteenth Amendment outlaws slavery.

Rights of Citizens The Fourteenth Amendment (1868) originally was intended to protect the legal rights of the freed slaves. Today it protects the rights of citizenship in general by prohibiting a state from depriving any person of life, liberty, or property without "due process of law." In addition, it states that all citizens have the right to equal protection of the law in all states.

Representation in Congress This section reduced the number of members a state had in the House of Representatives if it denied its citizens the right to vote. Later civil rights laws and the Twenty-fourth Amendment guaranteed the vote to African Americans.

Vocabulary

apportionment: distribution of seats in House based on population

abridge: to reduce

of the United States, shall have engaged in insurrection or rebellion against the same, or given aid or comfort to the enemies thereof. But Congress may by a vote of two-thirds of each House, remove such disability.

Section 4

The validity of the public debt of the United States, authorized by law, including debts incurred for payment of pensions and bounties for service in suppressing insurrection or rebellion, shall not be questioned. But neither the United States nor any State shall assume or pay any debt or obligation incurred in aid of insurrection or rebellion against the United States, or any claim for the loss or emancipation of any slave; but all such debts, obligations and claims shall be held illegal and void.

Section 5

The Congress shall have power to enforce, by appropriate legislation, the provisions of this article.

Amendment XV

Section 1

The right of citizens of the United States to vote shall not be denied or abridged by the United States or by any State on account of race, color, or previous condition of servitude.

Section 2

The Congress shall have power to enforce this article by appropriate legislation.

Amendment XVI

The Congress shall have power to lay and collect taxes on incomes, from whatever source derived, without apportionment among the several States and without regard to any census or enumeration.

Amendment XVII

Section 1

The Senate of the United States shall be composed of two Senators from each State, elected by the people thereof, for six years; and each Senator shall have one vote. The electors in each State shall have the qualifications requisite for electors of the most numerous branch of the State legislatures.

Public Debt The public debt acquired by the federal government during the Civil War was valid and could not be questioned by the South. However, the debts of the Confederacy were declared to be illegal. *Could former slaveholders collect payment for the loss of their slaves?*

Right to Vote The Fifteenth Amendment (1870) prohibits the government from denying a person's right to vote on the basis of race. Despite the law, many states denied African Americans the right to vote by such means as poll taxes, literacy tests, and white primaries. During the 1950s and 1960s, Congress passed successively stronger laws to end racial discrimination in voting rights.

Election of Senators The Seventeenth Amendment (1913) states that the people, instead of state legislatures, elect United States senators. *How many years are in a Senate term?*

Vocabulary

insurrection: rebellion against the government

emancipation: freedom from slavery

Section 2

When vacancies happen in the representation of any State in the Senate, the executive authority of such State shall issue writs of election to fill such vacancies: *Provided*, That the legislature of any State may empower the executive thereof to make temporary appointments until the people fill the vacancies by election as the legislature may direct.

Section 3

This amendment shall not be so construed as to affect the election or term of any Senator chosen before it becomes valid as part of the Constitution.

Amendment XVIII
Section 1

After one year from ratification of this article, the manufacture, sale, or transportation of intoxicating liquors within, the importation thereof into, or the exportation thereof from the United States and all territory subject to the jurisdiction thereof for beverage purposes is hereby prohibited.

Section 2

The Congress and the several States shall have concurrent power to enforce this article by appropriate legislation.

Section 3

This article shall be inoperative unless it shall have been ratified as an amendment to the Constitution by the legislatures of the several States, as provided in the Constitution, within seven years from the date of the submission hereof to the States by the Congress.

Prohibition The Eighteenth Amendment (1919) prohibited the production, sale, or transportation of alcoholic beverages in the United States. Prohibition proved to be difficult to enforce. This amendment was later repealed by the Twenty-first Amendment.

Amendment XIX
Section 1

The right of citizens of the United States to vote shall not be denied or abridged by the United States or by any State on account of sex.

Section 2

Congress shall have power by appropriate legislation to enforce the provisions of this article.

Woman Suffrage The Nineteenth Amendment (1920) guaranteed women the right to vote. By then women had already won the right to vote in many state elections, but the amendment put their right to vote in all state and national elections on a constitutional basis.

"Lame-Duck" Amendments The Twentieth Amendment (1933) sets new dates for Congress to begin its term and for the inauguration of the president and vice president. Under the original Constitution, elected officials who retired or who had been defeated remained in office for several months. For the outgoing president, this period ran from November until March. Such outgoing officials had little influence and accomplished little, and they were called lame ducks because they were so inactive. *What date was fixed as Inauguration Day?*

Succession This section provides that if the president-elect dies before taking office, the vice president-elect becomes president.

Amendment XX

Section 1

The terms of the President and Vice President shall end at noon on the 20th day of January, and the terms of the Senators and Representatives at noon on the 3d day of January, of the years in which such terms would have ended if this article had not been ratified; and the terms of their successors shall then begin.

Section 2

The Congress shall assemble at least once in every year, and such meeting shall begin at noon on the 3d day of January, unless they shall by law appoint a different day.

Section 3

If, at the time fixed for the beginning of the term of the President, the President elect shall have died, the Vice President elect shall become President. If a President shall not have been chosen before the time fixed for the beginning of his term, or if the President elect shall have failed to qualify, then the Vice President elect shall act as President until a President shall have qualified; and the Congress may by law provide for the case wherein neither a President elect nor a Vice President elect shall have qualified, declaring who shall then act as President, or the manner in which one who is to act shall be selected, and such person shall act accordingly until a President or Vice President shall have qualified.

Section 4

The Congress may by law provide for the case of the death of any of the persons from whom the House of Representatives may choose a President whenever the right of choice shall have devolved upon them, and for the case of the death of any of the persons from whom the Senate may choose a Vice President whenever the right of choice shall have devolved upon them.

Section 5

Section 1 and 2 shall take effect on the 15th day of October following the ratification of this article.

Vocabulary

president elect: individual who is elected president but has not yet begun serving his or her term

Section 6

This article shall be inoperative unless it shall have been ratified as an amendment to the Constitution by the legislatures of three-fourths of the several States within seven years from the date of its submission.

Amendment XXI

Section 1

The eighteenth article of amendment to the Constitution of the United States is hereby repealed.

Section 2

The transportation or importation into any State, Territory, or possession of the United States for delivery or use therein of intoxicating liquors, in violation of the laws thereof, is hereby prohibited.

Section 3

This article shall be inoperative unless it shall have been ratified as an amendment to the Constitution by conventions in the several States, as provided in the Constitution, within seven years from the date of the submission hereof to the States by the Congress.

Repeal of Prohibition The Twenty-first Amendment (1933) repeals the Eighteenth Amendment. It is the only amendment ever passed to overturn an earlier amendment. It is also the only amendment ratified by special state conventions instead of state legislatures.

Amendment XXII

Section 1

No person shall be elected to the office of the President more than twice, and no person who had held the office of President, or acted as President, for more than two years of a term to which some other person was elected President shall be elected to the office of the President more than once. But this Article shall not apply to any person holding the office of President when this Article was proposed by the Congress, and shall not prevent any person who may be holding the office of President, or acting as President, during the term within which this Article becomes operative from holding the office of President or acting as President during the remainder of such term.

Section 2

This article shall be inoperative unless it shall have been ratified as an amendment to the Constitution by the legislatures of three-fourths of the several States within seven years from the date of its submission to the States by the Congress.

Term Limit The Twenty-second Amendment (1951) limits presidents to a maximum of two elected terms. It was passed largely as a reaction to Franklin D. Roosevelt's election to four terms between 1933 and 1945.

Amendment XXIII

Section 1

The District constituting the seat of Government of the United States shall appoint in such manner as the Congress may direct:

A number of electors of President and Vice President equal to the whole number of Senators and Representatives in Congress to which the District would be entitled if it were a State, but in no event more than the least populous State; they shall be in addition to those appointed by the States, but they shall be considered, for the purposes of the election of President and Vice President, to be electors appointed by a State; and they shall meet in the District and perform such duties as provided by the twelfth article of amendment.

Section 2

The Congress shall have power to enforce this article by appropriate legislation.

Amendment XXIV

Section 1

The right of citizens of the United States to vote in any primary or other election for President or Vice President, for electors for President or Vice President, or for Senator or Representative in Congress, shall not be denied or abridged by the United States or any State by reason of failure to pay any poll tax or other tax.

Section 2

The Congress shall have power to enforce this article by appropriate legislation.

Amendment XXV

Section 1

In case of the removal of the President from office or his death or resignation, the Vice President shall become President.

Section 2

Whenever there is a vacancy in the office of the Vice President, the President shall nominate a Vice President who shall take the office upon confirmation by a majority vote of both Houses of Congress.

Section 3

Whenever the President transmits to the President pro tempore of the Senate and the Speaker of the House of Representatives his written declaration that he is unable to discharge the powers and duties of his office, and until he transmits to them a written declaration to the contrary, such powers and duties shall be discharged by the Vice President as Acting President.

Section 4

Whenever the Vice President and a majority of either the principal officers of the executive departments or of such other body as Congress may by law provide, transmit to the President pro tempore of the Senate and the Speaker of the House of Representatives their written declaration that the President is unable to discharge the powers and duties of his office, the Vice President shall immediately assume the power and duties of the office of Acting President.

Thereafter, when the President transmits to the President pro tempore of the Senate and the Speaker of the House of Representatives his written declaration that no inability exists, he shall resume the powers and duties of his office unless the Vice President and a majority of either the principal officers of the executive department or of such other body as Congress may by law provide, transmit within four days to the President pro tempore of the Senate and the Speaker of the House of Representatives their written declaration that the President is unable to discharge the powers and duties of his office. Thereupon Congress shall decide the issue, assembling within forty-eight hours for that purpose if not in session. If the Congress, within twenty-one days after receipt of the latter written declaration, or, if Congress is not in session, within twenty-one days after Congress is required to assemble, determines by two-thirds vote of both Houses that the President is unable to discharge the powers and duties of his office, the Vice President shall continue to discharge the same as Acting President; otherwise, the President shall resume the power and duties of his office.

Amendment XXVI

Section 1

The right of citizens of the United States, who are eighteen years of age or older, to vote shall not be denied or abridged by the United States or by any State on account of age.

Voting Age The Twenty-sixth Amendment (1971) lowered the voting age in both federal and state elections to 18.

Time & Life Images/Getty Images

Section 2

The Congress shall have power to enforce this article by appropriate legislation.

Amendment XXVII

No law, varying the compensation for the services of Senators and Representatives, shall take effect, until an election of representatives shall have intervened.

Congressional Pay Raises The Twenty-seventh Amendment (1992) makes congressional pay raises effective during the term following their passage. James Madison offered the amendment in 1789, but it was never adopted. In 1982 Gregory Watson, then a student at the University of Texas, discovered the forgotten amendment while doing research for a school paper. Watson made the amendment's passage his crusade.

▼ **Joint meeting of Congress**

The Federalist Era

1789–1800

ESSENTIAL QUESTIONS • *What are the characteristics of a leader?*
• *Why does conflict develop?* • *How do governments change?*

The Story Matters . . .

Abigail Adams is thoughtful and smart. Like other women of her day, she does not lead a public life. Yet to her husband—patriot and now President John Adams—she is a trusted adviser.

During her husband's presidency, she watches with a keen eye as the first political parties form. She helps her husband identify his true friends—and his secret enemies.

Her involvement in politics shocks some. For a time, it even costs her a dear friendship with Thomas Jefferson.

The division of the nation into different political parties was a trying time for the United States. It was one of the challenges facing the young nation in the Federalist Era.

◄ *Abigail Adams played a major role in the career of John Adams, one of the leading figures in early American history.*

The Granger Collection, NYC

Chapter 9

Place and Time: United States 1789 to 1800

In 1790 the United States occupied the eastern areas of the continent, but people were moving to the West. There were fewer states than today, but some were larger than they are now. Other countries controlled much of the land that now makes up the nation. Some areas were claimed by more than one country.

Step Into the Place

MAP FOCUS The United States in 1790 was concentrated on the East Coast and surrounding areas.

1 LOCATION Look at the map. Where is your state located? Did your state exist in 1790?

2 LOCATION What other countries had territory near the new United States?

3 CRITICAL THINKING
Making Inferences What does this map suggest about why settlers in the United States were moving west?

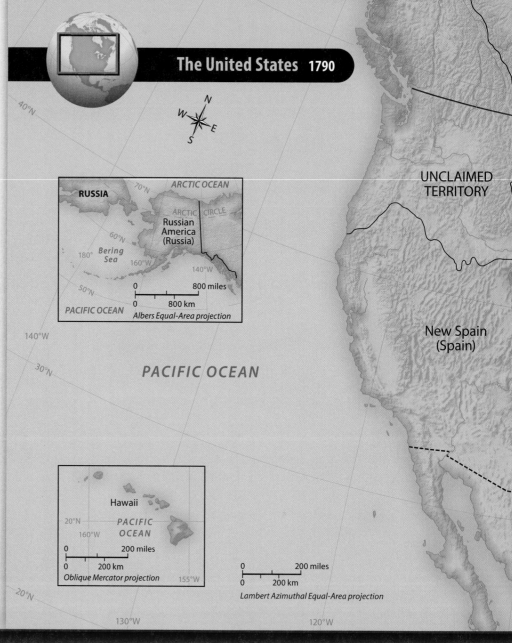

The United States 1790

RUSSIA

ARCTIC OCEAN

ARCTIC CIRCLE

Russian America (Russia)

Bering Sea

PACIFIC OCEAN

0   800 miles
0   800 km
Albers Equal-Area projection

PACIFIC OCEAN

Hawaii

PACIFIC OCEAN

0   200 miles
0   200 km
Oblique Mercator projection

0   200 miles
0   200 km
Lambert Azimuthal Equal-Area projection

UNCLAIMED TERRITORY

New Spain (Spain)

Step Into the Time

TIME LINE What events on this time line suggest that the United States was early in its history as a nation?

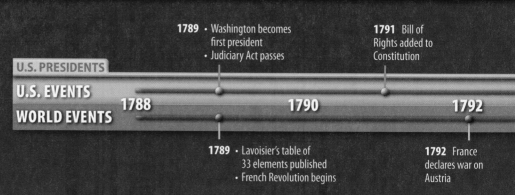

U.S. PRESIDENTS

U.S. EVENTS

WORLD EVENTS

1788

1790

1792

1789 • Washington becomes first president
• Judiciary Act passes

1791 Bill of Rights added to Constitution

1789 • Lavoisier's table of 33 elements published
• French Revolution begins

1792 France declares war on Austria

networks

There's More Online!

☑ **MAP** Explore the interactive version of this map on NETWORKS.

☑ **TIME LINE** Explore the interactive version of this time line on NETWORKS.

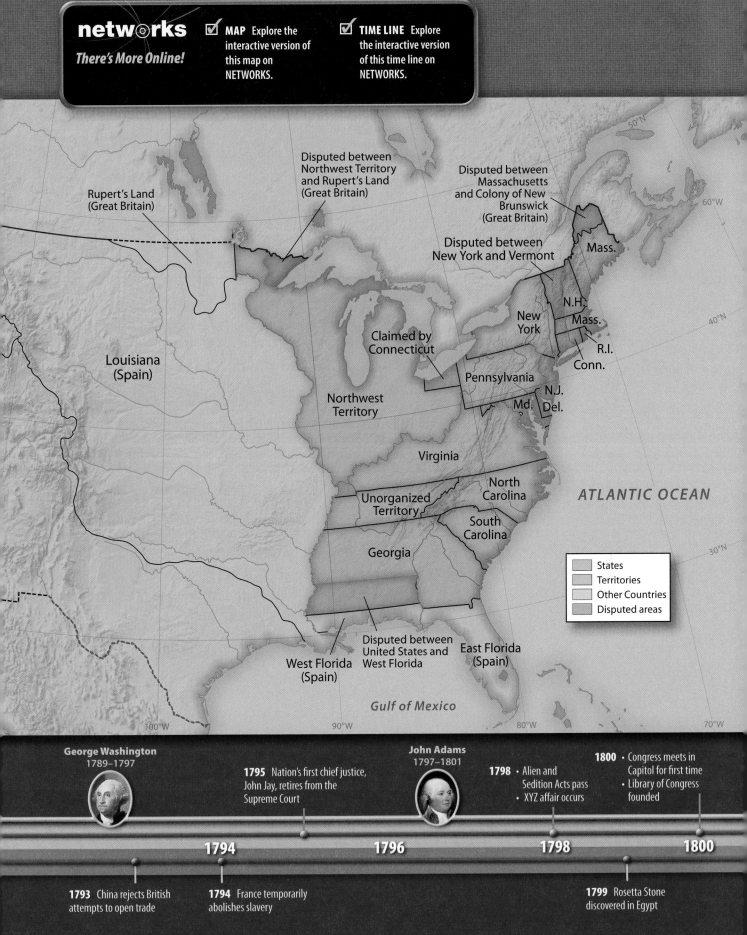

Rupert's Land (Great Britain)

Disputed between Northwest Territory and Rupert's Land (Great Britain)

Disputed between Massachusetts and Colony of New Brunswick (Great Britain)

Disputed between New York and Vermont

Mass.

N.H

Mass.

New York

R.I.

Conn.

Louisiana (Spain)

Claimed by Connecticut

Pennsylvania

N.J.

Md. Del.

Northwest Territory

Virginia

North Carolina

ATLANTIC OCEAN

Unorganized Territory

South Carolina

Georgia

States
Territories
Other Countries
Disputed areas

Disputed between United States and West Florida

West Florida (Spain)

East Florida (Spain)

Gulf of Mexico

50°N

60°W

40°N

30°N

70°W

100°W   90°W   80°W

George Washington
1789–1797

1795 Nation's first chief justice, John Jay, retires from the Supreme Court

John Adams
1797–1801

1798 • Alien and Sedition Acts pass
• XYZ affair occurs

1800 • Congress meets in Capitol for first time
• Library of Congress founded

1794   **1796**   **1798**   **1800**

1793 China rejects British attempts to open trade

1794 France temporarily abolishes slavery

1799 Rosetta Stone discovered in Egypt

Lesson 1

The First President

ESSENTIAL QUESTION *What are the characteristics of a leader?*

IT MATTERS BECAUSE

George Washington and his administration established many customs and processes that are still in place today.

Washington Takes Office

GUIDING QUESTION *What decisions did Washington and the new Congress have to make about the new government?*

Under the Articles of Confederation, the United States had several presidents. Their job was to lead Congress, and they were not strong chief executives. The government under the Articles was weak and ineffective. When delegates met to reform the government, they wrote a new Constitution that included a strong executive branch headed by a single president.

On April 30, 1789, George Washington took the oath of office as the first president of the United States under that new Constitution. John Adams became vice president.

Washington knew that his actions and decisions would set **precedents** (PREH•suh•duhnts), or traditions, that would help shape the nation's future. "No slip will pass unnoticed," he said. Washington worked closely with Congress to create an effective government. In those first years, the president and Congress created departments within the executive branch and set up the court system. Congress added the Bill of Rights to the Constitution. Washington set the standard for how long a president should serve and for how the nation should relate to other nations.

Reading HELPDESK

Taking Notes: *Describing*

As you read, use a table like this one to describe important figures in the nation's early years. Use as many as seven rows.

Name	Role
George Washington	
	Vice President

Content Vocabulary
- **precedent**
- **cabinet**
- **bond**

The Cabinet

The executive branch of government took shape during the summer of 1789. Congress set up three departments and two offices within the executive branch. Washington chose leading political figures to head them. He picked Thomas Jefferson to head the State Department, which handles relations with other nations. He named Alexander Hamilton to manage the nation's money at the Department of the Treasury. Henry Knox was the choice to look after the nation's defense as the secretary of the Department of War. To address the government's legal affairs, Washington chose Edmund Randolph to be attorney general. Congress also created the office of postmaster general.

The three department heads and the attorney general had many important duties. Among them was giving advice to the president. Together, this group of top executive advisers formed what is called a **cabinet**.

Congress was unsure how much power the president ought to have over the cabinet. In a vote on this question, senators were evenly divided. Vice President John Adams broke the tie. He voted to allow the president the power to dismiss cabinet officers without Senate approval. This established presidential power over the whole executive branch.

Establishing the Court System

The first Congress also faced the job of forming the nation's court system. Some favored a **uniform** legal system for the entire nation. Others favored keeping the existing state systems. The two sides reached an agreement in the Judiciary Act of 1789. This act established a federal court system. The states kept their own laws and courts, but the federal courts had the power to reverse state decisions. The act marked a first step in creating a strong and independent national judicial system.

President Washington (far right) relied on the expert advice of this cabinet. Henry Knox is seated at left. Next to him are Thomas Jefferson, Edmund Randolph (back turned), and Alexander Hamilton.

The Granger Collection, NYC

precedent something done or said that becomes an example for others to follow

cabinet a group of advisers to a president

Academic Vocabulary

uniform of the same form with others

Making Comparisons

In 1791 Congress created a federal court system with three levels. Those three levels today include the district courts at the lower level, the appeals courts in the middle, and the Supreme Court at the top. Use the Internet to research this system, and create a chart or diagram that compares the powers of each level. For more information about making comparisons, read *Thinking Like a Historian.*

The Constitution established the Supreme Court as the final authority on many issues. President Washington chose John Jay to lead the Supreme Court as chief justice. The Senate approved Jay's nomination.

The Bill of Rights

Americans had fought a revolution to gain independence from British control. They did not want to replace one unjust government with another one. As protection from the powers of a strong national government, many Americans wanted the Constitution to include a bill of rights. It would guarantee civil liberties. In fact, some states had agreed to ratify the Constitution only with the promise that a bill of rights be added.

To fulfill this promise, James Madison introduced a set of amendments during the first session of Congress. Congress passed 12 amendments, and the states ratified 10 of them. In December 1791, these 10 amendments, together called the Bill of Rights, became part of the Constitution.

The Bill of Rights limits the power of government. It protects individual liberty, including freedom of speech and the rights of people accused of crimes. The Tenth Amendment says that any power not listed in the Constitution belongs to the states or the people. Madison hoped this amendment would help protect Americans against a national government that was too powerful.

✅ PROGRESS CHECK

Listing What were three important actions taken by Washington and the first Congress?

The Supreme Court Building, built in 1935, is the seat of the Supreme Court of the United States.

Tom Brakefield / Getty Images

Reading Strategy: *Determining Cause and Effect*

A cause is an event that triggers some event. An effect is the event that occurs as a result of the cause. Read about the Bill of Rights. Identify the cause that triggered the effect—the ratification of the Bill of Rights.

bond certificate that promises to repay borrowed money in the future—plus an additional amount of money, called interest.

The New Economy

GUIDING QUESTION *How did the economy develop under the guidance of Alexander Hamilton?*

As president, Washington focused on foreign affairs and military matters. He rarely suggested new laws and almost always approved the bills that Congress passed. For the government's economic policies, the president depended on Alexander Hamilton, secretary of the treasury. Hamilton was in his early thirties when he took office, but he had bold plans and clear policies in mind.

Hamilton faced a difficult task. The federal and state governments had borrowed money to pay for the American Revolution. They now owed millions of dollars to other countries and to American citizens. As a result, the nation faced serious financial trouble. Hamilton tried to improve the government's finances and strengthen the nation at the same time.

Hamilton's Plan

The House of Representatives asked Hamilton to make a plan for the "adequate support of the public credit." This meant that the United States needed a way to borrow money for its government and economy. To be able to borrow in the future, the government had to prove it could pay back the money it already owed.

Hamilton proposed that the federal government take over and pay off the states' wartime debts. He argued that paying off the debt as a nation would build national credit and make it easier for the nation to borrow money. Hamilton also believed that federal payment of state debts would give the states a strong interest in the success of the national government.

The Plan Faces Opposition

Congress agreed to part of Hamilton's plan—to pay the money owed to other nations. However, Hamilton's plan to pay off the debt owed to American citizens caused protest.

When borrowing money from citizens during the American Revolution, the government issued **bonds**. These are notes that promise repayment of borrowed money in the future.

Alexander Hamilton shaped the new nation's economy.

▶ **CRITICAL THINKING**

Explaining Why did Hamilton propose that the federal government pay off the states' wartime debts?

PROTECTIVE TARIFFS

In the late 1700s, American industries lacked experience. As a result, it often cost American manufacturers more to make a product than it cost foreign makers. To raise the price of imported products, the U.S. government used tariffs. This helped protect American industries by making foreign-made goods more expensive and, therefore, less attractive to American buyers.

BREAKDOWN OF COST

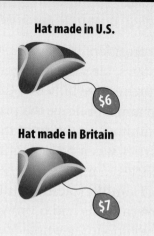

U.S.
- Profit: $1
- Cost to produce: $5

Britain
- Tariff: $2
- Profit: $1
- Cost to produce: $4

Hat made in U.S. $6

Hat made in Britain $7

ECONOMICS SKILL

Tariffs affected the price consumers paid for goods.

1 COMPARING Use the figures above to create a line graph for the cost of producing 100 hats in the United States and 100 hats in Britain. Which is greater?

2 COMPARING Now graph the cost of buying 100 American-made and 100 British-made hats with the tariff. Which is greater?

3 CRITICAL THINKING
Speculating How might the issue of U.S.-imposed tariffs impact U.S. relations with Britain?

While waiting for repayment, many bond owners—shopkeepers, farmers, and soldiers—sold their bonds. They accepted less money than the bonds' stated value. Often, the buyers of these bonds were speculators, people who risk money in hopes of making a large profit in the future.

Now, Hamilton was proposing to pay off the old bonds at full value. This would make the speculators rich. The original bondholders would get nothing. Many people were upset by this idea. One newspaper said Hamilton's plan was "established at the expense of national justice, gratitude, and humanity."

Even stronger opposition came from the Southern states. These states had **accumulated**, or built up, much less debt than the Northern states. Several had already repaid their debts. Yet Hamilton wanted the entire nation to pay all the debt together. Southern states complained about having to help pay other states' debts.

Compromise and a Capital

To win support for his plan, Hamilton worked out a **compromise** with Southern leaders. If they voted for his plan to pay off the state debts, he would support locating the nation's capital in the South.

Congress ordered a special district to be laid out between Virginia and Maryland along the banks of the Potomac River. There, George Washington chose the site for the new capital city, later named Washington, D.C., in his honor. While workers prepared the new city, the nation's capital shifted from New York to Philadelphia.

Reading **HELP**DESK

Academic Vocabulary

accumulate to build up or collect
compromise a settlement of a disagreement reached by each side giving up some of what it wants in order to reach an agreement

The Fight for a National Bank

Hamilton also asked Congress to create a national bank—the Bank of the United States. The proposed bank would hold government funds and make debt payments. It would also issue a single form of money for use throughout the nation. At that time, different states and banks issued their own currencies. Having a national currency would make trade and all other financial actions much easier.

Madison and Jefferson opposed a national bank, believing it would help the wealthy. They argued that the Constitution did not give Congress the power to create a bank. Hamilton believed the Constitution indirectly gave Congress power to create a bank when it gave Congress power to collect taxes and borrow money. Washington agreed, and Congress created the national bank.

Tariffs and Taxes

Hamilton believed that the United States needed more manufacturing. He proposed high tariffs—taxes on imports. The tariffs would raise money for the government and protect American industries from foreign competition. The South had little industry and opposed such tariffs. Congress passed only low tariffs. Hamilton also called for national taxes to help the government pay the national debt. Congress approved several taxes, including a tax on whiskey made in the United States.

Hamilton's ideas created conflict. Jefferson and Madison worried that Hamilton was building a dangerously powerful government run by the wealthy. They began to organize opposition to Hamilton and the policies he favored.

✓ PROGRESS CHECK

Explaining Why did some people oppose Hamilton's plan to pay off government bonds?

LESSON 1 REVIEW

Review Vocabulary

1. Use the following two words in a sentence about the first Washington presidency.

   a. precedent   **b.** cabinet

2. Explain the significance of the word *bond* to this era of United States history.

Answer the Guiding Questions

3. *Recalling* What decisions did Washington and the first Congress have to make about the new government?

4. *Summarizing* How did the economy develop under the guidance of Alexander Hamilton?

5. **EXPOSITORY WRITING** Why do you think George Washington's presidency was so important in the development of the young nation? Write a paragraph to explain.

networks

There's More Online!

☑ **BIOGRAPHY** John Jay

☑ **GAME** Fill in the Blank

☑ **GRAPHIC ORGANIZER** Effects of Treaties

☑ **MAP** Native American Campaigns

☑ **PRIMARY SOURCE** Treaty of Greenville

☑ **VIDEO**

Lesson 2
Early Challenges

ESSENTIAL QUESTION *Why does conflict develop?*

IT MATTERS BECAUSE
George Washington's strong leadership brought stability to the young government.

Trouble in the New Nation

GUIDING QUESTION *What challenges on the frontier did the new government face?*

Washington faced difficult challenges while in office. Britain and France were pushing the United States to get more involved in their conflicts. President Washington stood firm against this pressure. Native Americans, aided by the British and Spanish, fought the westward advance of American settlers. In addition, there was growing unrest from within the American population.

The Whiskey Rebellion

The new government wanted to collect taxes on some products made in the United States. In 1791 Congress passed a tax on the manufacture and sale of whiskey, a type of alcohol made from grain. Western Pennsylvania farmers were especially upset by this tax. Their anger turned into violence in July 1794. An armed mob attacked tax collectors and burned down buildings. This protest, called the Whiskey Rebellion, alarmed government leaders. They viewed it as a challenge to the power of the new government. Washington sent federal troops to meet the challenge. His action sent a strong message to the public: The government would use force to **maintain** order.

Reading **HELP**DESK

Taking Notes: *Determining Cause and Effect*

As you read, use a diagram like this one to describe how the treaties mentioned in this lesson affected the United States.

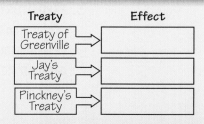

Treaty	Effect
Treaty of Greenville	
Jay's Treaty	
Pinckney's Treaty	

Content Vocabulary
• **impressment**

Challenges in the West

Washington worried about ongoing European interest in the Northwest Territory. The British and Spanish were trying to stir up Native American anger against American settlers in the region. To block these efforts, Washington signed treaties with Native American groups. Yet American settlers ignored the treaties and moved onto lands promised to Native Americans. Fighting broke out between the two groups.

Again, Washington decided to use force. He sent an army under General Arthur St. Clair to restore order in the Northwest Territory. In November 1791, St. Clair's army met a strong Native American force led by Little Turtle, a Miami chief. More than 600 U.S. soldiers died in the battle. It was the worst defeat U.S. forces had ever suffered against Native Americans.

Americans hoped an alliance with France would help them achieve full control in the West. The possibility of French involvement led Great Britain to take action. In 1794 the British urged Native Americans to destroy American settlements west of the Appalachians. The British also began building a new fort in Ohio.

Native Americans demanded that settlers who were living north of the Ohio River leave the area. In response, Washington sent Anthony Wayne, a Revolutionary War general, to the region.

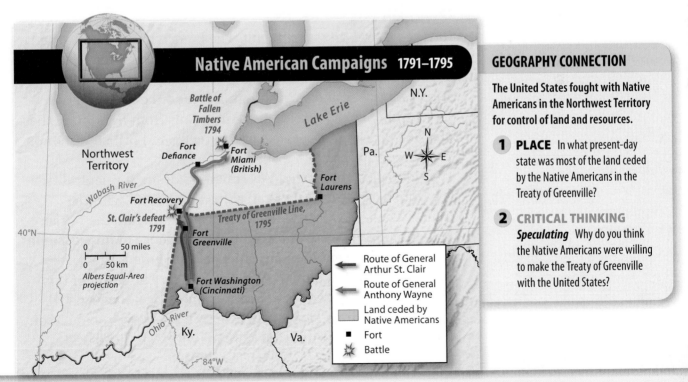

Native American Campaigns 1791–1795

Battle of Fallen Timbers 1794

Northwest Territory

Fort Defiance

Fort Miami (British)

Wabash River

Fort Recovery

St. Clair's defeat 1791

Fort Greenville

Treaty of Greenville Line, 1795

Fort Laurens

Fort Washington (Cincinnati)

Ohio River

Lake Erie

N.Y.

Pa.

Ky.

Va.

40°N

84°W

0   50 miles
0   50 km
Albers Equal-Area projection

Route of General Arthur St. Clair
Route of General Anthony Wayne
Land ceded by Native Americans
■ Fort
✳ Battle

GEOGRAPHY CONNECTION

The United States fought with Native Americans in the Northwest Territory for control of land and resources.

1 PLACE In what present-day state was most of the land ceded by the Native Americans in the Treaty of Greenville?

2 CRITICAL THINKING
Speculating Why do you think the Native Americans were willing to make the Treaty of Greenville with the United States?

Academic Vocabulary

maintain to keep

John Jay (1745–1829)

John Jay attended college at the age of 14 and the First Continental Congress at the age of 28. Later, with Alexander Hamilton and James Madison, he wrote essays for *The Federalist* defending the Constitution.

George Washington appointed Jay the first chief justice of the United States in 1789. To avoid war with Great Britain, Jay negotiated Jay's Treaty. This unpopular treaty ruined his chances for the presidency.

▶ **CRITICAL THINKING**
Making Inferences What can you infer about Jay based on his accomplishments in life?

In August 1794, Wayne's army defeated more than 1,000 Native Americans under Shawnee chief Blue Jacket. The Battle of Fallen Timbers, near present-day Toledo, Ohio, crushed the Native Americans' hopes of keeping their land. In the Treaty of Greenville (1795), Native American leaders agreed to surrender most of the land in what is now Ohio.

☑ **PROGRESS CHECK**

Analyzing Why did Washington's efforts to gain the peaceful cooperation of Native Americans in the West fail?

Problems with Europe

GUIDING QUESTION *Why did Washington want to remain neutral in foreign conflict?*

In 1789 France erupted in revolution. Americans cheered at first as the French rose up against their king. The French struggle against royal tyranny was familiar to them. By 1793, however, the revolution had turned terribly violent. Some Americans were horrified by the bloodshed. Public opinion became divided.

When Britain and France went to war in 1793, some Americans sympathized with France. Others supported Britain. Washington hoped that the United States could stay neutral and not take either side.

Washington Struggles to Stay Neutral

Staying neutral proved difficult. The French tried to draw the United States into their conflict with Britain. They sent Edmond Genêt (zhuh•NAY) to ask American volunteers to attack British ships. President Washington **issued** the Proclamation of Neutrality, which prohibited Americans from fighting in the war. The proclamation also barred French and British warships from American ports.

Britain also challenged Washington's desire for neutrality. The British captured American ships that traded with the French. Then, they forced the American crews into the British navy. Americans were outraged by this practice of **impressment**.

Washington sent John Jay, chief justice of the United States, to discuss a solution with the British. The result of this negotiation was called Jay's Treaty. In the treaty, the British agreed to withdraw from American soil. There was no mention of impressment or British interference with American trade.

Getty Images

Reading HELPDESK

impressment seizing people against their will and forcing them to serve in the military or other public service

Academic Vocabulary

issue to deliver or hand out

Build Vocabulary: *Multiple Meaning Words*

The word *issue* can also be a noun, meaning "a troublesome subject," as in the sentence, "I brought up the issue to the rest of the class."

Few Americans approved of this treaty. Washington also found fault with it but believed it would end the crisis. After fierce debate, the Senate approved Jay's Treaty in a close vote.

Pinckney's Treaty With Spain

Spanish leaders were nervous about Jay's Treaty. They feared that the United States and Great Britain would now work together against Spain in North America. Washington sent U.S. diplomat Thomas Pinckney to Spain to settle differences between the nations. In 1795 Pinckney's Treaty gave the Americans free navigation of the Mississippi River and the right to trade at New Orleans.

Washington Leaves Office

After eight years in office, Washington decided not to seek a third term as president. In his Farewell Address, Washington urged his fellow citizens to "observe good faith and justice toward all nations. ... It is our true policy to steer clear of permanent alliances." These parting words influenced the nation's foreign policy for more than 100 years.

Washington also warned against something he saw as a growing threat to the young nation: political parties. You will read about this threat in the next lesson.

When George Washington decided to step down after two terms as president, he set a precedent. No president served more than two terms until Franklin Roosevelt began his third term in 1941.

▶ **CRITICAL THINKING**
Analyzing Visuals What does this picture suggest about the public's feeling toward President Washington?

 **PROGRESS CHECK**

Explaining What was the significance of Jay's Treaty?

LESSON 2 REVIEW

Review Vocabulary

1. Use the word *impressment* in a sentence about the United States during Washington's presidency.

Answer the Guiding Questions

2. *Describing* Describe the Whiskey Rebellion and the government's actions in response to it.

3. *Explaining* What role did foreign nations play in President Washington's relations with Native American groups?

4. *Summarizing* What was Washington's approach to foreign policy, and why was it complicated?

5. **PERSONAL WRITING** A tribute is a speech showing respect and gratitude. Write a one-paragraph tribute that you might have delivered on President George Washington's retirement.

networks
There's More Online!

☑ **CHARTS** Jefferson and Hamilton

☑ **GRAPHIC ORGANIZER** Role of Federal Government

☑ **PRIMARY SOURCE** Jefferson and the Constitution Political Cartoon

☑ **SLIDE SHOW** The Two-Party System

Naturalization Act
Required that aliens be residents for 14 years instead of 5 years before they became eligible for U.S. citizenship

Alien Acts
Allowed the president to imprison aliens and to send those he considered dangerous out of the country

Lesson 3
The First Political Parties

ESSENTIAL QUESTION *How do governments change?*

IT MATTERS BECAUSE
Our nation's two-party political system developed from Americans taking opposing sides on political issues.

Opposing Parties

GUIDING QUESTION *How did different opinions lead to the first political parties?*

The American people generally admired President Washington and his service to the nation. Still, harsh attacks appeared from time to time in newspapers. One paper even called Washington "the scourge and the misfortune of his country."

Most of the attacks on Washington came from supporters of Thomas Jefferson. They hoped to weaken support for the policies of Alexander Hamilton, which the president seemed to favor. In fact, by 1796, the supporters of Jefferson and Hamilton were beginning to form the nation's first political parties.

At that time, many Americans thought political parties were harmful to good government. The Constitution made no mention of parties because its authors saw no good use for them. Washington disapproved of political parties, or "factions" as they were known. He warned that they would divide the nation.

To others, though, it seemed natural that people would disagree about issues. They also knew that people who hold similar views tend to band together.

Washington's cabinet was clearly divided on key issues. Alexander Hamilton and Thomas Jefferson had very different views. They disagreed on economic policy and foreign relations.

Reading **HELP**DESK

Taking Notes: *Comparing and Contrasting*

As you read, use a diagram like this one to compare and contrast the goals of the first two U.S. political parties.

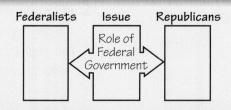

Federalists　Issue　Republicans

Role of Federal Government

Content Vocabulary

- **partisan**
- **caucus**
- **alien**
- **sedition**
- **nullify**
- **states' rights**

They did not share the same opinion on the power of the federal government or on the meaning of the Constitution. Even Washington was **partisan** (PAHR•tuh•zuhn)—clearly favoring one faction. The president believed he stood above politics, but he usually supported Hamilton's views.

Political Parties Emerge

The differences found in Washington's cabinet also existed in Congress and among the public. They formed the basis for two **distinct** political parties that emerged at this time.

One party was the Federalists. Led by Hamilton, this group favored a strong federal government. They believed the Constitution gave government "implied" powers. These implied powers are not enumerated, or listed clearly in the Constitution. Instead, Federalists believed the enumerated powers imply the power to do other things. Federalists believed Congress could make all laws "necessary and proper" to carry out its enumerated powers.

The Democratic-Republicans, or Republicans, stood against the Federalists. Jefferson and Madison led this faction. They believed in a strict reading of the Constitution. They rejected the Federalist idea of implied powers. They believed congressional powers were limited to what is absolutely necessary to carry out the enumerated powers.

Debate over the national bank highlighted these differences. The Constitution gave Congress specific powers to do such things as issue and borrow money. To Hamilton, this implied that the federal government could create a bank to help with these tasks. Jefferson disagreed.

The Role of the People

The two parties also disagreed about the role of ordinary citizens in government. Federalists supported representative government, in which elected officials ruled in the people's name. They did not believe it was wise to let the public become too involved in politics.

Federalists thought that educated, wealthier men should hold public office. They did not trust ordinary people to make good decisions. In Hamilton's words, "The people are turbulent and changing; they seldom judge or determine right."

Bettmann/Corbis

—Thinking Like a— HISTORIAN

Analyzing Political Cartoons

Newspapers that supported Washington and Hamilton ridiculed Thomas Jefferson in print and in cartoons. In this cartoon, Jefferson is throwing the U.S. Constitution into a fire. The eagle is a symbol of the United States. What is the eagle trying to do in this cartoon? For more information about analyzing primary sources, read *Thinking Like a Historian*.

partisan firmly favoring one party or faction

Academic Vocabulary

distinct clearly different from the others

Hamilton led the Federalist Party, which favored broad federal powers. They believed that wealthy, educated men should be elected to office and control the government.

Jefferson and the Republican Party wanted to limit federal powers and protect the powers of the states. They thought it was important for ordinary people to participate in government.

The Republicans feared a strong central government controlled by only a few people. They believed that democracy and liberty would be safe only if ordinary people took part fully in government. As Jefferson wrote in a letter, "I am not among those who fear the people. They, and not the rich, are our dependence [what we depend on] for continued freedom."

Washington's Reaction

The growing differences between the parties—and between Hamilton and Jefferson—troubled President Washington. He tried to get his two cabinet members to work out their differences. He wrote to Jefferson, trying to persuade him: "I . . . ardently wish that some line could be marked out by which both of you could walk."

Washington's efforts to get Jefferson and Hamilton to work together failed. The split was so strong that Jefferson left the cabinet and his job as secretary of state. Soon afterward, Hamilton resigned as secretary of the treasury. The rival groups and their points of view moved further apart. As the election of 1796 approached, the two parties each prepared to seek control of the presidency.

The Presidential Election of 1796

To prepare for the election, both parties held **caucuses** (KAW• kuhs•uhz). At these meetings, members of Congress and other leaders nominated, or chose, their parties' candidates for office.

Each party chose two presidential candidates, and the electors voted for any two. The Federalists chose John Adams and Charles Pinckney. The Republicans chose Thomas Jefferson and Aaron Burr. There was no candidate identified as a vice-presidential candidate on the ballot.

The Federalists carried the New England region. Republican strength lay in the Southern states. Adams got 71 electoral votes, winning the election. Jefferson finished second with 68 votes. Under the rules of the Constitution at that time, the person with the second-highest electoral vote total—Jefferson—became vice president. The administration that took office on March 4, 1797, had a Federalist president and a Republican vice president.

☑ PROGRESS CHECK

Contrasting How did the election of 1796 differ from the first presidential elections?

Reading **HELP**DESK

caucus a meeting of members of a political party to choose candidates for upcoming elections

Reading Strategy: *Identifying Points of View*

Most quotations express a person's point of view—what that person thinks or feels about a situation. Reread Hamilton's and Jefferson's quotations on the role of the people. Study the details. Try to restate the quotations in your own words. Then explain each person's point of view.

John Adams as President

GUIDING QUESTION *What important events occurred during the presidency of John Adams?*

John Adams spent most of his life in public service. He was well-known as one of Massachusetts's most active patriots in the period before and during the Revolutionary War. He served two terms as vice president under Washington before becoming president. His time in office, however, was troubled.

The XYZ Affair

The nation was in the middle of a dispute with France when Adams took office. The French viewed the 1794 Jay's Treaty as an American attempt to help the British in their war with France. To punish the United States, the French seized American ships that carried cargo to Britain.

President Adams sent a team to Paris to try to **resolve** the dispute in the fall of 1797. French officials chose not to meet with the Americans. Instead, the French sent three agents, who demanded a bribe and a loan for France from the Americans. The Americans refused.

When Adams learned what had happened, he was furious. The president urged Congress to prepare for war. In his report to Congress, Adams used the letters X, Y, and Z in place of the French agents' names. As a result, the event came to be called the XYZ affair.

Alien and Sedition Acts

When the public found out about the XYZ affair, many grew angry at foreign attempts to influence their government. They became more suspicious of **aliens**—residents who are not citizens. Many Europeans who had come to the United States in the 1790s supported the ideals of the French Revolution. Some Americans questioned whether these aliens would remain loyal if the United States went to war with France.

In response to these concerns, Federalists in 1798 passed the Alien and Sedition Acts. **Sedition** (sih•DIH•shuhn) means activities aimed at weakening the government. The Alien and Sedition Acts allowed the president to imprison aliens. The president could also deport—send out of the country—those thought to be dangerous. President Adams was a strong supporter of these laws.

Connections to — TODAY

Modern Political Parties

Today's Democratic Party started as the Democratic-Republican Party, which Thomas Jefferson and James Madison helped create in the 1790s. The Federalists no longer exist. The modern Republican Party was founded in the 1850s during the antislavery movement. These two political parties—Democrats and Republicans—now dominate the political process, filling most offices across the country. You can use the Internet to learn about the Democratic and Republican Parties of today.

alien a person living in a country who is not a citizen of that country

sedition activities aimed at weakening the established government by inciting resistance or rebellion to authority

Academic Vocabulary

resolve to find a solution; to settle a conflict

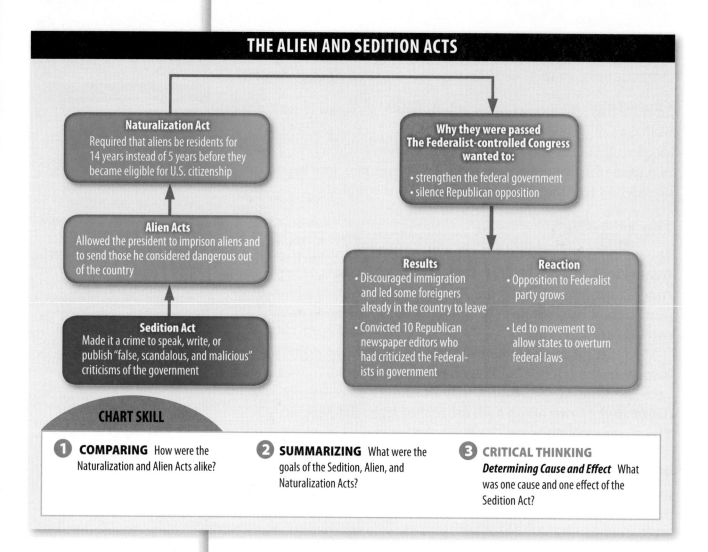

THE ALIEN AND SEDITION ACTS

Naturalization Act
Required that aliens be residents for 14 years instead of 5 years before they became eligible for U.S. citizenship

Alien Acts
Allowed the president to imprison aliens and to send those he considered dangerous out of the country

Sedition Act
Made it a crime to speak, write, or publish "false, scandalous, and malicious" criticisms of the government

Why they were passed
The Federalist-controlled Congress wanted to:
• strengthen the federal government
• silence Republican opposition

Results
• Discouraged immigration and led some foreigners already in the country to leave
• Convicted 10 Republican newspaper editors who had criticized the Federalists in government

Reaction
• Opposition to Federalist party grows
• Led to movement to allow states to overturn federal laws

CHART SKILL

① **COMPARING** How were the Naturalization and Alien Acts alike?

② **SUMMARIZING** What were the goals of the Sedition, Alien, and Naturalization Acts?

③ **CRITICAL THINKING**
Determining Cause and Effect What was one cause and one effect of the Sedition Act?

Domestic and Foreign Affairs

Democratic-Republicans saw the Alien and Sedition Acts as Federalist tyranny. They looked to the states to respond and protect people's liberties. Madison and Jefferson wrote statements of protest that the Virginia and Kentucky legislatures passed as resolutions.

The Virginia and Kentucky Resolutions of 1798 and 1799 claimed that the Alien and Sedition Acts violated the Constitution. They declared that the states should not put them into action. The Kentucky Resolution further said that states could **nullify** (NUH•luh•fy)—legally overturn—federal laws they thought were unconstitutional.

The resolutions supported the principle of **states' rights**. This principle held that the powers of the federal government were limited to those clearly granted by the Constitution. To

Reading **HELP**DESK

nullify to legally overturn
states' rights the idea that states should have all powers that the Constitution does not give to the federal government or forbid to the states

White House Historical Association

Abigail Adams was the first First Lady to occupy the White House. She lived there while the building was still under construction. Adams found the unfinished East Room so large that she used it for hanging the family laundry.

prevent the federal government from becoming too powerful, the states should have all other powers not expressly forbidden to them. The issue of states' rights would remain an important issue in American politics for many years.

Meanwhile, the Federalists urged Adams to declare war on France. Adams, however, resisted this pressure. Instead, he sent a representative to seek peace with France.

In 1800 the French agreed to a treaty and stopped their attacks on American ships. Though it had benefits for the United States, the agreement with France was unpopular and hurt Adams's chance for reelection. Rather than cheering the agreement, Hamilton and his supporters opposed their own president. The Federalists were now split. This improved Democratic-Republican hopes for winning the presidency in the 1800 election.

☑ **PROGRESS CHECK**

Specifying What was important about the Virginia and Kentucky Resolutions of 1798 and 1799?

LESSON 3 REVIEW

Review Vocabulary

1. Use the following words in a sentence about the development of political parties.

   a. partisan   **b.** caucus

2. Use the following terms in a paragraph about the presidency of John Adams.

   a. alien   **b.** sedition
   c. nullify   **d.** states' rights

Answer the Guiding Questions

3. *Contrasting* What was the belief of those who opposed the formation of political parties? What was the belief of those who supported them?

4. *Recalling* What happened in the XYZ affair?

5. **PERSONAL WRITING** Choose the candidate that you might have supported in the election of 1796 and make a campaign poster using words and illustrations to promote your candidate.

Write your answers on a separate piece of paper.

❶ Exploring the Essential Questions

EXPOSITORY WRITING Washington was the first of several generals who later became president. Think about this statement: A good general makes a good president. Is this an opinion or a fact? Do you agree or disagree? Explain.

❷ 21st Century Skills

COMPARING AND CONTRASTING Compare and contrast the views of the Federalists and the Democratic-Republicans.

❸ Thinking Like a Historian

DRAWING INFERENCES AND CONCLUSIONS In the first years of the United States under the Constitution, the first political parties started to develop. This ran against the hopes and expectations of many of the people who had written the Constitution. Write a brief essay in which you attempt to explain why the country may have been better off without political parties.

❹ GEOGRAPHY ACTIVITY

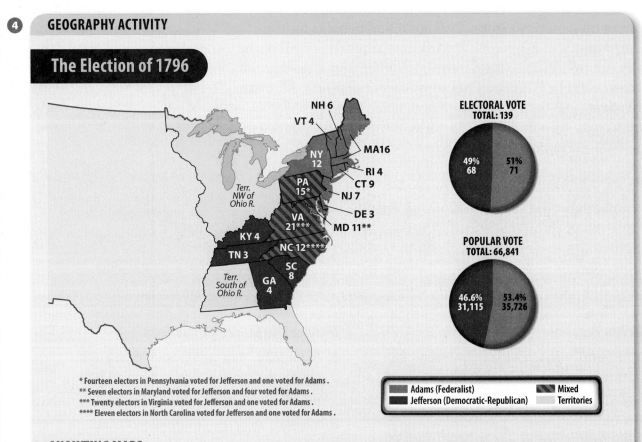

The Election of 1796

NH 6
VT 4
MA16
NY 12
RI 4
CT 9
PA 15*
NJ 7
Terr. NW of Ohio R.
VA 21***
DE 3
MD 11**
KY 4
NC 12****
TN 3
SC 8
Terr. South of Ohio R.
GA 4

ELECTORAL VOTE
TOTAL: 139
49% 68
51% 71

POPULAR VOTE
TOTAL: 66,841
46.6% 31,115
53.4% 35,726

* Fourteen electors in Pennsylvania voted for Jefferson and one voted for Adams .
** Seven electors in Maryland voted for Jefferson and four voted for Adams .
*** Twenty electors in Virginia voted for Jefferson and one voted for Adams .
**** Eleven electors in North Carolina voted for Jefferson and one voted for Adams .

Adams (Federalist)
Jefferson (Democratic-Republican)
Mixed
Territories

ANALYZING MAPS

The map and graphs give results of the election of 1796, in which John Adams was elected president. How many electoral votes did Jefferson get from his home state of Virginia? From which state did John Adams get his greatest electoral vote?

REVIEW THE GUIDING QUESTIONS

Choose the best answer for each question.

1 With the Judiciary Act of 1789, Congress

    A. placed state courts under federal courts.

    B. established a federal court system.

    C. blocked state laws in favor of federal laws.

    D. named judges for all federal and state courts.

2 What was one reason Madison and Jefferson opposed the idea of a national bank?

    F. They believed it was unconstitutional for Congress to create a bank.

    G. They wanted each state to create and form its own bank.

    H. They feared that banking activities would threaten the purchase of municipal bonds.

    I. They considered bank practices, such as charging interest, to be unethical.

3 The Whiskey Rebellion was

    A. an armed uprising by farmers in Ohio.

    B. a violent slave rebellion in Virginia.

    C. a skirmish between U.S. soldiers and Native Americans in the Ohio Valley.

    D. a protest by Pennsylvania farmers over a new tax.

4 Pinckney's Treaty allowed the U.S. to

    F. purchase the state of Alaska.

    G. use the Mississippi River and trade in New Orleans.

    H. take over lands in Florida and Georgia.

    I. defend against the British impressment of sailors.

5 Which of the following is true about the Federalists?

    A. They supported representative government.

    B. They thought that there could never be too much democracy.

    C. They believed it was wise for the public to be involved in politics.

    D. Thomas Jefferson was their leader.

6 The Virginia and Kentucky Resolutions

    F. were drafted by Federalists opposing Republican uses of federal power.

    G. claimed that the Alien and Sedition Acts violated the Constitution.

    H. distributed land to settlers in Virginia and Kentucky.

    I. rejected the principle of states' rights stated in the Constitution.

DBQ **DOCUMENT-BASED QUESTIONS**

The following passage is taken from the Treaty of Greenville.

"The Indian tribes who have a right to those lands, are quietly to enjoy them, hunting, planting, and dwelling thereon, ... but when those tribes ... shall ... sell their lands they are to be sold only to the United States; and until such sale, the United States will protect all the said Indian tribes ... against all citizens of the United States. ... "

—from the Treaty of Greenville, 1795

7 **Identifying** What does the United States government promise Native Americans in this document?

A. Money will be set aside from the sale of their lands.

B. United States citizens will share Native American hunting lands.

C. They will be protected until their lands are sold.

D. They have the right to make war against others.

8 **Analyzing** How does this document control the sale of Native American lands?

F. Native Americans must sell their land only to the United States.

G. Native Americans cannot sell their land to anyone.

H. Native Americans are free to sell their lands to the highest bidder.

I. Native Americans must share the profits from selling their land.

SHORT RESPONSE

This 1798 cartoon shows an exchange between a Republican and Federalist over the Sedition Act.

9 What is happening in the cartoon, and how are others reacting?

10 What does the cartoon suggest about politics of the era?

EXTENDED RESPONSE

11 **Personal Writing** You are a citizen of the United States in 1796. It is a presidential election year. Write a letter to a friend in another country in which you describe the political events of the Washington Administration and the upcoming election. Offer your thoughts about the two new political parties.

Need Extra Help?

If You've Missed Question	1	2	3	4	5	6	7	8	9	10	11
Review Lesson	1	1	2	2	3	3	2	2	3	3	3

The Jefferson Era

1800–1816

ESSENTIAL QUESTIONS · *How do governments change?*
· *How does geography influence the way people live?* · *Why does conflict develop?*

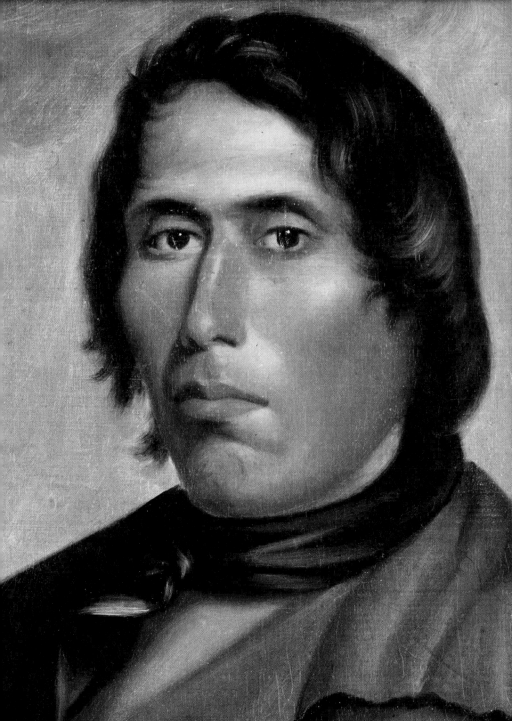

The Story Matters . . .

Shawnee leader Tecumseh grew up in what the Americans call the Northwest Territory. He fights to slow the advance of white settlers across the Appalachian Mountains. Tecumseh scoffs at the demands that his people give up their ancient homelands. "Sell a country!" he says. "Why not sell the air, the clouds and the great sea, as well as the earth?"

Tecumseh knows it will take the strength of many to stop the Americans. He hopes to build a great alliance of all the Native American groups in the region. Will he succeed in his plan?

◄ *Shawnee leader Tecumseh rallied Native Americans to resist American settlement in the early 1800s.*

The Granger Collection, NYC

Place and Time: America 1800 to 1816

During the Jefferson Era and the years immediately following it, the United States grew rapidly. The Louisiana Purchase roughly doubled the size of the country, and explorers probed the unknown lands beyond the frontier.

Step Into the Place

MAP FOCUS After the United States purchased the Louisiana Territory from France in 1803, it sent explorers into its new lands—and beyond.

1 LOCATION What part of the Louisiana Territory did Lewis and Clark explore? What other territory did they explore?

2 MOVEMENT In which direction did the Pike expedition travel when it started out?

3 CRITICAL THINKING
Analyzing What were the major geographic obstacles that Lewis and Clark encountered during their journey through the Louisiana Territory?

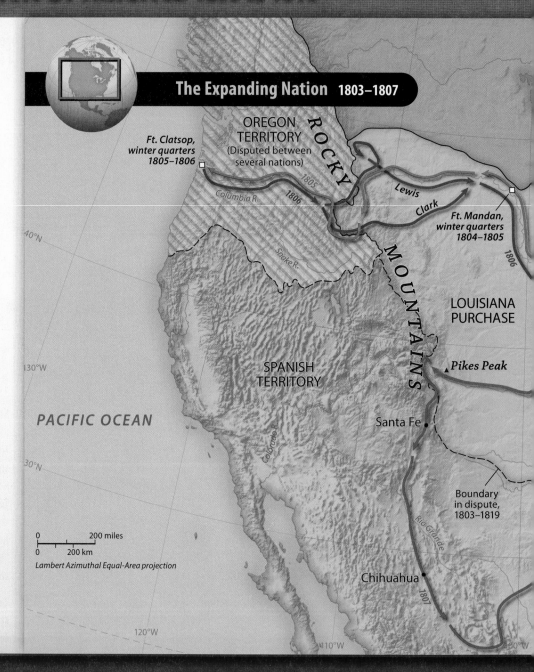

The Expanding Nation 1803–1807

OREGON TERRITORY
(Disputed between several nations)

Ft. Clatsop, winter quarters 1805–1806

ROCKY

Columbia R.

Lewis

Clark

Ft. Mandan, winter quarters 1804–1805

1805

1806

1806

Snake R.

MOUNTAINS

LOUISIANA PURCHASE

SPANISH TERRITORY

Pikes Peak

PACIFIC OCEAN

Santa Fe

Colorado R.

Boundary in dispute, 1803–1819

Rio Grande

40°N

130°W

30°N

120°W

110°W

100°W

Chihuahua

1807

0   200 miles
0   200 km
Lambert Azimuthal Equal-Area projection

Step Into the Time

TIME LINE Based on the time line, what conclusions can you draw about the relationship between the United States and Britain in the early 1800s?

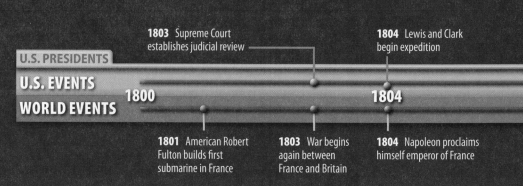

1803 Supreme Court establishes judicial review

1804 Lewis and Clark begin expedition

U.S. PRESIDENTS

U.S. EVENTS

WORLD EVENTS

1800

1804

1801 American Robert Fulton builds first submarine in France

1803 War begins again between France and Britain

1804 Napoleon proclaims himself emperor of France

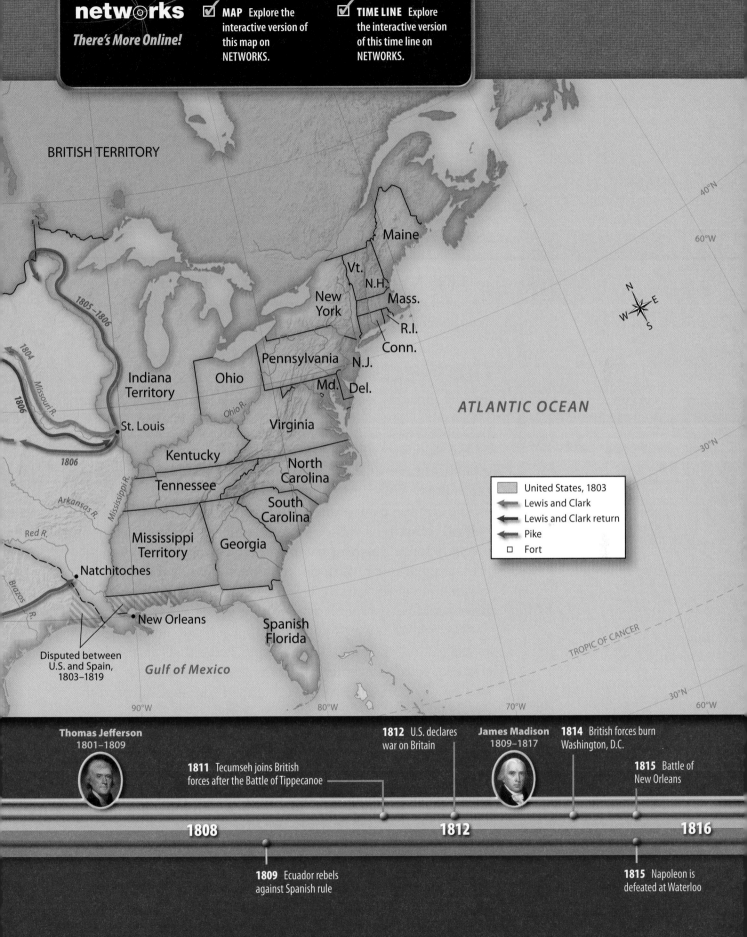

networks
There's More Online!

☑ **MAP** Explore the interactive version of this map on NETWORKS.

☑ **TIME LINE** Explore the interactive version of this time line on NETWORKS.

BRITISH TERRITORY

Maine

Vt.

N.H.

New York

Mass.

R.I.

Conn.

Pennsylvania

N.J.

Indiana Territory

Ohio

Md.

Del.

Ohio R.

Virginia

1805–1806

1804

Missouri R.

1806

• St. Louis

Kentucky

1806

North Carolina

Tennessee

Arkansas R.

Mississippi R.

South Carolina

Red R.

Mississippi Territory

Georgia

• Natchitoches

Brazos R.

• New Orleans

Spanish Florida

Disputed between U.S. and Spain, 1803–1819

Gulf of Mexico

ATLANTIC OCEAN

TROPIC OF CANCER

	United States, 1803
←	Lewis and Clark
←	Lewis and Clark return
←	Pike
☐	Fort

40°N

60°W

30°N

30°N

60°W

90°W   80°W   70°W

N E S W

Thomas Jefferson
1801–1809

1811 Tecumseh joins British forces after the Battle of Tippecanoe

1812 U.S. declares war on Britain

James Madison
1809–1817

1814 British forces burn Washington, D.C.

1815 Battle of New Orleans

1808

1812

1816

1809 Ecuador rebels against Spanish rule

1815 Napoleon is defeated at Waterloo

netw⊙rks

There's More Online!

☑ **CHART/GRAPH** The Supreme Court—Then and Now

☑ **GRAPHIC ORGANIZER** Republicans and the Role of Government

☑ **MAP** The Election of 1800

☑ **SLIDE SHOW** Monticello

Lesson 1

A New Party in Power

ESSENTIAL QUESTION *How do governments change?*

IT MATTERS BECAUSE

In the election of 1800, the nation experienced a peaceful transfer of power from one party to the other.

The Election of 1800

GUIDING QUESTION *What did the election of 1800 show about the nature of politics?*

In the election of 1800, Federalists supported President Adams for a second term and Charles Pinckney for vice president. Republicans nominated Thomas Jefferson for president and Aaron Burr as his running mate.

The election campaign of 1800 was very different from the political campaigns we see today. Neither Adams nor Jefferson traveled around the country to gather support. Many thought direct campaigning improper for a person who would be president. Instead, hundreds of letters were sent to leading citizens and newspapers to make candidates' views public.

The campaign was bitterly fought. Each side made personal attacks against the other. For example, Federalists accused Jefferson, who believed in freedom of religion, of being "godless." Republicans warned that the Federalists favored the wealthy and would bring back monarchy.

The Vote Is Tied

Under the Constitution, voters in a presidential election are really electing groups of people called electors. These electors meet in what is known as the Electoral College. There they cast

(tc) Private Collection, Peter Newark American Pictures/Bridgeman Art Library, (tr) imagebroker/Alamy Images

Reading **HELP**DESK

Taking Notes: *Analyzing*

As you read, use a diagram like this one to analyze the ways in which the Republicans changed the government.

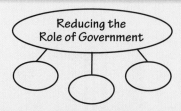
Reducing the Role of Government

Content Vocabulary

• **customs duty**
• **jurisdiction**

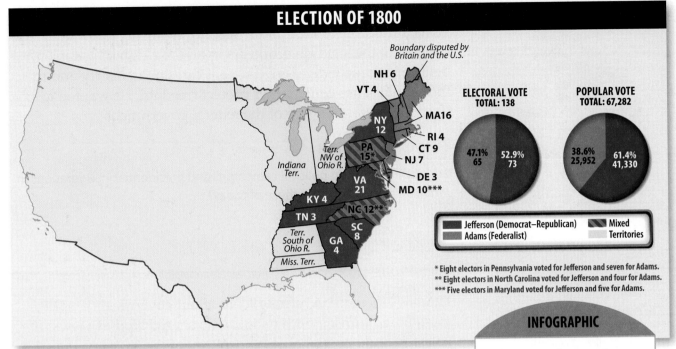

ELECTION OF 1800

Boundary disputed by Britain and the U.S.

NH 6
VT 4
MA16
NY 12
RI 4
CT 9
Terr. NW of Ohio R.
PA 15*
NJ 7
Indiana Terr.
DE 3
VA 21
MD 10***
KY 4
NC 12**
TN 3
SC 8
Terr. South of Ohio R.
GA 4
Miss. Terr.

ELECTORAL VOTE TOTAL: 138
47.1% 65 | 52.9% 73

POPULAR VOTE TOTAL: 67,282
38.6% 25,952 | 61.4% 41,330

Jefferson (Democrat–Republican) Mixed
Adams (Federalist) Territories

* Eight electors in Pennsylvania voted for Jefferson and seven for Adams.
** Eight electors in North Carolina voted for Jefferson and four for Adams.
*** Five electors in Maryland voted for Jefferson and five for Adams.

INFOGRAPHIC

Each state sent electors to the Electoral College. Territories (shown in yellow) did not.

1 IDENTIFYING Which areas tended to support Adams?

2 CRITICAL THINKING *Drawing Conclusions* Why do you think Adams and Jefferson both had their support concentrated in particular regions of the country?

the ballots that actually elect the president and vice president. Each state has as many electoral votes as it has members of Congress.

At that time, the Constitution said that electors were to cast two ballots—without indicating which was for president and which was for vice president. The candidate with the majority of votes became president, and the candidate with the next-largest number of votes became vice president. In 1800, 73 electors cast their ballots for Jefferson and Burr. Each candidate, therefore, got the same number of votes. Because of the tie vote, the House of Representatives had to decide the election.

In the House, Federalists tried to keep Jefferson from becoming president by supporting Burr. For 35 ballots, the election remained tied. Finally, one Federalist decided not to vote for Burr.

Because no one wanted to see another tie between a presidential and vice-presidential candidate, Congress passed the Twelfth Amendment to the Constitution in 1803. From then on, electors cast one of their votes for president and the other for vice president.

Jefferson's Inauguration

On the day he became president, Jefferson dressed in his everyday clothes. He walked to the Senate to take the oath of office. President Adams did not attend.

Reading Strategy: *Predicting*

Good readers think ahead as they are reading. They predict, or guess, what might happen next. Find a good stopping place, like the bottom of this page, and ask yourself a question about what might happen next. For example, you might ask, "Since Jefferson was a Republican who had just defeated the Federalists, how might he change the government?" Try to answer your question, then read ahead to see whether your predictions are correct.

Thomas Jefferson (1743–1826)

In addition to his many achievements in government and politics, Jefferson was a noted inventor and architect. His inventions include a plow that was twice as fast as older ones, a machine for making macaroni, and a device that encoded messages. He also designed the house on his plantation (Monticello) and founded the University of Virginia.

▶ **CRITICAL THINKING**

Analyzing Based on his interests and skills, what qualities do you think Jefferson might have had?

In his Inaugural Address, Jefferson outlined some of his goals, including "a wise and frugal government" and "the support of the state governments in all their rights." Jefferson believed a large federal government threatened liberty and that individual states could better protect freedom. He wanted to limit the power and size of the federal government.

✓ **PROGRESS CHECK**

Contrasting How did political campaigns and presidential inaugurations in Jefferson's day differ from those of today?

Jefferson as President

GUIDING QUESTION *What did Jefferson want to accomplish during his presidency?*

Thomas Jefferson had strong ideas about government and he surrounded himself with people who shared **similar** views. Jefferson and Albert Gallatin, secretary of the treasury, reduced the national debt and cut down on military expenses. Jefferson also limited the number of federal government workers to a few hundred people. At the same time, his government got rid of most federal taxes. They only collected **customs duties**, or taxes on imported goods. Under Jefferson, the government's income would come from customs duties and from the sale of western lands. He believed that these changes were needed to make the United States a great nation.

Judiciary Act of 1801

After the election and before Jefferson took office, the Federalists passed an act that set up a system of courts. John Adams used this act, the Judiciary Act of 1801, to make hundreds of appointments during his last days as president. Adams also asked John Marshall to serve as chief justice. Congress was then still under Federalist control and supported Adams's choices. In this way, Adams blocked Jefferson from making appointments and made sure the Federalists controlled the courts.

Adams's appointments could not take effect until these last-minute appointees, known as "midnight judges," received certain official papers, called commissions. When Jefferson became president, some of these appointees had not yet received their commissions. Jefferson told Secretary of State James Madison not to deliver them.

Private Collection, Peter Newark American Pictures/Bridgeman Art Library

Reading **HELP**DESK

customs duty tax collected on goods that are imported
jurisdiction the power or right to interpret and apply a law

Academic Vocabulary

similar sharing qualities, but not the same as; like
principle a fundamental, or basic, law or idea

The Growing Power of the Supreme Court

One of the appointees who did not get his commission was William Marbury. He asked the Supreme Court to force its delivery. The Court said it did not have the **jurisdiction** (jur•iss•DIK•shuhn)—the legal authority—to force delivery of Marbury's commission. Marbury had argued that an act of Congress gave the Court such authority, but the Court ruled that that act violated the Constitution.

Jefferson's home at Monticello in Charlottesville, Virginia, is considered an architectural masterpiece.

The ruling in *Marbury* v. *Madison* affected much more than William Marbury's career. In his opinion, Chief Justice John Marshall established the three **principles** of judicial review: (1) the Constitution is the supreme law of the land; (2) the Constitution must be followed when there is a conflict with any other law; and (3) the judicial branch can declare laws unconstitutional. In short, Marshall claimed for the courts the power to find acts of other branches unconstitutional. Judicial review is a key check on the legislative and executive branches.

In his 34-year term as chief justice, Marshall helped broaden the power of the Court. He also expanded federal power at the expense of the states. In *McCulloch* v. *Maryland* (1819), the Court held that Congress does have implied powers and that states cannot tax the federal government. In *Gibbons* v. *Ogden* (1824), the Court held that federal law overrules state law in matters affecting more than one state. In *Worcester* v. *Georgia* (1832), the Court decided that states could not regulate Native Americans. Only the federal government had that power.

☑ **PROGRESS CHECK**

Explaining What was the significance of the *Marbury* v. *Madison* ruling?

LESSON 1 REVIEW

Review Vocabulary

1. Write a sentence about the Jefferson administration that uses the term *customs duty*.

Answer the Guiding Questions

2. ***Contrasting*** How did the process of electing a president change after the election of 1800?

3. ***Discussing*** How did President Jefferson act on his beliefs about government?

4. ***Explaining*** Explain how the powers of the Supreme Court and federal law were extended by significant court cases during this period.

5. **EXPOSITORY WRITING** During John Marshall's term on the Supreme Court, federal and Court power expanded. Write a paragraph contrasting these decisions with Thomas Jefferson's stated views on the proper size and power of the federal government.

Lesson 2
The Louisiana Purchase

ESSENTIAL QUESTION *How does geography influence the way people live?*

IT MATTERS BECAUSE
The Louisiana Purchase changed the size and shape of the nation and helped hasten westward expansion.

Westward, Ho!

GUIDING QUESTION *How did Spain and France play a role in Americans moving west?*

In 1800 the territory of the United States extended as far west as the Mississippi River. The area west of the river—known as the Louisiana Territory—belonged to Spain. The Louisiana Territory was an enormous area of land, stretching south to the city of New Orleans and west to the Rocky Mountains. Its northern boundaries remained undefined.

During the early 1800s, Americans moved west in search of land and adventure. Pioneers, many of them farmers, traveled over the mountains into Kentucky and Tennessee. Many also set out for the less settled areas of the Northwest Territory. They made a long and exhausting journey over the Appalachian Mountains. Pioneers heading to the western lands had to travel along rough, muddy roads or cut their way through thick forests.

These westward-bound pioneers loaded their household goods into Conestoga (kah•neh•STOH•guh) wagons, sturdy vehicles topped with white canvas. The settlers traveled with their two most valued possessions: rifles and axes. They needed rifles for protection and to hunt animals for food. They used axes to cut paths for their wagons through the dense forests.

Reading **HELP**DESK

Taking Notes: *Describing*

As you read, use a diagram like this one to describe the areas that Lewis and Clark and Zebulon Pike explored.

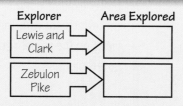

Explorer — Area Explored

Lewis and Clark →

Zebulon Pike →

Content Vocabulary
• secede

Many of the pioneers set up farms along rivers that fed into the Upper Mississippi River. Farmers needed access to the Mississippi to transport their crops to markets. Their goods traveled down the Mississippi to New Orleans, where workers loaded them onto other ships bound for markets on the East Coast. The Spanish controlled the region, but they allowed the Americans to sail on the Lower Mississippi and trade in New Orleans. For the western farmers, this agreement was vital to their economic survival.

The French Threat

For some years, the Spanish allowed American goods to move freely in their territory. In 1802, the Spanish suddenly changed their policy, no longer allowing American goods to move into and beyond New Orleans. President Jefferson learned that Spain and France had secretly agreed to transfer the Louisiana Territory to France. Jefferson believed that France had also gained Florida in its secret agreement with Spain.

This news alarmed Jefferson. The agreement between Spain and France posed a serious threat to the United States. France's leader, Napoleon Bonaparte, had plans to create empires in Europe and the Americas. French control would put American trade along the Mississippi River at risk. Congress authorized Robert Livingston, the new minister to France, to offer as much as $2 million for New Orleans and West Florida in order to gain control of the territory.

When Toussaint L'Ouverture defeated the French in Haiti, France lost interest in Louisiana.

Napoleon and Santo Domingo

Napoleon dreamed of a Western empire. He saw the Caribbean island of Santo Domingo as an important naval base from which he could control such an empire. Events in Santo Domingo, however, ended Napoleon's dream. Inspired by the ideas of the French Revolution, Toussaint L'Ouverture (too•SAN loo•vuhr•TOOR) led enslaved Africans and other laborers in Santo Domingo in a revolt against the island's plantation owners. After fierce fighting, the rebels won and declared the colony an independent republic. L'Ouverture established a new government.

In 1802, Napoleon sent troops to regain control of Santo Domingo, but they were not successful. By 1804, the French were driven out of Santo Domingo. The country took its original name, Haiti.

✔ **PROGRESS CHECK**

Explaining Explain why French control of the Louisiana Territory worried Jefferson.

Build Vocabulary: *Word Origins*

The Conestoga wagon took its name from Conestoga, Pennsylvania, the town where it was first made.

An Expanding Nation

GUIDING QUESTION *How did the Louisiana Purchase open an area of settlement?*

Napoleon had a problem: he needed money to finance his war against Britain. Without Santo Domingo, Napoleon had little use for Louisiana. In order to solve his money problem, he decided to sell the Louisiana Territory. A French official told U.S. representatives Robert Livingston and James Monroe that the entire Louisiana Territory was for sale. The offer took Livingston and Monroe by surprise. They did not have the **authority** to accept such an offer.

The deal, however, was too good to pass up. The new territory would provide plenty of cheap land for farmers for future generations. It would also give the United States control of the Mississippi River, which would protect domestic shipping interests. These benefits convinced Livingston and Monroe to close the deal, even though they did not have authorization to buy the whole territory. After a few days of negotiation, the parties agreed on a price of $15 million.

Jefferson worried that such a large **purchase** might not be legal. The Constitution said nothing about acquiring new territory. By what authority could he buy the land? He thought of seeking a constitutional amendment, but he realized there was no time for such a step. Jefferson decided the government's treaty-making powers allowed the purchase of the new territory. The Senate approved the purchase in October 1803. The purchase of the Louisiana Territory doubled the size of the United States.

The Lewis and Clark Expedition

Americans knew little about the land west of the Mississippi, and Jefferson wanted to learn more about the new territory he had just acquired. He persuaded Congress to sponsor an expedition to gather information about the new land. The expedition would document findings about the territory's people, plants, and animals and recommend sites for future forts.

The expedition had another goal: finding and mapping the fabled Northwest Passage, a water route across North America. In order to trade with Asia, Europeans had to sail around Africa. Because the trip was long and costly, European explorers searched, unsuccessfully, for a more direct route. Once the Americas were colonized, Americans and Europeans continued

Reading **HELP**DESK

Academic Vocabulary

authority the power to influence or command thought, opinion, or behavior
purchase the act of buying something

Build Vocabulary: *Related Words*

Meriwether Lewis kept a journal—a record of the experiences, ideas, and thoughts he had during the expedition. The word *journalism* generally means the collection or presentation of the news, but in particular the direct presentation of facts or events without the writer's interpretation.

to sail around Africa or around the tip of South America in order to reach Asia. Finding a water route across North America became more important than ever.

Jefferson chose Meriwether Lewis, his 28-year-old private secretary, to head the expedition. Lewis joined the militia during the Whiskey Rebellion and had been in the army when Jefferson hired him as his private secretary in 1801. Jefferson apparently looked forward to one day sending out an expedition to explore the continent, and hired Lewis with that in mind. William Clark was co-leader of the expedition. Clark was 32 years old and a friend of Lewis's. Clark also brought along York, an enslaved African American and lifelong companion of Clark's. York was a key member of the expedition. He was especially helpful building ties with Native Americans, many of whom had never before seen an African American and were drawn to him.

Lewis and Clark were well-informed, amateur scientists. They also had experience doing business with Native Americans. Together they assembled a crew of expert sailors, gunsmiths, carpenters, scouts, and a cook. Two men of mixed Native American and French heritage served as interpreters.

In the spring of 1804, the expedition left St. Louis and worked its way up the Missouri River. On May 5, 1805, Lewis described what they encountered along the trail in his journal:

PRIMARY SOURCE

66 Buffalo Elk and goats or Antelopes feeding in every direction . . . [T]he buffalo furnish us with fine veal and fat and beef. . . . We have not been able to take any fish for some time past. The country is as yesterday beautiful in the extreme. 99

—from the journals of Lewis and Clark

The expedition encountered many Native American groups on the journey. A Shoshone woman named Sacagawea (SA•kuh•juh•WEE•uh) joined their group as a guide.

After 18 months and nearly 4,000 miles (6,437 km), Lewis and Clark reached the Pacific Ocean. They spent the winter there. Then they headed back east, returning in September 1806. The explorers had collected valuable information about people, plants, animals, and the geography of the West. Perhaps most important, their journey inspired people to move westward.

BIOGRAPHY

Sacagawea (c. 1788–1812?)

Sacagawea was the daughter of a Shoshone chief. Lewis and Clark hired her and her husband, a French Canadian fur trader, as interpreters. Sacagawea proved extremely valuable. She negotiated the purchase of horses, found edible plants, and made moccasins and clothing. According to Clark, her presence helped calm the fears of Native Americans the group met during their journey.

▶ **CRITICAL THINKING**
Speculating What challenges might the expedition have faced without Sacagawea?

From 1804 to 1806, Meriwether Lewis and William Clark mapped and explored more than 7,000 miles (11,265 km).

(t) Hulton Archive/Getty Images, (b) David David Gallery/SuperStock

Pike's Expedition

Lewis and Clark were not the only people Jefferson sent to explore the wilderness. Lieutenant Zebulon Pike led two expeditions west between 1805 and 1807. He traveled through the Upper Mississippi River valley and into present-day Colorado. In Colorado, he found a snowcapped mountain he called Grand Peak, known today as Pikes Peak.

From Pike's travels, Americans learned about the Great Plains and Rocky Mountains. Pike also mapped part of the Rio Grande and traveled across northern Mexico and what is now southern Texas.

A Federalist Plan to Secede

The Louisiana Purchase troubled Federalists in the Northeast. They feared the westward expansion would weaken New England's power in political and economic affairs. A group of

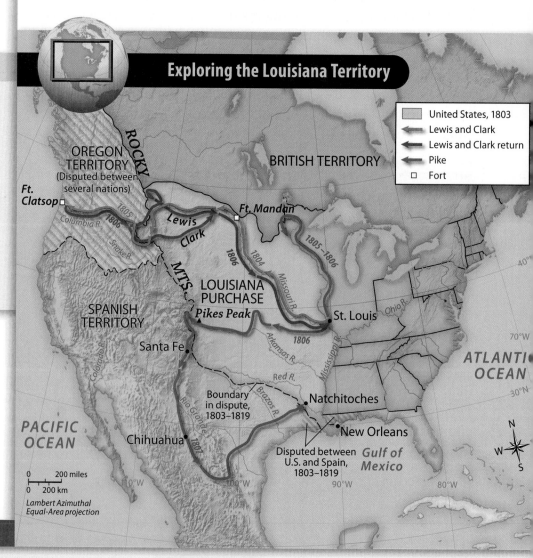

Exploring the Louisiana Territory

United States, 1803
Lewis and Clark
Lewis and Clark return
Pike
Fort

Federalists in Massachusetts plotted to **secede** (suh•SEED), or withdraw, from the Union. New England would become the "Northern Confederacy."

The plotters realized that if the confederacy were to last, it had to include New York as well as New England. The Massachusetts Federalists needed a powerful friend in New York who would support their plan. They turned to Aaron Burr.

Hamilton and Burr Duel

Alexander Hamilton was concerned about rumors of secession. He had never trusted Aaron Burr, and now he heard that Burr had secretly agreed to lead New York out of the Union. Hamilton accused Burr of plotting treason. Meanwhile, Burr was suffering setbacks in his political career. Blaming Hamilton for these troubles, Burr challenged him to a duel.

The two men—armed with pistols—met in Weehawken, New Jersey, in July 1804. Hamilton hated dueling, which was illegal but popular among upper-class Americans at the time. Hamilton pledged not to shoot at his rival, but Burr took no such pledge. He aimed to shoot Hamilton, and he was successful. Seriously wounded, Hamilton died the next day. Burr fled to avoid arrest.

After the duel, Aaron Burr fled to South Carolina. Never tried for Hamilton's death, Burr returned to Washington, D.C., and completed his term as vice president.

✓ PROGRESS CHECK

Drawing Conclusions Why was the Louisiana Purchase important for the United States?

LESSON 2 REVIEW

Review Vocabulary

1. Identify a word that means the opposite of *secede*.

Answer the Guiding Questions

2. ***Explaining*** How did the secret agreement between Spain and France over Louisiana affect American trade in the West?

3. ***Identifying Cause and Effect*** Name two effects of the Lewis and Clark expedition.

4. ***Summarizing*** How did the Federalists react to the Louisiana Purchase? Explain.

5. **PERSONAL WRITING** Write a one-paragraph journal entry from the perspective of a participant of the Lewis and Clark expedition, explaining your feelings and expectations as you set out on your journey.

networks

There's More Online!

☑ **BIOGRAPHY**
Stephen Decatur

☑ **CHART/GRAPH**
U.S. Policies Leading to
the War of 1812

☑ **GAME** Lesson Terms

☑ **GRAPHIC ORGANIZER**
U.S. Actions

☑ **VIDEO**

Lesson 3

A Time of Conflict

ESSENTIAL QUESTION *Why does conflict develop?*

IT MATTERS BECAUSE

As the United States grew, tensions emerged within and beyond the nation's borders.

American Ships on the High Seas

GUIDING QUESTION *How did the United States become involved in a conflict with Tripoli?*

In 1785 the ship *Empress of China* returned to New York from China. The ship's cargo of tea and silk sold for a great profit. The chance for similar profit inspired others to follow in the *Empress of China's* wake. Soon, American merchant ships were sailing regularly to China and India, as well as South America, Africa, and lands along the Mediterranean Sea.

In the mid-1790s, France and Britain were at war. French and British merchant ships stayed home to avoid capture by their enemies. American merchants took advantage of this opportunity. By 1800, the United States had almost 1,000 merchant ships trading around the world.

Piracy on the Seas

The practice of piracy, or robbery on the seas, made some foreign waters dangerous. Pirates from the Barbary States of North Africa—Morocco, Algiers, Tripoli, and Tunis—terrorized European ships sailing on the Mediterranean Sea.

The Barbary pirates demanded that governments pay **tribute,** or protection money, to allow their country's ships to pass safely. If tribute was not paid, the pirates attacked and took

(tl) Courtesy of the Naval Historical Foundation, Washington, DC, (tc) The Granger Collection, NYC, (tc) Private Collection, Photo © Christie's Images/Bridgeman Art Library, (tcr) The Granger Collection, NYC, (tr) Getty Images

Reading HELPDESK

Taking Notes: *Analyzing*

As you read, use a diagram like this one to analyze the actions the U.S. took in response to each of the following situations.

	Action Taken
Demand for Tribute	
Attacks on the Chesapeake	
Tecumseh's Confederation	

Content Vocabulary

• **tribute**
• **neutral rights**
• **embargo**
• **nationalism**

ships, and imprisoned their crews. European countries often paid this tribute. They believed that it was less expensive to pay the Barbary pirates than it was to go to war with them.

War With Tripoli

The Barbary States also demanded that the United States pay tribute. In 1801 the ruler of Tripoli asked the United States for even more money. When President Jefferson refused to pay, Tripoli declared war on the United States. In response, Jefferson sent ships to blockade Tripoli.

In 1804 pirates seized the U.S. warship *Philadelphia*. They towed the ship into Tripoli Harbor and threw the crew into jail. Stephen Decatur, a 25-year-old U.S. Navy captain, took action. He slipped into the heavily guarded harbor with a small raiding party. Decatur burned the captured ship to prevent the pirates from using it. A British admiral praised the deed as the "most bold and daring act of the age."

Stephen Decatur and crew attack one of Tripoli's gunboats.

▶ **CRITICAL THINKING**
Drawing Conclusions Why do you think Stephen Decatur was considered a national hero?

tribute money paid to a leader or state for protection

Predicting Consequences

As tensions between the United States and Great Britain worsened, the British warship *Leopard* attacked the American vessel *Chesapeake* off the coast of Virginia. How do you think the American people reacted to this violent conflict? For more information about predicting consequences, read *Thinking Like a Historian.*

Officers of the British ship *Leopard* impress American sailors from the *Chesapeake* in 1807.

The war ended with the signing of a peace treaty in June 1805. Tripoli agreed to stop demanding tribute, but the United States had to pay $60,000 for the release of the prisoners. Although the United States no longer had to pay tribute to Tripoli, it continued paying other Barbary States until 1816.

Violating Neutral Rights

Thomas Jefferson won reelection in 1804. The nation was at peace—but trouble was brewing. Across the Atlantic Ocean, Great Britain and France were fighting a war that threatened to interfere with American trade.

When Britain and France went to war in 1803, the United States traded with both countries. By not taking sides in the war, the United States was able to continue with this trade. A nation not involved in a conflict enjoyed **neutral rights**, meaning its ships could sail the seas and not take sides.

American merchants prospered for two years. By 1805, however, Britain and France were each trying to block the other from trading with the United States. Britain blockaded the French coast and threatened to search all ships trading with France. France then announced that it would search and seize ships caught trading with Britain.

The British Abuse American Shipping

The British desperately needed sailors for their naval war. Many of their own sailors had deserted due to the terrible living conditions—hard labor, harsh treatment, and terrible food— in the British Royal Navy. British naval ships began stopping American ships to search for suspected British deserters. The British then forced these deserters to return to the British navy. This practice of forcing people to serve in the navy was called impressment (ihm•PREHS•muhnt).

While some of the sailors taken were deserters from the British navy, the British also impressed hundreds of native-born and naturalized American citizens.

The British often waited for American ships outside an American harbor, where they boarded and searched them. In June 1807, the British warship *Leopard* stopped the American vessel *Chesapeake* off the coast of Virginia. The *Leopard's* captain demanded to search the American ship for British deserters, but the *Chesapeake's* captain refused. In reply, the British opened fire, crippling the *Chesapeake* and killing three crew members.

The Granger Collection, NYC

Reading **HELP**DESK

neutral rights privileges or freedoms that are granted to nations that do not choose a side in a conflict
embargo a prohibition or blocking of trade with a certain country

Academic Vocabulary

react to act in response to something

When news of the attack spread, Americans **reacted** with an anti-British fury not seen since the Revolutionary War. Secretary of State James Madison called the attack an outrage. Many Americans demanded war against Britain, but President Jefferson wanted to avoid war.

More Problems for American Trade

When Britain violated America's neutral rights, Jefferson banned some trade with Britain. After the attack on the *Chesapeake*, he took stronger measures.

Congress passed the Embargo Act in December 1807. An **embargo** (ihm•BAHR•goh) prohibits trade with another country. The act targeted Great Britain, but the embargo banned imports from and exports to *all* foreign countries. Jefferson wanted to prevent Americans from using other countries as go-betweens for forbidden trade.

The embargo of 1807 was a disaster. With ships confined to their harbors, unemployment rose in New England. Without European markets, the South could not sell its tobacco or cotton. The price for wheat fell in the West, and river traffic stopped. Britain, meanwhile, simply bought needed goods from other countries. Congress repealed the Embargo Act in March 1809. In its place, it passed the Nonintercourse Act. This act, which prohibited trade only with Britain and France, was also unpopular and unsuccessful.

ECONOMICS SKILL

Read the information and analyze the graph, then answer these questions.

1 ANALYZING VISUALS
Describe the imbalance of trade that occurred in the years after 1810.

2 CRITICAL THINKING
Determining Cause and Effect How did the conflict with the British affect American trade?

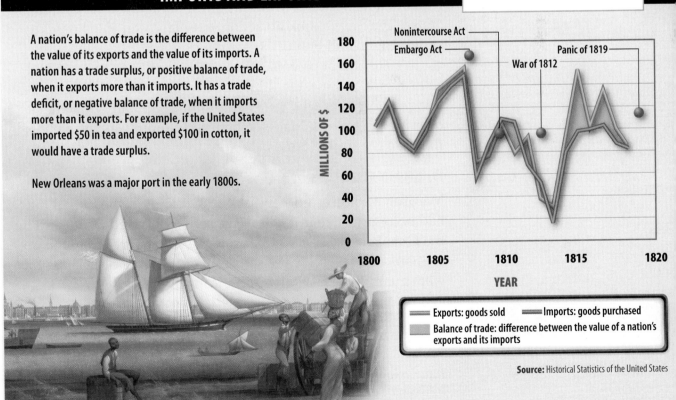

IMPORTS AND EXPORTS 1800–1820

A nation's balance of trade is the difference between the value of its exports and the value of its imports. A nation has a trade surplus, or positive balance of trade, when it exports more than it imports. It has a trade deficit, or negative balance of trade, when it imports more than it exports. For example, if the United States imported $50 in tea and exported $100 in cotton, it would have a trade surplus.

New Orleans was a major port in the early 1800s.

Nonintercourse Act
Embargo Act
War of 1812
Panic of 1819

MILLIONS OF $

180
160
140
120
100
80
60
40
20
0

1800   1805   1810   1815   1820

YEAR

Exports: goods sold   Imports: goods purchased
Balance of trade: difference between the value of a nation's exports and its imports

Source: Historical Statistics of the United States

Private Collection, Photo © Christie's Images/Bridgeman Art Library

Tecumseh called on Native Americans to unite in order to stop American expansion.

The Election of 1808

Jefferson, following Washington's precedent, made it clear that he would not be a candidate for a third term. The Republicans chose James Madison from Virginia as their candidate. The Federalists hoped that voter anger over the embargo would help them win. They nominated Charles Pinckney. Pinckney carried most of New England, but the Federalists gained little support from the other regions. Madison won the presidency with 122 electoral votes. Pinckney received just 47 votes.

✓ PROGRESS CHECK

Explaining Was the Embargo Act effective? Why?

War at Home and Abroad

GUIDING QUESTION *What issues challenged James Madison during his presidency?*

James Madison took office as president under unfavorable conditions. The nation was involved in the embargo crisis, and Britain continued to halt American ships. Cries for war with Britain grew louder.

War Looms

In 1810 Congress passed a new trade law. It would permit direct trade with either France or Britain, depending on which country first lifted its trade **restrictions**, or limits, against the United States. The British took no action, but Napoleon acted quickly, promising to end France's trade restrictions.

In spite of that promise, the French continued to seize and sell American ships. On the verge of war, Americans were divided only over who the enemy should be. Although angry over French actions, Madison believed Britain was the bigger threat to the United States.

Broken Treaties

Madison also received news about problems in the West. Ohio had become a state in 1803. White settlers wanted more land in the Ohio River valley. Native Americans had already given up millions of acres. Now the settlers were moving onto lands that were guaranteed to Native Americans by treaty.

The Granger Collection, NYC

Reading **HELP**DESK

nationalism a strong sense of devotion to one's country

Academic Vocabulary

restriction rule or regulation that limits something

As tensions grew, some Native Americans renewed their contacts with British agents and fur traders in Canada. Other Native Americans pursued a new strategy. Tecumseh (tuh•KUHM•suh), a powerful Shawnee chief, tried to build a confederacy among Native American nations in the Northwest.

Tecumseh wanted to halt white movement into Native American lands. He believed that a strong alliance—with the backing of the British in Canada—could achieve that goal. Tecumseh also thought the treaties the U.S. government made with individual Native American nations were worthless. "The Great Spirit gave this great island to his red children," he said. No one nation, he believed, had the right to give it away.

Working alongside Tecumseh was his brother, Tenskwatawa (ten•skwah•TAH•wuh). Known as the Prophet, Tenskwatawa urged Native Americans to return to their ancient customs. His message gained a large following. He founded Prophetstown in northern Indiana, near where the Tippecanoe and Wabash Rivers meet.

Tecumseh Meets the Governor

The governor of the Indiana Territory, William Henry Harrison, became alarmed by the growing power of the two Shawnee brothers. Fearing that they would form an alliance with the British, Harrison sent Tecumseh a letter. He warned Tecumseh that the United States had more warriors than all the Indian nations combined. Tecumseh replied to Harrison in person.

PRIMARY SOURCE

❝ Since the peace was made, you have killed some Shawnees, Delawares and Winnebagoes. You have taken land from us and I do not see how we can remain at peace if you continue to do so. You try to force red people to do some injury. It is you that are pushing them on to some mischief. . . . You try to prevent the Indians from doing as they wish—to unite and let them consider their lands common property of the whole. ❞

—from *The Centennial History of Oregon, 1811–1912,*
by Joseph Gaston

The Battle of Tippecanoe

Harrison attacked Prophetstown while Tecumseh was away trying to expand the confederacy. After more than two hours of battle, the Prophet's forces fled.

The Prophet lacked his brother's military skill and was badly defeated in the Battle of Tippecanoe.

MPI/Getty Images

The Battle of Tippecanoe was a victory for the Americans. Yet it came at a cost. After his people's defeat, Tecumseh joined forces with the British who, settlers believed, had supplied his confederacy with guns.

The War Hawks Call for War

Meanwhile, President Madison faced demands for a more aggressive policy toward Britain. The loudest voices came from a group of young Republican congress members known as the War Hawks. Led by Henry Clay of Kentucky and John Calhoun of South Carolina, they represented the West and South.

The War Hawks supported increases in military spending and were driven by hunger for land. War Hawks from the West wanted the fertile forests of southern Canada, whereas the southerners wanted Spanish Florida. The War Hawks also wanted to expand the nation's power. Their **nationalism** (NA•shuh•nuh•lih•zuhm)—or loyalty to their country—appealed to a renewed American patriotism.

Not everyone, however, wanted war. The Federalists in the Northeast remained strongly opposed to it.

The Eve of War

By the spring of 1812, Madison knew that he could no longer avoid war with Britain. In a message to Congress on June 1, Madison asked them to declare war.

The British had already decided to end their policy of search and seizure of American ships. Unfortunately, news of Britain's change in policy did not reach Washington, D.C., until it was too late. Once set in motion, the war machine could not be stopped.

☑ **PROGRESS CHECK**

Summarizing List three factors that led to war with Britain.

LESSON 3 REVIEW

Review Vocabulary

1. How do *tribute* and *neutral rights* affect shipping?

2. Explain the significance of the following terms:

   a. embargo **b.** nationalism

Answer the Guiding Questions

3. *Explaining* Explain why U.S. security was threatened as a result of the war between Britain and France.

4. *Summarizing* Why did conflict on the American frontier increase tensions between the United States and Britain?

5. *Contrasting* Describe how people from the South, Northeast, and West felt about going to war with Britain.

6. **EXPOSITORY WRITING** Which of the challenges that the United States faced in this period do you feel was the most serious? Write a paragraph explaining your choice.

Lesson 4
The War of 1812

ESSENTIAL QUESTION *Why does conflict develop?*

IT MATTERS BECAUSE

The War of 1812 changed how Americans felt about their country and how other countries viewed the United States.

Defeats and Victories

GUIDING QUESTION *In what ways was the United States unprepared for war with Britain?*

When the war began, the War Hawks were confident the United States would achieve a quick victory over the British. In reality, though, the Americans were unprepared for war.

The fighting force was small and ill-prepared. The regular army had fewer than 12,000 soldiers, 5,000 of whom were new recruits. Added to that were the state militias, with between 50,000 and 100,000 poorly trained soldiers. Commanders who had served in the American Revolution were now too old to fight. In addition, not everyone supported the conflict. Some states opposed "Mr. Madison's War." The Americans also **underestimated,** or misjudged, the strength of the British and their Native American allies.

In July 1812, the war began. General William Hull led the American army from Detroit into Canada, where they met Tecumseh and his warriors. Fearing a massacre by the Native Americans, Hull surrendered Detroit to the British. Several other American attempts to invade Canada also ended in failure. General William Henry Harrison led one of these unsuccessful efforts. He decided that the Americans could make no headway as long as the British controlled Lake Erie.

Reading **HELP**DESK

Taking Notes: *Describing*

As you read, use a graphic organizer like the one shown here to record and describe each battle's outcome.

Battle | Outcome
Lake Erie →
Washington, D.C. →
New Orleans →

Content Vocabulary
• **frigate**

Academic Vocabulary

underestimate to judge something below its actual value

U.S. Naval Strength

The U.S. Navy had three of the fastest **frigates** (FRIH • guhts), or warships, afloat. When the *Constitution* destroyed two British vessels early in the war, Americans rejoiced. Privateers, armed private ships, also captured many British vessels, boosting American morale.

Oliver Hazard Perry, commander of the Lake Erie naval forces, had his orders. He was to assemble a fleet and seize the lake from the British. The showdown came on September 10, 1813, when the British ships sailed out to face the Americans. In the bloody battle that followed, Perry and his ships destroyed the British naval force. After the battle, Perry sent General Harrison the message, "We have met the enemy and they are ours."

With Lake Erie in American hands, the British and their Native American allies tried to pull back from the Detroit area. Harrison and his troops cut them off. In the fierce Battle of the Thames, Tecumseh was killed.

American forces also attacked York (present-day Toronto), burning the parliament. Still, though America had won several victories by the end of 1813, Canada remained under British rule.

Defeat of the Creeks

Before his death in the Battle of the Thames, Tecumseh had talked with the Creeks in the Mississippi Territory about forming a confederation to fight the United States. With his death, hopes for such a confederation ended. The British-Native American alliance also came to an end.

In March 1814, Andrew Jackson led U.S. forces in an attack on the Creeks in the Battle of Horseshoe Bend. More than 550 Creek people died in that battle, and the Creeks were forced to give up most of their lands.

☑ PROGRESS CHECK

Evaluating Was the United States prepared to wage war? Explain.

The British Offensive

GUIDING QUESTION *Why were Americans instilled with national pride after the battle of New Orleans?*

Before fighting broke out with the United States, the British had already been at war with the French. Fighting two wars was difficult. Britain had to send soldiers and ships to both France

frigate a fast, medium-sized warship

Build Vocabulary: *Related Words*

The word *proceeded* in the quotation on the next page is similar to the word *preceded*. The prefixes *pro-* and *pre-* can both mean "before, or in front of." In this case *pro* means "forward," and the word *proceeded* means "to go forward." The word *preceded* means "to be or go in front of."

and the United States. In the spring of 1814, British fortunes began to improve. After winning the war against Napoleon, Britain was free to send more forces against the United States.

In August 1814, the British sailed into Chesapeake Bay and launched an attack on Washington, D.C. British troops quickly overpowered the American militia on the outskirts of the city. Then they marched into the American capital. "They proceeded, without a moment's delay, to burn and destroy everything in the most distant degree connected with the government," reported a British officer. Among the buildings set ablaze were the Capitol and the president's mansion. Fortunately, a thunderstorm put out the fires before they could completely destroy the buildings.

The British did not try to hold Washington, D.C. Instead, they headed north to Baltimore. They attacked that city in mid-September, but the people of Baltimore were ready and held firm. A determined defense and fierce artillery fire from Fort McHenry in the harbor kept the British from entering the city.

As the bombs burst over Fort McHenry during the night of September 13, local attorney Francis Scott Key watched. The next morning he saw the American flag still flying over the fort. Deeply moved, Key wrote a poem that became known as "The Star-Spangled Banner." Congress designated "The Star-Spangled Banner" as the national anthem in 1931.

GEOGRAPHY CONNECTION

During the War of 1812, approximately 286,000 Americans fought the British, and an estimated 2,200 were killed in battle.

1 MOVEMENT Based on this map, from what three places did the British attack the Americans?

2 CRITICAL THINKING
Drawing Conclusions Based on this map, in what area did the British have their greatest success? Explain your answer.

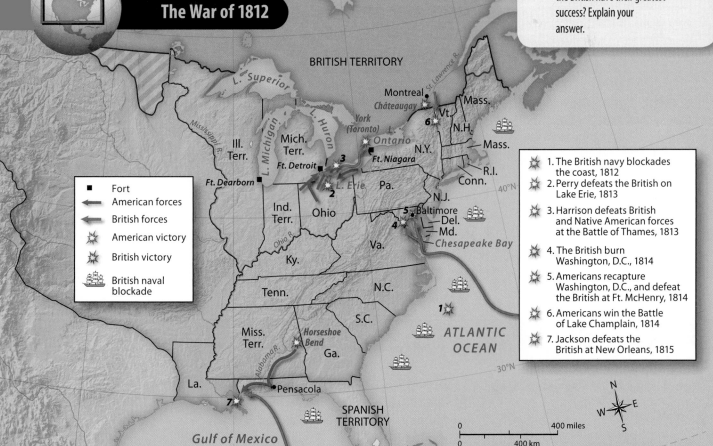

The War of 1812

Legend:
- ■ Fort
- ← American forces
- ← British forces
- ✺ American victory
- ✹ British victory
- ⛵ British naval blockade

1. The British navy blockades the coast, 1812
2. Perry defeats the British on Lake Erie, 1813
3. Harrison defeats British and Native American forces at the Battle of Thames, 1813
4. The British burn Washington, D.C., 1814
5. Americans recapture Washington, D.C., and defeat the British at Ft. McHenry, 1814
6. Americans win the Battle of Lake Champlain, 1814
7. Jackson defeats the British at New Orleans, 1815

0   400 miles
0   400 km
Albers Equal-Area projection

Dolley Madison (1768–1849)

Dolley Payne Todd married James Madison in 1794, several years after the death of her first husband. While James Madison served as President Jefferson's secretary of state, Dolley acted as hostess for the widowed president. During the War of 1812 she showed remarkable bravery. In 1814 as the British approached the capital, she refused to leave the White House until she had packed up many valuable items, a painting of George Washington, and other priceless valuables.

▶ **CRITICAL THINKING**
Drawing Conclusions Why do you think Dolley Madison risked danger to save White House valuables?

A Turning Point at Plattsburgh

While British forces were attacking Washington and Baltimore, British General Sir George Prevost was moving into New York from Canada. Leading more than 10,000 British soldiers, his **goal** was to capture Plattsburgh, a key city on the shore of Lake Champlain. An American naval force on the lake defeated the British fleet in September 1814. Fearing the Americans would surround them, the British retreated into Canada.

The Battle of Lake Champlain convinced the British that the war in North America was too costly and unnecessary. They had defeated Napoleon in Europe. To keep fighting the United States would result in little gain and was not worth the effort.

The End of the War

In December 1814, American and British representatives met in Ghent, Belgium, to sign a peace agreement. The Treaty of Ghent did not change any existing borders. There was no mention of the impressment of sailors. Even neutral rights had become a dead issue since Napoleon's defeat.

One final, ferocious battle occurred before word of the treaty reached the United States. On January 8, 1815, the British advanced on New Orleans. Waiting for them were Andrew Jackson and his troops. The redcoats were no match for Jackson's soldiers, who hid behind thick cotton bales. The bales absorbed the British bullets, while the British advancing in the open provided easy targets for American troops. In a short but gruesome battle, hundreds of British soldiers were killed. At the Battle of New Orleans, Americans achieved a decisive victory. Andrew Jackson became a hero whose fame would help him win the presidency in 1828.

Nationalism and New Respect

From the start, New England Federalists had opposed "Mr. Madison's War." These unhappy Federalists gathered in December 1814 at the Hartford Convention in Connecticut. A few favored secession, but most wanted to remain with the Union. To protect their interests, they made a list of proposed amendments to the Constitution.

Collection of the New-York Historical Society/Bridgeman Art Library

Reading **HELP**DESK

Academic Vocabulary

goal something one is trying to accomplish

The Federalists' grievances seemed unpatriotic in the triumph following the war. The party lost the public's respect and disappeared as a political force, leaving only one significant political party. The War Hawks took over leadership of the Republican Party and carried on the Federalist belief in a strong national government. The War Hawks favored trade, western expansion, the energetic development of the economy, and a strong army and navy.

Americans felt a new sense of patriotism and a strong national identity after the War of 1812. The young nation also gained new respect from other nations around the world.

Although it took place after the peace treaty had been signed in Ghent, the Battle of New Orleans made Andrew Jackson (above) a national hero, easing his entrance into politics.

▶ **CRITICAL THINKING**
Speculating Why do you think military success often leads to political success?

☑ **PROGRESS CHECK**

Identifying Cause and Effect Identify three effects of the War of 1812.

(t) The Granger Collection, NYC. (b) Stock Montage/Getty Images

LESSON 4 REVIEW

Review Vocabulary

1. Use the word *frigate* in a sentence about the developments of this era.

Answer the Guiding Questions

2. *Explaining* Why was the Battle of the Thames important for the United States in the War of 1812?

3. *Determining Cause and Effect* How did the outcome of the war affect the Federalist Party's efforts to change the Constitution?

4. *Summarizing* Describe how the War Hawks influenced the Republican Party after the War of 1812.

5. PERSONAL WRITING Consider the causes and costs of the war, the Treaty of Ghent, and the impact of the war on the American people. Was the War of 1812 worth fighting? Did it help or hurt the young United States? State your opinion in a brief essay.

Write your answers on a separate piece of paper.

1 Exploring the Essential Questions

EXPOSITORY WRITING What do you think were the two most significant changes in the United States during the Jefferson Era? Explain why you consider them important.

2 21st Century Skills

COMPARING AND CONTRASTING In a small group, discuss the similarities and differences between Jefferson's first term as president and Madison's first term as president. Consider the state of the nation and the challenges each man faced. Make a chart that summarizes the group's ideas.

3 Thinking Like a Historian

UNDERSTANDING CAUSE AND EFFECT Significant changes occurred during Thomas Jefferson's presidency. Some of those changes still affect us today. Use a chart like the one shown below to identify changes and note modern effects of those changes.

	Geography	Civics and Government
Jefferson Era		
Today		

4 Visual Literacy

ANALYZING POLITICAL CARTOONS During his presidency, Jefferson had to respond to British and French attacks on American shipping. Examine the political cartoon. What are Britain's King George and France's Napoleon Bonaparte doing? Explain whether the cartoon is critical or supportive of Jefferson and his response. Discuss whether political cartoons are an effective way of making comments about the government.

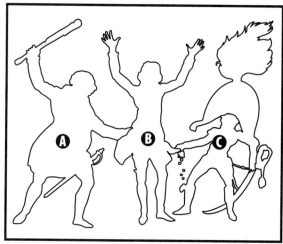

A King George of England
B Thomas Jefferson
C Napoleon Bonaparte of France

REVIEW THE GUIDING QUESTIONS

Choose the best answer for each question.

1 Which statement reflects a principle of judicial review?

  A. State law takes precedence over federal law.

  B. The Constitution is the supreme law of the land.

  C. Laws that conflict with the Constitution may stand.

  D. The executive branch must uphold the Constitution.

2 Which of the following factors influenced Napoleon's decision to sell the Louisiana Territory to the United States?

  F. the westward movement of American settlers

  G. his plans to invade Russia

  H. the loss of a naval base in Santo Domingo

  I. Spain's refusal to allow American goods to move into or past New Orleans

3 Why did Federalists oppose the Louisiana Purchase?

  A. They thought it was too expensive, and they feared new taxes.

  B. They worried about conflicts with Native Americans.

  C. They were concerned that they would lose political power as new states were created.

  D. They were afraid France would regret the sale and the nation would be forced into war with France.

4 What happened as a result of the Embargo Act of 1807?

  F. It made the nation's economy stronger as Americans had to buy and sell more American goods.

  G. It was effective in stopping Britain from violating America's neutral rights.

  H. It forced Americans to find new markets for their goods.

  I. It hurt the the U.S. economy by wiping out trade with other nations.

5 Why was the death of Tecumseh a setback for the British in the War of 1812?

  A. It caused Tenskwatawa to side with the Americans.

  B. Tecumseh was an ally of the British.

  C. Tecumseh was an enemy of the French.

  D. Tecumseh had a long history of besting Americans in battle.

6 Which of the following best describes an effect of the War of 1812?

  F. The Federalist Party gained strength.

  G. Other nations grew to despise the United States.

  H. American patriotism weakened.

  I. The United States gained status in the world.

DBQ **DOCUMENT-BASED QUESTIONS**

"The only way to stop this evil [white settlement of Indians' land], is for all the red men to unite in claiming a common and equal right in the land as it was at first, and should be now—for it never was divided, but belongs to all. ... Sell a country! Why not sell the air, the clouds, and the great sea, as well as the earth?"

—Tecumseh in a letter to President Harrison, 1810

7 **Identifying Main Ideas** What does Tecumseh suggest in this letter?

A. Native Americans should get a good price for selling their land.

B. Native Americans should give the land to white people.

C. Native Americans should work together to keep out white settlers.

D. Native Americans should sell the land and divide the profits equally.

8 **Identifying Main Ideas** What does this letter suggest about Tecumseh's views of earlier Native American agreements to sell their land?

F. He supports these agreements.

G. He believes Native Americans were misled.

H. He believes they had no right to sell the land.

I. He believes the prices received for the land were too low.

SHORT RESPONSE

"Third.—Congress shall not have power to lay any embargo on the ships or vessels of the citizens of the United States, in the ports or harbors thereof, for more than sixty days."

"Fifth.—Congress shall not make or declare war, or authorize acts of hostility against any foreign nation, without the concurrence of two-thirds of both Houses, except such acts of hostility be in defense of the territories of the United States when actually invaded."

—Amendments to the Constitution Proposed by the Hartford Convention, 1814

9 Do these changes suggest support or disapproval of the policies of Jefferson and Madison? Explain.

10 Why did these amendments fall out of favor after the War of 1812?

EXTENDED RESPONSE

11 **Expository Writing** Thomas Jefferson has just begun his first term as president of the United States. Write an article summarizing his views and explaining what you expect from his presidency.

Need Extra Help?

If You've Missed Question	❶	❷	❸	❹	❺	❻	❼	❽	❾	❿	⓫
Review Lesson	1	2	2	3	3	4	3	3	4	4	1

Growth and Expansion

1790–1840

ESSENTIAL QUESTIONS • *How does geography influence the way people live?*
• *Why does conflict develop?*

networks

There's More Online about the growth of the United States during the first part of the nineteenth century.

CHAPTER 11

The Story Matters . . .

American settlers have always preferred to live on rivers and other waterways. In these days before railroads and automobiles, water is the fastest, easiest way to move goods. When nature fails to provide a waterway, Americans take out their shovels—and take matters into their own hands.

The Erie Canal stretches 363 miles (584 km) and connects the Great Lakes of the Midwest to the Atlantic Ocean in New York City. Horses or mules tow boats loaded with 30 tons (27 t) of goods in both directions. The Erie Canal cuts the cost of shipping goods along this route from $100 per ton to $10 per ton. It shows that Americans can overcome great obstacles in their expansion to the West.

◄ *The Erie Canal opened for business in 1825.*

Bettmann/CORBIS

Place and Time: United States 1790 to 1840

In the early 1800s, United States industry and agriculture grew rapidly. Many Americans moved westward, created new settlements and cities, and improved methods of transportation.

Step Into the Place

MAP FOCUS During the early 1800s, industrialization grew. The map on the next page shows major industrial cities that emerged during this time.

1 PLACE Look at the map. Which cities near the Great Lakes saw industrial growth?

2 LOCATION Which industrial cities lie south of Virginia and Kentucky?

3 CRITICAL THINKING
Determining Cause and Effect
How do you think a region's geography influenced industrial growth in that region?

In 1818 General Andrew Jackson was ordered to stop the Native American raids coming from Florida. To accomplish this goal, he invaded areas of West Florida and Spanish East Florida. His actions helped Spain realize it could not defend or control Florida.

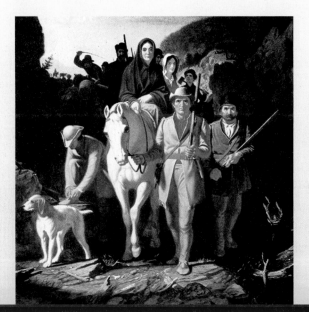

In the late 1700s, Daniel Boone helped lead American settlers into the lands beyond the Appalachian Mountains.

Step Into the Time

TIME LINE Look at the time line. Agriculture and industry grew rapidly during this period. How many years after Robert Fulton designed the first practical steamboat did workers complete the Erie Canal?

1790 Washington, D.C., founded

1793 Eli Whitney invents cotton gin

George Washington 1789–1797

John Adams 1797–1801

Thomas Jefferson 1801–1809

U.S. PRESIDENTS

U.S. EVENTS

WORLD EVENTS

1790

1800

1792 Russia invades Poland

1804 Haiti claims independence from France

(t) North Wind Picture Archives, (c) INTERFOTO / Alamy, (b) White House Historical Association

networks
There's More Online!

☑ **MAP** Explore the interactive version of this map on NETWORKS.

☑ **TIME LINE** Explore the interactive version of this time line on NETWORKS.

Growing Industrial Cities 1800–1840

L. Superior

Minnesota

Wisconsin

L. Michigan

L. Huron

Michigan
Detroit

Milwaukee

Iowa

Chicago

Illinois

Missouri R.

St. Louis

Missouri

Indiana

Cleveland

Ohio

Cincinnati

Ohio R.

Louisville

Kentucky

West Virginia

Vermont

Maine

New Hampshire

Manchester
Lowell
Boston
Pawtucket

New York

Mass.

Conn.

Rhode Island

Rochester

Buffalo

L. Ontario

L. Erie

Pennsylvania

Pittsburgh

New York City

New Jersey

Philadelphia

Baltimore

Delaware

Maryland

Richmond

Virginia

60°W

40°N

N
W   E
S

ATLANTIC OCEAN

Arkansas R.

Arkansas

Mississippi R.

Tennessee

Tennessee R.

North Carolina

South Carolina

30°N

Miss.

Alabama

Atlanta

Georgia

● Industrial city experiencing significant growth 1800-1840

Red R.

Louisiana

New Orleans

Florida

0 ———— 400 miles
0 ———— 400 km
Lambert Azimuthal Equal-Area projection

1807 Robert Fulton designs first practical steamboat

James Madison 1809–1817

James Monroe 1817–1825

1825 Erie Canal completed

John Q. Adams 1825–1829

Andrew Jackson 1829–1837

Martin Van Buren 1837–1841

1810

1820

1830

1840

1814 Francis Scott Key writes poem that becomes national anthem

1815 Napoleon defeated at Battle of Waterloo

1823 Mexico becomes a republic

1840 Workers in Lowell, Massachusetts, begin publishing the *Lowell Offering*

1820 Missouri Compromise passed

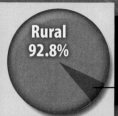

Lesson 1
A Growing Economy

ESSENTIAL QUESTION *How does geography influence the way people live?*

IT MATTERS BECAUSE
The Industrial Revolution of the late 1700s changed how people lived and worked.

Industrial Growth

GUIDING QUESTION *How did new technology affect the way things were made?*

In colonial times, most Americans lived in the same place that they worked, which was usually a farm. When they wanted or needed something, they made it. Using their hands and simple tools, people made much of their own furniture, farm equipment, household items, and clothing.

In the mid-1700s, people began producing goods through new methods. In Great Britain, inventors built machines that did some of the work involved in cloth making, such as spinning thread. These new machines ran on the power of flowing water. British cloth makers built factories, called mills, along rivers. In the mills, they installed large numbers of machines. To tend the machines, mill owners paid people wages, regular payment of money in return for work. People began to leave their homes and farms to work in the mills and collect wages. This historic change is so important that it is known as the Industrial Revolution.

The Industrial Revolution in the United States

The Industrial Revolution reached the United States around 1800. Changes began in New England because of its geography. First, New England's poor soil made farming difficult. People

(c) University of Massachusetts Lowell, Center for Lowell History, (r) Archive Photos/Kean Collection/Getty Images

Reading **HELP**DESK

Taking Notes: *Finding the Main Idea*
Use a diagram like this one to identify the major elements of the free enterprise system.

Free enterprise system

Content Vocabulary
- **cotton gin**
- **interchangeable part**
- **patent**
- **capitalism**
- **capital**
- **free enterprise**

willingly gave up farm work to earn wages elsewhere. Second, New England's many rivers and streams offered the waterpower needed to run factory machinery. Third, the area had many ports. These ports allowed the shipping in of raw materials, such as cotton, and the shipping out of finished goods, such as cloth.

New Inventions

At the heart of the Industrial Revolution was **technology.** First, new machines changed the way people made cloth. Inventions such as the water frame and spinning jenny spun thread, and the power loom wove the thread into cloth. Compared to making thread or cloth by hand, the machines saved time and money.

Other inventions followed. In 1793 Eli Whitney invented the **cotton gin.** The word *gin* is short for "engine." It quickly and easily removed the seeds from picked cotton and allowed a huge increase in cotton production.

Whitney later accepted the task of making 10,000 muskets in two years for the government. At that time, skilled workers made muskets and other items one at a time. They made each part individually, and each weapon was unlike any other. Whitney made musket parts in large numbers. Each part was identical to others of its type. Even unskilled workers could then assemble a musket quickly. Plus, if a musket broke, a soldier could quickly replace the bad part with another that fit. Whitney's idea of **interchangeable parts** changed manufacturing forever.

The Rise of Factories

In 1790 Congress passed a patent law to protect the rights of inventors. A **patent** gives an inventor the sole legal right to make money from an invention for a certain period of time.

The British also tried to protect their inventions. One law prohibited textile workers from sharing technology or leaving the country. Still, a few British workers brought these secrets to the United States. One such worker was Samuel Slater. He memorized the design of the machines used in the British factory in which he worked.

In the 1790s, Slater built copies in the United States of British machines that made cotton thread. Slater's mill marked an important step in the Industrial Revolution in the United States.

Francis Cabot Lowell improved on Slater's mill in 1814. Lowell's Massachusetts textile, or cloth, factory not only made thread, it also wove the thread into cloth. Lowell began the factory system, in which all manufacturing steps are combined in one place.

Thinking Like a HISTORIAN

Making Comparisons

Working in a factory was very different from working and living on a farm. Think about how working for wages changed the lives of people who had been used to making most of the goods they needed. How do you think life was different for the women in the picture below? For more about making comparisons, review *Thinking Like a Historian.*

These young factory workers from the 1840s, known as "Lowell Girls," lived and worked together.

cotton gin a machine that removes seeds from cotton fiber

interchangeable part a part of a machine or device that can be replaced by another, identical part

patent sole legal right to an invention and its profits

Academic Vocabulary

technology equipment that makes use of advanced knowledge and skill to solve a problem or do a task

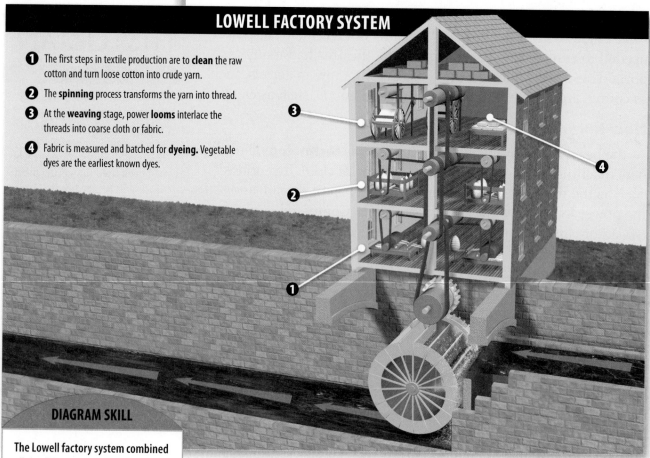

LOWELL FACTORY SYSTEM

❶ The first steps in textile production are to **clean** the raw cotton and turn loose cotton into crude yarn.

❷ The **spinning** process transforms the yarn into thread.

❸ At the **weaving** stage, power **looms** interlace the threads into coarse cloth or fabric.

❹ Fabric is measured and batched for **dyeing.** Vegetable dyes are the earliest known dyes.

DIAGRAM SKILL

The Lowell factory system combined all the different steps of making cloth under one roof.

❶ **IDENTIFYING** What is the source of the power in this mill?

❷ **CRITICAL THINKING**
Explaining How was this system an improvement over earlier technology?

Free Enterprise

The capitalist economic system of the United States helped spur industrial growth. In **capitalism,** individuals and businesses own property and decide how to use it. The people—not the government—control **capital,** which includes the buildings, land, machines, money, and other items used to create wealth.

We also use the term **free enterprise** to describe the American economic system. People are free to work wherever they wish and to buy, sell, and produce whatever they want. The major **elements** of free enterprise are economic freedom, profit, private property, and competition. Business owners produce the products they think will sell the best and make the most profit. Businesses compete for customers with low prices and high quality. This competition helps push businesses to improve.

✓ PROGRESS CHECK

Describing How did New England's physical geography support the growth of industries?

Reading **HELP**DESK

capitalism economic system in which people and companies own the means of production

capital money or other items, such as machines or buildings, used to create wealth

free enterprise a type of economy in which people are free to buy, sell, and produce whatever they want

Agriculture Grows

GUIDING QUESTION *Why did agriculture remain the leading occupation of Americans in the 1800s?*

While many New Englanders went to work in factories in the early 1800s, most Americans still lived and worked on farms. In the Northeast, farms were small, so a family could do all the necessary work. Farmers in the Northeast usually sold their products locally.

Agriculture moved west along with American settlers. Western farmers in the region north of the Ohio River found land that could support a thriving agriculture. Many of these farmers concentrated on raising pork and cash crops such as corn and wheat.

In the South, cotton production rose sharply. The demand for cotton grew steadily as textile factories appeared. In addition, the cotton gin allowed planters to grow cotton over a much wider area. Southern farmers seeking new land moved west to plant the valuable crop. Between 1790 and 1820, cotton production soared from 3,000 to 300,000 bales per year in the South.

The success and spread of cotton created a huge demand for enslaved workers. Trade in enslaved Africans expanded. Between 1790 and 1810, the number of enslaved Africans in the United States rose from about 700,000 to 1.2 million.

As farmers moved west, the crops they planted varied according to the climate. While cotton was the common choice in the warmer South, grain crops such as wheat (shown here) and corn dominated the cooler areas to the north.

✓ **PROGRESS CHECK**

Determining Cause and Effect What are some of the significant effects of increased cotton production in the South?

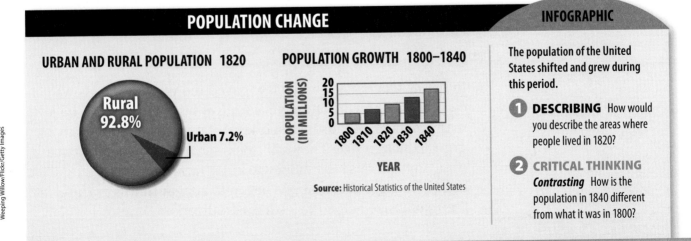

POPULATION CHANGE

URBAN AND RURAL POPULATION 1820

Rural 92.8%

Urban 7.2%

POPULATION GROWTH 1800–1840

POPULATION (IN MILLIONS)

20, 15, 10, 5, 0

1800, 1810, 1820, 1830, 1840

YEAR

Source: Historical Statistics of the United States

INFOGRAPHIC

The population of the United States shifted and grew during this period.

1 DESCRIBING How would you describe the areas where people lived in 1820?

2 CRITICAL THINKING *Contrasting* How is the population in 1840 different from what it was in 1800?

Weeping Willow/Flickr/Getty Images

Academic Vocabulary

element part of a larger whole

The area now known as the South Street Seaport in New York City offered hotels, restaurants, and businesses. The value of trade in the area increased from $84 million in 1825 to $146 million in 1836.

Economic Independence

GUIDING QUESTION *How did the growth of factories and trade affect cities?*

Small investors—such as shopkeepers, merchants, and farmers—provided the money necessary to build most new businesses. These people invested money in hopes of earning profits if the businesses were successful. Low taxes, minimum government regulations, and competition encouraged people to invest in new industries.

Growth of Corporations

In the 1830s, changes in the law paved the way for the growth of corporations. A corporation is a type of business that can have many owners. Because of their legal status, corporations can grow to a large size. They sell stock—shares of ownership in a company—to raise the money to build factories and expand their business. Large corporations began to appear in this era, and their great size helped drive industrialization.

Archive Photos/Kean Collection/Getty Images

Reading HELPDESK

Build Vocabulary: *Word Origins*

The word *corporation* comes from the Latin word *corpus*, which means "body." It is a group of people that acts together. A corporation continues to exist even after the people who first formed it have gone.

Cities Grow Up

The growth of factories and trade led to the growth of towns and cities. Many cities developed along rivers because factories could take advantage of the waterpower and easily ship goods to markets. Older cities such as New York, Boston, and Baltimore also grew as centers of commerce and trade.

Along New York City's South Street, shipping piers extended for 3 miles (5 km). One traveler wrote of the busy waterfront:

66 Every thought, word, look, and action of the multitude seemed to be absorbed by commerce. 99

—from *The Growing Years* by Margaret L. Coit

To the west, towns such as Pittsburgh, Cincinnati, and Louisville were located on major rivers. As farmers in the West shipped more products by water, these towns grew rapidly.

Cities and towns looked different from modern urban areas. They featured wood and brick buildings and unpaved streets. Barnyard animals often roamed freely. There were no sewers to carry away waste, so diseases such as cholera and yellow fever were a threat. Fire was another danger. Sparks from a fireplace could easily ignite wooden buildings. Fires could be disastrous since few cities had organized fire companies. Yet cities offered many opportunities, such as a variety of jobs and steady wages. As cities grew, residents built libraries, museums, and shops for people to enjoy during their leisure time. For many, the jobs and attractions of city life outweighed the dangers.

☑ **PROGRESS CHECK**

Analyzing Why were rivers important for the growth of cities?

LESSON 1 REVIEW

Review Vocabulary

1. Write a paragraph about Eli Whitney using the terms *cotton gin, patent,* and *interchangeable part.*

2. Explain in a paragraph the connection between *capital, capitalism,* and *free enterprise.*

Answer the Guiding Questions

3. *Explaining* How did the introduction of factories change the way goods were made in the colonies?

4. *Identifying* What economic activity was most widespread in the United States in the early 1800s?

5. *Determining Cause and Effect* How did industrialization affect the way people lived in the United States?

6. **PERSONAL WRITING** Imagine it is 1825 and you have recently moved from the family farm to New York City, where you work in a factory. Write a letter to a friend describing your new life.

netw⊙rks

There's More Online!

☑ **GRAPHIC ORGANIZER**
Transportation
Developments

☑ **MAP**
• The National Road
• Canals 1820–1860

☑ **SLIDE SHOW**
The Erie Canal

☑ **VIDEO**

Lesson 2

Moving West

ESSENTIAL QUESTION *How does geography influence the way people live?*

IT MATTERS BECAUSE

Settling the West led to improvements in transportation that helped the nation grow and prosper.

Headed West

GUIDING QUESTION *What helped increase the movement of people and goods?*

In 1790 the first **census**—the official count of a population—**revealed** that there were nearly 4 million Americans. At that time, most of these people still lived in the narrow strip of land between the Appalachian Mountains and the Atlantic Ocean. That pattern, however, was changing. For years, a few rugged American settlers had been crossing the Appalachian Mountains and settling in western lands. Now, a steady stream of settlers began moving west.

Daniel Boone and the Wilderness Road

Explorer and pioneer Daniel Boone was among the early western pioneers. In 1769 he explored a Native American trail through the Appalachian Mountains. Called Warriors' Path, it led Boone through a break in the mountains—the Cumberland Gap. Beyond the gap lay the gentle hills of a land now called Kentucky. For two years, Boone explored the area's dense forests and lush meadows.

In 1775 Boone rounded up 30 skilled foresters to make the trail easier to cross for pioneers migrating west. Boone's crew widened Warriors' Path, cleared rocks from the Cumberland

(cl) North Wind Picture Archives / Alamy, (c) Bettmann/Corbis, (r) Collection of the New-York Historical Society/Bridgeman Art Library

---

Taking Notes: *Sequencing*

Use a time line like this one to identify and place in chronological order the major developments in transportation during the early 1800s.

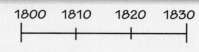

1800   1810   1820   1830

Content Vocabulary
• **census**   • **canal**
• **turnpike** • **lock**

Gap, cut down trees in Kentucky, and marked the trail. The new Wilderness Road, as it came to be known, served as the main southern highway from the eastern states to the West. More than 100,000 people traveled it between 1775 and 1790.

Building Roadways

The nation needed good inland roads for travel and to ship goods. Private companies built many **turnpikes,** or toll roads. Tolls, or fees paid by travelers, helped pay the cost of building them. Many roads had a base of crushed stone. In some areas workers built "corduroy roads." These roads had a surface made up of logs laid side by side, like the ridges of corduroy cloth.

Ohio became a state in 1803. The new state asked the federal government to build a road to connect it with the East. In 1806 Congress approved funds for a national road to the West, though it took five more years for members to agree on the route.

Work on the project began in 1811 in Cumberland, Maryland. The start of the War of 1812 with Great Britain halted construction. As a result, the road's first section, which ran from Maryland to Wheeling in present-day West Virginia, did not open until 1818.

Connections to
TODAY

The National Road

Drivers today can follow a modern road that closely follows the route of the National Road. It is U.S. Route 40, which continues past the end of the original National Road all the way to Utah. The Internet also offers a great deal of information about the route and key points along it.

GEOGRAPHY CONNECTION

The National Road was the nation's first federally funded highway. When completed in 1837, the gravel road extended from the eastern seaboard to Vandalia, Illinois.

1 **MOVEMENT** What towns did the National Road pass through on its way to Vandalia?

2 **CRITICAL THINKING**
Speculating In what ways do you think the National Road affected communities near which it passed?

The National Road 1811–1837

POPULATION IN OHIO, INDIANA, AND ILLINOIS			
Year	Ohio	Indiana	Illinois
1800	45,465	5,641	—
1810	230,760	24,520	12,282
1820	581,434	147,178	55,211
1830	937,903	343,031	157,445

Source: United States Census

census the official count of a population
turnpike road on which tolls are collected

Academic Vocabulary

reveal to show

Robert Fulton did not invent the technology of the steamboat, but his *Clermont* helped lead to the growth of steamboats in the United States. The 140-foot (43 m) *Clermont* was large, fast, and comfortable.

The route closely followed that of a military road George Washington had built in 1754. It eventually reached Ohio and then Vandalia, Illinois. Congress viewed the road as vital to military readiness but did not take on any other road-building projects.

Traveling on Rivers

River travel was far more comfortable than travel by road, which was often rough and bumpy. Also, boats or river barges could carry far larger loads of farm products or other goods.

River travel had two big drawbacks, however. First, most major rivers in the eastern **region** flowed in a north-south direction, while most people and goods were headed east or west. Second, while traveling downstream was easy, moving upstream against the current was slow.

In the 1780s and 1790s, boat captains were already using steam engines to power boats in quiet waters. These early engines, however, did not have enough power to overcome the strong currents and winds found in large rivers, lakes, or oceans.

The *Clermont*'s First Voyage

In 1802 Robert Livingston, a political and business leader, hired Robert Fulton to build a steamboat with a powerful engine. Livingston wanted the steamboat to carry cargo and passengers up the Hudson River from New York City to Albany.

In 1807 Fulton launched his steamboat, the *Clermont*. The boat made the 150-mile (241 km) trip from New York City to Albany in 32 hours. Using only sails, the trip would have taken four days.

The *Clermont* offered many comforts. Passengers could sit or stroll on deck or relax in sleeping compartments below deck. The engine was noisy, but its power provided a smooth ride.

Reading **HELP**DESK

canal an artificial waterway

lock separate compartment in which water levels rise and fall in order to raise or lower boats on a canal

Academic Vocabulary

region an area defined by a feature or characteristic

Steamboats ushered in a new age of river travel. Shipping goods and moving people became cheaper and faster. Regular steamboat service began along the Mississippi River, between New Orleans and Natchez, Mississippi, in 1812. Steamboats also contributed to the growth of river cities such as Cincinnati and St. Louis. By 1850 some 700 steamboats were carrying cargo and passengers within the United States.

New Waterways

Steamboats improved transportation but were limited to major rivers. No such river linked the East and the West.

Business and government officials led by DeWitt Clinton in New York developed a plan to connect New York City with the Great Lakes region. They would build a **canal**—an artificial waterway—across the state. The canal would connect the Hudson River with Buffalo on Lake Erie. From these points, existing rivers and lakes could connect a much wider area.

The Erie Canal

Thousands of workers, many of them Irish immigrants, helped build the 363-mile (584 km) Erie Canal. Along the way they built a series of **locks**—separate compartments in which workers could raise or lower the water level. The locks worked like an escalator to raise and lower boats up and down hills.

Canal building was a hazardous task. Many workers died as a result of cave-ins or blasting accidents. Another threat was disease, which bred in the swamps where the workers toiled.

After more than eight years of hard work, the Erie Canal opened on October 26, 1825. Clinton, who was now governor of New York, boarded a barge in Buffalo and traveled on the canal to Albany. From there he sailed down the Hudson River to New York City. As crowds cheered, officials poured water from Lake Erie into the Atlantic Ocean.

GEOGRAPHY CONNECTION

The Erie Canal was just one of many canals built between 1820 and 1860.

1 **HUMAN-ENVIRONMENT INTERACTION** Which canal helped connect Lake Michigan to the Mississippi River?

2 **CRITICAL THINKING**
Making Inferences Why do you think so many of the canals were built north of the Ohio River and in the Northeast?

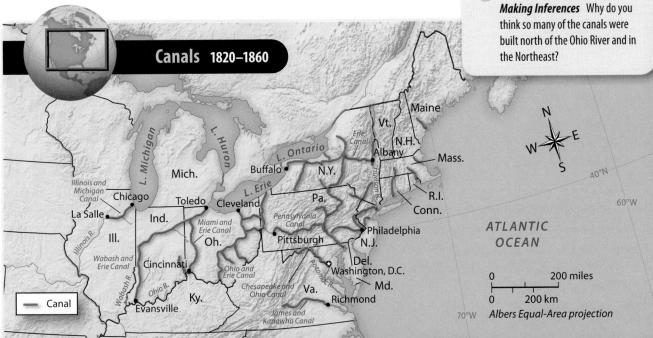

Canals 1820–1860

The Erie Canal brought industry and economic growth to communities all along its length.

▶ **CRITICAL THINKING**
Analyzing Why do you think the canal helped populations grow?

Canal Travel Expands

At first, the Erie Canal did not allow steamboats because their powerful engines could cause damage to the canal's earthen banks. Instead, teams of mules or horses hauled the boats and barges. A two-horse team pulled a 100-ton (91 t) barge about 24 miles (39 km) in one day. This was fast compared with travel by wagon. In the 1840s, workers strengthened the canal banks so that steam tugboats could pull the barges.

The Erie Canal's success did not go unnoticed. By 1850 the country had more than 3,600 miles (5,794 km) of canals. Canals lowered shipping costs and brought prosperity to towns along their routes. They also linked regions of a growing country.

☑ **PROGRESS CHECK**

Finding the Main Idea Why were canals built?

The Move West Continues

GUIDING QUESTION *Why did Americans tend to settle near rivers?*

The United States added four new states between 1791 and 1803— Vermont, and the western states of Kentucky, Tennessee, and Ohio. Then, between 1816 and 1821, Indiana, Illinois, Mississippi, Alabama, and Missouri also became states.

Collection of the New-York Historical Society/Bridgeman Art Library

Build Vocabulary: *Multiple Meaning Words*

Some words with the same spelling and sound have more than one meaning. The word *lock* also means "a device for keeping something (door, window, box) closed and unable to open."

The formation of new states reflected the dramatic growth of the region west of the Appalachians. In 1800 only 387,000 white settlers lived west of the Appalachian Mountains. By 1820 that number had grown to more than 2.4 million people. Ohio, for example, had only 45,000 settlers in 1800. By 1820 it had 581,000 residents.

Early pioneer families often settled in communities along the great rivers, such as the Ohio and the Mississippi. These waterways provided a highway for shipping crops and other goods to markets. The growth of canals also helped expand the area open to settlement. Canals allowed people to settle on lands farther from the large rivers.

People often preferred to settle with others from their original homes. It was mainly people from Tennessee and Kentucky who settled Indiana, for example. Michigan's pioneers came mostly from New England.

Western families often gathered together for social events. Men took part in sports such as wrestling. Women met for quilting and sewing parties. Both men and women took part in cornhuskings. These were gatherings where farm families shared the work of stripping the outer layers from corn.

Life in the West did not have many of the conveniences of Eastern town life. The pioneers had not traveled to the West to live a pampered life. They wanted to make new lives for themselves and their families.

At the same time, these new settlers brought with them many of the same hopes and dreams held by people in the East. In this way, the western migration of American pioneers helped spread an American culture and way of life.

☑ **PROGRESS CHECK**

Describing What was life like for families on the western frontier?

Connections to
TODAY

Moving West

Americans have always been on the move, searching for new opportunities or better climates. In recent years, leading destinations for American migrants have been states such as Florida, Arizona, and Nevada. This migration pattern represents a long-standing trend of Americans leaving the Northeast and Midwest for the South, West, and Southwest.

LESSON 2 REVIEW

Review Vocabulary

1. Use each of these terms in a different sentence that explains the term's meaning.

   a. census   **b.** turnpike

2. Write a sentence that explains how canals and locks are related.

Answer the Guiding Questions

3. *Summarizing* What did Americans do in the late 1700s and early 1800s to improve the movement of people and goods?

4. *Describing* How did rivers play a role in the settlement of the West?

5. **EXPOSITORY WRITING** Write a paragraph explaining how life in the West was different from life in the East.

netw⊚rks
There's More Online!

☑ **BIOGRAPHY**
Henry Clay

☑ **CHART**
Mississippi River Basin

☑ **GRAPHIC ORGANIZER**
Effects of the Missouri Compromise

☑ **MAP**
• The Missouri Compromise
• Acquisition of Florida

☑ **PRIMARY SOURCE**
From *Life on the Mississippi*

☑ **VIDEO**

Lesson 3
Unity and Sectionalism

ESSENTIAL QUESTION *Why does conflict develop?*

IT MATTERS BECAUSE
Although national pride was evident throughout the country, each region—North, South, and West—wanted to further its own economic and political interests.

National Unity

GUIDING QUESTION *How did the country change after the War of 1812?*

With the end of the War of 1812, the **intense** divisions that once split the nation seemed gone. In their place was a feeling of unity. In the 1816 presidential election, James Monroe, the Republican candidate, faced no serious opposition. The Federalists, weakened by doubts about their loyalty during the war, barely survived as a national party. Monroe won the election by an overwhelming margin.

A Boston newspaper called this time the Era of Good Feelings. The new president was a living, breathing symbol of this mood. Monroe had been involved in national politics since the American Revolution. He wore breeches, or knee-length pants, and powdered wigs—styles no longer in fashion. Yet with his sense of dignity, Monroe represented a united country, free of political strife.

Outgoing President James Madison's last message to Congress in 1817 expressed a growing nationalism, or strong loyalty to the nation. The War of 1812 had made clear that Jefferson's ideal of a limited central government could not meet the needs of a nation in times of crisis. Sounding more like a Federalist than a Republican,

---

Reading **HELP**DESK

Taking Notes: *Determining Cause and Effect*

Use a diagram like this one to show how the Missouri Compromise affected different parts of the country.

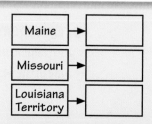

Maine	→	
Missouri	→	
Louisiana Territory	→	

Content Vocabulary
• **sectionalism** • **interstate commerce**
• **monopoly** • **cede**

Madison urged the federal government to guide the growth of trade and industry. The large Republican majority in Congress agreed. The Republicans, who had once strongly supported states rights, now promoted federal power.

Henry Clay's American System

Henry Clay, a Republican and speaker of the house, proposed a nationalist program to help the nation grow. Clay's American System aimed to help the economy in each section of the country and increase the power of the federal government. Clay called for higher tariffs, a new Bank of the United States, and **internal** improvements, including the building of roads, bridges, and canals.

Not all congressional leaders agreed with Clay, and they did not accept all of his ideas. Congress did not spend much money on internal improvements, but other parts of the American System did become law.

The Second Bank of the United States

The charter for the First Bank of the United States expired in 1811, and Congress let the bank die. In 1816 the Republican majority in Congress brought the national bank back to life. President Madison signed the bill creating the Second Bank of the United States.

After the First Bank closed, many state banks had acted unwisely. They made too many loans and allowed too much money into circulation. These actions led to inflation, a rise in the prices of goods. As prices rose, American families could buy less and less with each dollar. The absence of a national bank also meant the federal government had no safe place to keep its funds. The Second Bank of the United States restored order to the money supply, helping American businesses to grow.

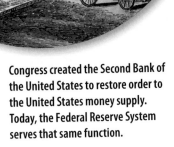

Competition From Britain

Another challenge facing the economy was a flood of British goods following the War of 1812. British factories often had more advanced technology and methods than American factories. The British turned out goods of higher quality and at a lower price than goods made in the United States. Naturally, buyers preferred these goods. By flooding the United States with their goods, the British hoped to keep American businesses from competing.

Congress created the Second Bank of the United States to restore order to the United States money supply. Today, the Federal Reserve System serves that same function.

▶ **CRITICAL THINKING**
Making Connections Is the idea of having a central bank for the nation consistent with the idea of free enterprise? Explain.

North Wind Picture Archives

Academic Vocabulary

intense very strong
internal within the country

New Tariffs

American manufacturers called for high tariffs to protect their growing industries. To address this problem, Congress passed the Tariff of 1816. Unlike earlier revenue tariffs, which were meant to provide income for the federal government, this tariff was designed to protect American manufacturers from foreign competition by placing high taxes on imports. Merchants who paid the tariff on imported goods simply added the cost of the tariff to their prices. This made imported items more expensive for consumers and encouraged them to buy cheaper, American-made goods.

When Congress passed protective tariffs in 1818 and 1824 that were even higher than the Tariff of 1816, some Americans protested. Southerners were especially angry. They felt that the tariff protected Northern manufacturers at their expense. The South had few factories, so people there saw little benefit from high tariffs. What the Southern states did see were higher prices for the goods they had to buy.

Growing Sectionalism

The tariff dispute illustrated a growing **sectionalism** (SEHK•shuh•nuh•lih•zuhm)—differences in the goals and interests of different parts of the country. Such differences had existed since colonial times. Now, it seemed, they were growing sharper. In fact, they soon brought an end to the Era of Good Feelings.

In the early 1800s, three distinct sections developed in the United States—the North, the South, and the West. The North included New England and the Mid-Atlantic states. The South covered what is now the Southeast. The West included the area between the Appalachian Mountains and the Mississippi River. Geography, economics, and history all contributed to sectional differences and differing ways of life in the United States. As the differences grew deeper, however, people began to wonder whether sectionalism might divide the nation.

Each section of the country had a strong voice in Congress in the early 1800s. Henry Clay of Kentucky represented the West. John C. Calhoun of South Carolina spoke for Southern interests. Daniel Webster of Massachusetts protected the interests of New England. Each leader, although nationalist, remained concerned with protecting the interests of his own section of the country.

Reading **HELP**DESK

sectionalism rivalry based on the special interests of different areas

Nationalism and the Supreme Court

In three decisions in the early 1800s, the Supreme Court backed the powers of the national government over the states. During this time, Chief Justice John Marshall provided strong leadership.

In the case of *Fletcher* v. *Peck* in 1810, the Court ruled that courts could declare acts of a state government void if they violated provisions of the Constitution. Then, in 1819, the Court decided the case of *McCulloch* v. *Maryland*. It said that the state of Maryland could not tax the local office of the Bank of the United States because it was the property of the national government. Allowing such a tax, the Court said, would give states too much power over the national government.

The Court also ruled that the national bank was constitutional, even though the Constitution did not specifically give Congress the power to create a bank. Marshall observed that the Constitution specifically gave Congress power to issue money, borrow money, and collect taxes. Congress could also, he reasoned, do whatever was "necessary and proper" to carry out those powers.

In 1824 the Court again ruled in favor of federal government power in *Gibbons* v. *Ogden*. The state of New York had granted a **monopoly** (muh•NAH•puh•lee)—sole control of an industry—to a steamship operator running ships between New York and New Jersey. Under New York's law, no other operator could run steamboats on the same route. The Supreme Court said that only Congress had the power to make laws governing **interstate commerce,** or trade between states.

Missouri Statehood

In 1819 the Missouri Territory asked Congress for admission as a state. Most Missouri settlers had come from Kentucky and Tennessee, which allowed slavery. They believed slavery ought to be legal in Missouri.

Representative James Tallmadge proposed that Missouri gradually abolish slavery in order to be admitted to the Union. The House passed this plan, but the Senate blocked it.

At the time, the population in the North was slightly larger than in the slave states of the South. Consequently, the North had 105 members in the House of Representatives compared to the South's 81 members. Representation in the Senate was balanced, with 11 slave states and 11 free states. The addition of Missouri as a free state would put the South in the minority in both houses of Congress.

BIOGRAPHY

Henry Clay (1777–1852)

Henry Clay had a long career in Congress that began when he was elected to fill a Senate vacancy when he was just 29, a year shy of the Constitution's age requirement. Clay's ability to resolve arguments earned him the nickname "The Great Compromiser." He believed strongly in the nation. In a speech on the Senate floor, he once said: "If the . . . sad event of the dissolution [breaking up] of this Union is to happen, . . . I shall not survive to behold the sad and heart-rending [upsetting] spectacle."

▶ **CRITICAL THINKING**
Analyzing Primary Sources How does Clay's statement reflect nationalist views?

monopoly a market where there is only one provider
interstate commerce economic activity taking place between two or more states

Christie's Images/Bridgeman Art Library

Missouri's application for statehood sparked a national debate that led to the Missouri Compromise.

1 REGION Under the Missouri Compromise, was the Unorganized Territory open or closed to slavery?

2 CRITICAL THINKING
Analyzing Do you think the Missouri Compromise was a permanent solution to the question of slavery in new states? Explain.

The Missouri Compromise 1820

CANADA

N.H.
Vt. Maine
free state
in 1820

Unorganized Territory

Michigan Territory

N.Y. Mass.
R.I.
Pa. Conn.

Ill. Ind. Ohio
N.J.
Del.
Md.

NEW SPAIN

Mo.
slave state
in 1821

Va.

Ky.

Missouri Compromise Line
36°30'N

Tenn.

N.C.

Arkansas Terr.

S.C.

ATLANTIC OCEAN

Miss. Ala. Ga.

La.

Fla.

Gulf of Mexico

0   400 miles
0   400 km
Albers Equal-Area projection

40°N

30°N

90°W   80°W

N E W S

Free state/territory

Closed to slavery by the Missouri Compromise

Slave state/territory

Territory opened to slavery by the Missouri Compromise

The Missouri Compromise

Debates in Congress heated to the boiling point. Fearing a split in the Union, Henry Clay suggested the Missouri Compromise. Clay proposed that Maine, in the Northeast, enter the Union as a free state. Missouri could then enter as a slave state. This would keep an even balance of power in the Senate—12 free states and 12 slave states.

The Missouri Compromise also addressed the question of slavery in the rest of the Louisiana Purchase territory. The compromise drew a line west from the southern boundary of Missouri—at 36°30′ N latitude. The compromise blocked slavery north of the line but permitted it south of the line.

The Missouri Compromise promised a temporary solution to sectional conflict. It did nothing to solve the basic problem, however. Americans who moved west took their different ways of life with them. White Southerners wanted to take an economy based on slavery to their new homes. Northerners believed in labor by free people and wanted to establish that in the West. It was a disagreement that seemed to have no peaceful solution.

☑ **PROGRESS CHECK**

Explaining Describe how the Supreme Court's decisions affected the power of the federal government.

Reading Strategy: *Summarizing*

When you summarize, you reduce the important content into short and simple form. Summarize the effects of the Missouri Compromise described on this page.

Foreign Affairs

GUIDING QUESTION *How did the United States define its role in the Americas?*

The War of 1812 heightened Americans' pride in their country. Americans also realized that the United States had to establish a new relationship with the "Old World"—the powers of Europe.

Relations with Britain

In the 1817 Rush-Bagot Agreement, the United States and Britain agreed to limit the number of armed naval vessels on the Great Lakes. Each country was to take apart or destroy other armed ships on the Great Lakes.

The Convention of 1818 set the northern boundary of the Louisiana Territory between the United States and Canada at the 49th parallel. The convention also created a secure border. Each country agreed to maintain its border without armed forces. Secretary of State John Quincy Adams also negotiated the right of Americans to settle in the Oregon Country.

Relations with Spain

Spain owned the colonies of East Florida and West Florida. In 1810 American settlers in West Florida rebelled against Spanish rule. The United States government then argued that West Florida was included in the Louisiana Purchase. In 1810 and 1812, the United States took control of sections of West Florida.

Acquisition of Florida 1819

Texas

La.

Miss.

Alabama

Georgia

Natchez

Baton Rouge

New Orleans

Pensacola

St. Augustine

ATLANTIC OCEAN

30°N

Gulf of Mexico

Florida

Annexed by U.S., 1810
Annexed by U.S., 1812
Ceded by Spain, 1819
Present-day boundaries

0   250 miles
0   250 km

Albers Equal-Area projection

95°W   90°W   85°W   80°W

GEOGRAPHY CONNECTION

The United States acquired Florida in 1819.

1 **PLACE** Which states include land that was once part of Florida?

2 **CRITICAL THINKING** *Drawing Conclusions* Why do you think Spain came to believe that keeping Florida was impossible?

Reading in the Content Area: *Lines of Latitude*

The map on this page shows a single line running horizontally—a line of latitude, or a parallel. Marked 30°N, this line runs close to the city of St. Augustine in Florida. Further north, not shown on this map, is the 49th parallel. This line became the boundary between Canada and the Louisiana territory in 1818.

At this 1813 meeting, the Congress of Chilpancingo, Mexican leaders declared independence from Spain and drafted a constitution calling for a republican government. Mexico would finally achieve independence in 1821.

The territory claimed by the United States reached west to the borders of Louisiana and Mississippi. Spain objected to losing part of West Florida but took no action against the United States.

Native Americans living in Spanish East Florida sometimes raided American settlements in Georgia. General Andrew Jackson was ordered to stop these Seminole raids. Jackson believed his order included pursuing the Seminoles into the Florida colonies. In the spring of 1818, another general, William McIntosh, led Creek allies against the Seminoles in Georgia. Meanwhile, Jackson followed fleeing Seminoles into Spanish West Florida. After pursuing the Seminoles, Jackson and his troops moved farther into West Florida. There they seized the Spanish forts at Pensacola and San Marcos. Secretary of State Adams had not authorized Jackson's actions, but he did nothing to stop them or to punish Jackson.

Jackson's raid demonstrated American military strength compared to that of Spain. Secretary of State Adams believed that the Spanish did not want war and wanted to settle the dispute. Adams was correct, and with the Adams-Onís Treaty of 1819, Spain **ceded,** or gave up control of, all claims and ownership to both East and West Florida. They also gave up claims to Oregon Country in the Pacific Northwest, while the United States agreed to Spanish control of Texas.

---

cede to transfer control of something

Reading in the Content Area: *Historical Maps*

Maps often use shading to show changes over time. To read a map of this type, point to each shaded area on the map as you read the map key. You may want to cover other areas, if possible.

Spain Loses Power

Meanwhile, Spain was losing power elsewhere in its vast empire. In 1810 a priest named Miguel Hidalgo (ee • DAHL • goh) led a rebellion in Mexico. Hidalgo called for racial equality and the redistribution of land. The Spanish captured and executed Hidalgo, but by 1821 Mexico had gained its independence from Spain.

Simón Bolívar, also known as "the Liberator," led the independence movement that won freedom for the present-day countries of Venezuela, Colombia, Panama, Bolivia, and Ecuador. José de San Martín successfully achieved independence for Chile and Peru. By 1824 Spain had lost control of most of South America.

The Monroe Doctrine

In 1822 four European nations—France, Austria, Russia, and Prussia—discussed a plan to help Spain regain its American holdings. The possibility of increased European involvement in the Americas troubled President Monroe. There were also concerns about Russia's intentions for controlling land in the Northwest.

The president issued a statement on December 2, 1823: The United States would not get involved in the internal affairs or wars in Europe. It also would not interfere with any existing European colonies in the Americas. At the same time, the statement said, North and South America "are henceforth not to be considered as subjects for future colonization by any European powers." The Monroe Doctrine, as the statement came to be known, served as a clear warning to European nations to keep out of the Americas. It became a guiding force in American foreign policy in the decades ahead.

✓ PROGRESS CHECK

Summarizing Why did Spain finally give up Florida to the United States?

LESSON 3 REVIEW

Review Vocabulary

1. Use each of these terms in a sentence that explains the term's meaning.

    a. monopoly   **b.** interstate commerce   **c.** cede

2. What does the term *sectionalism* mean?

Answer the Guiding Questions

3. ***Explaining*** What factors contributed to the rise of nationalism in the 1810s?

4. ***Making Inferences*** Why was the Monroe Doctrine issued?

5. ***Listing*** What issues divided the country at the end of the Era of Good Feelings?

6. ***Describing*** How did the United States role in the world change in the early 1800s?

7. **PERSUASIVE WRITING** Members of Congress agreed to the Missouri Compromise in an attempt to prevent serious conflict. Write a letter to a member of Congress arguing for or against this compromise.

Life on the Mississippi

by Mark Twain

Samuel Langhorne Clemens (1835–1910), known as Mark Twain, was born in Missouri. He spent his early years along the Mississippi River in the town of Hannibal.

Later, as a young man, Clemens trained as a river pilot's apprentice. He used his experiences as a basis for many of the stories in *Life on the Mississippi.* This book is a collection of humorous anecdotes and folktales, and it provides a glimpse into Twain's life before he became a famous author.

Mark Twain used memories of his youth in writing *Life on the Mississippi.*

" *I remember the annual processions of mighty rafts that used to glide by Hannibal when I was a boy,—an acre or so of white, sweet-smelling boards in each raft, a crew of two dozen men or more ...* "

—from *Life on the Mississippi*

Steamboats carried passengers and cargo up and down the Mississippi.

66 Between La Salle's opening of the river and the time when it may be said to have become the vehicle of anything like a regular and active commerce, seven **sovereigns** had occupied the throne of England, America had become an independent nation. . . .

The river's earliest commerce was in great barges—keelboats, broadhorns. They floated and sailed from the upper rivers to New Orleans, changed cargoes there, and were **tediously** warped and poled back by hand. A voyage down and back sometimes occupied nine months. In time this commerce increased until it gave employment to hordes of rough and hardy men; rude, uneducated, brave, suffering terrific hardships with sailor-like **stoicism** . . . , heavy fighters, reckless fellows, every one, **elephantinely** jolly, foul-witted, **profane; prodigal** of their money, bankrupt at the end of the trip, fond of barbaric finery, **prodigious** braggarts; yet, in the main, honest, trustworthy, faithful to promises and duty, and often picturesquely **magnanimous.**

By and by the steamboat intruded. Then for fifteen or twenty years, these men continued to run their keelboats down-stream, and the steamers did all of the upstream business, the keelboatmen selling their boats in New Orleans, and returning home as deck passengers in the steamers.

But after a while the steamboats so increased in number and in speed that they were able to absorb the entire commerce; and then keelboating died a permanent death. The keelboatman became a deck hand, or a mate, or a pilot on the steamer; and when steamer-berths were not open to him, he took a berth on a Pittsburgh coal-flat, or on a pine-raft constructed in the forests up toward the sources of the Mississippi.

In the **heyday** of the steamboating prosperity, the river from end to end was flaked with coal-fleets and timber rafts, all managed by hand, and employing hosts of the rough characters whom I have been trying to describe. I remember the annual processions of mighty rafts that used to glide by Hannibal when I was a boy,—an acre or so of white, sweet-smelling boards in each raft, a crew of two dozen men or more, three or four wigwams scattered about the raft's vast level space for storm-quarters,—and I remember the rude ways and the tremendous talk of their big crews . . . for we used to swim out a quarter or third of a mile and get on these rafts and have a ride. 99

Vocabulary

sovereign one who holds power
tedious boring
stoicism the quality of not reacting to pleasure or pain
elephantine having great size
profane not religious
prodigal wasteful
prodigious large in size or quantity
magnanimous noble, generous
heyday the peak of one's strength

Literary Element

Imagery is the use of descriptive and figurative language. It appeals to at least one of the five senses: hearing, seeing, tasting, smelling and touching. As you read, identify images that create a sensory experience. For example, how does Twain's description of the rafts appeal to your sense of smell?

Analyzing Literature   DBQ

❶ *Analyzing* What does Twain think of the men who worked on the barges?

❷ *Explaining* What happened to the keelboat operators once steamboats took over commerce on the river?

❸ *Expressing* How does Twain describe his impressions of the rafts and men he saw as a young boy? Which senses do these images appeal to?

Write your answers on a separate piece of paper.

1 Exploring the Essential Questions

EXPOSITORY WRITING How did the spread of the population in the United States over a wider area create challenges and tensions? Write an essay that answers this question.

2 21st Century Skills

COMMUNICATION Review what you know about the process that resulted in Missouri statehood and the Missouri Compromise. Then, create a summary of the compromise that describes its key features and key contributors. Organize your findings in a diagram, or write an essay with headings that clearly communicate the information.

3 Thinking Like a Historian

UNDERSTANDING CAUSE AND EFFECT Create a diagram such as the one below to explain the effects of innovations such as the factory system and the cotton gin on the South.

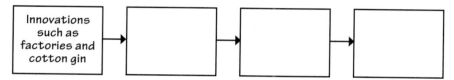

4 Visual Literacy

ANALYZING PAINTINGS This picture shows New York Governor DeWitt Clinton pouring water from Lake Erie into the Atlantic Ocean. What do you think is the meaning of Clinton's action?

REVIEW THE GUIDING QUESTIONS
Choose the best answer for each question.

1 What was the significance of interchangeable parts?
A. It made farming less profitable.
B. It made it possible to produce items in large numbers.
C. It increased the demand for slave labor.
D. It undermined the factory system.

2 The system in which all manufacturing steps are brought together in one place is called the
F. factory system.
G. patent system.
H. capital system.
I. corporation system.

3 Why did pioneer families tend to settle in communities along major rivers?
A. Rivers provided easy escape routes in the event of Native American attack.
B. It was easier for them to travel east along the rivers.
C. Rivers provided opportunities for recreation.
D. They could ship their crops to market more easily.

4 How was the National Road funded?
F. The federal government financed the road.
G. Private companies collected tolls from travelers.
H. Money was used from the canal fund.
I. Farmers were taxed on their crop production.

5 In the mid-1800s, which group was least likely to support tariffs?
A. Northeastern factory owners
B. Southern planters
C. Westerners living on the frontier
D. free African Americans living in the North

6 As a result of Andrew Jackson's 1818 actions in Florida,
F. the United States and Spain went to war.
G. East Florida was separated from West Florida.
H. Spain realized it could not maintain control of Florida.
I. Spain increased its presence in North America.

DBQ **DOCUMENT-BASED QUESTIONS**

The following are the words of President James Monroe:

"With the existing colonies ... of any European power we have not interfered and shall not interfere. But with the [Latin American] governments who have declared their independence and maintained it ... we could not view any [involvement] for the purpose of oppressing them ... by any European power in any other light than as the [showing] of an unfriendly disposition toward the United States."

—James Monroe, speech to Congress, December 1823

7 **Identifying** In this statement, Monroe is issuing the

A. American Plan.

B. Missouri Compromise.

C. Monroe Doctrine.

D. Latin American Doctrine.

8 **Identifying Central Issues** In this statement, Monroe pledges to

F. respect existing colonies but not new attempts to control Latin America.

G. open Latin America to colonization from European powers.

H. respect new European colonies but seek freedom for old ones.

I. be unfriendly toward Latin American governments.

SHORT RESPONSE

"Section 8. And be it further enacted, That in all that territory ceded by France to the United States, under the name of Louisiana, ... slavery and involuntary servitude ... shall be, and is hereby, forever prohibited."

—Missouri Compromise

9 Describe the issue that this portion of the Missouri Compromise is seeking to resolve.

10 Why was it necessary to make this agreement?

EXTENDED RESPONSE

11 **Expository Writing** Describe the forces that tended to unify Americans in the early 1800s as well as some of the important points of disagreement.

Your essay should include the Industrial Revolution and the growth of American cities; the settlement of the western United States; transportation systems in the early and mid-1800s; sectional conflicts and the American System; and relations of the United States with foreign nations.

Need Extra Help?

If You've Missed Question	**1**	**2**	**3**	**4**	**5**	**6**	**7**	**8**	**9**	**10**	**11**
Review Lesson	1	1	2	2	3	3	3	3	3	3	1–3

The Jackson Era

1824–1845

netw⊙rks

There's More Online about the people and events of the Jackson Era.

CHAPTER 12

ESSENTIAL QUESTIONS • *What are the characteristics of a leader?*
• *What are the consequences when cultures interact?* • *How do governments change?*

The Story Matters . . .

He has put up a strong fight to save the land he believes the United States had promised his people. Now, weakened by illness, Osceola is ready for peace. He arrives at Fort Peyton carrying a white flag of truce. There, United States soldiers arrest Osceola and send him as a prisoner to a South Carolina fort.

At the fort, Osceola senses death approaching. He prepares by dressing in his finest clothes. Luckily for history, artist George Catlin is at the prison that day. He asks Osceola's permission to paint him in his fine clothing. Within days of sitting for this portrait, Osceola is dead.

In this chapter you will learn more about Osceola and the fight that he and other Native Americans waged against the United States to protect their land, rights, and freedom.

◀ *This portrait of Seminole leader Osceola was painted shortly before his death in 1838.*

Superstock/Getty Images

321

Place and Time: United States 1820s and 1840s

As American settlement spread to the West, Americans came into conflict with the Native Americans who lived there. Over time, Native Americans were pushed even farther west.

Step Into the Place

MAP FOCUS During the Jackson Era, the Indian Removal Act forced the Seminole and other eastern Native Americans to move from their homelands to new homes west of the Mississippi River.

1 REGION Look at the map. In what part of Florida did the Seminole live?

2 MOVEMENT How did the removal route of the Seminole differ from that of the other groups?

3 HUMAN-ENVIRONMENT INTERACTION What kinds of challenges might Native Americans have encountered when traveling such long distances?

4 CRITICAL THINKING
Analyzing How might the removal of the Native Americans have enabled greater expansion of the United States?

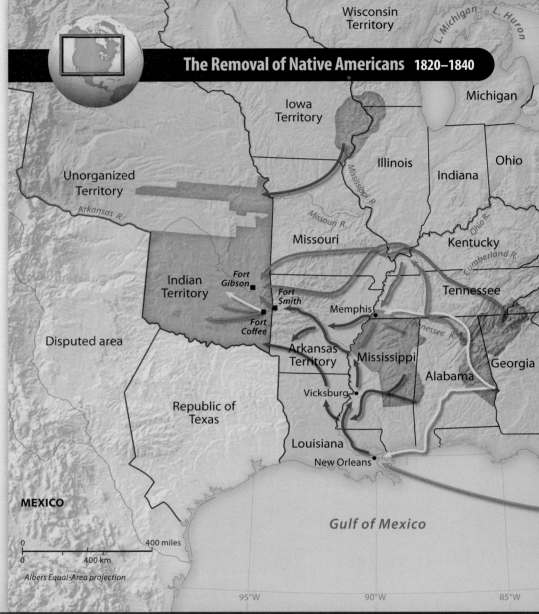

The Removal of Native Americans 1820–1840

Step Into the Time

TIME LINE Look at the time line. What events suggest a weakening of Spain's colonial empire in the Americas?

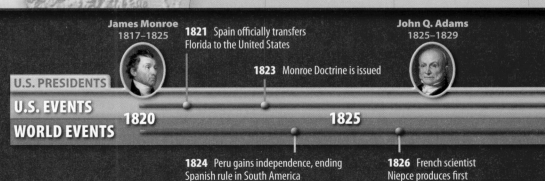

James Monroe 1817–1825

1821 Spain officially transfers Florida to the United States

1823 Monroe Doctrine is issued

John Q. Adams 1825–1829

U.S. PRESIDENTS
U.S. EVENTS
WORLD EVENTS

1820

1825

1824 Peru gains independence, ending Spanish rule in South America

1826 French scientist Niepce produces first photograph

White House Historical Association

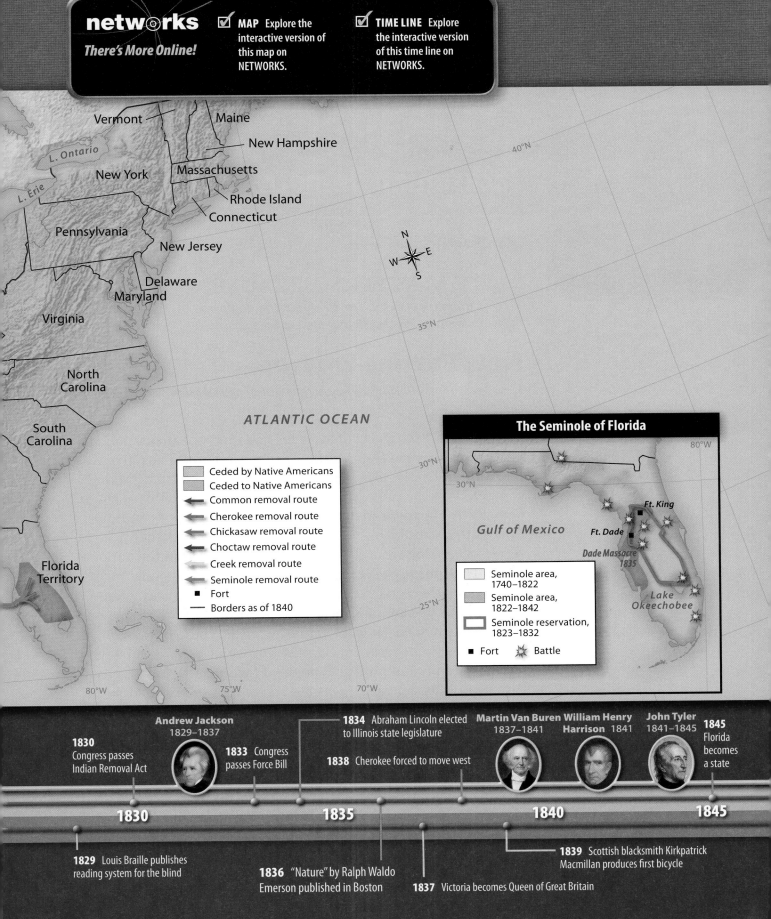

networks
There's More Online!

☑ **MAP** Explore the interactive version of this map on NETWORKS.

☑ **TIME LINE** Explore the interactive version of this time line on NETWORKS.

Vermont
Maine
New Hampshire
L. Ontario
New York
Massachusetts
L. Erie
Rhode Island
Connecticut
Pennsylvania
New Jersey
Delaware
Maryland
Virginia

North Carolina

South Carolina

ATLANTIC OCEAN

40°N

35°N

30°N

25°N

80°W   75°W   70°W

Florida Territory

Legend
- Ceded by Native Americans
- Ceded to Native Americans
- Common removal route
- Cherokee removal route
- Chickasaw removal route
- Choctaw removal route
- Creek removal route
- Seminole removal route
- ■ Fort
- — Borders as of 1840

The Seminole of Florida

80°W

30°N

Gulf of Mexico

Ft. King
Ft. Dade

Dade Massacre 1835

Lake Okeechobee

- Seminole area, 1740–1822
- Seminole area, 1822–1842
- Seminole reservation, 1823–1832
- ■ Fort   ✴ Battle

1830 Congress passes Indian Removal Act

Andrew Jackson 1829–1837

1833 Congress passes Force Bill

1834 Abraham Lincoln elected to Illinois state legislature

1838 Cherokee forced to move west

Martin Van Buren 1837–1841

William Henry Harrison 1841

John Tyler 1841–1845

1845 Florida becomes a state

1830   **1835**   **1840**   **1845**

1829 Louis Braille publishes reading system for the blind

1836 "Nature" by Ralph Waldo Emerson published in Boston

1837 Victoria becomes Queen of Great Britain

1839 Scottish blacksmith Kirkpatrick Macmillan produces first bicycle

networks

There's More Online!

☑ **BIOGRAPHY**
Andrew Jackson

☑ **GRAPHIC ORGANIZER**
Democrats and National Republicans

☑ **MAP**
• The Election of 1824
• The Election of 1828

☑ **VIDEO**

Lesson 1
Jacksonian Democracy

ESSENTIAL QUESTION *What are the characteristics of a leader?*

It Matters Because

During the Jackson Era, the American democracy expanded and our modern political system began to take shape.

New Parties Emerge

GUIDING QUESTION *What new ways of campaigning appeared during the elections of 1824 and 1828?*

From 1816 to 1824, the United States had only one major political party. This was the Democratic Republican Party. The party was far from united. In 1824, four Democratic Republican candidates competed for the presidency. Party leaders chose William H. Crawford, a former senator from Georgia, to be their candidate. Three other candidates were **favorite sons**—that is, they received backing from their home states rather than the national party. Their views reflected the interests of their regions.

Two favorite sons, Andrew Jackson and Henry Clay, were from the West. Clay, of Kentucky, was Speaker of the House of Representatives. Jackson, of Tennessee, was a hero of the War of 1812. Raised in poverty, he claimed to speak for Americans who had been left out of politics. The third favorite son, John Quincy Adams of Massachusetts, was the son of former president John Adams. He was popular with merchants of the Northeast.

The House Chooses the President

In the election, Jackson received a **plurality** (pluh•RA•luh•tee) of the popular vote—the largest share. No candidate received a **majority,** or more than half, of the electoral votes.

(c) CORBIS SYGMA, (r) Bettmann/CORBIS

Reading **HELP**DESK

Taking Notes: *Comparing*

As you read, use a diagram like this to compare political parties, their candidates, and their supporters.

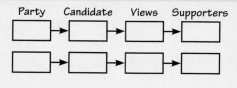

Content Vocabulary

• **favorite son** • **mudslinging** • **nominating**
• **plurality** • **bureaucracy** convention
• **majority** • **spoils system**

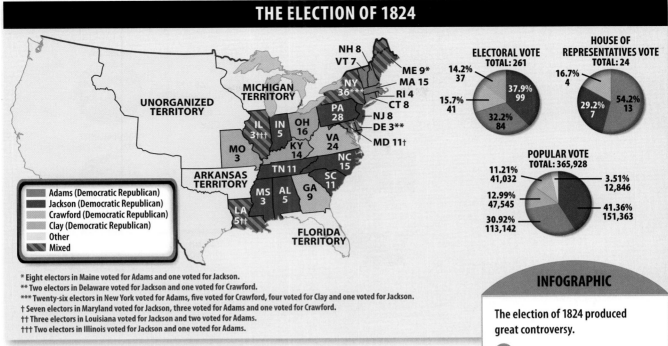

THE ELECTION OF 1824

NH 8
VT 7
ME 9*
NY 36***
MICHIGAN TERRITORY
MA 15
RI 4
CT 8
PA 28
NJ 8
DE 3**
MD 11†
IL 3†††
IN 5
OH 16
VA 24
MO 3
KY 14
NC 15
TN 11
SC 11
ARKANSAS TERRITORY
MS 3
AL 5
GA 9
LA 5††
FLORIDA TERRITORY
UNORGANIZED TERRITORY

Legend:
- Adams (Democratic Republican)
- Jackson (Democratic Republican)
- Crawford (Democratic Republican)
- Clay (Democratic Republican)
- Other
- Mixed

ELECTORAL VOTE TOTAL: 261
- 14.2% 37
- 37.9% 99
- 15.7% 41
- 32.2% 84

HOUSE OF REPRESENTATIVES VOTE TOTAL: 24
- 16.7% 4
- 54.2% 13
- 29.2% 7

POPULAR VOTE TOTAL: 365,928
- 11.21% 41,032
- 3.51% 12,846
- 12.99% 47,545
- 41.36% 151,363
- 30.92% 113,142

* Eight electors in Maine voted for Adams and one voted for Jackson.
** Two electors in Delaware voted for Jackson and one voted for Crawford.
*** Twenty-six electors in New York voted for Adams, five voted for Crawford, four voted for Clay and one voted for Jackson.
† Seven electors in Maryland voted for Jackson, three voted for Adams and one voted for Crawford.
†† Three electors in Louisiana voted for Jackson and two voted for Adams.
††† Two electors in Illinois voted for Jackson and one voted for Adams.

INFOGRAPHIC

The election of 1824 produced great controversy.

1 **CALCULATING** Where did the candidate who won the most electoral votes finish in the House vote?

2 **CRITICAL THINKING** *Drawing Conclusions* On what basis might Jackson have expected to win the presidency?

The Constitution requires that the House of Representatives select the president when no candidate has won a majority of the electoral vote.

As the House prepared to vote, Clay met with Adams. Clay agreed to use his influence as Speaker to defeat Jackson. With Clay's help, the House chose Adams for president. Adams quickly named Clay to be secretary of state. In the past this office had been the stepping-stone to the presidency. Jackson's followers accused the two men of making a "corrupt bargain" and stealing the election.

Adams as President

Adams and Clay denied any wrongdoing. No one ever uncovered any evidence of a bargain. Still, the charge cast a shadow over Adams's presidency.

In his first message to Congress, Adams announced his plans. In addition to improving roads and waterways, he wanted to build a national university and support scientific research.

Adams's proposals upset his opponents. They wanted a more limited role for the federal government. It would be wrong, they believed, for government to spend money on such projects. Congress finally approved funds for improving rivers, harbors, and roads, but this was far less than Adams wanted.

favorite son a candidate for national office who has support mostly from his home state
plurality the largest number of something, but less than a majority
majority greater than half of a total number of something

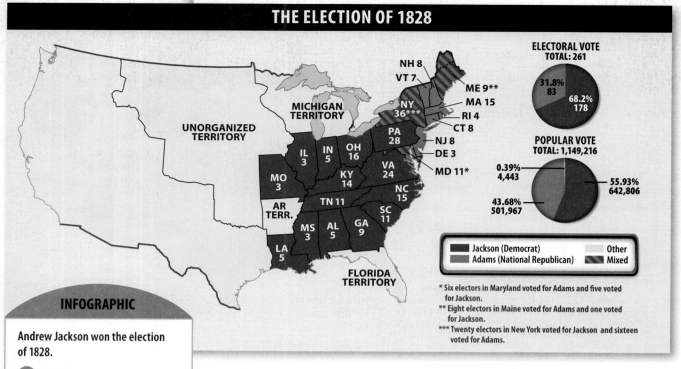

THE ELECTION OF 1828

MICHIGAN TERRITORY

UNORGANIZED TERRITORY

NH 8
VT 7
ME 9**
NY 36***
MA 15
RI 4
CT 8
PA 28
NJ 8
DE 3
MD 11*

IL 3
IN 5
OH 16
VA 24
MO 3
KY 14
NC 15
AR TERR.
TN 11
SC 11
MS 3
AL 5
GA 9
LA 5

FLORIDA TERRITORY

ELECTORAL VOTE
TOTAL: 261

31.8% 83
68.2% 178

POPULAR VOTE
TOTAL: 1,149,216

0.39% 4,443
55.93% 642,806
43.68% 501,967

■ Jackson (Democrat)   ▨ Other
■ Adams (National Republican) ▨ Mixed

* Six electors in Maryland voted for Adams and five voted for Jackson.
** Eight electors in Maine voted for Adams and one voted for Jackson.
*** Twenty electors in New York voted for Jackson and sixteen voted for Adams.

INFOGRAPHIC

Andrew Jackson won the election of 1828.

1 CALCULATING How many more electoral votes did Jackson get than he needed to win the election?

2 CRITICAL THINKING
Comparing How did having only two presidential candidates in 1828 affect the results of this election?

The Election of 1828

By 1828, the Democratic Republican Party had split. Jackson's supporters called themselves Democrats. The National Republicans supported Adams. Most Democrats favored states' rights and distrusted strong central government. The National Republicans wanted a strong central government. They supported measures such as building roads and a national bank to **facilitate** economic growth.

During the campaign, both sides resorted to **mudslinging,** or attempts to ruin their opponent's reputation with insults. The candidates also used slogans, buttons, and rallies. Such practices became a regular part of American political life.

In the election, Jackson received most of the votes cast in the frontier states. He also received many votes in the South, where his support for states' rights was popular. John C. Calhoun of South Carolina, who had been Adams's vice president, switched parties to run with Jackson. Calhoun also supported states' rights. Jackson won the election easily. Shortly after the election, Jackson's supporters officially formed the Democratic Party.

✓ PROGRESS CHECK

Making Connections What practices of the 1828 election are still used today?

Reading **HELP**DESK

mudslinging a method in election campaigns that uses gossip and lies to make an opponent look bad

bureaucracy a system of government in which specialized tasks are carried out by appointed officials rather than by elected ones

Academic Vocabulary

facilitate to help make happen
participate to take part in

Jackson as President

GUIDING QUESTION *How did Andrew Jackson make the American political system more democratic?*

Andrew Jackson had qualities most Americans admired. He was a patriot, a self-made man, and a war hero. Thousands of ordinary people came to Washington for his inauguration. Later, many attended a White House reception.

Expanded Voting Rights

President Andrew Jackson promised "equal protection and equal benefits" for all Americans—at least, all white American men. Jackson's promise reflected the spirit of the times.

In the nation's early years, only men who owned property or paid taxes could vote. By the 1820s, many states had loosened these requirements. White male sharecroppers, factory workers, and others could now **participate** in the political process. By 1828, nearly all states let voters, rather than state legislatures, choose presidential electors. Women still could not vote. African Americans and Native Americans had few rights of any kind.

Making Government More Democratic

Democrats wanted to further open government to the people. They argued that ordinary citizens could do most government jobs. They were disturbed that the federal government had become a **bureaucracy** (byuh•RAH•kruh•see), a system in which nonelected officials carry out laws.

Andrew Jackson's supporters gather outside the White House hoping to shake hands with a president who seemed to be just like them.

▶ **CRITICAL THINKING**
Drawing Conclusions Why do you think people identified so closely with Andrew Jackson?

Andrew Jackson (1767–1845)

Like many of his supporters, Andrew Jackson was born in a log cabin. A noted war hero, Jackson was called "Old Hickory" because he was said to be as tough as a hickory stick. Small farmers, craftspeople, and others who felt left out of the expanding American economy admired Jackson. They felt that his rise from a log cabin to the White House demonstrated the kind of success story possible only in the United States.

▶ **CRITICAL THINKING**
Making Inferences Why do you think voters would identify with a candidate who was from humble beginnings?

Soon after taking office in 1829, Jackson fired many federal workers and replaced them with his supporters. The fired employees protested. They charged that the president was acting like a tyrant.

One Jackson supporter said: "To the victors belong the spoils." In other words, because Jackson had won the election, his supporters had the right to the spoils, or benefits, of victory. This practice of replacing current government employees with supporters of the winner is called the **spoils system.**

Jackson's supporters also abandoned the unpopular caucus system, in which top party leaders chose the party's candidates for office. Instead, parties began using **nominating conventions** (NAHM•ih•nayt•ing kuhn•VEN•shuhnz), where delegates from the states chose the party's presidential candidate. This system allowed many more people to participate in the selection of candidates.

☑ **PROGRESS CHECK**

Analyzing How did nominating conventions make government more democratic?

The Tariff Debate

GUIDING QUESTION *How did a fight over tariffs become a debate about states' rights versus federal rights?*

A tariff is a tax on imported goods. The high tariff on European manufactured goods was pleasing to Northeastern factory owners. Tariffs made European goods more expensive. This encouraged Americans to buy American-made goods. Southerners disliked the tariff. They had a profitable trade selling their cotton to Europe. They feared that taxing European goods might hurt this trade. In addition, tariffs meant higher prices for the goods they bought from their European trading partners.

In 1828 Congress had passed a very high tariff law. Vice President Calhoun claimed that a state had the right to nullify, or refuse to accept, a federal law if it was not in that state's best interests. President Jackson disagreed with this reasoning. He feared that nullification would destroy the Union.

Bettmann/CORBIS

In 1830, at a Washington dinner marking Thomas Jefferson's birthday, Jackson had a chance to make his feelings on nullification known. He offered a toast. Looking directly at Calhoun, the president declared, "Our Union! It must be preserved!" Answering Jackson's challenge, the vice president rose with a toast of his own: "The Union, next to our liberty, most dear." To make sure his meaning was clear, Calhoun added, "It can only be preserved by respecting the rights of the states."

Not long after Jackson and Calhoun faced off at the dinner, Congress passed the Maysville Road bill. The bill provided federal funds for the building of a road in Kentucky. Jackson vetoed the bill. Jackson argued that because the road would be entirely within Kentucky, it should be a state project. In other words, the federal government should support only projects that benefited the entire nation.

In 1832 Congress passed a lower tariff. It was not enough to cool the protest. South Carolina passed the Nullification Act, declaring it would not pay "illegal" tariffs. The state threatened to secede, or break away, from the Union if the federal government interfered.

Jackson believed in a strong Union. He asked Congress to pass the Force Bill. This act allowed him to use the military to enforce federal law. South Carolina accepted the new tariff but nullified the Force Bill.

✓ PROGRESS CHECK

Making Inferences How might the workers at a factory in the Northeast react to the lowering of the tariff?

LESSON 1 REVIEW

Review Vocabulary

1. Show understanding of the following terms by using them in a sentence about the election of 1824.

   a. plurality   **b.** majority

2. Use the following terms in a sentence that illustrates how the terms are connected.

   a. bureaucracy   **b.** spoils system

Answer the Guiding Questions

3. ***Evaluating*** How do you think new election campaign methods affected American democracy?

4. ***Analyzing*** How did the election of 1828 show the growth of democracy?

5. ***Explaining*** How was the fight over tariffs related to the issue of states' rights?

6. **EXPOSITORY WRITING** Andrew Jackson once said, "One man with courage makes a majority." Write a paragraph explaining what you think Jackson meant by this quote and how this idea influenced his leadership.

networks

There's More Online!

☑ **GRAPHIC ORGANIZER**
Seminole and Cherokee Resistance

☑ **MAP** The Removal of Native Americans, 1820–1840

☑ **PRIMARY SOURCE** Osceola

☑ **VIDEO** The Trail of Tears

Lesson 2
Conflicts Over Land

ESSENTIAL QUESTION *What are the consequences when cultures interact?*

IT MATTERS BECAUSE
The forced removal and relocation of Native Americans in the 1830s largely ended the Native American presence in the eastern United States.

Removing Native Americans

GUIDING QUESTION *Why were Native Americans forced to abandon their land and move west?*

As the nation expanded west, many Native Americans still remained in the East. The Cherokee, Creek, Seminole, Chickasaw, and Choctaw peoples lived in Georgia, Alabama, Mississippi, and Florida. These groups had created successful farming communities that were much like many other American communities. As a result, Americans considered them "civilized" and referred to them as the "Five Civilized Tribes."

Though Americans recognized the success of the Five Civilized Tribes, they did not necessarily respect their rights. In fact, some white people wanted the Native Americans' lands for themselves. To make this possible, they wanted the **federal** government to force eastern Native Americans to **relocate** to lands west of the Mississippi River.

Andrew Jackson supported the white settlers' demand for Native American land. He had once fought the Creek and Seminole in Georgia and Florida to give the settlers more land. When he became president in 1829, he stated that he wanted to move all Native Americans to the Great Plains. Many people believed this region to be a wasteland

Reading HELPDESK

Taking Notes: *Describing*

As you read, use a graphic organizer like this one to describe how each group of Native Americans resisted removal, and the result.

(Cherokee)   (Seminole)

Content Vocabulary
• relocate

Like most people of the Americas in the early 1800s, the Seminole in this village lived off the land they farmed.

where American settlers would never want to live. Many people thought that if all Native Americans moved there, conflict with them would be ended.

The Cherokee Versus Georgia

In 1830 President Jackson pushed the Indian Removal Act through Congress. This law allowed the federal government to pay Native Americans to move west. Jackson then sent officials to make treaties with the Native Americans in the Southeast. In 1834 Congress established the Indian Territory. Most of the region was located in what is now the state of Oklahoma. This area was to be the new home for the Native Americans of the Southeast.

Most eastern Native American peoples felt forced to sell their land and move west. The Cherokee refused to do so. In treaties of the 1790s, the federal government had recognized the Cherokee as a separate nation. However, the state of Georgia, in which many Cherokee lived, refused to accept the Cherokee's status. In 1830 Georgia made Cherokee land part of the state. It also began to enforce state laws in the Cherokee Nation.

As pressure for relocation mounted, the Cherokee appealed to the American people:

PRIMARY SOURCE

66 We are aware, that some persons suppose it will be for our advantage to remove beyond the Mississippi. . . . Our people universally think otherwise. . . . We wish to remain on the land of our fathers. 99

—Appeal of the Cherokee Nation, 1830

relocate to move to another place

Academic Vocabulary

federal relating to a national government

Build Vocabulary: *Multiple Meaning Words*

The term *federal* applies to more than just the national government of the United States. It describes any system of government in which several smaller state or district governments unite but still keep control over their own internal affairs.

Lesson 2 **331**

This painting depicts the Cherokee on the Trail of Tears.

▶ **CRITICAL THINKING**

Analyzing Images What does this image suggest about the Native Americans' experience on the Trail of Tears? Use details from the painting to explain your answer.

Still, Georgia pressured the Cherokee. In response, the Cherokee turned to the U.S. Supreme Court. In *Worcester* v. *Georgia* (1832), Chief Justice John Marshall ruled that Georgia had no right to interfere with the Cherokee. President Jackson, who supported Georgia's efforts to remove the Cherokee, declared that he would ignore the Supreme Court's ruling. "John Marshall has made his decision," Jackson is said to have declared, "now let him enforce it." No one was willing or able to challenge the president's failure to enforce the Court's ruling.

The Trail of Tears

By 1835, the Cherokee were divided about what to do. That year the federal government convinced a small number of Cherokee— about 500 of them—to sign the Treaty of New Echota. In this treaty, the group agreed to give up all Cherokee land by 1838.

Cherokee Chief John Ross sent a protest to the U.S. Senate. Ross explained that the few Cherokee who signed the treaty did not speak for all the 17,000 Cherokee in the region. Many white Americans, including senators Daniel Webster and Henry Clay, also opposed the treaty as unfair. However, their pleas did not change the minds of President Jackson or the white settlers. In 1836 the Senate approved the treaty by a single vote.

Woolaroc Museum, Bartlesville, OK/SuperStock

Reading **HELP**DESK

Reading in the Content Area: *Bar Graphs*

Bar graphs often have vertical bars, but they may also appear with horizontal bars, as in the graph on the opposite page. In such graphs, the subject of each bar appears on the left. The item being measured—in this case, people—appears at the bottom of the graph.

When the treaty's 1838 deadline arrived, only about 2,000 Cherokee had moved west. Jackson's successor, President Martin Van Buren, ordered the army to move the rest of them. In May 1838, General Winfield Scott arrived in the Cherokee Nation with 7,000 troops to remove the remaining Cherokee by force. He told them that resistance and escape were hopeless. The Cherokee knew that fighting would lead to their destruction. Filled with sadness and anger, Cherokee leaders gave in.

Between June and December 1838, soldiers rounded up Cherokee in North Carolina, Georgia, Alabama, and Tennessee. Under guard, the Cherokee began their march to Indian Territory in the West.

The forced relocation of some 15,000 Cherokee was a terrible ordeal. Most people were not prepared for the journey. Trouble started even before they set out. As the Cherokee crowded in camps and awaited the command to begin their march, illness broke out. As many as 2,000 Cherokee died.

Once on the trail, the Cherokee suffered from hunger and from exposure to the weather. These conditions led to the deaths of another 2,000 people.

When the relocation was over, about one quarter of the Cherokee population was dead. The Cherokee came to call their forced journey west the Trail Where They Cried. Historians call it the Trail of Tears.

✔ PROGRESS CHECK

Assessing What was the purpose of the Indian Removal Act?

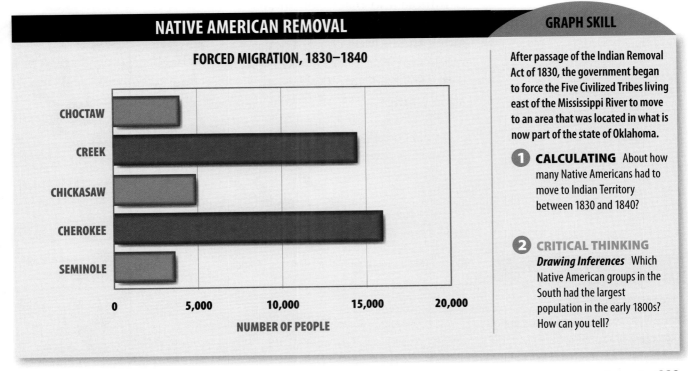

NATIVE AMERICAN REMOVAL

FORCED MIGRATION, 1830–1840

CHOCTAW

CREEK

CHICKASAW

CHEROKEE

SEMINOLE

0   5,000   10,000   15,000   20,000

NUMBER OF PEOPLE

GRAPH SKILL

After passage of the Indian Removal Act of 1830, the government began to force the Five Civilized Tribes living east of the Mississippi River to move to an area that was located in what is now part of the state of Oklahoma.

❶ **CALCULATING** About how many Native Americans had to move to Indian Territory between 1830 and 1840?

❷ **CRITICAL THINKING** *Drawing Inferences* Which Native American groups in the South had the largest population in the early 1800s? How can you tell?

Resistance and Removal

GUIDING QUESTION *Why did some Native Americans resist resettlement?*

Many Native American peoples did not want to give up their lands. However, the Seminole in Florida were the only group to successfully resist removal. They faced pressure in the early 1830s to sign treaties giving up their land, but the Seminole leader Osceola (ah•see•OH•luh) and his followers refused to leave. They decided to fight instead. Osceola was born a Creek but lived among the Seminole of Florida. "I will make the white man red with blood, and then blacken him in the sun and rain," Osceola vowed.

The Seminole Wars

In 1835 the U.S. Army arrived in Florida to force the removal of the Seminole. Instead, in December 1835, a group of Seminole attacked troops led by Major Francis Dade as they marched across central Florida. Only a few soldiers **survived.** The Dade Massacre prompted a call for additional troops to fight the Seminole.

Between 1835 and 1842, about 3,000 Seminole and African Americans known as Black Seminoles fought some 30,000 U.S. soldiers. The Black Seminoles were escaped slaves from Georgia and South Carolina. Some lived among the Seminole people. Others had built their own settlements. Like the Seminole, they did not want to move. One reason is that they feared the American soldiers would force them back into slavery. Together, the Seminole and Black Seminoles attacked white settlements along the Florida coast. They made surprise attacks and then retreated back into the forests and swamps.

This statue of Osceola is located in Tallahassee, Florida.

Dennis MacDonald/World of Stock

The war cost the U.S. government over $20 million and the lives of more than 1,500 soldiers. Many Seminole also died. Others were captured and forced to move west. In 1842, with most of the surviving Seminole now in Indian Territory, the fighting stopped.

War broke out again in 1855 over what little land in Florida the Seminole had left. By 1858, the few remaining Seminole had escaped into the Everglades, where their descendants still live today.

Life in the West

By 1842, only a few scattered groups of Native Americans remained east of the Mississippi River. Most of them now lived in the West. They had given up more than 100 million acres of land. In return, they received about $68 million and 32 million acres west of the Mississippi. There they lived, organized by tribes, on reservations. Eventually, white settlement would extend into these areas as well.

The Five Civilized Tribes relocated in the eastern half of Indian Territory on lands already claimed by several Plains peoples, including the Osage, Comanche, and Kiowa. The U.S. Army built forts in the area and promised to protect the Five Civilized Tribes and maintain peace in the area. The Choctaw police force, known as the Lighthorsemen, also helped maintain order and public safety.

Settled in their new homes, the Five Civilized Tribes developed their own constitutions and governments. They built farms and schools. However, the disputes over removal that arose within each tribal group during the 1830s continued to divide the groups for years to come.

✓ PROGRESS CHECK

Analyzing What effect did the Native Americans' use of surprise attacks have on the Seminole Wars?

Connections to TODAY

Oklahoma's Heritage

The state of Oklahoma gets its name from the Choctaw word *okla*—"people"—and *humma*—"red." Although Oklahoma today has a larger Native American population than any other state, only about 8 percent of present-day Oklahomans are Native American. Most Native American Oklahomans are descended from the 67 tribes who lived in what was once part of Indian Territory.

LESSON 2 REVIEW

Review Vocabulary

1. Use the term *relocate* to describe the relationship between the United States and Native Americans in the 1830s.

Answer the Guiding Questions

2. *Explaining* What reason did the government give for forcing the Native Americans to relocate?

3. *Analyzing* Why were the Cherokee forced to move in spite of the Supreme Court's ruling in *Worcester* v. *Georgia*?

4. *Describing* How did the Seminole resist removal?

5. **PERSONAL WRITING** Write a diary entry as a Cherokee traveling to Indian Territory on the Trail of Tears.

netw⊙rks

There's More Online!

☑ **GRAPHIC ORGANIZER**
The Bank War

☑ **MAP** Elections of 1836 and 1840

☑ **PRIMARY SOURCE**
• Jackson Political Cartoon
• Harrison Campaign Poster

Lesson 3

Jackson and the Bank

ESSENTIAL QUESTION *How do governments change?*

IT MATTERS BECAUSE
The ongoing struggle over the Bank of the United States represented the ongoing struggle over the role of the federal government.

Jackson's War Against the Bank

GUIDING QUESTION *What events occurred when President Jackson forced the National Bank to close?*

Andrew Jackson disliked the Second Bank of the United States long before he became president. Congress had set up the bank in 1816 to hold the federal government's money and to control the nation's money supply. Private bankers rather than elected officials ran the bank. Its president, Nicholas Biddle, represented everything Jackson disliked. Jackson prided himself on being a self-made western pioneer who had started with nothing. Biddle came from a wealthy Philadelphia family and had a good education and experience in financial matters.

In addition, the Bank's assigned duties made it a powerful **institution.** Many western settlers depended on being able to borrow money to run their farms. The Bank's strict policies made such loans difficult to obtain. Like many other westerners, Jackson viewed the Bank as a monopoly that favored wealthy Easterners and limited western growth.

The Bank and the Election of 1832

Jackson's opponents planned to use the Bank to defeat him in the 1832 presidential campaign. Senators Henry Clay and Daniel Webster were friends of Biddle. They persuaded Biddle to apply

(l) The Granger Collection, NYC,
(c) Library of Congress Prints & Photographs Division, [LC-USZ62-19198],
(r) David J. & Janice L. Frent Collection/CORBIS

Reading HELPDESK

Taking Notes: *Identifying*

Use a chart like this one to identify the actions taken by President Jackson that put the Bank of the United States out of business.

Bank of United States Closes

Content Vocabulary
• veto

early for a new charter—a government permit to run the Bank—even though the Bank's charter did not expire until 1836. They thought this would force Jackson to take action against the bank.

Clay and Webster believed the Bank had the support of the American people. They thought that if Jackson tried to **veto,** or reject, the renewal of the Bank's charter, he would lose support. Henry Clay wanted to run for president. He and Webster believed that Jackson's veto would help Clay defeat the president in the 1832 election.

Jackson was sick in bed when the bill to renew the Bank's charter came to him to sign. He told Secretary of State Martin Van Buren, "The bank is trying to kill me. But I will kill it." Jackson vetoed the bill. He argued that the Bank was unconstitutional despite the Supreme Court's decision to the contrary in *McCulloch* v. *Maryland* (1819).

Webster and Clay were right about one thing. The Bank did play a large part in the election of 1832. Instead of gaining support for Clay as president, however, their plan backfired. Most people supported Jackson's veto, and Jackson was reelected. Jackson then decided to "kill" the Bank even before its current charter ended. He ordered all government deposits withdrawn from the Bank and placed in smaller state banks. In 1836 he refused to sign a new charter for the Bank, and it closed.

The Panic of 1837

Jackson decided not to run for a third term in 1836. The Democrats chose Van Buren, Jackson's vice president during his second term. The Whigs, a new party that included former National Republicans and other anti-Jackson forces, were the opposition. The Whigs nominated three candidates. Each had support in a different part of the nation. The Whigs hoped this tactic would keep Van Buren from getting a majority of the electoral votes. Then the election would be decided by the House of Representatives, which the Whigs controlled. The Whigs' plan failed. Jackson's popularity and support helped Van Buren win both the popular and the electoral vote.

Van Buren had barely taken office when a financial panic hit the nation. The panic was in part an effect of Jackson's victory over the Bank of the United States. When the Bank ceased operations in 1836, control over state banks vanished.

Jackson's opponents compared him to a bad king—a tyrant with too much power.

▶ **CRITICAL THINKING**
Analyzing Primary Sources What is the meaning of the documents that appear at Jackson's feet?

veto to reject a bill and prevent it from becoming law

Academic Vocabulary

institution an organization that has an important purpose in society

Some of these banks began issuing huge amounts of banknotes. Concerned that these notes had little value, the government stopped accepting them as payment for purchasing public land. People began to question the value of their banknotes, leading to economic panic.

The Panic of 1837 led to a depression, a severe economic downturn. Land values dropped and banks failed. Thousands of businesses closed. Many workers lost their jobs, and farmers lost their land. In cities across the nation, many people could not afford food or rent.

President Van Buren did little to ease the crisis. He believed in the principle of *laissez-faire*—that government should interfere as little as possible in the nation's economy. However, Van Buren did persuade Congress to create an independent federal treasury in 1840. This meant that the government no longer had to deposit its money in private banks as it had been doing. It would keep its money in the federal treasury instead. This new system prevented state and private banks from using government money to back their banknotes. It helped prevent further bank crises.

Calling it a "second declaration of independence," Van Buren and his supporters hailed the passing of the federal treasury law. Still, members of Van Buren's own Democratic Party joined the Whigs in criticizing the act. The split in the Democratic Party gave the Whigs a chance to win the presidency in 1840.

This cartoon blames President Van Buren's policies for the Panic of 1837. Van Buren is standing, second from the right.

✓ **PROGRESS CHECK**

Explaining What was the purpose of the new treasury system?

Reading **HELP**DESK

Build Vocabulary: *Word Origins*

The French term *laissez-faire* is a combination of a form of the verb *laisser,* which means "to let or allow," and the verb *faire,* meaning "to do." In translation, the phrase literally means "let them do." As a policy, it has been translated as "let them do as they please," referring to the people. In practice, it refers to giving the government the smallest role possible.

The Whigs in Power

GUIDING QUESTION *What events occurred during the 1840s that led to the weakening of the Whig party?*

When Van Buren ran for reelection in 1840, Democrats had held the White House for 12 years. Now, with the country still in the depths of depression, the Whigs thought they had a chance to win the presidency.

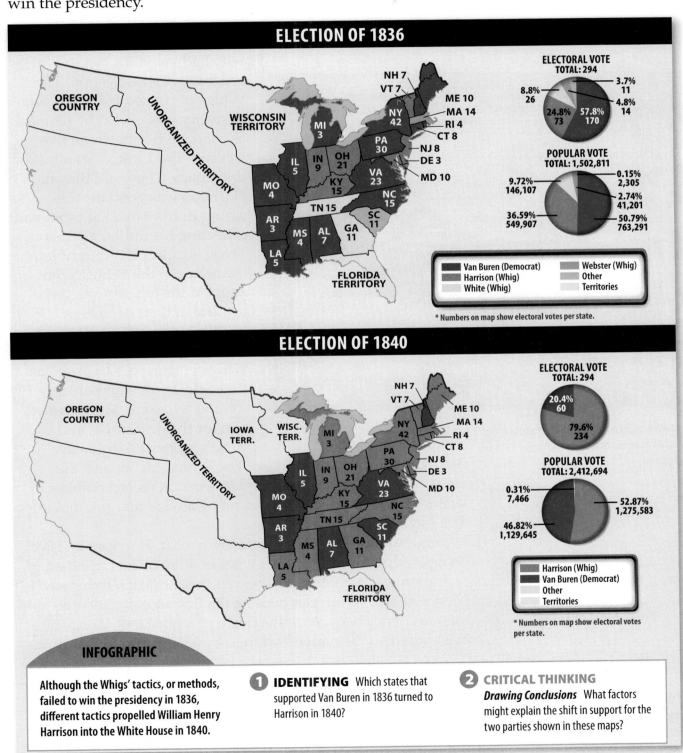

ELECTION OF 1836

ELECTORAL VOTE
TOTAL: 294

- 57.8% 170
- 24.8% 73
- 8.8% 26
- 3.7% 11
- 4.8% 14

POPULAR VOTE
TOTAL: 1,502,811

- 50.79% 763,291
- 36.59% 549,907
- 9.72% 146,107
- 0.15% 2,305
- 2.74% 41,201

Legend:
- Van Buren (Democrat)
- Harrison (Whig)
- White (Whig)
- Webster (Whig)
- Other
- Territories

* Numbers on map show electoral votes per state.

ELECTION OF 1840

ELECTORAL VOTE
TOTAL: 294

- 79.6% 234
- 20.4% 60

POPULAR VOTE
TOTAL: 2,412,694

- 52.87% 1,275,583
- 46.82% 1,129,645
- 0.31% 7,466

Legend:
- Harrison (Whig)
- Van Buren (Democrat)
- Other
- Territories

* Numbers on map show electoral votes per state.

INFOGRAPHIC

Although the Whigs' tactics, or methods, failed to win the presidency in 1836, different tactics propelled William Henry Harrison into the White House in 1840.

1 IDENTIFYING Which states that supported Van Buren in 1836 turned to Harrison in 1840?

2 CRITICAL THINKING
Drawing Conclusions What factors might explain the shift in support for the two parties shown in these maps?

The Log Cabin Campaign

To run against Van Buren, the Whigs united behind one of their 1836 candidates, William Henry Harrison. Like Andrew Jackson, Harrison was a hero of the War of 1812. John Tyler, a planter from Virginia, was Harrison's running mate. Harrison had first gained fame with his victory over Tecumseh's followers in the Battle of Tippecanoe in 1811. The Whigs made reference to this event in the campaign slogan: "Tippecanoe and Tyler Too."

Harrison needed the support of the workers and farmers who had voted for Jackson in order to win the election. The Whigs portrayed Harrison, who in reality was a wealthy Ohioan, as a simple frontiersman like Jackson. The Democrats attacked this image. They said that all Harrison was good for was sitting in front of a log cabin and collecting his military pension. These attacks played right into the hands of the Whigs, who adopted the log cabin as the **symbol** of their campaign.

During the campaign of 1840, the log cabin image appeared in paintings, banners, and political cartoons.

While presenting Harrison as a "man of the people," the Whigs portrayed Van Buren as a wealthy snob with perfume-scented whiskers. They blamed him for the depression and accused him of spending the people's money on expensive furniture for the White House. The Whigs' tactics and the effects of the depression seemed to work. A record number of voters turned out to elect Harrison by a wide margin, making him the first Whig president.

Inauguration day, 1841, was bitterly cold. Harrison insisted on delivering his long speech without a hat or coat. He died of pneumonia 32 days later. He served the shortest term of any president, and John Tyler became the first vice president to gain the presidency because of the death of a president. At age 50, Tyler was also the nation's youngest president up to that time.

David J. & Janice L. Frent Collection/CORBIS

Reading **HELP**DESK

Academic Vocabulary

symbol a word or object that stands for something else

Reading Strategy: *Summarizing*

A summary is a short restatement of the ideas in a text. Summarizing helps you digest and remember the main points in what you have read. Read the text about the Log Cabin Campaign. On a separate sheet of paper, write one or two sentences that capture the main ideas about the campaign.

John Tyler's Presidency

John Tyler won the vice presidential election as a Whig. However, he had once been a Democrat and had opposed many Whig policies. Whig party leaders had put him on the election ballot with Harrison mainly to attract Southern voters. Whig Party leaders Daniel Webster and Henry Clay had believed they could control Harrison and run the country behind the scenes. Harrison's death ruined that plan.

President Tyler vetoed several bills sponsored by Whigs in Congress. His lack of party loyalty outraged many Whigs. When he twice vetoed a bill to renew the charter of the Bank of the United States, all but one of his cabinet members resigned. Only Daniel Webster remained as secretary of state. Whig leaders actually expelled Tyler from the Whig Party.

The biggest success of the Tyler presidency came in the area of foreign relations. In 1842 the United States and Great Britain signed the Webster-Ashburton Treaty. This agreement settled a long dispute over the border between Maine and Canada and set a firm U.S.- Canadian boundary from Maine to Minnesota.

Except for opposing Tyler, the Whigs could not agree on their party's goals. Increasingly, they voted by region—North, South, and West—not party. This division may explain why the Whig candidate, Henry Clay, lost the election of 1844 to Democratic candidate James Polk. After only four years, the Whigs were out of power.

The Whigs elected just one more president, Zachary Taylor, in 1848. Taylor also died in office. By then, the Whig Party had become badly divided over the issue of slavery. By the early 1850s the party had nearly disappeared. Many Northern Whigs left the party and helped to form a new political party—the Republican Party that we have today.

✔ PROGRESS CHECK

Describing How did the Whigs lose power in the election of 1844?

LESSON 3 REVIEW

Review Vocabulary

1. Use the word *veto* in a sentence that demonstrates your understanding of the term.

Answer the Guiding Questions

2. ***Identifying Cause and Effect*** Describe the events that occurred as a result of the closing of the Second National Bank.

3. ***Describing*** Why did Tyler's policies differ from those of the Whig Party?

4. **PERSUASIVE WRITING** Write a campaign slogan for Martin Van Buren and for William Henry Harrison that each man could have used on campaign signs to attract voter support in 1840.

Write your answers on a separate piece of paper.

1 Exploring the Essential Questions

EXPOSITORY WRITING Why do you think Andrew Jackson was so popular in the 1820s and 1830s? Do you think he would be as popular a leader if he were president today? Research and examine information on the current and most recent past presidents. Then write an essay that examines Jackson's popularity and answers these questions.

2 21st Century Skills

COMPARING AND CONTRASTING Write an essay comparing the election of 1828 with a recent presidential election. Include information about how people got political information then and how they get it now.

3 Thinking Like a Historian

MAKING COMPARISONS Create a two-column chart in which you list Democrat Andrew Jackson's main ideas about government in one column and the ideas of the National Republican Party in the other column. Then research on the Internet the basic ideas of the Democratic and Republican parties today. Make a third column on your chart and check D or R to indicate which of Jackson's ideas would be more like the Democrats or Republicans of today.

Jackson's Ideas	National Republican Party Ideas	Political Parties Today

4 Visual Literacy

ANALYZING CAMPAIGN POSTERS This poster advertises a meeting on behalf of presidential candidate William Henry Harrison. What is the image of Harrison portrayed in this poster? What elements contribute to producing that image?

REVIEW THE GUIDING QUESTIONS

Choose the best answer for each question.

1 In the 1828 presidential election, Andrew Jackson's Democratic Party
A. wanted a strong central government.
B. supported setting up a national bank.
C. favored states' rights.
D. was dominated by wealthy merchants and farmers.

2 Jackson's ideas about political rights and equality included
F. all men.
G. only white women and white men.
H. everyone who lived in the United States.
I. only white men.

3 In the case of *Worcester* v. *Georgia* (1832), the United States Supreme Court ruled that
A. Georgia had no right to interfere with the Cherokee.
B. the spoils system was unconstitutional.
C. the federal government had no authority over Native Americans.
D. states had to support a national bank.

4 Why was the removal of the Cherokee people from Tennessee and Georgia called the Trail of Tears?
F. The Cherokee traveled mainly by water.
G. The Cherokee left a trail so other Native Americans could find them.
H. The Cherokee suffered and were unhappy when they had to leave their homeland.
I. The Cherokee's trail disappeared after they left.

5 Jackson attacked the Bank of the United States because
A. it was being run by corrupt elected officials.
B. it made too many loans to noncitizens.
C. it financed foreign business deals that put Americans out of work.
D. it was controlled by wealthy Easterners.

6 One reason the Whigs won the presidential election of 1840 was that
F. they made a "corrupt bargain" with Henry Clay to steal the presidency.
G. the Democrats split over supporting Martin Van Buren.
H. the depression caused by the Panic of 1837 had ended.
I. they gained support from people who had supported Andrew Jackson.

DBQ DOCUMENT-BASED QUESTIONS

John Ross, a chief of the Cherokee Nation, wrote the following in a letter to the House of Representatives in 1836:

> "A [false] Delegation, … proceeded to Washington City with this pretended treaty, and by the false and fraudulent representations [replaced] the legal and accredited Delegation of the Cherokee people, and obtained for this instrument, … the recognition of the United States Government. And now it is presented to us as a treaty, ratified by the Senate, and approved by the President."

7 **Making Inferences** What does Ross feel about the treaty?

A. He thinks Congress made a mistake and will correct it.

B. He believes it was not negotiated by true representatives of his people.

C. He is happy that the treaty was ratified by the Senate.

D. He favors the treaty and wants Congress to recognize and enforce it.

8 **Summarizing** Ross thinks the treaty is

F. a legal document.

G. the best the Cherokees can get.

H. false and illegal.

I. like previous U.S. treaties with the Cherokee.

SHORT RESPONSE

> "We had never sold our country. We never received any annuities [payments] from our American father! And we are determined to hold on to our village!"
>
> —Black Hawk, leader of a group of Sauk and Fox Native Americans

9 What do you think Black Hawk means when he states that his people "never sold our country"?

10 What does Black Hawk's statement suggest about Native Americans' level of trust toward the federal government?

EXTENDED RESPONSE

11 **Expository Writing** Use the two documents on this page and what you have learned in the chapter to write an essay evaluating the Indian Removal Act and its effect on America's development as a nation. Did it help the nation grow? Why or why not?

Need Extra Help?

If You've Missed Question	1	2	3	4	5	6	7	8	9	10	11
Review Lesson	1	1	2	2	3	3	2	2	2	2	2

Manifest Destiny

1818–1853

ESSENTIAL QUESTIONS · *How does geography influence the way people live?*
· *Why does conflict develop?* · *How do new ideas change the way people live?*

◄ Settlers traveled by wagon train along the Oregon Trail.

The Granger Collection, NYC

The Story Matters . . .

The six-month trip to the Oregon Country in the Northwest is hard and dangerous. Pioneers in "wagon trains" of up to 100 wagons wade or swim across swift rivers, climb steep mountains, face severe storms, and risk conflict with Native Americans.

Still, 12,000 people make the journey along the Oregon Trail in the 1840s. What prize lures them? Many, made poor by an economic crisis in 1837, are drawn by stories of rich land in Oregon.

These pioneers are also part of something bigger than themselves. They are helping the nation fulfill its "Manifest Destiny"—the idea that the United States should stretch from sea to shining sea.

Place and Time: North America 1800 to 1853

In the first half of the 1800s, the United States greatly expanded its territory. By 1853, it stretched clear across the continent, from coast to coast.

Step Into the Place

MAP FOCUS Note that the area controlled by the United States more than doubled in size during this period.

1 REGION After the Louisiana Purchase, from which country did the United States gain the most territory?

2 PLACE Which area of the country do you think was most densely populated in 1853? Why?

3 CRITICAL THINKING
Speculating As the United States grew, how do you think Native Americans were affected?

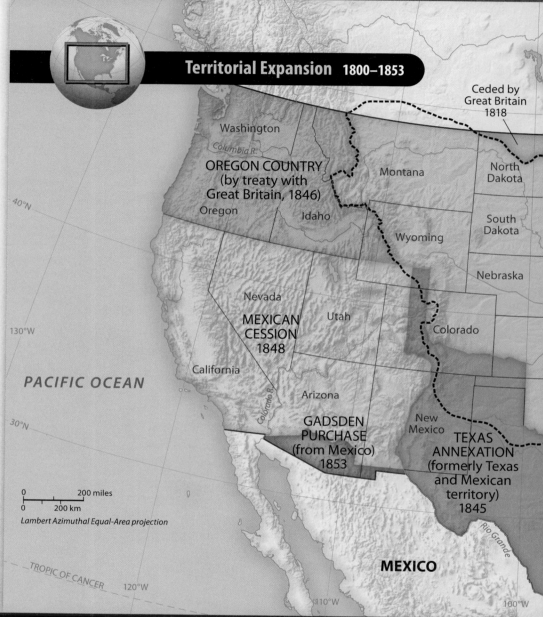

Territorial Expansion 1800–1853

Ceded by Great Britain 1818

Washington

Columbia R.

OREGON COUNTRY (by treaty with Great Britain, 1846)

Oregon

Montana

North Dakota

Idaho

South Dakota

Wyoming

Nebraska

Nevada

Utah

Colorado

MEXICAN CESSION 1848

California

Arizona

Colorado R.

New Mexico

GADSDEN PURCHASE (from Mexico) 1853

TEXAS ANNEXATION (formerly Texas and Mexican territory) 1845

PACIFIC OCEAN

MEXICO

Rio Grande

0   200 miles
0   200 km
Lambert Azimuthal Equal-Area projection

40°N
130°W
30°N
TROPIC OF CANCER
120°W
110°W
100°W

Step Into the Time

TIME LINE Identify events on the U.S. Events time line that you think might be related to one another, and explain how you think they may be related.

James Madison 1809–1817

James Monroe 1817–1825

U.S. PRESIDENTS

U.S. EVENTS

WORLD EVENTS

1818 The U.S. and Britain set the northern border of the Louisiana Purchase

1821 Spain transfers Florida to the United States

1810

1820

1821 Mexico declares independence from Spain

White House Historical Association

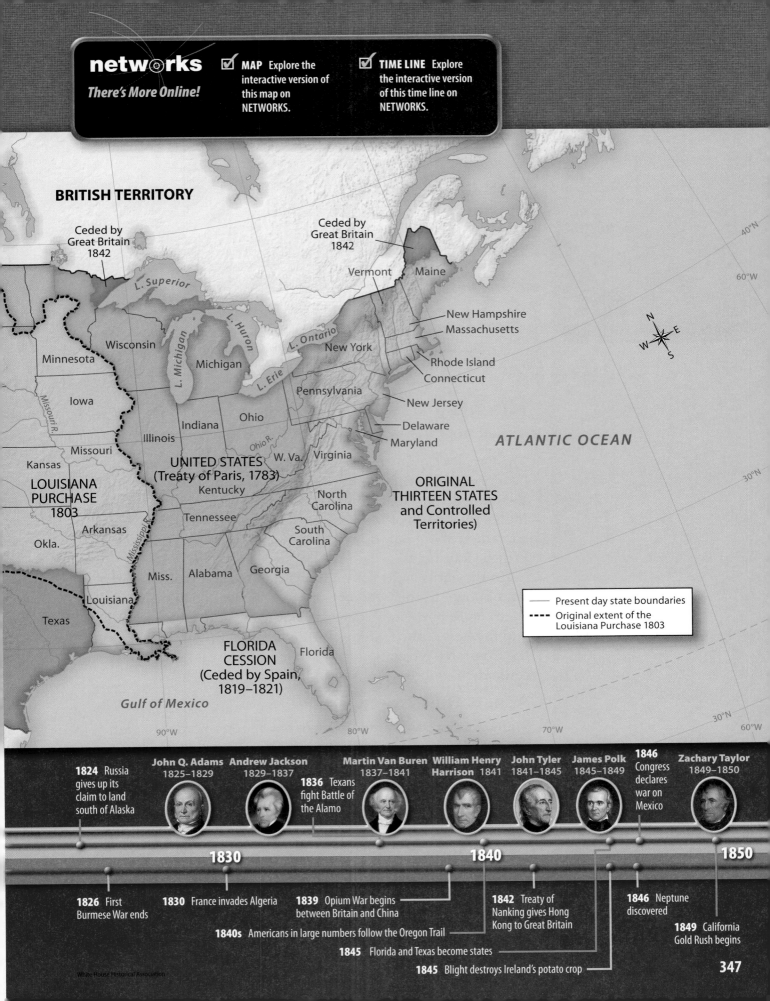

BRITISH TERRITORY

Ceded by Great Britain 1842

Ceded by Great Britain 1842

Vermont

Maine

L. Superior

New Hampshire

Massachusetts

L. Huron

L. Michigan

L. Ontario

New York

Rhode Island

Connecticut

Wisconsin

Michigan

L. Erie

Minnesota

Pennsylvania

New Jersey

Iowa

Missouri R.

Ohio

Delaware

Illinois

Indiana

Maryland

ATLANTIC OCEAN

Kansas

Missouri

Ohio R.

W. Va.

Virginia

UNITED STATES
(Treaty of Paris, 1783)

Kentucky

North Carolina

ORIGINAL THIRTEEN STATES and Controlled Territories)

LOUISIANA PURCHASE 1803

Arkansas

Tennessee

Mississippi R.

South Carolina

Okla.

Miss.

Alabama

Georgia

Louisiana

Texas

——— Present day state boundaries

- - - - Original extent of the Louisiana Purchase 1803

FLORIDA CESSION
(Ceded by Spain, 1819–1821)

Florida

Gulf of Mexico

90°W   80°W   70°W   60°W

40°N

60°W

30°W

30°N

30°N

N
E
W
S

1824 Russia gives up its claim to land south of Alaska

John Q. Adams 1825–1829

Andrew Jackson 1829–1837

1836 Texans fight Battle of the Alamo

Martin Van Buren 1837–1841

William Henry Harrison 1841

John Tyler 1841–1845

James Polk 1845–1849

1846 Congress declares war on Mexico

Zachary Taylor 1849–1850

1830

1840

1850

1826 First Burmese War ends

1830 France invades Algeria

1839 Opium War begins between Britain and China

1840s Americans in large numbers follow the Oregon Trail

1842 Treaty of Nanking gives Hong Kong to Great Britain

1846 Neptune discovered

1849 California Gold Rush begins

1845 Florida and Texas become states

1845 Blight destroys Ireland's potato crop

347

networks
There's More Online!

☑ **CHART** Oregon Trail Facts

☑ **GRAPHIC ORGANIZER** Event Time Line 1819–1846

☑ **MAP** Oregon Country

☑ **PRIMARY SOURCE** Osborne Russell, trapper

Lesson 1
The Oregon Country

ESSENTIAL QUESTION *How does geography influence the way people live?*

IT MATTERS BECAUSE
Thousands of pioneers moved west, adding their struggles and triumphs to the American story.

Rivalry in the Northwest

GUIDING QUESTION *Why did Americans want to control the Oregon Country?*

The Oregon Country was a huge area located north of California, between the Pacific Ocean and the Rocky Mountains. It included all of what are now Oregon, Washington, and Idaho, **plus** parts of Montana and Wyoming. The region also contained about half of what is now the Canadian province of British Columbia.

In the early 1800s, four nations claimed the vast, rugged land known as the Oregon Country. The United States based its claim on Robert Gray's discovery of the Columbia River in 1792 and the Lewis and Clark expedition. Great Britain had explored the Columbia River. Spain controlled California, and Russia had settlements south from Alaska into Oregon.

Adams-Onís Treaty

Many Americans wanted control of Oregon in order to gain **access** to the Pacific Ocean. In 1819 Secretary of State John Quincy Adams got Spain to approve the Adams-Onís Treaty. The Spanish agreed to set the limits of their territory at what is now California's northern border and to give up all claims to Oregon. In 1824 Russia also gave up its claim to the land south of Alaska.

(l) Image Club, (c) Courtesy National Park Service

Reading **HELP**DESK

Taking Notes: *Sequencing*

As you read, list key events on a time line such as this one.

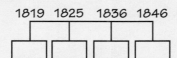

1819 1825 1836 1846

Content Vocabulary
- **joint occupation**
- **mountain man**
- **emigrant**
- **prairie schooner**
- **Manifest Destiny**

Dealing with Great Britain was more complicated. In 1818 Adams worked out an agreement with Britain for **joint occupation.** This meant that people from both the United States and Great Britain could settle there. When Adams became president in 1825, he proposed that the two nations divide Oregon along the 49° N line of latitude. Britain refused, and the countries extended the joint occupation.

Mountain Men in Oregon

Fur traders had been the first Americans to take up the challenge of living in the Oregon Country. They came to trap beaver, whose skins were in great demand in Europe. The British established trading posts in the region, as did merchant John Jacob Astor of New York. In 1808 Astor organized the American Fur Company. The country's leading fur company, it traded on the East Coast, in the Pacific Northwest, and in China.

At first the fur merchants traded with the Native Americans. Gradually others joined the trade. These tough, independent men spent most of their time in the Rocky Mountains and were known as **mountain men.** Many had Native American wives. They lived in buffalo-skin lodges and dressed in fringed buckskin pants, moccasins, and beads.

Over time, the mountain men could no longer make a living by trapping. Overtrapping limited the amount of pelts available, and changes in fashion reduced demand for pelts. Some moved to Oregon and settled on farms.

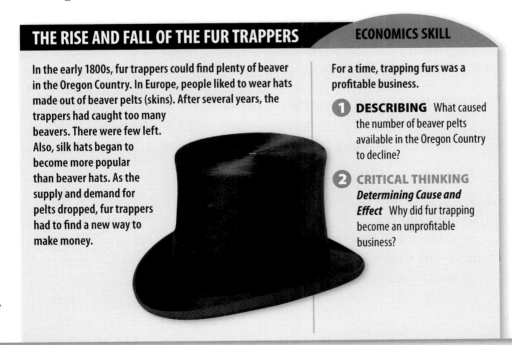

THE RISE AND FALL OF THE FUR TRAPPERS

ECONOMICS SKILL

In the early 1800s, fur trappers could find plenty of beaver in the Oregon Country. In Europe, people liked to wear hats made out of beaver pelts (skins). After several years, the trappers had caught too many beavers. There were few left. Also, silk hats began to become more popular than beaver hats. As the supply and demand for pelts dropped, fur trappers had to find a new way to make money.

For a time, trapping furs was a profitable business.

1 **DESCRIBING** What caused the number of beaver pelts available in the Oregon Country to decline?

2 **CRITICAL THINKING** *Determining Cause and Effect* Why did fur trapping become an unprofitable business?

Image Club

joint occupation situation in which people from two countries can occupy an area
mountain man an adventurer of the American West

Academic Vocabulary

plus in addition to
access a way into something or someplace

With their knowledge of the western lands, several mountain men, such as Jim Bridger and Kit Carson, found work as guides. They led the parties of settlers now streaming west. Beginning in the 1830s, the mountain men carved out several east-to-west passages that played a vital role in western settlement. The most popular route was the Oregon Trail. Others included the California Trail and the Santa Fe Trail.

✓ **PROGRESS CHECK**

Identifying What did America gain from the Adams-Onís Treaty?

Oregon and Manifest Destiny

GUIDING QUESTION *What is Manifest Destiny?*

In the 1830s, Americans began traveling to the Oregon Country to settle. Economic troubles in the East and reports of Oregon's fertile land drew many people.

Marcus and Narcissa Whitman

Among the first settlers were Dr. Marcus Whitman and his wife, Narcissa. They were missionaries who went to Oregon in 1836 and built a mission among the Cayuse people near the present site of Walla Walla, Washington. They wanted to provide medical care and convert the Cayuse to Christianity.

The new settlers unknowingly brought measles to the mission. Native Americans had never been exposed to this disease. An epidemic killed many of the Cayuse children. The Cayuse blamed the Whitmans. They attacked the mission in November 1847 and killed the Whitmans and 11 others.

Along the Oregon Trail

The Whitman massacre was a shocking event, but it did little to stop the flood of pioneers on their way to Oregon. Drawn by reports of fertile Oregon land, and driven by economic hard times in the East, many Americans took to the trail. These pioneers were called **emigrants**—people who leave their country—because they left the United States to go to Oregon.

Before the 1847 Cayuse attack, the Whitman Mission was a popular stopping point for settlers traveling along the Oregon Trail.

▶ **CRITICAL THINKING**
Drawing Conclusions Based on this picture, what do you think the Whitman Mission offered travelers on the way to the Oregon Country?

Courtesy National Park Service

Reading **HELP**DESK

emigrant person who leaves his or her country to live somewhere else
prairie schooner a canvas-covered wagon used by pioneers in the mid-1800s

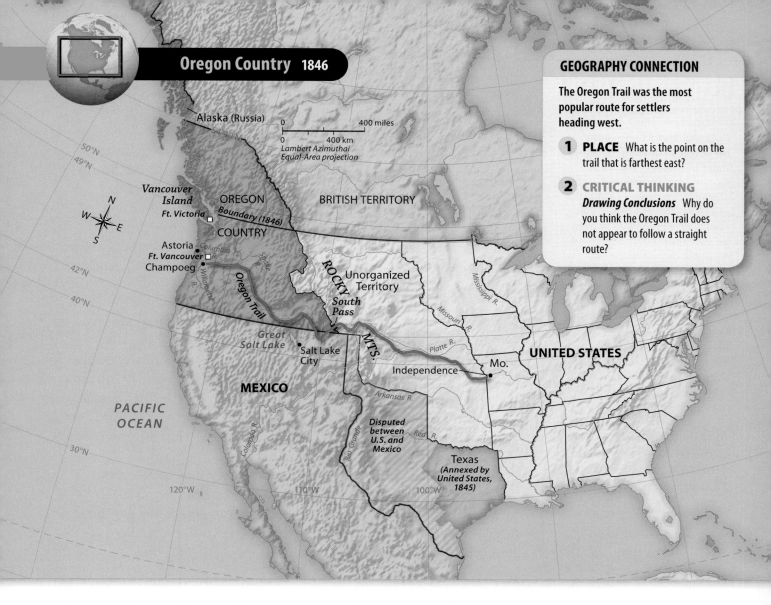

Oregon Country 1846

Alaska (Russia)

0   400 miles
0   400 km
Lambert Azimuthal
Equal-Area projection

Vancouver Island
Ft. Victoria
OREGON
Boundary (1846)
COUNTRY

BRITISH TERRITORY

Astoria
Ft. Vancouver
Champoeg
Columbia R.
Snake R.
Willamette R.

Oregon Trail

ROCKY

Unorganized Territory

South Pass

Great Salt Lake
Salt Lake City

MTS.

Missouri R.
Mississippi R.

Platte R.

UNITED STATES

Independence
Mo.

MEXICO

Arkansas R.

PACIFIC OCEAN

Colorado R.

Rio Grande

Red R.

Disputed between U.S. and Mexico

Texas
(Annexed by United States, 1845)

50°N
49°N
42°N
40°N
30°N
120°W   110°W   100°W

N W E S

GEOGRAPHY CONNECTION

The Oregon Trail was the most popular route for settlers heading west.

1 PLACE What is the point on the trail that is farthest east?

2 CRITICAL THINKING
Drawing Conclusions Why do you think the Oregon Trail does not appear to follow a straight route?

In 1843 about a thousand emigrants made the journey. Tens of thousands more would follow in the years ahead. Before the difficult 2,000-mile (3,219 km) journey, these pioneers packed all their belongings. They stuffed their canvas-covered wagons with supplies. From a distance these wagons looked like schooners, or ships at sea, and people called them **prairie schooners.** Gathering in Independence or other towns in Missouri, the pioneers followed the Oregon Trail across the Great Plains, along the Platte River, and through the South Pass of the Rocky Mountains. Then they turned north and west along the Snake and Columbia Rivers into the Oregon Country.

America Seeks Its Manifest Destiny

Since colonial times, many Americans had believed their nation's mission should be to serve as a model of freedom and democracy. In the 1800s that vision changed.

Push-pull factors are reasons for people to leave one area and move to another area. Push factors—such as lack of economic activity or a natural disaster such as a hurricane or flood—drive people away from an area. Pull factors—such as a desirable climate or the opportunity to own land— attract people to an area.

What were the push and pull factors affecting emigrants to Oregon? For more about understanding cause and effect, review *Thinking Like a Historian.*

Manifest Destiny   the belief that the United States was destined by God to extend its boundaries to the Pacific Ocean

Many believed that the nation's mission was to spread freedom by settling the entire continent. In 1819 John Quincy Adams expressed what many Americans were thinking when he said expansion to the Pacific was as certain as the Mississippi River flowing to the sea.

In the 1840s, New York newspaper editor John O'Sullivan expressed in more specific words the idea of a national mission. O'Sullivan declared it was America's "**Manifest Destiny** to overspread and to possess the whole of the continent which Providence has given us." O'Sullivan meant that the United States was clearly destined—set apart for a special purpose—by God to extend its boundaries all the way to the Pacific Ocean.

"Fifty-Four Forty or Fight"

Many Americans wanted the United States to take over all of Oregon. In the 1844 presidential election, James K. Polk, the Democratic nominee, supported this desire. Democrats used the slogan "Fifty-Four Forty or Fight," referring to the line of latitude they believed should be the nation's northern border in Oregon.

Polk's Whig opponent, Henry Clay, did not take a strong position on the Oregon issue. Polk won the election because Whig support was not united behind Clay.

A firm believer in Manifest Destiny, Polk was focused on acquiring Oregon. Britain would not accept a border at 54°40' N latitude. In 1846 the two countries compromised. They set the border at 49° N latitude. It was the same boundary the British had rejected 21 years before.

☑ **PROGRESS CHECK**

Summarizing   How did Polk's views differ from Clay's in the 1844 election?

LESSON 1 REVIEW

Review Vocabulary

1. Using the following words, write sentences that describe settlers traveling on the Oregon Trail.

   a. Manifest Destiny   **b.** emigrant
   c. prairie schooner

Answer the Guiding Questions

2. *Specifying*   Which nations claimed the Oregon Country? How did John Quincy Adams resolve the claims?

3. *Explaining*   In what way was the Oregon Trail part of Manifest Destiny?

4. *Defining*   What did "Fifty-Four Forty or Fight" mean?

5. *Analyzing*   During the 1840s, more Americans than British settled in the Oregon Country. How do you think this settlement influenced negotiations with the British over the territory?

6. **PERSUASIVE WRITING**   You are a scout in the 1830s who makes a living by guiding settlers to Oregon. Write a two-paragraph "advertisement" telling people why they should move to Oregon and why they should choose you to guide them.

networks

There's More Online!

☑ **BIOGRAPHY**
Davy Crockett

☑ **CHART** Florida's
Capitol Buildings

☑ **GRAPHIC ORGANIZER** Texas
History Time Line

☑ **MAP** Texas War for Independence

☑ **SLIDE SHOW** The Alamo

☑ **VIDEO**

Lesson 2
Statehood for Florida and Texas

ESSENTIAL QUESTION *Why does conflict develop?*

IT MATTERS BECAUSE

Through conflict and negotiations, the United States acquired Florida and Texas.

Florida

GUIDING QUESTION *How did Florida become a state?*

When Spain transferred Florida to the United States on July 17, 1821, Florida became an American territory. Under the terms of the Northwest Ordinance of 1787, Florida had an appointed territorial governor, a territorial legislature, and a nonvoting delegate to the United States Congress.

Tallahassee became the territorial capital in 1824. The capital was located about midway between St. Augustine and Pensacola, Florida's major cities at that time. Not counting Native Americans, fewer than 8,000 people lived in the territory, including enslaved people. Later, as news of the area's fertile land spread, thousands of new settlers streamed into Florida.

Many planters from Virginia, Georgia, and the Carolinas had worn out their soil with years of heavy use. They left their old plantations for new land in Florida. Here, the planters **established** cotton and tobacco plantations, especially in northern Florida and the narrow strip in the northwest called the Panhandle. In addition, small farms and cattle ranches dotted the region of central Florida. The leading planters of northern Florida played a major role in the government and politics of the area.

(l) State Archives of Florida, (cl) Bettmann/CORBIS,
(c) Archives and Information Services Division, Texas State Library and Archives Commission,
(cr) Burstein Collection/CORBIS, (r) Texas State Library & Archives Commission

Reading **HELP**DESK

Taking Notes: *Sequencing*

As you read, list key events on a time line like this one.

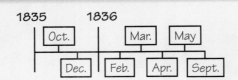

Content Vocabulary
- **Tejano**
- **decree**
- **barricade**
- **annex**

The Territory Grows

In 1837 the census for the territory of Florida reported that 48,000 people lived there. Enslaved people made up about one-half of Florida's population. Officials organized a vote to determine if Floridians wanted to form a state. Only white men over 21 years of age voted in this election. These voters chose to seek statehood. Now Floridians had to draw up a state constitution and submit it to the U.S. Congress.

Florida voters chose 56 people to attend the constitutional convention in St. Joseph, a small port city on the Gulf Coast. The first constitution provided for a governor elected for four years and an elected General Assembly, or legislature. The constitution also allowed slavery and called for a system of public schools. The delegates approved the constitution on January 11, 1839. Florida then sent the document to the U.S. Congress for final approval, or ratification.

Florida's desire to enter the Union as a slave state caused some difficulty. Congress had long struggled to maintain an equal balance between slave and free states. As a result, it would take six years for Congress to act on Florida's wish. Congress had to wait until another territory was ready to become a free state.

Statehood for Florida

Iowa finally emerged as a free state candidate. With the question of slavery **removed,** President John Tyler signed the Florida statehood bill. Florida became the twenty-seventh state in the United States on March 3, 1845. The next year, Iowa became a free state. Thus, the balance between the slave and free states in the nation remained the same in Congress.

☑ PROGRESS CHECK

Determining Cause and Effect What caused the population of Florida to grow?

The new capital in Tallahassee was chosen because it was about halfway between Florida's major cities at the time. This building was the second capitol, and it was in use from 1826 to 1839.

State Archives of Florida

Reading **HELP**DESK

Academic Vocabulary

establish to set up or create
remove to take away

Texas

GUIDING QUESTION *How did Texas become a state?*

In 1821 Mexico won independence from Spain. Mexico controlled the land that is now Texas. At the time, the non-Native American population of Texas was about 3,000. Most of these people were **Tejanos** (tay•HAH•nohs), or Mexicans who claimed Texas as their home. Wishing to increase settlement, Mexico offered vast tracts of land to people who would agree to bring families to settle there—as citizens of Mexico. Stephen F. Austin brought 300 American families to settle in Texas. Austin's success made him a leader among the American settlers.

Santa Anna hoped the fall of the Alamo would show the Texans their cause was hopeless. Instead, Texans rallied to the cry "Remember the Alamo!"

At first, Mexico encouraged Americans to settle in Texas. Before long, Americans greatly outnumbered Tejanos. Tensions with Mexico developed when Americans refused to follow Mexico's rules. These included learning Spanish and becoming Catholic. Many Americans also had enslaved African Americans, which Mexico threatened to ban. In 1830 Mexico issued a **decree,** or official order, closing its borders to further immigration. American settlers, led by Austin and Sam Houston, tried to make peace with Mexican leaders. These efforts failed. Texans—including Americans and Tejanos—began planning to break away from Mexico.

In 1835 the conflict grew violent. Mexican General Antonio López de Santa Anna took an army into Texas to punish the rebels. In December of that year, the Texans captured the city of San Antonio from a larger Mexican force. Santa Anna was enraged. His army reached San Antonio in late February 1836. There it found a small Texan force **barricaded,** or blocked off, inside a mission building called the Alamo.

The Alamo

The Texans had only about 180 soldiers to take on Santa Anna's army of several thousand. The Texans did have brave leaders, however, including folk hero Davy Crockett, commander William B. Travis, and a tough Texan named Jim Bowie.

Alamo defenders were inspired by their leader, William Barret Travis.

Tejano a Texan of Latin American, often Mexican, descent
decree official order
barricade to block off

Davy Crockett (1786–1836)

Davy Crockett was born in Tennessee and became known as a bear hunter, soldier, and scout. Stories of his daring deeds turned him into a folk hero. He served three terms in Congress and moved to Texas after he was defeated for re-election. He joined the Texas army to fight against Mexico and fought to the death at the Alamo.

▶ **CRITICAL THINKING**
Summarizing What were Crockett's major contributions to the United States?

GEOGRAPHY CONNECTION

Texas became an independent republic after winning its independence from Mexico.

1 **LOCATION** What battle took place northeast of Brazoria?

2 **CRITICAL THINKING**
Drawing Conclusions Which side was the aggressor in this war? Explain your answer.

Reading **HELP**DESK

annex to add a territory to one's own territory

For 13 long days, through several attacks, the defenders of the Alamo kept Santa Anna's army at bay with rifle fire. On March 6, 1836, Mexican cannon fire smashed the Alamo's walls.

The Mexican army was too large to hold back. They entered the fortress, killing all the defenders, including Travis, Crockett, Bowie, and a number of Tejanos. Only a few women and children and some servants survived to tell of the battle.

The Alamo defenders had been defeated, but they had bought the Texans time to gather troops and supplies. They had also provided the Texans with a rallying cry: "Remember the Alamo!"

Texas Declares Its Independence

During the siege at the Alamo, Texan leaders met at the town of Washington-on-the-Brazos. Among them were a number of Tejanos, who were also unhappy with Mexican rule. On March 2, 1836—four days before the fall of the Alamo—they declared independence from Mexico. They then established the Republic of Texas.

Texan leaders set up a temporary government. This government named Sam Houston commander in chief of the Texan forces. Houston gathered an army of about 900 at San Jacinto (san juh•SIHN•toh), near the site of present-day Houston. Santa Anna camped nearby with an army of more than 1,300. On April 21, the Texans launched a surprise attack, shouting, "Remember the Alamo!" They killed more

(t) Burstein Collection/CORBIS

Texas War for Independence 1835–1836

Legend:
- → Mexican forces
- ✸ Mexican victory
- → Texan forces
- ✸ Texan victory
- ▨ Austin's colony
- ▨ Disputed territory

UNITED STATES
Unorganized Terr.
Arkansas
Red R.
Brazos R.
Boundary claimed by Mexico
Colorado R.
REPUBLIC OF TEXAS
Louisiana
Washington-on-the-Brazos
1836
San Jacinto April 21, 1836
Alamo, March 6, 1836
Houston
San Antonio Bexar, Dec. 10, 1835
Gonzales, Oct. 2, 1835
Brazoria
Boundary claimed by Texas
Goliad, March 20, 1836
Refugio, March 14, 1836
Santa Anna 1836
Nueces R.
San Patricio Feb. 27, 1836
MEXICO
Urrea 1836
Rio Grande
Gulf of Mexico

N
W E
S

0   200 miles
0   200 km
Albers Equal-Area projection

96°W   94°W   92°W

than 600 soldiers and captured about 700 more—including Santa Anna. On May 14, 1836, Santa Anna signed a treaty that recognized the independence of Texas.

The Lone Star Republic

In September 1836, Texans elected Sam Houston as their president. Mirabeau Lamar, who had fought at the Battle of San Jacinto, served as vice president. Houston sent a delegation to Washington, D.C., to ask the United States to **annex,** or take control of, Texas.

Andrew Jackson, however, refused their request. The addition of another slave state would upset the balance of slave and free states in Congress. For the moment, Texas would remain an independent country.

Juan Seguín (above) and José Antonio Navarro were Tejanos who supported and worked for an independent Texas.

Texas Becomes a State

Many Texans wanted to join the United States. Southerners favored Texas annexation, but Northerners opposed admitting another slave state to the Union. President Martin Van Buren did not want to inflame the slavery issue or risk war with Mexico. He put off the question of annexing Texas. John Tyler, who became president in 1841, supported Texas annexation. The Senate remained divided over the slavery issue and failed to ratify the annexation treaty.

The situation changed with the 1844 presidential campaign. Manifest Destiny was a popular idea at the time. The South wanted Texas. The North favored gaining all of Oregon. Candidate James K. Polk supported both actions. After Polk won, Congress passed a resolution to annex Texas. In 1845 Texas joined the Union.

✅ **PROGRESS CHECK**

Identifying Central Issues Why did it take a long time for the United States to annex Texas?

(t) Mark Barnett, (b) Texas State Library & Archives Commission

LESSON 2 REVIEW

Review Vocabulary

1. Explain the significance of the following terms in Texas history.

   a. Tejano   **b.** annex
   c. decree   **d.** barricade

Answer the Guiding Questions

2. ***Explaining*** What factor explained Florida's six-year wait to have its request for statehood approved?

3. ***Specifying*** Why was the Battle of San Jacinto important?

4. ***Making Connections*** How did the battle at the Alamo help the cause of Texas independence?

5. **PERSUASIVE WRITING** Imagine you live in 1840 and are trying to encourage American settlement in Florida. Write an advertisement that might attract settlers to this land.

What Do You Think?

Was Manifest Destiny Justified?

In 1845 a magazine editor named John L. O'Sullivan declared that it was the "manifest destiny" of the United States to expand westward to the Pacific Ocean. Manifest Destiny did have its opponents, however. Long-time public servant Albert Gallatin expressed his opposition to Manifest Destiny.

No

PRIMARY SOURCE

ALBERT GALLATIN

❝ It is said, that the people of the United States have an hereditary superiority of race over the Mexicans, which gives them the right to **subjugate** and keep in bondage the inferior nation. . . .

Is it compatible with the principle of Democracy, which rejects every hereditary claim of individuals, to admit an hereditary superiority of races? . . . At this time the claim is but a pretext for covering and justifying unjust **usurpation** and unbounded ambition. . . .

Among ourselves, the most ignorant, the most inferior, either in physical or mental faculties, is recognized as having equal rights, and he has an equal vote with any one, however superior to him in all those respects. This is founded on the **immutable** principle that no one man is born with the right of governing another man. ❞

Emigrants often packed their wagons so full that they had to make the long trip on foot.

Texans celebrate as Texas becomes the 28th state in December 1845.

Yes

JOHN L. O'SULLIVAN

66 Texas is now ours. Already, before these words are written, her Convention has undoubtedly ratified the acceptance, by her Congress, of our **proffered** invitation into the Union. . . . The next session of Congress will see the representatives of the new young State in their places in both our halls of national legislation, side by side with those of the old Thirteen. . . .

Other nations have undertaken to intrude themselves [into the question of Texas. They have come] between us and the proper parties to the case, in a spirit of hostile intervention against us, for the avowed object of thwarting our policy and hampering our power, limiting our greatness and checking the fulfillment of our manifest destiny to overspread the continent allotted by Providence for the free development of our yearly multiplying millions. 99

Vocabulary

subjugate conquer

usurpation an unjust seizing of power

immutable does not change

proffered present for acceptance

What Do You Think? DBQ

❶ **Summarizing** According to O'Sullivan, what was Manifest Destiny?

❷ **Analyzing** What does Albert Gallatin think is the real motive underlying the idea of Manifest Destiny?

❸ **Contrasting** How do you think O'Sullivan might have responded to Gallatin's claims about the true motives of Manifest Destiny?

netw⊙rks
There's More Online!

☑ **BIOGRAPHY**
John C. Frémont

☑ **GRAPHIC ORGANIZER** Individual Achievements

☑ **MAP**
• Santa Fe Trail
• War With Mexico

☑ **PRIMARY SOURCE**
The Bear Flag

☑ **VIDEO**

Lesson 3
War With Mexico

ESSENTIAL QUESTION *Why does conflict develop?*

IT MATTERS BECAUSE
Mexican lands in the West became part of the United States.

The New Mexico Territory

GUIDING QUESTION *How did the Santa Fe Trail benefit the New Mexico Territory?*

In the early 1800s, the land called New Mexico was a vast region between the Texas and California territories. It included all of the land that is now the states of New Mexico, Arizona, Nevada, and Utah and parts of Colorado and Wyoming. Native Americans had lived in the area for thousands of years. Spanish conquistadors, or soldiers, arrived in the late 1500s. They made the region part of Spain's American colonies. In 1610 the Spanish founded the settlement of Santa Fe. Spanish missionaries soon followed the conquistadors into the area.

Mexico—including New Mexico—won its independence from Spain in 1821. Before that time, the Spanish had tried to keep Americans away from Santa Fe. They feared that Americans would want to take over the area. The new Mexican government, however, welcomed American traders. Mexico hoped trade would boost the economy.

William Becknell, the first American trader to reach Santa Fe, arrived in 1821. Becknell's route came to be known as the Santa Fe Trail. It was a big improvement over the trails that existed in the dry and rugged area at that time. As Becknell wrote: "I avoided the so much dreaded sand hills, where adventurers have frequently been forced to drink the blood of their mules, to allay [relieve] their thirst."

(c) The Granger Collection, NYC, (r) Photodisc/Getty Images

Reading **HELP**DESK

Taking Notes: *Describing*

As you read, describe the achievements of each individual in a chart like this one.

	Achievements
William Becknell	
John C. Frémont	
Winfield Scott	

Content Vocabulary
• **rancho**
• **ranchero**

The Santa Fe Trail

The Santa Fe Trail
Present-day state borders

Colorado

Kansas

Saline R.

Missouri R.

Independence

Bent's Fort   Ft. Lyon

Ft. Zarah

Ft. Dodge

Mountain Route

Arkansas R.

Council
Grove

Ft.
Larned

Route

Lower Spring

Missouri

Cimarron

Willow Bar

Santa Fe

Ft. Union

Canadian R.

Oklahoma

Arkansas

Pecos R.

Rio Grande

New
Mexico

Red R.

Arkansas R.

Texas

0   200 miles
0   200 km
Albers Equal-Area projection

The Santa Fe Trail started near Independence, Missouri, which was then on the western edge of the United States. It crossed the prairies to the Arkansas River. It followed the river west toward the Rocky Mountains before turning south. The trail was mostly flat, and Becknell used wagons to transport his goods.

Other Americans soon followed Becknell. The Santa Fe Trail became a busy trade route. As trade with New Mexico increased, Americans began settling in the area. Some began to believe that acquiring New Mexico was part of American Manifest Destiny.

☑ **PROGRESS CHECK**

Describing How did William Becknell influence the American settlement of New Mexico?

California's Spanish Culture

GUIDING QUESTION *How did the culture of California develop?*

Spanish explorers and missionaries from Mexico settled California in the 1700s. Captain Gaspar de Portolá and Father Junípero Serra (hoo•NIP•uh•roh SEHR•uh) began a chain of missions that eventually extended from San Diego to Sonoma.

The missions aimed to convert Native Americans to Christianity and the Spanish way of life. Native Americans learned to farm, and they worked at weaving and other crafts. American mountain man Jedediah Smith described the missions as "large farming and [cattle-ranching] establishments."

John C. Frémont (1813–1890)

John C. Frémont was a mapmaker who helped explore and settle the West. He led his third expedition to California in 1845. The United States was close to war with Mexico because of the conflict over Texas. In June 1846, he encouraged a small group of Americans during the Bear Flag Revolt. Frémont later wrote that he saw their actions as "movements with the view of establishing a settled and stable government, which may give security to their persons and property."

▶ **CRITICAL THINKING**
Drawing Conclusions Based on Frémont's quotation, how do you think the Mexican government treated American settlers?

After Mexico won independence from Spain in 1821, California became a Mexican state. Mexicans bought mission lands and set up huge ranches, or **ranchos.** Native Americans worked the land in return for food and shelter. **Rancheros**—ranch owners—treated Native Americans almost like slaves.

In the 1840s, more Americans reached California. John C. Frémont, an army officer, wrote of the region's mild climate and vast natural **resources.** Americans began to talk about adding California to the Union. They argued that the nation would then be safely bordered by the Pacific Ocean rather than by a foreign country. Shippers also hoped to build seaports on the Pacific coast for trade with East Asia.

✅ **PROGRESS CHECK**

Explaining Why did Americans want to make California part of the United States?

Conflict Begins

GUIDING QUESTION *Why did war break out between the United States and Mexico?*

President James K. Polk was determined to get the California and New Mexico territories from Mexico. After Mexico refused to sell the lands, Polk planned to gain them through war. To **justify** a war, Polk hoped to get Mexico to strike first.

Relations between the two countries were not friendly. The two nations disagreed about where the Texas-Mexico border was. The United States said that the Rio Grande formed the border. Mexico claimed that the border lay along the Nueces (nu•AY•sehs) River, 150 miles (241 km) farther north.

Polk sent a representative, John Slidell, to Mexico to propose a deal. Slidell could offer $30 million for California and New Mexico as long as Mexico accepted the Rio Grande as the Texas border. The United States would also pay what Mexico owed to American citizens. Mexican leaders refused to discuss the offer. They announced that they intended to reclaim Texas for Mexico.

To bring pressure, Polk ordered General Zachary Taylor to lead U.S. forces into the disputed area on the Rio Grande. To Mexican leaders, Taylor's action was an invasion of their country. On April 25, 1846, Mexican troops attacked Taylor's forces. President Polk told Congress that Mexico had "invaded our territory and shed American blood upon the American soil." On May 13, Congress passed a declaration of war against Mexico.

The Granger Collection, NYC

Reading **HELP**DESK

rancho ranch, especially the large estates set up by Mexicans in the American West
ranchero rancher, owner of a rancho

Academic Vocabulary

resource something that can be used for benefit, especially land, minerals, and water
justify to provide an explanation for

A War Plan

Polk planned to defeat Mexico by accomplishing three goals. First, the United States would drive Mexican forces out of Texas. Second, it would seize New Mexico and California. Finally, American forces would advance into Mexico and capture the capital, Mexico City.

By 1847, Zachary Taylor had accomplished the first goal. His army had captured all the important towns in the border area between Mexico and Texas. General Stephen Kearney made progress toward the second goal by marching his troops down the Santa Fe Trail. They captured New Mexico's capital, Santa Fe, in 1846 after the Mexican governor fled. Kearney then turned toward California.

California Uprising

Even before war with Mexico officially began, American settlers in northern California had begun an uprising. They were encouraged by American general John C. Frémont. The settlers had little trouble overcoming the weak official Mexican presence in the territory. On June 14, 1846, the Americans declared California independent. They renamed it the Bear Flag Republic. The name came from the flag the rebels had made for their new nation.

GEOGRAPHY CONNECTION

War between the United States and Mexico broke out in 1846 near the Rio Grande. Polk's party, the Democrats, generally supported the war. Many Whigs did not, calling Polk's actions unnecessary and unjust. Northerners accused Democrats of waging war to gain territory for the spread of slavery.

1 LOCATION Which battle was a Mexican victory?

2 CRITICAL THINKING
Making Inferences What information on the map can you use to infer which side won the war?

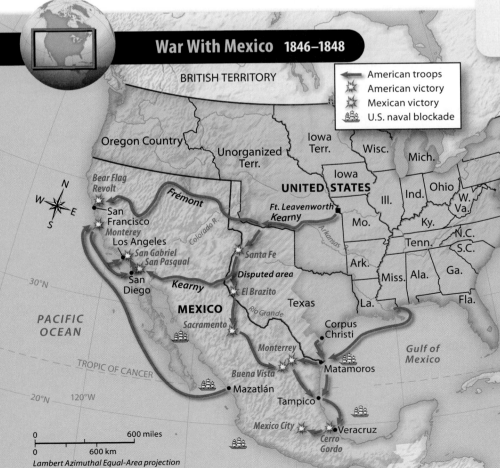

War With Mexico 1846–1848

The state flag of California today is based on the bear flag created during the Bear Flag Revolt in 1846.

CALIFORNIA REPUBLIC

The Bear Flag Republic did not exist for long. Within a month, American warships arrived at the ports of San Francisco and San Diego to claim the republic for the United States.

Mexico still refused to surrender, even though it had lost New Mexico, California, and Texas. President Polk sent General Winfield Scott and his troops to attack Mexico City. They landed in the port of Veracruz and captured it after three weeks of fighting. They still needed to travel 300 miles (483 km) to Mexico City, fighting Mexican troops along the way.

Finally, in September 1847, six months after Scott's forces landed in Veracruz, they captured Mexico's capital. Polk's plan for the war had succeeded.

Peace Terms

Defeated on February 2, 1848, Mexico's leaders signed the Treaty of Guadalupe Hidalgo (GWAH•duh•loop he•DAHL•goh). Mexico gave the United States more than 500,000 square miles (1,295,000 sq. km) of territory—what are now the states of California, Nevada, and Utah, as well as most of Arizona and New Mexico and parts of Colorado and Wyoming. Mexico accepted the Rio Grande as its border with Texas. In return, the United States paid Mexico $15 million and assumed $3.25 million in debts Mexico owed American citizens.

With Oregon and the former Mexican territories under the American flag, the dream of Manifest Destiny had been realized. The question of whether the new lands should allow slavery, however, would lead the country toward another bloody conflict.

☑ **PROGRESS CHECK**

Describing What did America gain from the Mexican War?

LESSON 3 REVIEW

Review Vocabulary

1. Describe the settlements established by the Spanish and by Mexicans in California using the following words.

   a. rancho   **b.** ranchero

Answer the Guiding Questions

2. *Specifying* What was the main purpose of the Santa Fe Trail?

3. *Explaining* Why did Americans want to acquire California?

4. *Identifying* What was the source of the conflict between the United States and Mexico before they went to war?

5. *Analyzing* Describe how trade contributed to United States territorial growth.

6. **PERSONAL WRITING** Write a brief national anthem for the Bear Flag Republic. Include details meant to inspire pride among its citizens.

There's More Online!

☑ **BIOGRAPHY**
Mariano G. Vallejo

☑ **GRAPH** San Francisco
Population Growth

☑ **GRAPHIC ORGANIZER**
Roles in the West

☑ **PRIMARY SOURCE**
Gold Rush Letter

☑ **VIDEO**

Lesson 4

California and Utah

ESSENTIAL QUESTION *How do new ideas change the way people live?*

IT MATTERS BECAUSE

Through the treaty ending the war with Mexico, the United States controlled Texas, California, and what was then New Mexico territory.

California Gold Rush

GUIDING QUESTION *How did the discovery of gold help California?*

When gold was discovered at Sutter's Mill in 1848, people from all over the world traveled to California in search of riches. Those who arrived in 1849 were called **forty-niners.** As one official reported, "The farmers have thrown aside their plows, the lawyers their briefs, the doctors their pills, the priests their prayer books, and all are now digging gold." Some people arrived by sea. Others traveled on the Oregon Trail or the Santa Fe Trail.

Americans made up about 80 percent of the forty-niners. Others came from Mexico, South America, Europe, and Australia. About 300 men arrived from China, the first large group of Asian immigrants to settle in America. Although some eventually returned to China, others remained and established California's Chinese American community.

The Californios

The Treaty of Guadalupe Hidalgo ended the war with Mexico and made Californios—Mexicans living in California—citizens of the United States. The treaty also guaranteed them the rights to their lands. The Land Law of 1851, however, established a group of reviewers who examined the Californios' land rights.

Reading **HELP**DESK

Taking Notes: *Describing*

As you read, take notes in a chart like this one. Describe what each person or group did and what their roles were in the settlement of California and Utah.

Forty-Niners	Role
Mormons	Role
Brigham Young	Role

Content Vocabulary
• forty-niner
• boomtown
• vigilante

A few forty-niners became rich from their work on the hillsides and streams of California, but most gained little or nothing.

When a new settler claimed land that was held by a Californio, the two parties would go to court. There, it was the Californio who had to prove his or her ownership of the land. Some Californios were able to prove their claims. Many others lost their cases and their land.

The Life of a Forty-Niner

As people rushed to a new area to look for gold, they built new communities. Towns and small cities appeared almost overnight. One site on the Yuba River had only two houses in September 1849. A year later, a miner arrived to find a bustling town of 1,000 people "with a large number of hotels, stores, groceries, bakeries, and ... gambling houses."

Cities also flourished during the Gold Rush. As ships arrived daily with gold seekers, San Francisco became a **boomtown,** growing quickly from a tiny village to a city of about 20,000 people.

Most forty-niners had no experience in mining. Whenever they heard that gold had been discovered at a particular site, they rushed to it and attacked the hillsides with pickaxes and shovels. They spent hours bent over streambeds, "panning" for gold dust and nuggets. Panning involved gently swirling water and gravel in a pan in order to remove dirt and, perhaps, reveal a small speck of gold.

Bettmann/CORBIS

Reading **HELP**DESK

forty-niner fortune-seeker who came to California during the Gold Rush
boomtown a fast-growing community

The California Gold Rush more than doubled the world's supply of gold. For all their hard work, however, very few forty-niners achieved lasting wealth. Most found little or no gold. Many of those who did find gold lost their riches through gambling or wild spending.

Boomtown merchants, however, made huge profits. They could charge whatever they liked for food and other essential items because there were no other nearby stores that sold these products. For example, an immigrant named Levi Strauss sold the miners sturdy pants made of denim. His "Levi's" made him rich.

Gold Rush Society

Mining camps contained men of all backgrounds but few women. Lonely and suffering hardships, many men spent their free hours drinking, gambling, and fighting. Mining towns had no police or prisons. As a result, citizens known as **vigilantes** (vih•juh•LAN•teez) formed committees to protect themselves. Vigilantes took the law into their own hands and acted as police, judge, jury, and sometimes executioner.

Economic and Political Progress

The Gold Rush had lasting effects on California. Agriculture, shipping, and trade grew to meet the demand for food and other goods. Many people who had arrived looking for gold stayed to farm or run a business.

Rapid growth brought the need for better government. In 1849, Californians applied for statehood and wrote a **constitution.** The constitution's ban on slavery, however, caused a crisis in Congress. Southern states opposed California's admission. Congress eventually worked out a compromise by which California became a free state in 1850.

☑ **PROGRESS CHECK**

Determining Cause and Effect How did the California Gold Rush lead to the expansion of cities?

A Religious Refuge in Utah

GUIDING QUESTION *Why did the Mormons settle in Utah?*

While the Gold Rush was transforming California, change was also taking place in nearby Utah. There, Mormons, or members of the Church of Jesus Christ of Latter-day Saints, were building a new community and fulfilling their vision of the godly life.

North Wind Picture Archives

---

vigilante person who acts as police, judge, and jury without formal legal authority

Academic Vocabulary

constitution a list of laws supporting a government

The Mormons Move On

The Church of Jesus Christ of Latter-day Saints was among a number of religious movements that sprang up during the religious awakenings of the 1830s and 1840s. The founder of the Mormon Church was Joseph Smith, a New Englander living in western New York. Smith said that he had received visions that led him to build a new church. He began preaching Mormon ideas in 1830.

Smith published *The Book of Mormon* that year, announcing that it was a translation of words written on golden plates that he had received from an angel. The text told of the coming of the Christ and the need to build a kingdom on Earth to receive him.

Smith hoped to use his visions to build an ideal society. He believed that property should be held in common, rather than belong to individuals. He also supported polygamy, the idea that a man could have more than one wife. This angered a large number of people. Mormons eventually gave up this practice.

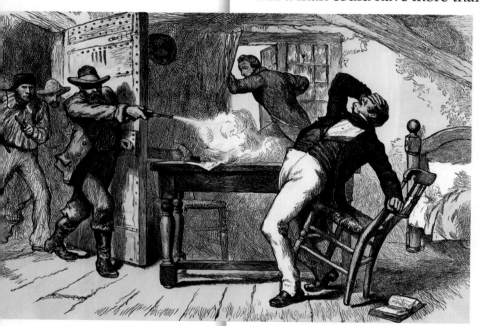

Joseph Smith was killed while being held in an Illinois jail.

Smith formed a community in New York, but neighbors disapproved of the Mormons' religion and forced them to leave. The Mormons eventually settled in Illinois. In 1839 they bought the town of Commerce, Illinois, and renamed it Nauvoo. Nauvoo became a prosperous community.

Still, the Mormons continued to suffer persecution, or mistreatment because of their beliefs. In 1844 a mob of local residents killed Joseph Smith. After Smith's death, Brigham Young took over as head of the Mormons. Young decided that the Mormons should move again to escape persecution and find religious freedom. This time, the Mormons would move west to the Great Salt Lake in present-day Utah. Although part of Mexico at the time, no Mexicans had settled in the region because of its harsh terrain.

North Wind Picture Archives

Reading **HELP**DESK

Academic Vocabulary

incorporate to include, absorb

A Haven in the Desert

The Mormon migration began in 1846. About 12,000 Mormons made the trek in the largest single migration in American history. The Mormons' route became known as the Mormon Trail and served as a valuable route to the western United States.

In 1847 the Mormons finally reached the Great Salt Lake. There, Young declared that the Mormons would build a new settlement. The Mormons staked a claim on the dry, wild land they called Deseret. Soon they had set up farming communities.

At first life was difficult for the settlers. The Mormons, however, made Deseret flourish through hard work and determination. They carefully planned towns, such as Salt Lake City, and built irrigation canals for their farms. They taxed property and regulated the use of water, timber, and other resources. Mormons also founded industries so they could be self-sufficient. Mormon merchants sold supplies to the forty-niners who passed through Utah on their way to California.

In 1848 the United States acquired the Salt Lake area from Mexico after the Mexican War. In 1850 Congress established the Utah Territory. Brigham Young was named governor.

By 1860 there were many Mormon communities, but Utah was not easily **incorporated** into the United States. Problems included the Mormon practice of polygamy and frequent conflicts with federal officials. In 1857 and 1858, war almost broke out between the Mormons and the United States Army. Utah did not become a state until 1896, after the Mormons officially gave up the practice of polygamy.

Mormons minted coins and printed paper money in the 1840s and 1850s.

Government Transfer: US DOTT, USM

☑ PROGRESS CHECK

Summarizing Why did the Mormons have to keep moving from one place to another?

LESSON 4 REVIEW

Review Vocabulary

1. Define each of the following words or terms, then use them to write a paragraph about the Gold Rush.

   a. forty-niner   **b.** boomtown   **c.** vigilante

Answer the Guiding Questions

2. *Explaining* Why was California's entry into the Union delayed?

3. *Explaining* What did Joseph Smith believe was the goal for Mormons?

4. *Making Connections* How did the Gold Rush affect California's population?

5. *Listing* Make a list of reasons that Deseret was able to flourish.

6. EXPOSITORY WRITING Consider the challenges and opportunities facing a forty-niner. What kinds of qualities do you think this kind of person would have to possess?

CHAPTER 13 Activities

Write your answers on a separate piece of paper.

1 Exploring the Essential Questions

EXPOSITORY WRITING Use examples from the history of Texas and the experiences of the Mormons to illustrate how geography, conflict, and new ideas change the way people live.

2 21st Century Skills

SEQUENCING EVENTS Put the following events on a time line in chronological (time) order: Florida becomes a state, the Adams-Onís Treaty, gold is discovered in California, the election of President James K. Polk, the battle of the Alamo, the Mormons reach the Great Salt Lake.

3 Thinking Like a Historian

PREDICTING CONSEQUENCES Imagine a large, uninhabited area in the Florida Panhandle. How would the environment change if Southern planters from other states came and settled there? Create a graphic organizer like the one below, and write the changes in the boxes provided.

landscape

4 Visual Literacy

ANALYZING PAINTINGS This painting shows a group of Mormons on the Mormon Trail to Utah in the 1850s. How does this painting portray the Mormons? What kind of life does the painting suggest the Mormons will be living when they reach their destination?

North Wind Picture Archives

REVIEW THE GUIDING QUESTIONS

Choose the best answer for each question.

1 Which of these is a reason that many Americans believed in Manifest Destiny?

A. They did not want to speak Spanish.

B. They liked to wear clothes made from beaver skins.

C. They believed it was God's plan for the country.

D. They did not like the British.

2 Which of these people was the biggest supporter of Manifest Destiny?

F. John Quincy Adams

G. Henry Clay

H. John Tyler

I. James K. Polk

3 What was the main problem that delayed the statehood of Texas and Florida?

A. Congress wanted to keep a balance of slave and free states in the Union.

B. Neither one had a large enough population.

C. They had no organized government.

D. They were in continual conflict with neighboring territories.

4 The Santa Fe Trail

F. was a disputed area between the United States and Mexico.

G. began as a route for bringing trade goods from the western edge of the United States to the territory of New Mexico.

H. was used by emigrants to get to Oregon.

I. was part of the Bear Flag Republic.

5 The population of California increased quickly after

A. the arrival of the Chinese.

B. people learned that they could get there by water.

C. the discovery of gold.

D. people heard about the mild climate.

6 The Mormons used irrigation to water crops at

F. Deseret.

G. California missions.

H. Sutter's Mill.

I. boomtowns in California.

DBQ DOCUMENT-BASED QUESTIONS

William Clayton, a Mormon emigrant, wrote the following in 1847:

"When I commune [discuss] with my own heart and ask myself whether I would choose to dwell here in this wild-looking country amongst the Saints [Mormons] surrounded by friends, though poor, … or dwell amongst the gentiles [in this context, non-Mormons] with all their wealth … to be eternally mobbed, harassed, hunted, our best men murdered … give me the quiet wilderness and my family to associate with."

7 Analyzing Primary Sources What choice did William Clayton make?

A. to live in the wild country, even though he would be poor

B. to gain wealth and good things

C. to reject his faith

D. to suffer persecution

8 Drawing Conclusions What was his reason for that choice?

F. He wanted to become powerful in the church.

G. He looked forward to a life of adventure.

H. He wanted to live quietly with people of his own faith.

I. He wanted to become a saint.

SHORT RESPONSE

"I allude to the question of slavery. Opposition to its further extension … is a deeply rooted determination … in what we call the non-slaveholding states. … How is it in the South? Can it be expected that they should expend in common their blood and their treasure in the acquisition of immense territory, and then willingly forego the right to carry thither [there] their slaves, and inhabit the conquered country … ? Sir, I know the feelings and opinions of the South … ."

—Senator Thomas Corwin, 1847, in a speech on the Mexican War

9 Based on the excerpt, what does Senator Corwin expect Southern whites to do if the United States wins the Mexican War?

10 Do you think Corwin is for or against the war? Explain.

EXTENDED RESPONSE

11 Expository Writing Write four separate reactions to the idea of Manifest Destiny from the perspective of each of these people: James K. Polk, General Santa Anna, a Native American of the Plains, a mountain man.

Need Extra Help?

If You've Missed Question	1	2	3	4	5	6	7	8	9	10	11
Review Lesson	1	1	2	3	4	4	4	4	3	3	1–4

North and South

1820–1860

ESSENTIAL QUESTIONS • How does technology change the way people live? • How do people adapt to their environment? • Why do people make economic choices?

The Granger Collection, New York

The Story Matters . . .

These women are like many other workers at the mills of Lowell, Massachusetts. They have come to earn wages and to live in the comfortable company town mill-owners have built. At Lowell, the women can earn good wages and enjoy the cultural offerings designed to help them grow into fine, upstanding members of society.

The women hear that other factories do less for their workers. Also, more and more immigrants are arriving each day. The immigrants are hungry—and willing to work longer hours for lower wages. Things are changing at Lowell. These women are wondering what the future holds for them and the rapidly industrializing North.

◀ *These women worked in one of the many booming industries of the North—a mill in Lowell, Massachusetts.*

Chapter 14

Place and Time: United States 1820 to 1860

The United States is an expanding nation in 1840. Settlement has moved westward, and new cities and industries are emerging in the North and South.

Step Into the Place

MAP FOCUS This is how the United States looked in 1840. Some areas were states, some were still territories, and some belonged to foreign nations. The 10 cities shown were the 10 largest cities at that time.

1 REGION In what regions of the country are all the organized states located?

2 LOCATION Where are the largest cities located?

3 CRITICAL THINKING
Drawing Conclusions What factors do you think helped these cities grow?

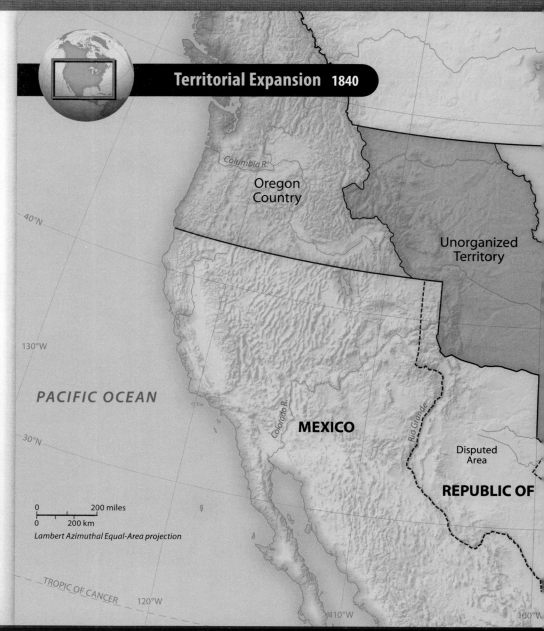

Territorial Expansion 1840

Columbia R.

Oregon Country

Unorganized Territory

40°N

130°W

PACIFIC OCEAN

30°N

Colorado R.

MEXICO

Rio Grande

Disputed Area

REPUBLIC OF

0 — 200 miles
0 — 200 km
Lambert Azimuthal Equal-Area projection

TROPIC OF CANCER   120°W

110°W   100°W

Step Into the Time

TIME LINE Review the time line. Identify an event on the time line that might help explain the growing immigration to the United States during this era. Explain your answer.

U.S. PRESIDENTS

James Monroe 1817–1825

1824 U.S. and Russia settle Northwest coast land claims

John Q. Adams 1825–1829

Andrew Jackson 1829–1837

U.S. EVENTS
WORLD EVENTS

1820

1830

1820 Antarctica is discovered

1825 World's first public railroad opens in England

1826 James Fenimore Cooper's *Last of the Mohicans* is published

1832 Greece recognized as independent state

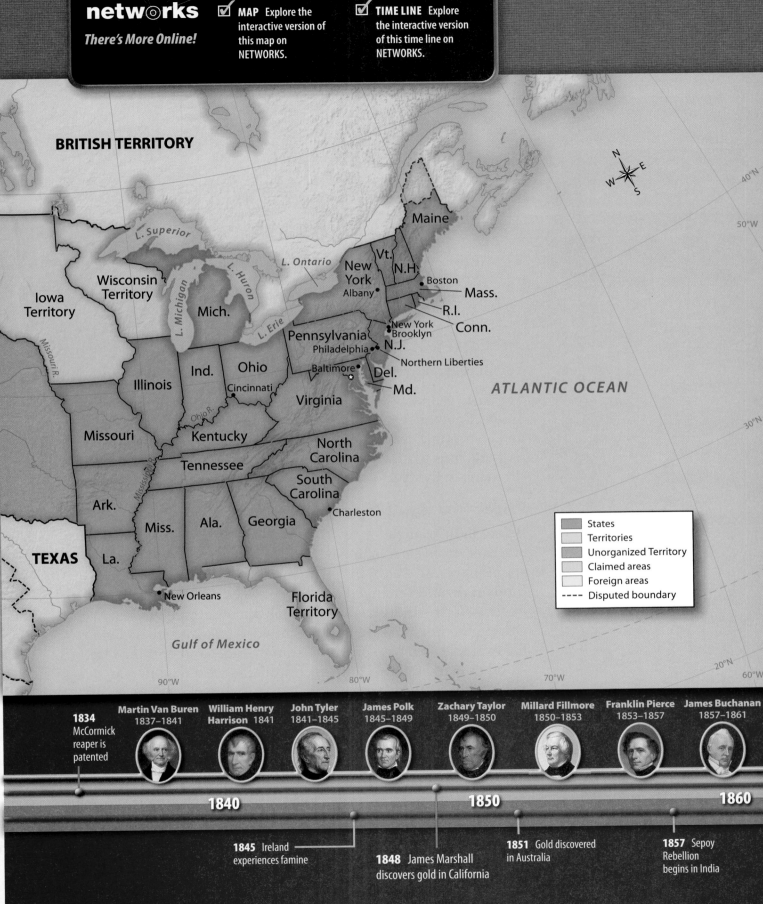

netw⊙rks
There's More Online!

☑ **MAP** Explore the interactive version of this map on NETWORKS.

☑ **TIME LINE** Explore the interactive version of this time line on NETWORKS.

BRITISH TERRITORY

Iowa Territory

Wisconsin Territory

L. Superior

L. Huron

L. Michigan

Mich.

L. Ontario

L. Erie

Maine

Vt.

New York

N.H.

Boston

Albany

Mass.

R.I.

Conn.

Illinois

Ind.

Ohio

Cincinnati

Pennsylvania

Philadelphia

New York
Brooklyn

N.J.

Northern Liberties

Baltimore

Del.

Md.

ATLANTIC OCEAN

Missouri

Kentucky

Virginia

Ohio R.

Missouri R.

Mississippi R.

Ark.

Tennessee

North Carolina

South Carolina

Miss.

Ala.

Georgia

Charleston

TEXAS

La.

New Orleans

Florida Territory

Gulf of Mexico

90°W

80°W

70°W

60°W

20°N

30°N

40°N

50°W

Legend:
- States
- Territories
- Unorganized Territory
- Claimed areas
- Foreign areas
- ---- Disputed boundary

1834 McCormick reaper is patented

Martin Van Buren 1837–1841

William Henry Harrison 1841

John Tyler 1841–1845

James Polk 1845–1849

Zachary Taylor 1849–1850

Millard Fillmore 1850–1853

Franklin Pierce 1853–1857

James Buchanan 1857–1861

1840

1850

1860

1845 Ireland experiences famine

1848 James Marshall discovers gold in California

1851 Gold discovered in Australia

1857 Sepoy Rebellion begins in India

Lesson 1
The Industrial North

ESSENTIAL QUESTION *How does technology change the way people live?*

IT MATTERS BECAUSE
Industry and innovation expanded the North's economy and power.

Technology and Industry

GUIDING QUESTION *How did technology and industry change during the 1800s?*

The early years of the 1800s saw much **innovation** in industry and technology. The ways in which Americans worked, traveled, and communicated underwent great change. The new ways of living affected the whole nation, but their effects were most dramatic in the North.

Three Phases of Industrialization

Before industrialization, workers made most goods one item at a time, from start to finish. To make clothes, a woman might spin the thread, weave the cloth, then cut and sew the fabric. Industrialization changed that way of working.

The North's industrialization took place in three phases. During the first phase, employers divided jobs into smaller steps. For example, one worker would spin thread—and nothing else. Another worker wove cloth. Each worker specialized in one step and became an expert in it. Two specialized workers could produce more cloth than if each worker did both tasks.

During the second phase of industrialization, entrepreneurs built factories to bring specialized workers together. This allowed the product to move quickly from one worker to the next.

(l) Ann Ronan Picture Library/ Heritage-Images/The Image Works
(r) The Granger Collection, NYC

Reading HELPDESK

Taking Notes: *Determining Cause and Effect*

As you read, use a diagram like the one shown to describe the three phases of the development of industrialization in the North.

Development of Industrialization

Phase 1
Phase 2
Phase 3

Content Vocabulary
• **clipper ship**
• **telegraph**
• **Morse code**

In the third phase, workers used machines to complete tasks. For example, machines called looms wove cloth using the power of flowing water. The machines worked much faster than any human could. The worker's job changed from weaving to tending the machine.

Mass production of cloth began in New England in the early 1800s. Then, Elias Howe invented the sewing machine in 1846. Workers could now make clothing in mass quantities by using machine-made fabrics and sewing machines.

Similar changes were transforming other industries and affecting the North's economy. By 1860, the Northeast's factories made at least two-thirds of the country's manufactured goods.

Changing Transportation

Improvements in transportation contributed to the success of the new American industries. Between 1800 and 1850, crews built thousands of miles of roads and canals. By connecting lakes and rivers, canals opened new shipping routes. In 1807 inventor Robert Fulton launched his first steamboat, the *Clermont*, on the Hudson River. Steamboats made fast upstream travel possible. They carried goods and passengers more cheaply and quickly along inland waterways than flatboats or sail-powered vessels did.

In the 1840s, builders began to widen and deepen canals to make space for steamboats. By 1860, about 3,000 steamboats traveled the country's major rivers and canals, as well as the Great Lakes. This encouraged the growth of cities such as Cincinnati, Buffalo, and Chicago.

Sailing technology also improved in the 1840s. The new clipper ships featured tall sails and sleek hulls. They could sail 300 miles (483 km) per day, as fast as most steamships at that time. **Clipper ships** got their name because they "clipped" time from long journeys. Before the clippers, the voyage from New York to Great Britain took about 21 to 28 days. A clipper ship could usually cut that time in half.

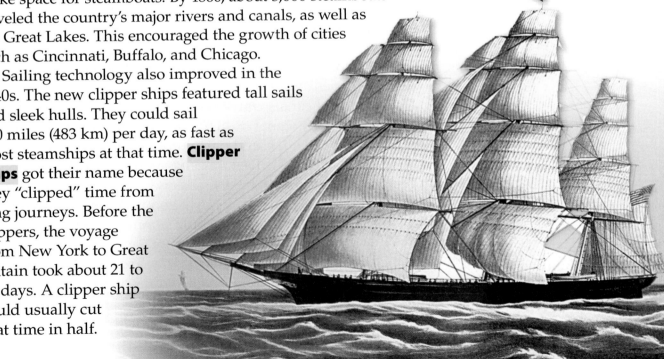

In 1851 the *Flying Cloud*, a famed clipper ship, sailed from New York City to San Francisco in 89 days.

clipper ship ship with sleek hulls and tall sails that "clipped" time from long journeys

Academic Vocabulary

innovation a new development or invention

The Railroads Arrive

The first railroads in the United States ran along short stretches of track that connected mines with nearby rivers. Horses pulled these early trains. The first steam-powered passenger locomotive began running in Britain in 1829.

A year later, Peter Cooper designed and built the first American steam-powered locomotive. The *Tom Thumb*, as it was called, got off to a slow start. It actually lost a race staged against a horse-drawn train when its engine failed. Before long, however, engineers had improved the technology. By 1840, steam locomotives were pulling trains in the United States. In 1840 the United States had almost 3,000 miles (4,828 km) of railroad track. By 1860, the nation's tracks totaled about 31,000 miles (49,890 km), mostly in the North and Midwest.

The new rail lines connected many cities. One line linked the cities of New York and Buffalo. Another connected Philadelphia and Pittsburgh. Railway builders connected these eastern lines to lines being built farther west in Ohio, Indiana, and Illinois. By 1860, the nation's railroads formed a network that united the Midwest and the East.

Moving Goods and People

The impact of improved transportation was felt deeply in the western areas of the country. Before canals and railroads, farmers sent their crops down the Mississippi River to New Orleans. From there, goods sailed to the East Coast or to other countries. This took a considerable amount of time and often caused goods to be more expensive.

Railways and canals **transformed** trade in these regions. The opening of the Erie Canal in 1825 and later the railroad networks allowed grain, livestock, and dairy products to move directly from the Midwest to the East. Improvements in transportation provided benefits to both businesses and consumers. Farmers and manufacturers could now move goods faster and more cheaply. As a result, consumers could purchase them at lower prices than in the past.

The railroads also played an important role in the settlement of the Midwest and the growth of its industry. Fast, affordable train travel brought people into Ohio, Indiana, and Illinois. The populations of these states grew. New towns and industries developed as more people moved into the area.

telegraph a device that used electric signals to send messages

Academic Vocabulary

transform to change significantly

Build Vocabulary: *Multiple Meaning Words*

The word *engineer* has many meanings. As a verb, it can mean to use science and math to make certain complex products. As a noun, it often means someone who applies those skills—for example, someone who builds buildings or electrical systems. The word also refers to the people who operate and drive trains.

Progress with Problems

As more people moved more quickly along railways and waterways, the possibility of disaster also increased. Some tragic events occurred.

The SS *Central America* was a 270-foot side-wheel steamer that carried passengers and cargo between New York and the Central American country of Panama. The ship traveled one part of a widely traveled route between the East Coast and California. In September 1857, the *Central America* was carrying a full load of passengers and a large amount of gold when it steamed into a hurricane. The ship sank off the coast of the Carolinas, and hundreds of people drowned.

The Great Train Wreck of 1856 occurred between Camp Hill and Fort Washington, Pennsylvania, on July 17, 1856. Two trains slammed head-on into each other. An estimated 60 people were killed, and more than 100 were injured. At that point in time, it was considered one of the worst accidents in railroad history. The tragic news horrified the nation. Newspapers demanded that railroad companies improve their methods and equipment and make the safety of passengers their first concern.

Communications Breakthroughs

The growth of industry and the new pace of travel created a need for faster methods of communication. The **telegraph** (teh•luh•graf)—a device that used electric signals to send messages—filled that need.

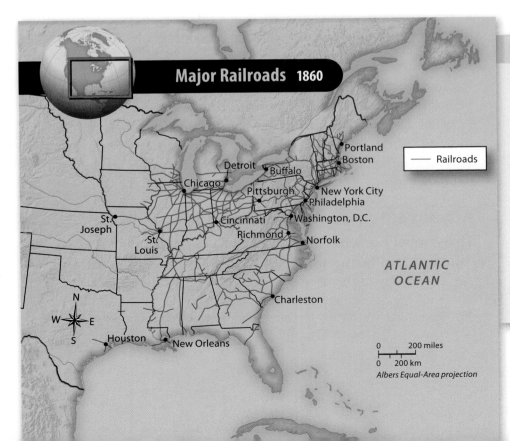

Major Railroads 1860

— Railroads

ATLANTIC OCEAN

Portland
Boston
Detroit
Buffalo
Chicago
Pittsburgh
New York City
Philadelphia
Cincinnati
Washington, D.C.
St. Joseph
Richmond
St. Louis
Norfolk
Charleston
Houston
New Orleans

N W E S

0   200 miles
0   200 km
Albers Equal-Area projection

GEOGRAPHY CONNECTION

Railroads were important not only for transporting people across the country, but they also allowed goods to be shipped greater distances than ever before.

1 **REGION** Which regions were least served by railroads in 1860?

2 **CRITICAL THINKING**
Making Connections Looking at the map, you can see that most of the railroad mileage runs between eastern and western points. Why do you think that is?

John Deere (1804–1886)

John Deere was born in Vermont. He trained as a blacksmith but found it difficult to make a living in his home state. He traveled to the state of Illinois in the 1830s. There he learned that farmers were having a difficult time plowing the region's rich but sticky soil with the rough iron plows of the day. Deere began making a polished steel plow that performed much better. Within 10 years, Deere was selling 1,000 plows per year. He was quoted as saying, "I will never put my name on a product that does not have in it the best that is in me."

▶ **CRITICAL THINKING**
Drawing Conclusions What can you conclude about the benefit of Deere's invention for his farmer customers?

Morse code a system of dots and dashes that represent the alphabet

Samuel Morse, an American inventor, developed a system for sending coded messages instantly along electrical wires. After Morse showed his system could send messages over a short distance, Congress gave him money to test the device over a wider area. Morse strung wires between Washington, D.C., and Baltimore, Maryland. On May 24, 1844, he was ready to try out his system. A crowd of people watched as Morse tapped out the words "What hath God wrought" on his telegraph system. A few moments later, the operator in Baltimore sent the same message back in reply. Morse's telegraph had worked!

Telegraph operators sent messages quickly by using **Morse code.** This code uses different arrangements of short and long signals—dots and dashes—to represent letters of the alphabet. Telegraph companies formed, and workers put up telegraph lines across the country. By 1852, there were about 23,000 miles (37,015 km) of telegraph lines in the United States.

The telegraph allowed information to be communicated in minutes rather than days. People could quickly learn about news and events from other areas of the United States. The telegraph also allowed businesses to become more efficient with production and shipping.

✅ **PROGRESS CHECK**

Explaining How did canals and railways transform trade in the interior of the United States?

Farming Innovations

GUIDING QUESTION *What changes made agriculture more profitable in the 1830s?*

In the early 1800s, few farmers were willing to settle in the treeless Great Plains west of Missouri, Iowa, and Minnesota. Even areas of mixed forest and prairie west of Ohio and Kentucky seemed too difficult for farming. Settlers worried that their old plows could not break the prairie's matted sod. They also worried that the soil would not be fertile enough to support fields of crops.

Advancements in Agriculture

Three inventions of the 1830s helped farmers overcome difficulties in farming the land. As a result, settlement expanded throughout wider areas of the Midwest.

One of these inventions was the steel-tipped plow developed by John Deere in 1837. This allowed farmers to cut through the hard-packed prairie sod. Knowing that they would be able to farm the land on the prairies helped people make the decision to move west. Equally important to the transformation of farming were the mechanical reaper, which sped up the harvesting of wheat, and the thresher, which quickly separated the grain from the stalk. Each of these innovations reduced the labor required for farming.

McCormick's Reaper

Cyrus McCormick was the genius behind the invention of the mechanical reaper. Before this invention, farmers had harvested grain with handheld cutting tools. McCormick's reaper greatly increased the amount of crop a farmer could harvest. Because farmers could harvest more wheat, they could plant more of it. Growing wheat became profitable. Raising wheat became and would remain the main economic activity on the Midwestern prairies.

New machines and the ease of access to railroads allowed farmers to plant more acres with cash crops. Midwestern farmers grew wheat and shipped it east by train and canal barge. Northeast and Middle Atlantic farmers increased their production of fruits and vegetables.

In spite of improvements in agriculture, the North was steadily becoming more industrial and urban. Agriculture in the region was still growing, but industry was growing faster.

✔ PROGRESS CHECK

Identifying What innovation sped up the harvesting of wheat?

LESSON 1 REVIEW

Review Vocabulary

1. Use these two words in a sentence that shows their importance to American life in the early 1800s.

    a. telegraph b. Morse code

Answer the Guiding Questions

2. *Explaining* How was water transportation improved in the 1800s?

3. *Summarizing* How were messages sent by telegraph?

4. *Identifying* List innovations in farming methods in the 1830s.

5. **EXPOSITORY WRITING** Which individual do you think created the invention with the greatest impact on the nation's development, and why?

    - Samuel Morse
    - John Deere
    - Cyrus McCormick

networks

There's More Online!

☑ **CHART/GRAPH**
• Immigration Sources
• Immigration, 1820–1860

☑ **GRAPHIC ORGANIZER**
Growth of Cities

☑ **PRIMARY SOURCE** Life in Lowell

☑ **SLIDE SHOW** Child Labor

Lesson 2

People of the North

ESSENTIAL QUESTION *How do people adapt to their environment?*

IT MATTERS BECAUSE

Industrialization in the North changed the way people lived and worked as well as where they lived and worked.

The Factories of the North

GUIDING QUESTION *Why did many Americans push for reform in the workplace during this era?*

The factory system combined several steps of an item's production under one roof. In the mid-1800s, machines took over more and more manufacturing tasks. The range of goods manufactured this way also increased. American factories began to turn out everything from fabric and clothing to shoes, watches, guns, sewing machines, and agricultural machinery.

Conditions for Factory Workers

Working conditions worsened as the factory system developed. Employees worked long hours. By 1840, the average workday was 11.4 hours. Longer days caused fatigue—and on-the-job accidents. Many factory machines had rapidly moving belts and other parts. These belts had no shields for protection, and many workers, especially children, suffered injuries from these belts. Belts were just one of the many hazards of factory work.

Employees often worked under harsh conditions. In the summer, factories were hot and stifling. The machines gave off heat, and there was no such thing as air-conditioning at that time. Likewise, in the winter workers were often cold because most factories had no heating.

(l) North Wind Picture Archives, (c) The Granger Collection, NYC

Reading **HELP**DESK

Taking Notes: *Identifying*

As you read, use a diagram like the one here to list two reasons that cities grew.

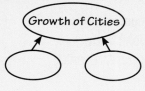

Content Vocabulary

• **trade union**   • **famine**
• **strike**   • **nativist**
• **prejudice**
• **discrimination**

No laws existed to control working conditions or protect workers. Factory owners were often more concerned about profits than about employees' comfort and safety.

Child labor was also a serious problem. Children in factories often worked six days a week and 12 hours or more a day. The work was dangerous and hard. Young workers tended machines in mills and worked underground in coal mines. Reformers called for laws to regulate child labor, shorten work hours, and improve conditions. Many years passed before child labor regulations became law.

Workers' Attempts to Organize

Workers tried various ways to gain better conditions in the workplace. By the 1830s, they began organizing into unions. Skilled workers formed **trade unions.** These were groups of workers with the same trade, or skill. The idea was that by working together, union members would have more power than they would as individuals.

In New York City, skilled workers wanted to receive higher wages and limit their workday to 10 hours. Groups of skilled workers formed the General Trades Union of the City of New York. The workers staged a series of **strikes** in the mid-1830s. A strike is a refusal to work in order to put pressure on employers.

Going on strike was illegal in the early 1800s. In addition to the threat of losing their jobs, workers who went on strike faced punishment for breaking the law. In 1842 a Massachusetts court ruled that workers did have the right to strike. However, workers would not receive other legal rights for many more years.

African Americans in the North

In the North, slavery had largely disappeared by the 1830s. Still, racial **prejudice** (PREH•juh•duhs)—an unfair opinion of a group—and **discrimination** (dihs•krih•muh•NAY•shuhn)—unfair treatment of a group—remained. White men in New York no longer had to own property in order to vote. Few African Americans enjoyed this right. Rhode Island and Pennsylvania passed laws to keep African Americans from voting.

In addition, most **communities** in the North did not allow African Americans to attend public schools. Many communities also kept them from using other public services. African Americans often had to attend poor-quality schools and go to hospitals that were reserved only for them.

North Wind Picture Archives

Connections to TODAY

Child Labor Laws

In the United States today, federal laws place strict limits on the work children can do. The Fair Labor Standards Act limits the hours that a child under the age of 16 can work. It also prohibits children from certain dangerous jobs, such as working in logging or operating a crane. States also have child labor laws, which are sometimes even more strict than federal law.

Manufacturers often hired children because they could pay children lower wages than adult workers.

trade union group of workers with the same trade, or skill

strike a work stoppage by employees as a protest against an employer

prejudice an unfair opinion not based on facts

discrimination unfair treatment

Academic Vocabulary

community group of people who live in the same area

Lesson 2 **383**

In the business world, a few African Americans found success. In New York City, Samuel Cornish and John B. Russwurm founded *Freedom's Journal,* the first African American newspaper, in 1827. In 1845 Macon B. Allen became the first African American **licensed,** or given official authority, to practice law in the United States. Most African Americans, however, lived in poverty in the mid-1800s.

Women Workers

Women also faced discrimination in the workplace. Employers often paid women half as much as they paid male workers. Men kept women from joining unions and wanted them kept out of the workplace.

In the 1830s and 1840s, some female workers tried to organize. Sarah G. Bagley, a weaver from Massachusetts, founded the Lowell Female Labor Reform Organization. In 1845 her group petitioned for a 10-hour workday. Because most of the workers were women, the legislature did not consider the petition. However, movements like the one Sarah Bagley led paved the way for later movements to help working women.

☑ **PROGRESS CHECK**

Describing How did conditions for workers change as the factory system developed?

The Growth of Cities

GUIDING QUESTION *What challenges did European immigrants face in Northern cities?*

Industrialization had a big impact on cities. Factories were usually in urban areas. Because factories drew workers, Northern cities grew in size in the early 1800s.

Urban Populations Grow

Some major cities developed between 1820 and 1840 from Midwestern villages located along rivers. St. Louis sits on the banks of the Mississippi River just south of where that river meets the Illinois and Missouri Rivers. By the mid-1800s, steamboats from north and south lined up along the docks of St. Louis. Pittsburgh, Cincinnati, and Louisville also profited from their locations on waterways. These cities became centers of trade that linked Midwest farmers with cities of the Northeast.

The women who worked at the Lowell mills communicated—and shared grievances—through a publication called the *Lowell Offering.* It included creative works on many topics, including the hardships facing factory workers.

The Granger Collection, NYC

Reading HELP DESK

famine an extreme shortage of food
nativist person opposed to immigration

Academic Vocabulary

license to give an official authority to do something

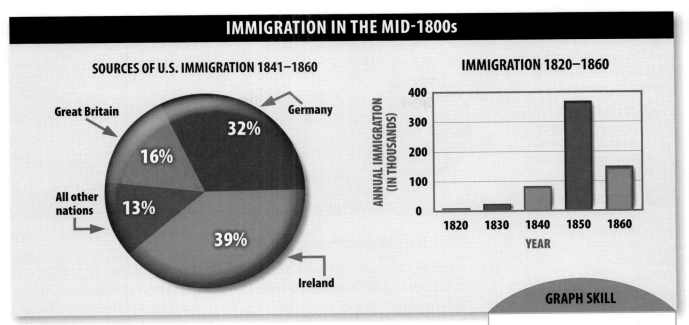

IMMIGRATION IN THE MID-1800s

SOURCES OF U.S. IMMIGRATION 1841–1860

Germany 32%
Great Britain 16%
All other nations 13%
Ireland 39%

IMMIGRATION 1820–1860

ANNUAL IMMIGRATION (IN THOUSANDS) — YEAR: 1820, 1830, 1840, 1850, 1860

Increased Immigration

Between the years 1840 and 1860, immigration to the United States grew sharply. The greatest number of immigrants came from Ireland. A plant disease, the potato blight, destroyed most of the Irish food supply in the 1840s. The people of Ireland faced **famine,** an extreme shortage of food. More than a million people died during what was called the Great Irish Famine. Another 1.5 million Irish emigrants—people who leave their home to move elsewhere—left for the United States between 1846 and 1860.

The second largest group of immigrants in the United States between 1820 and 1860 came from Germany. Some sought work and opportunity. Others fled to escape political problems at home.

Immigration's Impact

European immigrants brought languages, customs, religions, and traditions to their new country. Some of their ways of living changed American culture.

Immigrants Face Prejudice

In the 1830s and 1840s, some people began to resist immigration. They were known as **nativists** (NAY•tih•vihsts). Nativists believed that immigration threatened the future of "native"—American-born—citizens. They often blamed immigrants for problems in society. Some nativists accused immigrants of taking jobs from "real" Americans and were angry that immigrants would work for lower wages. Others accused immigrants of bringing crime and disease to U.S. cities.

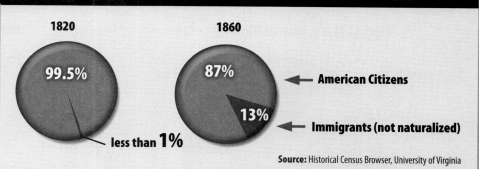

IMMIGRANTS AS A PERCENTAGE OF POPULATION

Immigration to the United States had a noticeable effect on the country's population.

1 **CALCULATING** How much larger was the immigrant population as a share of the overall population in 1860 compared to 1820?

2 **CRITICAL THINKING** *Speculating* How might a nativist react to this information?

1820

99.5%

less than **1**%

1860

87%

13%

← **American Citizens**

← **Immigrants (not naturalized)**

Source: Historical Census Browser, University of Virginia

The Know-Nothing Party

In 1849 nativists formed a new political party. Because party members often answered questions about their group with the statement "I know nothing," the party came to be known as the Know-Nothing Party. The Know-Nothings called for stricter citizenship laws. In 1854 the Know-Nothings became known as the American Party.

PRIMARY SOURCE

❝ Americans must rule America; and to this end native-born citizens should be selected for all State, Federal and municipal offices of government employment, in preference to all others. ❞

—American Party platform, from the American National Convention, 1856

☑ **PROGRESS CHECK**

Identifying From which two nations did most immigrants come in the mid-1800s?

LESSON 2 REVIEW

Review Vocabulary

1. Use these terms in a sentence that explains their meaning.

    a. trade union **b.** strike

2. Write a brief statement about life in the mid-1800s using the following terms.

    a. prejudice **b.** discrimination
    c. famine **d.** nativist **e.** emigrant

Answer the Guiding Questions

3. *Listing* What were some of the early attempts at work reform in the North?

4. *Discussing* Why did some Americans object to immigration?

5. *Explaining* What were conditions like for African Americans in the North in the mid-1800s?

6. **PERSONAL WRITING** Take the role of a young person working in a factory in the North in the mid-1800s. Write a letter in which you tell a friend what you like and dislike about your job.

1840

51.6%

networks

There's More Online!

☑ **GRAPHIC ORGANIZER**
The Southern Economy

☑ **MAP** Cotton Production
1820–1860

Lesson 3
Southern Cotton Kingdom

ESSENTIAL QUESTION *Why do people make economic choices?*

IT MATTERS BECAUSE

The demand for cotton deepened the white South's commitment to slavery and a slave-based economy.

Rise of the Cotton Kingdom

GUIDING QUESTION *How were the economies of the South and North different?*

In the early years of the United States, the South had an economy based almost entirely on farming, despite the fact that settlers had developed only a small part of the region. Most Southerners lived in the Upper South, an area along the Atlantic coast in Maryland, Virginia, and North Carolina. A few people had also settled in Georgia and South Carolina.

By 1850, the South had changed. Its population had spread inland to the Deep South. This region includes Georgia and South Carolina, as well as Alabama, Mississippi, Louisiana, and Texas. The economy of the South was thriving. That economy depended, however, on slavery. In fact, slavery grew stronger than ever in the South, while it all but disappeared in the North.

Cotton Is King

Southern planters grew mainly rice, indigo, and tobacco in colonial times. After the American Revolution, demand for these crops decreased. European mills now wanted Southern cotton.

Raising a cotton crop took a large amount of time and labor. After the harvest, workers had to carefully separate the plant's sticky seeds from the cotton fibers.

(c) SSPL/The Image Works

Reading **HELP**DESK

Taking Notes: *Determining Cause and Effect*

As you read, use a diagram like this one to show the reasons cotton production grew but industrial growth was slower in the South.

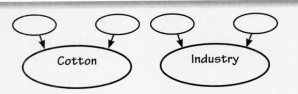

Content Vocabulary
• **productivity**
• **domestic slave trade**

Lesson 3 **387**

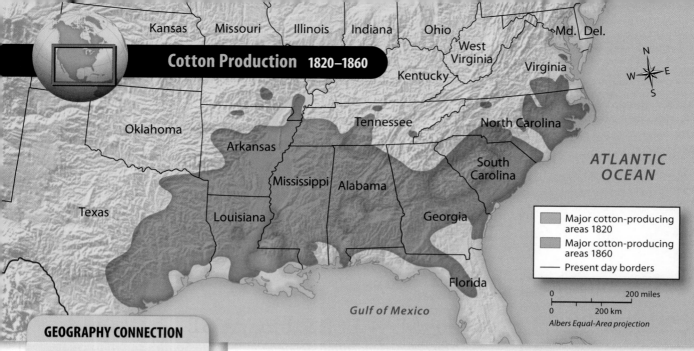

Cotton Production 1820–1860

Kansas　Missouri　Illinois　Indiana　Ohio　Md. Del.

West Virginia

Kentucky　Virginia

Oklahoma

Arkansas　Tennessee　North Carolina

Mississippi　Alabama　South Carolina

Texas　Louisiana　Georgia

ATLANTIC OCEAN

Florida

Gulf of Mexico

Legend:
- Major cotton-producing areas 1820
- Major cotton-producing areas 1860
- Present day borders

0　200 miles
0　200 km
Albers Equal-Area projection

GEOGRAPHY CONNECTION

Agriculture was very profitable in the South. By 1860, much of the South was devoted to raising cotton.

1 REGION In which region did cotton expand most, the Upper South or Deep South?

2 CRITICAL THINKING
Making Connections How might the expansion of slavery in the Deep South affect slavery in the Upper South?

Eli Whitney solved this problem with his invention of the cotton gin in 1793. Whitney's gin quickly and easily removed seeds from cotton fibers. With a cotton gin, **productivity** (proh•duhk•TIH•vuh•tee)—the amount a worker can produce in a given time—shot up. The cotton gin helped workers **process** 50 times more cotton each day than they could by hand.

The use of the cotton gin had important **consequences.** It encouraged farmers to grow more cotton in more places. Because Southern planters relied on enslaved workers to plant and pick their cotton, the demand for slave labor increased. Slavery spread across a larger area of the South.

By 1860, the Deep South and Upper South remained agricultural, but each region concentrated on different crops. The Upper South grew more tobacco, hemp, wheat, and vegetables. The Deep South produced more cotton, as well as rice and sugarcane.

Because more workers were needed to produce cotton and sugar, the sale of enslaved Africans became a big business. The Upper South became a center for the sale and transport of enslaved people. This trade became known as the **domestic slave trade.**

✓ **PROGRESS CHECK**

Describing What effect did the cotton gin have on the South's economy?

Southern Industry

GUIDING QUESTION *Why did industry develop slowly in the South?*

Industry developed more slowly in the South than in the North. Why was this so? One reason was the boom in cotton. Agriculture, especially cotton farming, produced great profits. Building new industry is costly. Planters would have had to sell enslaved people or land to raise the money to build factories. They chose instead to invest in profitable agriculture—including enslaved Africans.

In addition, the market for manufactured goods in the South was small. Enslaved people, who made up a large share of the population, had no money to buy goods. This limited local market discouraged industries from developing.

For these reasons, some white Southerners simply did not want industry. One Texas politician, Louis Wigfall, summed up that Southern point of view:

PRIMARY SOURCE

❝ We want no manufactures: we desire no trading, no mechanical or manufacturing classes. As long as we have our rice, our sugar, our tobacco and our cotton, we can command wealth to purchase all we want. ❞

—quoted in *Louis T. Wigfall, Southern Fire-Eater*

ECONOMICS SKILL

Cotton's role in the economy of the South—and the nation—increased in the 1800s.

1 **CONTRASTING** How did cotton's share of the U.S. export market change between 1800 and 1860?

2 **CRITICAL THINKING** *Determining Cause and Effect* How do you think increases in productivity affected the demand for enslaved labor? Explain.

INCREASES IN PRODUCTIVITY

New inventions helped increase worker productivity in the 1800s. Increased productivity meant farmers could grow more cotton to sell. By the mid-1800s, cotton made up more than one-half of U.S. exports.

Elias Howe's sewing machine drove up worker productivity by enabling workers to make large amounts of clothing in a day.

SSPL/The Image Works

COTTON PRODUCTION AS A PERCENTAGE OF U.S. EXPORTS

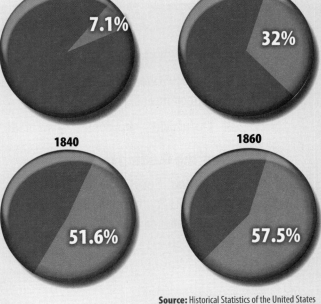

1800 — 7.1%

1820 — 32%

1840 — 51.6%

1860 — 57.5%

Source: Historical Statistics of the United States

Factories in the South

Some Southern leaders wanted to develop industry in the region. They thought that the South depended too much on the North for manufactured goods. These leaders also argued that factories would improve the economy of the Upper South.

William Gregg of South Carolina shared this view. He opened his own textile factory. Georgia's Augustin Clayton also went into textiles, opening a cotton mill. In Virginia, Joseph Reid Anderson made Tredegar Iron Works one of the nation's leading iron producers. The Alabama Iron Works also included a sawmill for producing lumber. These industries, however, were not typical of the South.

Southern Transportation

In general, farmers and the few manufacturers of the South relied on natural waterways to transport their goods. Most towns were located on coasts or along rivers because canals were scarce and roads were poor.

Southern rail lines were short, local, and not linked together. The South had fewer railroads than the North. This caused Southern cities to grow more slowly than Northern cities, where railways were major routes of commerce and settlement. The rail networks in the North also gave Northern manufacturers an advantage over their Southern competitors. Lower shipping costs allowed Northerners to charge less for their goods. By 1860, only about one-third of the nation's rail lines lay within the South. This rail shortage would hurt the South in the years to come.

☑ **PROGRESS CHECK**

Explaining How did slavery affect the development of the Southern economy?

LESSON 3 REVIEW

Review Vocabulary

1. Use these two words in a sentence in a way that shows their meaning and relationship.

   a. productivity **b.** domestic slave trade

Answer the Guiding Questions

2. *Comparing* Discuss ways the economies of the Upper South and the Deep South became dependent on each other around 1860.

3. *Explaining* How did some Southerners contribute to industrial growth in the region?

4. *Identifying* What were the barriers to Southern transportation?

5. **PERSUASIVE WRITING** Look again at the words of Texas politician Louis Wigfall, who said, "We want no manufactures." Add a second paragraph to this quotation that explains why, in words you imagine Wigfall might use, he opposes industry for the South.

Lesson 4
People of the South

ESSENTIAL QUESTION *How do people adapt to their environment?*

IT MATTERS BECAUSE

Enslaved Africans faced many hardships but were able to establish family lives, religious beliefs, and a distinct culture.

Southern Agriculture

GUIDING QUESTION *How were Southern farms different from Southern plantations?*

Slavery was at the heart of the Southern economy, but that did not mean that every white person owned large numbers of enslaved people. White society in the South was complex and had many levels. Most white Southerners fit into one of four categories: yeomen, tenant farmer, rural poor, or plantation owner.

Small Farmers and the Rural Poor

Most white people in the South were **yeomen** (YOH•muhn), farmers who generally owned small farms of 50 to 200 acres (20–81 ha). These yeomen lived mostly in the Upper South and in the hilly areas of the Deep South. They did not practice plantation-style agriculture. They grew crops to use themselves and to trade with local merchants. Yeomen generally owned few or no enslaved African Americans.

Another group of Southern whites worked as tenant farmers. They rented land from property owners.

These classes of white Southerners made up the majority of the white population of the South. They lived in simple homes—cottages or log cabins. The poorest of these groups lived in crude cabins.

(l) Collection of the New-York Historical Society/Bridgeman Art Library, (cl) CORBIS, (c) Carlos Barria/Reuters/CORBIS, (cr) CORBIS, (r) CMH/UIG/Universal Images Group/age fotostock

Reading **HELP**DESK

Taking Notes: *Describing*

As you read, use a diagram like the one here to describe the work that was done on Southern plantations.

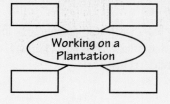

Working on a Plantation

Content Vocabulary

• **yeoman**
• **overseer**
• **spiritual**
• **slave codes**
• **Underground Railroad**
• **literacy**

SOUTHERN POPULATION 1860

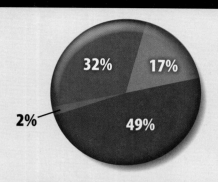

32%   17%

2%   49%

This picture shows the Legree Plantation, Capers Island, South Carolina.

African Americans
- Enslaved
- Free

Whites
- Slaveholders
- Not Slaveholders

*Total population = 12 million
Source: Geospatial and Statistical Data Center

GRAPH SKILL

In 1860 about 400,000 households in the South held enslaved workers. Nearly 4 million African Americans remained in slavery.

1 **IDENTIFYING** What percentage of the total Southern population was African American?

2 **CRITICAL THINKING**
Making Inferences Given the size of the African American population, how do you think white Southerners were able to control African Americans?

These rural poor were often stubborn and independent. Though they were looked down upon by many, they were proud of their ability to provide for their families.

A few free African Americans also held enslaved workers. Some free African Americans bought members of their own families to free them, although others worked their enslaved workers in the same manner as white Southern planters.

Plantation Owners

The larger plantations covered several thousand acres. In addition to the land they owned, plantation owners measured their wealth by the number of enslaved people they had. In 1860 only about 4 percent of slaveholders held 20 or more enslaved workers.

Earning profits was the main goal for owners of large plantations. To make a profit, they needed to bring in more money than they spent to run their plantations.

Large plantations had fixed costs. These are operating costs that remain much the same year after year. For example, the cost of housing and feeding workers is a fixed cost. There is no easy way to reduce a fixed cost.

On the other hand, the price of cotton changed from season to season. A change in price often meant the difference between a successful year for a plantation and a bad one.

Collection of the New-York Historical Society/Bridgeman Art Library

Reading **HELP**DESK

yeoman farmer who owns a small farm

Reading in the Content Area: *Circle Graphs*

Circle graphs show how a whole is divided into parts. In the graph above, what is the whole being shown, and what is the largest share of that whole?

Plantation owners—who were almost always men—traveled often in order to ensure fair dealings with traders. Their wives often led difficult and lonely lives. They took charge of their households and supervised the buildings. They watched over the enslaved domestic workers and sometimes tended to them when they became ill. Women also often kept the plantation's financial records.

Keeping a plantation running involved many tasks. Some enslaved people cleaned the house, cooked, did laundry and sewing, and served meals. Others were trained as blacksmiths, carpenters, shoemakers, or weavers. Still others tended livestock. Most enslaved African Americans, however, were field hands. They worked from sunrise to sunset to plant, tend, and harvest crops. An **overseer** (OH•vuhr•see•uhr), or plantation manager, supervised them.

✓ PROGRESS CHECK

Identifying What group made up the largest number of whites in the South?

The Lives of Enslaved People

GUIDING QUESTION *How did enslaved African Americans try to cope with their lack of freedom?*

The fate of most enslaved African Americans was hardship and misery. They worked hard, earned no money, and had little hope of freedom. They lived with the threat that an owner could sell them or members of their family without warning. In the face of these brutal conditions, enslaved African Americans tried to build stability. They kept up their family lives as best they could. They developed a culture all their own that blended African and American elements. They came up with clever ways to resist slavery.

African American Family Life

The law did not recognize slave marriages. Still, enslaved people did marry and raise families, which provided comfort and support. Uncertainty and danger, however, were always present. There were no laws or customs that would stop a slaveholder from breaking a family apart. If a slaveholder chose to—or if the slaveholder died—families could be and often were separated.

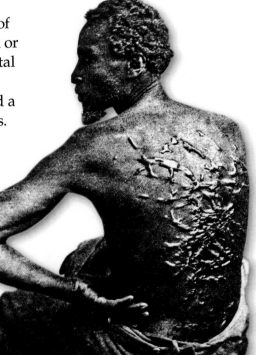

The punishments used against enslaved people included whipping, which could leave terrible scars.

CORBIS

overseer plantation manager

From the rhythmic patterns and themes of work songs and spirituals arose a new musical form—the blues. The blues influenced later styles, including jazz, rock and roll, and rap.

Wynton Marsalis is a modern-day jazz musician whose music has its roots in work songs and spirituals.

In the face of this threat, enslaved people set up a network of relatives and friends. If an owner sold a father or mother, an aunt, an uncle, or a close friend stepped in to raise the children left behind. These networks were a source of strength in the lives of enslaved people. Large, close-knit extended families became an important part of African American culture.

African American Culture

In 1808 Congress banned the import of slaves. Slavery remained **legal,** but traders could no longer purchase enslaved people from other countries. Some illegal slave trading continued, but by 1860, almost all the enslaved people in the South had been born there.

Though most enslaved people were born in the United States, they tried to preserve African customs. They passed traditional African folk stories on to their children. They performed African music and dance.

Enslaved people also drew on African rhythms to create musical forms that were uniquely American. One form was the work song, or field holler. A worker led a rhythmic call-and-response song, which sometimes included shouts and moans. The beat set the tempo for their work in the fields.

African American Religion

Many enslaved African Americans followed traditional African religious beliefs and practices. Others, however, accepted the Christian religion that was dominant in the United States. Christianity became for enslaved people a religion of hope and resistance. Enslaved people prayed for their freedom. They expressed their beliefs in **spirituals,** African American religious folk songs. The spiritual below, for example, refers to the biblical story of Daniel, whom God saved from being eaten by lions:

> **PRIMARY SOURCE**
>
> 66 Didn't my Lord deliver Daniel
> Deliver Daniel, deliver Daniel
> Didn't my Lord deliver Daniel
> An' why not-a every man. 99
>
> —from *Didn't My Lord Deliver Daniel*

Carlos Barria/Reuters/CORBIS

spiritual an African American religious folk song

Academic Vocabulary

legal permitted by law

On large plantations, enslaved people might live in small communities such as this.

Spirituals helped enslaved people express joy—but also sadness about their suffering here on Earth. Enslaved people also used spirituals as a way to communicate secretly among themselves.

Slave Codes

The **slave codes,** sometimes called black codes or Negro Laws, were laws in the Southern states that controlled enslaved people. Such laws had existed since colonial times.

One purpose of the codes was to prevent what white Southerners dreaded most—a slave rebellion. For this reason, slave codes prohibited enslaved people from gathering in large groups. The codes also required enslaved people to have written passes before leaving the slaveholder's property.

The slave codes made teaching enslaved people to read or write a crime. White Southerners feared that an educated enslaved person might start a revolt. They thought an enslaved person who could not read and write was less likely to rebel.

Fighting Back

Enslaved African Americans did sometimes rebel openly against their owners. One who did was Nat Turner.

Turner, who had taught himself to read and write, was a popular religious leader among the enslaved people in his area. In 1831 he led a group of followers on a **brief,** violent rampage in Southhampton County, Virginia. Turner and his followers killed at least 55 whites.

Copper slave tags identified enslaved workers when they were away from their home plantation.

► **CRITICAL THINKING**
Drawing Conclusions Why do you think enslaved Africans might need identification tags when they were away from their plantations?

(t) CORBIS, (b) CMH/UIG/Universal Images Group/age fotostock

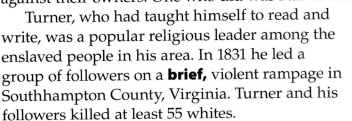

slave codes laws in a Southern state that controlled enslaved people

Academic Vocabulary
brief short

**Harriet Tubman
(c. 1820–1913)**

Harriet Tubman was born into slavery in Maryland. She escaped in 1849 and fled to Philadelphia. The following year Tubman returned to free her family. This began a career during which she made 19 trips to the slaveholding South and helped about 300 slaves escape to freedom. During the Civil War, Tubman helped the Union Army. In June 1863, she led a squad of African American soldiers on a South Carolina mission the led to the freeing of 800 enslaved African Americans. After the war, Tubman became an active women's suffragist and created the Home for the Aged in Auburn, New York. She died there in 1913.

▶ **CRITICAL THINKING**
Drawing Conclusions Why do you think Tubman was willing to risk her own freedom to help free other enslaved African Americans?

Reading **HELP**DESK

Underground Railroad a system of cooperation to aid and house enslaved people who had escaped
literacy the ability to read and write

Two months after the uprising began, authorities captured and hanged Turner. Still, his rebellion terrified white Southerners. White mobs killed dozens of African Americans, many of whom had nothing to do with the rebellion. Whites also passed more severe slave codes, making life under slavery even harsher.

Armed revolts such as Turner's were rare because enslaved African Americans realized they had little chance of winning. For the most part, enslaved people resisted slavery by working slowly or by pretending to be ill. Sometimes they might set fire to a plantation building or break tools. Such acts helped enslaved African Americans cope with their lack of freedom. Even if they were not free, they could strike back at the slaveholders.

Escaping Slavery

Enslaved people also resisted by running away from their owners. Often their goal was to find relatives on other plantations. Sometimes they left to escape punishment.

Less often, enslaved African Americans tried to run away to freedom in the North. Getting to the North was very difficult. Among those who succeeded were Harriet Tubman and Frederick Douglass, two African American leaders.

Most who succeeded escaped from the Upper South. A runaway might receive aid from the **Underground Railroad,** a network of "safe houses" owned by people opposed to slavery.

Moses Grandy, who did escape, spoke about the hardships runaways faced:

PRIMARY SOURCE

❝ They hide themselves during the day in the woods and swamps; at night they travel. … In these dangerous journeys they are guided by the north-star, for they only know that the land of freedom is in the north. ❞

—from *Narrative of the Life of Moses Grandy*

The big danger, of course, was capture. Most runaways were caught and returned to their owners. The owners punished them severely, usually by whipping.

✓ **PROGRESS CHECK**

Explaining How did the African American spirituals develop?

North Wind Picture Archives

Southern Cities

GUIDING QUESTION *What changes did urbanization introduce in the South by the mid-1800s?*

Though mostly agricultural, the South had several large cities by the mid-1800s, including Baltimore and New Orleans. The 10 largest cities in the South were either seaports or river ports. Cities located where the region's few railroads crossed paths also began to grow. These included Chattanooga, Montgomery, and Atlanta.

Free African Americans formed their own communities in Southern cities. They practiced trades and founded churches and institutions, yet their rights were limited. Most states did not allow them to move from state to state. Free African Americans did not share equally in economic and political life.

In the early 1800s, there were no statewide public school systems in the South. People who could afford to do so sent their children to private schools. By the mid-1800s, however, education was growing. North Carolina and Kentucky set up and ran public schools.

The South lagged behind other parts of the country in **literacy** (LIH•tuh•ruh•see), the ability to read and write. One reason was that the South was thinly populated. A school would have to serve a wide area, and many families were unwilling or unable to send children great distances to school. Many Southerners also believed education was a private matter.

☑ **PROGRESS CHECK**

Identifying What factors made possible the growth of the few Southern cities?

LESSON 4 REVIEW

Review Vocabulary

1. Use the following words in a brief paragraph about slavery in the South.

   a. overseer   **b.** slave codes
   c. spiritual   **d.** Underground Railroad

2. Explain the significance of the following terms:

   a. yeoman   **b.** literacy

Answer the Guiding Questions

3. *Discussing* How did the family structure of enslaved African Americans help them survive life under slavery?

4. *Explaining* How did African American culture develop in cities in the South?

5. **PERSONAL WRITING** From the perspective of an enslaved person, write about whether it is worth the risk to seek freedom.

Write your answers on a separate piece of paper.

❶ Exploring the Essential Questions

EXPOSITORY WRITING Describe how improved transportation affected trade for farmers and manufacturers in the Midwest. Use examples from the chapter to help you organize your essay.

❷ 21st Century Skills

USING BAR GRAPHS Use this chapter and information from outside sources to collect data about the number of enslaved African Americans in the United States between 1800 and 1860. Create a series of bar graphs showing the changes in the enslaved population. Write a paragraph that explains what factors are behind the information shown in the graphs.

❸ Thinking Like a Historian

UNDERSTANDING CAUSE AND EFFECT Use a diagram like this one to show and briefly describe the factors that encouraged the growing settlement of the Midwest in the early and mid-1800s.

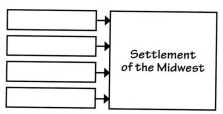

Settlement of the Midwest

❹ Visual Literacy

ANALYZING POLITICAL CARTOONS Many Irish immigrants journeyed to the United States in the mid-1800s. Castle Garden was the processing facility for immigrants at that time. According to this cartoon, how do the British feel about the migration? How do you know?

A UNCLE SAM (UNITED STATES)　　**C** JOHN BULL (BRITAIN)

B IRISH IMMIGRANTS　　**D** BRITISH LION

REVIEW THE GUIDING QUESTIONS

Choose the best answer for each question.

1 What happened in the first phase of industrialization in the North?

A. Factory workers used machinery to perform some work.

B. Manufacturers made products by dividing the tasks among the workers.

C. Waterpower and steam power were used to produce more products in less time.

D. Manufacturers built factories to bring specialized workers together.

2 The Underground Railroad helped enslaved people who

F. wanted to smuggle enslaved people from Africa into the United States.

G. wanted to expand transportation routes in the South.

H. had escaped from their owners.

I. were too weak to walk.

3 The American Party was once called the Know-Nothing Party because

A. party members knew nothing about the important issues.

B. party members did not support education.

C. party members responded to questions about the group by saying, "I know nothing."

D. party members were mainly Catholics who knew nothing about Protestants.

4 Which of the following inventions were most important to the growth of cities in the interior of the United States?

F. the clipper ship and telegraph

G. the cotton gin and Underground Railroad

H. the locomotive and steamship

I. the sewing machine and the slave codes

5 What was the main reason that the Southern economy remained largely agricultural?

A. Southerners did not know how to start industries.

B. Cotton sales were very profitable.

C. Southerners refused to work in factories.

D. There were no railroads in the South.

6 The largest group of white people in the South were

F. yeomen.

G. tenant farmers.

H. enslaved.

I. plantation owners.

DBQ DOCUMENT-BASED QUESTIONS

The following is an excerpt from a work contract from around 1830.

"We ... agree to work for such wages per week, and prices by the job, as the Company may see fit to pay. ...We also agree not to be engaged in any [labor union], whereby the work may be [delayed], or the company's interest in any work [harmed]."

Source: Cocheco Manufacturing Company

7 **Making Inferences** This excerpt suggests that labor unions at this time

A. were not very active.

B. did not have many members.

C. were a cause of worry for employers.

D. were not helpful to employees.

8 **Drawing Conclusions** What does this contract suggest about the relationship between employees and employers in factories in the early 1800s?

F. The relationship was close.

G. Employers had deep respect for their workers.

H. There was conflict between workers and employers.

I. Employers were having trouble getting enough people to take their factory jobs.

SHORT RESPONSE

A Southern newspaper publisher wrote the following in 1856.

"Every Roman Catholic in the known world is under the absolute control of the Catholic Priesthood. ... And it is ... this power of the Priesthood to control the Catholic community, and cause a vast multitude of ignorant foreigners to vote as a unit."

Source: William G. Brownlow, *Americanism Contrasted with Foreignism, Romanism, and Bogus Democracy*

9 What did the writer believe about Catholic immigrants to the United States?

10 What did the writer find dangerous about Catholics being controlled by priests?

EXTENDED RESPONSE

11 **Persuasive Writing** Take the role of an immigrant to America in 1840. Would you decide to settle in the North or the South? Describe the conditions in both sections of the country that led to your decision.

Need Extra Help?

If You've Missed Question	1	2	3	4	5	6	7	8	9	10	11
Review Lesson	1	4	2	1	3	4	2	2	2	2	1–4

The Spirit of Reform

1820–1860

ESSENTIAL QUESTIONS • Why do societies change?
• What motivates people to act? • How do new ideas change the way people live?

netw⊙rks

There's More Online about the issues that American reformers tackled in the mid-1800s.

CHAPTER 15

The Story Matters . . .

Young Emily Dickinson excels at school, especially in Latin, science, and writing. Dickinson even takes the then-unusual step of attending college for a year, but she finds its strict rules unsuited for her creative energy.

As an adult, she spends less and less time in public. After the age of 40, she dresses only in white. She does not travel and chooses not to meet most visitors. She spends much of her time writing, eventually producing 1,800 brilliant gems of poetry. She is a literary pioneer—though few people at the time know it. Only 10 of her poems ever appear in print during her lifetime. Only in death is she recognized among the era's many women of achievement.

◄ *Emily Dickinson was a brilliant poet of the mid-1800s.*

The Granger Collection, NYC

401

Place and Time: United States 1820 to 1860

During this period, many men and women, including whites and African Americans, worked to abolish slavery. Other people wanted to reform laws and customs that limited women's choices and created harsh conditions for the poor and people with disabilities.

Step Into the Place

MAP FOCUS One of the main reforms people sought in the mid-1800s was the abolition of slavery. Reformers also tried to help enslaved people escape to freedom in the North or outside the country. Some of the routes to freedom are noted on the map.

1 LOCATION On the map, locate the cities of Toledo, Cleveland, and Buffalo. Why do you think these cities became important points for people trying to escape slavery?

2 CRITICAL THINKING
Speculating Why do you think some enslaved people traveled to Canada instead of stopping when they reached a free Northern state?

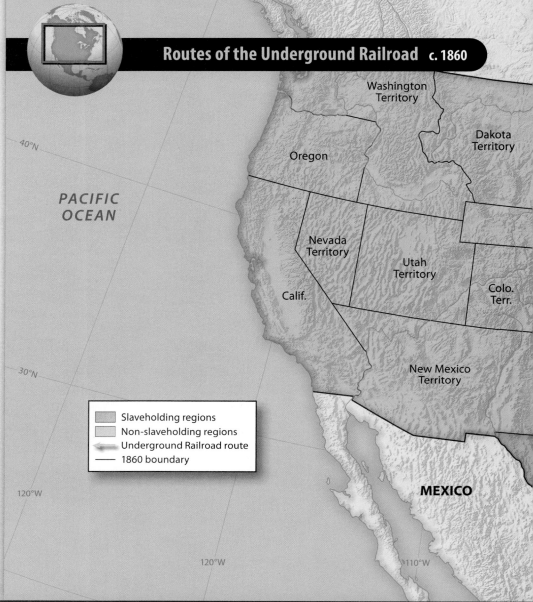

Routes of the Underground Railroad c. 1860

Washington Territory

Dakota Territory

Oregon

PACIFIC OCEAN

40°N

Nevada Territory

Utah Territory

Calif.

Colo. Terr.

30°N

New Mexico Territory

Slaveholding regions
Non-slaveholding regions
Underground Railroad route
1860 boundary

120°W

MEXICO

120°W

110°W

Step Into the Time

TIME LINE Look at the time line. Who was president when New York banned slavery?

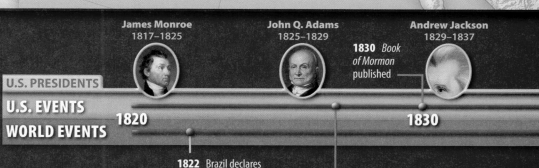

James Monroe
1817–1825

John Q. Adams
1825–1829

Andrew Jackson
1829–1837

1830 *Book of Mormon* published

U.S. PRESIDENTS
U.S. EVENTS
WORLD EVENTS

1820

1830

1822 Brazil declares independence from Portugal

1827 New York bans slavery

White House Historical Association

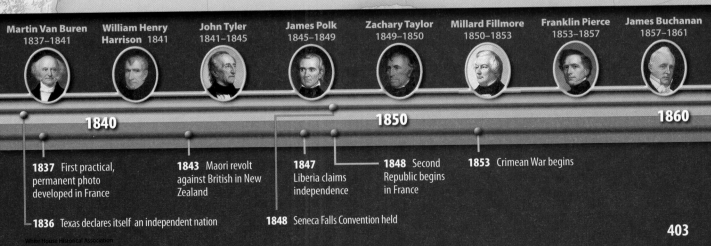

networks
There's More Online!

☑ **MAP** Explore the interactive version of this map on NETWORKS.

☑ **TIME LINE** Explore the interactive version of this time line on NETWORKS.

CANADA

Great Lakes

Dakota Territory

Minn.

Wis.

Mich.

N.H.

Vt.

Maine

Portland

Oswego

Rochester

N.Y.

Boston

Mass.

Milwaukee

London

Buffalo

Albany

Providence

R.I.

Iowa

Chicago

Windsor

Cleveland

Conn.

Des Moines

Toledo

Pa.

New York City

Nebraska Territory

Percival

Ind.

Ohio

Cumberland

N.J. Philadelphia

Del.

Quincy

Indianapolis

Columbus

Md.

Kansas

Springfield

Ill.

Cincinnati

Marietta

ATLANTIC OCEAN

Lawrence

Mo.

Ohio R. Ironton

Richmond

Chester

Evansville

Jeffersonville

Va.

Norfolk

Cairo

Ky.

Nashville

N.C.

Indian Territory

Ark.

Tenn.

New Bern

Little Rock

S.C.

Miss.

Ala.

Atlanta

Charleston

La.

Georgia

Savannah

Texas

Jackson

Montgomery

Okefenokee Swamp

Austin

Tallahassee

Fla.

New Orleans

Everglades

Mississippi R.

Missouri R.

Platte R.

Arkansas R.

Red R.

0   400 miles
0   400 km
Albers Equal-Area projection

N
W   E
S

Gulf of Mexico

90°W   80°W   70°W

40°N

30°N

Martin Van Buren
1837–1841

William Henry Harrison 1841

John Tyler
1841–1845

James Polk
1845–1849

Zachary Taylor
1849–1850

Millard Fillmore
1850–1853

Franklin Pierce
1853–1857

James Buchanan
1857–1861

1840   **1850**   **1860**

1837 First practical, permanent photo developed in France

1843 Maori revolt against British in New Zealand

1847 Liberia claims independence

1848 Second Republic begins in France

1853 Crimean War begins

1836 Texas declares itself an independent nation

1848 Seneca Falls Convention held

Lesson 1
Social Reform

ESSENTIAL QUESTION *Why do societies change?*

IT MATTERS BECAUSE
Developments in the early 1800s helped shape the social and cultural fabric of the United States.

Religion and Reform

GUIDING QUESTION *What was the effect of the Second Great Awakening?*

Reverend James B. Finley described the scene this way:

PRIMARY SOURCE

❝The noise was like the roar of Niagara [Falls]. The vast sea of human beings seemed to be agitated as if by a storm. . . . Some of the people were singing, others praying, some crying for mercy. . . . While witnessing these scenes, a peculiarly strange sensation, such as I had never felt before, came over me. My heart beat tumultuously [violently], my knees trembled, my lip quivered, and I felt as though I must fall to the ground.❞

—from *Autobiography of Rev. James B. Finley*

Finley was describing an early nineteenth-century religious meeting called a **revival.** At this time, people traveled great distances to hear preachers speak and to pray, sing, weep, and shout. This wave of religious interest—known as the Second Great Awakening—stirred the nation. The first Great Awakening had spread through the colonies in the mid-1700s.

Also at this time, a new spirit of reform took hold in the United States. This spirit brought changes to American religion, education, and literature. Some reformers sought to improve society by forming

Reading **HELP**DESK

Taking Notes: *Identifying*

As you read, use a diagram like this one to identify the reformers' contributions.

Reformer		Contribution
Thomas Gallaudet	→	
Dorothea Dix	→	

Content Vocabulary

• **revival**
• **utopia**
• **temperance**
• **normal school**
• **civil disobedience**

utopias (yu•TOH•pee•uhs)—communities based on a vision of the perfect society. Most of these communities did not last. A few groups, such as the Mormons, did form lasting communities.

The Impact of Religion

Attending revivals often made men and women eager to reform their own lives and the world. Some people became involved in missionary work or social reform movements. Among those movements was the push to ban alcohol.

Connecticut minister Lyman Beecher was a leader of this movement. He wanted to protect society from "rum-selling, tippling folk, infidels, and ruff-scuff." Beecher and other reformers called for **temperance**, or drinking little or no alcohol. They used **lectures**, pamphlets, and revival-style rallies to warn people of the dangers of liquor.

The temperance movement persuaded Maine and some other states to outlaw the manufacture and sale of alcohol. States later repealed most of these laws.

Changing Education

Reformers also wanted to improve education. Most schools had little money, and many teachers lacked training. Some people opposed the idea of compulsory, or required, education.

Religious revivals could attract thousands of people for days of prayers and song.

▶ **CRITICAL THINKING**
Analyzing Images Who are the people standing and sitting on the platform?

The Granger Collection, NYC

revival religious meeting
utopia community based on a vision of the perfect society

temperance drinking little or no alcohol

Academic Vocabulary

lecture speech meant to provide information, similar to what a teacher presents

In addition, some groups faced barriers to schooling. Parents often kept girls at home. They thought someone who was likely to become a wife and mother did not need much education. Many schools also denied African Americans the right to attend.

Massachusetts lawyer Horace Mann was a leader of educational reform. He believed education was a key to wealth and economic opportunity for all. Partly because of his efforts, in 1839 Massachusetts founded the nation's first state-supported **normal school**—a school for training high school graduates to become teachers. Other states soon adopted Mann's reforms.

New colleges and universities opened their doors during the age of reform. Most of them admitted only white men, but other groups also began winning access to higher education. Oberlin College of Ohio, for example, was founded in 1833. The college admitted both women and African Americans.

This picture shows students with hearing impairments receiving specialized instruction. The education of people with disabilities greatly advanced during the early and mid-1800s.

Helping People with Disabilities

Reformers also focused on teaching people with disabilities. Thomas Gallaudet (ga•luh•DEHT) developed a method to teach those with hearing impairments. He opened the Hartford School for the Deaf in Connecticut in 1817. At that same time, Samuel Gridley Howe was helping people with vision impairments. He printed books using an alphabet created by Louis Braille, which used raised letters a person could "read" with his or her fingers. Howe headed the Perkins Institute, a school for the visually impaired in Boston.

Schoolteacher Dorothea Dix began visiting prisons in 1841. She found some prisoners chained to the walls with little or no clothing, often in unheated cells. Dix also learned that some inmates were guilty of no crime. Instead, they were suffering from mental illnesses. Dix made it her life's work to educate the public about the poor conditions for prisoners and the mentally ill.

☑ **PROGRESS CHECK**

Describing How did Samuel Howe help people with vision impairments?

The Granger Collection, NYC

normal school state-supported school for training high school graduates to become teachers

civil disobedience refusing to obey laws considered unjust

Academic Vocabulary

author writer of books, articles, or other written works

Culture Changes

GUIDING QUESTION *What type of American literature emerged in the 1820s?*

Art and literature of the time reflected the changes in society and culture. American **authors** and artists developed their own style and explored American themes.

Writers such as Margaret Fuller, Ralph Waldo Emerson, and Henry David Thoreau stressed the relationship between humans and nature and the importance of the individual conscience. This literary movement was known as Transcendentalism. In his works, Emerson urged people to listen to the inner voice of conscience and to overcome prejudice. Thoreau practiced **civil disobedience** (dihs•uh•BEE•dee•uhns)—refusal to obey laws he found unjust. For example, Thoreau went to jail in 1846 rather than pay a tax to support the Mexican American War.

In poetry, Henry Wadsworth Longfellow wrote narrative, or story, poems such as the *Song of Hiawatha*. Walt Whitman captured the new American spirit and confidence in his *Leaves of Grass*. Emily Dickinson wrote hundreds of simple, deeply personal poems, many of which celebrated the natural world.

American artists also explored American topics and developed a purely American style. Beginning in the 1820s, a group of landscape painters known as the Hudson River School focused on scenes of the Hudson River Valley. Print-makers Nathaniel Currier and James Merritt Ives created popular prints that celebrated holidays, sporting events, and rural life.

✓ **PROGRESS CHECK**

Describing How did the spirit of reform influence American authors?

Ralph Waldo Emerson's house in Concord, Massachusetts, was a gathering place for many of the leaders of the Transcendentalist movement.

David Lyons/Alamy

LESSON 1 REVIEW

Review Vocabulary

1. Examine the three terms below. Then write a sentence or two explaining how these terms were related to each other during the period of social reform.

   a. revival   **b.** utopia   **c.** temperance

Answer the Guiding Questions

2. *Analyzing* What was the relationship between the Second Great Awakening and the reform movements of the early 1800s?

3. *Explaining* What themes did the transcendentalists focus on in their writings?

4. *Comparing and Contrasting* How was the work of Dorothea Dix similar to that of Thomas Gallaudet? How was it different?

5. **PERSUASIVE WRITING** Create a brochure about the newly established Oberlin College to send to potential students. Explain why the college differs from others, and describe the advantages of this college experience.

☑ **BIOGRAPHY**
Sojourner Truth

☑ **GRAPH** Slavery in the
United States

☑ **GRAPHIC ORGANIZER**
Prominent Abolitionists

☑ **MAP** Liberia

☑ **SLIDE SHOW** Farm Labor in the
United States

☑ **VIDEO**

Lesson 2

The Abolitionists

ESSENTIAL QUESTION *What motivates people to act?*

IT MATTERS BECAUSE

The growing demands of abolitionists helped deepen the divide between North and South.

The Start of the Abolition Movement

GUIDING QUESTION *How did Americans' attitudes toward slavery change?*

Among the reformers of the early 1800s were **abolitionists** (a•buh•LIH•shuhn•ihsts), who sought the end of slavery. Though their voices were growing, their cause was not a new one.

The Early Movement

Even before the Revolution, some Americans had tried to limit or end slavery. Early antislavery societies generally believed slavery had to be ended gradually. First they wanted to stop the slave trade. Then they would phase out slavery itself. Supporters believed that ending slavery gradually would give the South's economy time to adjust to the loss of enslaved labor.

At the Constitutional Convention in 1787, delegates debated slavery and its future. The delegates reached a compromise, allowing each state to decide whether to allow the practice.

By the early 1800s, the Northern states had officially ended slavery there. The practice continued in the South. In fact, the rise of the Cotton Kingdom increased the use of enslaved labor.

The reform movement of the early and mid-1800s gave new life to the antislavery cause. A growing number of Americans were coming to believe slavery was wrong and that the practice should end.

(c) The Granger Collection, NYC.
(c) Library of Congress, Prints & Photographs Division, LC-USZ62-119343,
(r) North Wind Picture Archives

Reading **HELP**DESK

Taking Notes: *Identifying*

As you read, use a diagram like this one to identify five abolitionists. Below each name, write a brief description of his or her role in the movement.

Abolitionists

Content Vocabulary

• abolitionist

Many who led the antislavery movement came from the Quaker faith. One Quaker, Benjamin Lundy, founded a newspaper in Ohio in 1821 called the *Genius of Universal Emancipation*. Its purpose was to spread the abolitionist message. "I heard the wail of the captive," he wrote. "I felt his pang of distress, and the iron entered my soul."

The Colonization Plan

There were many barriers to ending slavery. Many white Northerners still supported the practice. Even some white abolitionists worried about the effect free African Americans would have on society. They did not like the idea of hundreds of thousands of former enslaved people living in the United States.

In 1816 a group of powerful whites formed the American Colonization Society. They planned to send free African Americans to Africa to start new lives. The society raised money to send free African Americans out of the country. Some went to the west coast of Africa, where the society acquired land for a colony. The first settlers arrived in Liberia ("place of freedom") in 1822. In 1847 Liberia declared itself an independent republic.

The American Colonization Society did not stop the growth of slavery. It helped resettle only about 10,000 African Americans by the mid-1860s. Only a few African Americans wanted to go to Africa, while most wanted to be free in America

✔ **PROGRESS CHECK**

Identifying What was the purpose of the American Colonization Society?

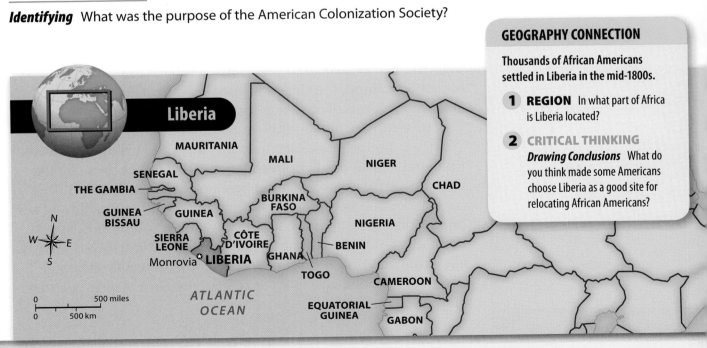

GEOGRAPHY CONNECTION

Thousands of African Americans settled in Liberia in the mid-1800s.

1 **REGION** In what part of Africa is Liberia located?

2 **CRITICAL THINKING**
Drawing Conclusions What do you think made some Americans choose Liberia as a good site for relocating African Americans?

abolitionist person who sought the end of slavery in the United States in the early 1800s.

The Movement Builds Strength

GUIDING QUESTION *Why did the reform movement gain momentum?*

Gradualism and colonization remained the main goals of antislavery groups until the 1830s. At this time, abolitionists began arguing that enslaved African Americans should be freed immediately. Slavery became America's most pressing social issue.

Making the Case Against Slavery

Massachusetts abolitionist William Lloyd Garrison had a great influence on the antislavery movement. In 1831 he started a newspaper called *The Liberator*.

Garrison was one of the first white abolitionists to call for an immediate end to slavery. He rejected a slow, gradual approach. In the first issue of *The Liberator*, he wrote, "I *will be* as harsh as truth, and as uncompromising as justice. . . . I will not retreat a single inch—AND I WILL BE HEARD."

Garrison was heard. He attracted enough followers to start the New England Anti-Slavery Society in 1832 and the American Anti-Slavery Society the next year. By 1838, the groups Garrison started had more than 1,000 local branches.

Sarah and Angelina Grimké were two other early abolitionists. The sisters were born in South Carolina to a wealthy slaveholding family. They both moved to Philadelphia in 1832. While living in the North, the Grimké sisters spoke out for both abolition and women's rights.

To show their commitment to abolition, the Grimkés asked their mother to give them their family inheritance early. Instead of money or land, the sisters wanted several of the family's enslaved workers. The sisters immediately freed them.

The Grimkés, along with Angelina's husband Theodore Weld, wrote *American Slavery As It Is* in 1839. This book collected firsthand stories of life under slavery. The book was one of the most powerful abolitionist publications of its time.

Harriet Beecher Stowe was another writer who made a major impact on public opinion. Her 1852 novel, *Uncle Tom's Cabin*, became a wildly popular best-seller. The book portrayed slavery as a cruel and brutal system. Some people, however, strongly opposed the book and its message. Sale of *Uncle Tom's Cabin* was banned in the South.

Reading **HELP**DESK

Reading Strategy: *Summarizing*

When you summarize a reading, you find the main idea of the passage and restate it in your own words. Read about the work of William Lloyd Garrison. On a separate sheet of paper, summarize the information in one or two sentences.

African American Abolitionists

Free African Americans in the North especially supported the goal of abolition. Most lived in poverty in cities and had trouble getting good jobs and decent housing. They were often subject to violent attacks. Yet these African Americans were proud of their freedom. They sought to help those who remained enslaved.

African Americans helped organize and lead the American Anti-Slavery Society. They subscribed to *The Liberator*. They also did their own writing and publishing. In 1827 Samuel Cornish and John Russwurm started the country's first African American newspaper *Freedom's Journal*.

Born free in North Carolina and settling in Boston, writer David Walker published a powerful pamphlet against slavery. He challenged African Americans to rebel and overthrow slavery. He wrote, "America is more our country than it is the whites'—we have enriched it with our blood and tears."

In 1830 free African American leaders held a convention in Philadelphia. Delegates met "to devise ways and means for the bettering of our condition." They discussed starting an African American college and encouraging free African Americans to move to Canada.

The Role of Frederick Douglass

Frederick Douglass is the best-known African American abolitionist. Born into slavery in Maryland, Douglass escaped in 1838. He settled first in Massachusetts.

Frederick Douglass speaks while disorder breaks out at this 1860 abolitionist meeting in Boston, Massachusetts.

▶ **CRITICAL THINKING**
Drawing Conclusions Why do you think this abolitionist meeting in a northern city became disorderly?

Sojourner Truth (1797–1883)

Sojourner Truth was a powerful voice for abolition. Truth worked with William Lloyd Garrison, Frederick Douglass, and others to bring about the end of slavery. She traveled throughout the North and spoke about her experiences in slavery. Sojourner Truth was also an active supporter of the women's rights movement.

▶ **CRITICAL THINKING**

Making Connections Why do you think Sojourner Truth later became involved with the women's rights movement?

As a runaway, Douglass faced the danger of capture and a return to slavery. Still, he joined the Massachusetts Anti-Slavery Society. He traveled widely to speak at abolitionist meetings. He even appeared at events in London and the West Indies. Douglass was a powerful speaker who often moved listeners to tears. He also edited the antislavery newspaper *North Star*.

Douglass made his home in the United States because he believed abolitionists must fight slavery at its source. He insisted that African Americans receive not just freedom but full equality with whites as well. In 1847 friends helped Douglass buy his freedom from the slaveholder from whom he had fled in Maryland.

Sojourner Truth

"I was born a slave in Ulster County, New York," Isabella Baumfree began when she told her story to audiences. After a childhood and youth filled with hardship, she escaped in 1826. Then, she officially gained her freedom in 1827 when New York banned slavery. Baumfree later settled in New York City with her two youngest children. In 1843 Baumfree chose a new name. In the biography *Sojourner Truth: Slave, Prophet, Legend*, she explained: "The Lord [named] me Sojourner … Truth, because I was to declare the truth to the people."

The Underground Railroad

Abolitionists sometimes risked prison and death to help African Americans escape slavery. They helped create a network of escape **routes** from the South to the North called the Underground Railroad.

Underground Railroad "passengers"—that is, escaping African Americans—traveled by night, often on foot. The North Star guided them in the direction of freedom. During the day they rested at "stations"—barns, basements, and attics—until the next night. The railroad's "conductors" were whites and African Americans who guided the runaways to freedom in the northern United States or Canada. Harriet Tubman was the most famous conductor.

The Underground Railroad helped as many as 100,000 enslaved people escape. It gave hope to many more.

☑ **PROGRESS CHECK**

Identifying What were Underground Railroad "stations"?

Library of Congress, Prints & Photographs Division, LC-USZ62-119343

Build Vocabulary: *Origins of Sayings*

"Underground Railroad" is a metaphor. A metaphor describes one thing by calling it something else. Readers imagine a train track that is literally underground. This helps them understand that the Underground Railroad was a method for moving people that was not visible to the public.

Academic Vocabulary

route line of travel

Reaction to the Abolitionists

GUIDING QUESTION *Who opposed the abolition of slavery?*

Abolitionists stirred strong reactions. Most white Southerners believed abolition threatened their way of life, which required enslaved labor.

Even in the North, only a few white people supported abolition. Many white Northerners worried that freed African Americans would never blend into American society. Others feared that abolitionists could begin a war between the North and South.

Opposition to abolitionism sometimes led to violence. In Philadelphia a bloody race riot followed the burning of an antislavery group's headquarters. Police had to jail William Lloyd Garrison to protect him from a Boston mob.

Elijah Lovejoy in Illinois was not so lucky. Angry whites invaded his antislavery newspaper offices and wrecked his presses three times. Three times Lovejoy installed new presses. The fourth time the mob attacked, it set fire to the building. When Lovejoy came out of the blazing building, someone shot and killed him.

In 1837 a mob attacked and killed newspaper editor Elijah Lovejoy.

▶ **CRITICAL THINKING**
Explaining Why did anti-abolitionists attack Elijah Lovejoy?

North Wind Picture Archives

The White South Reacts

White Southerners fought abolitionism with arguments in defense of slavery. They claimed that slavery was necessary to the Southern economy and had allowed Southern whites to reach a high level of culture. As anti-abolitionist Senator James Henry Hammond said in an 1858 speech to Congress: "In all social systems there must be a class to do the menial duties, to perform the drudgery of life. ... Such a class you must have, or you would not have that other class which leads progress, civilization, and refinement."

White Southerners also argued that they treated enslaved people well. They claimed that Northern workers were worse off than enslaved workers because they worked in factories for long hours at low wages. Also, Northern workers had to pay for their own goods and services from their small earnings, while enslaved African Americans received food, clothing, and **medical** care.

Other defenses of slavery were based on racism. Many whites believed that African Americans were better off under white care than on their own.

The conflict between pro-slavery and antislavery groups continued to mount. At the same time, a new women's rights movement was growing.

☑ **PROGRESS CHECK**

Identifying Points of View How did many Southerners defend the institution of slavery?

Academic Vocabulary

medical relating to medicine and help given to people who are sick or injured

---

LESSON 2 REVIEW

Review Vocabulary

1. Use the term *abolitionist* in a sentence about the mid-1800s.

Answer the Guiding Questions

2. *Identifying Points of View* What concern about ending slavery did the American Colonization Society seek to address?

3. *Discussing* How did African Americans help the abolitionist movement gain strength?

4. *Comparing and Contrasting* How did Northerners and Southerners view abolition differently?

5. **PERSONAL WRITING** Take the role of a conductor on the Underground Railroad. Write an explanation for why you are willing to help African Americans escape from slavery to freedom.

networks

There's More Online!

☑ **GRAPHIC ORGANIZER**
Women's Rights Leaders

☑ **PRIMARY SOURCE**
William Lloyd Garrison
on Frederick Douglass

☑ **TIME LINE** Opportunity and
Achievement for Women

☑ **VIDEO**

Lesson 3
The Women's Movement

ESSENTIAL QUESTION *How do new ideas change the way people live?*

IT MATTERS BECAUSE
Women began the long quest for expanded rights, including the right to vote, in the mid-1800s.

Reform for Women

GUIDING QUESTION *What did women do to win equal rights?*

For women such as Lucretia Mott, causes such as abolition and women's rights were linked. Like many other women reformers, Mott was a Quaker. Quaker women enjoyed an unusual degree of equality in their communities. Mott was actively involved in helping runaway enslaved workers. She organized the Philadelphia Female Anti-Slavery Society. At an antislavery convention in London, Mott met Elizabeth Cady Stanton. The two found they also shared an interest in women's rights.

The Seneca Falls Convention

In July 1848, Stanton and Mott helped organize the first women's rights convention in Seneca Falls, New York. About 300 people, including 40 men, attended.

A highlight of the convention was debate over a Declaration of Sentiments and Resolutions. These resolutions called for an end to laws that discriminated against women. They also demanded that women be allowed to enter the all-male world of trades, professions, and businesses. The most controversial issue, however, was the call for woman **suffrage,** or the right to vote in elections.

Reading HELPDESK

Taking Notes: *Summarizing*

As you read, use a diagram like this one to summarize the contributions each individual made to the women's movement.

Individual	Contribution
Lucretia Mott →	
Elizabeth Cady Stanton →	
Susan B. Anthony →	

Content Vocabulary
• **suffrage**
• **coeducation**

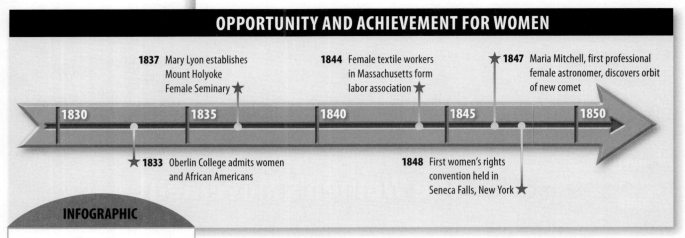

OPPORTUNITY AND ACHIEVEMENT FOR WOMEN

1837 Mary Lyon establishes Mount Holyoke Female Seminary

1844 Female textile workers in Massachusetts form labor association

1847 Maria Mitchell, first professional female astronomer, discovers orbit of new comet

1830 · 1835 · 1840 · 1845 · 1850

1833 Oberlin College admits women and African Americans

1848 First women's rights convention held in Seneca Falls, New York

INFOGRAPHIC

In the mid-1800s, women began to argue for—and earn—their own rights and an equal place in society.

1 IDENTIFYING Which items on the time line reflect growing opportunities for women to learn and gain skills?

2 CRITICAL THINKING
Analyzing Which items on the time line suggest women were using their education to achieve great things?

Elizabeth Stanton insisted the resolutions include a demand for woman suffrage. Some delegates worried that the idea was too radical. Mott told her friend, "Lizzie, thee will make us ridiculous." Standing with Stanton, Frederick Douglass argued powerfully for women's right to vote. After a heated debate, the convention voted to include in their declaration the demand for woman suffrage in the United States.

The Seneca Falls Declaration

The first women's rights convention called for women's equality and for their right to vote, to speak publicly, and to run for office. The convention issued a Declaration of Sentiments and Resolutions modeled on the Declaration of Independence. Just as Thomas Jefferson had in 1776, women are announcing the need for revolutionary change based on a claim of basic rights:

PRIMARY SOURCE

❝ When, in the course of human events, it becomes necessary for one portion of the family of man to assume among the people of the earth a position different from that which they have hitherto [before] occupied, but one to which the laws of nature and of nature's God entitle them, a decent respect to the opinions of mankind requires that they should declare the causes that impel them to such a course. ❞

In this passage, two important words—*and women*—are added to Thomas Jefferson's famous phrase:

❝ We hold these truths to be self-evident: that all men and women are created equal; that they are endowed by their Creator with certain inalienable rights; that among these are life, liberty, and the pursuit of happiness. . . . ❞

Reading **HELP**DESK

suffrage the right to vote

The women's declaration called for an end to laws that discriminated against women. It demanded that women be free to enter the all-male world of trades, professions, and businesses.

66 The history of mankind is a history of repeated injuries and [wrongful takings of power] on the part of man toward woman, having in direct object the establishment of an absolute tyranny over her. To prove this, let facts be submitted to a candid world. . . .

Now, in view of this entire [withholding of rights] of one-half the people of this country, their social and religious degradation,—in view of the unjust laws above mentioned, and because women do feel themselves aggrieved, oppressed, and fraudulently deprived of their most sacred rights, we insist that they have immediate admission to all the rights and privileges which belong to them as citizens of the United States. 99

—Seneca Falls Convention Declaration of Sentiments

The Women's Movement Grows

The Seneca Falls Convention helped launch a wider movement. In the years to come, reformers held several national conventions, with the first taking place in Worcester, Massachusetts, in 1850. Both male and female reformers joined the cause.

Among the movement's leaders was Susan B. Anthony. Anthony was the daughter of a Quaker abolitionist. She called for equal pay and college training for women, and **coeducation** (coh•eh•juh•KAY•shuhn)—the teaching of males and females together. Anthony also organized the country's first women's temperance association, the Daughters of Temperance. Anthony met Elizabeth Cady Stanton at a temperance meeting in 1851. They became lifelong friends and partners in the struggle for women's rights and suffrage.

Opportunities for women increased greatly in the late 1800s. Beginning with Wyoming in 1890, several states granted woman suffrage. Yet not until 1920 and the Nineteenth Amendment to the Constitution did women gain the right to vote everywhere.

✔ **PROGRESS CHECK**

Describing What is suffrage?

Elizabeth Cady Stanton (left), seen here with Susan B. Anthony, was an organizer of the Seneca Falls Convention.

coeducation the teaching of males and females together

National Portrait Gallery, Smithsonian Institution/Art Resource, NY

Maria Mitchell was the first woman to work as a professional astronomer. "It seems to me that the needle is the chain of woman. . . . Emancipate her from the 'stitch, stitch, stitch,' . . . and she would have time for studies which would engross as the needle never can."

▶ **CRITICAL THINKING**
Paraphrasing Restate the quote from Mitchell above using your own words.

Mount Holyoke Female Seminary in South Hadley, Massachusetts, was the first women's college in the United States.

▶ **CRITICAL THINKING**
Analyzing Primary Sources What do you think Lyon meant when she referred to women's education as "the great secret"?

(t) National Oceanic and Atmospheric Administration/Department of Commerce,
(b) The Granger Collection, NYC

Women Make Gains

GUIDING QUESTION *In what areas did women make progress in achieving equality?*

Pioneers in women's education began to call for more opportunity. Early champions such as Catherine Beecher believed that women should be educated for their traditional roles in life. The Milwaukee College for Women used Beecher's ideas "to train women to be healthful, intelligent, and successful wives, mothers, and housekeepers."

Other people thought that women could be trained to be **capable** teachers and to fill other professional roles. These pioneers broke down the barriers to female education and helped other women do the same.

One of these pioneers, Emma Willard, educated herself in subjects considered suitable only for males, such as science and mathematics. In 1821 Willard set up the Troy Female Seminary in upstate New York. Willard's seminary taught mathematics, history, geography, and physics, as well as the usual homemaking subjects.

Mary Lyon, after working as a teacher for 20 years, began raising funds to open a women's college. She established Mount Holyoke Female Seminary in Massachusetts in 1837, modeling its curriculum on that of nearby Amherst College. Lyon became the school's first principal, believing that "the great secret . . . is female education."

Reading **HELP**DESK

Academic Vocabulary

capable skillful
ministry the job of a religious leader

Marriage and the Family

Prior to the mid-1800s, women had few rights. They depended on men for support. Anything a woman owned became the property of her husband if she married. She had few options if she was in an unhappy or abusive relationship.

During the mid- to late-1800s, women made some gains in marriage and property laws. New York, Pennsylvania, Indiana, Wisconsin, Mississippi, and the new state of California recognized the right of married women to own property.

Some states passed laws allowing divorced women to share guardianship of their children with their former husbands. Indiana was the first of several states that allowed women to seek divorce if their husbands abused alcohol.

Breaking Barriers

In the 1800s, women had few career choices. They could become elementary teachers—often at lower wages than a male teacher received. Jobs in professions dominated by men were even more difficult. Women had to struggle to become doctors or work in the **ministry**. Some strong-minded women succeeded.

Elizabeth Blackwell tried and failed repeatedly to get into medical school. Finally accepted by Geneva College in New York, Blackwell graduated first in her class and achieved fame as a doctor.

Maria Mitchell was another groundbreaking woman. Mitchell received an education from her father. In 1847 she became the first person to discover a comet with a telescope. The next year, she became the first woman elected to the American Academy of Arts and Sciences. In 1865 Mitchell joined the faculty of Vassar College.

Women's gains in the 1800s were remarkable—but far from complete. Women remained limited by social customs and expectations. In fact, women had just begun the long struggle to achieve their goal of equality.

✓ PROGRESS CHECK

Describing What gains did women make in the field of education?

Connections to
TODAY

Women's Colleges

Mount Holyoke is one of the Seven Sisters—a group of outstanding colleges founded to educate women. Today, Mount Holyoke and several of the Seven Sisters still provide a woman-only educational experience. Some of the Seven Sisters now admit men.

LESSON 3 REVIEW

Review Vocabulary

1. Explain ways that *suffrage* and *coeducation* could offer women in the 1800s new ways to participate in society.

Answer the Guiding Questions

2. ***Analyzing*** What did the Seneca Falls Convention do to help the women's movement grow?

3. ***Explaining*** Describe the rights within marriage that women gained in the 1800s.

4. **EXPOSITORY WRITING** What arguments might a woman have used to support suffrage? You are a female pioneer traveling west. Write a paragraph explaining why women should have the right to vote.

Narrative of the Life of Frederick Douglass, an American Slave

Frederick Douglass

Frederick Douglass (c. 1818–1895) was born and raised in slavery in Maryland. One of his owners broke the law by teaching Douglass to read and write. Frederick escaped from slavery in 1838 and made his way to freedom in the North. There he began to speak against slavery.

This passage comes from Chapter 1 of Frederick Douglass's autobiography. He wrote the autobiography because many people doubted his story. They heard him speak against slavery and thought he spoke too well to have been a slave. Douglass decided to tell his life story as a way to quiet these critics.

Frederick Douglass escaped a life of slavery to become a leading abolitionist.

❝ I was born in Tuckahoe, near Hillsborough, and about twelve miles from Easton, in Talbot County, Maryland. I have no accurate knowledge of my age, never having seen any authentic record containing it. By far the larger part of the slaves know as little of their ages as horses know of theirs, and it is the wish of most masters within my knowledge to keep their slaves thus ignorant. I do not remember to have ever met a slave who could tell of his birthday. They seldom come nearer to it than planting-time, harvest-time, cherry-time, spring-time, or fall-time. A want of information concerning my own was a source of unhappiness to me even during childhood. The white children could tell their ages. I could not tell why I ought to be deprived of the same privilege. I was not allowed to make any inquiries of my master concerning it. . . . The nearest estimate I can give makes me now between twenty-seven and twenty-eight years of age. I come to this, from hearing my master say, some time during 1835, I was about seventeen years old. . . .

My mother and I were separated when I was but an infant—before I knew her as my mother. It is a common custom, in the part of Maryland from which I ran away, to part children from their mothers at a very early age. Frequently, before the child has reached its twelfth month, its mother is taken from it, and hired out on some farm a considerable distance off, and the child is placed under the care of an old woman, too old for field labor. For what this separation is done, I do not know, unless it be to **hinder** the development of the child's affection toward its mother, and to blunt and destroy the natural affection of the mother for the child. This is the inevitable result.

I never saw my mother, to know her as such, more than four or five times in my life; and each of these times was very short in duration, and at night. She was hired by a Mr. Stewart, who lived about twelve miles from my home. She made her journeys to see me in the night, traveling the whole distance on foot, after the performance of her day's work. She was a field hand, and a whipping is the penalty of not being in the field at sunrise . . . I do not recollect of ever seeing my mother by the light of day. . . . Death soon ended what little [relationship] we could have while she lived, and with it her hardships and suffering. She died when I was about seven years old . . . I was not allowed to be present during her illness, at her death, or burial. . . . Never having enjoyed, to any considerable extent, her soothing presence, her tender and watchful care, I received the **tidings** of her death with much the same emotions I should have probably felt at the death of a stranger. ❞

Literary Element

First-Person Point of View occurs when a story's narrator tells his or her own experiences. First-person narrators use the pronouns *I, me,* and *we*. These narrators tell readers a lot about their own experience but very little about the experiences of other people or characters in their stories. As you read, think about what you learn because Douglass tells his own story—and what you don't learn.

Vocabulary

hinder
prevent

tidings
news

Analyzing Literature   DBQ

❶ Recalling How old was Frederick Douglass when he wrote this narrative?

❷ Analyzing How does Douglass feel about his age? Explain.

❸ Making Inferences How does Douglass feel about his mother and her death? Explain.

Write your answers on a separate piece of paper.

1 **Exploring the Essential Questions**

EXPOSITORY WRITING Take on the role of a mid-1800s reformer and explain your goals for American society. Write an essay in which you describe the changes you hope to achieve and the challenges you face in getting people to change their ideas over time.

2 **21st Century Skills**

DRAWING INFERENCES AND CONCLUSIONS Review the chapter for information about the reasons that people opposed abolition, temperance, and women's rights. Then select a current problem or injustice that you feel deeply about. Use the information from the chapter to draw conclusions about who in society today might be opposed to your cause and why.

3 **Thinking Like a Historian**

UNDERSTANDING CAUSE AND EFFECT Review the events related to the Second Great Awakening. Create a diagram like the one to the right to show some changes that resulted from this period of reform. Add additional spokes if you need to. Then explain the role that religion had in promoting these reforms.

Second Great Awakening

4 **Visual Literacy**

ANALYZING PAINTINGS This picture is called *The Hunters' Shanty in the Adirondacks,* by Currier and Ives. Describe the subject of this painting. What kind of feeling or mood do you think the artists are trying to create? Is it an appealing image? Explain.

Corbis

REVIEW THE GUIDING QUESTIONS
Choose the best answer for each question.

1 A major subject of transcendentalist literature was

A. realism.

B. the importance of inner knowledge and individual conscience.

C. anti-abolitionism.

D. the relationship between humans and technology.

2 What was the main goal of the temperance reformers?

F. improve public schools

G. increase church attendance

H. reduce alcohol drinking

I. teach the hearing impaired

3 Which of the following arguments did pro-slavery Southerners use against abolitionists?

A. Many abolitionists were also secretly slaveholders.

B. Slave labor was essential to the South, allowing Southern whites to reach a high level of culture.

C. Abolitionists only wanted to free enslaved workers so that they could work in Northern factories.

D. Abolitionists wanted to steal Southerners' farms.

4 What happened at the Seneca Falls Convention in 1848?

F. Delegates called for an end to child labor.

G. Delegates passed a resolution in favor of voting rights for all African Americans.

H. Delegates demanded that women be given the right to vote.

I. Delegates petitioned the states to add an Equal Rights Amendment to the Constitution.

5 William Lloyd Garrison influenced the antislavery movement by

A. using inherited money to buy and free enslaved workers.

B. starting the American Anti-Slavery Society.

C. giving speeches about his experiences as an enslaved man.

D. publishing an African American newspaper.

6 How did the Troy Female Seminary improve women's education?

F. It was open to African American men.

G. It taught them housekeeping skills.

H. It allowed them to study with men.

I. It taught subjects such as science.

DBQ **DOCUMENT-BASED QUESTIONS**

Horace Mann wrote this excerpt in an 1848 report.

> *"According to the European theory, men are divided into classes,—some to toil and earn, others to seize and enjoy. According to the Massachusetts theory, all are to have an equal chance for earning, and equal security in the enjoyment of what they earn. ... Education, then, beyond all other devices of human origin, is the great equalizer of the conditions of men."*

> —from "Report No. 12 of the Massachusetts School Board"

7 **Analyzing** Which describes the European theory according to Mann?

A. People in Europe are better than others.

B. Everyone has an equal chance.

C. Opportunity is determined at birth.

D. Massachusetts has good laws.

8 **Understanding Cause and Effect** According to Mann, what is the greatest cause of equality among men?

F. education

G. job security

H. class at birth

I. where you were born

SHORT RESPONSE

This statement reflected the goals of the temperance movement.

> *"We hold these truths to be self-evident; that all men are created temperate [without the need to drink alcohol]; that they are endowed by their Creator with certain natural and innocent desires; that among these are the appetite for cold water and the pursuit of happiness!"*

> —from *Manifesto of the Washington Total Abstinence Societies,* 1841

9 Which American document does this passage imitate? How can you tell?

10 Why do you think the writers chose this style? Explain.

EXTENDED RESPONSE

11 **Expository Writing** Write a short essay that describes the roots, goals, and accomplishments of the social reform, education reform, and women's rights movements. Explain the similarities and differences. Give an example of a change each movement achieved that affects your life today.

Need Extra Help?

If You've Missed Question	1	2	3	4	5	6	7	8	9	10	11
Review Lesson	1	1	2	3	2	3	1	1	1	1	1–3

Toward Civil War

1840–1861

ESSENTIAL QUESTION · *Why does conflict develop?*

netw⊙rks

There's More Online about the people and events that led the nation into civil war.

CHAPTER **16**

Lesson 1
The Search for Compromise

Lesson 2
Challenges to Slavery

Lesson 3
Secession and War

The Story Matters . . .

His is a complicated story that raises many questions about slavery and freedom. Dred Scott was born into slavery in Virginia. He has been bought and sold like a piece of furniture. He has been taken against his will to live in many places—including, for a time, a place where slavery is illegal. Now Scott is wondering: Did his time in "free" territory turn him into a free man? He decides to take his question to a court for a judge to decide.

Other people wonder if Scott—an enslaved African American—even has the right to go to court.

The answers to these questions are of great interest to the people of the United States. Emotions run high as the debate over slavery rages.

◄ *Dred Scott was at the center of a controversial Supreme Court ruling in the 1850s.*

The Granger Collection, NYC

Place and Time: United States 1840 to 1861

The divide between North and South, which had been deepening for decades, split wide following the election of 1860. States of the South decided they must break away from the Union and form their own nation.

Step Into the Place

MAP FOCUS The map shows the states that seceded from the Union.

1 REGION To which side did the states in the far West belong?

2 LOCATION Describe the location of the Union slave states relative to the other Union states and the seceding states.

3 CRITICAL THINKING
Speculating How do you think the location of the Union slave states affected their decision not to secede?

135,000 SETS, 270,000 VOLUMES SOLD.

UNCLE TOM'S CABIN

FOR SALE HERE.

AN EDITION FOR THE MILLION, COMPLETE IN 1 Vol., PRICE 37 1-2 CENTS.
"   "   IN GERMAN, IN 1 Vol., PRICE 50 CENTS.
"   "   IN 2 Vols., CLOTH, 6 PLATES, PRICE $1.50.
SUPERB ILLUSTRATED EDITION, IN 1 Vol., WITH 153 ENGRAVINGS,
PRICES FROM $2.50 TO $5.00.

The Greatest Book of the Age.

After the Southern states seceded, Union attempts to maintain control of Fort Sumter at Charleston, South Carolina, triggered armed conflict. The first shots of the Civil War were fired here on April 12, 1861.

This pictures shows a scene from the book *Uncle Tom's Cabin*. The book played a powerful role in an increasingly emotional debate over slavery in the 1850s.

Step Into the Time

TIME LINE Look at the time line. Which world event suggests that other nations were also debating the issue of slavery?

William Henry Harrison 1841

John Tyler 1841–1845

James Polk 1845–1849

U.S. PRESIDENTS		
U.S. EVENTS		
WORLD EVENTS		

1840

1845

1846 Congress establishes the Smithsonian Institution

1843 Charles Dickens's *A Christmas Carol* published

1845 Many Irish emigrate to escape famine

1848 Marx publishes *The Communist Manifesto*

(t) Thinkstock /Getty Images, (c) Bettmann/CORBIS, (b) White House Historical Association

networks

There's More Online!

☑ MAP Explore the interactive version of this map on NETWORKS.

☑ TIME LINE Explore the interactive version of this time line on NETWORKS.

A Nation Divided 1861

CANADA

130°W

Washington Territory

Salem

Oregon

Nevada Terr.

Sacramento

California

Utah Territory

New Mexico Territory

Dakota Territory

Nebraska Territory

Colorado Territory

Kansas
Topeka

Indian Territory

Texas

Austin

MEXICO

Minn.

St. Paul

Wisc.

Iowa
Des Moines

Madison

Ill.

Mo.

Jefferson City

Springfield

Ark.

Little Rock

La.

Baton Rouge

Mich.
Lansing

Ind.
Indianapolis

Ohio
Columbus

Ky.
Frankfort

Tenn.
Nashville

Miss.
Jackson

Ala.
Montgomery

Ga.

Atlanta

Tallahassee

Florida

N.H. Maine

Vt.
Augusta

Montpelier

Concord
Mass.

Albany
Boston
Providence

N.Y.
Hartford
R.I.
Conn.

Penn.
Harrisburg
Trenton
N.J.
Wheeling
Dover
Md.
Washington, D.C.
Del.
Annapolis

W. Va.
Richmond

Va.

Raleigh
N.C.

Columbia
S.C.
Ft. Sumter

PACIFIC OCEAN

ATLANTIC OCEAN

40°N

70°W

30°N

120°W

110°W

90°W

80°W

Legend
- Union territories
- Union free state
- Union slave state
- Seceding state
- Boundary between Union & Confederacy

0   300 miles
0   300 km

Lambert Azimuthal Equal-Area projection

Zachary Taylor
1849–1850

Millard Fillmore
1850–1853

1854 Congress passes the Kansas-Nebraska Act

Franklin Pierce
1853–1857

1857 U.S. Supreme Court makes *Dred Scott* decision

James Buchanan
1857–1861

1861 Civil War begins

Abraham Lincoln
1861–1865

1850   1855   1860   1865

1855 Florence Nightingale improves health care during Crimean War

1856 Henry Bessemer introduces his steelmaking process

1859 The Drake Well becomes first U.S. oil well

1861 Alexander II frees Russia's serfs, or bound servants

Lesson 1
The Search for Compromise

ESSENTIAL QUESTION *Why does conflict develop?*

IT MATTERS BECAUSE
The decision whether to allow slavery in new territories was a heated issue that divided the nation.

Political Conflict Over Slavery

GUIDING QUESTION *What political compromises were made because of slavery?*

The question of slavery had long fueled debate in the United States. Each time this debate flared, the nation's leaders struck some form of compromise.

For example, in 1820 the Missouri Compromise preserved the balance between slave and free states in the Senate. It also brought about a temporary stop in the debate over slavery.

New Territory Brings New Debates

In the 1840s, the debate over slavery in new territories erupted again. In 1844 the Democrats nominated James K. Polk of Tennessee for president and called for the annexation of Texas at the earliest possible time. After Polk's election, Texas was admitted to the Union in December 1845.

Texas's entry into the Union angered the Mexican government. Matters worsened when the two countries disputed the boundary between Texas and Mexico. At the same time, support was growing in the South for taking over California and New Mexico. President Polk tried to buy these territories from the Mexican government, but failed. All these issues helped lead to the Mexican War.

(c) Smithsonian American Art Museum, Washington, DC/Art Resource, NY

Reading **HELP**DESK

Taking Notes: *Describing*

As you read, use a diagram like the one shown to note reactions to the Kansas-Nebraska Act. Explain the reasons for these reactions.

Kansas-Nebraska Act

Antislavery: Pro-slavery:

Content Vocabulary
• **fugitive**   • **civil war**
• **secede**
• **border ruffian**

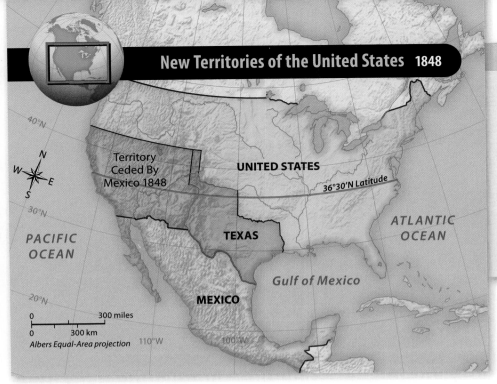

New Territories of the United States 1848

40°N

Territory Ceded By Mexico 1848

UNITED STATES

36°30'N Latitude

30°N

PACIFIC OCEAN

TEXAS

ATLANTIC OCEAN

Gulf of Mexico

20°N

MEXICO

0   300 miles
0   300 km
Albers Equal-Area projection   110°W   100°W

GEOGRAPHY CONNECTION

The territory of the United States expanded in the mid-1800s.

1 LOCATION How might location play a part in whether New Mexico and California became slave or free states?

2 CRITICAL THINKING
Explaining How does this map help explain the growing divide over slavery in the United States?

Differing Views

Soon after the war with Mexico began, Representative David Wilmot of Pennsylvania introduced the Wilmot Proviso. This proposal would ban slavery in any lands the United States might acquire from Mexico.

Southerners protested. They wanted the new territory to remain open to slavery. Senator John C. Calhoun of South Carolina offered another idea, saying that neither Congress nor any territorial government could ban slavery from a territory or **regulate** it.

Neither bill passed, but both caused heated debate. By the 1848 presidential election, the United States had taken California and New Mexico from Mexico but took no action on slavery in those territories.

In 1848 the Whigs picked General Zachary Taylor as their presidential candidate. The Democrats chose Senator Lewis Cass of Michigan. Both candidates ignored the slavery issue, which angered some voters.

Those who opposed slavery left their parties and formed the Free-Soil Party. Its slogan was "Free Soil, Free Speech, Free Labor, and Free Men." The party chose former president Martin Van Buren as its candidate. Taylor won, but the Free-Soil Party gained several seats in Congress.

Academic Vocabulary

regulate to control

James Michael Newell painted this mural, *The Underground Railroad,* in the post office of Dolgeville, New York, in 1940.

▶ **CRITICAL THINKING**

Analyzing Visuals What methods does the painter use to show the danger and difficulties facing the runaway family?

A New Compromise

Concerned over growing abolitionism, Southerners wanted a strong national **fugitive** (FYOO•juh•tihv), or runaway, slave law. Such a law would require every state to return runaway slaves.

In 1849 California applied to become a state—without slavery. If California became a free state, however, slave states would be outvoted in the Senate. Even worse, antislavery groups wanted to ban slavery in Washington, D.C. Southerners talked about **seceding** (sih•SEED•ihng) from, or leaving, the Union.

In 1850 Senator Henry Clay of Kentucky suggested a compromise. California would be a free state, but other new territories would have no limits on slavery. In addition, the slave trade, but not slavery itself, would be illegal in Washington, D.C. Clay also pushed for a stronger fugitive slave law.

A heated debate took place in Congress. Senator Calhoun opposed Clay's plan. Senator Daniel Webster supported it. Then President Taylor, who was against Clay's plan, died unexpectedly. Vice President Millard Fillmore, who favored the plan, became president.

Senator Stephen A. Douglas of Illinois solved the problem. He divided Clay's plan into parts, each to be voted on separately. Fillmore had several Whigs abstain, or not vote, on the parts they opposed. In the end, Congress passed the Compromise of 1850.

Smithsonian American Art Museum, Washington, DC/Art Resource, NY

Reading **HELP**DESK

fugitive person who is running away from legal authority
secede to officially leave an organization

Academic Vocabulary

network interconnected system

The Fugitive Slave Act

Part of the Compromise of 1850 was the Fugitive Slave Act. Anyone who helped a fugitive could be fined or imprisoned. Some Northerners refused to obey the new law. In his 1849 essay "Civil Disobedience," Henry David Thoreau wrote that if the law "requires you to be the agent [cause] of injustice to another, then I say, break the law." Northern juries refused to convict people accused of breaking the new law. People gave money to buy freedom for enslaved people. Free African Americans and whites formed a **network,** or interconnected system, called the Underground Railroad to help runaways find their way to freedom. Democrat Franklin Pierce became president in 1853. He intended to enforce the Fugitive Slave Act.

✅ **PROGRESS CHECK**

Explaining Who formed the Free-Soil Party and why?

The Kansas-Nebraska Act

GUIDING QUESTION *What is the Kansas-Nebraska Act?*

In 1854 Senator Stephen A. Douglas of Illinois introduced a bill to settle the issue of slavery in the territories. It organized the region west of Missouri and Iowa as the territories of Kansas and Nebraska. Both were north of 36°30′ N latitude, the line that limited slavery. Before the law they would have been free, giving the free states more votes in the Senate and angering the South.

Douglas hoped to make his plan acceptable to both the North and South. He proposed repealing the Missouri Compromise and letting the voters in each territory vote on whether to allow slavery. He called his proposal "popular sovereignty."

GEOGRAPHY CONNECTION

As the United States grew, so did the debate over slaveholding.

1 **PLACE** Which territories did not allow slavery in 1854?

2 **CRITICAL THINKING**
Analyzing Which side in the slavery debate lost territory because of the Kansas-Nebraska Act in 1854?

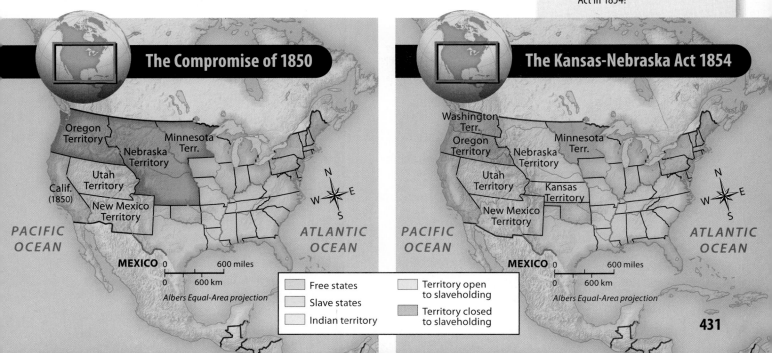

The Compromise of 1850

Oregon Territory • Minnesota Terr. • Nebraska Territory • Utah Territory • Calif. (1850) • New Mexico Territory

PACIFIC OCEAN • ATLANTIC OCEAN • MEXICO

0 — 600 miles
0 — 600 km
Albers Equal-Area projection

The Kansas-Nebraska Act 1854

Washington Terr. • Oregon Territory • Minnesota Terr. • Nebraska Territory • Utah Territory • Kansas Territory • New Mexico Territory

PACIFIC OCEAN • ATLANTIC OCEAN • MEXICO

0 — 600 miles
0 — 600 km
Albers Equal-Area projection

Free states
Slave states
Indian territory
Territory open to slaveholding
Territory closed to slaveholding

This idea, which is central to the American system of government, means that the people are the source of all government power. Douglas's *popular sovereignty* came to mean a particular method for deciding the question of slavery in a place.

Northerners protested. The plan allowed slavery in areas that had been free for years. Southerners supported the bill. They expected Kansas to be settled mostly by slaveholders from Missouri. They would, of course, vote to keep slavery legal. With some support from Northern Democrats and the backing of President Pierce, the Kansas-Nebraska Act passed in 1854.

Conflict in Kansas

Supporters of both sides rushed to Kansas. Armed pro-slavery supporters known as **border ruffians** (BOHR•duhr RUH•fee•uhns) crossed the border from Missouri just to vote. When elections took place, only about 1,500 voters lived in Kansas, but more than 6,000 people voted. The pro-slavery group won.

Kansas established laws supporting slavery. Slavery opponents refused to accept the laws. They armed themselves, held their own elections, and adopted a constitution banning slavery. By January 1856, Kansas had two rival governments.

In May 1856, slavery supporters attacked the town of Lawrence, an antislavery stronghold. Antislavery forces retaliated. John Brown led an attack that killed five supporters of slavery. Newspapers wrote about "Bleeding Kansas" and "the Civil War in Kansas." A **civil war** is war between citizens of the same country. In October 1856, federal troops arrived to stop the bloodshed.

☑ PROGRESS CHECK

Identifying Cause and Effect What events led to "Bleeding Kansas"?

border ruffian armed pro-slavery supporter who crossed the border from Missouri to vote in Kansas

civil war conflict between citizens of the same country

LESSON 1 REVIEW

Review Vocabulary

1. Explain the significance of the following terms.

    a. fugitive   **b.** secede

2. Use the following terms in a short paragraph about Kansas in the 1850s.

    a. border ruffians   **b.** civil war

Answer the Guiding Questions

3. *Describing* How did the Compromise of 1850 address the question of slavery?

4. *Analyzing* What was the Wilmot Proviso? Why was it so controversial?

5. *Explaining* How did Stephen Douglas help win approval of the Compromise of 1850?

6. *Listing* What were some ways that Northerners defied the Fugitive Slave Act?

7. **NARRATIVE WRITING** Write a dialogue between two people in Nebraska who are expressing their views on the issue of popular sovereignty. Have one person defend the policy and the other oppose it.

netwⓞrks

There's More Online!

☑ **GRAPHIC ORGANIZER**
Political Parties
1848–1856

☑ **MAP** The Election
of 1856

☑ **PRIMARY SOURCES**
• The *Dred Scott* Decision
• "A Plea for Captain John Brown"

Lesson 2
Challenges to Slavery

ESSENTIAL QUESTION *Why does conflict develop?*

IT MATTERS BECAUSE
As feelings over slavery intensified, the chance for compromise disappeared.

Birth of the Republican Party

GUIDING QUESTION *How did a new political party affect the challenges to slavery?*

After the Kansas-Nebraska Act, the Democratic Party began to divide along sectional lines. Northern Democrats left the party. Differing views over slavery also split the Whig Party.

The 1854 Congressional Elections

Antislavery Whigs and Democrats joined with Free-Soilers to form the Republican Party. One of the party's major goals was the banning of slavery in new territories. In 1854 the Republicans chose candidates to challenge the pro-slavery Whigs and Democrats in state and congressional elections.

The Republicans quickly showed strength in the North. In the election, they won control of the House of Representatives and several state governments. Unlike the Republicans, almost three-fourths of the Democratic candidates from free states lost in 1854.

In contrast, Republican candidates received almost no support in the South. At the same time, the Democrats, having lost members in the North, were becoming a largely Southern party. This division would be even more apparent in the presidential election of 1856.

Reading **HELP**DESK

Taking Notes: *Describing*

As you read, use a diagram like the one shown to note each party's candidate and platform in the 1856 presidential election. Also record the election result.

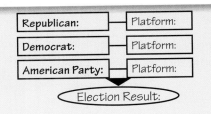

Republican:	—	Platform:
Democrat:	—	Platform:
American Party:	—	Platform:

Election Result:

Content Vocabulary
• **arsenal**
• **martyr**

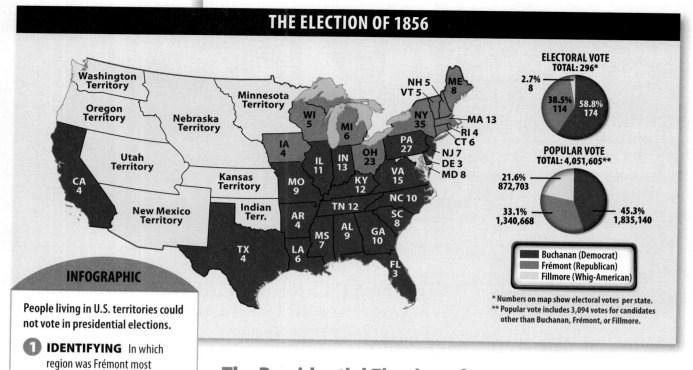

THE ELECTION OF 1856

ELECTORAL VOTE TOTAL: 296*

- 2.7% 8
- 38.5% 114
- 58.8% 174

POPULAR VOTE TOTAL: 4,051,605**

- 21.6% 872,703
- 33.1% 1,340,668
- 45.3% 1,835,140

- ■ Buchanan (Democrat)
- ■ Frémont (Republican)
- ■ Fillmore (Whig-American)

* Numbers on map show electoral votes per state.
** Popular vote includes 3,094 votes for candidates other than Buchanan, Frémont, or Fillmore.

INFOGRAPHIC

People living in U.S. territories could not vote in presidential elections.

1 IDENTIFYING In which region was Frémont most successful? Which states in that region did he not win?

2 CRITICAL THINKING
Drawing Conclusions A landslide is an overwhelming victory. Do you think Buchanan's victory was a landslide? Why or why not?

The Presidential Election of 1856

The Whig Party, torn apart over slavery, did not offer a candidate in 1856. Republicans chose Californian John C. Frémont, a famed western explorer. The party platform called for free territories. Its campaign slogan was "Free soil, Free speech, and Frémont."

The Democratic Party nominated James Buchanan of Pennsylvania. He was a diplomat and former member of Congress. Buchanan tried to appeal to Southern whites. The Democratic Party endorsed the idea of popular sovereignty.

The American Party, or Know-Nothings, grew quickly between 1853 and 1856 by attacking immigrants. The party nominated former president Millard Fillmore as its candidate. Yet this party was also divided over the issue of the Kansas-Nebraska Act. When the Know-Nothings refused to call for a repeal of the act, many northern supporters left the party.

The vote in 1856 was divided along **rigid** sectional lines. Buchanan took all Southern states except Maryland. Frémont won 11 of the 16 free states but did not get any electoral votes from south of the Mason-Dixon Line. With 174 electoral votes compared to 114 for Frémont and 8 for Fillmore, Buchanan won.

☑ **PROGRESS CHECK**

Explaining Why did the Republican Party form?

Reading **HELP**DESK

Reading Strategy: *Context Clues*

When you find an unknown word, look at surrounding text for clues to the meaning. Clues to the meaning of the unknown word may be:

- a definition: The word is defined immediately following its use.
- a synonym: A word or expression that has the same meaning as another word or expression. (For example, huge, big, and enormous are synonyms.)
- inference: Hints are given to help you figure out the meaning.

Dred Scott v. Sandford

GUIDING QUESTION *Why was the* Dred Scott *case important?*

Dred Scott was an enslaved African American bought by a doctor in Missouri, a slave state. In the 1830s, the doctor moved with Scott to Illinois, a free state, then to the Wisconsin Territory. The Northwest Ordinance of 1787 banned slavery there. Later the doctor returned with Scott to Missouri.

In 1846 antislavery lawyers helped Scott sue for his freedom. Scott claimed he should be free since he had lived in areas where slavery was illegal. Eleven years later, the case reached the Supreme Court. At issue was Scott's status, but the case also gave the Court a chance to rule on the question of slavery itself.

The Court Rules

Chief Justice Roger B. Taney (TAW•nee) wrote the Court's opinion: Dred Scott was still an enslaved person. As such, he was not a citizen and had no right to bring a lawsuit. Taney wrote that living on free soil did not make Scott free. A slave was property. The Fifth Amendment prohibited the taking of property without "due process."

Finally, Taney wrote that Congress had no power to ban slavery. The Missouri Compromise, that banned slavery north of 36°30′ N latitude, was unconstitutional, and so was popular sovereignty. Not even voters could ban slavery because it would mean taking someone's property. In effect, Taney said that the Constitution protected slavery.

Reaction to the Decision

The Court's decision upheld what many white Southerners believed: Nothing could legally stop slavery. It ruled limiting the spread of slavery, the Republicans' main issue, unconstitutional.

Republicans and other antislavery groups were outraged. They called the decision "a wicked and false judgment" and "the greatest crime" ever committed in the nation's courts.

✓ PROGRESS CHECK

Explaining Why did the *Dred Scott* decision say voters could not ban slavery?

Academic Vocabulary

rigid firm and inflexible

CORBIS

Many newspapers announced the *Dred Scott* decision on their front pages. Scott is pictured at bottom left, next to a picture of his wife.

▶ **CRITICAL THINKING**

Analyzing Visuals Do these images present a positive view of Scott? Explain your answer.

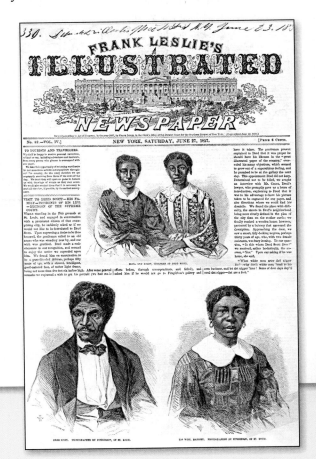

Abraham Lincoln (1809–1865)

Just a few years before becoming a national leader, Lincoln was relatively unknown. From a poor rural family, Lincoln knew the importance of education to success. As a young man, he had mostly taught himself and in time became a lawyer. Lincoln was intensely opposed to slavery. He served in the Illinois state legislature and the U. S. Congress. In 1858, he ran for the Senate against Stephen A. Douglas. Although Lincoln lost the election, he gained national attention as a leading Northern voice against slavery.

▶ **CRITICAL THINKING**
Speculating Why do you think Lincoln won fame in spite of losing the race for the Senate?

Lincoln and Douglas

GUIDING QUESTION *How did Abraham Lincoln and Stephen A. Douglas play a role in the challenges to slavery?*

The Illinois Senate race of 1858 was the center of national attention. The contest pitted the current senator, Democrat Stephen A. Douglas, against a rising star in the Republican Party named Abraham Lincoln.

People considered Douglas a possible candidate for president in the 1860 election. Lincoln, far less known outside of his state, challenged Douglas to a series of debates. Douglas reluctantly agreed.

The Lincoln-Douglas Debates

Lincoln and Douglas debated seven times. The face-offs took place in Illinois cities and villages during August, September, and October of 1858. Thousands of spectators came to the debates. Newspapers provided wide coverage. The main **topic,** or subject of discussion, was slavery.

During the debate at Freeport, Lincoln pressed Douglas about his views on popular sovereignty. Lincoln asked whether the people of a territory could legally exclude slavery before becoming a state.

Douglas replied that voters could exclude slavery by refusing to pass laws that protected the rights of slaveholders. Douglas's response, which became known as the Freeport Doctrine, satisfied antislavery followers, but it cost Douglas support in the South.

Douglas claimed that Lincoln wanted African Americans to be fully equal to whites. Lincoln denied this. Still, Lincoln insisted that African Americans should enjoy rights and freedoms:

PRIMARY SOURCE

❝ But in the right to eat the bread . . . which his own hand earns, [an African American] is my equal and the equal of [Senator] Douglas, and the equal of every living man. ❞

—Abraham Lincoln, August 21, 1858

The real issue, Lincoln said, was "between the men who think slavery a wrong and those who do not think it wrong. The Republican Party think it wrong."

MPI/Archive Photos/Getty Images

Reading HELPDESK

Academic Vocabulary

topic subject of discussion

Following the debates, Douglas won a narrow victory in the election. Lincoln lost but did not come away empty-handed. He gained a national reputation as a man of clear thinking who could argue with force and persuasion.

John Brown and Harpers Ferry

After the 1858 election, Southerners felt threatened by Republicans. Then, an act of violence added to their fears.

On October 16, 1859, the abolitionist John Brown led a group on a raid on Harpers Ferry, Virginia. His target was a federal **arsenal** (AHRS•nuhl), a storage site for weapons. Brown hoped to arm enslaved African Americans and start a revolt against slaveholders. Abolitionists had paid for the raid.

PRIMARY SOURCE

❝ Now if . . . I should forfeit my life for the furtherance of the ends of justice and MINGLE MY BLOOD . . . with the blood of millions in this slave country whose rights are disregarded by wicked, cruel, and unjust enactments—I submit; so LET IT BE DONE. ❞

—John Brown's statement to the Virginia Court

The Lincoln-Douglas debates have been described as "the most famous war of words in history."

▶ **CRITICAL THINKING**
Analyzing Visuals How does the artist of this picture portray the audience of the debate?

arsenal a place to store weapons and military equipment
martyr a person who dies for a great cause

Colonel Robert E. Lee and federal troops crushed Brown's raid. More than half of Brown's group, including two of his sons, died in the fighting. Lee's troops captured Brown and his surviving men.

▶ **CRITICAL THINKING**
Analyzing Primary Sources
Why do you think Brown's raids were so controversial in the United States of the late 1850s?

Local citizens and federal troops defeated Brown's raid. Tried and convicted of treason and murder, Brown received a death sentence. His hanging shook the North. Some antislavery Northerners rejected Brown's use of violence. Others saw him as a **martyr** (MAHR•tuhr)—a person who dies for a cause.

John Brown's death rallied abolitionists. When white Southerners learned of Brown's abolitionist ties, their fears of a great Northern conspiracy against them were confirmed. The nation was on the brink of disaster.

✓ **PROGRESS CHECK**

Identifying Why did John Brown raid the arsenal at Harpers Ferry?

LESSON 2 REVIEW

Review Vocabulary

1. Use the word *arsenal* in a sentence about Harpers Ferry.

2. Explain the meaning of *martyr* as it relates to John Brown.

Answer the Guiding Questions

3. *Specifying* What issue led to the formation of the Republican Party, and what stand did the party take on the issue?

4. *Explaining* What reasons did Taney give for why he believed Dred Scott was an enslaved person?

5. *Identifying* How did the Lincoln-Douglas debates benefit Lincoln?

6. *Making Inferences* Why do you think the raid on Harpers Ferry by just a few men was so threatening to Southerners?

7. **PERSONAL WRITING** Imagine you live at the time of John Brown's raid on Harpers Ferry. Write a letter to the editor of a local paper expressing your feelings about his methods.

networks

There's More Online!

☑ **BIOGRAPHY**
Jefferson Davis

☑ **GRAPHIC ORGANIZER**
November 1860 to
March 1861

☑ **MAP** Seceding States 1860–1861

☑ **POLITICAL CARTOON**
Secessionists Leaving the Union

Lesson 3
Secession and War

ESSENTIAL QUESTION *Why does conflict develop?*

IT MATTERS BECAUSE

When Abraham Lincoln was elected president, the Southern states decided to break away from the Union.

The 1860 Election

GUIDING QUESTION *What was the importance of the election of 1860?*

In the presidential election of 1860, the big question was whether the Union would continue to exist. Regional differences divided the nation.

The issue of slavery split the Democratic Party. Northern Democrats supported popular sovereignty. They nominated Stephen Douglas. Southern Democrats vowed to uphold slavery. Their candidate was John C. Breckinridge.

Moderates from the North and South formed the Constitutional Union Party. The Constitutional Unionists took no position on slavery. They chose John Bell as their candidate.

The Republicans nominated Abraham Lincoln. They wanted to leave slavery alone where it existed—but also to ban it in the territories. Still, white Southerners feared that a Republican victory would promote slave revolts as well as interfere with slavery.

With the Democrats divided, Lincoln won a clear majority of electoral votes. Voting followed sectional lines. Lincoln's name did not even appear on the ballot in most Southern states. He won every Northern state, however. So in effect, the more populous North outvoted the South.

(l) Chicago Historical Society, (c) The Granger Collection, NYC
(cr) Stock Montage/Archive Photos/Getty Images, (r) Library of Congress

Reading **HELP**DESK

Taking Notes: *Sequencing*

As you read, list the major events on a time line like the one shown.

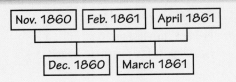

Content Vocabulary
• **secession**
• **states' rights**

Looking for Compromise

The Republicans had promised not to stop slavery where it already existed. Yet white Southerners did not trust the Republicans to protect their rights. On December 20, 1860, South Carolina voted to secede from the Union.

In other Southern states, leaders debated the question of **secession,** or withdrawal from the Union. Meanwhile, members of Congress tried to find ways to prevent it. Senator John Crittenden of Kentucky suggested a series of amendments to the Constitution. They included a protection for slavery south of 36°30′ N latitude—the line set by the Missouri Compromise—in all territories "now held or hereafter acquired."

Republicans **rejected,** or refused to accept, Crittenden's idea. They had just won an election by promising to stop slavery's spread into any territories. "Now we are told …" Lincoln wrote, "the government shall be broken up unless we surrender to those we have beaten."

Leaders in the South also rejected the plan. "We spit upon every plan to compromise," exclaimed one Southern leader. "No human power can save the Union," wrote another.

The Confederacy Established

By February 1861, Texas, Louisiana, Mississippi, Alabama, Florida, and Georgia had joined South Carolina and seceded. Delegates from these states met to form a new nation. Calling themselves the Confederate States of America, they chose Jefferson Davis as their president.

Southerners used **states' rights** to **justify** secession. Each state, they argued, had voluntarily chosen to enter the Union. They defined the Constitution as a contract among the independent states. They believed the national government had broken the contract by refusing to enforce the Fugitive Slave Act and by denying Southern states equal rights in the territories. As a result, Southerners argued, the states had a right to leave the Union.

The Public Reacts to Secession

Not all white Southerners welcomed secession. Church bells rang and some people celebrated in the streets. To other Southerners, the idea of secession was alarming. Virginian Robert E. Lee expressed concern about the future. "I only see that a fearful calamity is upon us," he wrote.

Some Southerners wore ribbons like this to show their support for secession from the Union. The ribbons carried slogans, such as this one used in the American Revolution—"Liberty or Death."

▶ **CRITICAL THINKING**
Analyzing Why do you think secessionists used the same slogans as those used in the Revolutionary War?

Chicago Historical Society

secession withdrawal
states' rights theory that individual states are independent and have the right to control their most important affairs

Academic Vocabulary

reject to refuse to accept
justify to find reasons to support

Some Northerners approved of the Southern secession. If the Union could survive only by giving in to slavery, they declared, then let the Union be destroyed. Still, most Northerners believed that the Union had to be preserved. As Lincoln put it, the issue was "whether in a free government the minority have the right to break up the government whenever they choose."

Lincoln Takes Over

As always, several months passed between the November election and the start of the new president's term. Buchanan would remain in office until March 4, 1861. In December 1860, Buchanan sent a message to Congress. He said that the Southern states had no right to secede from the Union. He added that he had no power to stop them from doing so.

As Lincoln prepared for his inauguration, people throughout the United States wondered what he would say and do. They wondered, too, what would happen in Virginia, North Carolina, Kentucky, Tennessee, Missouri, Delaware, Maryland, and Arkansas. These slave states had not yet seceded, but their decisions were not final. If the United States used force against the Confederates, the remaining slave states also might secede.

GEOGRAPHY CONNECTION

Some slaveholding states and territories did not secede from the Union.

1 **LOCATION** Which states seceded before the attack on Fort Sumter? Which seceded after the attack on Fort Sumter?

2 **CRITICAL THINKING**
Speculating Which side controlled more territory, and how might the answer affect a military conflict between the two sides?

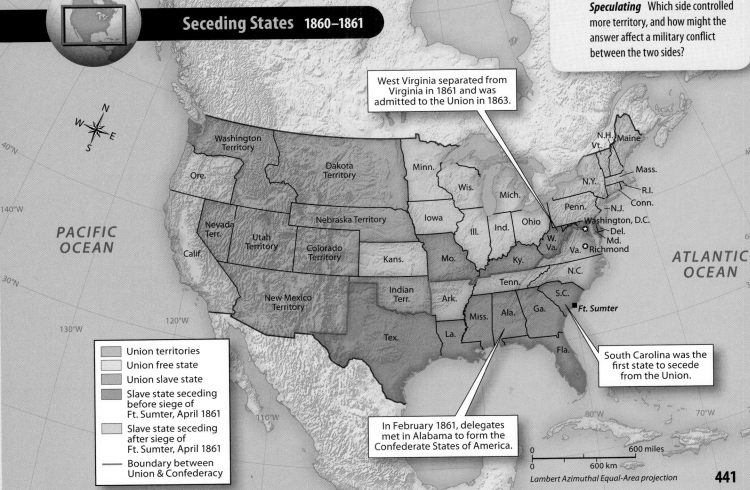

Seceding States 1860–1861

West Virginia separated from Virginia in 1861 and was admitted to the Union in 1863.

South Carolina was the first state to secede from the Union.

In February 1861, delegates met in Alabama to form the Confederate States of America.

- Union territories
- Union free state
- Union slave state
- Slave state seceding before siege of Ft. Sumter, April 1861
- Slave state seceding after siege of Ft. Sumter, April 1861
- Boundary between Union & Confederacy

Lambert Azimuthal Equal-Area projection

441

This cartoon was created in 1861, just before the Civil War began. At that time, secession was breaking apart the United States.

1 **INTERPRETING** What do the men in the cartoon represent?

2 **CRITICAL THINKING**
Drawing a Conclusion What do you think the cartoonist is predicting will happen because of the men's action?

SECESSIONISTS LEAVING THE UNION

In his Inaugural Address, Lincoln spoke to the seceding states directly. He said that he could not allow secession and that "the Union of these States is perpetual [forever]." He vowed to hold federal property in the South, including a number of forts and military installations, and to enforce the laws of the United States. At the same time, Lincoln pleaded with the South:

PRIMARY SOURCE

66 In your hands, my dissatisfied fellow countrymen, and not in mine, is the momentous issue of *civil war*. The Government will not assail you. You can have no conflict without being yourselves the aggressors. . . .

. . . We are not *enemies*, but *friends. We must not be enemies.* Though passion may have strained, it must not break our bonds of affection. 99

—Abraham Lincoln, First Inaugural Address

✓ **PROGRESS CHECK**

Explaining What was John Crittenden's proposal to save the Union?

Build Vocabulary: *Word Parts*

The suffix -*ist* on the word *cartoonist* tells you that a cartoonist is a person. The same is true of the words *pianist* (a person who plays the piano) and *essayist* (a person who writes essays). Can you think of other examples with the suffix -*ist*?

Fighting at Fort Sumter

GUIDING QUESTION *What did the attack on Fort Sumter signify?*

The day after taking office, Lincoln received a message from the commander of Fort Sumter, a U.S. fort on an island guarding Charleston Harbor. The message warned that the fort was low on supplies and the Confederates demanded its surrender.

Lincoln responded in a message to Governor Francis Pickens of South Carolina that he was sending an unarmed group to the fort with supplies. He promised Union forces would not "throw in men, arms, or ammunition" unless they were fired upon.

Jefferson Davis ordered his forces to attack Fort Sumter before the Union supplies could arrive. Confederate guns opened fire on April 12, 1861. Union captain Abner Doubleday witnessed the attack from inside the fort:

PRIMARY SOURCE

66 Showers of balls . . . and shells poured into the fort in one incessant stream, causing great flakes of masonry to fall in all directions. 99

—quoted in *Fort Sumter*

Meanwhile, high seas kept Union ships from reaching the fort. Facing a hopeless situation, the Union surrendered the fort on April 14. Despite heavy bombardment, no one had died.

With the loss of Fort Sumter, Lincoln decided he had to act. He issued a call for troops. Volunteers quickly signed up. In reaction to Lincoln's call, Virginia, North Carolina, Tennessee, and Arkansas voted to join the Confederacy. The Civil War had begun.

✓ **PROGRESS CHECK**

Explaining Why did Lincoln decide not to send armed troops to Fort Sumter?

LESSON 3 REVIEW

Review Vocabulary

1. Use the word *secession* in a sentence about Florida.

2. Explain the meaning of *states' rights* as it relates to the U.S. Constitution.

Answer the Guiding Questions

3. *Specifying* What did South Carolina do after Lincoln won the election of 1860? Why?

4. *Explaining* What was the impact of the attack on Fort Sumter?

5. *Drawing Conclusions* What was President Lincoln's priority when he took office in March 1861?

6. *Analyzing* What role did the idea of states' rights play in the Civil War?

7. **NARRATIVE WRITING** Write a brief newspaper article about the attack on Fort Sumter that describes the battle in an objective way, without bias for one side or the other.

What Do You Think?

Did the South Have the Right to Secede?

When Abraham Lincoln began his first term as president on March 4, 1861, seven Southern states had already voted to secede from the Union and formed the Confederate States of America.

The Confederacy's president, Jefferson Davis, had taken office earlier, on February 18, 1861. Each man's inauguration address presented a different view on whether any state had the right to secede.

Yes

PRIMARY SOURCE

JEFFERSON DAVIS

❝ Our present position . . . illustrates the American idea that government rests upon the consent of the governed, and that it is the right of the people to alter or abolish a government whenever it becomes destructive of the ends for which it was established. The declared purpose of the compact of Union from which we have withdrawn was to 'establish justice, insure domestic tranquility, to provide for the common defence, to promote the general welfare, and to secure the blessings of liberty for ourselves and our posterity'; and when in the judgment of the sovereign States now comprising this Confederacy it [no longer meets] the purposes for which it was **ordained**, and ceased to answer the ends for which it was established, a peaceful appeal to the ballot box declared that, so far as they are concerned, the government created by that compact should cease to exist. In this they merely asserted a right which the Declaration of Independence of July 4, 1776, defined to be inalienable. ❞

—Jefferson Davis

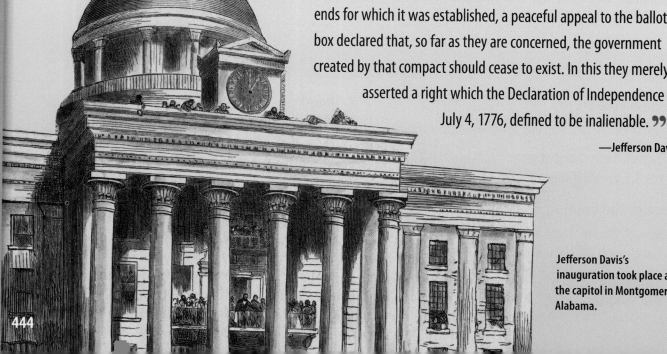

Jefferson Davis's inauguration took place at the capitol in Montgomery, Alabama.

Abraham Lincoln's inauguration took place at the United States Capitol in Washington, D.C.

No

PRIMARY SOURCE

ABRAHAM LINCOLN

❝ The [president] derives all his authority from the people, and they have referred none upon him to fix terms for the separation of the States. The people themselves can do this if also they choose, but the executive as such has nothing to do with it. His duty is to **administer** the present government as it came to his hands and to transmit it **unimpaired** by him to his successor. . . .

. . . The mystic chords of memory, stretching from every battlefield and patriot grave to every living heart and hearthstone all over this broad land, will yet swell the chorus of the Union, when again touched, as surely they will be, by the better angels of our nature. ❞

—Abraham Lincoln

(t) Library of Congress [LC-US2C4-4583]. (b) Stock Montage/Archive Photos/Getty Images

Vocabulary

ordained
established

administer
manage, direct

unimpaired
not harmed, not damaged

What Do You Think?   DBQ

1 **Identifying** What are Abraham Lincoln's and Jefferson Davis's basic arguments against or in favor of secession?

2 **Making Inferences** What issue seems most important to Lincoln? To Davis?

3 **Evaluating** In your opinion, which of the two makes the more powerful appeal to emotions? Explain your answer in a short essay.

Write your answers on a separate piece of paper.

① Exploring the Essential Question

EXPOSITORY WRITING Make a list of five important events you read about in this chapter. Select the two events you think did the most to increase the conflict between the North and South. Write an essay in which you explain how these events led to war.

② 21st Century Skills

IDENTIFYING PROBLEMS AND SOLUTIONS Working with a small group, think of a controversial issue that is a source of disagreement among the public today. Possible examples include health care reform or immigration reform. Research opposite sides of the issue; then work together to come up with a list of compromises that might make the solution to this problem acceptable to different sides.

③ Thinking Like a Historian

PREDICTING CONSEQUENCES What do you think would have happened to the Confederacy if Lincoln had made no effort to prevent it from seceding? Provide reasons to support your answer.

④ Visual Literacy

COMPARING ARTIFACTS Below are campaign posters produced during political campaigns. The poster on the left is from a presidential campaign from the mid-1800s; the poster on the right is from more recent times. What features do the two items share in common? How are they different from one another?

REVIEW THE GUIDING QUESTIONS

Choose the best answer for each question.

1 Which of the following was a proposal to ban slavery in any lands acquired from Mexico?

   A. Compromise of 1850
   B. Wilmot Proviso
   C. Missouri Compromise
   D. Freeport Doctrine

2 What resulted from the Fugitive Slave Act?

   F. Passage of the law stopped violence in Kansas.
   G. Most Northerners respected slaveholders' rights.
   H. Abolitionists were jailed in the North.
   I. The law convinced many Northerners to help runaways.

3 The Supreme Court's *Dred Scott* decision stated that

   A. enslaved persons could bring lawsuits.
   B. the slave trade should be abolished.
   C. Congress had no power to ban slavery in any territory.
   D. the Missouri Compromise was constitutional.

4 Which was included in the Republican Party platform in the election of 1860?

   F. The question of slavery should be decided by popular sovereignty.
   G. In a free society, the minority has the right to break up the government.
   H. Slavery should be left where it existed but be excluded from the territories.
   I. Slavery should be protected in all territories south of 36°30' N latitude.

5 The armed pro-slavery groups of Missourians who went to Kansas to vote were called

   A. Kansas Crusaders.
   B. Border Breakers.
   C. Missouri Militia.
   D. Border Ruffians.

6 What event officially started the Civil War?

   F. the raid on Harpers Ferry
   G. the attack on Fort Sumter
   H. the burning of Lawrence, Kansas
   I. the election of Abraham Lincoln

DBQ DOCUMENT-BASED QUESTIONS

7 **Identifying** According to the map, in 1860 Kentucky and Missouri were both

A. Confederate states.

B. Union free states.

C. Union territories.

D. Union slave states.

8 **Making Generalizations** What generalization can you make about the Union slave states?

F. They share a border with free states to the north.

G. They all border the Mississippi River.

H. They are all in New England.

I. They are farther south than Alabama.

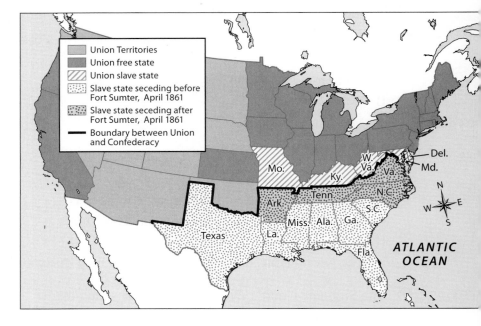

SHORT RESPONSE

Erastus D. Ladd described voters from Missouri crossing the border to vote in an 1855 election in Kansas.

"They claimed to have a legal right to vote in the Territory [Kansas], and that they were residents by virtue of their being then in the Territory. They said they were free to confess that they came from Missouri; that they lived in Missouri, and voted as Missourians."

Source: Albert Bushnell Hart, *Source-Book of American History*

9 Did Ladd think the actions of these voters were legal? Explain your answer.

10 What is Ladd suggesting about the elections in Kansas?

EXTENDED RESPONSE

11 **Personal Writing** Take the role of an African American living in the United States in the 1850s. Write a journal entry expressing your thoughts after the *Dred Scott* decision is issued.

Need Extra Help?

If You've Missed Question	**1**	**2**	**3**	**4**	**5**	**6**	**7**	**8**	**9**	**10**	**11**
Review Lesson	1	1	2	3	1	3	3	1	1	1	2

The Civil War

1861–1865

ESSENTIAL QUESTION *Why does conflict develop?*

◄ Abraham Lincoln was president during the nation's greatest crisis.

Library of Congress [LC-DIG-ppmsca-19241]

The Story Matters . . .

In November 1860, voters elect a self-educated lawyer from Illinois named Abraham Lincoln to be president of the United States. Even before Lincoln is inaugurated, South Carolina and six other Southern states secede from the Union. As he waits to take office, Lincoln sees the nation he is to lead spiral downward toward civil war—a war that will prove to be the deadliest in U.S. history.

Lincoln does not give up. He believes "[a] house divided against itself cannot stand," and he guides the nation until it is once again united.

CHAPTER 17

Place and Time: United States 1861 to 1865

In December 1860, South Carolina announced that it was seceding from the United States. Within a few months, six other states had followed South Carolina out of the Union. After the battle at Fort Sumter, a total of 11 Southern states joined together in the Confederate States of America.

Step Into the Place

MAP FOCUS In 1861 soldiers fired the first shots of the Civil War. Armies of the Confederacy and the Union did battle in locations all across the country.

1 LOCATION On this map, which Union states have Civil War battle sites?

2 PLACE What clue can you find on the map that might explain why so many battles took place in Virginia?

3 CRITICAL THINKING
Drawing Conclusions Why do you think most of the battles of the Civil War took place in the Confederate states?

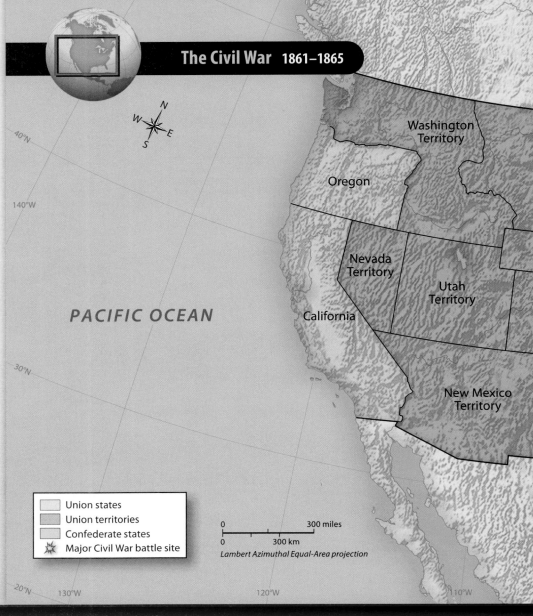

The Civil War 1861–1865

PACIFIC OCEAN

Washington Territory

Oregon

Nevada Territory

Utah Territory

California

New Mexico Territory

Union states
Union territories
Confederate states
Major Civil War battle site

0 ——— 300 miles
0 ——— 300 km
Lambert Azimuthal Equal-Area projection

Step Into the Time

TIME LINE Look at the time line. For how many years after the Emancipation Proclamation did the Civil War continue?

Abraham Lincoln
1861–1865

U.S. PRESIDENTS

U.S. EVENTS

WORLD EVENTS

1861

1862

1861 Robert E. Lee takes command of Virginia's Confederate forces

1862 International Red Cross established (American Red Cross organized 10 years later)

networks
There's More Online!

☑ **MAP** Explore the interactive version of this map on NETWORKS.

☑ **TIME LINE** Explore the interactive version of this time line on NETWORKS.

CANADA

New Hampshire
Vermont
Maine

Minnesota

Wisconsin

Dakota Territory

Massachusetts

Michigan

New York

Susquehanna R.

Rhode Island
Connecticut

Pennsylvania

Delaware R.

Nebraska Territory

Iowa

Philadelphia

New Jersey

Potomac R.

Baltimore

Delaware
Maryland

Ohio

Illinois

Ind.

Cincinnati

W. Va.

Washington, D.C.

Missouri

St. Louis

Ohio R.

Richmond

Colorado Territory

Kansas

Arkansas R.

Kentucky

Virginia

Indian Territory

Arkansas

Tennessee

Tennessee R.

North Carolina

South Carolina

Charleston

Ala.

Atlanta

Savannah R.

Miss.

Alabama R.

Georgia

Red R.

Texas

La.

Vicksburg

Mississippi R.

Tallahassee

Florida

New Orleans

ATLANTIC OCEAN

MEXICO

Gulf of Mexico

60°W
40°N
30°N
70°W
80°W
90°W

Andrew Johnson
1865–1869

1863 • Emancipation Proclamation issued
• Grant named commander of Union armies

1864 Sherman's March to the Sea begins

1865 Civil War ends

1863

1864

1865

1863 London subway opens

1864 First Geneva Convention establishes rules for treatment of prisoners of war

1865 French writer Jules Verne publishes novel about a trip to the moon

Lesson 1
The Two Sides

ESSENTIAL QUESTION *Why does conflict develop?*

IT MATTERS BECAUSE
Both the North and the South had strengths and weaknesses that helped determine their military strategies.

Two Very Different Sides

GUIDING QUESTION *What were the goals and strategies of the North and the South?*

The war divided many families. Neither side imagined, however, that the four years of fighting would lead to so much suffering. By the end of the war, 600,000 Americans had lost their lives. Many thousands more were wounded in battle.

Division in the Border States

For most states, choosing sides in the Civil War was easy. The **border states** of Delaware, Maryland, Kentucky, and Missouri, however, were bitterly divided. Slavery existed in all four states, though it was generally not as widespread as in the Confederate states. All four of these states had close ties to the North and the South.

The border states were vital to the **strategy** of the Union. Missouri could control parts of the Mississippi River and major routes to the West. Kentucky controlled the Ohio River. Delaware was close to the key Union city of Philadelphia. Maryland, perhaps the most important of the border states, was close to Richmond, the Confederate capital. Most significantly, Washington, D.C., lay within the state. If Maryland seceded, the North's capital would be surrounded.

(c) Bettmann/CORBIS, (c) Library of Congress, (cr) North Wind Picture Archives, (r) StockTrek/SuperStock

Reading **HELP**DESK

Taking Notes: *Comparing and Contrasting*

As you read, note the differences and similarities between the North and the South in a Venn diagram like this one.

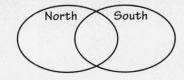

North   South

Content Vocabulary
• **border state**
• **enlist**

President Lincoln worked tirelessly to keep the four border states in the Union. In September 1861, he wrote:

66 I think to lose Kentucky is nearly the same as to lose the whole game. . . . We would as well consent to separation at once, including the surrender of this capitol. 99

—from *Abraham Lincoln: His Speeches and Writings*

In the end, Lincoln was successful. Still, many border state residents supported the Confederacy. The president had to work hard to restrain these opponents of the war.

Strengths and Weaknesses

When the war began, each side had advantages and disadvantages compared to the other. How each side used its strengths and weaknesses would determine the war's outcome.

The North had a larger population and more resources than the South. The South had other advantages, such as excellent military leaders and a strong fighting spirit. Also, because most of the war was fought in the South, the Confederacy knew the land and had the will to defend it.

The Goals of War

Each side had different goals in fighting the Civil War. The Confederacy wanted to be an independent nation. To do this, it did not have to invade the North or destroy the Union army. It just needed to fight hard enough and long enough to convince Northerners that the war was not worth its cost.

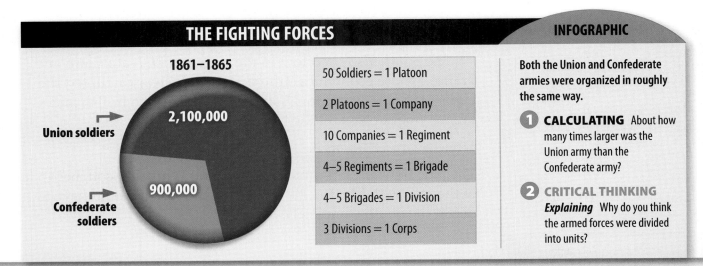

THE FIGHTING FORCES

INFOGRAPHIC

1861–1865

2,100,000

Union soldiers

900,000

Confederate soldiers

50 Soldiers = 1 Platoon	
2 Platoons = 1 Company	
10 Companies = 1 Regiment	
4–5 Regiments = 1 Brigade	
4–5 Brigades = 1 Division	
3 Divisions = 1 Corps	

Both the Union and Confederate armies were organized in roughly the same way.

1 **CALCULATING** About how many times larger was the Union army than the Confederate army?

2 **CRITICAL THINKING** *Explaining* Why do you think the armed forces were divided into units?

border state state on the border between the North and South: Delaware, Maryland, Kentucky, and Missouri

Academic Vocabulary

strategy a careful plan or method

RESOURCES IN THE NORTH AND SOUTH

The North and South went into the war with very different strengths and weaknesses.

1 **SUMMARIZING** How would you summarize the status of the North and South at the start of the war?

2 **CRITICAL THINKING**
Comparing In what areas did the North have the greatest advantage over the South?

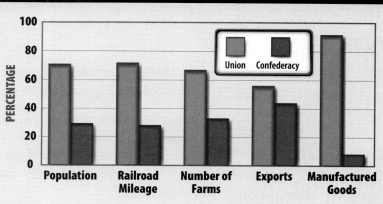

Source: U.S. Census Bureau, *Historical Statistics of the United States*

In **contrast,** the North wanted to restore the Union. Its forces had to invade the South and force the breakaway states to give up their quest for independence. Although slavery helped drive a wedge between Northerners and Southerners, President Lincoln's original aim was not to defeat slavery. He wrote in 1862:

PRIMARY SOURCE

66 If I could save the Union without freeing *any* slave I would do it, and if I could save it by freeing *all* the slaves I would do it; and if I could save it by freeing some and leaving others alone I would also do that. 99

—from *Abraham Lincoln: His Speeches and Writings*

Confederate Strategies

The Confederacy's basic strategy was to conduct a defensive war. This meant that it would hold as much territory as possible. Southerners felt that if they showed determination to be independent, Northerners would tire of the war.

The South also tried to win the support of Great Britain and France, whose economies suffered when the war disrupted the export of Southern cotton. Southerners hoped the British and French might pressure the North to end the war.

Union Strategies

The North's war plan came from General Winfield Scott, hero of the war with Mexico. He knew that the North would have to defeat the South completely.

Reading **HELP**DESK

enlist to formally join a military force

Academic Vocabulary

contrast to compare with respect to differences

Reading in the Content Area: *Bar Graphs*

Bar graphs are often used to compare and contrast information about two groups. The large bars and different colors make them easy to read and interpret.

To do this, Scott proposed the so-called Anaconda Plan, which took its name from a type of snake that squeezes its prey to death. First, the Union would blockade, or close, Southern ports. This strategy would keep supplies from reaching the Confederacy and prevent the South from exporting its cotton crop. Second, the North would seek to gain control of the Mississippi River. This would split the Confederacy in two and cut Southern supply lines. Another goal of the Union forces was the capture of Richmond, Virginia—the Confederate capital.

☑ **PROGRESS CHECK**

Explaining Why did the South use a defensive strategy?

Americans Against Americans

GUIDING QUESTION *What was war like for the soldiers of the North and the South?*

The Civil War was more than a war between the states. It turned brother against brother and neighbor against neighbor. Kentucky senator John Crittenden had two sons who became generals. One fought for the Confederacy, the other for the Union. Even President Lincoln's wife, Mary Todd Lincoln, had relatives in the Confederate army.

Men of all ages rushed to **enlist** (ihn•LIHST) in, or join, the Union or Confederate army. Some did so out of patriotism. Others thought they would be called cowards if they did not serve. Still others were looking for excitement. The sister of William Stone of Louisiana wrote that her brother was eager:

PRIMARY SOURCE

❝ to be off to Virginia [to join the Confederate army]. He so fears that the fighting will be over before he can get there. ❞

—from *Brokenburn: The Journal of Kate Stone*

Though the average Civil War soldier was in his mid-20s, many recruits on both sides were hardly adults. Tens of thousands of soldiers were under 18. Some were younger than 14. To get into the army, many teenagers ran away from home or lied about their ages.

Although teenage boys were accepted into service, one group of men was not allowed to fight in the early days of the war. The Union refused at first to let free African Americans enlist. Union leaders worried that white troops would not accept African American soldiers.

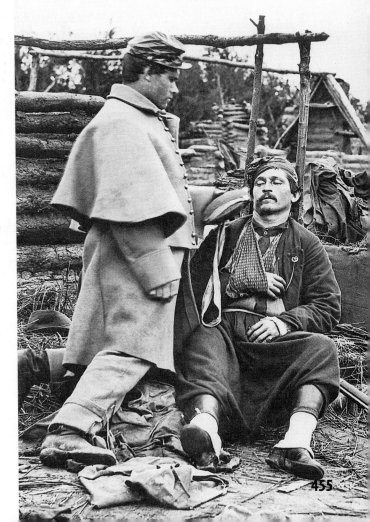

Though they fought bitterly, the two sides in the Civil War shared close bonds. Often families had soldiers on each side of the conflict.

Bettmann/CORBIS

455

A SOLDIER'S PAY

ARMY SALARIES (MONTHLY)				
Rank	Civil War	World War II 1942	Vietnam War 1965	Iraq War 2007
Private	*$13	$50	$85	$1,203–1,543.20
Corporal	$14	$66	$210	$1,699.50
Sergeant	$17	$78	$261	$1,854–2,339.10
Sergeant Major	$21	$138	$486	$4,110

*Until 1864, African Americans in the Civil War were paid only $7 per month
Source: Bureau of Economic Analysis; Princeton Review; www. militaryfactory.com

To get more men to enlist, Union recruiters put up posters offering a sign-up bonus, or bounty.

CHART SKILL

Although many volunteered to serve, soldiers in both the Union and Confederate armies received monthly pay. Compare their pay rates to those in later wars.

1 DESCRIBING What happens to a soldier's pay as he or she moves up in rank?

2 CRITICAL THINKING
Making Connections Name some items you could buy today with a Civil War private's monthly salary.

Later in the war, the Union army changed this policy. The Confederacy refused to consider having African Americans fight until the war's final, desperate days. They did not want to give enslaved people weapons.

High Hopes

When the war began, each side expected a quick victory. Northerners could not imagine the Confederates holding out for long against the Union's greater resources. Confederates believed the North could never subdue the fighting spirit of the South. Both sides were wrong. In the end, the war lasted far longer than most Americans could have guessed.

Who Were the Soldiers?

Soldiers came from every region of the country and all walks of life. Most came from farms. Almost half of the North's troops and more than 60 percent of the South's had owned or worked on farms.

By the summer of 1861, the Confederate army had about 112,000 soldiers. They were sometimes called Rebels. The Union had about 187,000 soldiers, also known as Yankees. By the end of the war, about 900,000 men fought for the Confederacy and about 2.1 million men bore arms for the Union. The Union army included just under 200,000 African Americans. About 10,000 Mexican Americans served in the war.

Library of Congress

Reading **HELP**DESK

Reading Strategy: *Finding the Main Idea*

Paragraphs and sections have main ideas and details that support that main idea. Make an outline of the section "A Soldier's Life" by writing down the main idea and listing the supporting details under it.

A Soldier's Life

Soldiers of the North and the South described what they saw and how they felt in letters to family and friends. Many wrote about their boredom, discomfort, sickness, fear, and horror.

Most of the time the soldiers lived in camps. Camp life had its pleasant moments of songs, stories, letters from home, and baseball games. At other times, a soldier's life was a dull routine of drills, bad food, marches, and rain.

Between battles, soldiers on both sides sometimes forgot they were enemies. A private described his wartime experiences:

PRIMARY SOURCE

❝ A part of Co [company] K and some of the enemy came together and stacked arms and talked for a long time. Our men cooked coffee and treated them and [afterward] ... each one took up his position again and they began to fire at each other again, but not as hard as before. ❞

—from *The Life of Billy Yank*

The Horrors of War

In spite of fleeting moments of calm, the reality of war was always close by. Thousands of casualties overwhelmed medical facilities. After the Battle of Shiloh, the wounded lay in the rain for more than 24 hours waiting for treatment. A soldier recalled, "Many had died there, and others were in the last agonies as we passed. Their groans and cries were heartrending."

Faced with these terrible realities, many men deserted. About one of every eleven Union soldiers and one of every eight Confederates ran away because of fear, hunger, or sickness.

✓ **PROGRESS CHECK**

Comparing and Contrasting How did the expectations of the war compare with the reality for both sides?

The picture above shows a Union artillery unit during the Civil War. The photograph below shows a U.S. artillery unit in Iraq in 2010.

▶ **CRITICAL THINKING**
Comparing and Contrasting How is the artillery that soldiers used during the Civil War like the artillery they use today? How is it different?

LESSON 1 REVIEW

Review Vocabulary

1. Use the following terms in sentences about the Civil War that demonstrate your understanding of the terms.

   a. border state   **b.** enlist

Answer the Guiding Questions

2. *Contrasting* How was the North's strategy different from the South's?

3. *Comparing and Contrasting* Compare and contrast attitudes in the Union and the Confederacy about enlisting African American soldiers.

4. *Evaluating* What was the goal of the Anaconda Plan?

5. **PERSONAL WRITING** You are a young Southern or Northern man in 1861. You have left home to join the army. Write a letter to your family explaining your reasons for joining the Union or Confederate army.

Lesson 2
Early Years of the War

ESSENTIAL QUESTION *Why does conflict develop?*

IT MATTERS BECAUSE
Neither side gained a strong advantage during the war's early years.

War on Land and at Sea

GUIDING QUESTION *What was the outcome of the first major battle of the war?*

While the Union and the Confederacy mobilized their armies, the Union navy began operations against the South. In April 1861, President Lincoln announced a blockade of all Confederate ports. The stage was set for fighting at sea as well as on land.

First Battle of Bull Run

Tension mounted in the summer of 1861, leading to the first major battle of the Civil War. On July 21, about 30,000 Union troops commanded by General Irvin McDowell attacked a smaller Confederate force led by General P.G.T. Beauregard.

The fighting took place in northern Virginia, near a small river called Bull Run. Hundreds of spectators from Washington, D.C., watched the battle from a few miles away.

Both sides lacked battle experience. At first, the Yankees drove the Confederates back. Then the Rebels rallied, inspired by General Thomas Jackson. Another Confederate general noted that Jackson was holding his position "like a stone wall." This earned him the nickname "Stonewall" Jackson. The Confederates then unleashed a savage counterattack that broke the Union lines. As they retreated, Union troops ran into civilians fleeing in panic.

(l) Library of Congress/08101,
(c) Bettmann/CORBIS,
(r) SuperStock/SuperStock

Reading **HELP**DESK

Taking Notes: *Sequencing*

As you read about the early Civil War battles, note them on a time line, and take notes on what happened during each of them.

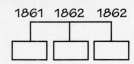

1861 1862 1862

Content Vocabulary

• **tributary**
• **ironclad**
• **casualty**

• **Emancipation**
  Proclamation

The loss shocked Northerners, who now realized that the war could be long and difficult. President Lincoln named a new general, George B. McClellan, to head the Union army in the East—called the Army of the Potomac—and to train the troops.

Although dismayed over Bull Run, President Lincoln was also determined. He put out a call for more army volunteers. He signed two bills requesting a total of 1 million soldiers to serve for three years. In addition, victories in the West would soon give a boost to Northern spirits and also increase enlistment.

Control of the West

In the West, the major Union goal was to control the Mississippi River and its **tributaries** (TRIH•byuh•tehr•eez), the smaller rivers that fed it. With control of the river, Union ships could prevent Louisiana, Arkansas, and Texas from supplying the eastern Confederacy. Union gunboats and troops would also be able to use the rivers to move into the heart of the South.

The battle for the rivers began in February 1862. Union forces captured Fort Henry on the Tennessee River. Naval commander Andrew Foote and army general Ulysses S. Grant led the assault. Soon afterward, Grant and Foote moved against Fort Donelson on the Cumberland River. The Confederates realized they had no chance of saving the fort. They asked Grant what terms he would give them to surrender. Grant replied, "No terms except an unconditional and immediate surrender can be accepted." "Unconditional Surrender" Grant became the North's new hero.

A Battle Between Ironclads

The Union blockade of Confederate ports posed a real threat to the Confederacy. Southerners hoped to break it with a secret weapon—the *Merrimack*. The *Merrimack* was a damaged frigate that had been **abandoned** by the Union. The Confederates rebuilt the wooden ship and covered it with iron. They renamed their new **ironclad** (EYE•uhrn•klad) the *Virginia*.

On March 8, 1862, the *Virginia* attacked Union ships in the Chesapeake Bay. Union shells just bounced off its sides. Some Union leaders feared the *Virginia* would destroy the Union navy, steam up the Potomac River, and bombard Washington, D.C.

By this time, however, the North had an ironclad of its own. The *Monitor* rushed southward to face the *Virginia*. On March 9, the two ironclads met in battle. Neither ship won, but the stirring clash raised spirits in both the North and the South.

To create the *Virginia*, the Confederate navy took what remained of a burned Union warship, covered it in iron, and equipped it with 10 guns. On its bow they placed an iron ram so the ship could steer into another ship and puncture its hull.

tributary stream or smaller river that feeds into a larger river
ironclad a warship equipped with iron plating for protection

Academic Vocabulary

abandon to leave behind or give up

Just two months after their March 1862 battle, the crew of the *Virginia* (on the right) destroyed their ship rather than let it fall into Union hands. The *Monitor* sank in a storm in December 1862.

▶ **CRITICAL THINKING**
Analyzing Visuals Why do you think neither ship was able to seriously damage the other?

The Battle of Shiloh

Meanwhile, in the West, General Grant and about 40,000 troops headed south toward Corinth, Mississippi, a major railroad junction. In early April 1862, the Union army camped at Pittsburg Landing, 20 miles (32 km) from Corinth, near Shiloh Church. Additional Union forces joined Grant from Nashville.

Confederate leaders decided to strike before more troops arrived to **reinforce** the Union. Early on the morning of April 6, Generals Albert Sidney Johnston and P.G.T. Beauregard led Confederate forces in a surprise attack. The battle lasted two days. It was a narrow victory for the Union, but the losses were enormous. Together, the two armies suffered more than 23,000 **casualties** (KA•zhuhl•teez)—people killed, wounded, captured, or missing.

After Shiloh, Union troops laid siege to Corinth, forcing the Confederates to withdraw. The Union army occupied the town on May 30. Memphis, Tennessee, fell to Union forces on June 6. The North seemed well on its way to controlling the Mississippi River.

Capturing New Orleans

A few weeks after Shiloh, the North won another key victory. On April 25, 1862, Union naval forces under David Farragut captured New Orleans, Louisiana, the largest city in the South. Farragut, who was of Spanish descent, grew up in the South but remained loyal to the Union. The capture of New Orleans meant

Bettmann/CORBIS

that the Confederacy could no longer use the Mississippi River to carry its goods to sea. The city's fall also left the Confederate stronghold of Vicksburg, Mississippi, as the only major obstacle to the Union's strategy in the West.

✓ PROGRESS CHECK

Explaining How did the loss of New Orleans affect the Confederacy?

War in the Eastern States

GUIDING QUESTION *How did the Union respond to important defeats in the East in 1862?*

While the two sides fought for control of Tennessee and the Mississippi River, the Union was trying to capture the Confederate capital at Richmond, Virginia. Close to the Union, Richmond was vulnerable to attack. Confederate armies fought hard to defend it. Confederate forces in the East enjoyed much more success than their western counterparts.

Confederate Victories

Southern victories in the East were largely the result of the leadership of Robert E. Lee and Stonewall Jackson. The two generals knew the terrain and could move forces quickly. They were also expert at inspiring troops. As a result, Confederate forces managed to defeat much larger Union forces.

> **GEOGRAPHY CONNECTION**
>
> Gaining control of the West was a key part of the Union's war strategy.
>
> **1 PLACE** Where did the South win battles in the West?
>
> **2 CRITICAL THINKING**
> ***Making Inferences*** What important cities remained for the North to capture after 1863?

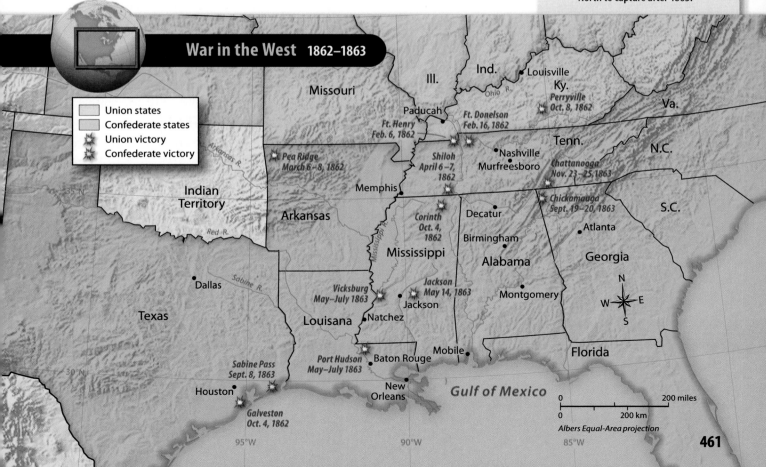

War in the West 1862–1863

Union states
Confederate states
Union victory
Confederate victory

Louisville
Ky.
Perryville
Oct. 8, 1862
Va.
Ind.
Ill.
Missouri
Ohio R.
Paducah
Ft. Donelson
Feb. 16, 1862
Ft. Henry
Feb. 6, 1862
Tenn.
N.C.
Pea Ridge
March 6–8, 1862
Shiloh
April 6–7, 1862
Nashville
Murfreesboro
Chattanooga
Nov. 23–25, 1863
Arkansas R.
Indian Territory
Memphis
Chickamauga
Sept. 19–20, 1863
S.C.
Arkansas
Corinth
Oct. 4, 1862
Decatur
Atlanta
Red R.
Birmingham
Georgia
Mississippi
Alabama
Dallas
Sabine R.
Jackson
May 14, 1863
Montgomery
N
Vicksburg
May–July 1863
Jackson
W · E
Texas
Natchez
S
Louisana
Mobile
Florida
Sabine Pass
Sept. 8, 1863
Port Hudson
May–July 1863
Baton Rouge
Houston
New Orleans
Gulf of Mexico
0   200 miles
Galveston
Oct. 4, 1862
0   200 km
Albers Equal-Area projection
95°W   90°W   85°W

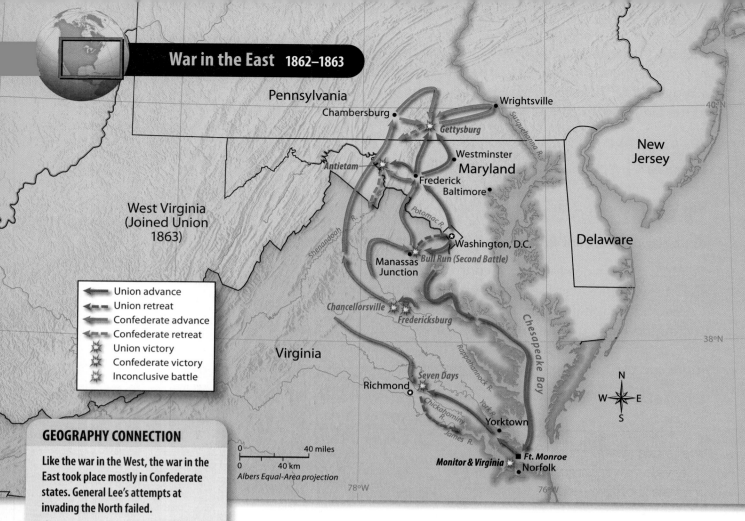

Pennsylvania
Chambersburg
Wrightsville
Gettysburg
Westminster
Maryland
Frederick
Antietam
Baltimore
New Jersey
West Virginia (Joined Union 1863)
Potomac R.
Shenandoah R.
Washington, D.C.
Delaware
Manassas Junction
Bull Run (Second Battle)
Chancellorsville
Fredericksburg
Virginia
Chesapeake Bay
Rappahannock R.
York R.
Seven Days
Richmond
Chickahominy R.
James R.
Yorktown
Monitor & Virginia
Ft. Monroe
Norfolk

Union advance
Union retreat
Confederate advance
Confederate retreat
Union victory
Confederate victory
Inconclusive battle

0   40 miles
0   40 km
Albers Equal-Area projection

GEOGRAPHY CONNECTION

Like the war in the West, the war in the East took place mostly in Confederate states. General Lee's attempts at invading the North failed.

1 PLACE Which battle took place closest to the Union capital at Washington, D.C.?

2 CRITICAL THINKING
Making Generalizations What does this map suggest about the difficulty of invading enemy territory? Explain your answer.

In 1862 Confederate forces enjoyed a string of impressive victories in Virginia, each over a different Union general. The Confederates turned back General George B. McClellan at the Seven Days' Battle, General John Pope at the Second Battle of Bull Run, and General Ambrose Burnside at Fredericksburg. In May 1863, at Chancellorsville, Virginia, Lee's army defeated a Union force twice its size. "My God, my God," Lincoln said when he learned of the defeat, "What will the country say!" The mood in the Union grew grim.

Lee Invades Maryland

Confederate president Jefferson Davis urged Lee to move his troops into western Maryland—Union territory. His goal was to move into Pennsylvania and to bring the war deeper into the Northern states. Though he knew McClellan was following him with a sizable force, Lee's forces crossed into Maryland and began the invasion of Union territory.

Reading HELPDESK

Reading Strategy: *Taking Notes*

Taking notes about what you are reading can help you remember facts and prepare effectively for tests. As you read the section "War in the Eastern States," make a list of each battle, the date, the location, and which side won.

The Battle of Antietam

Once in Maryland, Lee split his army into four parts. To confuse McClellan, he ordered each part to move in a different direction. Lee's plan never had a chance to work. A Confederate officer lost his copy of the orders describing it. Two Union soldiers found the orders and brought them to McClellan.

McClellan did not attack immediately. This gave Lee time to gather his troops. On September 17, 1862, the two sides met at a place called Antietam (an•TEE•tum) near Sharpsburg, Maryland.

Antietam was a key victory for the Union. It was also the deadliest single day of fighting in the war. About 6,000 soldiers died. About 17,000 more suffered wounds. Because of the great losses, Lee retreated to Virginia after the battle. For the time being, his strategy of invading the North had failed.

✓ **PROGRESS CHECK**

Summarizing What was the outcome of the Battle of Antietam?

The Emancipation Proclamation

GUIDING QUESTION *What was the effect of the Emancipation Proclamation?*

At first, Lincoln viewed the Civil War as a battle for the Union, not a fight against slavery. As the war went on, Lincoln changed the way he thought about the role of slavery in the war.

The Debate Over Ending Slavery

Lincoln hated slavery, yet he was reluctant to make the Civil War a battle to end it. Early in the war, Lincoln hesitated to move against slavery for fear of losing the border states. Even many white Northerners who disapproved of slavery were not eager to risk their lives to end it.

Meanwhile, abolitionists, including Frederick Douglass and newspaper editor Horace Greeley, urged Lincoln to make the war a fight to end slavery. The abolitionists described slavery as a moral wrong that needed to be abolished. They also pointed out that slavery was the root of the divisions between North and South. Finally, they argued that if Lincoln presented the war as a fight to abolish slavery, Britain and France would be less willing to support the South. Confederate hopes were increasingly linked to this European support.

SuperStock/SuperStock

Emancipation Proclamation
decree issued by President Lincoln freeing enslaved people in those parts of the Confederacy still in rebellion on January 1, 1863

A Call for Emancipation

The Constitution did not give Lincoln the power to end slavery, but it did give him the power to take property from an enemy in wartime. By law, enslaved people were considered property. On September 22, 1862, Lincoln announced that he would issue the **Emancipation Proclamation** (ih•mant•suh•PAY•shuhn prah•kluh•MAY•shuhn). This decree freed all enslaved people in rebel-held territory on January 1, 1863.

The Emancipation Proclamation did not change the lives of all enslaved people overnight. For example, enslaved people living in the loyal border states remained in bondage. Others remained under the direct control of their holders in the South and would have to wait for a Union victory before gaining their freedom.

Yet the Emancipation Proclamation had a strong impact. With it, the government declared slavery to be wrong. It was clear that a Union victory would end slavery in the United States.

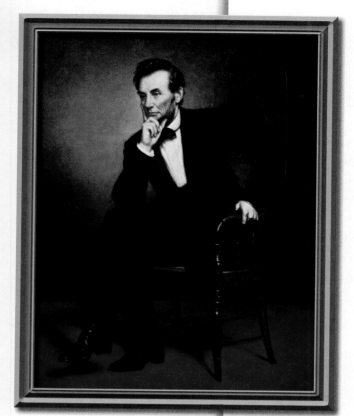

Lincoln's Emancipation Proclamation sent a clear message to enslaved people and the Confederacy about the future of slavery.

PRIMARY SOURCE

❝ I never in my life felt more certain that I am doing right than I do in signing this paper. . . . If my name ever goes into history it will be for this act, and my whole soul is in it. ❞

—Abraham Lincoln, 1863

✓ **PROGRESS CHECK**

Explaining How did the Emancipation Proclamation change the focus of the war?

LESSON 2 REVIEW

Review Vocabulary

1. Identify the significance of the following terms to the subject of the Civil War.

   a. tributary   **b.** ironclad   **c.** casualty

Answer the Guiding Questions

2. *Analyzing* Why was the outcome of the Battle of Bull Run surprising to Northerners?

3. *Explaining* Why was it important for the Confederacy to defend Richmond?

4. *Evaluating* How did the Emancipation Proclamation affect enslaved people in the South?

5. **PERSUASIVE WRITING** Choose one of Douglass' and Greeley's arguments for making abolition an aim of the war. Write a short paragraph expanding on the argument.

SuperStock/Getty Images

Lesson 3

Life During the Civil War

ESSENTIAL QUESTION *Why does conflict develop?*

IT MATTERS BECAUSE
Those who lived through the Civil War experienced many challenges and hardships.

A Different Way of Life

GUIDING QUESTION *How did life change during the Civil War?*

When the Civil War began, many young people left their homes to serve in the military. This meant leaving family and friends, and jobs or school.

Almost everyone who stayed home was touched in some way by the war. Only about half of the school-age children attended school because many had to stay home to help their families. Schools closed during the war in some areas, especially those near battles and skirmishes. Many schools and churches served instead as hospitals for the wounded.

Hardships in the South

Although the war affected everyone, life in the South changed most dramatically. Both armies spent the majority of their time on Southern soil. Because the fighting took place there, the South suffered the most destruction. Southerners who lived in the paths of marching armies lost their crops and sometimes their homes. Thousands of Southern civilians became refugees—people displaced by war.

Even those who lived outside the war zones suffered. As the war dragged on, many areas faced shortages of food and everyday supplies. Common household items became scarce.

Reading **HELP**DESK

Taking Notes: *Identifying*

As you read, complete a diagram like this one to catalog the ways that women in the North and the South contributed to the war effort.

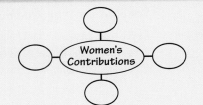

Women's Contributions

Content Vocabulary
• **habeas corpus**
• **draft**
• **bounty**

Frances Clayton disguised herself as a man to fight in the Civil War. As many as 400 other women did the same.

As one observer noted, the South depended on the outside world "for everything from a hairpin to a toothpick, and from a cradle to a coffin." Most people had to learn to do without.

✓ **PROGRESS CHECK**

Summarizing Why did many children stop going to school during the Civil War?

New Roles for Women

GUIDING QUESTION *What were the new roles for women in the Civil War?*

Against the advice of family and friends, Kate Cumming, a young woman from Mobile, Alabama, left home to begin a career as a nurse with the Confederate Army of the Mississippi. Cumming was one of the many women whose lives changed because of the Civil War.

In both the North and the South, women kept the farms and factories going. They ran offices, taught school, and kept government records. Women suffered the stress of having husbands away at war and the pain of losing family members. They struggled to keep their families together. With little money available, they cut back on expenses and went without many things they were used to.

Caring for the Wounded

In the Civil War, thousands of women on both sides served as nurses. The idea of women nurses on the battlefield was a relatively new one. Many doctors did not welcome them. They said that women were too delicate for the bloody work of wartime hospitals. Some men also felt it was improper for women to tend the bodies of men they did not know.

Strong-minded women disregarded these objections. Serving with the Union army, Mary Edwards Walker became the first female army surgeon and later received the Congressional Medal of Honor. Dorothea Dix helped persuade officials to let women work as nurses. She became the superintendent of nurses for the Union army and recruited large numbers of women to serve. Another Northerner, Clara Barton, became famous for her work helping wounded soldiers. In the South, Sally Tompkins set up a hospital for soldiers in Richmond, Virginia. Tompkins held the rank of captain in the Confederate army and was the only female officer in the Confederate forces.

Reading **HELP**DESK

Build Vocabulary: *Related Words*

The word *spy*, which means "to watch secretly," is related to the word *espionage*, which means "spying."

Reading Strategy: *Finding the Main Idea*

As you read "New Roles for Women," jot down the main idea in each paragraph in your notebook. Using your notes, write a sentence that summarizes this section.

The women who served in wartime hospitals came face to face with terrible brutality. After the Battle of Shiloh, Kate Cumming wrote, "Nothing that I had ever heard or read had given me the faintest idea of the horrors witnessed here."

Spying

Women on both sides served as spies. For example, Rose O'Neal Greenhow entertained Union leaders in Washington, D.C. From them, she gathered information about Union plans and passed it to the South. Greenhow eventually was caught and convicted of treason—the crime of betraying one's country. Belle Boyd of Front Royal, Virginia, informed Confederate generals of Union troop movements in the Shenandoah River valley.

Harriet Tubman, a leading "conductor" on the Underground Railroad, also served as a spy and scout for the Union. In 1863 Tubman led a mission that freed many enslaved people and disrupted Southern supply lines.

Some women disguised themselves as men and became soldiers. Loreta Janeta Velázquez fought for the South at the First Battle of Bull Run and at the Battle of Shiloh. She later became a Confederate spy.

☑ **PROGRESS CHECK**

Explaining Why did some people object to women working as nurses during the war?

In 1861 Dorothea Dix became superintendent of woman nurses for the Union army. Part of her job was to set up military hospitals like the brick building shown here. Dix served till the end of the war without pay.

The Captured and the Wounded

GUIDING QUESTION *What were the conditions of hospitals and prison camps during the Civil War?*

For many soldiers, battle could be a terrifying experience. For those with wounds or for those taken prisoner, the misery was just beginning.

Prisoners of War

Each side treated its enemy soldiers with a mixture of sympathy and hostility. At first the two sides exchanged prisoners. After this system broke down over issues such as Confederate treatment of African American prisoners, each side set up prison camps. A prisoner typically kept his blanket and a cup or canteen. These possessions were all he had during his imprisonment. Food shortages made the suffering worse. Volunteers **distributed** bread and soup to the wounded. In the prisons, though, there was little or nothing to eat.

Andersonville prison opened in Georgia in early 1864. It was built to hold 10,000 prisoners. By August, 33,000 crammed its grounds. The men slept in shallow holes dug in the ground. All they received to eat each day was a teaspoon of salt, three tablespoons of beans, and eight ounces of cornmeal. They drank and cooked with water from a stream that also served as a sewer. Almost 13,000 Union prisoners died there, mostly from disease.

The Union prison in Elmira, New York, was no better. Captured soldiers from the South suffered through the winter months without blankets and warm clothes. The hospital was located in a flooded basement. A pond within the compound served as both toilet and garbage dump. Almost one quarter of all prisoners at Elmira died.

Field Hospitals

Surgeons set up hospitals near battlefields. There, with bullets and cannonballs flying by, they bandaged wounds and amputated limbs. Nurse Kate Cumming recalled:

PRIMARY SOURCE

❝ We have to walk, and when we give the men anything kneel, in blood and water; but we think nothing of it. ❞

—from *Kate: The Journal of a Confederate Nurse*

CORBIS

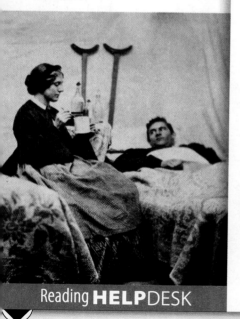

In the Civil War, more than 2,000 women served as nurses in hospitals on both sides. Most were volunteers.

Academic Vocabulary

distribute to hand out, spread around

Reading Strategy: *Context Clues*

When you find an unknown word, look at surrounding text for clues to the meaning. Clues may be:
• The word is defined immediately following its use.
• A synonym or an antonym is used that explains the meaning.
• Hints appear in the surrounding passage to help you figure out the meaning.

Disease was another medical threat. Crowded together in camps and drinking unclean water, many soldiers got sick. Disease spread quickly—and could be deadly. Some regiments lost half their men to illness before they ever went into battle.

✅ **PROGRESS CHECK**

Explaining Why were prison camps set up?

Political and Economic Change

GUIDING QUESTION *What political and economic changes occurred during the Civil War?*

Doctors in the Civil War did not have many modern medicines. To prevent deadly infections, they often amputated wounded limbs with tools such as these.

In the South, many white people opposed the war. The fighting was costly not just in terms of lives lost or damaged, but in food, material, and money. Everywhere, people suffered from shortages. Bread riots broke out throughout the South as hungry people took to the streets. In Richmond, a group of mostly women and children gathered peacefully to protest but soon started smashing shop windows and stealing food.

In the North, the Democratic Party was split down the middle. War Democrats supported the war while criticizing Lincoln's handling of it. Peace Democrats argued for an immediate end to fighting and a reunion of the states through negotiation. Most Peace Democrats came from the Midwestern states of Ohio, Illinois, and Indiana. Critics of the Peace Democrats called them Copperheads. A copperhead is a type of deadly snake. Rather than take offense, the Copperheads proudly embraced this label. They wore copper pennies as badges on their clothing.

As in the South, some Northerners who opposed the war discouraged people from enlisting. A few even helped Confederate prisoners of war escape. Opponents claimed that the Peace Democrats encouraged the South to keep fighting. They said the war dragged on because Confederates believed the Peace Democrats would eventually prevail in the North.

Jail Without Trial

As a way of dealing with war opponents in the North, President Lincoln suspended **habeas corpus** (HAY•bee•uhs KAWR•puhs)—a legal process that helps ensure the government has a legal right to keep someone in jail. The Constitution says government can suspend habeas corpus, but only "when in cases of rebellion or invasion, the public safety may require it."

A Northern newspaper ran this cartoon in 1863. It shows Lady Liberty warding off an attack of the Peace Democrats, or Copperheads.

▶ **CRITICAL THINKING**
Analyzing Images What does this cartoon suggest about the artist's view of Copperheads? Explain your answer.

THE COPPERHEAD PARTY.——IN FAVOR OF *A VIGOROUS PROSECUTION OF PEACE!*

With this act, Lincoln's government was able to jail thousands of Northerners without putting them on trial. Some of these people were likely traitors to the Union. Others did nothing more than use their right of free speech to criticize the government.

In the South, President Davis also suspended habeas corpus. He, too, believed he needed to deal harshly with opponents of the war. Still, Davis's action upset many loyal supporters.

Draft Laws

Both the North and the South had trouble getting troops to sign up. In 1862 the Confederate Congress passed a **draft** that required able-bodied white men between ages 18 and 35 to serve for three years. Later the requirement included men from ages 17 to 50. Several exceptions were allowed. A man with enough money could hire a **substitute** to serve for him. Later, a man with 20 or more enslaved people did not have to serve.

At first, the North offered a **bounty** (BAUN•tee), or a sum of money, to encourage volunteers. In March 1863, it also passed a draft. Men aged 20 to 45 had to register. As in the South, a man could avoid the draft by hiring a substitute or paying $300. Many workers earned less than $500 a year and could not afford these options. In the North and the South, people complained it was "a rich man's war and a poor man's fight."

People rioted to protest the draft in several Northern cities. The New York City draft riots in July 1863 were the worst. As the first names were drawn, rioters attacked government and military buildings. Then mobs turned their attacks against

Reading **HELP**DESK

habeas corpus a legal writ, or order, that guarantees a prisoner the right to be heard in court
draft a system of selecting people for required military service
bounty reward or payment

Visual Vocabulary

greenback
paper money issued by the United States government

Academic Vocabulary

substitute an alternate or replacement

African Americans. Many white workers had opposed the Emancipation Proclamation, fearing freed African Americans would take their jobs. After four days, more than 100 people were dead. Federal troops finally stopped the riots.

War and the Economy

The war strained the economies of the North and the South. However, the North, with its greater resources, was better able to cope with the costs of the war.

The two sides had three ways of paying for the war. First, they borrowed money. Second, they passed new taxes, including income taxes. Third, they printed money. Northern bills became known as **greenbacks** because of their color.

In the North, industry profited from the war effort. It made guns, ammunition, shoes, and uniforms. Farmers prospered, too. They sold their crops to feed the troops. Because goods were in high demand, prices went up—faster than workers' wages. This inflation caused hardship for working people.

The white South felt the economic strain even more sharply than the North. Many of the battles of the Civil War took place on Confederate soil, destroying farmland and railroad lines. The Union naval blockade prevented the shipping of trade goods. Vital materials could not reach the Confederacy. Salt was in such short supply that women scraped the floors of smokehouses to recover it. Food shortages led to riots in Atlanta, Richmond, and other cities.

The South also suffered much worse inflation. As early as 1862, citizens were begging Confederate leaders for help.

✅ **PROGRESS CHECK**

Comparing How did the war affect the economy in the North and South?

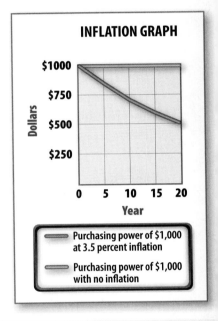

Thinking Like a
HISTORIAN

Analyzing and Interpreting Information

Inflation, a rise in prices, hurts people by reducing the buying power of money. The graph below shows that with just 3.5 percent inflation, the buying power of $1,000 drops sharply. In 20 years, the $1,000 will have about half its original buying power. To learn more about analyzing and interpreting information, review *Thinking Like a Historian*.

INFLATION GRAPH

Dollars / Year

— Purchasing power of $1,000 at 3.5 percent inflation

— Purchasing power of $1,000 with no inflation

LESSON 3 REVIEW

Review Vocabulary

1. Use each of these terms in a complete sentence that explains the term's meaning.

   a. habeas corpus   **b.** draft   **c.** bounty

Answer the Guiding Questions

2. *Explaining* How did the roles of women change during the Civil War?

3. *Evaluating* How did the Civil War affect children?

4. *Comparing* What challenges and threats did prisoners and wounded soldiers face?

5. *Summarizing* Who were the Copperheads? What was their position on fighting the war?

6. **PERSUASIVE WRITING** President Lincoln and President Davis suspended habeas corpus to deal with opponents of the war. Do you think suspending civil liberties is justified in some situations? Write a short essay in which you state and defend your position.

Across Five Aprils

by Irene Hunt

A Union soldier might wear a cap like this.

Irene Hunt (1907–2001) was born in Pontiac, Illinois, more than 40 years after the Civil War ended. Her father died when she was seven years old. Hunt graduated from the University of Illinois in 1939. She taught French and English in Illinois public schools until she retired to write full-time in 1969. She wrote many books for young people and won a Newberry Medal for her second novel, *Up a Road Slowly*. Hunt died in 2001.

First published in 1965, *Across Five Aprils* was Irene Hunt's first novel. It is the story of Jethro Creighton, a nine-year-old boy living in Indiana during the Civil War. In this excerpt, he and his mother are at home when a letter arrives from one of Jethro's older brothers, who is fighting for the Union.

> **❝I miss yore good cookin Ma. You tell Jeth that bein a soljer aint so much.❞**
>
> —from Irene Hunt's *Across Five Aprils*

In February 1862, Brigadier General Ulysses S. Grant demanded and received unconditional surrender of Confederate Fort Donelson on the Cumberland River.

66 Finally one day Ed Turner brought them a letter from Tom. Ed looked pinched with cold after his long drive, but he wouldn't stop for coffee.

"A fam'ly needs to be alone when one of these letters comes," he said in answer to Ellen's invitation. "I'd be pleased if you'd let me know what the boy has to say—later on when Matt has the time to drop over."

Jenny had gone with her father to see about some **stock,** and Jethro was alone in the cabin with his mother. When Ed Turner was gone, she handed the letter to Jethro.

"My hands is shakin', Son," she said. They were, indeed, but both she and the boy knew that the real reason she was forced to hand the letter over was the fact that she could not read.

The envelope was crumpled and stained, the letter written in pencil in a round, childish hand. It was probably among the first three or four letters that young Tom had ever written.

Dere Fokes:

I take pencle in hand to let you no that Eb and me is alright.

I expect you no by now how we took Fort Henry down here. Mebby I oughtnt say we took it becus it was the ironclads that done it. Old admiral Foote had what it took and he give the rebs a **dressin down** but some of his iron-clads got hit hard. A boy I no was on the Essex and he was burned so bad he dide when that boat got nocked out of the fite.

Us boys didn't do much fitin at Fort Henry but at Donelson I can tell you we made up fer it. We had done a foolish thing on our way to Donelson and I will rite you about it. When we was marchin tord the fort the weather was like a hot april day back home. We was feelin set-up about Fort Henry and when some of the boys got tard of carryin hevey blanket rolls they jest up and throwed em away. Then more and more of us acted like crazy fools and we throwed away hevey cotes and things to make our lodes a littel liter. As soon as we got to Donelson the wether turned cold as Billy Sideways and some of the boys that was sick or bad hurt they froze to deth in the snow. Things was awful bad with so many kilt and others froze. I felt sick when I looked at them and so I am, not so proud about Donelson as mebby I ought to be. I miss yore good cookin Ma. You tell Jeth that bein a soljer aint so much.

yrs truley
Tom 99

Text: From ACROSS FIVE APRILS Copyright © 1964 by Irene Hunt. Used by permission of Pearson Education, Inc. All Rights Reserved.

Vocabulary

stock
livestock

dressin down
(incorrect spelling of "dressing down") a serious punishment or scolding

Literary Element

Dialect refers to the language, speech patterns, spelling, grammar, and sounds used by people from a particular area or from a particular social or economic group. As you read, note the ways Irene Hunt uses dialect to reveal information about her characters. If you have trouble following the dialect, try reading the text aloud.

Analyzing Literature   DBQ

1. *Explaining* Why didn't Ed Turner accept Mrs. Creighton's invitation to stay for coffee?

2. *Analyzing* What does the dialect used in Tom's letter reveal about him? Use examples from the text to support your answer.

3. *Interpreting* What has Tom learned about the reality of war?

Lesson 4

The Strain of War

ESSENTIAL QUESTION *Why does conflict develop?*

IT MATTERS BECAUSE

Union victories at Gettysburg and Vicksburg marked a turning point in the war.

Southern Victories

GUIDING QUESTION *What factors contributed to the early success of the Confederate forces?*

The military leadership of Generals Robert E. Lee and Stonewall Jackson was a key factor in the Confederates' military success in the East. With their knowledge of the land and ability to inspire troops, these two generals often defeated larger Union forces.

The Battle of Fredericksburg

After Antietam, Robert E. Lee moved his army out of Maryland into Virginia. This encouraged the newly named Union commander, General Ambrose Burnside, to march his troops toward the Confederate capital at Richmond. Lee intercepted the Union army near Fredericksburg. Lee's forces dug trenches in hills south of the town. This gave them the advantage of higher ground from which to fight. On December 13, 1862, Union forces attacked. Lee's **entrenched** (ihn•TREHNCHT) troops drove them back with heavy losses. Devastated, Burnside resigned.

Victory at Chancellorsville

In May 1863, Lee met Union forces led by General Joseph Hooker in the Battle of Chancellorsville. General Lee again showed daring and a brilliant command of tactics. Although Hooker had

(l) North Wind Picture Archives, (cl) Archive Photos/Getty Images,
(c) Kean Collection/Getty Images,
(r) The Granger Collection, NYC

Reading **HELP**DESK

Taking Notes: *Categorizing*

As you read, use a chart like this one to keep track of who won which battles.

Union Victories	Confederate Victories

Content Vocabulary
- **entrench**
- **flank**

twice as many men, Lee divided his forces. Some Confederate troops confronted the main Union force. Others under the leadership of Stonewall Jackson secretly marched to a spot at the far end of the Union line. The risky plan worked perfectly. Jackson's army surprised the Union force with a crushing attack on its **flank** (FLANGK), or side. Lee struck from the front. Caught between the two Confederate forces, Hooker eventually withdrew his men.

The Confederate victory came at a high cost. In the confusion of battle, Confederate soldiers fired on and wounded Stonewall Jackson by mistake. Surgeons amputated Jackson's arm, prompting Lee to say, "He has lost his left arm, and I have lost my right." Worse, Jackson developed pneumonia. After a week of suffering, he died. His death cost the South one of its great leaders. It also affected the morale of its army and its citizens.

Problems With Union Leadership

In contrast, Union leadership in the East disappointed the president. In less than a year, a frustrated Lincoln saw three different generals try and fail to lead the Union to victory.

The first, Major General George McClellan, commanded the Union forces at the Battle of Antietam in March 1862. Although he was expert at preparing for battle, he was overly careful and slow to act. Said Lincoln, "If McClellan doesn't want to use the army, I'd like to borrow it for a while." The last straw came when, after victory at Antietam, McClellan failed to obey Lincoln's order to follow the retreating Confederate troops and destroy them.

Lincoln pushed his next commander, General Ambrose Burnside, to take aggressive action. Burnside quickly lost the president's favor after his crushing loss at Fredericksburg.

Next, Lincoln appointed Major General Joseph Hooker, who had often been critical of other generals. Hooker's attitude matched the president's. "May God have mercy on General Lee, for I will have none," he declared. Despite Hooker's confidence, Lee's much smaller army crushed Hooker's forces at Chancellorsville. Hooker soon resigned.

Lincoln's next commander needed to prove himself quickly. Major General George Meade took command three days before one of the war's great battles, at Gettysburg, Pennsylvania.

North Wind Picture Archives

✓ **PROGRESS CHECK**

Explaining Why was Lincoln frustrated with the Union generals?

BIOGRAPHY

Thomas Jonathan "Stonewall" Jackson (1824–1863)

Thomas Jackson was born in Virginia. At the age of 18, he moved north to attend the military academy at West Point. He went on to a short and unremarkable career in the United States Army. During the 1850s, he taught at the Virginia Military Institute. At that time, he showed more interest in art than in war. When the Civil War started, Jackson was not widely known in the military. That changed at the First Battle of Bull Run, when Jackson won his nickname "Stonewall." By 1863 he had become one of the Confederacy's top leaders.

▶ **CRITICAL THINKING**
Speculating What does Jackson's nickname—Stonewall—suggest about his personal qualities?

---

entrench to place within a trench, or ditch, for defense; to place in a strong defensive position
flank the side or edge of a military formation

Build Vocabulary: *Metaphor*

Entrench is often used metaphorically to refer to ideas that are firmly held and cannot be easily changed. Here's an example: "Thanks to my parents, the belief that I would succeed as long as I studied hard became entrenched in my mind."

Beginning with the Revolutionary War, African Americans have had a long history of serving with distinction in the U.S. military. When the draft ended in 1973, African American enrollment in the armed forces increased. Today, African Americans make up about 17 percent of the active forces and 15 percent of the Reserves and National Guard.

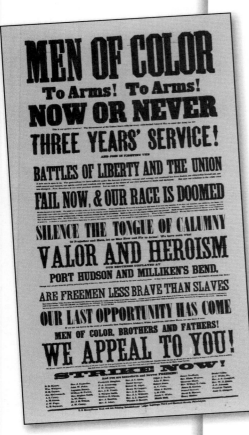

The Union army actively recruited African Americans through posters like this.

Reading HELPDESK

Academic Vocabulary

reverse to go in the opposite direction

African Americans in the Civil War

GUIDING QUESTION *What role did African Americans play in military efforts?*

At first, both the North and the South barred African Americans from serving in their armies. As time passed, the North relaxed its rules.

Excluded in the South

Even though African Americans made up more than 30 percent of the smaller Southern population, Confederate leaders would not allow them to enlist. Only in the last days of the war, when defeat drew near, did they consider it. Confederate leaders feared that once armed, African American soldiers would attack their fellow troops or even begin a general revolt.

Enlisted in the North

At first, President Lincoln resisted calls to enlist African Americans in the Union army. He feared that such a policy would be unpopular in the border states.

By 1862, though, it was clear that the North needed more soldiers in order to defeat the Confederacy. Many African Americans were eager to fight. As a result, Congress decided to **reverse** past policy and allow the formation of all-African American regiments.

These new Union soldiers were in a tough position. Many white Union regiments doubted their fighting ability. Others resented them. Many Southern troops also especially hated the Union's African American soldiers. They often focused their fiercest fire on African American regiments.

Despite this, African Americans joined. By the end of the war, they made up about 10 percent of the Union army. Some were freed people from the North. Others had fled enslavement in the South. These men fought hard and effectively, too. As one white Union officer wrote about an all-African American Kansas regiment:

PRIMARY SOURCE

66 They make better soldiers in every respect than any troops I have ever had under my command. 99

—Union General James G. Blunt

COME AND JOIN US BROTHERS.

PUBLISHED BY THE SUPERVISORY COMMITTEE FOR RECRUITING COLORED REGIMENTS
1210 CHESTNUT ST. PHILADELPHIA.

This picture, showing troops in a camp near Philadelphia, served as a Union recruiting poster.

▶ **CRITICAL THINKING**

Analyzing Visuals What do you think is the purpose of this poster? Explain your answer.

The 54th Massachusetts

The best-known African American regiment was the 54th Massachusetts. Founded in 1863, the 54th was under the command of Colonel Robert Gould Shaw, who came from a Boston abolitionist family. Later that year, the 54th served on the front lines in an assault on Fort Wagner in South Carolina. Confederate gunfire caused nearly 300 casualties in the 54th alone, including Colonel Shaw. Though the Union could not capture the fort, the 54th became famous for the courage and sacrifice of its members. It would also serve with distinction in other battles, such as the Battle of Olustee in Florida.

☑ **PROGRESS CHECK**

Determining Cause and Effect Why did Lincoln hesitate to enlist African Americans?

The Tide Turns

GUIDING QUESTION *How was the Battle of Gettysburg a turning point in the war?*

In spring of 1863, the Confederates had the upper hand. Their victory at Chancellorsville ruined Union plans to attack Richmond. Lee was emboldened. He decided to take the war once more into the North, hoping to impress France and Britain.

The Confederate strategy was similar to that of the colonies in the Revolutionary War. Though far outnumbered, the colonies won the support of France—and the war. Now, France and Britain missed the goods, especially cotton, that Southern planters had once supplied. If the Confederates appeared to be winning, those nations might help their cause.

GEOGRAPHY CONNECTION

After two days of heavy fighting at Gettysburg, the Confederates mounted a heavy attack on the Union lines.

1 LOCATION Where did the Confederates concentrate their attack?

2 CRITICAL THINKING
Drawing Conclusions What about the Union position as shown on this map might have given Union forces an advantage?

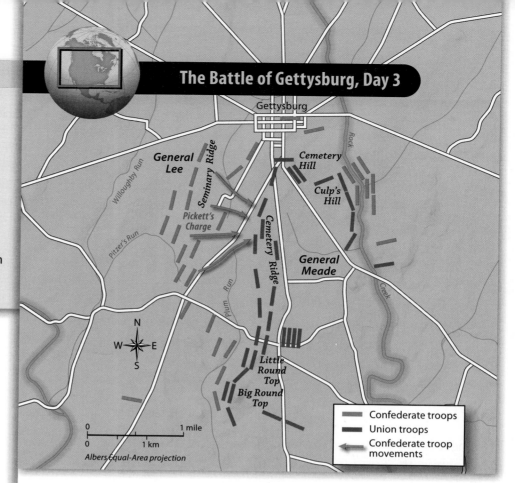

The Battle of Gettysburg, Day 3

The Battle of Gettysburg

In July 1863, a small town in southern Pennsylvania became the site of one of the most decisive battles in the Civil War. Gettysburg was not a capital, a key port, or the location of a fort. It was almost an accident that such serious fighting took place there.

The Confederates entered the town looking for supplies. General Lee hoped to avoid fighting in a landscape he did not know well. It was there, however, that he **encountered** the enemy. When Lee's troops crawled out of Gettysburg four grueling days later, they had suffered 25,000 casualties. The Union—the victor—lost 23,000.

The battle started at 7:30 A.M. on July 1. Outnumbered Union troops retreated to a section of high ground called Cemetery Ridge. Reinforcements arrived for both sides. On the second day of fighting, Southern generals tried to drive Union forces from hills named Round Top and Little Round Top. In furious fighting, Union forces under General George Meade held their positions.

The next day, Lee ordered an attack designed to "create a panic and virtually destroy the [Union] army." First, the Confederates fired nearly 140 cannons at the Union lines. Then, General George Pickett led thousands of Confederate troops in an attack on the Union's position at Cemetery Ridge. Putting themselves directly in the line of fire, they advanced across open land in what came to be remembered as Pickett's Charge.

At first, it seemed that Pickett's Charge might work. The Confederates broke the first line of Union defense. In the end, however, half of those who started the attack lay dead or wounded on the ground. Lee later wrote, "The army did all it could. I fear I required of it impossibilities."

Gettysburg ended the Confederates' hope of gaining help from Britain and France. The South had hoped to receive two ironclads from the British and use them to sweep Union shipping from the Atlantic. However, in October 1863, the British government decided not to release the ships.

The Siege of Vicksburg

On July 4, the day that Lee retreated from Gettysburg, the Confederacy suffered another major blow. The important river city of Vicksburg, Mississippi, fell under the control of Union troops led by Ulysses S. Grant.

Grant had first attacked Vicksburg in April. His army surrounded the 30,000 Confederate troops there. In May Grant began a siege of the town, preventing food and supplies from reaching the Confederates. Union gunships on the river supported Grant's 77,000 troops by firing thousands of shells into the city.

This painting shows Union forces fighting their way to the Confederate lines at Vicksburg, Mississippi, in May 1863.

▶ CRITICAL THINKING
Analyzing Visuals Do you think this painting was meant for a Union audience or a Confederate audience? Explain your answer.

The siege lasted 47 days. There were more than 9,000 Confederate and 10,000 Union casualties, and many soldiers died of disease or starvation. Despite heavy losses of soldiers, fewer than 20 citizens of Vicksburg were killed in the long siege.

A few days after Vicksburg fell, the Confederacy lost Port Hudson in Louisiana, its last stronghold on the Mississippi River. The Union had split the South in two. Arkansas, Louisiana, and Texas were now cut off. The tide of the Civil War had turned.

Lincoln's Address at Gettysburg

On November 19, 1863, officials and citizens gathered to dedicate the Soldiers' National Cemetery at Gettysburg. At the ceremony, former governor of Massachusetts Edward Everett delivered a two-hour speech. After him, President Abraham Lincoln spoke for about two minutes. In 272 words, Lincoln honored the soldiers and their cause, and stated his vision for the country.

PRIMARY SOURCE

66 These dead shall not have died in vain. . . . Government of the people, by the people, for the people shall not perish from the earth. 99

—from the Gettysburg Address

Reactions to Lincoln's Gettysburg Address were mixed. Everett, along with the *New York Times, Chicago Tribune,* and *Springfield* (Mass.) *Republican,* thought the speech was a success. The *Republican* wrote, "His little speech is a perfect gem; deep in feeling, compact in thought and expression, and tasteful ... in every word and comma." It remains one of the most enduring and powerful speeches in American history.

✓ PROGRESS CHECK

Summarizing How did the events at Vicksburg change the tide of the war?

LESSON 4 REVIEW

Review Vocabulary

1. Use the following terms in sentences about the Civil War.

   a. entrench   b. flank

Answer the Guiding Questions

2. *Explaining* Why was the Battle of Chancellorsville important?

3. *Making Inferences* Why do you think some leaders called for African Americans to be allowed to fight in the Civil War?

4. *Evaluating* Why was Gettysburg a turning point for the South?

5. **PERSONAL WRITING** You are a soldier who fought at Gettysburg. Write a letter to a loved one at home, describing the battle scene, how you felt, and what the outcome was.

Lesson 5
The War's Final Stages

ESSENTIAL QUESTION *Why does conflict develop?*

IT MATTERS BECAUSE
With each side determined to win, the bloodiest months of the Civil War were still to come.

The Union Closes In

GUIDING QUESTION *What events occurred at the end of the war?*

By 1864 Union forces had the South surrounded. Union ships blocked the Confederate coast, reducing the trade goods getting out and supplies getting in. The Union also controlled the Mississippi River, cutting off the western Confederate states from those in the East. The South seemed ready to fall—if the Union could come up with the right plan of attack. General Grant would be the one to draw up such a plan.

General Grant Takes Charge

Ulysses S. Grant had been only an average student. He failed as a farmer and in business. Yet he became a brilliant soldier. He led Union troops to victory at Shiloh and Vicksburg and at another key battle in Chattanooga, Tennessee. In March 1864, President Lincoln put General Grant in charge of all the Union armies.

President Lincoln liked that Grant was a man of action. Now in charge, Grant wasted little time coming up with a plan to finish the war. He would deliver killing blows from all sides. His armies would move on to Richmond, the Confederate capital. At the same time, General William Tecumseh Sherman would lead attacks across the Deep South.

(l) Library of Congress/LC-USZC4-678, (c) Bettmann/CORBIS, (r) Library of Congress LC-B8184-10575

Reading **HELP**DESK

Taking Notes: *Determining Cause and Effect*

As you read, keep track of the chain of events that led to the end of the Civil War using a diagram like this one.

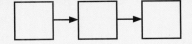

Content Vocabulary
• **resistance**
• **total war**

Ulysses S. Grant (1822–1885)

Ulysses S. Grant was born and raised in Georgetown, Ohio. As a young man, his father pressured him to attend the U.S. Military Academy at West Point. Grant was not interested in military service, but he went because it was his only chance at further education. Yet Grant became a fearless soldier and an expert rider at a time when soldiers rode horses in battle. Grant's military strategy seemed ruthless at times, but he said, "I have never advocated [war] except as a means of peace."

▶ **CRITICAL THINKING**
Explaining What do you think Grant meant in the quotation?

Grant soon put his strategy into action. In May and June of 1864, Grant's army confronted Lee's smaller force in a **series** of three battles near Richmond, Virginia. These were the Battles of the Wilderness, Spotsylvania Court House, and Cold Harbor. At each battle, Confederate lines held at first, but Grant quickly renewed the attack. "Whatever happens, there will be no turning back," Grant promised Lincoln. He was determined to march southward, attacking Lee's forces relentlessly and in spite of heavy losses until the Confederacy surrendered.

Grant Moves South Toward Richmond

The Wilderness was a densely wooded area about halfway between Washington, D.C., and Richmond, Virginia. Here, on May 5, 1864, the six bloodiest weeks of the war began. For two days, Union and Confederate forces struggled among a tangle of trees through which they could hardly see. A Union private said, "It was a blind and bloody hunt to the death."

At the Battle of the Wilderness, Lee had only about 60,000 men, while Grant had more than 100,000. Both sides suffered huge casualties. Grant, who lost 17,000 men, cried in his tent at the end of the second day. Meanwhile, brushfires raged through the forest. The fires burned alive 200 wounded men. On the morning of the third day, with no clear winner, Grant moved his forces south toward Richmond.

The next battles took place at nearby Spotsylvania Court House and at Cold Harbor. On June 2, the night before the third battle began, a Union general observed that men were "writing their names and home addresses on slips of paper and pinning them to the backs of their coats" to help people identify their bodies. The war seemed hopeless. Grant, however, was determined. He explained to the White House, "I propose to fight it out on this line, if it takes all summer."

In a space of 30 days, Grant lost 50,000 of his troops. His critics in the North called him a "butcher." Lincoln, however, stood by his general. "I can't spare this man," Lincoln is reported to have said. "He fights." As he fought, the Confederates were also losing men—losses their smaller army could not survive.

Siege at Petersburg

Grant made steady progress. He next arrived at Petersburg, a railroad center vital to the Confederate movement of troops and supplies. If Grant could take Petersburg, Richmond would be

Library of Congress/LC-USZC4-678

Reading **HELP**DESK

Academic Vocabulary

series events that occur one after the other

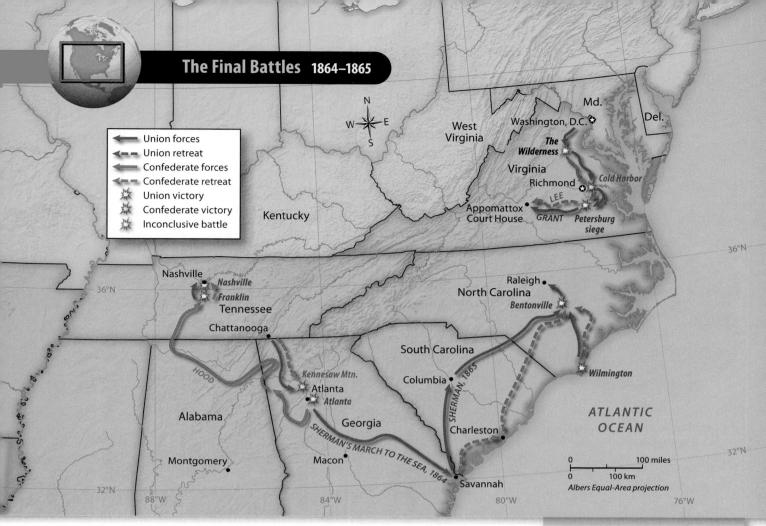

The Final Battles 1864–1865

Union forces
Union retreat
Confederate forces
Confederate retreat
Union victory
Confederate victory
Inconclusive battle

cut off from the rest of the Confederacy. Grant laid siege. The Confederates defended the city, but they could not break the Union's grip. Trains brought food and more troops to the Union side. The Confederates could get neither. Determined, they refused to give up.

Sherman in Georgia

Meanwhile, William Tecumseh Sherman headed for Georgia. In early July, his troops circled Atlanta. There they faced the brilliant Confederate general, John Hood. Hood's forces put up major **resistance** (rih•ZIHS•tuhnts). Sherman laid siege, finally forcing Hood to abandon the city on September 1. Among white Southerners, the mood became desperate as the prospect of defeat became more certain. Mary Chesnut, a South Carolinian who kept a diary throughout the war, wrote, "There is no hope, but we will try to have no fear."

GEOGRAPHY CONNECTION

During the final year of the war, Union troops moved through the heart of the Confederacy.

1 LOCATION Where did Sherman's March to the Sea begin and end?

2 CRITICAL THINKING
Analyzing Visuals What information on the map helps explain why Sherman was able to cause such destruction on his March to the Sea?

resistance refusal to give in

Farragut Blockades Mobile Bay

The highest-ranking officer in the Union navy was David Farragut. The son of a Spanish military man, Farragut had joined the navy when he was only 12 years old. In August 1864, he led a fleet of 18 ships through a narrow channel into Mobile Bay in Alabama. His mission was to gain control of the bay. Faced with stiff resistance, Farragut prepared for battle. To make sure he had a good view, he climbed high into the ship's rigging and had himself tied in place.

The Confederates had forts on both sides of the channel, and they had mined the water with torpedoes. Unwilling to back down, Farragut shouted his famous order: "Damn the torpedoes, full speed ahead!" The mission succeeded in blocking the last Southern port east of the Mississippi.

The Election of 1864

In the North, opposition to the war grew stronger through much of 1864. It seemed unlikely that Lincoln could win reelection in November. His loss could mean an end to the war and recognition of the Confederacy as an independent country. White Southerners clung to this hope.

After Union troops captured Atlanta and blocked Mobile Bay, however, weary Northerners began to believe again that victory was possible. In November, President Lincoln won a second term. He took 55 percent of the popular vote and 212 to 21 electoral votes over the Democratic candidate, General George B. McClellan.

Many **interpreted** Lincoln's reelection as a clear sign from the voters: They wanted a permanent end to slavery. On January 31, 1865, Congress passed the Thirteenth Amendment, which banned slavery in the United States.

☑ **PROGRESS CHECK**

Explaining Why did it seem unlikely that Lincoln would be reelected in the early part of 1864?

The War Ends

GUIDING QUESTION *What is total war?*

From the beginning of the war, a goal of the Union was to capture the Confederate capital at Richmond. Petersburg had been the last roadblock in Grant's path. After a nine-month siege, Grant finally drove Lee's army out of that city. Jefferson Davis knew that Richmond was doomed.

David Farragut led the U.S. Navy to some of its greatest victories in the Civil War.

Bettmann/CORBIS

Sherman's March to the Sea

Still, the Confederacy fought on. The Union was determined to break the South's will to continue the fight. To break this will, Sherman burned much of the city of Atlanta in November 1864. Sherman then had his troops march across Georgia toward the Atlantic, burning cities and crops as they went. This trail of destruction is known as Sherman's March to the Sea.

Sherman continued his march through the Carolinas to join Grant's forces near Richmond. Union troops took food, tore up railroad lines and fields, and killed livestock. General Sherman's march was part of a strategy called **total war.** Total war involves targeting not only the enemy's army, but also its land and people. Sherman hoped that by bringing the horrors of the war to the Southern population, he could help end the war.

White Southerners were outraged by Sherman's march. Thousands of African Americans, however, left their plantations to follow the protection of his army. For them, the March to the Sea was a march to freedom.

Richmond Falls

Meanwhile, Grant continued the siege of Petersburg. Lee and his troops defended the town, but sickness, casualties, and desertion weakened them. Finally, on April 2, 1865, the Confederate lines broke and Lee withdrew.

Word of Lee's retreat soon reached the Confederate president. As the Union army marched toward Richmond, Davis and his cabinet prepared to leave. They gathered documents and ordered that bridges and weapons useful to the enemy be burned. Then they fled the city. An observer wrote:

When the Union army marched into the Confederate capital after the 11-month siege, they found the city in ruins and still burning.

PRIMARY SOURCE

❝The trains came and went, wagons, vehicles, and horsemen rumbled and dashed to and fro. . . . As night came on . . . rioting and robbing took place. ❞

—from *Battles and Leaders of the Civil War*

The armory, with its stores of ammunition, exploded. Boom after boom rang through the city, and fires raged out of control.

On April 3, President Lincoln visited the captured town of Petersburg. Later, Lincoln confided to naval officer David Porter, "Thank God I have lived to see this. It seems to me that I have been dreaming a horrid nightmare for four years, and now the nightmare is gone."

President Lincoln, his son Tad, and a group of military officials arrived in Richmond on April 4 to tour the fallen Confederate capital. As Lincoln walked through the streets, joyful African Americans followed—singing, laughing, and reaching out to touch the president.

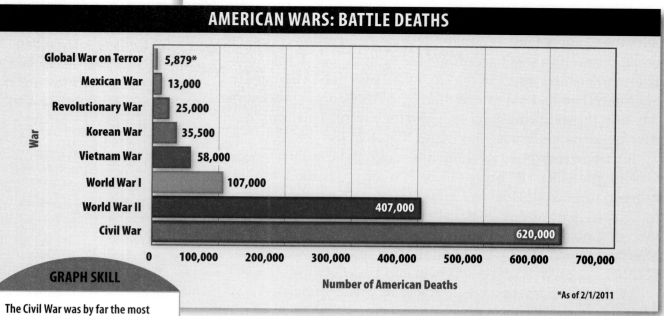

AMERICAN WARS: BATTLE DEATHS

War

War	Number of American Deaths
Global War on Terror	5,879*
Mexican War	13,000
Revolutionary War	25,000
Korean War	35,500
Vietnam War	58,000
World War I	107,000
World War II	407,000
Civil War	620,000

Number of American Deaths

*As of 2/1/2011

GRAPH SKILL

The Civil War was by far the most costly war in terms of lives lost of any conflict in American history.

1 CALCULATING How many more Americans died in the Civil War than in the second-most-costly war?

2 CRITICAL THINKING
Analyzing What makes the Civil War different from the other wars in this graph besides the higher number of war dead?

When one man knelt down to thank him, Lincoln told him, "Don't kneel to me. You must kneel to God only, and thank Him for your freedom."

At the home of Confederate president Davis, Lincoln sat wearily for a while on a chair in the president's office. After visiting two prisons for Confederate prisoners, Lincoln replied to a question about what to do with captured Confederates: "If I were in your place, I'd let 'em up easy, let 'em up easy."

As a child, Dallas Tucker witnessed the arrival of Union troops in his hometown of Richmond, Virginia. He later recalled:

PRIMARY SOURCE

❝[There was] a tremendous shock, which rocked the house and rattled the windows. At first we thought it was an earthquake, but very soon concluded . . . it must be an explosion of some kind. . . . It was, in fact, the blowing up of the government powder magazine just beyond the city limits. . . . Richmond was on fire. . . . In sheer despair, warehouse after warehouse was thrown open, and the gathered crowd of hungry, despairing people were told to go in and help themselves.

. . . Just as I reached the Washington Monument, I [saw] the troops entering [Capital] Square. . . . It was then only a few minutes later . . . that I saw the United States flag appear on the flag-pole above, where the Stars and Bars [the Confederate flag] had floated for years.❞

— Reverend Dallas Tucker, writing in the *Richmond Dispatch*, February 3, 1902

Reading **HELP**DESK

Build Vocabulary: *Word Origins*

The word *compassion* was first used in the fourteenth century. Its origin is a compound word from Latin: *compati*. The prefix *com* means "with," and the root *pati* means "suffer" or "bear."

A Meeting at Appomattox Court House

The formal end of the war came on April 9, 1865. Two days earlier, Grant had asked Lee to surrender, writing, "The result of last week must convince you of the hopelessness of further resistance." At first, Lee had believed he must fight on. Then, the Union captured the train carrying food to his starving troops and completely surrounded his army. Lee knew it was over.

Grant met with Lee in a small Virginia town called Appomattox Court House. The two men shook hands and talked a little. Then Grant offered his terms: Lee's officers could keep their small firearms, and any soldier with a horse could keep it. No one would disturb the soldiers as they made their way home. Grant also gave 25,000 rations to feed Lee's troops. America's deadliest war ended with dignity and compassion.

The Toll of War

More lives were lost in the Civil War than in any other conflict in American history. The war cost billions of dollars and left many Southern cities and farms in ruins.

The North's victory saved the Union. The war also made clear that the national government was more powerful than the states. Finally, the war freed millions of African Americans. As you will read, however, the end of slavery left unsettled many of the problems that newly freed African Americans were to face.

Many questions remained. No one yet knew how to bring the Southern states back into the Union, nor what the status of African Americans would be in Southern society. Americans would struggle to answer these questions in the years ahead—an era known as Reconstruction.

Nearly 4 million people served in the military forces during the Civil War.

☑ **PROGRESS CHECK**

Explaining Why did General Lee finally surrender?

Library of Congress LC-B8184-10575

LESSON 5 REVIEW

Review Vocabulary

1. How did total war affect civilians of the Confederacy?

Answer the Guiding Questions

2. ***Explaining*** How did events on the battlefield affect Lincoln's reelection?

3. ***Identifying Cause and Effect*** Why did Sherman burn and destroy the South's land?

4. ***Evaluating*** Why did the war leave the U.S. government stronger than ever before?

5. **NARRATIVE WRITING** You are a reporter covering Lee's army at the time of his surrender. Write a brief article describing the events surrounding his meeting with Grant.

Write your answers on a separate piece of paper.

1 Exploring the Essential Question

EXPOSITORY WRITING Write a short essay that describes the impact civilians had on the war effort. Include references to the North and the South.

2 21st Century Skills

COMMUNICATING Assume the point of view of an adviser to President Lincoln. Write an argument in favor of enlisting African Americans in the Union cause.

3 Thinking Like a Historian

DRAWING INFERENCES AND CONCLUSIONS Based on the events leading up to the end of the war, how do you think soldiers on each side felt about Lee's surrender at Appomattox? How might enslaved African Americans have felt? Write a paragraph that addresses these questions.

4 Visual Literacy

ANALYZING POLITICAL CARTOONS Look at the images and read the caption of this cartoon. What do the men on either side of Lincoln represent? What are the "two difficulties" the president faces?

LINCOLN'S TWO DIFFICULTIES.

Lin. "WHAT? NO MONEY! NO MEN!"

CORBIS

REVIEW THE GUIDING QUESTIONS
Choose the best answer for each question.

1 What was one advantage the Southern states had during the Civil War?

A. They received military support from Britain and France.

B. The largest weapons factories were located in the South.

C. They were more familiar with the places where most battles occurred.

D. Most people in the North and South supported the Confederacy's effort to form an independent country.

2 Gaining control of the Mississippi River enabled the Union to

F. surround the Confederacy.

G. force the Confederacy to surrender.

H. defeat the Confederate forces at Gettysburg.

I. split the Confederacy into smaller parts.

3 During the war, the economy of the Confederacy was

A. severely strained by the Union blockade and the destruction of Southern land and property.

B. unchanged because most of the battles took place on Northern soil.

C. strengthened due to inflation.

D. strengthened by bounties paid to army recruits.

4 Which of the following is one advantage the Union had over the South?

F. They had greater numbers of troops.

G. They knew the terrain better than the Southern troops did.

H. They had stronger military leadership.

I. They had a strong fighting spirit.

5 The city of Atlanta was burned

A. as the result of an accident caused by Union troops marching through.

B. as part of Sherman's total war strategy.

C. by Confederate troops trying to stop Union forces from taking the city.

D. after a freak lightning strike set the docks on fire.

6 Control of the sea was significant during the Civil War because

F. the Union was able to block France and Britain's attempts to send arms to the Confederacy.

G. the Union was able to cut off the Confederates' ability to export goods.

H. the Confederacy was able to stop the Union from trading with Europe.

I. President Lincoln was a former navy officer.

DBQ DOCUMENT-BASED QUESTIONS

Frederick Douglass led the movement to allow African American men to enlist in the Union armed forces.

> "Once let the black man get upon his person the brass letters U.S. ... and a musket on his shoulder and bullets in his pocket, and there is no power on earth that can deny that he has earned the right to citizenship."
>
> —from James M. McPherson, *Battle Cry of Freedom*

7 **Identifying Main Ideas** How does Douglass think enlisting will help African Americans?

A. He believes they would enjoy having a uniform to wear.

B. He believes that it will earn African Americans the right to citizenship.

C. He thinks that only African Americans can free enslaved people.

D. Serving in the army will give them the experience to fight slaveholders.

8 **Making Inferences** From this excerpt, you can infer that Douglass believes that African Americans

F. have not earned the right to citizenship.

G. must fight to prove themselves worthy of citizenship.

H. will prove to be an unstoppable force in battle.

I. already deserve citizenship.

SHORT RESPONSE

> "With malice toward none, with charity for all, with firmness in the right as God gives us to see the right, let us strive on to finish the work we are in, to bind up the nation's wounds, to care for him who shall have borne the battle and for his widow and his orphan—to do all which may achieve and cherish a just and lasting peace among ourselves and with all nations."
>
> —from Abraham Lincoln's Second Inaugural Address

9 State two reasons Lincoln did not focus on Union victory in the war.

10 What do you think Lincoln's main goal is in this speech?

EXTENDED RESPONSE

11 **Expository Writing** Write an essay predicting what will happen in the United States in the years following the war.

Need Extra Help?

If You've Missed Question	**1**	**2**	**3**	**4**	**5**	**6**	**7**	**8**	**9**	**10**	**11**
Review Lesson	1	2, 4	3	1	5	2	4	4	5	5	1–5

The Reconstruction Era

1865–1896

ESSENTIAL QUESTION: *How do new ideas change the way people live?*

In the years leading up to the Civil War and after, Frederick Douglass was a leading voice for African American rights.

Bettmann/CORBIS

networks

There's More Online about events of the Reconstruction era.

CHAPTER 18

Lesson 1
Planning Reconstruction

Lesson 2
The Radicals Take Control

Lesson 3
The South During Reconstruction

Lesson 4
The Post-Reconstruction Era

The Story Matters . . .

Frederick Douglass has done as much as any American in winning freedom for African Americans. Formerly enslaved, Douglass became a powerful voice for the abolitionist cause. During the Civil War, he shared his advice with President Lincoln himself. Now, he is looking forward to the rebuilding of the nation—Reconstruction. He says, "Whether the tremendous war so heroically fought and so victoriously ended shall pass into history a miserable failure . . . must be determined one way or another by the present session of Congress." In this chapter, you will read about Congress's response to Douglass's challenge.

Place and Time: United States 1865 to 1896

After the Civil War, the federal government faced the task of putting the nation back together. At the same time, the nation continued to grow and confront a variety of challenges all across the continent.

Step Into the Place

MAP FOCUS The federal government admitted Southern states back into the Union, and the nation sought to establish control of the West.

1 **PLACE** Which former Confederate state was the first to rejoin the Union?

2 **HUMAN-ENVIRONMENT INTERACTION** Which states and territories are likely to be impacted by completion of the transcontinental railroad? Explain your answer.

3 **CRITICAL THINKING** *Making Inferences* Why do you think different states reentered the Union at different times?

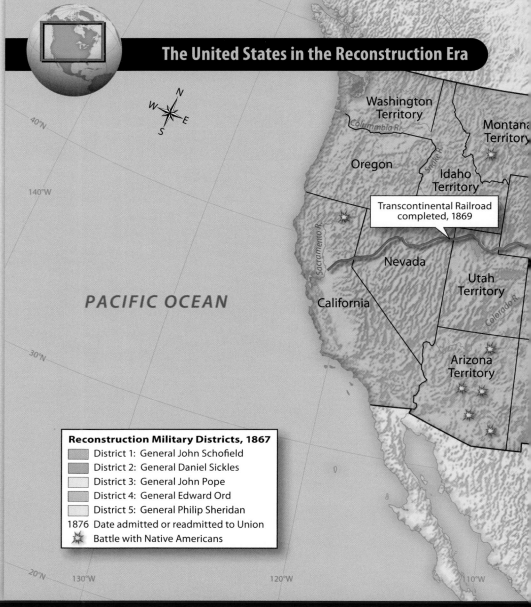

The United States in the Reconstruction Era

Washington Territory
Columbia R.
Montana Territory
Oregon
Idaho Territory
Transcontinental Railroad completed, 1869
Snake R.
Sacramento R.
Nevada
Utah Territory
Colorado R.
California
PACIFIC OCEAN
Arizona Territory

Reconstruction Military Districts, 1867
District 1: General John Schofield
District 2: General Daniel Sickles
District 3: General John Pope
District 4: General Edward Ord
District 5: General Philip Sheridan
1876 Date admitted or readmitted to Union
Battle with Native Americans

Step Into the Time

TIME LINE Look at the time line. When was the First Reconstruction Act passed? How much longer did Reconstruction last?

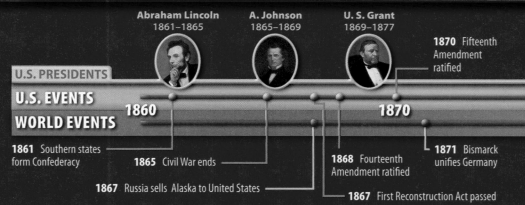

Abraham Lincoln 1861–1865
A. Johnson 1865–1869
U. S. Grant 1869–1877

U.S. PRESIDENTS
U.S. EVENTS
WORLD EVENTS

1860
1870

1870 Fifteenth Amendment ratified

1861 Southern states form Confederacy

1865 Civil War ends

1867 Russia sells Alaska to United States

1868 Fourteenth Amendment ratified

1867 First Reconstruction Act passed

1871 Bismarck unifies Germany

White House Historical Association

networks

There's More Online!

☑ **MAP** Explore the interactive version of this map on NETWORKS.

☑ **TIME LINE** Explore the interactive version of this time line on NETWORKS.

CANADA

New Hampshire — Maine

Vermont

Massachusetts

Missouri R.

Minnesota

L. Superior

New York

Rhode Island

Connecticut

Dakota Territory

Wisconsin

L. Huron

L. Michigan

Michigan

L. Ontario

Pennsylvania

New Jersey

Wyo Terr.

L. Erie

Iowa

Great Chicago Fire, 1871

Mississippi R.

Delaware

Maryland

Nebraska 1867

Ohio

Platte R.

Illinois

Ind.

W. Va.

Virginia 1870

Colorado 1876

10th Cavalry, Buffalo Soldiers

Exodusters, 1879

Kansas

Missouri

Kentucky

Ohio R.

North Carolina 1868

ATLANTIC OCEAN

New Mex. Terr.

Arkansas R.

Indian Territory

Arkansas 1868

Tennessee 1866

Tennessee R.

South Carolina 1868

9th Cavalry, Buffalo Soldiers

Miss. 1870

Alabama 1868

Georgia 1870

Mississippi R.

Texas 1870

La. 1868

Florida 1868

Rio Grande

Gulf of Mexico

MEXICO

| 0 | 300 miles |
| 0 | 300 km |

Lambert Azimuthal Equal-Area projection

60°W

40°N

30°N

90°W   80°W   70°W

| R. B. Hayes 1877–1881 | James Garfield 1881 | Chester Arthur 1881–1885 | Grover Cleveland 1885–1889 | Benjamin Harrison 1889–1893 | Grover Cleveland 1893–1897 |

1880   **1890**   **1900**

1877 Reconstruction ends

1882 Egypt comes under British control

1891 Famine spreads across Russia

1896 Ethiopia defeats invading Italians

1879–1880 Edison perfects the electric incandescent lightbulb

1889 Hull House opens in Chicago

networks
There's More Online!
- ☑ **GRAPHIC ORGANIZER** Reconstruction Plans
- ☑ **SLIDE SHOW**
  - Reconstruction in the South
  - Lincoln's Funeral Procession

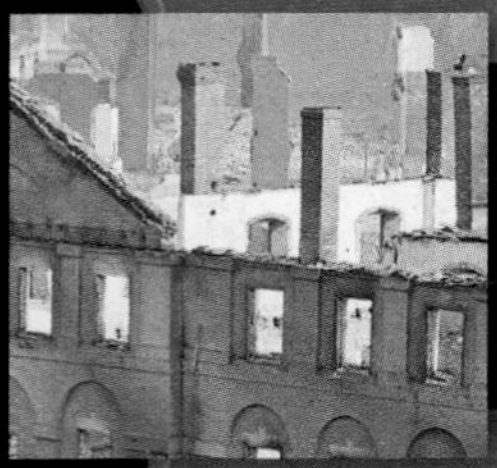
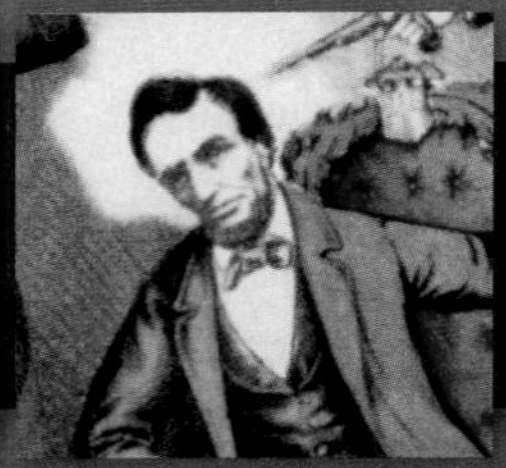
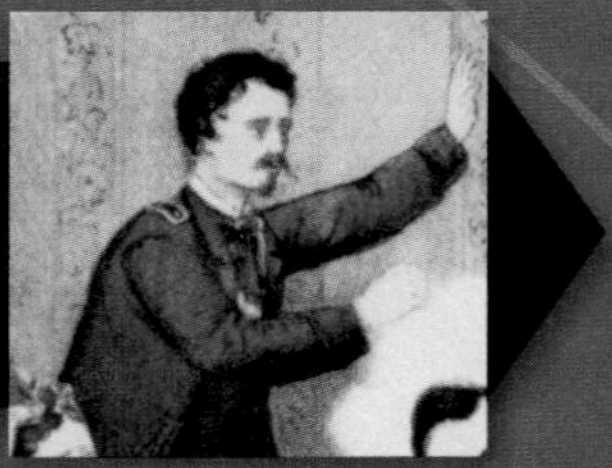

Lesson 1
Planning Reconstruction

ESSENTIAL QUESTION *How do new ideas change the way people live?*

It Matters Because
Plans for Reconstruction after the Civil War proved difficult and divisive.

The Reconstruction Debate

GUIDING QUESTION *Why did leaders disagree about the South rejoining the Union?*

The Confederate states tried and failed to break away from the United States. Now, they had to rejoin that Union. In addition, the war left the South's economy and society in ruins. It would take much effort to restore the states that had experienced so much destruction during the war.

The task of rebuilding the former Confederate states and readmitting them to the Union was called **Reconstruction** (ree•kuhn•STRUHK•shuhn). The president and members of Congress had different ideas about how to achieve these goals. The debate over Reconstruction led to bitter conflict in the years following the Civil War.

Lincoln's Ten Percent Plan

President Lincoln offered the first plan for bringing Southern states back into the Union. In December 1863, while the Civil War still raged, Lincoln presented his ideas. Lincoln's plan required voters in each Southern state to take an oath of loyalty to the Union. When 10 percent of the voters in a state had taken the oath, the state could form a new state government. The state would also be required to adopt a new constitution that banned

(l) Library of Congress [LC-DIG-cwpb-03370], (c & r) Library of Congress LC-USZC4-1155

Reading **HELP**DESK

Taking Notes: *Summarizing*

Using a graphic organizer like the one shown here, write short summaries of the Reconstruction plans proposed by Abraham Lincoln, the Radical Republicans, and Andrew Johnson.

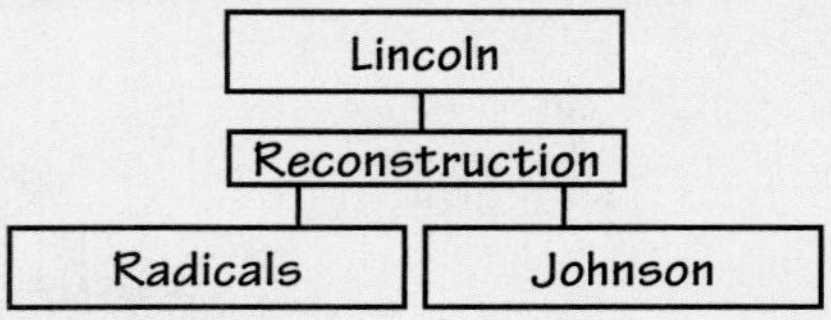

Content Vocabulary
- **Reconstruction**
- **amnesty**

slavery. Once a state had met these conditions, it could send representatives to Congress. Lincoln's proposal was known as the Ten Percent Plan.

Lincoln did not want to punish the South after the war ended. He believed that punishment would accomplish little and would slow the nation's healing from the war. Lincoln wanted to see white Southerners who supported the Union take charge of their state governments. He offered **amnesty** (AM•nuh•stee)—forgiveness for any crimes committed—to those who would swear loyalty to the Union. Only Confederate leaders would not be offered amnesty.

In 1864, three states—Louisiana, Arkansas, and Tennessee—set up new governments under Lincoln's plan. Congress, however, was not willing to accept the new states. It refused to seat their senators and representatives.

The Radical Republicans

Some members of Congress thought Lincoln's plan went too easy on the South. A group of Republican representatives favored a more **radical** approach to Reconstruction. This group was known as the Radical Republicans, or the Radicals. Radical leader Thaddeus Stevens said that Southern institutions "must be broken up and relaid, or all our blood and treasure have been spent in vain." The Radicals were powerful. The Republican Party controlled Congress, and the Radicals had much influence in the party. Congress could—and did—vote to deny seats to any state that sought to reenter the Union under Lincoln's plan.

The city of Richmond, Virginia, shown here, was the capital of the Confederacy and an industrial center.

▶ **CRITICAL THINKING**
Determining Cause and Effect What challenges do you think this type of destruction presented to the economy of Virginia?

Library of Congress [LC-DIG-cwpb-03370]

Reconstruction the period of rebuilding the South and readmitting Southern states into the Union
amnesty the granting of a pardon to a large number of persons

Academic Vocabulary
radical extreme

Acting on his sympathies for the Confederacy, John Wilkes Booth assassinated President Lincoln on April 14, 1865. Lincoln had had less than a week to celebrate the Union victory.

▶ **CRITICAL THINKING**
Analyzing Images How does the artist use actions of the people in this picture to create a mood? Explain your answer.

In July 1864, Congress passed its plan for Reconstruction. The Wade-Davis Bill stated that to rejoin the Union, a state must meet three requirements. First, a majority of the state's white male adults had to pledge loyalty to the Union. Second, only white males who swore they had not fought against the Union could vote for delegates to a state constitutional convention. Third, all new state constitutions had to ban slavery. The bill also barred former Confederates from holding public office.

Lincoln objected to the harshness of this plan. Lincoln wanted new state governments to be quickly established and the rebuilding of the South to get underway. Because Congress was about to end its session, he was able to "pocket veto" the bill: He refused to sign it, and the bill died after Congress adjourned. Still, the Wade-Davis Bill made President Lincoln realize that he would have to compromise with the Radicals.

Founding the Freedmen's Bureau

In March 1865, Lincoln and Congress together created the Freedmen's Bureau. Its main purpose was to help African Americans **adjust** to life after slavery. The Freedmen's Bureau provided food, clothing, and medical care to poor Southerners, especially those freed from slavery. It set up schools, some staffed with teachers from the North. The bureau helped some people get their own land to farm or find work for fair pay.

☑ **PROGRESS CHECK**

Listing What were the three requirements for rejoining the Union stated in the Wade-Davis Bill?

Reading **HELP**DESK

Academic Vocabulary

adjust to become more suited to new conditions

Johnson's Reconstruction Plan

GUIDING QUESTION *How did Lincoln's assassination change the plans for the South rejoining the Union?*

Events took a dramatic turn on the night of April 14, 1865. As the president enjoyed a play at Ford's Theater in Washington, D.C., actor and Confederate sympathizer John Wilkes Booth shot Lincoln in the head. Hours later, Lincoln died.

News of the president's assassination swept across the nation. African Americans mourned the death of the man who helped bring an end to slavery. White Northerners grieved for the president who had restored the Union.

Vice President Andrew Johnson became president. Although he was a Southerner, Johnson had supported the Union during the Civil War. Johnson had his own ideas about rebuilding the South. His Reconstruction plan gave amnesty to most Southerners who swore loyalty to the Union. However, high-ranking Confederates could receive pardons only by appealing to the president. This part of his plan was meant to humiliate Confederate leaders. He believed that they had tricked other Southerners into secession. Johnson also opposed equal rights for African Americans. "White men alone must manage the South," he stated.

President Johnson's plan did require that Southern states outlaw slavery before they could rejoin the Union. They also had to ratify the Thirteenth Amendment to the Constitution. Passed by Congress in January 1865, the Thirteenth Amendment abolished slavery in the United States. By the end of 1865, all former Confederate states except Texas had set up new governments under Johnson's plan. These newly reformed states were now ready to rejoin the Union.

☑ **PROGRESS CHECK**

Specifying What did the Thirteenth Amendment accomplish?

LESSON 1 REVIEW

Review Vocabulary

1. Explain the meaning of the term *Reconstruction*.

2. Use the word *amnesty* in a sentence.

Answer the Guiding Questions

3. *Explaining* What was the nature of the disagreement about the terms under which former Confederate states might rejoin the Union after the Civil War?

4. *Speculating* How would Lincoln's assassination affect the debate over Reconstruction?

5. **EXPOSITORY WRITING** You have been hired by the newly formed Freedmen's Bureau to promote the new organization. Write a brief description of the bureau, its work, and why it is important to the future of the nation.

Lesson 2

The Radicals Take Control

ESSENTIAL QUESTION *How do new ideas change the way people live?*

IT MATTERS BECAUSE

Reconstruction under the Radical Republicans advocated rights for African Americans and harsh treatment of former Confederates.

Protecting African Americans' Rights

GUIDING QUESTION *How did the North attempt to assist African Americans in the South?*

In 1865 former Confederate states began creating new governments based on President Johnson's plan. These states elected leaders to again represent them in the Congress. When the new senators and representatives arrived in Washington, D.C., Congress would not seat them. The Radical Republicans were not willing to readmit the Southern states on Johnson's easy terms. Radicals were determined to make the former Confederacy's return to the Union difficult for the white South.

Black Codes and Civil Rights

Events in the South strengthened the Radicals' determination. By early 1866, legislatures in the Southern states had passed laws called **black codes.** These laws were designed to help control the newly freed African Americans. Some black codes made it illegal for African Americans to own or rent farms. The laws also made it easy for white employers to take advantage of African American workers. Some black codes allowed officials to fine or

---

Reading HELPDESK

Taking Notes: *Determining Cause and Effect*

As you read, take notes on the impact of the Fourteenth and Fifteenth Amendments on African Americans. Use a diagram like the one shown here to organize your notes.

| Fourteenth Amendment | → | |
| Fifteenth Amendment | → | |

Content Vocabulary
• **black codes**
• **override**
• **impeach**

even arrest African Americans who did not have jobs. To freed men and women and their supporters, life under the black codes was little better than slavery.

At the same time, Congress tried to protect the rights of the South's African Americans. In 1866 it passed a bill that gave the Freedmen's Bureau new powers. The Bureau could now set up special courts to try persons charged with violating African Americans' rights. African Americans could sit on the juries in these courts and judge accused white Southerners.

To combat the black codes, Radical Republicans pushed the Civil Rights Act of 1866 through Congress. This law gave the federal government power to get involved in state affairs to protect African Americans' rights. It also granted citizenship to African Americans. This act was meant to counter the Supreme Court decision in the 1857 case *Dred Scott* v. *Sandford*. The Supreme Court had ruled that African Americans were not citizens.

President Johnson vetoed both bills. He claimed that the federal government was exceeding its authority. Johnson also argued that both bills were unconstitutional. He reasoned that they had been passed by a Congress that did not include representatives from all the states. By raising this issue, he was warning that he would veto any law passed by a Congress in which the South was not represented.

Republicans in Congress were able to **override,** or defeat, both vetoes, and the bills became law. Radical Republicans began to see that Congress and Johnson would not be able to work together on Reconstruction. They gave up hope of compromising with the president and began to create their own plan for dealing with the South.

The Fourteenth Amendment

Congress did worry that the courts might overturn the Civil Rights Act. It proposed another amendment to the Constitution, which the states ratified in 1868. The Thirteenth Amendment had ended slavery. The Fourteenth Amendment took the next step by stating that:

PRIMARY SOURCE

❝ All persons born or naturalized in the United States, and subject to the jurisdiction thereof, are citizens of the United States and of the State wherein they reside. ❞

—the Fourteenth Amendment

Radical Republicans such as Charles Sumner of Massachusetts were determined not only to rebuild the South but also to remake Southern society.

Stock Montage/Archive Photos/Getty Images

black codes laws passed in the South just after the Civil War aimed at controlling freed men and women, and allowing plantation owners to take advantage of African American workers

override to reject or defeat something that has already been decided

This language protected the citizenship extended to African Americans by the Civil Rights Act of 1866. It guaranteed that citizenship could not later be taken away by passing another law. The amendment made it clear that if a state barred any adult male citizen from voting, that state could lose some representation in Congress.

Another part of the Fourteenth Amendment said that no state could take a person's life, liberty, or property "without due process of law." It stated that every person was entitled to "equal protection of the laws." It also **excluded** former Confederate leaders from holding any national or state office unless Congress had pardoned them.

Some people considered amending the Constitution to protect African Americans to be an extreme measure. Increasing violence toward African Americans across the South convinced moderate Republicans that an amendment was necessary. Congress required that the Southern states ratify the Fourteenth Amendment as another condition of rejoining the Union. Because most refused to do so at first, this delayed the amendment's ratification until 1868.

✓ PROGRESS CHECK

Defining Identify two key features of the Civil Rights Act of 1866.

North Wind Picture Archives

White mobs killed nearly 50 African Americans and burned their homes, churches, and schools in Memphis, Tennessee, in May 1866. Reactions to such violence helped Republicans win an overwhelming victory in the 1866 elections.

▶ **CRITICAL THINKING**
Making Connections Why would such violent acts have helped Republicans win elections?

Reading **HELP**DESK

Academic Vocabulary

exclude to prevent from being involved in something

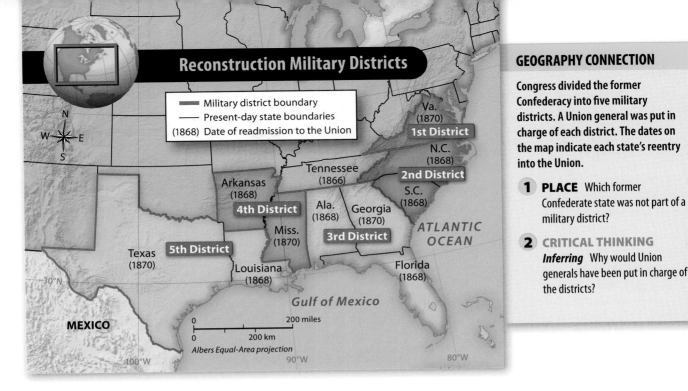

Reconstruction Military Districts

Military district boundary
Present-day state boundaries
(1868) Date of readmission to the Union

Va. (1870)
1st District
N.C. (1868)
Tennessee (1866)
2nd District
S.C. (1868)
Arkansas (1868)
4th District
Ala. (1868)
Georgia (1870)
3rd District
Miss. (1870)
Texas (1870)
5th District
Louisiana (1868)
Florida (1868)
ATLANTIC OCEAN
Gulf of Mexico
MEXICO

0   200 miles
0   200 km
Albers Equal-Area projection

GEOGRAPHY CONNECTION

Congress divided the former Confederacy into five military districts. A Union general was put in charge of each district. The dates on the map indicate each state's reentry into the Union.

1 PLACE Which former Confederate state was not part of a military district?

2 CRITICAL THINKING
Inferring Why would Union generals have been put in charge of the districts?

Radical Republicans in Charge

GUIDING QUESTION *What elements were included in the Radical Republican idea of Reconstruction?*

President Johnson campaigned against the Radical Republicans in the congressional elections of 1866. He attacked the Fourteenth Amendment and made it a major issue in the campaign. Many Northerners disliked Johnson's tone. Some feared the clashes between whites and African Americans that were taking place in the South. Voters rejected Johnson's views, and the Republicans won an overwhelming majority in Congress. This meant that Johnson could no longer prevent them from overriding his vetoes. A period known as Radical Reconstruction began.

The Reconstruction Acts

By 1867, 10 of the former Confederate states had not ratified the Fourteenth Amendment. In response, Congress passed the First Reconstruction Act. This law required that those states form new governments. Only Tennessee, which had ratified the amendment, kept its government and rejoined the Union.

The act divided the 10 defiant states into five military districts. Each district would be governed by an army general until new state governments were formed. Former Confederate leaders were banned from serving in these new governments. Each state also had to submit a new state constitution to Congress for approval. Finally, the act guaranteed African American men the right to vote in state elections. A Second Reconstruction Act empowered the army to register voters in each district and to help organize state constitutional conventions.

Many white Southerners refused to take part in the elections for constitutional conventions and new state governments. Thousands of newly registered African Americans did cast ballots. These developments favored the Republicans, who took control of Southern state governments. By 1868, Alabama, Arkansas, Florida, Georgia, Louisiana, North Carolina, and South Carolina had set up new governments, ratified the Fourteenth Amendment, and rejoined the Union. By 1870, the remaining three states—Mississippi, Virginia, and Texas—had also been readmitted.

Impeaching the President

The Constitution makes the president the commander in chief of the military. This gave President Johnson control over the military governors created by the First Reconstruction Act.

Because Johnson strongly opposed the Reconstruction Acts, Congress passed a series of laws to limit his power. One of these laws was the Tenure of Office Act. This law stated that the president could not remove government officials, including members of his own cabinet, without the Senate's approval. Congress wanted to protect Secretary of War Edwin Stanton. Stanton was the cabinet official in charge of the military and a supporter of Radical Reconstruction.

Tensions between Johnson and the Radical Republicans continued to grow. In August 1867, while Congress was not in session, Johnson **suspended** Stanton—temporarily stopped him from working—without the Senate's approval. When the Senate met again, it refused to approve the suspension. Johnson then fired Stanton. This action deliberately violated the Tenure of Office Act. Johnson also appointed people the Radical Republicans opposed to command some of the military districts in the South.

The House of Representatives voted to **impeach** (ihm•PEECH) President Johnson—that is, formally charge him with wrongdoing. In 1868 the case went to the Senate for a trial. The trial lasted almost three months. Johnson's defenders claimed that the president had exercised his right to challenge laws he considered unconstitutional. They argued that the House had impeached Johnson for political reasons. Johnson's critics said that Congress had supreme power to make the laws and that Johnson's use of the veto interfered with that power.

This ticket entitled the holder to attend the impeachment trial of President Johnson.

▶ **CRITICAL THINKING**
Speculating Why might Johnson's conviction and removal have weakened the office of president?

North Wind Picture Archives

The Senate did not get the two-thirds majority it needed to convict President Johnson. Some moderate Republicans supported the president, arguing that he should not be removed from office for political reasons. As a result, Johnson remained president until Lincoln's second term ended in 1869. During that time, President Johnson did little to interfere with Congress's Reconstruction plans.

The Fifteenth Amendment

Most Southern states had rejoined the Union by the time the presidential election of 1868 drew near. Most Americans hoped that the turbulent period of Reconstruction was over. The Republican Party rejected Johnson and instead nominated Civil War hero Ulysses S. Grant. The Democrats chose New York governor Horatio Seymour as their candidate. Most African American voters supported Grant, and he won the presidency. The election results also showed that voters continued to support Radical Reconstruction.

Congress took one more major step in Reconstruction in 1869 when it proposed the Fifteenth Amendment. This amendment guaranteed that state and federal governments could not deny the right to vote to any male citizen because of "race, color, or previous condition of servitude."

When the states ratified the Fifteenth Amendment in 1870, Republicans thought their job was largely done. They believed that they had succeeded in giving African American men the right to vote. They also thought the power of the vote would allow African Americans to better protect themselves against unfair treatment by white people. Both beliefs would prove to be too optimistic.

☑ PROGRESS CHECK

Describing How did Congress organize the South during Reconstruction?

LESSON 2 REVIEW

Review Vocabulary

1. Define each of the following terms, then use each term in a sentence.

   a. suspend   b. impeach   c. override

Answer the Guiding Questions

2. *Describing* What threats did African Americans continue to face in the South, and what measures did Congress take to deal with these threats?

3. *Analyzing* What measures did the Radical Republicans take to make Reconstruction harder for the white South?

4. **PERSUASIVE WRITING** Assume the role of President Andrew Johnson. Write a short speech to give at your trial, explaining why senators should not convict you of wrongdoing.

Lesson 3
The South During Reconstruction

ESSENTIAL QUESTION *How do new ideas change the way people live?*

IT MATTERS BECAUSE
Reconstruction brought significant—but not necessarily lasting—change to the South.

Republicans in Charge

GUIDING QUESTION *How were African Americans discouraged from participating in civic life in the South?*

Republicans controlled Southern politics during the Reconstruction period. Groups in charge of state governments supported the Republican Party. These groups included African Americans, some white Southerners, and white newcomers from the North.

African Americans in Government

Though they had fewer rights than white Southerners, African Americans greatly influenced Southern politics. During Reconstruction, African Americans played important roles as voters and as elected officials. In some states their votes helped produce victories for Republican candidates—including African American candidates. For a short time, African Americans held the majority in the lower house of the South Carolina legislature. Overall, the number of African Americans holding top positions in most Southern states during Reconstruction was small. African Americans did not control any state government. At the national level, 16 African Americans served in the House of Representatives and 2 served in the Senate between 1869 and 1880.

(l) Library of Congress/3b49620, (c & r) The Granger Collection, NYC

Reading **HELP**DESK

Taking Notes: *Classifying*

As you read, use a diagram like the one shown here to describe improvements in the education of African Americans in the South during Reconstruction.

Improvements in Education

Content Vocabulary
• **scalawag**　　• **sharecropping**
• **corruption**
• **integrate**

At the center of this picture of leading Reconstruction politicians is Frederick Douglass. Beside him are Hiram Revels (right), who in 1870 became the first African American elected to the United States Senate, and Blanche K. Bruce, who became the first African American to serve a full term in the Senate.

▶ **CRITICAL THINKING**
Making Inferences Why do you think Douglass appears at the center of this picture?

Carpetbaggers and Scalawags

Some Southern whites supported the Republican Party. These were often pro-Union business leaders and farmers who had not owned enslaved people. Former Confederates who held resentment against those who had been pro-Union called these people **scalawags** (SKA•lih•wagz), a term meaning "scoundrel" or "worthless rascal."

Republicans also had the support of many Northern whites who moved to the South after the war. White Southerners called these Northerners carpetbaggers. The term referred to cheap suitcases made of carpet fabric—what white Southerners might have thought untrustworthy newcomers might carry. White Southerners were suspicious of the Northerners' intentions. Some carpetbaggers were dishonest people looking to take advantage of the South's difficulties, but most were not. Many sincerely wanted to help rebuild the South.

White Southerners accused Reconstruction governments of **corruption** (kuh•RUHP•shuhn)—dishonest or illegal actions. Some officials did make money illegally. Yet there is no evidence that corruption in the South was greater than in the North.

Library of Congress/3b49620

scalawag name given by former Confederates to Southern whites who supported Republican Reconstruction of the South
corruption dishonest or illegal actions

Build Vocabulary: *Word Origins*

Today the term *carpetbagger* is used to criticize candidates who run for office in a place where they have not lived for long.

This picture shows a school for African American children in Charleston, South Carolina.

Resistance to Reconstruction

Life during Reconstruction was difficult for African Americans. Most Southern whites did not want African Americans to have more rights. White landowners often refused to rent land to freed people. Store owners refused them **credit.** Many employers would not hire them. Many of the jobs available to African Americans were those that whites were unwilling to do.

A more serious danger to the freed people in the South was secret societies such as the Ku Klux Klan. These groups used fear and violence to deny rights to freed men and women. Disguising themselves in white sheets and hoods, Klan members threatened, beat, and killed thousands of African Americans and the whites who supported them. Klan members burned African American homes, schools, and churches. Many Democrats, planters, and other white Southerners supported the Klan. Some saw violence as a way to oppose Republican rule.

In 1870 and 1871, Congress passed several laws to try to stop the growing Klan violence. These laws were not always effective. White Southerners often refused to testify against those in their own communities who attacked African Americans and their white supporters.

✓ **PROGRESS CHECK**

Explaining Why did many Southerners resent scalawags and carpetbaggers?

The Granger Collection, NYC

Reading **HELP**DESK

integrate to unite, or to blend into a united whole
sharecropping system of farming in which a farmer works land for an owner who provides equipment and seeds and receives a share of the crop

Academic Vocabulary

credit a loan, or the ability to pay for a good or service at a future time rather than at the time of purchase
academy a school or college for special training

Education and Farming

GUIDING QUESTION *What were some improvements and some limitations for African Americans?*

During the early days of Reconstruction, African Americans built their own schools. Many Northerners came south to teach. In the 1870s, Reconstruction governments created public schools for both races. Soon about 50 percent of white children and 40 percent of African American children attended school in the South.

African Americans also made gains in higher education. Northerners set up **academies** in the South. These academies grew into a network of colleges and universities for African Americans.

African American and white students usually went to different schools. Few states had laws requiring schools to be **integrated** (IHN•tuh•grayt•uhd). Schools that are integrated have both white and African American students. Often, integration laws were not enforced.

In addition to education, freed people wanted farmland. Having their own land would enable them to support their families. Some African Americans bought land with the help of the Freedmen's Bank. Many freed people, however, had no choice but to farm on land owned by whites.

In the **sharecropping** (SHEHR•krah•peeng) system, landowners rented land to sharecroppers, or farmers. Sharecroppers gave a percentage of their crops to the landowner. Landowners often demanded an unfairly large percentage that left sharecroppers with almost nothing to support themselves. For many, sharecropping was little better than slavery.

☑ PROGRESS CHECK

Describing How did sharecroppers get land to farm?

LESSON 3 REVIEW

Review Vocabulary

1. Use the following terms in sentences that illustrate the meaning of these terms.

   a. integrate   **b.** sharecropping

2. How are the terms *corruption* and *scalawag* connected?

Answer the Guiding Questions

3. *Explaining* In what ways was life during Reconstruction difficult for African Americans?

4. *Describing* How did education improve in the South during Reconstruction?

5. **NARRATIVE WRITING** Charlotte Forten was an African American who moved from the North to teach freed children in South Carolina. Of her students, she wrote, "The long, dark night of the Past, with all its sorrows and its fears, was forgotten; and for the Future—the eyes of these freed children see no clouds in it." Write an explanation of what you think Forten meant.

networks
There's More Online!

☑ **GRAPHIC ORGANIZER**
The New South

☑ **MAP** Election of 1876

☑ **PRIMARY SOURCE**
Sharecropper Contract

☑ **SLIDE SHOW**
Southern Textile Industry

Lesson 4
The Post-Reconstruction Era

ESSENTIAL QUESTION *How do new ideas change the way people live?*

IT MATTERS BECAUSE

After Reconstruction, a "New South" emerged, but African Americans steadily lost freedoms.

Reconstruction Ends

GUIDING QUESTION *How did Democrats regain control of Southern governments?*

As a general, Ulysses S. Grant had led the North to victory in the Civil War. His reputation as a war hero carried him into the White House in the election of 1868 and to reelection in 1872. Unfortunately, Grant had little experience in politics.

Scandal and corruption plagued Grant's presidency. In addition, a severe economic depression began during his second term. A crisis arose when a powerful banking firm declared bankruptcy. This triggered a wave of fear known as the Panic of 1873. It set off a depression that lasted much of the decade.

The depression and the scandals in the Grant administration hurt the Republican Party. In the 1874 congressional elections, the Democrats won back control of the House of Representatives. Democrats also made gains in the Senate. These changes cost the Radical Republicans much of their power.

Meanwhile, Southern Democrats worked hard to regain control of their state governments. They got help from groups such as the Ku Klux Klan, which terrorized African Americans and other Republican voters. The Democrats who came to power in the South called themselves "redeemers." They claimed to have redeemed, or saved, their states from "black Republican" rule.

(c & r) The Granger Collection, NYC

Reading **HELP**DESK

Taking Notes: *Summarizing*

As you read, use a diagram like this one to summarize the main ideas about the New South.

The New South
Goal for Industry:
Goal for Agriculture:

Content Vocabulary
• poll tax
• literacy test
• grandfather clause
• segregation
• lynching

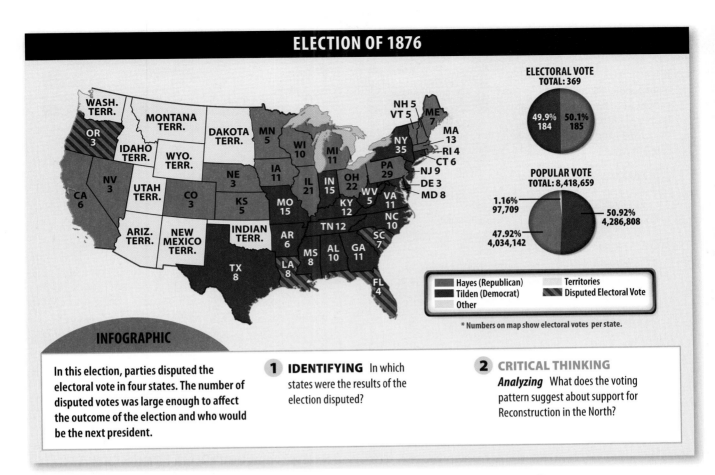

ELECTION OF 1876

ELECTORAL VOTE TOTAL: 369

49.9% 184 | 50.1% 185

POPULAR VOTE TOTAL: 8,418,659

1.16% 97,709
50.92% 4,286,808
47.92% 4,034,142

Hayes (Republican)
Tilden (Democrat)
Other
Territories
Disputed Electoral Vote

* Numbers on map show electoral votes per state.

INFOGRAPHIC

In this election, parties disputed the electoral vote in four states. The number of disputed votes was large enough to affect the outcome of the election and who would be the next president.

1 IDENTIFYING In which states were the results of the election disputed?

2 CRITICAL THINKING
Analyzing What does the voting pattern suggest about support for Reconstruction in the North?

The Election of 1876

Republicans attempted to keep control of the White House by choosing Ohio Governor Rutherford B. Hayes as their candidate for president in 1876. Hayes held moderate views on Reconstruction. Republicans hoped he would appeal to voters in both the North and the South.

Hayes ran against Democrat Samuel Tilden, the governor of New York, in a very close election. Neither got a majority of the electoral votes, mainly because of confusing election returns from three Southern states. These states—Florida, South Carolina, and Louisiana—were still under Republican rule. Republicans insisted that many voters in these states favored Hayes, but their votes had not been counted. Congress named a **commission** to decide which candidate should receive the disputed electoral votes. The commission recommended giving them all to Hayes. Doing this would make Hayes president by one electoral vote.

Connections to
TODAY

The Election of 2000

A voting dispute in Florida also affected the 2000 presidential election. An extremely close vote count led to a bitter dispute between Republican George W. Bush and Democrat Al Gore over whether and how to recount the ballots. The dispute kept either party from gaining enough electoral votes to win the election. This time, a U.S. Supreme Court ruling helped make Bush the winner and president.

Academic Vocabulary

commission a group of officials chosen for a specific responsibility

INDUSTRY IN THE NEW SOUTH

Before the Civil War, the backbone of the Southern economy was agriculture. It remained so through the rest of the nineteenth century, though industry in the region made dramatic gains.

1 **CALCULATING** About how many more manufacturing establishments did Florida have in 1900 than in 1860?

2 **CRITICAL THINKING**
Analyzing Which two Southern states experienced the greatest growth in manufacturing between 1860 and 1900? Explain.

MANUFACTURING IN THE SOUTHERN STATES 1860–1900*			
State	**1860**	**1880**	**1900**
Alabama	1,459	2,070	5,602
Arkansas	518	1,202	4,794
Florida	185	426	2,056
Georgia	1,890	3,593	7,504
Louisiana	1,744	1,553	4,350
Mississippi	976	1,479	4,772
North Carolina	3,689	3,802	7,226
South Carolina	1,230	2,078	3,762
Tennessee	2,572	4,326	8,016
Texas	983	2,996	12,289
TOTAL	**15,246**	**23,525**	**60,371**

*Number of manufacturing establishments

To ensure that Congress accepted this **outcome,** Republicans made many promises to the Democrats. One of these was a pledge to withdraw the troops who had been stationed in the South since the end of the Civil War. Shortly after Hayes took office in 1877, the last troops left the South.

Rise of the "New South"

By the 1880s, forward-looking Southerners were convinced that their region must develop an industrial economy. They argued that the South had lost the Civil War because its industry did not match the North's. Atlanta newspaper editor Henry Grady headed a group that urged Southerners to "out-Yankee the Yankees" and build a "New South." This "New South" would have industries based on the region's coal, iron, tobacco, cotton, and lumber resources. Southerners would create this new economy by embracing a spirit of hard work and regional pride.

Southern industry made great gains in the 1880s. Textile mills sprang up across the region. The American Tobacco Company, developed largely by James Duke of North Carolina, came to control nearly all of the tobacco manufacturing in the country. By 1890, the South produced nearly 20 percent of the nation's

Reading **HELP**DESK

poll tax a tax a person must pay in order to vote

Academic Vocabulary

outcome the effect or result of an action or event

iron and steel. Much of the industry was in Alabama, near deposits of iron ore. In Florida, port cities Jacksonville and Pensacola prospered because of strong demand for lumber and other products.

The South possessed a cheap and reliable supply of labor. A railroad-building boom also helped development. By 1870, the railroad system, destroyed by the war, was nearly rebuilt. Between 1880 and 1890, track mileage more than doubled.

The New South's Rural Economy

In spite of these gains, the South did not develop an industrial economy as strong as the North's. Agriculture remained the South's main economic activity.

Supporters of the New South hoped to promote small, profitable farms that grew a variety of crops instead of relying on cotton. A different economy emerged, however. Many landowners held on to their large estates. When estates were divided, much of the land went to sharecropping and tenant farming. Neither of these activities was profitable.

Debt also caused problems. Poor farmers used credit to buy supplies. Merchants who provided credit also charged high prices, and farmers' debts rose. To repay debts, farmers turned to cash crops. As in the past, the main cash crop was cotton. Higher cotton production drove cotton prices down. Lower prices led farmers to plant even more cotton. The growth of sharecropping and the heavy reliance on a single cash crop helped prevent improvements in the conditions of Southern farmers.

By 1880, a third of the South's farmers were sharecroppers or tenant farmers, systems that helped keep African Americans in a condition not much better than slavery.

 **PROGRESS CHECK**

Describing Why did Southern industry grow in the late 1800s?

A Divided Society

GUIDING QUESTION *Why did freedom for African Americans become a distant dream after Reconstruction ended?*

As Reconstruction ended, African Americans' dreams for justice faded. Laws passed by the redeemer governments denied Southern African Americans many of their newly won rights.

Voting Restrictions

The Fifteenth Amendment barred a state from denying someone the right to vote because of race. White Southern leaders found ways to get around the amendment. One way was by requiring a **poll tax,** a fee required for voting. Many African Americans could not afford to pay the tax, so they could not vote.

After Reconstruction, white Southern leaders used a variety of means to deny African Americans their right to vote.

Another means of denying voting rights was the **literacy test** (LIH•tuh•ruh•see TEHST). This approach required potential voters to read and explain difficult parts of state constitutions or the federal Constitution. Because most Southern African Americans had little education, literacy tests prevented many from voting.

Both poll taxes and literacy tests also kept some whites from voting. To prevent this, some states passed **grandfather clauses** (GRAND•fah•thuhr KLAHZ•ihz). These laws allowed people to vote if their fathers or grandfathers had voted before Reconstruction. Because African Americans could not vote until 1867, they were excluded. Such laws and the constant threat of violence caused African American voting to decline sharply.

Jim Crow Laws

By the late 1800s, segregation had also become common across the South. **Segregation** (seh•grih•GAY•shuhn) is separation of the races. Southern states passed so-called Jim Crow laws that required African Americans and whites to be separated in almost every public place. In 1896 the Supreme Court upheld segregation laws in *Plessy* v. *Ferguson*. The case involved a Louisiana law that required separate sections on trains for African Americans and whites. The Court ruled that segregation was legal as long as African Americans had access to public places equal to those of whites.

In practice, the separate facilities for African Americans were far from equal. Southern states spent much more money on schools and other facilities for whites than on those for African Americans. Still, this "separate but equal" doctrine gave legal support to segregation for more than 50 years.

Violence against African Americans also rose. One form of violence was **lynching** (LIHN•cheeng), in which angry mobs killed people by hanging them. Some African Americans were lynched because they were suspected of crimes—others because they did not act as whites thought they should.

Reading **HELP**DESK

literacy test a method used to prevent African Americans from voting by requiring prospective voters to read and write at a specified level

grandfather clause a device that allowed persons to vote if their fathers or grandfathers had voted before Reconstruction began

segregation the separation or isolation of a race, class, or group

lynching putting to death by the illegal action of a mob

Exodusters and Buffalo Soldiers

Formerly enslaved people began to leave the South during Reconstruction. They called themselves "Exodusters." This name came from the biblical book of Exodus, which describes the Jews' escape from slavery in Egypt.

During the exodus of the 1870s, more than 20,000 African Americans migrated to Kansas. They hoped their journey would take them far from the poverty that they experienced in the South. Other African Americans escaped the South by becoming soldiers. They served in segregated army units and fought in the western Indian Wars from 1867 until 1896. According to legend, the men were called "buffalo soldiers" by the Apache and Cheyenne. The soldiers adopted the name as a sign of honor and respect. Units of Buffalo Soldiers answered the nation's call to arms not only in the West, but also in Cuba, the Philippines, Hawaii, and Mexico.

Reconstruction's Impact

Reconstruction was a success in some ways and a failure in others. It helped the South rebuild its economy. Yet much of the South remained agricultural and economically poor. African Americans gained greater equality and shared power in government, but their advances did not last. In the words of the great African American writer and civil rights leader W.E.B. Du Bois, "The slave went free; stood a brief moment in the sun; then moved back again toward slavery." Yet the seeds of freedom and equality had been planted. For a long time, African Americans struggled to gain their full rights.

✓ PROGRESS CHECK

Explaining What were Jim Crow laws?

LESSON 4 REVIEW

Review Vocabulary

1. Explain the meaning of the terms by using them in a sentence.

    a. literacy test   b. poll tax

2. What was the purpose of grandfather clauses?

Answer the Guiding Questions

3. ***Describing*** In what ways was the economy of the New South different from—and similar to—the economy of the past?

4. ***Summarizing*** How did Democrats regain control of Southern governments from the Republican Party?

5. ***Explaining*** Why did freedom for African Americans become a distant dream after Reconstruction ended?

6. **EXPOSITORY WRITING** How did the South after Reconstruction compare to the South before the Civil War? Write a paragraph that answers this question.

Write your answers on a separate piece of paper.

1 Exploring the Essential Question

EXPOSITORY WRITING Would Reconstruction have taken a different course if Lincoln had not been assassinated? Write an essay to explain your answer.

2 21st Century Skills

INFORMATION LITERACY Review this chapter and draw a time line of key events during Reconstruction. Identify the event that you think had the most impact and write a short essay justifying your choice.

3 Thinking Like a Historian

MAKING COMPARISONS How were poll taxes and literacy tests similar? How were they different?

4 Visual Literacy

ANALYZING PHOTOGRAPHS Look at the image of workers processing tobacco. Write a caption for the image that explains what is happening and how it reflects the new realities of the post-Civil War South.

CORBIS

REVIEW THE GUIDING QUESTIONS

Choose the best answer for each question.

1 Which was a reason that Northern leaders disagreed over the South rejoining the Union?

A. Some leaders wanted the South to pay for damage done during the Civil War.

B. Some leaders wanted harsher treatment of the South for leaving the Union.

C. Some leaders wanted to keep slavery legal in the South.

D. Some leaders felt that allowing Southern states back into the Union would delay westward expansion.

2 Which of the following protected the rights of African Americans in the South?

F. the Civil Rights Act of 1866

G. black codes

H. Jim Crow laws

I. sharecropping and tenant farming

3 Which of the following was a method used by state governments to prevent African Americans from voting?

A. the Ten Percent Plan

B. the Wade-Davis bill

C. the Freedmen's Bureau

D. literacy tests

4 Which of the following brought major improvement to the lives of African Americans in the South?

F. sharecropping

G. the Fourteenth Amendment

H. segregation laws

I. redeemer governments

5 How did the scandals surrounding the Grant administration and the Panic of 1873 affect politics in the United States?

A. Democrats regained control of Southern governments.

B. Republicans retained control of Southern governments.

C. President Grant was impeached.

D. Jim Crow laws were enforced.

6 For many African Americans in the South, sharecropping was

F. forbidden to them.

G. highly profitable.

H. more desirable that factory work.

I. not much better than slavery.

DBQ **DOCUMENT-BASED QUESTIONS**

The following are examples of Jim Crow laws in the South.

"The schools for white children and the schools for negro children shall be conducted separately." (Florida)

"Books shall not be interchangeable between the white and colored schools, but shall continue to be used by the race first using them." (North Carolina)

—Martin Luther King, Jr., National Historic Site

7 **Specifying** Which statement best represents the purpose of these laws?

A. The laws forced separation of the races.

B. The laws denied African Americans any access to schools.

C. The laws required inferior facilities for African Americans.

D. The laws made it difficult for African Americans to get an education.

8 **Analyzing** Which of the following was an effect of the North Carolina law?

F. African American schools were not permitted to have textbooks.

G. White schools could not give textbooks to African American schools.

H. Only white schools received new textbooks.

I. No money was set aside to buy textbooks for African American schools.

SHORT RESPONSE

"I have confidence ... in the endurance, capacity and destiny of my people [African Americans]. We will ... seek our places, sometimes in the field of letters, arts, science and the professions. More frequently mechanical pursuits will attract and elicit our efforts; more still of my people will find employment ... as the cultivators of the soil. The bulk of this people—by surroundings, habits, adaptation, and choice will continue to find their homes in the South. ... Whatever our ultimate position in the ... republic ... we will not forget our instincts for freedom nor our love for country."

—Senator Blanche K. Bruce, from a speech in 1876

9 How did Bruce expect most African Americans to earn a living?

10 According to Bruce, how did African Americans feel about their country?

EXTENDED RESPONSE

11 **Expository Writing** What do you think was Reconstruction's greatest success? What was its greatest failure? Explain your answer.

Need Extra Help?

If You've Missed Question	**1**	**2**	**3**	**4**	**5**	**6**	**7**	**8**	**9**	**10**	**11**
Review Lesson	1	2	4	2	4	3	4	4	3	3	1-4

GLOSSARY/GLOSARIO

NOTE Page numbers listed below refer to the page numbers shown on the reduced student edition pages.

- Content vocabulary are words that relate to American history content.
- Words that have an asterisk (*) are academic vocabulary. They help you understand your school subjects.
- All vocabulary words are **boldfaced** or highlighted in yellow in your textbook.

abandon • amend

ENGLISH	A	ESPAÑOL

*abandon to give up; to leave behind (p. 178; p. 459)

abolitionist person who sought the end of slavery in the United States in the early and mid-1800s (pp. 408–409)

*academy a school or college for special training (pp. 506–507)

*access a way into something or someplace (pp. 348–349)

*accumulate to build up or collect (p. 250)

*acquire to get possession or control of (pp. 31–32)

*adapt to change in response to a new set of conditions (p. 97)

*adjust to become more suited to new conditions (p. 496)

*administer manage; direct (p. 445)

*administrate to carry out (p. 213)

*advocate to support (pp. 126–127)

*aid to help (p. 152)

alien a person living in a country who is not a citizen of that country (p. 259)

*allay to reduce in strength (p. 91)

alliance a partnership; system in which countries agree to defend each other or to advance common causes (p. 102)

*alter to change (pp. 38–39)

ambush an attack in which the attacker hides and surprises the enemy (p. 168)

*amend to change or revise (p. 188)

*abandonar rendirse; dejar atrás (pág. 178; pág. 459)

abolicionista persona que buscaba el fin de la esclavitud a principios y mediados del siglo XIX en Estados Unidos (págs. 408–409)

*academia escuela o universidad donde se brinda enseñanza especializada (págs. 506–507)

*acceso entrada a un objeto o un lugar (págs. 348–349)

*acumular juntar o reunir (pág. 250)

*adquirir tomar posesión o control de algo (págs. 31–32)

*adaptarse cambiar como respuesta a una nueva serie de condiciones (pág. 97)

*ajustarse hacerse más apropiado para una nueva condición (pág. 496)

*administrar gerenciar; dirigir (pág. 445)

*administrar llevar a cabo (pág. 213)

*defender respaldar (págs. 126–127)

*ayudar auxiliar (pág. 152)

extranjero persona que vive en un país sin ser ciudadano de ese país (pág. 259)

*mitigar perder fuerza (pág. 91)

alianza sociedad; sistema en el cual los países acuerdan defenderse mutuamente o promover causas comunes (pág. 102)

*alterar cambiar (págs. 38–39)

emboscada ofensiva en el que el atacante se esconde y sorprende al enemigo (pág. 168)

*enmendar cambiar o modificar (pág. 188)

amendment a change, correction, or improvement added to a document (pp. 198–199)

amnesty the granting of a pardon to a large number of persons (p. 495)

***animosity** hostility; ill will; hatred (p. 127)

annex to add a territory to one's own territory (pp. 356–357)

apprentice a person who learns a trade from a skilled craftsperson (p. 97)

***approach** to get closer to something (p. 123)

archaeology the study of material remains of ancient peoples (pp. 4–5)

armada a fleet of warships (p. 50)

arsenal a place to store weapons and military equipment (p. 437)

artifact a tool, weapon, or other object left behind by early peoples (pp. 4–5)

astrolabe an instrument used to plan a course, using the stars (pp. 30–31)

***author** writer of books, articles, or other works (pp. 406–407)

***authority** the power to influence or command thought, opinion, or behavior (p. 274)

enmienda cambio, corrección o mejora que se hace a un documento (págs. 198–199)

amnistía perdón otorgado a un gran número de personas (pág. 495)

***animosidad** hostilidad; antipatía; odio (pág. 127)

anexar agregar un territorio al propio (págs. 356–357)

aprendiz persona que aprende un oficio de un artesano experto (pág. 97)

***aproximarse** acercarse a algo (pág. 123)

arqueología estudio de los restos materiales de pueblos antiguos (págs. 4–5)

armada flota de barcos de guerra (pág. 50)

arsenal lugar para almacenar armas y equipo militar (pág. 437)

artefacto instrumento, arma u otro objeto dejado por los pueblos primitivos (págs. 4–5)

astrolabio instrumento usado para planear un recorrido valiéndose de las estrellas (págs. 31–32)

***autor** escritor de libros, artículos u otras obras (págs. 406–407)

***autoridad** facultad de influir o imponer la forma de pensar, opinar o comportarse (pág. 274)

B

barricade to block off (p. 355)

bicameral having two separate lawmaking chambers (p. 177)

black codes laws passed in the South just after the Civil War aimed at controlling freed men and women, and allowing plantation owners to take advantage of African American workers (pp. 498–499)

blockade actions that keeps a country from communicating and trading with other nations (p. 159)

bond certificate that promises to repay borrowed money with interest by a certain date (pp. 248–249)

boomtown a fast-growing community (p. 366)

barricada bloqueo (pág. 355)

bicameral que tiene dos cámaras legislativas separadas (pág. 177)

códigos negros leyes aprobadas en el Sur después de la Guerra Civil, cuyo objetivo era controlar a los hombres y mujeres libertos, y permitir a los dueños de las plantaciones aprovecharse de los trabajadores afroamericanos (págs. 498–499)

bloqueo acción que evita que un país se comunique y comercie con otras naciones (pág. 159)

bono certificado en el que se promete pagar un préstamo con intereses en una fecha determinada (págs. 248–249)

ciudad en auge comunidad de rápido crecimiento (pág. 366)

border ruffian armed supporter of slavery who crossed the border from Missouri to vote in Kansas during the mid-1850s (p. 432)

bandido de la frontera individuo armado, partidario de la esclavitud, que cruzaba la frontera desde Missouri para votar en Kansas, a mediados de la década de 1850 (pág. 432)

border state state between the North and South that was divided over whether to remain in the Union or join the Confederacy: Delaware, Maryland, Kentucky, and Missouri (pp. 452–453)

estado fronterizo estado entre el Norte y el Sur que estaba dividido con respecto a si debía permanecer en la Unión o incorporarse a la Confederación: Delaware, Maryland, Kentucky y Missouri (págs. 452–453)

bounty reward or payment (p. 470)

recompensa retribución o pago (pág. 470)

boycott to refuse to buy items in order to protest or to force acceptance of one's terms (pp. 114–115)

boicot negarse a comprar productos para protestar o con el fin de presionar para que acepten las condiciones de una persona (págs. 114–115)

*brief short (p. 395)

*breve corto (pág. 395)

bureaucracy a system of government in which specialized tasks are carried out by appointed officials rather than by elected ones (pp. 326–327)

burocracia sistema de gobierno en el cual algunas tareas especializadas son realizadas por funcionarios designados, no elegidos (págs. 326–327)

burgess elected representative to an assembly (pp. 62–63)

burgués representante elegido a una asamblea (págs. 62–63)

C

cabinet a group of advisors to a president (p. 247)

gabinete grupo de asesores de un presidente (pág. 247)

canal an artificial waterway (pp. 304–305)

canal vía fluvial artificial (págs. 304–305)

*capable skillful (p. 418)

*capaz hábil (pág. 418)

cape a point of land that sticks out into water, much like a peninsula (p. 36)

cabo punta de tierra que sobresale en el agua, semejante a una península (pág. 36)

capital money or other resources used to create wealth (p. 298)

capital dinero y demás recursos usados para generar riquezas (pág. 298)

carbon dating a scientific method of determining the age of an artifact (pp. 6–7)

datación por carbono método científico para determinar la edad de un artefacto (págs. 6–7)

cash crop a crop raised for sale in markets (p. 85)

cultivo para la venta cultivo realizado para su venta en el mercado (pág. 85)

casualty a soldier who is killed, wounded, captured, or missing in battle (p. 460)

baja soldado que es asesinado, herido, capturado o desaparecido en combate (pág. 460)

caucus a meeting of members of a political party to choose candidates for upcoming elections (p. 258)

asamblea partidista reunión de miembros de un partido político para elegir candidatos a las próximas elecciones (pág. 258)

cede to transfer control of something (p. 314)

ceder transferir el control de algo (pág. 314)

census the official count of a population (pp. 302–303)

censo conteo oficial de una población (págs. 302–303)

Glossary/Glosario

*channel a long, narrow gutter or groove (p. 16)

*canal surco largo y estrecho (pág. 16)

charter a document granting the holder the right to settle a colony (p. 61)

carta constitucional documento que da al tenedor el derecho a establecer una colonia (pág. 61)

checks and balances a system by which each branch of government limits the powers of other branches so that one branch does not become too powerful (p. 197)

equilibrio de poderes sistema en el cual cada rama del gobierno limita los poderes de las otras ramas de manera que ninguna se vuelva demasiado poderosa (pág. 197)

circumnavigate to travel completely around something (pp. 40–41)

circunnavegar viajar rodeando por completo algo (págs. 40–41)

civic virtue the democratic ideas, practices, and values that are at the heart of citizenship in a free society (p. 100)

virtud cívica ideas, prácticas y valores democráticos que son fundamentales para la ciudadanía en una sociedad libre (pág. 100)

civil disobedience refusing to obey laws considered unjust as a nonviolent way to push for change (pp. 406–407)

desobediencia civil negativa a obedecer las leyes que se consideran injustas como una forma no violenta de presionar para que haya un cambio (págs. 406–407)

civil war conflict between citizens of the same country (p. 432)

guerra civil conflicto entre ciudadanos del mismo país (pág. 432)

civilization highly developed society (pp. 8–9)

civilización sociedad altamente desarrollada (págs. 8–9)

clan a group of people who have a common ancestor (p. 20)

clan grupo de personas que tienen un ancestro común (pág. 20)

classical related to the culture of ancient Greece and Rome (p. 29)

clásico relativo a la cultura de la Grecia antigua y Roma (pág. 29)

*clause a special condition in a formal document (pp. 180–181)

*cláusula condición especial en un documento formal (págs. 180–181)

clipper ship a fast ship with sleek hulls and tall sails that "clipped" time from long journeys (p. 377)

navío rápido barco rápido con cascos pulidos y mástiles altos que "ahorraba" tiempo en viajes largos (pág. 377)

coeducation the teaching of male and female students together (p. 417)

coeducación sistema en el que se enseña a hombres y mujeres en la misma institución (pág. 417)

*commission a group of officials chosen for a specific responsibility (p. 509)

*comisión grupo de funcionarios escogidos para una responsabilidad específica (pág. 509)

committee of correspondence an organization that spread political ideas and information through Britain's American colonies (p. 117)

comité de correspondencia organización que difundía ideas políticas e información en las colonias americanas de Gran Bretaña (pág. 117)

*community group of people who live in the same area (p. 383)

*comunidad grupo de personas que viven en la misma área (pág. 383)

compass an instrument that shows the direction of magnetic north (pp. 30–31)

brújula instrumento que muestra la dirección del norte magnético (págs. 30–31)

*complex highly detailed (pp. 8–9)

*complejo sumamente detallado (págs. 8–9)

*compromise a settlement of a dispute or disagreement reached by each side giving up some of what it wants in order to reach an agreement (p. 190; p. 250)

*compromiso resolución de una disputa o discrepancia a la que se llega cuando cada parte renuncia a algo de lo que desea para llegar a un acuerdo (pág. 190; pág. 250) *concurrence* agreement (p. 193)

concurrent power power shared by the states and federal government (p. 207)

conquistador Spanish explorer in the America's during the 1500s (pp. 42–43)

consequence effect or result of (p. 388)

constitution a detailed written plan for a government; a list of basic laws that support a government (p. 76; p. 367)

contact when two or more groups or objects come together (pp. 43–44)

contradict to go against or state the opposite (p. 208)

contrast to compare in terms of differences (p. 454)

convention a formal or official meeting (p. 187)

convert to change from one belief, form, or use to another (p. 102)

corruption dishonest or illegal actions (p. 505)

cotton gin a machine that removes seeds from cotton fiber (p. 297)

credit a loan, or the ability to pay for a good or service at a future time rather than at the time of the purchase (p. 506)

Crusade one of a series of expeditions Europeans made to regain control of Christian holy sites in the Middle East from the A.D. 1000s to the 1200s (pp. 28–29)

culture a people's shared values, beliefs, traditions, and behaviors (pp. 6–7)

customs duty tax collected on goods that are imported (p. 270)

concurrencia acuerdo (pág. 193)

poder concurrente poder que comparten los gobiernos estatales y el gobierno federal (pág. 207)

conquistador explorador español de América durante el siglo XVI (págs. 42–43)

consecuencia efecto o resultado (pág. 388)

Constitución plan escrito y detallado de un gobierno; conjunto de leyes básicas que respaldan un gobierno (pág. 76; pág. 367)

hacer contacto cuando dos o más grupos u objetos se acercan (págs. 43–44)

contradecir ir en contra o afirmar lo contrario (pág. 208)

contrastar comparar diferencias (pág. 454)

convención reunión formal u oficial (pág. 187)

convertir cambiar de una creencia, forma o uso a otro (pág. 102)

corrupción acciones deshonestas o ilegales (pág. 505)

almarrá máquina que elimina las semillas de la fibra de algodón (pág. 297)

crédito préstamo, o capacidad de pagar un bien o servicio en el futuro, no en el momento de la compra (pág. 506)

Cruzada una de una serie de expediciones europeas llevadas a cabo para recuperar el control de los lugares sagrados cristianos en el Medio Oriente entre los siglos XI y XIII A.D (págs. 28–29)

cultura valores, creencias, tradiciones y comportamientos que comparte un pueblo (págs. 6–7)

arancel aduanero impuesto que se cobra a los bienes importados (pág. 270)

D

debate a discussion by opposing points of view (pp. 130–131)

debtor person or country that owes money (pp. 76–77)

decree an order given by a person in authority (p. 355)

debate controversia en la que se presentan puntos de vista opuestos (págs. 130–131)

deudor persona o país que debe dinero (págs. 76–77)

decreto orden impartida por una persona que tiene autoridad (pág. 355)

depreciate to fall in value (p. 182)

depression a period when economic activity slows and unemployment increases (pp. 184–185)

*desert to leave without permission or intent to come back (p. 154)

*devote to commit oneself or one's resources to something (p. 38)

*diminish to reduce, make smaller (pp. 214–215)

*discipline the ability to follow rules and procedures (p. 130)

discrimination unfair treatment based on prejudice against a certain group (p. 383)

*distinct clearly different from the others (p. 257)

*distribute to hand out; spread around (p. 468)

diversity variety, such as of ethnic or national groups (p. 85)

domestic slave trade the trade of enslaved people among states in the United States (p. 388)

*dominate to control (p. 74–75)

draft a system of selecting people for required military service (p. 470)

*dress down a serious punishment or scolding (p. 473)

due process the legal rules and procedures established by law and guaranteed by the Constitution that the government must observe before depriving a person of life, liberty, or property (p. 214)

depreciar perder valor (pág. 182)

depresión periodo en el cual la actividad económica disminuye y el desempleo aumenta (págs. 184–185)

*desertar abandonar sin permiso ni intención de regresar (pág. 154)

*dedicar comprometerse a sí mismo o comprometer los recursos propios en algo (pág. 38)

*disminuir reducir, hacer más pequeño (págs. 214–215)

*disciplina capacidad de seguir reglas y procedimientos (pág. 130)

discriminación trato injusto basado en un prejuicio contra un grupo determinado (pág. 383)

*distinto claramente diferente de los demás (pág. 257)

*distribuir entregar; dispersar (pág. 468)

diversidad variedad, por ejemplo de grupos étnicos o nacionales (pág. 85)

comercio interno de esclavos comercio de personas esclavizadas entre los estados de Estados Unidos (pág. 388)

*dominar controlar (págs. 74–75)

reclutamiento sistema de selección de personas para el servicio militar obligatorio (pág. 470)

*reprimenda castigo o reprensión severos (pág. 473)

debido proceso reglas y procedimientos establecidos por la ley y que avala la Constitución, que el gobierno debe cumplir antes de privar a una persona de la vida, la libertad o la propiedad (pág. 214)

E

effigy a mocking figure representing an unpopular individual (pp. 114–115)

Electoral College a group of people named by each state legislature to select the president and vice president (pp. 196–197)

*element part of a larger whole (pp. 298–299)

efigie figura burlesca que representa a un individuo impopular (págs. 114–115)

colegio electoral grupo de personas designado por el órgano legislativo de cada estado con el fin de elegir al presidente y al vicepresidente (págs. 196–197)

*elemento parte de un todo (págs. 298–299)

*elephantine having great size (p. 317)

*elefantino de gran tamaño (pág. 317)

Emancipation Proclamation decree issued by President Abraham Lincoln freeing slaves in those parts of the Confederacy still in rebellion on January 1, 1863 (pp. 463–464)

Proclamación de la Emancipación decreto expedido por el presidente Abraham Lincoln el 1o. de enero de 1863 ordenando liberar a los esclavos de las regiones de la Confederación que aún estaban sublevadas (págs. 463–464)

embargo a prohibition or blocking of trade with a certain country (pp. 280–281)

embargo prohibición o bloqueo del comercio con un país determinado (págs. 280–281)

emigrant person who leaves his or her country to live elsewhere (p. 350)

emigrante persona que abandona su país para vivir en otro lugar (pág. 350)

*emphasis placing of stress or special importance on something (p. 99)

*enfatizar resaltar o dar especial importancia a algo (pág. 99)

*encounter to meet, come face-to-face with (p. 117; p. 478)

*encontrar reunirse, estar frente a frente (pág. 117; pág. 478)

*enforce to apply a rule or law; to carry out by force (p. 67)

*hacer cumplir aplicar una regla o ley; llevar a cabo una acción mediante el uso de la fuerza (pág. 67)

enlist to formally join a military force (p. 454)

enlistarse unirse formalmente a una fuerza militar (pág. 454)

entrench to place within a trench, or ditch, for defense; to place in a strong defensive position (pp. 474–475)

atrincherarse situarse dentro de una trinchera, o zanja, para defenderse; ubicarse en una fuerte posición de defensa (págs. 474–475)

enumerated power power specifically given Congress in the Constitution (p. 207)

poder enumerado poder conferido específicamente al Congreso en la Constitución (pág. 207)

epidemic an illness that affects large numbers of people (pp. 96–97)

epidemia enfermedad que afecta a un gran número de personas (págs. 96–97)

equal protection the equal application of the law regardless of a person's race, religion, political beliefs, or other qualities (p. 214)

igualdad ante la ley la misma aplicación de la ley sin importar la raza, la religión, las creencias políticas u otras cualidades (pág. 214)

*establish to set up or create (pp. 353–354)

*establecer instaurar o crear (págs. 353–354)

*estate a large area of land that has one owner (p. 74)

*finca gran extensión de tierra que tiene un único propietario (pág. 74)

*estimate a rough calculation of a number (pp. 6–7)

*estimado cálculo aproximado de un número (págs. 6–7)

*ethnic of or relating to national, tribal, racial, religious, language, or cultural background (p. 70)

*étnico perteneciente o relativo al origen nacional, tribal, racial, religioso, lingüístico o cultural (pág. 70)

*exclude to prevent from being involved in something; to shut out (p. 500)

*excluir evitar involucrarse en algo; dejar fuera (pág. 500)

executive branch the branch of government that executes, or carries out, the law and that is headed by the president (pp. 196–197)

poder ejecutivo rama del gobierno que ejecuta, o hace cumplir, las leyes y que está encabezada por el presidente (págs. 196–197)

*expand to increase in size or number (pp. 62–63)

*ampliar aumentar de tamaño o número (págs. 62–63)

export to sell goods to other countries; a good made in one country and then sold to another (p. 94)

exportar vender bienes a otros países; bien que se produce en un país y se vende a otro (pág. 94)

F

facilitate to help make happen (p. 326)

facilitar ayudar a que suceda (pág. 326)

famine an extreme shortage of food (pp. 384–385)

hambruna escasez extrema de alimentos (págs. 384–385)

favorite son a candidate for national office who has support mostly from his home state (pp. 324–325)

hijo predilecto candidato para un cargo nacional que tiene el respaldo de su estado de origen (págs. 324–325)

*federal relating to a national government (pp. 330–331)

*federal relativo al gobierno nacional (págs. 330–331)

federalism a form of government in which power is divided between the federal, or national, government and state government (p. 195)

federalismo forma de gobierno en la cual el poder se divide entre el gobierno federal o nacional y el gobierno estatal (pág. 195)

federation a government that links and unites different groups (p. 19)

federación gobierno que vincula y une a diferentes grupos (pág. 19)

flank the side or edge of a military formation (p. 475)

flanco lado o borde de una formación militar (pág. 475)

forty-niner fortune seeker who came to California during the Gold Rush of 1849 (pp. 365–366)

los del cuarenta y nueve buscadores de fortuna que llegaron a California durante la fiebre del oro de 1849 (págs. 365–366)

*found to start; to establish (p. 46)

*fundar iniciar; establecer (pág.46)

free enterprise a type of economy where people and businesses are free to buy, sell, and produce whatever they want, with a minimum of government intervention (p. 298)

libre empresa tipo de economía en el cual las personas y las empresas son libres de comprar, vender y producir lo que quieren, con una intervención gubernamental mínima (pág. 298)

frigate a warship (p. 286)

fragata barco de guerra (pág. 286)

fugitive person who is running away from legal authority (p. 430)

fugitivo persona que se encuentra huyendo de las autoridades (pág. 430)

*function to be in action; to operate (pp. 71–72)

*funcionar estar en acción; operar (págs. 71–72)

G

*goal something one is trying to accomplish (p. 288)

*meta algo que se trata de alcanzar (pág. 288)

grandfather clause part of southern state constitutions after the Civil War that placed high literacy and property requirements on voters whose fathers and grandfathers did not vote before 1867 (p. 512)

cláusula del abuelo parte de las constituciones estatales sureñas después de la Guerra Civil que fijaba exigentes requisitos de alfabetismo y propiedad a los electores cuyos padres y abuelos no votaban antes de 1867(pág. 512)

H

habeas corpus court order that requires police to bring a prisoner to court to explain why they are holding the person (pp. 469–470)

headright a 50-acre grant of land given to colonial settlers who paid their own way (pp. 62–63)

*heyday the peak of one's strength (p. 317)

hieroglyphics a form of writing that uses symbols or pictures to represent things, ideas, and sounds (p. 9)

*hinder to prevent (p. 421)

hábeas corpus orden judicial que exige que la policía traiga a un prisionero ante un tribunal para explicar por qué ha sido detenido (págs. 469–470)

concesión de tierras por cabeza 50 acres de tierra que se entregaban a los colonos, quienes pagaban a su manera (págs. 62–63)

*apogeo cima de la fortaleza de una persona (pág. 317)

jeroglífico forma de escritura que usa símbolos o imágenes que representan cosas, ideas y sonidos (pág. 9)

*dificultar evitar (pág. 421)

I

immigration the permanent movement of people into a country from other countries (pp. 96–97)

immunity resistance of an organism to infection or disease (p. 43)

*immutable does not change (pp. 358–359)

*impact an effect (p. 160)

impeach to formally charge a public official with misconduct in office (p. 502)

implied power authority not specifically mentioned in the Constitution but suggested in its language (pp. 210–211)

import to bring in goods from foreign countries (pp. 94–95)

*impose to force on others (p. 93)

impressment seizing people against their will and forcing them to serve in the military or other public service (p. 254)

*incorporate to include, absorb (pp. 368–369)

indentured servant laborer who agrees to work without pay for a certain period of time in exchange for passage to America (pp. 73–74)

*infallibly without fail (p. 127)

inmigración desplazamiento permanente hacia un país de personas de otros países (págs. 96–97)

inmunidad resistencia de un organismo a infecciones y enfermedades (pág. 43)

*inmutable que no cambia (págs. 358–359)

*impacto efecto (pág. 160)

recusar denunciar formalmente a un funcionario público por mala conducta en el ejercicio de su cargo (pág. 502)

poder implícito autoridad que no se menciona específicamente en la Constitución pero se sugiere en su redacción (págs. 210–211)

importar traer productos de otros países (págs. 94–95)

*imponer obligar a otros (pág. 93)

leva reclutamiento de personas contra su voluntad para obligarlas a servir en el Ejército o en otra entidad pública (pág. 254)

*incorporar incluir, absorber (págs. 368–369)

sirviente por contrato trabajador que acuerda trabajar sin un salario durante cierto tiempo a cambio de transporte hacia América (págs. 73–74)

*infaliblemente sin falla (pág. 127)

Glossary/Glosario

inflation when it takes more and more money to buy the same amount of goods; a continuous rise in prices of goods and services (p. 156)

inflación cuando se necesita cada vez más dinero para comprar la misma cantidad de bienes; aumento continuo en el precio de bienes y servicios (pág. 156)

*innovation a new development or invention (pp. 376–377)

*innovación nuevo desarrollo o invento (págs. 376–377)

*institution an organization that has an important purpose in society (pp. 336–337)

*institución organización que tiene un propósito importante en la sociedad (págs. 336–337)

integrate to unite, or to blend into a united whole (pp. 506–507)

integrar unir o mezclar en una unidad (págs. 506–507)

*intense very strong (pp. 308–309)

*intenso muy fuerte (págs. 308–309)

interchangeable part a part of a machine or device that can be replaced by another, identical part (p. 297)

parte intercambiable parte de una máquina o aparato que se puede reemplazar por otra; parte idéntica (pág. 297)

*internal within the country (p. 309)

*interno dentro del país (pág. 309)

*interpret to explain the meaning of something (p. 484)

*interpretar explicar el significado de algo (pág. 484)

interstate commerce economic activity taking place between two or more states (p. 311)

comercio interestatal actividad económica que tiene lugar entre dos o más estados (pág. 311)

*investigate to search for facts and other information about something (p. 61)

*investigar buscar hechos y otra información sobre algo (pág. 61)

*involve to include (p. 210)

*implicar incluir (pág. 210)

ironclad a warship equipped with iron plating for protection (p. 459)

acorazado barco de guerra equipado con capa de hierro para su protección (pág. 459)

Iroquois Confederacy a group of Native American nations in eastern North America joined together under one general government (p. 102)

Confederación Iroquesa grupo de naciones indígenas americanas del este de Norteamérica que se unieron bajo un gobierno general (pág. 102)

irrigate to supply water to crops by artificial means (p. 16)

irrigar suministrar agua a los cultivos por medios artificiales (pág. 16)

*issue a subject that people have different views about; to deliver or hand out (pp. 156–157; p. 254)

*asunto tema sobre el cual las personas tienen diferentes perspectivas; el término en inglés "issue" también significa "expedir" o "entregar" (págs. 156–157; pág. 254)

J

joint occupation the control and settlement of an area by two or more countries or groups (p. 349)

ocupación compartida control y establecimiento de un área por parte de dos o más países o grupos (pág. 349)

joint-stock company a business in which investors buy stock in return for a share of its future profits (p. 62)

sociedad por acciones empresa en la cual los inversionistas compran acciones a cambio de una parte en sus ganancias futuras (pág. 62)

judicial branch the branch of government that interprets the law; it includes courts that settle disputes and questions of the law (p. 197)

poder judicial rama del gobierno que interpreta las leyes; incluye los tribunales que resuelven las disputas y los asuntos relacionados con la ley (pág. 197)

judicial review power of the Supreme Court to say whether any federal, state, or local law or government action goes against the Constitution (p. 213)

revisión judicial facultad de la Corte Suprema de declarar si una ley federal, estatal o local, o una acción del gobierno van en contra de la Constitución (pág. 213)

jurisdiction a court's power or right to hear and decide cases (pp. 270–271)

jurisdicción facultad o derecho que tiene un tribunal de oír los casos y decidir sobre ellos (págs. 270–271)

*justify to provide an explanation for; to find reasons to support (p. 362; p. 440)

*justificar dar una explicación; hallar razones para sustentar (pág. 362; pág. 440)

L

*lecture speech meant to provide information, similar to what a teacher presents (p. 405)

*conferencia discurso que busca proporcionar información, similar a una presentación de un profesor (pág. 405)

*legal permitted by law (p. 394)

*legal permitido por la ley (pág. 394)

legislative branch the lawmaking branch of government (pp. 196–197)

poder legislativo rama del gobierno encargada de crear las leyes (págs. 196–197)

*license to give official authority to do something (p. 384)

*autorizar conferir autoridad oficial para hacer algo (pág. 384)

limited government idea that a government may only use the powers given to it by the people (p. 207)

gobierno limitado idea según la cual un gobierno solo puede usar los poderes que le confiere el pueblo (pág. 207)

*link to connect (p. 10)

*vincular conectar a (pág. 10)

literacy the ability to read and write (pp. 396–397)

alfabetismo capacidad de leer y escribir (págs. 396–397)

literacy test a method used to prevent African Americans from voting by requiring prospective voters to read and write at a specific level (p. 512)

prueba de alfabetismo método usado para evitar que los afroamericanos voten exigiendo que los posibles electores lean y escriban a un nivel específico (pág. 512)

lock in a canal, separate compartment with gates at each end used in which water levels rise and fall in order to raise or lower boats (pp. 304–305)

esclusa en un canal, compartimento separado con puertas en los extremos en el cual el nivel del agua sube y baja para que los barcos se levanten o desciendan (págs. 304–305)

Loyalist an American colonist who remained loyal to Britain and opposed the war for independence (pp. 124–125)

leal colono americano que permanecía fiel a Gran Bretaña y se oponía a la guerra de independencia (págs. 124–125)

lynching putting to death by the illegal action of a mob (p. 512)

linchar provocar la muerte mediante la acción ilegal de una turba (pág. 512)

M

magnanimous noble; generous (p. 317)

magnánimo noble; generoso (pág. 317)

*maintain to keep or uphold (pp. 252–253)

maize a variety of corn (pp. 6–7)

majority a number that is more than 50 percent of the total (pp. 324–325)

Manifest Destiny the belief popular in the United States during the 1800s that the country must extend its boundaries to the Pacific Ocean (p. 352)

manumission the freeing of individual enslaved persons (p. 186)

martyr a person who sacrifices his or her life for a principle or cause (pp. 437–438)

*medical relating to medicine; help given to people who are sick or injured (p. 414)

mercantilism an economic theory that a nation's power depends on its ability to increase wealth by increasing exports and receiving precious metals (p. 94)

mercenary paid soldier who serves in the armed forces of a foreign country (p. 146)

migration the movement of a large number of people into a new area (p. 6)

militia a military force made of ordinary citizens who are trained to fight in emergencies (p. 102)

*ministry the office and duties of a religious leader (p. 418–419)

minuteman a civilian during Revolutionary era who was ready to fight with only one minute's notice (p. 122)

mission a religious community where farming was carried out and Native Americans were converted to Christianity (pp. 45–46)

monopoly a market where there is only one provider of a good or service (p. 311)

Morse code a system for sending messages that uses a series of dots and dashes to represent the letters of the alphabet, numbers, and punctuation (p. 380)

mosque a Muslim house of worship (pp. 32–33)

mountain man an adventurer of the American West (p. 349)

*mantener conservar o sostener (págs. 252–253)

maíz elote (págs. 6–7)

mayoría número superior al 50 por ciento del total (págs. 324–325)

Destino Manifiesto creencia popular en Estados Unidos durante el siglo XIX según la cual el país debía ampliar sus fronteras hacia el océano Pacífico (pág. 352)

manumisión liberación de personas esclavizadas (pág. 186)

mártir persona que sacrifica su vida por un principio o una causa (págs. 437–438)

*médico relativo a la medicina; ayuda que se brinda a los enfermos y heridos (pág. 414)

mercantilismo teoría económica según la cual el poderío de una nación depende de su capacidad de aumentar sus riquezas incrementando las exportaciones y recibiendo metales preciosos (pág. 94)

mercenario soldado remunerado que sirve en las fuerzas armadas de un país extranjero (pág. 146)

migración desplazamiento de un gran número de personas en un área nueva (pág. 6)

milicia fuerza militar compuesta por ciudadanos comunes que están entrenados para combatir en situaciones de emergencia (pág. 102)

*ministerio cargo y deberes de un líder religioso (págs. 418–419)

miliciano civil que estaba listo para combatir en cuestión de minutos durante el periodo revolucionario (pág. 122)

misión comunidad religiosa donde se practicaba la agricultura y los indígenas americanos se convertían al cristianismo (págs. 45–46)

monopolio mercado en el que solo hay un proveedor de un bien o servicio (pág. 311)

código morse sistema de transmisión de mensajes que consta de una serie de puntos y rayas para representar las letras del abecedario, los números y la puntuación (pág. 380)

mezquita casa musulmana de adoración (pags. 32–33)

hombre de montaña aventurero del oeste americano (pág. 349)

mudslinging a method in election campaigns that uses gossip and lies to make an opponent look bad (p. 326)

calumnia método de las campañas electorales en el que se usan el rumor y las mentiras para hacer quedar mal al adversario (pág. 326)

N

nationalism a strong sense of devotion to one's country (p. 282; p. 284)

nacionalismo fuerte sentido de devoción al país propio (pág. 282; pág. 284)

nativist person opposed to immigration (pp. 384–385)

nativista persona que se opone a la inmigración (págs. 384–385)

naturalization the process of becoming a citizen of another country (pp. 214–215)

naturalización proceso para hacerse ciudadano de otro país (págs. 214–215)

*network interconnected system (pp. 430–431)

*red sistema interconectado (págs. 430–431)

*neutra l taking no side (p. 102)

*neutral que no toma partido (pág. 102)

neutral rights privileges or freedoms that are granted to nations that do not choose a side in a conflict (p. 280)

derechos neutrales privilegios o libertades que se otorgan a naciones que no toman partido en un conflicto (pág. 280)

nomad a person who moves from place to place (p. 6)

nómada persona que se traslada de un lugar a otro (pág. 6)

nominating convention a meeting in which representative members of a political party choose candidates to run for important elected offices (p. 328)

convención de nominación reunión en la cual los representantes de un partido político eligen candidatos para importantes cargos de elección (pág. 328)

normal school state-supported school for training high school graduates to become teachers (p. 406)

escuela normal escuela apoyada por el Estado en la que se educa a los estudiantes de secundaria para que sean profesores (pág. 406)

Northwest Passage a sea route between the Atlantic and Pacific Oceans, located along the north coast of North America (pp. 50–51)

Paso del Noroeste ruta marítima entre los océanos Atlántico y Pacífico, localizada en la costa norte de América del Norte (págs. 50–51)

nullify to legally overturn; to cancel (p. 260)

anular invalidar legalmente; cancelar (pág. 260)

O

*occupy to move into and take control of a place, especially by force (pp. 116–117)

*ocupar desplazarse a un lugar y tomar control de él, en especial mediante un enfrentamiento entre fuerzas (págs. 116–117)

*ordained established (p. 445)

*ordenado establecido (pág. 445)

ordinance a law or regulation (p. 180)

ordenanza ley o norma (pág. 180)

*outcome the effect or result of an action or event (p. 510)

*resultado efecto o producto de una acción o un evento (pág. 510)

override to reject or defeat something that has already been decided (p. 499)

anular rechazar o derrotar algo que ya se ha decidido (pág. 499)

overseer a plantation manager (p. 393)

supervisor administrador de una plantación (pág. 393)

P

pacifists people opposed to the use of war or violence to settle disputes (p. 71)

pacifista persona que se opone al uso de la guerra o la violencia para resolver disputas (pág. 71)

*participate to take part in (pp. 326–327)

*participar tomar parte (págs. 326–327)

partisan firmly favoring one party or faction (p. 257)

partidario que favorece firmemente un partido o facción (pág. 257)

patent sole legal right to an invention and its profits (p. 297)

patente derecho legal exclusivo sobre un invento y las ganancias que este produce (pág. 297)

Patriot American colonist who favored American independence (pp. 124–125)

patriota colono americano partidario de la independencia americana (págs. 124–125)

patroon landowner in the Dutch colonies who ruled over large areas of land (pp. 69–70)

patrón terrateniente de las colonias holandesas que dominaba grandes áreas de tierra (págs. 69–70)

persecute to mistreat a person or group on the basis of their beliefs (pp. 64–65)

perseguir maltratar a una persona o un grupo por sus creencias (págs. 64–65)

petition a formal request for government action (p. 129)

petición solicitud formal de una acción gubernamental (pág. 129)

pilgrimage a journey to a holy place (pp. 32–33)

peregrinación viaje a un lugar sagrado (págs. 32–33)

plantation a large farm (pp. 46–47)

plantación granja grande (págs. 46–47)

plurality the largest number of something, but less than a majority (pp. 324–325)

pluralidad mayor número de algo, inferior a la mayoría (págs. 324–325)

*plus in addition to (pp. 348–349)

*además en adición (págs. 348–349)

*policy a statement of ideals or plan of action (pp. 67–68)

*política declaración de ideales o plan de acción (págs. 67–68)

poll tax a tax a person must pay in order to vote (pp. 510–511)

impuesto al sufragio impuesto que una persona debe pagar para votar (págs. 510–511)

popular sovereignty the belief that government is subject to the will of the people (pp. 206–207)

soberanía popular creencia de que el gobierno está sujeto a la voluntad del pueblo (págs. 206–207)

*pose to present; to offer (pp. 52–53)

*plantear presentar; ofrecer (págs. 52–53)

prairie schooner a canvas-covered wagon used by pioneers in the mid-1800s (pp. 350–351)

carromato vagón cubierto de lona que usaban los pioneros a mediados del siglo XIX (págs. 350–351)

preamble the introduction to a formal document that often tells why the document was written (p. 132)

preámbulo introducción a un documento formal que con frecuencia indica por qué se escribió (pág. 132)

precedent something done or said that becomes an example for others to follow (pp. 246–247)

precedente algo que se hace o se dice y se vuelve un ejemplo para los demás (págs. 246–247)

prejudice an unfair opinion not based on facts (p. 383)

prejuicio opinión injusta que no se basa en los hechos (pág. 383)

presidio a fort (pp. 45–46)

presidio fuerte (págs. 45–46)

*previous earlier (pp. 146–147)

*previo anterior (págs. 146–147)

*principal most important (p. 86)

*principal lo más importante (pág. 86)

*principle a fundamental, or basic, law or idea (pp. 270–271)

*principio ley o idea fundamental o básica (págs. 270–271)

privateer a privately owned ship outfitted with weapons (p. 159)

corsario barco privado equipado con armamento (pág.159)

*process to prepare (p. 388)

*procesar preparar (pág. 388)

*prodigal wasteful (p. 317)

*derrochador despilfarrador (pág. 317)

*prodigious large in size or quantity (p. 317)

*prodigioso de gran tamaño o cantidad (pág. 317)

productivity a measure of how much a worker can produce within a given amount of time and effort (p. 388)

productividad medida de cuánto puede producir un trabajador en una cantidad de tiempo y con un esfuerzo determinados (pág. 388)

*profane not religious (p. 317)

*profano no religioso (pág. 317)

*proffer to present for acceptance (p. 359)

*proponer presentar para su aceptación (pág. 359)

*prohibit to prevent or forbid (pp. 112–113)

*prohibir evitar o proscribir (págs. 112–113)

propaganda ideas or information intentionally spread to harm or help a cause (p. 117)

propaganda ideas o información que se difunden intencionalmente para perjudicar o apoyar una causa (pág. 117)

proportional having the proper size in relation to other objects or items (p. 188)

proporcional que tiene el tamaño apropiado en relación con otros objetos o elementos (pág. 188)

Protestantism a form of Christianity that began in opposition to the Catholic Church (pp. 49–50)

protestantismo forma del cristianismo que nació en oposición a la Iglesia católica (págs. 49–50)

*pueblo a communal Native American structure; a town in Spanish-ruled lands (p. 16; p. 46)

*pueblo ciudad en tierras bajo el dominio español (pág. 16; pág. 46)

*purchase the act of buying something (p. 274)

*comprar acción de adquirir algo (pág. 274)

*pursue to proceed with (p. 167)

*proseguir continuar (pág. 167)

R

*radical extreme (p. 495)

*radical extremo (pág. 495)

ranchero a Mexican ranch owner (p. 362)

ranchero propietario de un rancho mexicano (pág. 362)

rancho a ranch, especially the large estates set up by Mexicans in the American West (p. 362)

ratify to vote approval of (p. 167)

*react to act in response to something (pp. 280–281)

rebellion open defiance of authority (pp. 116–117)

reconciliation settlement; understanding (pp. 126–127)

Reconstruction the period of rebuilding the South after the Civil War and readmitting the former Confederate states into the Union (pp. 494–495)

recruit to enlist in the military (p. 146)

*Reformation a sixteenth-century religious movement rejecting or changing some Roman Catholic teachings and practices and establishing the Protestant Churches (pp. 49–50)

*reformation change (p. 193)

*region an area defined by a feature or characteristic (p. 304)

*regulate to control or govern (p. 429)

*reinforce to make stronger (p. 460)

*reject to refuse to accept (p. 440)

*relinquish to give up (pp. 192–193)

relocate to move to another place (pp. 330–331)

*rely to depend upon (p. 86)

*remove to take away (p. 354)

Renaissance a reawaking of culture and intellectual curiosity in Europe from the 1300s to the 1600s (p. 30)

*renounce to give up; to abandon (pp. 126–127)

repeal to cancel an act or law (pp. 114–115)

representative government a system in which citizens elect a smaller group to make laws and conduct government on their behalf (p. 93)

republic a government in which citizens rule through elected representatives (p. 177)

reserved power authority belonging only to the states (p. 207)

rancho hacienda, en especial las grandes propiedades que los mexicanos establecieron en el oeste de Estados Unidos (pág. 362)

ratificar aprobar por votación (pág. 167)

*reaccionar actuar en respuesta a algo (págs. 280–281)

rebelión desafío abierto a la autoridad (págs. 116–117)

reconciliación acuerdo; entendimiento (págs. 126-127)

Reconstrucción periodo de reconstrucción del Sur después de la Guerra Civil y readmisión de los antiguos estados confederados en la Unión (págs. 494–495)

reclutar enlistar en las fuerzas militares (pág. 146)

*Reforma movimiento religioso del siglo XVI que rechazó o modificó algunas enseñanzas y prácticas de la Iglesia católica romana y estableció las iglesias protestantes (págs. 49–50)

*reforma cambio (pág. 193)

*región área definida por un rasgo o característica (pág. 304)

*regular controlar o gobernar (pág. 429)

*reforzar fortalecer (págs. 460)

*rechazar rehusarse a aceptar (pág. 440)

*abdicar ceder (págs. 192–193)

reubicar trasladar a otro lugar (págs. 330–331)

*confiar depender (pág. 86)

*quitar sacar (pág. 354)

Renacimiento renacer de la cultura y la curiosidad intelectual en Europa entre los siglos XIV y XVII (pág. 30)

*renunciar ceder, abandonar (págs. 126–127)

revocar cancelar un acto o una ley (págs. 114–115)

gobierno representativo sistema en el cual los ciudadanos eligen un grupo más pequeño para que legisle y dirija el gobierno en su nombre (pág. 93)

república gobierno en el cual los ciudadanos gobiernan por medio de representantes elegidos (pág. 177)

poder reservado autoridad que pertenece solo a los estados (pág. 207)

*reside to exist or live in (p. 197)

resistance refusal to give in (p. 483)

resolution an official expression of opinion by a group (pp. 114–115)

*resolve to find a solution; to settle a conflict (p. 259)

*resource something that can be used for benefit, especially land, minerals, and water (p. 362)

*restriction rule or regulation that limits something (p. 282)

*reveal to show (pp. 302–303)

revenue incoming money from taxes or other sources (pp. 112–113)

*revere to deeply love and respect (pp. 192–193)

reverse to go in the opposite direction (p. 476)

revival religious meeting (pp. 404–405)

*rigid firm and inflexible (pp. 434–435)

*route line of travel (p. 412)

*residir existir o vivir en un lugar (pág. 197)

resistencia negativa a darse por vencido (pág. 483)

resolución expresión oficial de la opinión por parte de un grupo (págs. 114–115)

*resolver hallar una solución; dirimir un conflicto (pág. 259)

*recurso algo que se puede usar para obtener beneficios, en especial tierra, minerales y agua (pág. 362)

*restricción norma o regulación que limita algo (pág. 282)

*revelar mostrar (págs. 302–303)

renta dinero que ingresa por concepto de impuestos o de otras fuentes (págs. 112–113)

*reverenciar amar y respetar profundamente (págs. 192–193)

invertir ir en la dirección contraria (pág. 476)

asamblea evangélica encuentro religioso (págs. 404–405)

*rígido firme e inflexible (págs. 434–435)

*ruta línea de viaje (pág. 412)

S

scalawag name given by former Confederates to Southern whites who supported Republican Reconstruction of the South (p. 505)

secede to withdraw or break away from a nation or organization; to officially leave an organization (pp. 276–277; p. 430)

secession withdrawal; to leave the Union (p. 440)

sectionalism rivalry based on the special interests of different areas (p. 310)

sedition activities aimed at weakening the established government by inciting resistance or rebellion to authority (p. 259)

segregation the separation or isolation of a race, class, or group (p. 512)

separation of powers the division of authority among executive, legislative, and judicial branches to make sure no one branch has too much power (p. 208)

bribón nombre dado por los antiguos confederados a los blancos sureños que apoyaban la reconstrucción republicana del Sur (pág. 505)

separarse retirarse o apartarse de una nación u organización; dejar oficialmente una organización (págs. 276–277; pag. 430)

secesión retiro; acción de abandonar la Unión (pág. 440)

faccionalismo rivalidad que surge de tener intereses en áreas diferentes (pág. 310)

sedición actividades que buscan debilitar el gobierno establecido incitando a la resistencia o a la rebelión contra la autoridad (pág. 259)

segregación separación o aislamiento de una raza, clase o grupo (pág. 512)

separación de poderes división de la autoridad entre las ramas ejecutiva, legislativa y judicial para garantizar que ninguna de ellas tenga demasiado poder (pág. 208)

*series events that occur one after the other (p. 482)

*serie eventos que ocurren uno tras otro (pág. 482)

sharecropping system of farming in which a farmer works land for an owner who provides equipment and seeds and receives a share of the crop (pp. 506–507)

aparcería sistema en el cual un agricultor trabaja la tierra para un propietario que suministra el equipo y las semillas y recibe una parte de la cosecha (págs. 506–507)

siege attempt to force surrender by blocking the movement of people or goods into or out of a place (p. 165)

sitio intento de obligar al enemigo a rendirse bloqueando el movimiento de personas y bienes desde y hacia un lugar (pág. 165)

*similar sharing qualities, but not the same as; like (p. 270)

*similar que comparte cualidades pero no es igual; parecido (pág. 270)

slave codes rules focusing on the behavior and punishment of enslaved people; laws in Southern states that controlled enslaved people (pp. 88–89; p. 395)

códigos esclavistas reglas que se enfocaban en la conducta de los esclavos y los castigos que recibían; leyes de los estados del Sur que controlaban a los esclavos (págs. 88–89; pág. 395)

*so-called known as (p. 124)

*llamado conocido como (pág. 124)

*source a supply (pp. 6–7)

*fuente suministro (págs. 6–7)

*sovereign one who holds power (p. 317)

*soberano quien ostenta el poder (pág. 317)

spiritual an African American religious folk song (p. 394)

espiritual canción tradicional religiosa afroamericana (pág. 394)

spoils system practice of rewarding government jobs to political supporters; replacing government employees with the winning candidate's supporters (p. 328)

sistema de botín práctica de recompensar con cargos en el gobierno a los seguidores políticos; reemplazar a los empleados del gobierno por los seguidores del candidato ganador (pág. 328)

states' rights the idea that states should have all powers that the Constitution does not give to the federal government or forbid to the states; theory that individual states are independent and have the right to control their most important affairs (p. 260; p. 440)

derechos de los estados idea de que los estados deberían tener todas las facultades que la Constitución no le confiere al gobierno federal o les prohíbe a estos; teoría según la cual los estados individuales son independientes y tienen derecho a controlar sus asuntos más importantes (pág. 260; pág. 440)

*status rank or place as compared to others (pp. 132–133)

*estatus posición o lugar en comparación con otros (págs. 132–133)

*stock livestock (p. 473)

*ganado semovientes (pág. 473)

*stoicism the quality of not reacting to pleasure or pain (p. 317)

*estoicismo cualidad de no reaccionar frente al placer o el dolor (pág. 317)

strait a narrow passage of water between larger bodies of water (p. 5)

estrecho paso de agua angosto entre grandes masas de agua (pág. 5)

*strategy a plan of action; a careful plan or method (p.165; pp. 452–453)

*estrategia plan de acción; plan o método cuidadosos (pág. 165; págs. 452–453)

strike a work stoppage by employees as a protest against an employer (p. 383)

huelga interrupción del trabajo por parte de los empleados como protesta contra el empleador (pág. 383)

*structure a building (p. 16)

*estructura construcción (pág. 16)

*subjugate conquer (pp. 358–359)

*subyugar conquistar (págs. 358–359)

subsistence farming producing just enough to meet immediate needs (pp. 84–85)

agricultura de subsistencia producir solo lo suficiente para satisfacer las necesidades inmediatas (págs. 84–85)

substitute an alternate or replacement (p. 470)

sustituto alternativa o reemplazo (pág. 470)

suffrage the right to vote (pp. 415–416)

sufragio derecho al voto (págs. 415–416)

survive to continue existing or living after nearly being destroyed (p. 334)

sobrevivir seguir existiendo o vivir después de haber estado a punto de ser destruido (pág. 334)

suspend to temporarily set aside or stop operation of something (p. 93; p. 502)

suspender dejar de lado o detener temporalmente el funcionamiento de algo (pág. 93; pág. 502)

sustain to suffer or experience (pp. 162–163)

soportar sufrir o experimentar (págs. 162–163)

symbol a word or object that stands for something else (p. 340)

símbolo palabra u objeto que representa otra cosa (pág. 340)

T

technology the use of scientific knowledge for practical purposes (p. 30; p. 297)

tecnología uso del conocimiento científico para propósitos prácticos (pág. 30; pág. 297)

tedious boring (p. 317)

tedioso aburrido (pág. 317)

Tejano a Texan of Latin American, often Mexican, descent (p. 355)

tejano descendiente texano de un latinoamericano, por lo general mexicano (pág. 355)

telegraph a device that used electric signals to send messages (pp. 378–379)

telégrafo aparato que envía mensajes mediante señales eléctricas (págs. 378–379)

temperance drinking little or no alcohol (p. 405)

abstinencia beber poco o nada de alcohol (pág. 405)

tenant farmer a farmer who pays a landowner an annual rent and worked for that person for a fixed number of days each year (pp. 52–53)

granjero arrendatario granjero que paga a un terrateniente una renta anual y trabaja para él un número determinado de días al año (págs. 52–53)

terrace a broad platform of flat land cut into a slope (p. 12)

terraza plataforma ancha de tierra plana excavada en una pendiente (pág. 12)

theocracy a society that is ruled by religious leaders (p. 9)

teocracia sociedad gobernada por líderes religiosos (pág. 9)

tidings news (p. 421)

novedades noticias (pág. 421)

tolerance the ability to accept and respect different views or behaviors (p. 67)

tolerancia capacidad de aceptar y respetar puntos de vista o comportamientos diferentes (pág. 67)

topic subject of discussion (p. 436)

asunto tema de análisis (pág. 436)

torrent fast-moving liquid (p. 127)

torrente líquido que corre rápidamente (pág. 127)

total war a strategy of bringing war to the entire society, not just the military (pp. 484–485)

guerra total estrategia de llevar la guerra a toda la sociedad, no solo al estamento militar (págs. 484–-485)

Glossary/Glosario

Glossary/Glosario

trade union group of workers with the same trade, or skill (p. 383)

sindicato grupo de trabajadores con el mismo oficio o destreza (pág. 383)

*tradition a long-standing cultural belief and practice (pp. 194–195)

*tradición creencia o práctica cultural de larga data (págs. 194–195)

*transfer to move (p. 146)

*transferir mover (pág. 146)

*transform to change significantly (p. 378)

*transformar cambiar significativamente (pág. 378)

triangular trade pattern of trade that developed in colonial times among the Americas, Africa, and Europe (p. 88)

comercio triangular patrón de comercio desarrollado durante la Colonia entre América, África y Europa (pág. 88)

tributary stream or smaller river that feeds into a large river (p. 459)

tributario corriente de agua o río pequeño que desemboca en un río más grande (pág. 459)

tribute money paid to a leader or state for protection (pp. 278–279)

tributo dinero que se paga a un líder o Estado para obtener protección (págs. 278–279)

turnpike a road that one must pay to use (p. 303)

autopista de peaje camino por el que se debe pagar para su uso (pág. 303)

U

*underestimate to judge something below its actual value (p. 285)

*subestimar juzgar algo por debajo de su valor real (pág. 285)

Underground Railroad a system of cooperation to aid and house enslaved people who had escaped (p. 396)

Tren Clandestino sistema de cooperación para ayudar y albergar a los esclavos que habían escapado (pág. 396)

*uniform identical; unchanging (p. 247)

*uniforme idéntico; constante (pág. 247)

*unimpaired not harmed; not damaged (p. 445)

*intacto que no se ha deteriorado; sin daño (pág. 445)

*usurpation an unjust seizing of power (pp. 358–359)

*usurpación toma injusta del poder (págs. 358–359)

utopia community based on a vision of a perfect society (p. 405)

utopía comunidad basada en una visión de una sociedad perfecta (pág. 405)

V

veto to reject a bill and prevent if from becoming law (p. 337)

vetar rechazar un proyecto y evitar que se convierta en ley (pág. 337)

*victual food (p. 91)

*víveres alimento (pág. 91)

vigilante person who acts as police, judge, and jury without formal legal authority (p. 367)

vigilante persona que actúa como policía, juez y jurado sin autoridad legal formal (pág. 367)

*violate to disregard or go against (p. 114)

*violar ignorar o ir en contra (pág. 114)

W

*widespread over a wide area (p. 50)

writ of assistance court document allowing customs officers to enter any location to search for smuggled goods (p. 113)

*generalizado en un área amplia (pág. 50)

interdicto de despojo documento judicial que permite a los funcionarios de aduana entrar a un lugar en busca de productos de contrabando (pág. 113)

Y

yeoman a farmer who owns a small farm (pp. 391–392)

pequeño terrateniente agricultor que posee una granja pequeña (págs. 391–392)

Glossary/Glosario

The following abbreviations are used in the index: m=map, c=chart, p=photograph or picture, g=graph, crt=cartoon, ptg=painting, q=quote

---
A

B

Index

X

Y

Z

Index